SADHANA

[THE TEXT-BOOK OF THE PSYCHOLOGY AND PRACTICE OF THE TECHNIQUES TO SPIRITUAL PERFECTION]

Sri Swami Sivananda

Published by
THE DIVINE LIFE SOCIETY
P.O. SHIVANANDANAGAR—249 192
DISTT. TEHRI-GARHWAL, UTTARAKHAND, HIMALAYAS, INDIA

Price]   2010   [Rs. 300/-

Dedicated
to
The Seekers of Truth

SRI SWAMI SIVANANDA

Born on the 8th September, 1887, in the illustrious family of Sage Appayya Dikshitar and several other renowned saints and savants, Sri Swami Sivananda had a natural flair for a life devoted to the study and practice of Vedanta. Added to this was an inborn eagerness to serve all and an innate feeling of unity with all mankind.

His passion for service drew him to the medical career; and soon he gravitated to where he thought that his service was most needed. Malaya claimed him. He had earlier been editing a health journal and wrote extensively on health problems. He discovered that people needed right knowledge most of all; dissemination of that knowledge he espoused as his own mission.

It was divine dispensation and the blessing of God upon mankind that the doctor of body and mind renounced his career and took to a life of renunciation to qualify himself for ministering to the soul of man. He settled down at Rishikesh in 1924, practised intense austerities and shone as a great Yogi, saint, sage and Jivanmukta.

In 1932 Swami Sivananda started the Sivanandashram. In 1936 was born The Divine Life Society. In 1948 the Yoga-Vedanta Forest Academy was organised. Dissemination of spiritual knowledge and training of people in Yoga and Vedanta were their aim and object. In 1950 Swamiji undertook a lightning tour of India and Ceylon. In 1953 Swamiji convened a 'World Parliament of Religions'. Swamiji is the author of over 300 volumes and has disciples all over the world, belonging to all nationalities, religions and creeds. To read Swamiji's works is to drink at the Fountain of Wisdom Supreme. On 14th July, 1963 Swamiji entered Mahasamadhi.

PUBLISHERS' NOTE

Outlines of Sadhana in Sivananda Literature

To inspire, to awaken and to guide the seekers after Truth and God-realisation, has been the unique life-work of the great sage, Swami Sivananda. In this Note, let us gain a grasp of the broad outlines upon which Swami Sivananda would have us proceed, if we make God-realisation or search after Truth, the main aim and goal of life. He has given us certain working methods, in as much as practical ways and means are more to be attended to, rather than mere theory. The spiritual life is to be built upon and sustained by three important supports, i.e., a well-conceived ideal, a definite programme of life and a background of thought.

For any of us, to proceed upon the spiritual life, the first requisite naturally goes without saying is that the individual should have an ideal. He should want something definite, he should aim at getting something concrete. There are ideas and ideals. One makes up his mind to develop extraordinary physique, to be the perfect figure; the second has the ideal of going round the world as many times as possible; the third to amass a million. At the back of every human effort, there is some unconsciously accepted ideal. For the aspirant, there is the spiritual ideal which he has set before himself to achieve and realise. This setting of some definite ideal before oneself, is the first requisite.

The second requisite is a well-laid and well-regulated plan of procedure or programme. After having conceived of the ideal which the aspirant wants to reach, as haphazard procedure will not only take him nowhere but will also mean a fruitless waste of his precious energies, he should chalk out a definite and well-marked programme. Without such a programme it is difficult to achieve any progress. The whole process of working out this programme will be experienced to be one not smooth-sailing but very rough-going. Many a time the aspirant will be compelled by overwhelming adverse forces to seek temporary refuge just as a ship when caught up in a terrible storm has to seek some port as an escape from the storm.

There is a way by which the aspirant may, while struggling hard to realise the ideal, and when faced with danger, seek the refuge. It is as Swami Sivananda has advocated, to cultivate what is termed as a concrete background of thought, because the aspirant's struggles are endless and he should have a background of thought into which he can immediately take refuge whenever occasion arises and these occasions are many, many not merely during the course of his spiritual Sadhana but many every day, every minute, even in a moment he will have to take refuge four or five times.

A well-conceived ideal and a definite programme of life and then a concrete background of thought to sustain him in his struggle to work out that programme—these are the three requisites which Swami Sivananda has advocated. While working out this programme of life there are certain facts which are worth remembering, i.e., spiritual progress is very gradual and it is in the nature of a twofold conflict. As Swamiji has said that though physical wars have ended on earth between nations, the war which has caused these external wars—man's struggle against his lower nature—has not been concluded properly. If man were to attain victory over his lower nature then he should have possession of himself and he will not be the slave of his passions which lead him to external war. This inner war has two aspects: one, of offence and the other of defence. Many a time a spiritual aspirant has got to carry on his fight against these two positive and negative sides. While he progresses on the path, he has consistently to protect himself from forces which assail him from inside. There is a class of insects called the coleoptera. They have two sets of wings. The external wings will be stiff like thick parchment. They are not fit for flying. There are two film-like wings inside, which are used for flying. They serve the beetle wonderfully well. They take the beetle up and forward, but they are so delicate that these external wings are the protecting armour—protecting these internal wings. That set of wings which takes the Sadhaka forward on the path is intense aspiration and constant Sadhana. Unless real fire of aspiration is maintained, one cannot progress. And to protect this aspiration against temptations, one must have the other set of wings in the shape of Vairagya and Satsanga and constantly keep up the current of Vichara or discrimination. Vichara is the chief anchor of protection for the aspirant. It is only discrimination which can protect the aspirant against temptations. With aspiration and the protective covering of Vairagya and Satsanga, you will have to work out the programme of life. While working out the programme of life, you should have a background of thought. Unless the aspirant is established in this background, he will not be able to habituate his mind to slip back automatically into this background.

In the case of the Bhakti Yogi, this background thought will be the Lord; in the case of a Jnana Yogi it may be Mahavakya that he is the Soul; for the Japa Yogi, it may be the Name. Thus to habituate himself to become established in the background of thought he should have what the Lord has prescribed in the Gita—constant Abhyasa. Without constant Abhyasa you cannot expect to have any success in spiritual life. This constant Abhyasa is necessary for marching forward and yet forward. In order to console the aspirant, sometimes Swamiji may say, "If you cannot progress much do not be depressed. It does not matter much." That is but only a consolation because the mind should never be depressed. An aspirant should always be wary to see that he always proceeds upwards, and has the protecting armour of Vichara, Vairagya and Satsanga to achieve the ideal, while working out the programme of life, in order to protect himself. There is the tortoise. The moment an enemy approaches to harm it, it withdraws itself into the shell. This is the exact purpose which the background of thought serves the aspirant. He has to withdraw himself into it. There is one difference in this particular case—the tortoise goes into the shell and comes out in the same condition as when it went, but every time as the aspirant takes refuge in the background he comes out with added strength.

To sum up, in order to tread the path of spiritual life: (1) let the aspirant conceive of an ideal; (2) let him put up a general programme of life; (3) let him have Abhyasa and Vairagya and (4) let him take to a background of thought into which he can take refuge at times of external stress. And for all this, the help of this book is most invaluable; it is in fact, the greatest boon that we could offer to the aspirant-world. There is no aspect of Sadhana which has not been dealt with, no path which has not been presented, and no point of guidance that the aspirant's peculiar difficulties need, which has not been elaborately dealt with. —THE DIVINE LIFE SOCIETY

PREFACE

Om! Salutations to that adorable Lord Hari, than Whom there is nothing greater, and Who is above all this universe.

The term "Sadhana" comes from the root "Sadh," which means to "exert," "to endeavour to get a particular result or Siddhi." He who does the practices or attempts is called a Sadhaka. If he achieves the desired result, Siddhi, he is called Siddha. A fully-developed Siddha is one who has attained full knowledge of Brahman. Self-realisation or Darshan of God is not possible without Sadhana. Any spiritual practice is called Sadhana. Sadhana and Abhyasa are synonymous terms. That which is obtained through Sadhana is Sadhya or Goal—the realisation of God or Brahman. Most comprehensive in its scope, this book presents almost every known form of Sadhana for the Experience of the Divine or Brahman.

If you want to evolve quickly you must have the right kind of Sadhana. If you are a student of the path of Self-reliance, you can yourself select the Sadhana for your daily practice. If you are a student of the path of self-surrender, you should get the right kind of Sadhana from a Guru and practise the same with intense faith.

Why should you prolong the bondage unnecessarily? Why should you not claim your divine birthright right now? Why should you not break your bondage now? Delay means prolongation of your sufferings. You can break it at any moment. This is in our power. Do it now. Stand up. Gird up your loins. Do rigorous and vigorous Sadhana and attain freedom, which is immortality or eternal bliss.

Make the lower nature the servant of the higher through discipline, Tapas, self-restraint and meditation. This is the beginning of your freedom.

The divine within you is stronger than anything that is without you. Therefore, be not afraid of anything. Rely on your own

Inner Self, the Divinity within you. Tap the source through looking within.

Without renunciation you can never be happy. Without renunciation you can never be at your ease. Therefore renounce everything. Make happiness your own. Hold renunciation as the foremost of things.

Improve yourself. Build your character. Purify your heart. Develop divine virtues. Eradicate evil traits. Conquer all that is worthy and noble.

Only when you have purified the heart, silenced the mind, stilled the thoughts and surging emotions, withdrawn the outgoing senses, thinned out the Vasanas, you can behold the glorious Atman during deep meditation.

There are five means by which perfect tranquility or emancipation can be attained. These form the highest happiness. They are Satsanga or association with the wise, discrimination between the real and unreal, dispassion, enquiry of 'Who am I?' and meditation. These are called heaven. These are religion. These form the highest happiness.

Become a good man first. Then control the senses. Then subdue the lower mind by the higher mind. Then the divine light will descend. Only then the vessel will be able to receive and hold the divine light.

Practise meditation persistently and calmly without haste. You will soon attain Samadhi or the Nirvikalpa state.

Spiritual life is toilsome and laborious. It demands constant vigilance and long perseverance before substantial progress is made.

You have yourself built the walls of your prison-house through ignorance. You can demolish the walls through discrimination and enquiry of 'Who am I?'

Sufferings purify the soul. They burn up the gross material, sins and impurities. The Divinity becomes more and more manifest. They give inner spiritual strength and develop the will-force, the power of endurance. Hence sufferings are blessings in disguise.

Even a ray of inner light during meditation will lighten your path. It will give you great deal of encouragement and inner strength. It will goad you to do more Sadhana. You will experience this ray of light when the meditation becomes more deep and when you rise above body-consciousness.

Life is the unfolding of the latent capacities of the soul. Lead the divine life. Generate sublime divine thoughts in your mind through meditation, Japa, Kirtan and study of sacred scriptures.

Bathe in the river of life everlasting. Plunge in it. Take a dip in it. Swim in it. Float in it. Rejoice.

Bask the body in the physical sunlight. Bask the soul in the sunlight of the Eternal. You will have good health and everlasting life.

Worship is the unfolding of the bud of the flower of the soul. Worship is life. Worship bestows life eternal. You may conquer millions of persons in a battle, but you will become the greatest conqueror only if you can conquer your own lower self or mind.

So long as your senses are not subdued or weakened, you will have to practise Tapas or self-restraint, Dama or Pratyahara.

When the electric lamp is covered by many wrappings of cloth, there will be no bright light. When the cloth is removed one by one, the light grows brighter and brighter. Even so, when the self-resplendent Atman which is covered by the five sheaths is stripped off the sheaths by meditation on the pure Self and the practice of 'Neti Neti' doctrine, the Self-luminous Atman reveals Itself to the meditator.

Sit down with a composed mind. Assert your mastery over the body and mind. Plunge deep into the chambers of your heart, and enter into the stupendous ocean of Silence. Listen to the voice which is soundless.

Purify the heart first and then climb the ladder of Yoga steadily with courage and undaunted spirit. Climb onwards swiftly. Attain Ritambhara Prajna and reach the summit of the ladder, the temple of wisdom, where the cloud of virtue or nectar dribbles from Dharmamegha Samadhi.

Build your spiritual life on a sure foundation, on the rock of the divine grace and strength of character. Take refuge in the Lord and His eternal law. There is no power in heaven or on earth that can bar your path now. Success in Self-realisation is certain. Failure exists not for you. There is light on your path. All is brilliant.

Sadhana means any spiritual practice that helps the Sadhaka to realise God. Abhyasa and Sadhana are synonymous terms. Sadhana is a means to attain the Goal of human life. Without Sadhana no one can achieve the purpose of life. Sadhana differs in different individuals according to the capacity, temperament and taste. Every one must take to some kind of Sadhana to attain the state of final beatitude. Sadhya is that which is attained through Sadhana. It is God or Atman or Purusha. If you want to evolve quickly you must have the right kind of Sadhana. If you are a student of the path of self-reliance, you can yourself select the Sadhana for your daily practice. If you are a student of the path of self-surrender, you should get right kind of Sadhana from a Guru and practise the same with intense faith.

Those who follow the path of devotion should do Japa, read the holy scriptures such as the Bhagavata or the Ramayana. By the practice of Nava Vidha Bhakti, the Bhakta should develop Bhakti to a very high degree. Sravana, Smarana, Kirtana, Vandana, Archana, Padasevana, Sakhya, Dasya and Atma-Nivedana are the nine methods to develop Bhakti. Bhaktas should observe Vrata, Anushthana and do prayers and Manasic Puja. They should serve others, realising that the Lord recides in the hearts of all. This is the Sadhana for those who tread the path of Bhakti Yoga.

Those who follow the path of Karma Yoga should do disinterested selfless service to the suffering humanity and society in various ways. They should surrender the fruits of action to the Lord as Isvararpana. They should give up agency by realising that they are the instruments in the hands of God. They should get rid of their selfishness and control their Indriyas. They should completely consecrate their lives in the service of humanity. they should consider that the whole world is a manifestation of the Lord. If they serve people with such a Bhava, their hearts get purified in the long run. Eventually they get knowledge of the Self through Chitta Suddhi. This is the Sadhana for the Karma Yogins. This is very important for all beginners in the spiritual path. This is not the goal itself. Many erroneously think so and neglect the higher courses of Sadhana. They should advance still further and through Dharana, Dhyana and Samadhi reach the highest goal.

A Raja Yogi slowly ascends the Yogic ladder through the eight steps. He gets ethical training in the beginning to purify himself by the practice of Yama and Niyama. Then he steadies his posture. Then he practises Pranayama to steady his mind and to purify the Nadis. Then by the practice of Pratyahara, Dharana and Dhyana, he gets Samadhi. Through Samyama, he gets different Siddhis. He restrains all the mental modifications that arise from the mind.

Those who take up the path of Vedanta or Jnana Yoga should acquire first the four means of salvation (Sadhana Chatushtaya)—Viveka, Vairagya, Shat-Sampat and Mumukshutva. Viveka is discrimination between the real and unreal. Vairagya is indifference to sensual enjoyments. Shat-Shampat is the sixfold virtues, Sama, Dama, Uparati, Titiksha, Sraddha and Samadhana. Then they approach a Brahma-Nishtha guru who has realised the Supreme Self and hear the Srutis from him. Then they reflect and meditate on the Self and attain eventually Atma-Sakshatkara. Then the Jnani exclaims with joy: "The Atman alone is, one without a second. Atman alone is the one Reality. I am Brahman, *Aham Brahma Asmi. Sivoham. Sarvam Khalvidam Brahma.*" The liberated Jivanmukta sees the Self in all beings and all beings in the Self.

The students of Hatha Yoga should try to awaken the Kundalini Sakti that lies dormant in the Muladhara Chakra by Mudras, Bandhas, Asanas and Pranayamas. They should try to unite the Prana and Apana and send the united Prana-Apana through the Sushumna Nadi. Heat is increased by retention of breath and Vayu ascends up along with Kundalini to the Sahasrara Chakra through the different Chakras. When Kundalini is united with Lord Siva at the Sahasrara Chakra, the Yogi attains supreme peace, bliss and immortality.

PRAYERS

I

O All-pervading, hidden and homogeneous Essence! O adorable Lord of the Universe! Thou art witnessing the drama of this world from behind the screen. Thou art self-luminous. Thou art the basis of all these names and forms. Thou art one without a second. Thy glory is ineffable. Thou art the source of all sciences, knowledge and beauty.

I do not know how to worship Thee. I have no strength to do any kind of Sadhana. I am full of weaknesses and Doshas. My mind is wavering. Indriyas are powerful and restless. Some say: "Thou art Nirakara and Nirguna." I don't want to indulge in fighting, discussions and debates. Give me peace and devotion. Give me strength to resist temptations and to control this enemy and thief, the mind. Let me utilise my body in Thy service. Let me remember Thee always. Let me be ever looking at Thy sweet, loving face. Grant me this prayer, O ocean of Love!

Give me true Viveka and lasting Vairagya. The Vairagya cometh and goeth. Let me be established in Para Vairagya. My self-surrender is not perfect and sincere, too. I admit my faults. Not a drop of tear comes out of my eyes. Make me weep in solitude, when I am alone. Let me not shed crocodile tears. Then only I can see Thee in my tears. My heart is harder than flint, steel and diamond. How can I make it as soft as butter? Give me the heart of Prahlada or Gouranga. This is my fervent prayer. O Lord of Love! Grant me this humble prayer of mine. I am suppliant to Thee. I am Thy disciple. Thou art my Guru.

II

O Preceptor of Wisdom Infinite, grant me the boon to serve untiringly the sick, the poor and the afflicted, not to associate with evil, never to tell lies and not to succumb to the love of sense-objects.

O Lord! I am in You and You are in me.
I am He whom I love, and He whom I Love is I.

O Light, illumine my intellect.
O Love, fill my heart.
O Power, give me strength.
O Lord, Thou art Courage! Fill me with courage.

Thou art mercy, fill me with mercy. Thou art Peace, fill me with peace. Thou art Effulgence, fill me with effulgence.

O Lord, Thou art the river. Thou art the cloud. Thou art the Ocean. Thou art the plant. Thou art the patient. Thou art the doctor. Thou art the disease. Thou art the medicine.

All belong to the Lord! I am doing His work. I am an instrument in His hands. His Will be done.

III

O Lord! Make my will strong to resist all temptations, to control my Indriyas and lower nature, to change my old evil habits, to make my surrender complete and real. Enthrone Thyself in my heart. Do not leave this place even for a second. Use my body, mind and organs as instruments. Make me fit to dwell in Thee for ever.

IV

THE UNIVERSAL PRAYER

O Adorable Lord of Mercy and Love!
Salutations and prostrations unto Thee.
Thou art Satchidananda (Existence-Knowledge-Bliss).
Thou art Omnipresent, Omnipotent and Omniscient.
Thou art the Indweller of all beings.
    Grant us an understanding heart,
    Equal vision, balanced mind,
    Faith, devotion and wisdom.
    Grant us inner spiritual strength
    To resist temptations and to control the mind.
    Free us from egoism, lust, greed, anger and hatred.
    Fill our hearts with divine virtues.
Let us behold Thee in all these names and forms.
Let us serve Thee in all these names and forms.
Let us ever remember Thee.
Let us ever sing Thy glories.
Let Thy Name be ever on our lips.
Let us abide in Thee for ever and ever.

CONTENTS

Publishers' Note . . . . (7)
Preface . . . . (10)
Prayers . . . . (15)

INTRODUCTORY

A Survey of the Evolution of the Ancient Indian
  Spiritual Techniques 31

CHAPTER ONE
FOUNDATIONS OF SADHANA

Prerequisites of Spiritual Sadhana 51
The Three Governing Factors of Sadhana 58
Primary Principles of Sadhana and Their Perversions . 60
Abhyasa: The First Phase of Sadhana 66
Four Points for Memory in Sadhana. 66
Bases of Spiritual Sadhana 67
Aspects of Spiritual Sadhana 69
Sadhana: Its Techniques of Applied Psychology . . . 81
Easy Method of Sadhana in Worldly Environment . . . 82
Some Secrets of Sadhana. 83
The Essence of Sadhana 85

CHAPTER TWO
SIGNIFICANT PROCESSES IN SADHANA

The Movement of Vasanas in Sadhana 86
Role of Restraint in Sadhana 90
Repression in Sadhana and Its Effects 94
Triple Withdrawal in Sadhana 100
Patience in Sadhana 101
Perseverance in Sadhana. 106
Continuity in Sadhana. 108
Four Progessive Stages in Sadhana 108

CHAPTER THREE
TYPES OF SADHANA

Fourfold Sadhana 109

The Simple Sadhana	113
Most Important Sadhana	115
A Dynamic Sadhana	116
Antaranga Sadhana	118
Ethical Sadhana	118
Mouna Sadhana	120
Brahmacharya Sadhana	126
Sadhana of the Antarmukha Vritti	128
Sadhana by Circumspection	129
Sadhana in Self-analysis	129
Sadhana of Pratipaksha Bhavana	130
Sadhana of Spiritual Vision	131
The Disciplines of Universal Love	131

CHAPTER FOUR
SADHANA IN THE PRASTHANATRAYA

The Sadhana of the Veda	133
Sadhana in the Brahma Sutras	134
Sadhana of the Upanishads	139
Sadhana of the Bhagavad-Gita	145

CHAPTER FIVE
SADHANA IN THE SMRITIS, EPICS AND PURANAS

Sadhana in the Manusmriti	152
Sadhana in the Ramayana	153
Sadhana in the Mahabharata	157
Sadhana in the Bhagavata Purana	159
Vishnupurana: Sadhana for Liberation	171
Sadhana in Garuda Purana	173
The Sadhana of the Yogavasishtha	173

CHAPTER SIX
SADHANA IN THE VARIOUS SCHOOLS

Sadhana in Veerasaivism	177
Sakti Yoga Sadhana	177
Sadhana in Saivasiddhanta	179
Sadhana in Kashmir Saivism	180

Sadhana in Pasupata Yoga 181

CHAPTER SEVEN
SADHANA IN SIVANANDA SUTRAS

Sadhana of Sivananda Upadesamritam. 182
Sivananda Mano-Vijnana Sadhana Sutras 187
Sivananda Hatha Yoga Sadhana Sutras 188
Sivananda Karma Yoga Sadhana Sutras 189
Sivananda Bhakti Yoga Sadhana Sutras 189
Sivananda Yoga Sadhana Sutras 190
Sivananda Vedanta Sadhana Sutras 190
Integral Yoga Sadhana 191

CHAPTER EIGHT
SARVA-SADHANA-SANGRAHA

Triplets in the Four Main Paths of Sadhana 194
Svara Sadhana 194
Laya Yoga Sadhana. 198
Pranava Sadhana 201
Soham Sadhana. 203
Vichara Sadhana 205
Dhyana Yoga Sadhana 211
Japa Yoga Sadhana 221
Gayatri Sadhana. 226
Mantra Yoga Sadhana. 230
Sankirtan Sadhana 236
Tantra Yoga Sadhana 237
Sava Sadhana. 238
Kriya Yoga Sadhana. 239
Sangita Sadhana 241
Sadhana by Prayer 246
Sadhana of the Yoga of Synthesis 248

CHAPTER NINE
IMPORTANCE OF SADHANA

Spiritualisation of Human Nature 254
Life's Supreme Purpose. 258
The Struggle for Perfection 260
Need for Sadhana. 260

Outgoing Tendencies of the Senses
and the Need for Self-control 263
Qualification for Sadhana 264
Sadhana—The Main Purpose of Life 267
Brahmamuhurta: The Best for Sadhana. 269
A Sermon on Sadhana 270

CHAPTER TEN
SADHANA FOR THE CONQUEST OF LOWER NATURE

Sadhana for Mastering the Mind 272
Various Methods of Mind-control 277
Sadhana for Controlling the Ten Senses 278
Sadhana for Developing Vairagya. 280
Sadhana for Elimination of Egoism 281
Six Sadhanas for Eradicating Jealousy 289
Sadhana for Annihilation of Arrogance 292
Sadhana for the Subjugation of Hatred 294
Sadhana for Controlling Anger 295
Sadhana for the Conquest of Fear 296

CHAPTER ELEVEN
SADHANAS FOR VARIOUS SIDDHIS

Four Sadhanas for God-realisation 299
Sadhana for Developing Will-power 299
Sadhana for Sense-control 302
Sadhana for Conquest of Raga-Dvesha. 304
Sadhana for Freedom from Accidents. 309
Sadhana for Success, Prosperity and Enlightenment . . 310
The Nineteen Factors of Sadhana for Peace 311
Sadhana for Samadhi in Six Months 314
Sadhana for Awakening Kundalini. 315
Sadhana for Realisation of Oneness 315

CHAPTER TWELVE
OBSTACLES TO PROGRESS IN SADHANA

The Mind of the Aspirant: A Psychological Study 317
Sadhana and the Vagaries of the Practitioner. 321
Temptations in Sadhana. 321

The Difficulty of Progress in Sadhana 322
Main Impediments to Sadhana 324

CHAPTER THIRTEEN
KARMA YOGA SADHANA

Service Is Essential 327
Karma Can Be Transformed into Yoga 331
Results of Karma Yoga Sadhana 333

CHAPTER FOURTEEN
BHAKTI YOGA SADHANA

Outlines of Bhakti Yoga Sadhana 336
A Few Facets of Bhakti Yoga Sadhana 340
Faith, Aspiration and Self-surrender. 343
Nine Modes of Bhakti Yoga Sadhana 344
Essentials in Bhakti Yoga Sadhana 349
The Role of Faith in Bhakti Sadhana 351
Important Sadhana in Bhakti Yoga 352
The Gist of Bhakti Yoga Sadhana 355

CHAPTER FIFTEEN
YOGA SADHANA

Yoga Sadhana: Introductory 357
Yoga Sadhana Explained 360
Yoga Sadhana: Its Eight Fundamentals 361
Mental Purification: An Essential Condition 365
Need for Yoga Sadhana 365
Structure of Yoga Sadhana 368
Practice of Yoga Sadhana 373
Practical Yogic Instructions 374
Inner Yogic Discipline 383
Light on Yoga Sadhana 393
Main Obstacles in Yoga Sadhana 394

CHAPTER SIXTEEN
VEDANTIC SADHANA

Vedantic Sadhana: Introductory 401
Aspects of Jnana Sadhana 402
The Seven Stages of Jnana 403

Methods of Vedantic Sadhana. 405
Obstacles in Vedantic Sadhana 406
The Nature of the Jnani 407
Hints on Vedantic Sadhana 407
Vedantic Aphorisms 424
Essence of Vedantic Sadhana. 429

CHAPTER SEVENTEEN
COURSES OF PRACTICAL SADHANA

Twelve Aspects of Saguna Dhyana Sadhana 431
A Programme of Sadhana. 431
Practical Sadhana: A Discussion 434
Sadhana for Ten Days. 449
Sadhana for Forty Days 450
Daily Routine 450
Ten Minutes Sadhana on Twelve Virtues 454
Twenty Important Spiritual Instructions 455
The Science of Seven Cultures 457
Everyday Guide to Sadhakas 460
Importance of Spiritual Diary 463
Resolves for Quick Spiritual Progress. 468
The Resolve Form. 468
Secret of Success in Sadhana 470
An Ideal Grihastha Sadhaka. 470
Some Hints on Sadhana. 471
Kabir's Method of Sadhana 475

CHAPTER EIGHTEEN
QUESTIONS AND ANSWERS ON SADHANA

Religion, Saint and Yogi. 476
Prerequisites for Realisation. 477
The Science of Mantra Repetition 477
Japa Yoga 482
Problems of Sadhana 482
What should Be Our Goal? 484
Methods of Mental Purification 485
Problems of Self-realisation 486
Hatha Yoga 487
The Need for a Spiritual Guide 489

Definition of Faith and Development of Devotion 491
Questions in Bhakti Yoga 492
Questions in Vedanta 498
Questions in Raja Yoga 499
Yoga and the Life Divine 500
World and Renunciation 501

CHAPTER NINETEEN
INTIMATE ADVICE TO ASPIRANTS

Aspirants—A Distinct Class by Themseves 503
Advice to Sadhakas 506
Instructions to Sannyasins 512
Guiding Lights 518
Sweetness in Sadhakas 521
Spiritual Guidance for Aspirants 522
Need for Great Vigilance 524
The Voice of Spiritual Aid 526
Sadhana and Samadhi 528
Some Spiritual Don'ts 531
Sadhana and the Guide 531
Guidance from the Scriptures 536
Sadhana Panchakam of Sri Sankaracharya 542

CHAPTER TWENTY
INSPIRING SVADHYAYA FOR ASPIRANTS

Physical Body and Life Divine 543
Repetition of Divine Name 543
Man and His Stepping Stones 543
Peace, Salt of Life and Sankirtan 543
The Sage, Happiness and Power 544
Life, The Melting Heart and Divine Grace 544
Humanity, Love and Goodness 545
Purity, Aspiration, Realisation 545
Sadhana and Sakti 545
Anger, Mind and Self-conquest 546
Compassion, Satsanga and Discrimination 546
Truth, Vedanta and Human Imagination 547
Inner Happiness and Omnipresence of the Lord 547
God and His Name 548

The Body and the Blessing of Human Birth	549
The Main Supports in Sadhana	549
The Demands of Yoga and the Worldly-minded	550
Difficulties in Life and the Messages of the Saint	550
God-consciousness and Sat-Chit-Ananda	550
Patience, Contentment and Divine Light	551
Love and Secret of God-realisation	552
Wisdom and Perfection	553
The Lord, His Form and His Presence	554
Analogies and Some Forms of Blessing	555
Life on Earth and the Liberated Sage	556
Self-control and Brahma Jnana	556
Virtues and Bhakti	557
Rewards of Japa and Upanishadic Study	558
Vairagya, Abhyasa and Meditation	558
Ignorance and the Corroding Human Passion	559
Representatives of the Divine Beauty	560
Pathway to Purity	560
The Sage and Equal Vision	561
Thoughtfulness and Sweet Dispostion	561
Cheerfulness and the Oneness with the Divine	562
Man, The Architect of Circumstances	562
Yoga, The Epitome of Religious Experience	563
The Origin of Desire and Brahmic Realisation	563
Good Conduct and Obstacles on the Path	564
The Pervasive Brahman, the Astral Body	564
Vedanta, The Path of Wisdom	565
Faith and the Love of God	565
The Inner Light and the Truly Wise	566
Definition of Religion and a Life in the Lord	566
Obstacles to Spiritual Progress and the Value of Suffering	567
World, Mind and Prayer	568
Attributes of the Divine Consciousness	569
Indiscrimination, Anger and the Language of the Heart	570
Saintliness and the Tender in Heart	570
Art, Life and Bhakti	571
A Rational Knowledge of the Divine	572

The Search for Immortality 573
Gauranga and the Miracles of Name 573
Ethical Life and Control of Emotions 574
Ideals in Nature 575
Importance of Virtue and Prem 575
Silence, Its Meaning and Its Place 576
The Middle Path 576
Steps of Aspiration. 577
Byways of Blessedness 577
Manasic Puja Sloka by Sri Sanakaracharya. 578
Excellent Slokas from Avadhuta Gita for Meditation. . . 578
The Life Triumphant 579
The Tree of Self, Sadhana and Samadhi 579

CHAPTER TWENTY-ONE
SONGS OF SADHANA

The Gist of Sadhana. 580
Practice of Real Sadhana 584
Intimate Advice 584
Song of Sadhana Week 584
Song of a Sadhaka 586
Phases of Sadhana 587
Twenty Precepts for Practice 587

CHAPTER TWENTY-TWO
SOME EXPERIENCES OF ASPIRANTS

Purpose of Sadhana. 590
Experiences of Sadhakas 593
Collective Sadhana 594
Instructions to Sadhakas 597

APPENDIX—I
A DRAMA IN SADHANA

The Path of a Sadhaka 603

APPENDIX—II
A GARLAND OF PRECEPTS IN SADHANA

Foundations of the Life Divine 614
The Discipline of Detachment 614

Practice of Yoga Sadhana	614
The Easiest Form of Sadhana	615
Qualifications of Aspirants	615
Sense-control and Self-purification	617
Obstacles in Sadhana	619
Egoism—The Seed for Birth and Death	619
Desire—The Root-cause of All Miseries	621
The Three Principal Enemies	622
Selfishness—A Deadly Vice	626
Cardinal Principles of Practical Sadhana	626
The Inner Spiritual Discipline	627
Jnana Yoga Sadhana	628
Light on the Path	633
Special Spiritual Insructions	635
Nivritti Sadhana	639
Science of Yoga Sadhana	641
Self-effort and Destiny	642
Brahmacharya—The Basis of All Sadhana	643
Goodness, Purity and Truthfulness	644
Charity—An Aspect of Sadhana	646
Suffering—A Stepping-stone to Success	647
Sadhana and Self-realisation	648
Essentials of Spiritual Life	648
Importance of Spiritual Practice	649
Important Sadhanas	650
Secret of Success in Sadhana	652
Overcome Temptations	653
Meditate and Realise	655
The Ideal Aspirant	656
Light on Sadhana	657
Advice to Aspirants	660
Realisation of the Self	661
The Way to Kaivalya	662
Progress on the Path	664
Sadhana—The Only Purpose of Life	666
Concentration and Meditation	667
Brahmic Consciousness	668
The Key to Blessedness	671

Sadhana and Some Experiences 672

APPENDIX—III
SIVANANDA SADHANA SARA

Fundamental Aspects of Sadhana 674
The Nature and Processes of Sadhana 675
Concentration and Need for Vigilance. 676
Conditions for Yoga Sadhana 677
Sadhana, The Divine Name and Equanimity 678
The Results of Real Love 679
Formula in Higher Sadhana 680
Sadhana and the Spiritual Destiny 681
Sadhana and the Mind 681
Requisites for Spiritual Progress 682
Guidance in Sadhana 684
The Principles of Spiritual Progress 686
Elements of Sadhana 687
Background of Thought 688
Sadhana and Samadhi 689
Phases of Spiritual Practice 690

APPENDIX—IV

Only with an Invincible and Powerful Arrow of Yogic
    Concentration Can You Kill the Seven Faculties
    that Trouble You 692

APPENDIX—V

Sivananda's Synthesis of Sadhanas
    (Sri K.S. Ramaswami Sastri) 695

ॐ श्रीसद्गुरुपरमात्मने नमः

SADHANA

असतो मा सद्गमय ।
तमसो मा ज्योतिर्गमय ।
मृत्योर्मा अमृतं गमय ।

INTRODUCTORY

A SURVEY OF THE EVOLUTION OF THE ANCIENT INDIAN SPIRITUAL TECHNIQUES

Hinduism, through the passage of several centuries, has come in for diverse criticisms and been subject to a wide range of different opinions. It has had praise in plenty and disparagement in plenty, too. There are those who praise its wisdom and there are quite as many, too, who would regard Hinduism as a mast of out-dated superstition accumulated by a race of illiterate and uncultured people. And religion being the main governing influence with the Hindu, he is superstition-bound and has consequently remained backward when other people have progressed by leaps and bounds. The above charge is supported by statistics on literacy, knowledge of hygiene, sanitation, science, psychology, etc. The Hindu race gets 'fail' marks in such ultra-modernistic 'efficiency test' that scientific minds of today would conduct. It seems as though centuries of culture, development, study and research have not gained much for the Hindu in the shape of knowledge of this grand universe of countless things which are visible before us. Yes, to a great extent this is so, and more wonder, the true Hindu does not seem to regret greatly that it is so. This is so far a special reason, and this reason it is that forms the distinctive quality of the Hindu genius, marking it out as completely different from the enlightened scientific hierarchy of the Twentieth Century. The reason is this:

The Hindu mind is assured that the invisible is the real. His scientific curiosity and thirst for knowledge (he has his full measure of this) is diverted towards the realm of invisible things. The grosser and the more external the things, the lesser is its value to the seeking Hindu. The Hindu may be seriously suffering from the baneful results of 'blind-faith', yet he had no such faith in wasting his precious life and faculties in research into things which he was convinced are absolutely transitory, evanescent. But, on the other hand the Hindu has spared himself no pains to get at the thing that is permanent, imperishable; that is true. He has brought to bear all his wisdom, his keen observation, his powerful logic, deep research and searching analysis and scientific calculation in his all out attempt to pierce beyond the veil of passing appearance and to come face to face with the Truth, the Eternal Fact. The Hindu lavished his genius upon this field which he regarded as worth his while, as it was concerned with eternal values. All other territory he considered it idle to waste too much effort upon; for to him it seemed absurd to run too seriously after shadows. Such labours of our ancient stalwarts resulted in the evolution of the marvellous system of Yoga for realising the Truth. The Yoga Sadhanas constitute the practical methodology for the great attainment. These Sadhanas are the outcome of the deepest psychological research. This psychology is not merely that of the mind but is something more. It is a supramental psychology. Spiritual psychology is the term by which I would prefer to refer to it.

To get an insight into this spiritual psychology let us sum up shortly the basic conception of the Indian Philosophy. The very core and essence of it all has been presented in a nutshell by the greatest of philosophers, Sri Sankara in the couplet, *"Sloka-ardhena pravakshyami yaduktam granthakotibhih; Brahma satyam jaganmithyaa jivo brahmaiva naaparah."* The Transcendent Being alone is real, phenomena are false, the (apparently separate) individual self is the Transcendent alone, and none other. Then, whence arose this feeling of being something different from That which is one Transcendent Being? Whence this sense of a limited finite existence, with its resultant deluded perception of the manifold variety of phenomena? Whence this little limited individuality with its distant separatist consciousness? This indeed is Maya. This sense of human individuality it is that obstructs the experience of Truth. This Ahankara or ego-sense is the outcome of nescience and is the root-cause of all bondage at the root of this deluded perception of passing phenomena. Ahankara or egoism is the chief bar to the experience of the inner Reality.

The thought of "I" is the cause of destructive bondage, declares the Yoga-Vasishtha. Then again,

अहमित्येव संकल्पो बन्धायातिविनाशिने।

Then again,

द्वे पदे बन्धमोक्षस्य न ममेति ममेति च।
ममेति बध्यते जन्तुर्न ममेति विमुच्यते॥

Says the Mahabharata, "Two words indicate Freedom and Bondage. They are 'not mine' and 'mine'. Through 'mineness' a creature is bound and through 'not-mineness' it is freed." This is powerfully expressed in the Mahopanishad wherein we find:

अहंकारवशादापदहंकारदुराधयः।
अहंकारवशादीहा नाहंकारात्परो रिपुः॥

'Calamity is due to being subject to Ahankara, bad agonies are due to Ahankara, desire is due to subjection to Ahankara, there is no greater enemy than Ahankara.'

In alluding to this, the root-cause of Samsara, and the main obstacle to Self-knowledge, the Great Sri Sankara, in the 'Vivekachudamani', states repeatedly that the arch-enemy of the seeker is the "EGO".

तेषामेव मूलं प्रथमविकारो भवत्यहंकारः।

The root of them all (i.e. obstacles) is the first modification (of nescience), called egoism. Freed from the clutches of egoism, man attains his real nature. The precious treasure of the Brahmic Bliss is closely guarded by the powerful deadly serpent of egoism. The aspirant is advised to kill this ego-serpent first if he desires to obtain the treasure of transcendent bliss.

This being the case, methods had to be evolved to annihilate this arch-enemy of Self-realisation. But, this ego-principle by itself is totally abstract and subtle beyond comprehension. It is too elusive a factor to be got at easily. This set the Hindu mind thinking, observing, probing, searching out and determining all its ramifications, its modifications, its manifestations and its grosser by-products. The Hindus found these rampant everywhere in the human personality. They found the ego leering with innumerable faces through one's thoughts, one's feelings, one's behaving, speaking and acting. In fact man was a monument of egoism. He was filled with ego-sense from the top of his head to the tip of his toe-nails. A tough task it seems to root out the ego. The discovery set the Hindu genius working still further. One by one the different aspects of man, the intellectual, the mental, the emotional, the physical were taken up and the play of the ego in each of the planes was studied, classified and tabulated.

This done, they next started formulating effective methods, direct as well as indirect, for dealing with each one of all these numerous ego-aspects in the individual, which were as so many formidable hurdles and barriers in the path of the Jiva's self-perfection. These constituted the numerous items of the Hindu Sadhakas that have come in for so much of ridicule at the hands of uncomprehending alien observers, and what is more deplorable, at the hands of its own narrow-visioned inheritors.

Now to start with a consideration of the methods evolved for dealing with the ego-barrier as expressed on the intellect plane, the Buddhi. This cognising principle, the Hindu found, was at the bottom of an endless chain of erroneous cognitions due to a fundamental error or wrong identification. He gave to it the name 'Adhyasa'. This Adhyasa was, he found in the nature of the basic error of identification with the body. This identification of "I am such and such" gave rise to a whole host of consequent identifications such as "I am Brahmin" or "I am non-Brahmin," "I am an aristocrat" or "I am a commoner," "I am rich" or "I am poor," "I am learned" or "I am ignorant," "I am healthy" or "I am unhealthy"; "fair or dark, lean or fat, handsome or ugly, clever or dull, tall or short, old or young," etc., etc. By a careful observation of the typical 'man-in-delusion,' the Hindu genius discovered that these Adhyasas had so insidiously woven themselves into the man's consciousness that they had got themselves established as a fundamental part of the normal awareness of the being. They are part and parcel of his personality and consciousness. This was due to the fact that the identification commenced right from the moment of birth and was present there already even before the intelligence had commenced functioning in the infant. Thus starting life itself with this false consciousness, the individual grew up into this self-hypnotism. The Hindu genius perceived now that powerful, persistent 'counter-hypnotism', if this term may be used, could alone effectively dehypnotise the individual of his deluded identification and clear up the way for the manifestation of his true consciousness. To this end, he was made to start the Sadhana with a regular, systematic, continuous reception of the counter-ideas that were to serve as the vanguard to the forces that were to be got ready to storm and to break up the bastion of the delusive Adhyasa. This continuous reception thus formed the first Anga of Jnana Yoga Sadhana, namely Sravana. Day after day, the seeker was made to sit by his preceptor and constantly hear such declarations as:

शुद्धोऽसि बुद्धोऽसि निरञ्जनोऽसि संसारमायापरिवर्जितोऽसि। नामरूपं न ते न मे। कथं रोदिषि रे वत्स। वासांसि जीर्णानि यथा विहाय नवानि गृह्णाति नरोऽपराणि। तथा शरीराणि विहाय जीर्णान्यन्यानि संयाति नवानि देही॥ न जायते म्रियते वा कदाचित्॥

"Thou art not this body; thou art not this mind; thou art neither the sleeping, waking, nor the slumbering self; thou art That which continues even during deep sleep and wakes up at dawn; thou art the innermost consciousness."

The prescription of this constant Sravana as the first step in Jnana Yoga Sadhana was based upon the sound psychology that is behind the principle of auto-suggestion. These ideas were constantly hammered again and again into the mind of the aspirant. This repetition through constant Sravana constituted the main secret of the working of this Sadhana and has been practised with unfailing success for centuries upon centuries by the Indian seeker long before the world had even dreamt about any being like Emile Coue. When the mind was thus being saturated with these spiritual counter-suggestions, the seeker was led on to the next stage of Jnana Sadhana which again was based upon the sound psychological knowledge of the principle, "as a man thinketh, so he becometh." *"Mana eva manushyanam karanam bandhamokshayoh"* declared the ancient sage. "What the mind is, that man is—this is the eternal secret" (Panchadasi ii-13). Thus we have Manana or constant reflection over and over again upon the truths continuously being heard during Sravana. Now the de-hypnotisation is well under way. On the constant reception of counter-ideas, they begin to make themselves felt and the Adhyasa begins to weaken. Continued Manana further thins out the false Adhyasa and all its resultant by-products. The aspirant begins now to feel gradually that he is something distinct from the body and mind and feelings, etc. He begins to tell himself *"Mano-buddhi-ahankara-chittani na aham."* To keep up this thought-current well boosted, the seeker is given an

Upasadhana, i.e., an auxiliary or a complementary practice (still another tribute to the masterly psychology of the ancient Hindu genius) of Svadhyaya or daily compulsory reading of Vedantic scriptures. This daily Svadhyaya works as a powerful fresh-up of the Adhyatmic counter-thought current that is being generated to exterminate Adhyasa. When this work has progressed the seeker arrives at Nididhyasana, the ultimate stage in Jnana Sadhana which means deep and intense meditation upon a single Truth. The Sadhana of Nididhyasana was based upon the full knowledge of the mighty power of a concentrated mind. The continuous and intense holding on to a single thought to the exclusion of all else resulted in the crystallisation of the thought into actual fact. The ancients had reduced it to a law to which they gave the name 'Bhramarakita Nyaya'. For this Sadhana they picked out a handful of terse and pithy formulae from the most inspiring portion of the Vedas, viz., the Upanishads. These are the Mahavakyas, to be intensely meditated upon. Call it wisdom or superstition; yet these Sadhanas based upon the soundest psychological knowledge have proved to be effective enough for bestowing Self-knowledge and Cosmic Consciousness to the practitioner.

In knowing this process the ancients perceived that man's ego was being continuously stimulated and excited into expression by innumerable factors that operated upon the individual externally. These were the Upadhis, such as profession, wealth, dress, habits, physical appetites, indulgences like smoking, gambling, fashion, talent, praise, authority, his environments, company, etc. These further augmented the identification by further limiting the consciousness of the individual. To inhibit these countless limiting adjuncts or Upadhis a series of auxiliary disciplines were shrewdly and carefully thought out and laid down for the seeker. The seeker should give up all sensuality (Vairagya), control his senses (Dama), control his mind (Sama), give up gross physical comforts (Titiksha), ignore wealth, give up all physical adornments, by wearing simple apparel, shave his head, give up flowers, scents, dancing, music, and live a simple, hard life in humble submission to the preceptor before whom he had to bow down his ego. Despite this, the old Adhyasas cropped up through the force of habit; and they were summarily dealt with by yet another shrewd method developed by the Hindu genius, the method of sharp denial. Such ideas, if they cropped up, were denied out of existence through the method of Neti-Neti-Sadhana. These Upa-sadhanas effectively safeguard the progress of the mainstream through its stages of Sravana, Manana, Nididhyasana, leading from Adhyasa to Svarupa Jnana, when the seeker would declare "Chidananda-Rupah Sivoham," "Svarupoham," "Sivoham," "Soham."

Next we have the fruit of research into the modes that the ego-principle takes in man's emotional part. Here it was found as deep attachments, multifarious sentiments, infatuation. Here we find that due to its play and through the field of emotion the ego-principle tends to express itself more and more as affections, attachments and feelings of love to human personalities and things of this physical world. There is a never-ceasing succession of manifestation of 'Mamata' or ego as 'Mineness'. It works havoc through the power of Moha. Sentiment plays a great part in holding the Jiva in bondage in this manner. By far the greater majority of mankind is enslaved in the snare of such earthly sentiments and deluded attachment. Hence, there is the universal need for a technique by which one could effectively deal with the individual ego-consciousness caught up in the meshes of Moha, Maya and Mamata. The methodology for the control of attachments and affections to discipline and training of sentiments and emotions, and their diversion and channellisation towards a supramundane ideal (by whose positive force alone the individual would be successful in withdrawing his strong Mayaic attachments to earthly objects) and the total refinement and the sublimation of his love was indispensable if this was to be achieved. This need is most adequately met by what is well-known as the Bhakti Yoga. It is the Prema Marga of the Vaishnavites and the path of mystical love and ecstasy of the Sufis, the western mystics and the lovers of God, and others of their elk. In India the earliest origin of this path of devotion may be traced back to Narada and Sandilya Sutras. From thence it has progressed through the centuries and through the hands of successive God-intoxicated and love-maddened saints and mystics who appeared in various parts of India in different periods. It has now developed in a very thorough, scientific and highly evolved system of the spiritualisation and divinisation of human emotion and love. The emotional temperament forming a vast majority of mankind, the path of Bhakti Yoga provides a masterly, psychological process to suit their need.

Now, here the problem presented was not so much one of the driving out certain erroneous ideas and substituting them by right thought; but it was one of diverting attachments, sublimating sentiments, affection and emotions and in diverting the flow of the heart's love from mundane objects to a supramundane ideal. For this purpose the method of Ishta-Upasana was formulated through which was achieved a complete and comprehensive change-over of the individual's emotional allegiance from the human plane to the divine realm. In trying to work out this method the formulators of this system did not fail to reckon with the limitation and common weakness of the human nature and therefore provided that this change-over was not abrupt, violent or revolutionary. It was made gradual, natural and evolutionary. How was this done? By a very unique method of first initiating the individual to conceiving of the Ishta upon a purely normal human basis, thus for instance the neophyte Bhakta was trained to look upon the Ishta as a being related to him in a human way. According to the person's object of love upon the human plane the Ishta is to be regarded as a master (the Bhakta being His servant or slave), as a friend, as a child, or again as the beloved (the Bhakta being the pining lover). Through these attitudes or Bhavas as they are termed, which in the beginning are purely human to start with, the Bhakta progresses up to such a degree of intensification of his devotion that at a point it becomes supra-physical and culminates in an experience where even the sense of separation between the Bhakta and his love's ideal becomes dissolved in ecstatic union. Para Bhakti merges into Jnana.

The adoption of the particular Bhava becomes the starting point for the Bhakti Yoga Sadhana. This Bhava or relative attitude is taken up spontaneously and instinctively in accordance with the basic temperament of the devotee. The laying down of the Pancha-Bhavas of Santa, Dasya, Sakhya, Vatsalya and Madhurya is clearly indicative of a careful observation and study of the main types of human temperament. They indicate the extent of psychological insight into the predominant attachments, the attraction centres of love, loyalty and allied emotions that hold in sway the vast majority of individuals in this world of human relationship. They were found to be classifiable into the calm and composed state of emotional balance, the element of admiring hero-worship, the strong ties of companionship between friend and friend, the maternal instinct (doting) or motherly love and the erotic element expressed as all-absorbing, intense Prema or the passion of pure love between the lover and the beloved. It will be found that with the shrewdest and most unerring insight they had isolated the main and strongest of the emotional trends in the human nature. Each one of these is such a force under the strong impelling power of which the individual goes to the extent of readily sacrificing his or her very life itself. It is an observed phenomenon that the loyal servitor is ever ready to give up his life in his duty of carrying out the behests of his master and leader whom he worships. The mother regards her own life as of no importance before that of her beloved child. A friend will sacrifice himself with joy for the sake of his friend. As for the true lover and the beloved they are indeed as one soul in two bodies. The extent of their self-effacement, self-sacrifice and the intensity of their love has been immortalised by many an ancient classic, both of East and West.

In summing up these five main emotion-patterns these ancient propounders of the Bhakti Marga have covered, as it were, all mankind. One or the other of these five Bhavas or emotion-patterns will be found present in greater or lesser degree in the human individual the world over. Thus this analysis and classification of the "emotional-man" is universal in scope. The human being is instinct with love. Upon this earthly plane, in this externalised gross physical life, the human individual, the eternal lover, manifests love as the expectant, confident and trusting supplicant or as admiring, adoring, self-dedicating hero-worship or again as the sweet and intense attachment of friendship. Love is expressed also as doting parent or the all-consuming, self-offering passion of the lover.

In Bhakti Yoga, we find formulated the admirable technique for gradually transferring this emotional adhesion from an outward physical object to an inward spiritual ideal. To this end, for an effective concentration of the emotional flow, proper and satisfactory focus is provided in the institution of the Ishta Devata. It is the tutelary deity or one's favourite chosen ideal. To ensure a full and perfect switch over and concentralisation of your emotional content, the factor of NISHTHA was insisted upon as one of the indispensable desiderata in Bhakti Yoga. Nishtha is a *sine qua non*. Bhakti Yoga thus envisages a well-conceived process of the diversion and transference of the love of man from the physical to the spiritual, from the outward to the inward, from the mundane to the Supra-Mundane. It may be tersely summarised in the two terms of "detach" and "attach." It is the detaching of the emotional adherence from the earthly objects and attaching the same to the spiritual personality of the Ishta. This is neither to be abrupt nor in any way unnatural and forced but through a rationally designed method where the emotional structure of the individual is not injured or shocked by any sudden breakaway from its habitual emotional mode, but rather on the contrary, the habitual emotion-pattern of the being is itself made use of as the special medium and the means of an extension of the emotional field into a hitherto untouched inward realm. The more you progress into this inward realm of love, the more complete does your detachment to the evanescent, perishable physical love-object becomes until it reaches the state of a total severance of this gross attachment and the all-consuming, whole-soul, passionate adoration of pure Prema or intense love, self-forgetting and self-dedicative in its nature, to the Divine Ideal or the Ishta. The emotional being is thus purified and sublimated, spiritualised and advanced, culminating in the supervention of the highest superconsciousness. To initiate, nurture and perfect this transformation and guide it through its gradual development from the earlier external stages to its later subtle inward fruition, the practice of the ninefold mode of devotional Sadhana was laid down. Sravana or delighting in daily listening to the Divine Lilas and the glorification of one's chosen deity is one mode. For this purpose various Puranas and Epics have been provided, chief among them being the Srimad Bhagavata, the Ramayana, the Siva Purana, the Vishnu Purana, the Skanda Purana and the Devi Bhagavata and Mahatmya. Through the constant listening to the Lilas and the glories of the Lord, keen admiration is evoked. Satsanga or the company of the wise is another means by which the devotee is enabled to converse on the glories of the Lord with persons with similar devotional temperament. Through Satsanga and Svadhyaya or study of devotional books, comes admiration for the Lord. From admiration comes Sraddha or faith. From Sraddha comes devotion to the Lord. Then the devotee practises Sadhana Bhakti, viz., Japa, Smarana and Kirtana. He burns the sins and obstacles to his devotion by the above practices. From Sadhana Bhakti he develops Nishtha (devoutness). From Nishtha comes Ruchi or taste for hearing and chanting themes about the Lord. Then comes Rati or intense attachment. Rati softens the heart. When Rati is intensified it is called Sthayi Bhava or steadiness or permanent form of Bhakti Rasa. When Sthayi Bhava is intensified, it is called Maha Bhava or Prema-Maya. Now the devotee drinks the Prema Rasa and lives in the Lord.

The second mode, Kirtan or the singing of hymns and devotional songs embodying sweet and touching sentiments of adoration, prayerfulness, supplication and the like serves to make the devotee's relation more intimate with the Ishta Devata and to intensify the bond of gradually progressive affection and love. The third mode of Smarana connoting a constant recollection of and dwelling upon God's Lilas serves to further deepen the Yogi's attachment to the chosen ideal, thus helping to further fulfil the requirement of Nishtha. The above two serve to saturate the mind with ideas of the Ishta and a wealth of associated thoughts. Their work is augmented by regular formalistic worship (Sakara Upasana) like Padasevana, Archana, etc., that leads on to the culminating stages of Bhakti when the devotee's life blooms out into a constant, intense and practical living of one or the other of the attitudes which takes up the entire emotional field of the seeker's personality and fully dominates his consciousness entering into and colouring every one of even its minutest phases and fluctuations. A vital transformation is wrought in the life and personality of the devotee in all its parts. A whole-soul dedication characterises the Sadhana at this stage. The seeker lives in a beatific world of his own, entirely made up of his all-absorbing, all-consuming love for his heart's ideal. He attains an exalted consciousness where all selfish love is extinct, the emotional personality is totally sublimated and with the consequent absolute self-evanescence, the seeker's consciousness soars high into the empyrean of Cosmic Consciousness at once transcendent and perfect, sublime, glorious, all-blissful and everlasting.

But however, in the case of by far the vast majority of mankind the combating of the ego as expressed in and through the realm of the intellect was found to be impracticable. The vast major section of human beings were too deeply immersed and too inextricably enmeshed and bound up in the snares and toils of deluding nescience in its extremely gross form, so that in them the ego-consciousness rarely rose up and made itself felt to any effect upon the intellect plane at all. They were fully bound up and absorbed in their purely physical and sensual rounds of life and in them the ego found its play in far grosser forms like gross clinging to the body and its creature comforts, constant anxiety and fear for its safety and animal well-being, rank selfishness and intense attachment arising out of the former. At this stage the unregenerate individual is selfishness personified, the being of overweening vanity, who thirsts for self-recognition, self-satisfaction and self-adulation. His ego swells with each and every feather added on to his cap of vanity. A thorough overhauling of his unregenerate, self-bound, egocentric personality is indicated here as a first concern to one who would seek redemption from this state.

Accordingly a practical course of vigorous "personality overhaul" was outlined. This is Karma Yoga, the path of selfless, humble, self-abnegating, motiveless service of all beings. This is an active disciplined work-out through the external day-to-day life and activities of the individual where he is trained to set aside self and put service before self. He is taught to deny his personal pleasure and work for the happiness of others. He is made to shed off all Abhimana or personal vanity arising out of circumstances incidental to his birth and environment. The Abhimanas of man are truly legionary. They are fetters that bind him down to his limited individuality. Ego is their substratum and main support. Pride of high birth, pride of learning, vanity of good looks and accomplishments, arrogance of status or of wealth, the sense of superiority due to innumerable factors connected with the body, consequent sense of false prestige and dignity, sense of shame, are some of the commonest forms of Abhimana present in the average individual. To cast out such vain Abhimana of birth, rank, wealth, learning, etc., is the task behind the Sadhanas of the Karma Yoga. The seeker is first asked to forget his notions of superiority and to consider himself a humble servant. But the idea is not sufficient. He must start to work. He starts to do the most menial manual work without the least repugnance or unwillingness. He is taught work as worship. Serve all. Behold the Lord in all. Serve them with the feeling that you are worshipping the Lord in and through such service. Give up selfishness. Control your senses. Trample over all sense of superiority. Be humble. Be simple. Be selfless. Sacrifice your comforts. Share with others what you have. Give, give, give. Love all. Work ceaselessly for the happiness and the good of all. Offer up your body, mind, wealth and everything in this process. In this way, the gross egoism immersed in Tamas and filled with unnatural Abhimana, pride, arrogance, selfishness, greed, shame, fear and superiority is put into the furnace of Karma Yoga Sadhana and it emerges as a purified, refined principle full of humility, sweet with selflessness, compassion and spirit of worshipful service devoid of vanity and arrogance, simple and loving. This refinement of the ego and change from Tamoguna to Sattvaguna makes it fit for the taking up of other higher modes of Yoga for total perfection.

It must be noted that in the case of Karma Yoga we cannot trace back its origin to any specific treatise or scripture which could be regarded as an exclusive and authoritative textbook upon which this Yoga has its basis. But, however we find that there is a general tendency to regard Karma Yoga as owing its genesis in the Gospel of the Gita as expounded to Arjuna by Bhagavan Sri Krishna. It is acknowledged that the gospel of selfless, unattached dynamism as found in certain parts of the Bhagavad Gita supplies the fundamentals upon which the system of Nishkama Karma Yoga in the form that we find it today has been built up. Therefore, it is usual to refer to the Gita as the scripture which expounds the doctrine of selfless, worshipful activity, worshipful because of the Lord's injunction "to offer up all actions unto Me," even as all worship is naturally offered at the feet of the deity. Without entering into the relative merits of the conflicting claims upon the philosophy of the Gita by Jnanis, Bhaktas, Yogis, philanthropists and altruistic social workers alike, the main point to be grasped here is that there was a vital need for a doctrine of vigorous activism, having for its basis utter selflessness, calm detachment and a total absence of personal passion and desire. The Gita has supplied the nucleus for such a doctrine. The passage of centuries, the advent of numerous God-men and compassionate saint-reformers did the rest.

The great need of such a doctrine was discovered by the men of wisdom from their researches into the nature of man. The knowledge of the operation of the three Gunas in the individual nature is something unique and distinctive to the spiritual psychology known to the Hindu sages. In the course of their observation and practical study of man they had found out that these Gunas had to be transcended one after another in their order of progression. Tamoguna did not easily allow of conversion and transformation directly into the pure Sattvaguna. It had necessarily to be first converted from the gross Tamas into active Rajas. From Rajas it could be later transformed into the purity of Sattva. Herein is found the need for a system of Sadhana that could in the first instance assail and break down the gross Tamasic aspects of the ego-sense in the individual. The Asuric ego of the Tamoguna Prakriti was found to have strong hold and play in the individual in the form of Sthula Abhimana or a gross self-arrogating sense of doership which would insist upon vaingloriously taking the credit (in its deep ignorance) for all movements of the cosmic Prakriti expressing itself in and through the instrumentality of the human monad. "It is I who did this," "By me alone was done that," "All this I have done." Thus asserts the strong Abhimana of the extremely unregenerate Tamasic ego in man in his early days of darkness and constricted ego-centered living. The gradual renunciation of this strong, vain, self-arrogating sense of doership or Asuric Kartritva Abhimana forms the rock-bottom of Karma Yoga psychology.

Abhimana is a fattened state assumed by the ego due to its association and unconscious identification (through nescience) with factors distinct from or external to its native state of simple self-awareness. This associated factor or limiting Upadhi may be anything from some subjective inborn talent to a purely objective possession. "I am aristocratic," "I am wealthy," "I am handsome," "I am learned," "I am clever," "I am accomplished," "I am strong," "I am influential," "I am a collector," "I am a political leader," "I am a great philanthropist," "I am intellectual," "I am highly cultured". In such and other similar ways does Abhimana exist in the individual. "I am nothing," "I am a servant of servants," "I am a humble instrument, I want no praise," "I seek no gain," "I wish for neither name nor fame," "I know nothing," "I live to learn". With such Bhava or mental-cum-emotional attitude held persistently and practised actively, the Karma Yogi is trained to batter down the citadel of Abhimana.

Karma Yoga constitutes a masterly system of self-purification and preliminary preparation which lays the sure foundation for all Yoga and spiritual life. The ancient seers well knew that without purification of the heart no divine experience is ever possible. In the absence of such purification of man's nature, the forced adoption and practice of other techniques of Yoga are seen to be ineffective and powerless to lead to any lasting good; whereas with the nature thoroughly purified and regenerated by the practice of Karma Yoga, the other higher aspects of Yoga when taken up and practised yield gratifying results very quickly and rapidly lead to higher spiritual unfoldment.

It has been said already that extreme selfishness, greed and the desire for personal gain and selfish enjoyment characterise the lowest self of man. Karma Yoga is an effective attempt to bring out an 'about-turn' in this disposition of the human mentality. The laws of Karma Yoga lay down that the Yogi casts aside all desires for selfish enjoyment and personal gain. He is made to simplify his life and to control his senses. Strict discipline is the keynote of Karma Yoga. He is trained to think and feel that he does nothing but he is merely an instrument in the hands of the Divine. In humility he worships the Divine Spirit enshrined in all beings as the Antaryamin through his selfless, motiveless, loving services. He has to shed his superiority complex and move about with equal vision amongst all people. His angularities are to be rounded off once and for all. He must learn to subserve his personal notions in all matters and develop adaptability with others. He should control anger for he should ever remember that he is the servant of humanity. While thus moving constantly in the midst of multifarious natures and individuals, the Karma Yogi shall not take any offence, at any injury or insult done to him by antagonistic people. He must ever readily forgive and forget. The Karma Yogi is made to be devoid of vengeful spirit. He shall not retaliate.

This training, these rules and discipline, are the psychological machinery brought into operation in working out the technique of Karma Yoga. Gradually his nature is chastened. His ego is purified. This ceaseless activity in the spirit of pure worshipfulness effectively shakes him up and out from the sloth of gross Tamas. It fits him to take up one or other of the higher Yogas for the further unfoldment of the now comparatively purified ego. Karma Yoga, as it were, is a well-conceived psycho-physical, all-out direct attack upon a wide front against the entire series of soul-constricting and limiting Adhyasas (psycho-physical identifications) present in and binding down the individual through his contact and association with the innumerable Upadhis (psycho-physical adjuncts) that constitute the world around him. In the arsenal supplying this attack the most prominent items of the 'sinews of war' to be borne in mind are, Nishkama Karma, or selfless action, Abhimana Tyaga or renunciation of egoism, Akarta-Abhokta, Nimitta Bhava or the feeling of non-doership, non-enjoyership and being an instrument merely, Raga-dvesha Rahita Karma or action freed from attachment and hatred, Anaasakti or non-attachment, Karmaphala Tyaga or renunciation of the fruit of action, Puja Bhava, Bhagavadarpana.

The fourth technique that was perfected is the Raja Yoga, the Yoga of will, completely and lucidly expounded by Maharshi Patanjali in his Yoga Sutras. Raja Yoga is at once a most scientific, direct and summary "root technique." It may be compared to attacking the lion in his very den or drying up the river at its very source. We have already seen that the ego-consciousness has its play through the medium of the mind. It can be said that it is primarily the mind movement that makes possible the manifestation of the Ahankara. This led on logically to the conclusion that if the very mind movement itself is totally arrested, this ought naturally to bring about a cessation of the play of Ahankara. Hence they argued, if the initial mind wave or Vritti is made the target of attack, then, the battle is taken, as it were, into the very camp of the enemy and it becomes direct and summary. Upon this firm premise was built up the technique of Raja Yoga. It constituted a process of nipping in the *bud* all ideation itself. It effectively stifled out and annihilated the primary movement of the very mentation itself. Thus we have as the first Sutra: "*Yogas-chittavritti-nirodhah.*"

But then the above process was indeed an extremely subtle one. It was purely an inner process carried on within the realm of the mind. Could any one directly take to this process with any measure of success? This is the question. No. This was not possible. A careful preparation was necessary before the individual could become fit to take up this process of Vritti-Nirodha. Herein again they have displayed their deep knowledge of the nature and the behaviour of the mind and its relation and connection with the other aspects of the man's being. They know of the existence of the threefold factor of Mala or gross impurity, Vikshepa or tossing of the mind and Avarana or the veil of ignorance within the consciousness of the human monad. Before one could assay to remove the Avarana he is to first overcome Mala and Vikshepa. The gross Tamoguna and Rajoguna supply is, as it were, the stuff for the fabric of Mala or psycho-vital impurity in the structure of man's personality. The first four Angas of Patanjali's Ashtanga Yoga were therefore directed at the total elimination of Tamoguna and Rajoguna from the individual Prakriti. This effectively achieved the removal of Mala and Vikshepa. Observing that Tamoguna tyrannised the personality in the form of various impure and vicious tendencies, gross desire and disbeliefs, the first two steps in Raja Yoga, Yama and Niyama, were formed to counter this deficiency by the cultivation of the sublime virtues of truth, compassion, purity, non-stealing, desirelessness and the like, together with the active observance of external and internal cleanliness, contentment and cheerfulness in all matters, austerity, daily scripture-study and worship.

Next, based upon the knowledge of the close interrelation between the mysterious Prana and the mental fluctuations (Vikshepa) they formulated the third and the fourth Angas of Raja Yoga, the steady Asana and the rhythmic Pranayama. The maintenance of steady, unshaken posture for a prolonged period of time was prescribed to achieve the marvellous result of controlling and toning down the vibratory tempo of the body cells from the Tamasic and Rajasic to a state of pure and harmonious Sattva. With Asana-jaya, Tamoguna is overcome, Rajoguna is controlled and Sattva supervenes in the system of the practicant. His whole nature is comparatively refined. The ancients knew that mind and Prana were the obverse and reverse of the self-same coin and they were interconnected. By the discipline of the one you could discipline the other. By the control of the one you would control the other. Upon this psychological fact was conceived the fourth part of the Raja Yoga Sadhana, i.e., Pranayama, the training and discipline of the mysterious vital force, Prana, through a system of breath-control. This went a long way in reducing the Vikshepa or the mind oscillation. These four steps are therefore the preparation leading up to the actual Yoga of "Vritti-Nirodha," whereby you give battle to the mind in its own element. The higher Yogic processes of Pratyahara, Dharana and Dhyana comprising the fifth, sixth and the seventh stages in Raja Yoga, constitute a triple yet unitary process, a sort of three-in-one Sadhana by which the Yogi rings the death-knell to all Vrittis or mind movements. Mano-Nasa or Mano-Laya is the aim of the Yogi, by which he cuts the very ground from under Ahankara. Devoid of support or stay, the ego-consciousness has nothing to stand upon. Its sole support withdrawn, it meets its extinction. The extinction of the mind is a terrible prospect to the modern man who fears it as leading to the loss of personality. But this prospect did not worry the ancient Yogic Scientist who has assured that the transitory personality enabled by the mind (which was itself perishable) was a false and illusory personality and that its extinction would give rise to the awakening of the true and glorious spiritual personality of the being, with its exalted consciousness of Immortality and Supreme Plenitude. With the annihilation of the mind, there is the dawn of supramental-supra-consciousness to which hitherto the mind, the ego, constituted the sole bar.

Mind is the breeding ground for the germ of Ahankara, wherein it grows and develops into legion. Mind is the soil as it were, for the seed of Ahankara, wherein it sprouts, grows and develops into countless million branches and offshoots. The principle of Ahankara or the separatist individualistic consciousness is supported by the mind. And *vice versa*; the mind is supported by Ahankara. They are inseparable companions. The one cannot exist without the other. Because the Ahankara is there the mind principle springs into functioning. Because the mind is there it becomes possible for Ahankara to manifest. Thus they are interdependent. Upon the mind the dancer Ahankara dances variously. The ego-mind combination finds expression in nescience in the form of ceaselessly recurring mental Vrittis, deluded Adhyasa, Mamata and Abhimana. The technique of Yoga with its various processes (Sadhanas) liquidates this root-cause of all Samsara, i.e., the demon of ego-consciousness in its manifold expressions as Adhyasa, Vritti, Mamata and Abhimana. Though it is a fact that all the four Yogas are complementary to one another, and ultimately work out one integral process, yet without having any watertight compartmentalisation, they are, at the same time, found to direct their special attention and the attack, towards someone of these four prominent aspects in which the ego-consciousness actively operates in the field of the individual's personality. The originators of the science and technique of Yoga formulated the four broad methods of

Jnana Marga, Raja Yoga, Bhakti Marga and Karma Yoga as psychological-cum-spiritual processes for freeing the Jiva from the bonds of Adhyasa, Chittavritti, Mamata and Abhimana, all of which constitute different modes or variants of the root principles of nescience manifest as the individualistic ego-consciousness. In doing this they have demonstrated a deep and wonderful insight into even the obscurest operations of the fourfold mind and the three Gunas that sway it. They have based the technique upon a full awareness of the existence of the laws of auto-suggestion, ceaseless positive assertion (Sajatiya-Vritti-Pravaha) of association of ideas, of Pratipaksha Bhavana (interaction of thought and counter-thought), creative power of concentrated thought, annihilation through inhibition (Vijatiya-Vritti-Nirodha), sublimation through psycho-spiritual superimposition and of nullification of the world-experience through dissociation of ego-consciousness from all extra personal objective factors impinging upon it from the field of phenomenal existence, the operation of the three Gunas as also the interrelation between Prana and mind. These have become enduring techniques for the attainment of self-perfection and their scope has been found to be universal because of the fact that the sage-seers responsible for them based them upon their intuitive knowledge of the fundamental composition of the human being and his physical, mental, psychic and spiritual nature.

It is to be clearly borne in mind that the final attainment of Yoga is fully supramental and purely spiritual in content. But through its ultimate reaches the process culminates in a true and entirely unalloyed spiritual experience, yet in its basal anatomy the process of Yoga is doubtless psychological. There is no definite or sharp dividing line between its earlier phases that are well grounded in the field of psychology and its later evolution into a higher realm when with the advancement in spirituality the individual draws progressively closer to the experience of pure consciousness *per se* shorn and devoid of all the lower and lesser limiting modes of the Tamoguna-ridden and Rajoguna-ridden fourfold mind. The one gradually merges into the other smoothly and naturally at some stage in the spiritual life of the seeker, which stage may and does start differently from individual to individual and for which no arbitrary period can be laid down. And even here throughout the life of Yoga, elements of both phases, psychological, as well as spiritual are found to be present and encroaching upon each other in varying degrees all the while. Thus we may find a purely spiritual item of Yoga Sadhana form part of the routine Abhyasa of the raw neophyte. Similarly, too, it may be that a highly advanced spiritual practicant and Yogi makes use of a very ordinary and seemingly trifling psychological expedient to aid him in some advanced spiritual process. Thus it will be seen that the technique of the different systems of Yoga, far from being any superstitious process blindly followed by an unenlightened people, is in effect a well-conceived set of vital and psycho-spiritual practices based upon sound knowledge of the nature and workings of the mysterious human mind and the 'Gunas' in all the varied phases in which they have their play in the individual. The above is an attempt made to throw some light upon the inner anatomy of certain of the prominent aspects of Yoga, Bharatavarsha's ancient yet enduring system of spiritual perfection and Self-realisation. It is not claimed as being either final or exhaustive, but its main purpose is to bring to the modern man a correct estimation and the realisation of the true worth of the Great System of Yoga.

CHAPTER ONE
FOUNDATIONS OF SADHANA

PREREQUISITES OF SPIRITUAL SADHANA

I

I will dwell here upon the main qualifications necessary for launching upon the actual Sadhana. All the ancient saints, seers, men of God that have had intuitive experience of the Truth have been declaring to all mankind the great bliss, the vast power and knowledge that can be experienced if only man would turn from sensual sinful life and strive for the higher divine life. Yet we see today that man is as much immersed—if not more—in worldliness as he was centuries ago and the state of mankind is as apathetic and lethargic towards these questions of a life in the spirit as it was at the beginning of creation. Why is it that in spite of the clarion call of very many great seers, the confident assurance of the scriptures, the repeated experiences of man himself in failing miserably to attain happiness amidst external physical world, man is again and again being deceived? Why is it that man has not yet learnt to take to Sadhana? We read hundreds of spiritual books; we attend discourses; we convene gatherings as during the Sadhana Week. After years of intense study of spiritual books, contact with saints, after hearing these things again and again, yet man does not actually do anything. Because he does not have a deep and abiding faith in the admonitions of saints, in the scriptures, in the words of those who have trodden the path and attained bliss. His faith in external objects is something more real to him. If only man did really believe in these great ones he would certainly be induced to act up to their words. It is this basic lack of faith in man that is at the root of his failure to do Sadhana. Sadhana is necessary; but man will not do it because he does not really believe in its necessity. Man believes that for his happiness money is required. Man believes that if only he will get a good job he will get money. Man believes that if he has good college education he will get this job; and through that money; and through that, happiness that he desires. Believing in it every parent sends his child to school and from a young age he is taught to believe that if he passes his examinations creditably he will get a good job, salary, motor cars, etc. The child believes in the words; he studies, passes the examinations and the remuneration he expects comes. Because he had a feeling, because he thought all these things were necessary he desired them. But ultimately, of course, it is the unfortunate experience of all men that this happiness they get is mixed up more than tenfold with pain. Man gets an anna of happiness and with it fifteen annas of pain, suffering, for which he did not bargain when he first set about searching for this happiness. Thus if man has faith in spiritual course of action he will act up to it. Lacking this faith he does not do Sadhana. If a man has to take up to Sadhana, if he really wants to obtain this bliss which is not mixed with pain, he will certainly have to repose faith. It may be called blind faith; but there is nothing like blind faith because all things on this earth go upon faith only and if man lives today it is on account of mutual trust and faith. A ten rupee note is a piece of paper and it is because you have the Asoka Chakra ensign on it, it will immediately get you whatever you want if presented at the bazaar. Because you have the faith in this piece of paper. If you do not have faith upon this paper, you would not have the confidence to start from the house; you would never be sure of reaching your destination. The doctor gives you a prescription on a piece of paper. If you do not have faith you will not take it from him. But the faith upon which all society is based makes you take his word, pay him money for his advice, take it to the chemist, get the medicine and you are cured. The entire social structure and order upon which mankind smoothly runs is based upon faith and trust. When you are prepared to put faith in mankind which is but a passing phenomena—those in whom you put your faith are dying before your eyes—when you are prepared to put faith upon these passing entities like mankind, why should you not put faith upon the very Creator of these things? Having first of all full faith in the words of the seers and known the necessity of Sadhana, what is the procedure, what is to be done next? You may have faith. Thousands of well-wishers may suggest good lines of action for your welfare and you may believe in them fully. If you do not put them into practice—if you do not begin to translate them into function—they will ever remain plans in the blue-print stage. If you don't set about procuring money, cement, bricks, various other building materials and labour, the whole construction will remain in blue-print only. It will not see the light of the day. After faith in Sadhana comes practice. You must set about *doing*. No question of believing. A *belief* must become an *act*. One must set about doing. Having reposed faith in the words of sages, you begin doing Sadhana. Once you commence Sadhana, the next important thing you should bear in mind is you should not easily give it up. *Perseverance* is of the utmost importance. All processes in this universe are gradual. They have got stages. Agriculture is gradual; it takes twelve months. You have to sow, water the field, cut out the weeds, and in course of time you will be able to take the grain. If you are impatient—if you sow the seed and as soon as it sprouts forth, you take it out—it will perish. If you want to go through all the stages and attain the end you must have patience and perseverance. A man who wants to lift a vessel from the well-water when the vessel is full, he begins to draw up the water upon the wheel; suddenly if he stops pulling, the vessel will fall back into the well. He will have to proceed with the drawing motion until the vessel is at the top. Persevere till the ultimate fruit is obtained. You must not give up. There is another important point that in spiritual Sadhana, man does not merely have to contend with the positive force. There are active forces that oppose him, that actually assail him and pull him down. Herein comes the necessity of the fourth important weapon in the hand—that is fortitude. While persevering, man has to have a little courage not to be easily shaken by the obstacles that assail him. He will have to brave the storm and proceed in spite of the difficulties and adverse conditions trying to cow him down, to push him off from the path of Sadhana. It is with fortitude he refuses to be discouraged and, relying upon the inner Self, he proceeds with the Sadhana. Ultimately he will attain the ideal for which he has been born upon earth; and while going through this process he will have to see that he keeps in mind the necessity of giving minute attention to all the small details upon the path because in every process all such small details of the process are to be attended to carefully. If any small detail is left out, thinking that it is superfluous, he will find that ultimately he has lost valuable time and labour. This delays progress. It is the conglomeration of small things that go up to achieve high ideals.

Therefore with firm faith, practical application, perseverance, careful attention to even small details and fortitude in trials, you must set foot and proceed on the path of Sadhana.

II

When we consider any question, a number of different aspects of the same question will have to be thought over if we are dealing with the matter so as to be complete. Usually it is some one of the aspects that gets the emphasis and others are missed because, according to the particular disposition of those who take up the subject, they lay stress upon certain aspects. It is natural when so many different Rishis have dealt in general about life—human life—what it constitutes, how it is impermanent, how its real goal is the achievement of Self-realisation or the vision of God, now, for instance, taking the Name of God, as the means to achieve this end, how Patanjali Maharshi has pointed out Yama, Niyama, Sama, Dama, etc., have to be practised, how we have to build the walls of Yama, Niyama, and the doors and windows of Sama, Dama to raise this mansion of Immortality. There is nothing you can call your own; everywhere life is impermanent; there is insecurity. Now these are all aspects; but then they have presented only the problem-side of the subject. There is the solution-aspect and here, too, the *theory* of the solution is one sub-aspect of this and the *practice* of the solution is yet another sub-aspect. When dealing with life, we put it as the problem of life, that is, sorrow, suffering, pain, and how to get rid of it, we should consider the solution, touch upon the various methods of Satsanga, taking His Name, Sama, Dama and Dharana. In the solution-aspect, the theory of the solution is present; but as spiritual aspirants, as sincere seekers, as all of you are, you want the practical side of the solution-aspect more than anything else. There are the two aspects. In books, for instance, there is the book that says, if you have got a certain trouble it can be cured by a course of such and such a medicine. This is like saying, "Vikshepa can be removed by Japa and Upasana." But there is another book which says—if you have got this trouble, procure so many grams of this medicine, purify it in this manner, mix it in this proportion, heat it up, let it be on the oven for so many minutes, mix it with such and such a thing—the detailed process of the solution is given so that anyone who reads it at once is able to act up to it. Information is different and complete explanation of the detail is different. Having now said that this practical aspect of the solution is all-important for earnest seekers, I shall put before you one or two points which are found to be most useful equipments for putting into practice this solution. When you actually start doing Sadhana, you find that various practical difficulties crop up. When you get the ingredients, supposing you grind them and find they do not mix properly, when you actually do certain things, some practical difficulties arise. These practical difficulties have to be dealt with on the spot. Thus, when we consider the aspect of Sadhana, we find one big difficulty for seekers, that is, they have to contend more with forces that are interior than forces that are exterior. For instance, among diseases we find that certain external conditions bring about certain diseases. We remove the external conditions by means of external forces—we clean the gutter; we spray the drain with anti-mosquito solution; we burn up refuse; we disinfect water; we inject people with anti-cholera vaccine; and we get over that disease. But here most of the forces you have to contend with are mental. Thus the big difficulty is that we cannot easily take the help of external agents to constantly keep a watch on these enemies as the Sanitary Department, for instance, and call them when they rise up. Therefore, while you carry on these spiritual practices like taking the Name of God, developing virtues, you have to develop a mental monitor; you have to train up a portion of the mind to act as a sort of ever vigilant guide. Immediately any forces come up to obstruct you; any bad thought, any anti-spiritual force; anything that is detrimental to your Sadhana crops up in your mental field; this mental monitor should be so trained that it should immediately strike and put down the adverse factor. This can come only through diligent cultivation and practice. Mind is so bad that every time you turn or direct it to a particular direction, the old Samskaras or Vrittis will ever be troubling you. Therefore, we have to put it down in a more severe manner. We have to get a mental monitor ready—which will at once check the anti-spiritual force that rises in him. If this mental monitor is kept, the process of Sadhana will be smoother; it will be greatly facilitated. This is like going through deep waters. This ship of a seeker is like the ship that goes into enemy waters which are sown with depth-charges and mines. These mines are under the surface of the water; they are potential destructive weapons. We have heard that early in the War the Germans used the magnetic mine. The enemy ship would at once attract it as the ship is constructed with metal—the mine would be drawn towards it and destroy the ship. There are magnetic mines without number in this deep ocean of Samsara where we have to steer the ship. For this the only method is we have to take the precautions as they did towards the magnetic mine. What they did was—they perfected a method of completely insulating the ship which rendered it safe against the magnetic mine. This insulation made the magnetic mine useless. It was not attracted, even though it was there and even though the ship passed near it. Thus, while going through the path of Sadhana, we have to see that we have insulated ourselves with the insulation of aspiration and trust in God. If ever your aspiration is always climbing upwards, these forces fail to be attracted towards you. Only when your aspiration is not upwards, when you are still in the plane of sensual pleasures and desires that it easily attracts the sense-objects towards you and the sense-objects destroy the spiritual progress that you are trying to make. Having insulated, there is another precaution we have to take. We should make that ideal the main interest of our life. The seeker may have a hundred interests according to the position in which he is placed, his family circumstances, the society, the environments; yet, if he will do what the military experts do—supposing they wished to direct the course of a certain apparatus—say a torpedo, rocket bomb—to a certain destination, they set its course before it starts. Thus, in whatever circumstances the seekers are placed, in whatever professions, in whatever society, family environments, by God, let them fix the purpose of their life as Moksha, to attain Self-realisation; let them so set up this dial, so strongly implant this idea into their mind and constantly remember it day and night as the setting of the compass in this machine. They will see even though here and there ups and downs may come, there may be temporary obstacles to the flight in that course, due to overwhelming external circumstances, this one being established in his ideal and constantly remembering it he is not shaken by the vicissitudes of life in his march towards the goal. While in this passing towards the goal, in spite of insulation against external forces we have to see through the whole process. Man has got to be constantly in the field of activity. Because circumstances are like that. Man has to work. While working naturally it is the tendency of the human mind to take the colouring of that thing with which it comes into contact—a man living in a smoky room will be affected by the smoke. He will have his clothing blackened. But there is one thing: even though the currents of Raga and Dvesha affect man, let us see that there is a constant force which will keep our inner state always divine, equipoised, spiritual; actions will be there and the forces will act upon you, but you must so develop the technique that you must not react. It is when the man reacts to the action of external forces that he fails. Therefore, trouble comes. You have the rapidity of the machine gun, an incredible number of shots are fired within the split-second and the barrel gets terribly heated. If there were no device to keep down the temperature of the barrel the machine gun would at once melt. They have perfected the technique of warfare—a flow of cold oil is made to circulate round the barrel and the temperature of the machine gun is kept down. While coming in contact with Raga, Dvesha, lust, anger and greed, we have to see the friction does not ignite us. Let us always keep handy the cooling balm of Bhagavan's Divine Name, and His reflection. Let us constantly keep this cooling balm ever close to us. Thus, it will ever keep our natures cool. It will not allow our natures to get heated. It will see that the spiritual equipoise is always kept. If there are certain vicious traits in man which he cannot escape, such things let him by a mere technique of transformation turn to his own use. During war the prisoners of war were caught; they were all enemies; but once they were caught as prisoners, they were made to work for our own benefit so that the soldiers of this nation may be fit. They were turned to the use of the victorious nation. We have got the nature of fault-finding. Everywhere we do not see the good. We always try to pick out defects. This is a great defect in spiritual aspirants; it retards spiritual progress. But this practice is there. Supposing the spiritual aspirant has it, let him not be very much upset about it. Supposing he turns this practice upon himself, he will see that this practice far from being an enemy, becomes his friend. He will have no time to think about the defects of others. He will be stunned in dealing with his own defects. Then he will see that even a mustard-seed of goodwill appear before his eyes because instituting a comparison with himself which is full of defects and shortcomings, he will find even small things in others a virtue.

THE THREE GOVERNING FACTORS OF SADHANA

Many people even after studying classic works on religion and philosophy, do not know what they should do in practice to attain the goal of life, viz., God-realisation, and they seek enlightenment on this. The three things essential for God-realisation are: (1) constant remembrance of God, (2) cultivation of virtues and (3) spiritualisation of all activities.

(1) **Constant remembrance of God:** There may be breaks in the beginning, but by repeated practice, gradually you can have constant remembrance. Constant *Namasmarana*, mental repetition of God's Name, alone is possible for the vast majority of people. Awakening of Kundalini and raising of *Brahmakara Vritti* are very, very difficult, but when the mind is purified, they would come automatically.

(2) **Cultivation of virtues:** Of all virtues Ahimsa (non-injury), Satya (truthfulness) and Brahmacharya (celibacy) are the most important. If one is established in one virtue, all other virtues will cling to him. Watch the *Vrittis*. Introspect. Develop purity in thought, word and deed. In the beginning, practise at least physical purity. Then mental purity will come by itself.

(3) **Spiritualisation of all activities:** Feel you are an instrument in the Lord's hands and that all the Indriyas (senses) belong to Him. Repeat the formula: "I am Thine; all is Thine; Thy Will be done." It is a beautiful formula for self-surrender. You may forget this formula and egoism may assert itself. But introspect again and again and find out your weakness. Try to be established in the feeling, "I am an instrument in the hands of the Lord." Remember the Gita verse:

SELF-SURRENDER

Yat karoshi yadasnasi yajjuhoshi dadasi yat;
Yat tapasyasi kaunteya tat kurushva madarpanam.

(Whatever you do, or eat, or offer in sacrifice, or give, or practise as austerity, do it as an offering unto Me.)

Praseeda devesa jagannivasa: "O God of gods! Resort for the world, have mercy." It is a formula more potent than or as potent as *pahi mam, palaya mam, prachodayat*—these are all tremendous formulae. They are very powerful. So again and again remember them and their significance.

Sri Ramah saranam mama, Sri Krishnah saranam mama, Harih saranam—these are potent Saranagati Mantras.

FOUNDATIONS OF SADHANA

Saranagati is taking refuge in the Lord, or self-surrender unto Him.

Karpanyadoshopahatasvabhavah
Prichchhami tvam dharmasammudhachetah;
Yat sreyah syat nischitam bruhi tanme
Sishyasteham sadhi mam tvam prapannam.

(My heart is overpowered by the taint of weakness; my mind is confused about duty. I ask Thee. Tell me decisively what is good for me. I am Thy disciple. Instruct me, who has taken refuge in Thee.—Gita II-7). This is a Satguru-Saranagati Mantra.

Sarvadharman parityajya mamekam saranam vraja,
Aham tva sarvapapebhyo mokshayishyami ma suchah.

(Abandoning all duties, take refuge in Me (the Lord) alone; I will liberate thee from all sins, grieve not.—Gita XVIII-66)

These are all Saranagati formulae. In the Eighteenth Chapter of the Gita there is a Sloka:

INSTRUMENTALITY

Yasya nahamkrito bhavo buddhiryasya na lipyate,
Hatvapi sa iman lokan na hanti na nibadhyate.

(He who has no egoism, whose intelligence is not tainted by (the obsession of) good or evil, even if he kills the whole world, he neither kills nor is bound by the action.—Gita XVIII-17) Krishna said this to Arjuna when the latter shied away from the battle to which he was duty-bound as a soldier when challenged by the aggressor.

Remember these Slokas. You will have the spirit of Saranagati. You will feel that the Lord is in you, and you are in the Lord.

After the day's work, offer whatever you have done to God. Do not identify yourself with actions. Feel that you are doing your duty as a detached instrument of the Lord's benevolence.

Kayena vacha manasendriyairva buddhyatmana va
                    prakritessvabhavat,
Karomi yadyat sakalam parasmai Narayanayeti
                    samarpayami.

Offer all actions and their fruits to God. Then you will not be bound. In this way you should spiritualise all your activities. Feel that the whole world is a manifestation of the Lord and you are serving the Lord in all names and forms, and whatever you do—your actions and the results thereof consecrate to the Lord. Then your heart will be purified and will be ready to receive the divine light and grace.

SUREST METHOD

Therefore, practise the three requisites—constant remembrance of God, spiritualising your activities and cultivating virtues.

These three are very important. Practise them. This is the easiest, the quickest and the surest method for attaining God-realisation.

Esha sarveshu bhuteshu gudhatma na prakasate;
Drisyate tvagryaya buddhya sukshmaya
sukshmadarsibhih.

(This Atman is hidden in all beings, but it is seen only by subtle seers through their sharp and subtle intellect.)

The intellect should be razor-sharp if you wish to understand the *Brahma Sutras* properly. All are not meant for it. Even then practical experience is essential. Therefore, to the vast majority, constant remembrance of the Lord, spiritualisation of all activities and cultivation of virtues—Ahimsa, Satya, Brahmacharya—form the most important part of Sadhana. These also constitute the noble eightfold path of Lord Buddha. These also correspond to the "Sermon on the Mount" of Lord Jesus. These are the essentials in all religions. So, kindly practise these, and attain God-relisation. Love all. Be good and do good. May Lord bless you all!

PRIMARY PRINCIPLES OF SADHANA AND THEIR PERVERSIONS

The path of the spiritual aspirant verily lies through a bewildering jungle of difficulties and dilemmas of problems and paradoxes. One of such vexing paradoxes is that your mind is both your best friend as also your bitter enemy. Mind becomes a true friend only after being gradually trained to be so. Mind begins to be really helpful after the aspirant has progressed sufficiently in spiritual Sadhana. Until then it should be regarded as a troublesome and treacherous enemy inside us. It is extremely diplomatic, cunning and crooked. It is an arch-deceiver. One of the master-strokes of the mind's artfulness is to make the aspirant feel and smugly imagine that he knows his mind perfectly well and cannot be led away by it and at the same time to delude him totally. The mind has the knack of making the unwary aspirant confidently think himself its master, while it makes a hopeless fool of him. Its deceptions are subtle.

You have heard the saying, "The devil can quote scriptures for its purpose." Similarly the mind can use a virtue to indulge in a vice. It has an inborn inclination to perversion. It can even take the support of a perfectly good principle seemingly to justify the most unprincipled sort of action. Unless it is scrutinised dispassionately its tricks are never fully discovered.

Certain of the perversions usually noticeable are described below. This will be valuable to sincere aspirants who are eager to study their minds and eliminate defects and shortcomings. These are extremely useful tips specially in the working field, for aspirants engaged in active Seva in the midst of other people.

Sadhakas are told, "Keep up Matri-bhava or Devi-bhava when you move with women." This is a grand principle to safeguard your purity and spiritual progress. But this does not tell you, "Move with women;" nor does this advice mean that if you try to have this attitude then you may go on freely mixing with the opposite sex without any limit or restraint. The mind will ask, "Why not? What if I do? To retreat from their presence is sheer timidity. No fear when you do so with Devi-Bhava!" Beware, O Aspirant, beware of this tendency! Divine Bhava is not a licence to throw away all restrictions of the Sadhaka's path. The permanent injunction for Sadhakas is to totally eschew all contact with the opposite sex. When unavoidably such contact becomes necessary, then, "Have Matri-bhava; have Devi-bhava" etc., are prescribed. Also this is to caution the aspirant not to hate women or become a misogynist. Women should be reverenced but from a safe distance. Let not Devi-bhava, etc., be taken to mean that you should be all the time in the midst of them. Watch your mind!

Then there is the advice which says, "You may hiss but not bite." This safe counsel was given to a fabulous snake which in a too extreme excess of piety became so totally docile and harmless that it got severely man-handled by a set of mischievous urchins. It was given as an example to over-timid householders and people struggling in the very midst of the harsh *realities* of competitive 'Vyavaharic' life. Here an overdose of 'Avanty-brahmin'-like humility might well make life impossible amidst the Asuric elements abounding in the world. Therefore, just an outward show of pugnacity may be countenanced in so far as this does not affect your basic goodness and brotherhood. *But this policy is not for the spiritual aspirant in the path of Sadhana and Nivritti.* Definitely no. Let aspirants take heed of these words. The Sadhaka is neither to 'bite' nor is he to 'hiss' even. This 'hissing' business will soon become a part of your nature. You will soon find yourself hissing for everything, at everything, at everyone, in and out of season. This hiss will include every variety of rudeness ranging from hot argument, sharp retort, curt reply to angry glaring, shouting and abuse. Thus, short of physical violence and fight, every type of verbal brutality will be put into the "hissing" category. This will ultimately lead to spiritual ruin. The mind is ever waiting to take advantage of even the least concession shown to it. Its natural tendency is to go downward. O Aspirant, do not bite or even 'hiss.' Be humble, be sweet, be gentle. Be firm but be soft, polite and courteous. If you wish to 'hiss' then 'hiss' at your own mind. Thrash the ego. Fight the Shadripus. Watch the mind!

Another victim to perversion is the piece of advice: "Be resolute. Stick to your principles. Never budge an inch"—the best possible advice to a sincere Sadhaka, but unfortunately often made the basis for the worst possible trait, i.e., obstinacy. This is a Tamasic trait. But the mind will make believe that you are manifesting Atma-bala or a divine determination. This is its work—to make him cling tightly to his ego. Hence this deception. But the careful aspirant must discern the difference between Sattvic Nishtha and sheer stubbornness. Atma-bala is not a cheap commodity to be got without a great deal of earnest struggle, discipline and will-culture. Determined adherence is advocated in respect of truly high and noble principles and not of self-conceited notions. By all means stick to spiritual Yogic Niyamas but avoid becoming obdurate in nature. Do not be deceived. Watch your mind!

"Speak the truth always. Be frank." Thus is the Upadesa. This means when you are required to talk then speak only the truth. It does not at all mean that you must go about telling everyone to his face what exactly you think of him or her. This is unwarranted behaviour. Under the garb of frankness to give free expression of opinions without caring for other peoples' feelings is not 'Arjava' or frankness or straightforwardness. At the least it is thoughtlessness; at its height it is sheer brutality. It does not bespeak well of an aspirant. The same teacher who tells you "Speak the truth; be frank!" also tells you to have *"Mita Bhashana, Madhura Bhashana"* moderate and sweet speech. Mind can even make you utilise frankness in order to express mild insult. An unpleasant truth is better left unsaid. If it becomes absolutely necessary and unavoidable then say it sweetly and with humility. "Not to hurt and wound others' feelings" is as equally important as speaking truth. Satya and Ahimsa must go together. Study thyself. Watch the mind!

Then there is the truism i.e., "Vairagya is really a mental state, mental detachment." The mind takes hold of this definition to justify a heedless sensual life without self-restraint or principle. The argument will always be, "Oh, I am not attached to all this. I can rise above it in a moment. I enjoy it as a master. Mentally I am detached." Contact with Vishayas has toppled down even Tapasvins like Visvamitra. Therefore, do not take Vairagya lightly. Cultivate Vairagya diligently. Safeguard your Vairagya carefully. Be vigilant. Watch the mind!

The caution not to go to extremes in Tapasya also gets a like fate. Man's normal nature is sensuous. The mind wants comforts and hates austerity. The indiscriminating aspirant conveniently ignores the qualifying adjective "extremes" in the advice quoted above and views all 'Tapasya' with disfavour. The result is to degenerate into luxury, lose even the minimum Titiksha and become a slave to a hundred wants. The warning is against *foolish extremes* but to a Sadhaka in the early stages a certain degree of austerity is essential for development. The mind will suggest so many justifications. It will bring the Gita to its side and show that Lord condemned Tapas. O aspirant, the Lord condemned '*Tamasic* Tapas'. He recommended Sattvic austerity of body, speech and mind. Reflect carefully. Always watch the mind!

"Take care of essentials. Do not pay too much attention to non-essentials." The above too serves as a handle for the mind to deceive the aspirant. If you have to follow this advice, first try to understand what is essential and what is non-essential. The idle nature of man is to loath following any sort of Niyama and set-lines of Sadachara. Therefore, everything is dismissed at a stroke as 'non-essential'. Then what remains, God only can say. The only 'essential' would seem to be to do what the mind likes. The Sadhaka must think what a spiritual instruction really means and then why it is given. Moreover essentials and non-essentials vary according to the stage of development of the spiritual aspirant. What may be unnecessary for an aspirant at a later stage may well be essential to him now. Do not throw away precious grain with the chaff. Watch the mind!

Finally the most dangerous deception played by the mind is in connection with Sadhana itself. The very Sadhana that is adopted by the aspirant to transfigure and divinise his life is converted into a prop and a field for the play of ego and senses. It is very difficult to break out of this ensnaring net without great earnestness and sincere endeavour. It is this vitiation of Sadhana that keeps the Sadhaka 'struck', as it were, on the path, arresting progress for years together. For example a youthful Sadhaka with sweet voice and musical talent naturally takes to Kirtan and Bhajan as his Sadhana. Art always attracts admirers. He is in demand at all auspicious functions. He gets popular amongst Satsangas. The subtle mind now spreads the net. The Kirtan becomes sweeter day by day. New songs and tunes are added to his musical repertory. Without his being aware the Kirtan has become a means to attract others to himself and to maintain the popularity. Thus the Sadhana becomes double-purposed—primarily for God's Darshan and side by side for worldly attraction. The result is the extraordinary phenomenon of the Sadhaka caught in his Sadhana and instead of Mochana (liberation) the quality of Sadhana becomes Bandhana (bondage). Maya is wonderful, indescribable. Her ways are mysterious and inscrutable.

Take Nishkamya Karma Yoga. Serving and helping others for no return is something unheard of in the purely Vyavaharic world. Naturally the disinterested Sevak is regarded as an exceptional being. All doors are open unto him. Many bring their troubles to him, open their hearts and freely confide even intimate problems. They, of course, take it for granted that the spiritual aspirant is perfectly pure in every respect. Here the Sadhaka walks upon the 'razor-edge' of life. The mind is the devil. Through the very intimacy of contacts in the Seva field, pleasure-centres are created and sensuousness gets scope in this Seva 'Sadhana'. Vanity and carnality get catered to and the aspirant appears to take a keen interest in the Nishkama Seva. But a ruthless search of the mind will reveal that the keenness and interest in the Karma Yoga Seva is as much for the sense-indulgence to be had in the Seva as for the Seva itself. So the mind destroys the Sadhana.

Aspirants practising Titiksha many a time stick on to the Titiksha for similar subconscious reasons. His endurance will earn for him a reputation. He will be regarded as extraordinary. So even after the Titiksha Sadhana *has served its purpose* he will keep on with it for continuing the status it has granted him. Another Sadhaka will under the idea of being indifferent towards the body and its needs, neglects to shave even. This will be quite sincere and bonafide in the beginning. But the long hair and beard that results out of this 'Udasinata' will prove the instrument for Maya to lay hold of the aspirant. The hair will be found to beautify his appearance. He loathes to part with it. Thus the former 'Udasinata' will be replaced by careful combing of the hair, application of oil, peeps into the mirror, dressing to suit the style of the hair, new mannerisms, etc. Thus in a trice will delusion spring upon you and overpower you like the tiger does its prey. Likewise Hatha Yogic exercises get misused to sustain gluttony; Vajroli is used for Vyabhichara and Yoga is made to serve Bhoga. All these perversions arise out of the mischief of the unregenerate mind. Therefore *watch* the *mind*.

The most extraordinary part of all this is that the mind will not allow you to take the above lessons seriously. It will still say, "O you are all right. This is not meant for *you*. Don't mind all this. Carry on as you are." O aspirant, do not listen to it. Non-cooperate with the rogue. Take the lessons to heart.

To know where exactly one stands on the path is very difficult. The tricks of the mind are most subtle. Only constant Vichara will keep you alert and safe. Deep introspection alone can reveal a little of the mysterious workings. Probe and probe into the mind. Do not be lenient to the mind. The mind will try to compromise with you. Relentlessly hunt out its hidden motives. Subject yourself to keen self-analysis every day without fail. Oust all sentiments in this process. Become an intelligent, serious and earnest self-C.I.D. Carry on a ceaseless search and a vigorous enquiry inwardly. Put your mind on the dissecting table of Vichara. Pray for the Grace of the Guru who alone can vanquish the mind and enable you to master it. Pray to the Lord to illumine your intellect with the light of knowledge. Watch the mind. Watch and pray. Thus alone, through introspection, analysis, discrimination, vigilance and prayer can you understand the subtle jugglery of this wonderful thing called 'mind' and transcend its deceptions and tricks.

ABHYASA: THE FIRST PHASE OF SADHANA

Abhyasa or practice is the effort to secure steadiness of the modifications of the mind. The effort to restrain all the Vrittis of the mind and to make the mind steady like the jet of a lamp in a windless place is called Abhyasa. To drive back the mind to its source—Hridaya Guha and get it absorbed in Atman is Abhyasa. To make the mind inward and to destroy all its outgoing tendencies is Abhyasa. And this practice should be done for a long time without any break and with perfect devotion.

Through Abhyasa you will have to change the outgoing Vishaya Vrittis of the mind. Without the Vrittis of the mind you cannot enjoy sensual objects, and if the Vrittis along with Samskaras are controlled, Manonasa or the annihilation of the mind follows.

Abhyasa becomes fixed and steady when practised for a long time without any break and with perfect devotion. Constant, steady application is indispensable for perfect control of the mind and attainment of Asamprajnata Samadhi which alone can fry all the seeds of Samskaras. Therefore, constant and intense practice is needed for a long time. Then alone the wandering mind will come under your perfect control. Then alone wherever it is directed it will be ever at rest. Without practice nothing can be achieved. The practice should be accompanied by perfect faith and devotion. If there is no faith and regularity, success is impossible. Abhyasa should be continued till you get perfection.

FOUR POINTS FOR MEMORY IN SADHANA

1. REMEMBER THE PAINS OF SAMSARA.
2. REMEMBER DEATH.
3. REMEMBER THE SAINTS.
4. REMEMBER GOD.

1 and 2 will produce Vairagya. 3 will bring inspiration. 4 will

cause attainment of God-consciousness. Every aspirant should constantly bear these most important four points in memory.

BASES OF SPIRITUAL SADHANA

A man abandoning society and activity as evil and shutting himself up in seclusion, isolated from mankind so that he might grow in virtue and into sainthood through meditation, will in all probability be found to be less ready to overlook the transgressions of an erring brother than a practical humanitarian earnestly exerting himself in the field of sincere selfless service. If a monkey or a stray dog happens to enter his Kutir and upset his water-pot or run away with his rottis, the Ekantavasi Virakta will perhaps shout and curse the animal and nurse a grudge against it to the end of his days! Then, again, the admirable virtue of adaptability comes only by mixing and moving among men in many moods and dealing with different peoples of diverse temperaments. It is through selfless activity and service that one acquires the ability to accommodate oneself to the peculiarities of personalities and of places. If, thinking to experience oneness of Self and to feel universal brotherhood, you confine yourself to a solitary cell and take to repeating Vedantic formulae, you run the risk of becoming Tamasic instead and turning eccentric and intolerant. Slowly you will lose what good traits you had previously. It is to guard against this risk that we have the wise counsel "Let not virtue wither for want of its exercise."

It is evident that the recluse in retreat and the Sannyasi in seclusion may well learn a useful point or two from the Nishkama Karma Yogi and the humble Svayam Sevak. No doubt through the method of meditation one may develop several virtues of a subjective type, subjective in that they centre round and concern the Sadhaka's own immediate personality. Through constant contemplation subjectively one may acquire non-attachment to one's body, and imperviousness to environment or a victory over the Rajasic urge to wander aimlessly, etc. Restraint and self-denial too could be acquired to some degree.

On the other hand, it is only through selfless activity, unattached work and loving service that one can acquire precious gems of purity, patience and humility. Humility especially comes through service alone. In this connection it is of a great profit to remember one point of immense practical value, i.e., of all virtues humility forms the basis. It is only when a man is humble and feels that there is much that he does not possess and has to acquire that, there arises in him the eager desire to grow into those noble qualities he is deficient in. Here begins his systematic endeavour and attempt to acquire and possess them. The proud and arrogant man has little scope for growth, because he feels he knows everything. There is that self-sufficiency in his pride which leads him to think that there remains nothing for him to strive for and to acquire. Therefore it is said that humility is the fruitful source of all virtues and that everything that is kind and good naturally grows from it.

Generosity and kindness too are the outcome of active contact with the suppliant and the needy, the helpless, the wretched and the distressed. Herein lies the unique distinctive quality of Nishkamya Karma, works reverently done as worship of the Almighty. Moreover, certain noble traits exist in man in dual aspects, latent and manifest. For example, the latent quality of purity is manifest as chastity in actual life. Fearlessness becomes manifest as positive courage when a sudden crisis calls it forth, when a dangerous emergency arises. A habitual state of self-restraint manifests itself as a deliberate act of self-control in the face of an actual temptation or trait. So far as complete and balanced development of both the aspects is concerned, Karma Yoga becomes indispensable.

Again subjective virtues developed by a life of seclusion and isolation, to attain to fullness and perfection should be actively exercised. One must not rest satisfied in merely eliminating evil, in being virtuous in a negative way. There must be a positive passion for putting into practice the good in us for the enhancement of the joy and welfare of all creatures. Then alone these virtues justify themselves; they become, as it were, ripe fruits, fully blossomed flowers.

They will then expand in their breadth and from the individual circle gradually extend to all humanity, then of the whole universe and finally become all-embracing and cosmic.

Development and progress if they are to extend thus into infinity must be dynamic. On the path of moral and spiritual happiness, a life of quiescence carries with it the danger of stagnation setting in at some stage or other. This is the reason why many fail to reach ethical perfection even after years of seclusion and meditation. Selfless activity and loving service should therefore never be underestimated and neglected.

Finally one would do well to bear in mind an important point. It has been seen how humility forms the fundamental basis of all good. Then, to the virtues that are acquired with great toil and patient effort, it is humility, again, that acts as the sustainer and vigilant preserver. Humility is the shield and armour against the arch-enemy of the aspirant, moral and spiritual pride. For having progressed considerably in the path of virtue, the virtuous man will unconsciously fall a prey to vanity. An insidious feeling of self-approbation will creep in unnoticed. This will later manifest itself in the form of a sort of indulgent attitude and a lofty contempt for those who are not following a similar life. A constant humility kept alive by a ceaseless exercise of it in service is the only sure armour against this foe. It vigilantly protects the striving seeker in his quest after true and abiding happiness. He who effaces his little "self" through a life of motiveless, humble and loving service with Narayana Bhava obtains a unique happiness and bliss. Who can gauge the exquisite joy that he experiences! May all therefore realise the supreme importance of cultivating noble virtues.

May all clearly perceive the indispensable necessity of actively exercising them and readily and cheerfully become Nishkama Karma Yogins.

ASPECTS OF SPIRITUAL SADHANA

I

When your house is on fire how daringly you enter the house to take your child who is sleeping in the room! Even so you must be very courageous when you tread on the spiritual path. You must be absolutely fearless. You must not have the least attachment to your body. Then only you will have Self-realisation quickly. Timid people are absolutely unfit for the spiritual line.

If there are mangoes on the top of a big tree you do not jump all at once to pluck them. It is impossible. You gradually climb up the tree by getting hold of different branches and then reach the top of the tree. Even so you cannot jump all at once to the summit of the spiritual ladder. You will have to place your foot with caution in each rung of the ladder. You will have to practise Yama, Niyama, Asana, Pranayama, Pratyahara, Dharana and Dhyana. Then only you will reach the highest rung of the ladder of Yoga viz., Samadhi. If you are a student of Vedanta you will have to equip yourself with the four means first. Then you will have to do Sravana, Manana and Nididhyasana. Then only you will attain Brahma-Sakshatkara. If you are a student of Bhakti Yoga, you will have to practise the nine modes of Bhakti viz., Sravana, Kirtana, Smarana, Padasevana, Archana, Vandana, Dasya, Sakhya and Atma-Nivedana. Then only you will attain the state of Para-Bhakti.

If the chicken and fowl run hither and thither to eat various sorts of rubbish, what does the owner of the poultry do? He gives a slight tap on their heads and throws before them some grains to eat. Gradually they leave their habit of eating filth. Even so this mind runs hither and thither to eat filthy things and enjoy the five kinds of sensual objects. Give a tap on its head and make it taste gradually the spiritual bliss by practice of Japa and Meditation.

A Jivanmukta or a Bhagavata has lustrous eyes. He has a protrusion on the top of the head and Trikuti, the space between the two eyebrows. Whatever he says will be indelibly impressed in your mind. You cannot forget it till the end of your life. He possesses tremendous power of attraction. He will clear all your doubts in a marvellous manner. You will enjoy a peculiar joy and peace in his presence. All your doubts will be cleared in his presence. Silence is his language. He is very compassionate and free from selfishness, anger, greed, egoism, lust and pride. He is an embodiment of truth, peace, knowledge and bliss.

It takes a long time for the charcoal to catch fire but gun-powder can be ignited within the twinkling of an eye. Even so it takes a long time for igniting the fire of knowledge for a man whose heart is impure. But an aspirant with great purity of heart gets knowledge of the Self within the twinkling of an eye, within the time taken to squeeze a flower by the fingers.

Maya is a very huge saw. Lust, anger, greed, delusion, pride, jealousy, hatred, egoism etc., are the teeth of this huge saw. All-worldly minded persons are caught up in the teeth of this saw and are crushed. Those who are endowed with purity, humility, love, dispassion, devotion and enquiry are not hurt.

They escape through the divine grace. They pass smoothly below the saw and reach the other side of immortality.

A piece of ordinary white paper or coloured paper has no value. You throw it away. But if there is the stamp or the picture of the Asoka Chakra on the paper (currency notes) you keep it safe in your money purse or trunk. Even so an ordinary piece of stone has no value for you. You throw it away. But if you behold the stone-Murthy of Lord Krishna at Pandharpur or any other Murthy in shrines, you bow your head with folded hands, because there is the stamp of the Lord in the stone. The devotee superimposes on the stone-Murthy, his own Beloved and all the attributes of the Lord. Image-worship is very necessary for beginners.

II

Some Sadhakas do constant Sadhana in a mild manner; some do intense Sadhana for two hours in the morning and two hours at night. If you want to attain Self-realisation quickly you must do intense and constant Sadhana for a protracted period.

You may have Darshan of Lord Krishna face to face. You may talk to Him also several times. You may play and eat with Him also. But if you want to have final liberation you must have Atma-Sakshatkara. Nama Deva had Darshan of Lord Krishna several times and yet he was declared to be a half-baked saint by the potter-saint Gora Kumbhar. He had to go to Vishoba Khesar for attaining perfection and Kaivalya.

When you sit on an Asana for meditation you want to get up soon, not on account of pain in the legs but on account of impatience. Conquer this undesirable negative quality by developing patience gradually. Then you will be able to sit for three or four hours at a stretch.

During meditation you will be frequently talking to somebody mentally. Stop this evil habit. Have a careful watch over the mind.

An aspirant writes to me: "Somebody tapped at my door at 3 a.m. I woke up and opened the door. I saw Lord Krishna with crown on His head. He disappeared soon. I went through the lane in search of Him. I was not able to find Him out. Then I came back to my house and sat in front of my door till day-break to see Him again."

Cases of somnambulists or sleep-walkers are not uncommon. They dream even while standing and walking also. The above case might have been a pure case of somnambulism. You will have to be very careful in ascertaining the true nature of your spiritual experiences, whether it is a dream or an actual reality. Darshan of Lord Krishna is not so very cheap. Aspirants make mistakes in the beginning.

Just as you remove at once a pebble in your shoe that troubles you, so also you must be able to remove any tormenting thought from your mind at once. Then only you have gained sufficient strength in control of thought. Then only you have attained some real progress in the spiritual path.

An aspirant says: "I am able to meditate on one Asana for three hours. In the end I become senseless but I do not fall down to the ground." If there is real meditation you will never become senseless. You will experience perfect awareness. This is a negative undesirable mental state. You will have to get over this state by keeping up perfect vigilance.

Suppose the mind runs outside during meditation forty times within one hour. If you can make it run only 38 times, it is a decided improvement. You have gained some control over the mind. It demands strenuous practice for a long time to check the mind-wandering. Vikshepa Sakti is very powerful. But Sattva is more powerful than Vikshepa Sakti. Increase your Sattva. You can very easily control the oscillation of the mind.

When there is deep concentration, you will experience great joy and spiritual intoxication. You will forget the body and the surroundings. All the Prana will be taken up to your head.

If you find it difficult to concentrate your mind within a room come outside and sit in an open place or terrace or by the side of a river, or in a quiet corner of a garden. You will have good concentration.

When you are lying down in your bed, sometimes a big light will pass along your forehead. As soon as you try to behold the light by meditating on the sitting posture it may disappear. You may ask "How is it that I fail to catch the light by exertion, whereas it comes by itself when I am lying down without an effort?" The reason is you lost the concentration as soon as you sat for meditation by entry of Rajas.

Find out your centre. Dwell always in the centre. The centre is Atman or Immortal Soul. This centre is the Garden of Eden. This is your original abode. This is Param Dhama. You can be above care, worry and fear now. How sweet is this home wherein there is eternal sunshine and perennial joy!

O friend! wake up! sleep no more. Meditate. It is Brahma-muhurta now! Open the gate of the temple of the Lord in your heart with the key of love. Hear the music of the soul. Sing the song of Prem to your Beloved. Play the melody of the Infinite. Melt your mind in His contemplation. Unite with Him. Immerse yourself in the ocean of Love and Bliss.

III

The moment you think during meditation, "I am pure now. I do not get any evil thoughts as before," a whole battalion of evil thoughts will enter the conscious surface of the mind. But they will pass off soon. You are in the struggling stage now. A time will come when you will not entertain even a single evil thought. Meditation is a powerful enemy of evil thoughts. The evil thoughts think "We will be quelled soon. Our host has started the meditation. Let us pounce upon the man once more." Continue your meditation vigorously. Mists and clouds cannot stand before the sun.

It is difficult to fix your mind in the beginning on the whole picture of Lord Krishna, because all the rays of the mind are not collected. Sometimes you can visualise the face, sometimes the feet, sometimes the eyes. Fix the mind on any part of the picture which the mind likes best.

The mind has attraction for certain new words or names of towns or persons. Suppose you have come across certain new words or names of towns or persons such as "ecstasy," "Fyzabad," "John Herbert." If you sit for meditation the mind will repeat "ecstasy," "Fyzabad," "John Herbert." Sometimes it will sing some songs, repeat some old poems or Sanskrit Slokas which you got by heart during your boyhood. Watch the mind carefully and try to bring it back to the point or centre.

Winter is very congenial for vigorous meditation. You will not get tired even if you meditate for hours together, at a stretch. But in the morning hours laziness tries its level best to overpower you. If you cover yourself with one or two warm blankets you will feel quite comfortable. You do not want to get up in the early morning, even though the repeated alarm wakes you up again and again. You decide now "Let me sleep for fifteen minutes more and then let me start my meditation." Then you begin to cover nicely with the blanket certain exposed parts of the feet. You feel quite pleasant now. What is the net result? You begin to snore nicely and get up only after the sun has risen. Days, weeks and months will roll on like this. Every winter also passes away in this manner. Just at that time which is quite favourable for meditation, mind deceives you and overpowers you by sleep. Mind is a master-magician. He knows several tricks and illusions. Maya operates through mind. Mysterious is mind. Mysterious is Maya. Be on your alert. Be vigilant. You can control mind and Maya. Throw the blanket as soon as you hear the alarm. Sit on Vajra Asana. Do a few Pranayamas. Drowsiness will disappear.

When you meditate with open eyes you may see a friend in front of you and hear his voice also; but you may not be able to make out the person and his voice; because the mind is not attached to the ears or the eyes. If the mind is entirely withdrawn from the sensual objects, if the thoughts are annihilated, if likes and dislikes are destroyed, how can you perceive the world at all? You will become mindless. You will behold the Self only everywhere. All names and forms will vanish.

It is very difficult to fix the mind all at once on a point. The mind moves with a tremendous velocity. Just as the horse in a circus runs in a circle again and again, so also the mind runs in a circle again and again. Instead of allowing the mind to run in a big circle, make it run in smaller and smaller circles. Eventually it can be fixed on a point. You will have to catch hold of the mind through intelligent methods. Mere coercion and force will not do. It will make matters worse.

Sometimes you may become despondent and feel, "I have many weaknesses and defects. How can I eradicate them? How can I control this strong and impetuous mind? Will I get liberation or Nirvikalpa Samadhi in this very birth? I have not gained much even though I have practised meditation for the last 8 years." Do not be disheartened. Even if you have controlled one or two Indriyas, even if you have controlled some thoughts, half the battle is won. Control of even one thought or destruction of even one Vasana will give you mental strength. Every thought that is controlled, every desire that is destroyed, every Indriya that is subdued, every defect or weakness that is eradicated will add strength to the mind, will develop your will and take you one step nearer to the goal. Friend! Why then lamentation and despair? Fight bravely in the Adhyatmic battle-field. Become a spiritual soldier. Come out victorious and wear the spiritual laurels of divine wisdom, eternal peace and supreme bliss.

IV

Sometimes the mind will be sluggish or slothful. You cannot concentrate. It will refuse to work. The same vigorous mind may become sluggish in the latter part of concentration, just as the horse that was running with good speed in the beginning of the journey becomes sluggish in the end. Just as the driver freshens the horse by giving a little grass and water, so also you will have to freshen the mind with some elevating thoughts and discipline with undistracted attention.

If the mind is restless or wandering, sit in a quiet room. Or lie down in Savasana like a dead man for 15 minutes and relax the body and mind completely. Entertain some pleasant thoughts. Think of some beautiful flowers, the glaciers of the Himalayas, the blue expansive sky, the vast ocean or some beautiful scenery in Himalayas, or Kashmir or in any other place. Now you can sit again for meditation.

Sometimes the mind will revolt seriously. You will feel, "I have not gained much through Tapas, discipline and meditation. Let me break the vow of Brahmacharya. Let me give up entirely all dietetic discipline. Let me revel in sensual objects. Let me eat sumptuously." Do not yield. Coax or cajole the mind. Do vigorous Japa and Kirtan. Study the book "How to get Vairagya" or "Bhartrihari's Vairagya Sataka" again and again. Remember the pains of Samsara and the defects of sensual life. Remember the saints and their teachings again and again. Stand adamant. Be cautious. Be vigilant. Watch and pray. The rebellious mind will cool down gradually.

Sometimes the mind will be in a total passive state. There will be diversion of attention. The mind will be in a perfect blank state. If this state is continued for a short time you will merge into sleep. This is the state called Laya. This is a serious obstacle in meditation. Do 10 or 20 Pranayamas vigorously. Then chant Om loudly for 10 minutes. This state will vanish rapidly.

Even a pure Brahmachari will be troubled in the beginning by curiosity. He will be curious to know and feel what sort of enjoyment will the sexual enjoyment be. He thinks sometimes, "Let me have the carnal knowledge of a woman once. Then I will be able to root out this sexual impulse and desire completely. This sexual curiosity is troubling me very much." Mind wants to delude this Brahmachari. Maya havocs through curiosity. Curiosity is transmuted into a strong desire. Enjoyment cannot bring up satisfaction of a desire. Just as a tiger, man-eater, runs after human flesh even if it tastes once human blood, so also the mind which has once tasted sexual pleasure will be ever hankering after it. The wise way is to kill the wave of curiosity by Vichara or enquiry of that pure sexless Atman, renunciation of sexual desire totally and constant meditation, by thinking over the glory of Brahmacharya and the defects of an impure life.

Even in a blind man who is a celibate who has not seen the face of a woman, the sexual impulse is very strong. Why? This is due to the force of Samskaras or impressions of previous births which are embedded in the subconscious mind. Whatever you do, whatever you think, is lodged or printed or indelibly impressed in the layers of the Chitta or subconscious mind. These impressions can be burnt or obliterated only by the dawn of knowledge of Atman or the Supreme Self. When the sexual Vasana fills the whole mind and body the Samskaras assume the form of big Vrittis or waves and torment the poor blind man. This clearly proves that there is transmigration of soul.

Thought is the real action. But there is a great deal of difference between actually shooting a man and thinking to shoot a man, between actual copulation and thinking to have coitus with a woman.

Philosophically speaking, thinking to shoot a man, thinking to have copulation is the real act. Desire is more than the act. God gives fruits according to the motives of the man. Be pure in your thoughts. Then only you can enter the kingdom of God within. Then only the Lord will be enthroned in your heart.

The aspirant or Yogi in the cave in the Himalayas or a silent meditator in the plains thinks that he is very much advanced in spirituality. He looks with contempt at his brother who is plodding to reach the goal through untiring selfless service and meditation combined. The former may be rich in Vairagya and Titiksha. He may be proficient in the study of scriptures. He may be able to bear cold. He may be able to live on bread and *dhal* alone. He may be able to sit on one Asana at a stretch for a longer time. But he may be lacking in mercy, cosmic love, broad tolerance, generosity, courage, etc. He may not be able to bear heat, he may complain of strong Vikshepa, he may not be able to keep up a balanced mind when he comes to the plains. While the latter may possess his own special virtues and balanced mind and may excel the Yogi of Himalayas or the silent meditator of the plains in many respects. One should have excellence in all virtues. One should be able to bear heat and cold. Then only he will become a perfect sage. Equanimity is Yoga.

A worldly man has Abhimana for his wealth and position. He has great Moha for his children and wife. But a Sannyasi or a Yogi has very great spiritual and moral pride. He thinks and feels "I am superior to a householder. I am a great Yogi. I can meditate for 12 hours. I possess great purity, renunciation and dispassion." The Abhimana of a Sannyasi is more dangerous and powerful than the Abhimana of a worldly man and so more difficult for eradication.

The enquiry of 'Who am I?' is a difficult Sadhana. It can only be practised by one who has a strong, pure and subtle intellect, who is equipped with the fourfold means, who has a sound knowledge of the Vedantic Prakriyas, Pancheekarana, Neti-Neti doctrine, the processes of Anvaya-Vyatireka, Bhaga-Tyaga Lakshana, Adhyaropa Apavada, Dharmas of the five Kosas, nature of Atman, etc. The qualified student only will get the proper answer for the question 'Who am I?' during meditation. Otherwise the mind will delude the aspirant.

V

Just as the light is burning within the hurricane lantern, so also the divine light is burning within the heart. You can behold the divine light through your inner third eye or the eye of intuition by withdrawing the senses and stilling the mind.

In a cage of nine doors there dwelleth the little bird Jiva, the little illusory 'I'. He can come out of the cage of flesh if he annihilates 'I'-ness and 'mine'-ness and the Vasanas.

Even the stone can melt sometimes. But the heart of an egoistic man cannot melt. It is harder than flint or diamond or granite. But it can melt sometimes. It can be rendered soft as butter by constant, untiring service of humanity, Satsanga, Japa of God's Name and meditation.

How sweet is the Name of the Lord! How soothing and elevating are the Names of Hari, Rama, Krishna, Siva! The Name drives away your fear, anguish, sorrow and pain, and fills your heart with joy, peace, strength and courage. The Name is a healing balm to your wounded heart and tired nerves. The Name is manna or panacea or divine elixir that confers immortality and eternal bliss. Remember the Name of the Lord always. Sing His Name and associate it with your breath; you will be freed from the round of births and deaths.

The fruit of concentration is meditation. The fruit of meditation is realisation. The fruit of realisation is liberation. In concentration you gather all thoughts and fix the mind on one point or one idea. In meditation you have a continuous flow of one idea.

He who provides for the frog that lives inside the rock will look after you. Why this lack of faith! Have living, unshakable faith in the Lord and His Grace and be at ease, O beloved Ram!

He who speaks does not know. He who knows does not speak. Empty vessels make much sound. He who talks much, thinks little, does little.

Be cautious. Study the nature of people. Move very carefully with people. Do not be deceived. Have a knowledge of psychology. Know people by their behaviour, talks, looks, smile, gait. Know them by the food they take, the books they study, and the companions they keep.

You can gauge your spiritual growth by the careful study of your dreams. If you have no evil thoughts in dreams, if you get frequent visions of your Ishta Devata in dreams, if you repeat your Ishta Mantra even in dreams, if you do worship or Puja even in dreams, you have made great advance in the spiritual path.

There is no mention of either Kundalini or will in Yoga Sutras by Patanjali Maharshi or in any Vedantic book. A Jnana Yogi enters into Nirvikalpa Samadhi by raising the Brahmakara Vritti through meditation on the significance of Maha Vakyas such as *"Tat Tvam Asi,"* or *"Aham Brahma Asmi."* He never attempts to awaken the Kundalini Sakti. He can enter into Samadhi without awakening the Kundalini. But if he wants to manifest some physical Siddhis he awakens the Kundalini. By mere willing he awakens the Kundalini. He never practises

Pranayama, Asanas, Bandhas, Mudras or any Hatha Yogic Kriyas for this purpose.

You can have perfect or absolute non-attachment only when you realise the Self. During the course of Sadhana the mind will try its best to cling to one form or the other. Again and again you will have to cut ruthlessly all sorts of attachments with the sword of non-attachment—*Asanga Sastrena Dridhena Chhitva* (Gita XV-3).

You must have the Bhava that Atman, Isvara, Devata, Mantra are one. With this Bhava you will have to repeat your Guru Mantra or Ishta Mantra. Then alone you will have Mantra-Siddhi or God-realisation quickly.

The best flower that can be offered to the Lord is your heart. Penetrate more deeply into the infinite domain of Kailasa, the Kingdom of illimitable bliss and boundless peace within.

May you be in direct communion with the Lord, thy Ishtam, guide, supreme refuge and solace!

VI

Pure as the snow of Himalayas, bright as sun-light, expansive as the sky, all-pervading as the ether, unfathomable as the ocean, cool as the waters of the Ganga in Rishikesh, is the Immortal Atman, the Substratum for this world, body, mind and Prana. Nothing is sweeter than this Atman.

Purify your heart and meditate. Plunge deep in your heart. Dive deep into the innermost recesses. You will find it. If you search in deep water only you will find the pearl of Atman. If you keep only to the shore, you will find broken shells only.

Just as rain exists in clouds, butter in milk, fragrance in flowers, so also this Atman lies hidden in all these names and forms. He who has a pure, one-pointed, sharp, subtle intellect will behold the Self through constant and intense meditation.

He who looks upon a woman as a son does his mother and also keeps aloof from her, he who has controlled lust and anger, he who has no attraction for the perishable objects of this universe, he who is practising meditation regularly will soon reach the Param Dhama or the Abode of Supreme Peace from where there is no return to this Mrityuloka or the world of death.

The sugar and the sugar toys, pot and the earth, iron nail and the sword, water and foam, the earrings and gold are not two things. They are one. Even so when real knowledge dawns, the manifold universe is nothing but Atman; the individual soul and Supreme Soul become identical.

Self fills the whole world. All is Self. There is nothing which is not in you. What should you desire, then, when you have realised the Self, because for you there is no object to be desired?

The old vicious Samskaras can be changed and destroyed. Mind is nothing but a bundle of Samskaras. Fight with them bravely. Fight bravely not for bread, nor for money, nor for name and fame, but for acquiring the Kingdom of Self or the vast domain of eternal peace, through destruction of worldly Samskaras. Chivalrous soldier is he who fights in the Adhyatmic inner battle-field with his old Samskaras with the sword of dispassion and armour of discrimination but not he who fights in the battle-field with his enemies with machine-guns. Fight with the Samskaras is more serious, more dangerous, more frightful than the external physical fight. The basis for the spiritual soldier is Sattva but the basis for the worldly soldier is a mixture of Rajas and Tamas. Rama and Ravana fought. Rama was Sattvic but Ravana was Tamasic. It is easy to go on an expedition to ascend the summit of Mount Everest. It is easy to scale the heights of Nanda Parvat. It is easy to reach the peak of Mandhata. But it is difficult to ascend the peak of the spiritual Himalayas of the soul. The undaunted aspirant armed with patience, perseverance, tranquillity, and courage slowly ascends peak after peak, subdues the Indriyas one by one, controls the thoughts one by one, eradicates the Vasanas one by one and eventually reaches the summit of Self-realisation or divine glory. Glory to such exalted souls or spiritual heroes!

Neophytes should not sit for meditation in a room just by the side of the kitchen. The mind will think of palatable dishes and cause distraction. The sweet aroma of certain preparations will tickle the olfactory nerves of the nose and glossopharyngeal nerves of the tongue.

If you keep a cup of hot tea and some sweetmeats in front of you and if you begin to study Upanishads or meditate, you will not have deep concentration. A portion of the mind will be ever thinking of the tea or sweetmeats. Neophytes should remove all such minor causes of distraction before they sit for meditation.

Treat all alike. Serve the poor and the sick. Cut off all sorts of attachment. Help the needy. Crush appetites. Eradicate the Vasanas and egoism. Abandon carnal pleasures. Meditate and realise the oneness of the Self. Help others also to acquire the knowledge of the Supreme Being.

The sage or a Jivanmukta inspired with Divine Spirit, intoxicated with the immortal nectar, filled with the infinite Atman, endowed with an equal vision and balanced mind beholds only the Self everywhere and embraces all with pure love.

SADHANA: ITS TECHNIQUES OF APPLIED PSYCHOLOGY

Watch all your feelings very carefully. Suppose you get a gloomy feeling. Take a small cup of milk or tea. Sit calmly. Close your eyes. Find out the cause for the depression and try to remove the cause. The best method to overcome this feeling is thinking of the opposite. Positive overcomes negative. This is a grand effective Law of Nature. Now think strongly of the opposite of gloom. Think of cheerfulness. Feel that you are in the actual possession of this quality. Again and again repeat this formula: 'Om Cheerfulness' mentally. Feel "I am ever cheerful." Begin to smile and laugh several times. Sing; sometimes that can elevate you quickly. Singing is very beneficial to drive off gloom. Chant OM loudly several times. Run in the open air. The depression will vanish soon. This is the Pratipaksha Bhavana method of Raja Yogins. This is the easiest method. The method of driving gloom by force—by willing, by assertion, by command—taxes the 'will' very much although it is the most efficient method. It demands great strength of will. Ordinary people will not succeed. The method of displacing or dislocating the negative feeling by substituting the opposite, positive feeling, is very easy. Within a very short time, the undesirable feeling vanishes. Practise this and feel. Even if you fail several times, continue. You will be successful after some sittings and some practice.

You can treat in the same manner other negative feelings as well. If there is the feeling of anger, think of love. If there is harshness of heart, think of mercy. If there is dishonesty, think of honesty, integrity. If there is miserliness, think of generosity and generous persons. If there is Moha (infatuation), think of discrimination and ATMIC VICHARA. If there is pride, think of humility. If there is hypocrisy, think of frankness and its invaluable advantages. If there is jealousy, think of nobility and magnanimity. If there is timidity, think of courage, and so on. You will drive off the negative feelings and will be established in a positive state. Practice of a continued type is essential. Be careful in the selection of your companions. Talk very little and that, too, on useful matters.

EASY METHOD OF SADHANA IN WORLDLY ENVIRONMENT

It is due to the veil of ignorance that man has forgotten his essential Divine Nature—Sat-Chit-Ananda State. It is not necessary for him to renounce the world and hide himself in the Himalayan caves to regain his lost Divinity. Here I present a very easy method of Sadhana by which, he can attain God-consciousness even while he is living in the world amidst multifarious activities. You need not have a separate place or room and time for meditation. Close your eyes for a minute or two once in every two or three hours and think of God and His Divine Qualities such as Mercy, Love, Peace, Joy, Knowledge, Purity, Perfection and so forth during work and repeat mentally Hari Om or Sri Ram, or Rama Rama or Krishna Krishna or any Mantra according to your taste. You should do this even during night time, whenever you happen to get up from bed to pass urine or on any other account. Though you are unable to get up during sleep specially for this purpose, you should do this practice at least occasionally when you slightly change your posture of sleep. This sort of habit will come only by practice. Feel that the body is a moving temple of God, your office or business house is a big temple or Brindavan, and every activity, walking, talking, writing, eating, breathing, seeing, hearing, etc., are offerings unto the Lord. Work is worship. Work is meditation.

Give up expectation of fruits and idea of agency, the feeling of "I am the doer," "I am the enjoyer." Feel that you are an instrument in the hands of God. He works through your organs. Feel also that this world is a manifestation of the Lord or Visva Brindavan and your children, wife, father, mother are the images or children of the Lord. See God in every face and in every object. Have a cool, balanced mind always. If you develop this changed angle of vision and Divine Bhava in daily life by protracted and constant practice, all actions will become Yogic activities. All actions will become worship of the Lord. This is quite sufficient. You will get God-realisation quickly. This is dynamic Yoga. This is a very powerful Sadhana. I have given you a very easy Sadhana. Hereafter you should not bring your lame excuse and say, "Swamiji, I have no time to do spiritual practices." Even if you have a little practice of the above Sadhana for three months you will notice that you are a changed being altogether.

Write daily for half an hour in a notebook your Ishta Mantra observing Mouna and without turning to the other sides. Write down in bold types in slips of paper "Speak Truth," "OM Courage," "OM Purity," "I must realise God now," "Time is most precious," "I will be a true Brahmachari," "Brahmacharya is Divine Life," "I am an embodiment of Courage, Purity, Mercy, Love and Patience" and fix them in the bedroom, dining hall, front-rooms and verandahs. Keep some slips in your pocket and diary also. This is an easy way for developing virtuous Divine Qualities.

SOME SECRETS OF SADHANA

Through the practice of Pranayama, the Sadhaka can attain long life. A healthy man takes 14 or 16 breaths in a minute. The number of breaths increases during sleep, exercise, running, etc. Retention of breath through the practice of Kumbhaka bestows longevity to the Yogic student. The lesser the number of breaths, the more is the duration of life.

The number of breaths is more in a dog and a horse. It is nearly fifty in a dog and so its duration of life is about 14 years. It is thirtyfive in a horse. So its duration of life is 29 to 30 years. An elephant breathes about 20 times in a minute and so it lives about a hundred years. A tortoise breathes five times in a minute and therefore it lives about four hundred years. A snake breathes twice or thrice in a minute. It lives for 500 to 1000 years.

The fewer the desires and wants, the lesser the number of breaths and *vice versa*. He who practises Japa, meditation, Brahmacharya and studies religious books or holy scriptures will have lesser number of breaths and more concentration. Lesser number of breaths means increase in concentration, rich inner spiritual life in Atman and more peace.

The Surya Mandal or the fire is in the Nabhi or the navel. The Chandra Mandal or the sphere of Amrita is a little below Ajna Chakra. Amrita or nectar dribbles and the Agni devours it, consumes it. So you have a short duration of life. If you practise Vipareetakarani Mudra or Sarvanga Asana you can conquer death, you can attain long life. In this posture the fire Mandal comes above. The nectar that dribbles from the Chandra Mandal cannot be swallowed by the Agni. Hence the nectar nourishes the Nadis and the body, and life is prolonged. Therefore it is essential that everybody should practise this vital Asana for keeping up good health and attaining longevity.

This is physical Vipareetakarani Mudra. Through the practice of Jnana Vipareetakarani Mudra you can attain immortality and eternal bliss. You can have Brahma Jnana. What is the Jnana Vipareetakarani Mudra? Have a changed angle of vision. Have a changed outlook. Behold Brahman or the one Self everywhere by negating the names and forms. Practise this again and again.

Man cannot have a strong mind unless the rays of the mind which go in diverse ways are stopped and made to converge to a point, as in the case of the rays of the sun through a magnifying glass. You can burn many things by centralising the rays of the sun through the magnifying glass. In the same way by centralising the scattered or dissipated rays of the mind and converging them on one point, through dispassion, discrimination and concentration, you can work wonders. You can perceive the marvels of the hidden innermost Self or the Supreme Atman.

Decrease in urine, faeces and phlegm, Tejas or brilliance in the eyes and face, beautiful complexion, lightness of body, sweet voice, abundance of vigour, visions of lights, freedom from disease and sloth are the first signs of progress in Yoga (Prathama Lakshana).

Clairvoyance, clairaudience are the signs that indicate the second stage in the onward march in the path of Yoga (Dviteeya Lakshana).

The Yogi can walk over the fire, water and a sharp sword. He can move in the skies. He has knowledge of the three periods of time (Trikala Jnana). These indicate that he is in the third, fourth and fifth stage of Yoga. Eventually he frees himself from Prakriti and the three Gunas and attains Kaivalya or Absolute Independence through Nirvikalpa or Nirbhaya Samadhi.

THE ESSENCE OF SADHANA

A Raja Yogi slowly ascends the Yogic ladder along the eight steps, viz., Yama, Niyama, Asana, Pranayama, Pratyahara, Dharana, Dhyana and Samadhi. He gets ethical training in the beginning to purify himself by the practice of Yama and Niyama. Then he steadies his posture, Asana. Then he practises Pranayama to steady his mind and purify the Nadis. Then by the practice of Pratyahara, Dharana and Dhyana he gets Samadhi. Through Samyama he gets different Siddhis. He restrains all the mental modifications that arise from the mind.

Hatha Yoga concerns with the physical body and control of breath. Raja Yoga deals with the mind. Raja Yoga and Hatha Yoga are interdependent. Raja Yoga and Hatha Yoga are necessary counterparts of each other. No one can become a perfect Yogi without a knowledge of and the practice of both. Proper Raja Yoga begins where properly practised Hatha Yoga ends. A Hatha Yogi starts his Sadhana with his body and Prana, while a Raja Yogi with his mind; a Jnana Yogi with his Buddhi and will. This is the chief difference. To get success in Raja Yoga, one should have a thorough knowledge of the mysteries of the mind and the way by which it is controlled.

The student of Hatha Yoga should try to awaken the Kundalini Sakti that lies dormant in the Muladhara Chakra by Asana, Pranayama, Mudra and Bandha. He should try to unite the Prana-Apana and send the united Prana-Apana through the Sushumna Nadi. Heat is increased by retention of breath and Vayu ascends up along with Kundalini to the Sahasrara Chakra through the different Chakras. When Kundalini is united with Lord Siva at the Sahasrara Chakra, the Yogi attains Samadhi and enjoys supreme peace, bliss and immortality.

CHAPTER TWO
SIGNIFICANT PROCESSES IN SADHANA

THE MOVEMENT OF VASANAS IN SADHANA

The aspirant is struggling on amidst the rough and tumble of the Vyavaharic world. Troubles and difficulties crop up at every step. Temptations, trials and tests assail him ever and anon. He strives and fights manfully against the heavy odds and at last thinks it high time that he segregated and tried to pursue his Sadhana away from these upsetting factors. He retires from the bustle of worldly Vyavaharic activity and goes into comparative seclusion of some spiritual institution where he spends some time in selfless service and does Sadhana systematically. But he is horrified to find that after a time instead of feeling a gradual and progressive purification, moral, mental and spiritual, he experiences more impurity, evil and undesirable emotions and thoughts. What is this strange phenomenon? Is he slipping backwards? What is this queer stage he is passing through? Is he indeed moving towards Light or getting more and more into darkness? These considerations begin to seriously trouble his mind. His natural anxiety and grave concern over his inexplicable state is quite understandable. If he reflects a little and patiently tries to introspect and analyse his condition and the change that is going on within him, he will soon know the actual truth and will at once be reassured. His mind will be at rest.

This is not a degenerating process but actually a purifying process. The course of spiritual development at times appears as the contrary of what it really is. This has a reason for it. Extreme things that are diametrically opposite and contradictory tend to seem identical at times. Very low rates of vibration the ear cannot catch and even so extremely high rates the ear cannot hear. A static object appears motionless. The same object set rotating at a tremendous velocity appears to the eye to be perfectly still. Thus when during a stage in Sadhana the extreme reverse process of purification and the getting rid of 'Mala' takes

SIGNIFICANT PROCESSES IN SADHANA

place, it seems alarming akin to that of the obverse positive process of acquiring Asubha-Vasana.

It is here that an important note of caution has to be vividly borne in mind. When these inner Vasanas begin to cast out themselves then the Sadhaka should with great alertness and vigilance see that they are not afforded any scope to have active physical manifestation. There must be only an abortive rush and dissolution. Like the excess water in the dam that is released out of the barrage by the periodical opening of a few sluice gates these Vasanas must harmlessly flow out. Then the Sadhaka is all right and he will soon proceed with his Sadhana as before. Else these outflowing Vasanas will get translated into actions and forge further bonds in the Karmic cording that holds the individual in thralldom here. Instead of becoming a release process it will be the reverse of it.

There are two processes in this connection that will be of great help and reassurance to the Sadhaka if he remembers and makes proper timely use of them with wise Vichara. Namely, it is not always necessary or even desirable that all such 'spending-out' forces should indeed be allowed to flow out abortively or that they should issue forth at all. Where they are, imbedded in the Chitta or the subconscious mind, these can be directly sublimated and nullified. Just as the heat of the sun shining upon the barrage waters reduces them by direct evaporation, thus too regular meditation by the aspirant directly sublimates a portion of the Vasana-store day by day as the Sadhana proceeds. Then with those forces that actually sally out there is a very profitable alternative the Sadhaka can and really should employ, namely sublimating upon the external physical plane and transforming them into some profitable spiritual activity. This latter can be employed either subjectively with beneficial repercussions upon himself or also objectively to the advantage of others. Subjectively for instance should the subtle lust-Vasana endeavour to manifest itself, then the Sadhaka, if he is alert, must transform it at once into a dozen Suryanamaskaras or a vigorous round of his favourite Pranayama, a course of Asanas or a full-throated chant of the sublime Purushasukta, Vishnusahasranama, Siva-mahimna, etc. Thus sublimation also gets profitably turned into Sadhana, precious life-transforming Sadhana.

Should the Vasana of anger commence this spending-out process then repair to a quiet room and have a good loud hearty laugh and make it effervesce into pure upsurge of good cheer and laughter. Or sit still and send out wave after wave of love, blessing and goodwill to the entire universe from the bottom of your heart. Repeat again and again the sublime verses of Santipatha of the Upanishads. You will simply be filled with overflowing cosmic love. All anger Vasanas will vanish *in toto*, leaving in their stead a continuous thrill of motiveless love. This feeling is indeed indescribable. This Sadhana will give you a positive asset of Sattva and Prema. You will find yourself a tangibly different being after even a single genuine attempt at this process of deliberate sublimation.

This subjective method is preferable and is to be adopted particularly with regard to such Rajoguna and Tamoguna-Vasanas that become activated through external contact and by association, such as for instance, anger, lust, etc. Then there are such tendencies as one's suppressed social nature, Rajasic urge to aimless activity, the erotic sentiment to manifest affection—an effusion that becomes manifest in acute form in very many inebriates as also Sadhakas that have elements of the effeminate in their nature. It will be well if these are sublimated through the objective way.

When a fit of social nature assails you, do not allow yourself to be driven out into the bazaar for gossiping or into the nearest reading-room, tea-shop or post-office to dissipate your diligently conserved energy in sundry politics, topical news or table-chat. Go among the poor and the afflicted instead and see if you can serve them in any way. Go to the road or the high-way among the pilgrims and the wayfarers and seek to relieve them of their loads and lessen their burdens with pleasant and elevating conversation. Thus in the very process of giving enrich yourself too.

When sentimentality assails you from inside, be wary, be still. Do not foolishly rush amidst your friends and colleagues. Rather go and commune with nature. Address endearingly the squirrel and the little lamb. Talk and laugh lovingly with the little birds among the bushes and bright butterfly flitting from flower to flower. Thus safely spend out the unwinding threads of Vasanas from the reel of Chitta. You will be quite safe.

So, when these inner Vasanas "break ice" as it were and

strike the surface, do not be dismayed. Understand what is happening and deal with them calmly. Adopt the methods outlined above to suit the case and with variations to fit in particular situations and temperaments. Overcome them wisely and be a gainer. This experience will enrich you and you will be more firmly established in Sadhana.

Now one point has to be noted in this connection. There is a similar process that appears like this *spontaneous uprising* of inner Vasanas but which it isn't. It is something different and hence has to be differently dealt with. This is the outrush of Vasanas, stimulated by an external agency or impulse. This situation is what is called temptation or test. This is dangerous, for here you are faced with two forces both of which you have to combat—the innate potency of the Vasanas and the active mechanism of the external stimulating agency.

Adopt a combination of several methods for this. Follow the already outlined sublimation methods and augment it with prayer, fasts, a little bit of aggressive self-restraint, changing of the place where the temptation is, taking of a resolute vow etc. You will succeed in overcoming the test.

The individual consciousness is made to pass through varying strata of mental and emotional states, pure, neutral as also impure as the muddy water made to pass through a tray of sand, charcoal and some germicidal medium, for the task of filtration and purification. For the filtering away of gross Mala the rough grains of the sands of Vyavaharic experiences suit and suffice admirably. But for the subtler impurities (like the gaseous ones in water) a medium like black charcoal is required. This is the recrudescence of disturbingly unspiritual thoughts and tendencies that dismay and upset the Sadhakas in the onward course of their spiritual development. This process takes place almost entirely upon the mental and emotional planes. Their inner working is very curious and interesting. They take place in both the waking as well as the dream states and in the latter in two slightly different shades of dream consciousness rather difficult to distinguish.

The various positive and negative and subjective and objective sublimatory methods detailed already are for use when the spending-out process is in the waking state. In dream state the Sadhaka has only to depend upon the subconscious mind to guard him and to effect a proper self-adjustment inside. More often than not the thought influence of his Guru as also the Grace of the Ishta-Devata (both are in reality the same thing) bring the Sadhaka safe out of the dream state processes. It leaves only a slight vague impression on the mind that retains it the next morning in the form of some mood either depressing or exhilarating as the case may be. And at times this process in the dream state takes place in a curious way.

The person dreams and the Vasanas spend themselves out but the consciousness of the Sadhaka is not aware of the fact that he has dreamed. Thus he wakes up in the morning with a curious feeling, a different man from the time he retired to bed the previous night, yet unable to explain it or attribute it to anything that he can recollect. This is somewhat like the process you adopt when you have unknowingly drunk impure water and later on to disinfect it you take charcoal tablets orally. The medicated tablets enter the stomach and there carry out their purifying work invisibly and unknowingly. You are unconscious of what is going on inside, as in the case of those Vasanas that expended themselves in your unconscious dreams. Thus proceeds this process of purification and the wise and vigilant Sadhaka raises himself upwards and progresses onward even as the clever boatman skilfully takes immediate advantage of each uprising wave and sails ahead making his little boat leap as it were from crest of the waves of this ocean of Adhyatmic life.

Victory is to the vigilant and success surely attends upon the sincere Sadhaka firm in his faith in the Guru's feet!

ROLE OF RESTRAINT IN SADHANA

About one hundred and fifty miles above the Sannyasins' colony of Rishikesh, in the Himalayan interior there is an outpost, Chamauli by name. Here they have built a sort of dam or barrage across the flow of the mountain Ganga. One fine day something happened there and the water was likely to get out of hand and burst out in an excessive flow. At once wires began to hum. A telegram was given to all the lower regions, warning them of a likely flood in the Ganga and asking them to shift higher up from the Ganga bank.

Now Ganga water is the very life and the soul for the people living by the side of the Ganga bank. But what is this strange phenomenon—people are now fleeting away from its life-giving waters. What is the reason for this? So long as its flow was within the limits, so long as its volume was restrained to a safe margin, it was most beneficial and very desirable. When the self-same natural and legitimate function of the dam (of supplying waters) exceeded, these waters became dangerous and terrible. Thus excess rendered a blessing into a menace. Now consider a similar state of things in the life of man.

The average man is the slave of his senses. Usually his life is one constant whirl amidst the numerous varieties of Vishayas that hem in upon his day-to-day life. His appetites goad him on to do two things, viz., they go out towards certain external pleasing and attractive things and they also desire to draw in certain things inward themselves. Thus man's slavery to his senses takes these two forms of going out towards certain things and drawing in certain things. At times in the case of certain types of objects both these processes are present combined together, viz., indulgence and consumption. It will not be wrong to say that both these are but the two aspects of the quality of sensuality.

Now sensuality is a broad, general term. It includes all and every variety of indulgence through the avenue of the senses. However it is not all indulgence that is totally unethical, immoral or criminal. Certain forms of indulgence like drunkenness, debauchery, adultery etc., are manifestly immoral and criminal. They are ruthlessly condemned. Some others, though not actually criminal, are yet extremely harmful either physically or mentally or both to the individual and at times to others near him as well. Tobacco chewing, snuffing or smoking, betting, gambling etc., come under this class. Such practices are strictly forbidden and stigmatised in unequivocal terms. Thirdly, there are still others (and it is with this class we are particularly concerned) that are of a natural character and within limits are even tolerated and legalised by convention. Consuming food and drink and indulging in sleep, rest and proper apparel for covering the body—these and the allied routine physical necessities are of this last mentioned category. They are to some extent amoral. There is basically nothing unethical in doing these actions, but when they are overdone they immediately assume the nature of moral issues. They lose their neutral nature and become directly or indirectly (at times directly and indirectly both) immoral. Thus for instance, to sleep is normal to all creatures on earth. Animal and man, sinner and saint alike do it. But then there is a limit within which it is a desirable and beneficial necessity. Too much sleeping makes a man lazy, lethargic, dull and ultimately, useless to both society and himself. To the Sadhaka it is one of the most dangerous habits. To him it is a vice to be eradicated. Habitual oversleep increases Tamas and makes Sadhana nullified and retards his progress.

Take another process—eating. Eating is recognised as an indispensable necessity so long as the physical sheath lasts. The lowest vermin to the highest realised saint, all take food. Overdo it, then indirectly as well as directly it becomes wrong, improper, unethical and positively criminal. It is a wrong and harmful practice from the health and medical point of view; improper from the point of social etiquette which regards gluttony with disfavour and disapproval; it is unethical, for by overfeeding man fattens his lustful propensities and becomes gross and sensual; and it is criminal from the economic point of view, for the wanton overfeeding of a section of people transgresses all canons of distribution and deprives the starving masses of their sorely needed food.

Now it is precisely here that we perceive the vital role of restraint in giving the proper balance, proportion and direction to such functions of variable moral implications. Inasmuch as their classification as moral or otherwise directly depends upon limit and extent of their indulgence or consumption, it is the equality of restraint and self-control in the individual that acts as the regulator that keeps them within the limits of the good, the proper. Thus it is the presence and absence of this element of self-control and restraint that makes the identical action of eating praiseworthy in one and blameworthy in another. It is laudable in the saintly persons of simple and Spartan habits, and culpable in the shameless voracious gourmand. And this is different in the quality of the self-same action in two persons which is due to the factor of restraint.

Why the role of restraint has been dealt with particular reference to this third class of neutral amoral function will be apparent when we consider that the other two categories are matters for eschewment *in toto*, wherein, strictly speaking, no question of restraint need arise at all. These actions are unnatural, unnecessary and dispensable. They are never to be done. Whereas the third class of inevitable routine items of sensual consumption and indulgence have got to be done, yet not to be overdone. And it is restraint that achieves this. It is restraint that supplies the guarantee and insurance against over-indulgence.

This function of restraint in guarding against and countering the urge for overdoing of consumption and indulgence, operates in two forms that of moderation and deliberate selection. Where over-consumption takes the shape of going beyond limits in point of quantity then restraint manifests as the principle of moderation to check it. When the error is in the nature of an indulgence in an injurious and undesirable quality, then restraint operates in the form of a rational sense of sane selection. Thus this latter makes the aspirant to choose Sattvic articles of diet and abstain from Rajasic and Tamasic eatables, even though they may be tastier than the Sattvic diet. Then again it makes the Sadhaka prefer to sleep for half an hour or one hour longer at night time rather than indulge in day-time sleep.

Moderation and selection form a dual-process whose exercise brings about a mutual, favourable reaction upon each other. When the quality of your consumption, the nature of the things taken in through the avenue of the senses, is non-exciting and Sattvic then this establishes a rhythm and harmony in the system. This state of harmony is an immense help in the exercise of restraint; for restraint is dependent on inner strength or Atma-bala. The greater the Sattva in man, so much more is the development of this inner force. Likewise the habitual adherence to the principle of moderation keeps the body and mind light and free of toxins. In such a state of health and purity all faculties are keen and alert, facilitating a great deal the exercise of Viveka and Vichara (discrimination and enquiry) upon which wise selection and restraint depend.

Thus it will be seen that the faculty of and the ability in restraint is the greatest friend of man. It guards against man's natural sensual propensities, getting the better of him and turning into excess. Restraint plays the important part of keeping the processes of consumption and indulgence within the bounds of their beneficial maximum or safe ceiling-limit. Make full and judicious use of this factor and you will reap a harvest, health, well-being, progress and spiritual attainments.

Restraint makes life worth living. Be restrained and become a Jitendriya-Yogisvara. Restraint makes you real emperor of the three worlds. Restraint leads to Realisation of the Self!

All hail to Restraint the supreme Regulator! All Glory to the quality of restraint which is truly a divine Vibhuti, veritable manifestation of the Lord Himself!

REPRESSION IN SADHANA AND ITS EFFECTS

Conquest of senses and self-mastery is well recognised as the prime indispensable condition for true progress in spiritual Sadhana. Now, while attempting at sense-control it should be borne in mind that the real and effective method lies in concentrating your attention at the control of the mind. Because the actual senses are not the Karmendriyas or the fleshy external situated in the physical body, but are the Jnanendriyas that have their seat in the Manomaya Kosa. The outward physical sense-organs are merely the vehicles through which the Jnanendriyas get their cravings satisfied. They form as it were the executive or labour corps, carrying out the bidding of their subtle counterparts in the mental sheath. Therefore, if through control of mind and Pratyahara the clamour of the inner-five is subdued, then the Karmendriyas become as mere fleshy appendages with no power to incite or to excite the person. Upon the indrawn mind the sound entering through the avenue of the ear fails to register. The nose inhales and draws in different odours but all unaware to the mind. The man with self-absorbed mind gazes with vacant unseeing eyes, for though the wide-open eyes gaze outward, yet the mind perceives naught. Tap a man on the back while he is intently engaged in deep study, he will not heed you, for he fails to feel the tap. Thus it is essentially the craving and goading of the inner quintuplet of subtle organs that sets up the agitation and turbulence in the physical senses of man.

This gives the clear clue as to where the wise Sadhaka ought to direct his efforts when aiming at the conquest of senses, eradication of cravings and self-mastery. Yet it is forgotten by most Sadhakas with the result that you frequently find that in a sudden fit of extreme austerity they try to wrestle with the outward senses in an intense effort to stifle them, starve them and trample them into submission. They seemingly succeed very well in the beginning and thus encouraged they even intensify the erroneous process. And when the outer physical repression thus assumes a degree of violence, its repercussions upon the individual's psyche begin to manifest in a series of disastrous symptoms. The person commences to exhibit reactionary tendencies in a variety of ways. The prominent form that the sum-total of these reactionary symptoms assumes is a total breaking away from the hitherto rigidly maintained self-control, or to put it rightly, auto-violent physical repression. It is marked by a loosening of all restraint and going headlong into a period of indulgence. Together with this a number of minor upheavals also take place which have the unfortunate effect of leaving a lasting impression upon the person. They work themselves into his subconscious system and get lodged as certain vague complexes and indefinable neurosis that baffle the routine analysis.

When the Sadhaka has undergone this experience while living a life of seclusion, then his case becomes all the more difficult. The scope and opportunity for caution, criticism and correction by others is absent. He is left all to himself and when a person is being swept away by a sudden strong current of extreme sensuousness and Rajas, then discrimination and sane analysis are rendered inoperative. Whereas if the Sadhaka happens during this period to be amongst many others, in a community or an institution, the beholders themselves being Sadhakas, familiar with this line of life, will not fail to observe his gradual change and the progressive intensification of his thoughtless repression till the breaking point is reached. Those with a little experience and insight will easily read the symptoms and diagnose his gradual heading towards the apex of his auto-violence and warn him in time of the inevitable reaction and its unenviable consequences. Thus where the concerned person himself cannot analyse his case, the observers point out to him what the matter is and analyse it for him to a certain extent.

But here too it has been observed that more often than not when such well intentioned warning and advice is offered, it is met with a distinct hostility and a spirit of aggressive defiance on the part of the Sadhaka. His aggressive attitude, when analysed, will be found to proceed from three factors, namely, an unconscious fear, a curious perversion of reasoning and a compensation process.

In the first case even though he knows and feels that his conduct is improper, yet he aggressively repels all advice and suggestion, for if he listens to them and follows accordingly, then it would mean the recovery of his poise and self-control again. This would deprive him of the pleasures that he is determined to taste. That part of his self, dominated for the period by the Bhoga-Vritti, is afraid that if he is submitted to their good counsels and admonitions, he would have to forego the pleasures, he is about to plunge into. This fear builds up a defence reaction of the protest which manifests itself as the attitude of aggression, which is so invariably present in the majority of such cases. This forms the exasperating feature which the external witnesses find it hardly possible to understand or to tolerate. It becomes so strong and marked that at times it ends the patience and actually antagonises those very well-wishers who seek to warn and draw him out of the slough he has fallen into.

In the second case by an extraordinary twist of logic the person convinces himself that he is justified in his actions. He feels that the period of restraint and abstinence has somehow entitled him to have a round of indulgence now and he resents any suggestion to the contrary. This very resentment itself is the sure indication, for his innermost self knows that he is totally wrong. But this is suppressed in the subconscious. This is a delusion, purely the outcome of the individual's mind clouded by passion.

A little thought will clearly show that he is plunging into indulgence because he had convinced himself beforehand that it was his due, but in spite he himself was plunged into it by the force of the revolting Indriyas, so long repressed by the aspirant's auto-violence. Then justification of it comes later on after the mischief is done. Thus it is not so much in the nature of an explanation as to why he is doing it, but rather a perverse attempt in asserting that he is right in what he is doing. It is the justification that follows the misconduct. To try to convince yourself, at such times, that you are acting thus because you know what you are going to do is right is just like putting the cart before the horse. You do wrong and say that you are right.

In the third case it is a compensation process. The aspirant is acutely aware that he has fallen in the estimation of the others who thought much of him and his self-control and austerity. His 'reputation' has suffered. He feels inferior. To cover this up and to make up for it in the eyes of others, he unconsciously adopts this aggression which is closely akin to Dutch-courage.

It might be thought that the analysis and statement of this third 'Compensation' factor is a matter of purely academic psychological interest and unnecessary in the investigation into a spiritual aspirant's inner movement and development. This is not so. This analysis has a definite bearing upon and significance to the Sadhaka. For this desire of 'compensation' and the consequent aggressiveness arises from the fact that the aspirant has not turned away from his old allegiance to his lower egoistic self. He is still identified with it. He wants to keep up its prestige. Hence the urge towards compensation as a face-saving device. This is unbecoming of an aspirant who is expected to willingly place himself in the hands of the higher Sattvic part in him right from the moment he enters the spiritual path. He has failed to subjugate his Asuric ego to the dictates of his higher mind. As an alternative he should at least surrender to his Guru. This too he has not done. Also, besides this he has totally neglected even the fundamentals of the path. The prime qualifications of Yama and Niyama provide these. If he had tried to develop humility this aggressive compensation would never have been necessitated. The fault would be readily accepted and the lesson learnt. Neither having the humility nor the intellectual honesty to admit one's own error, he adopts this perverted method. Now it will be clear how this analysis of 'compensation,' though purely psychological, yet throws much light upon the inner neglect and defect in the very build-up of his spiritual life. It reveals the lack of the very elements of ethics in him. Ethics is the very basis of spiritual life. Therefore, in handling such cases much tact, delicacy and understanding insight become necessary. How to deal exactly with them is a very difficult matter and depends to a great extent upon the particular circumstances and the particular person concerned.

Here the doubt will be raised that how can this method be erroneous? Is it not stated that if you withdraw the fuel, the fire will die down by itself and are not the sense-objects and their enjoyment the fuel for the fire of the senses? Yes, true. If the senses are the 'fire', then the objects may be called the fuel. A little careful reflection will show that actually the senses are not the real 'fire'. The above analogy has to be pushed one more step inward into the next circle of the beings, five-circled field of individualised consciousness. The outer orgy and vulgar whirling of the senses amidst the objects is in fact analogous to the crackling and heat generated by the inner fire. The real fire is actually the intense irritation and restlessness of the subtle Jnanendriyas whose heat, blaze and crackle are manifested as the rampaging of the Karmendriyas in the field of sense-objects. It is the Jnanendriyas that derive the satisfaction from indulgence. The actual enjoyment of taste is not done by the boneless piece of flesh inside the mouth nor does the rough and criss-crossed skin of the palm experience the pleasurable feeling of sensuous fleshly contacts. The tongue does not taste. It conveys the taste. Likewise the external dermis just conveys contactual feelings.

The Jnanendriyas constitute the 'fire' and it is fed by the fuel of memory (of previous enjoyments), imagination, brooding and deliberate dwelling mentally (upon tastes, pleasurable sensations and the attractive nature of sense-objects), and constant hoping and a keen, eager expectation and anticipation. All these constitute the fuel. The supply of this fuel is to be put an end to by strictly restricting the extent and nature of past memory, checking all imagination, resolutely stopping all mental indulgence or dwelling, and readily giving up hoping, anticipation and expectation. This is the reason for the advice 'Forget the past, give up planning the future, live in the solid present.' This is again the basis of the declaration that real Tyaga lies in the renunciation of Sankalpa-vikalpa. This is precisely why you are told 'Mano Jayam Eva Maha Jayam' and 'Man Jita Jagat Jita.'

The above control of the mental Vikaras is to be achieved more through positive non-violent methods than by the negative auto-violent process of forcible repression. Establishing of harmony and inner rhythm (as opposed to agitation) through Asanas and Sattvic diet, thinning the mind by Pranayama, diverting the imagination into higher and nobler super-sensual channels by regular Svadhyaya (study of scriptures and spiritual books) and Sravana, the practice of dwelling upon a definite Lakshya, acquired and strengthened through Upasana are some of the important methods to be actively employed by every earnest aspirant to succeed in self-restraint.

You must set up a guard over the mind. There must be

continuous discrimination and firm checking. Vichara and ready 'Nirodha' should never be stopped. Man is morally lazy and unwilling to take up this important task. Moreover, vanity also is at the back of this reluctance to employ this inner method of restraint. Because this is purely a subjective inner training. It does not get advertised and acquires no publicity. Whereas physical austerity and forcible methods appear heroic for all to see and admire. This vanity is very subtle and not realised easily. But, however, moral indolence and lethargy is the main cause, coupled with the lukewarm nature of the Sadhaka's aspiration. If you are truly eager for progress you will make sincere attempts at practising this real mental control. You must shake off all mental indolence and cooperate willingly with the higher mind in its task of non-cooperation with the sensuous self. Without doing this you fail miserably in your auto-violent methods and blame other sundry factors and persons or turn totally averse and heedless to spiritual practices and progress. This is a great blunder and also you will be the greatest loser thereby.

In concluding this topic there is one point to be taken note of. It may be asked, is there absolutely no virtue in or no use of controlling the external senses at all? Surely there is. It is quite necessary to control them also. It is good. But its implications and limitations have to be properly grasped and understood first. A fetish is not to be made of it. Done with commonsense, it becomes a helpful training. As modes of Titiksha such tussle with the senses is to be recommended. An occasional total downright 'starving' of one or more of the senses is quite all right. As for instance a complete waterless fast and all-night vigil once in a month or even twice on Ekadasi days is indeed most helpful. But then it is to be known in its true light, i.e., as a method—not as the ultimate objective. Also mistake should not be made of considering it as the one and the only method in Yoga. Its place in the spiritual path is as one among the various methods in attaining self-mastery. As an auxiliary means of getting established in the inner process of true self-control it is necessary. As a method of developing Titiksha, it is admirable. Doubtless it has its utility and equally also it has its limitations, and when foolishly carried to irrational extremes, definitely it has its dangers. It turns into a harmful auto-violent process that at times permanently breaks down the practitioner's capacity for Sadhana. Then its logic would be as bad as that of a man who wishing to arrest the rapid swelling-up of a toy rubber balloon grasps it with both hands and forcibly squeezes and presses it inward. The result will not be difficult to guess. The correct procedure will be to arrest the inflow of air being pumped in by the inflater. This latter technique of control is precisely what is achieved when you set about to subdue and restrain the Jnanendriyas by checking and arresting all the thoughts, memories, imaginations, hankerings and sensuous anticipations, that inflame the Jnanendriyas into a blaze of irresistible desire and fierce passion.

External sense-restraint is an important and effective instrument for the acquisition of a prize. But itself, it is not the prize. It is a sharp instrument and improper use of it will hurt the user. Understand its proper place in Sadhana and become wise. Make use of it in the proper way and master the mind. You will be successful. You will be crowned with glory.

May the Gita, the revealer of rational restraint guide thee in thy efforts at self-control and mind-mastery! May the Master Yogins like Lord Krishna and Gautama Buddha bestow upon thee true insight into the science of sense-subdual! May the Lord inspire thee to rightly use this knowledge and attain Perfection!

TRIPLE WITHDRAWAL IN SADHANA

Kathopanishad says, "The Self-existent Brahman created the senses with outgoing tendencies and so man beholds the external universe but not the internal Atman. But some wise persons with a steadfast mind who are desirous of attaining immortality behold the internal Atman by turning the gaze inward."

"Turning the gaze inward" means abstraction of all the Indriyas. All the senses are withdrawn from their respective objects through Pratyahara and the practice of Dama.

Sit on any comfortable Asana. Close the eyes. Concentrate on Trikuti or the space between the two eyebrows.

Practise Mulabandha by contracting the anus and inhale. Retain the breath and practise Jalandhara Bandha, by putting chin lock to attain one-pointedness (Ekagrata).

Withdrawal of Prana, withdrawal of mind from the sense-objects and withdrawal of senses at one and the same time constitute the triple withdrawal in Yoga Sadhana. It is more effective or potent than single withdrawal of either sense, mind or Prana. All the three withdrawals must be practised simultaneously. The mind will be controlled very easily by this potent Yoga Sadhana.

Gradually the breath will move within the nostrils. The velocity of the mind will be checked. The mind will attain one-pointedness (Ekagrata). The Vasanas will be thinned out. The turbulent senses will be made quiet. There will be harmony and peace. Yoga Nishtha will result. Nirvikalpa Samadhi will supervene.

PATIENCE IN SADHANA

The foundation-stone of Yoga, the first rung in the spiritual ladder is ethical perfection. Therefore, try to remove all negative qualities. Introspect and analyse your mind. When you remove one evil quality another one may crop up. Have patience and one by one tackle all the negative qualities. You are bound to succeed if you are patient. We spend much time in reading newspapers. You may, by all means, read newspapers to know what is going on in the world, but the object in reading newspapers should not be to rouse your emotions. Real peace can ensue only when you control your lower emotions. Then only spiritual life will be possible for you.

You have not a disciplined mind and that is the reason why there is suffering. You do not think or do Vichara as to wherefrom real bliss can be derived. You do not enquire "What good actions have I done on this earth?" We do not remember the definite promise we have made to the Lord when we left Him and entered the mother's womb. We do not remember the ideals. Try to lead a good virtuous life and leave off vain discussions like whether there exists God or not. All these are useless discussions. Becoming angry is awfully bad. Try to control anger. If a man says something unpleasant at once you begin to retaliate. We have not got the power or strength to bear patiently. We are weak. A man may be a muscular sandow. He might have devoted 6 to 12 hours a day in the development of his muscles. He might be able to break a big stone, but he may not have the strength to bear a harsh word. He is mentally weak. So we will have to develop mental strength and cultivate virtues. But, what a pity! We soon forget. We do not remember the ideal or the goal before us. We do a little Japa here and there, and at once expect Siddhis. This is not enough. You must do intense work.

Select a separate room in your house. This is necessary. Continuous practice of getting up at four o'clock is necessary. People practise for some time, then leave off the practice, and then resume again. This habit should be entirely given up. If you practise at Brahma Muhurta the mind can easily be fixed in meditation. It will facilitate much if you can be absolutely regular in your meditation. Then, with practice, meditation comes by itself, at the proper time. Even if you are ailing, at the usual time of meditation the mind will be in the most receptive mood. If you feel drowsy, sing loudly some of the philosophical songs like *Chidananda, Chidananda* and you will feel refreshed. Again and again hammer this mind with *Chidananda, Chidananda Hum*, I am the Immortal Atman. Sing this song. Take a little walk. All diseases will get cured. Feel the Divine presence within you. Every name is filled with Divine potency and utterance of Divine Names elevates you to glorious heights. This by itself clearly proves that God exists.

You must cultivate a regular habit of doing charity. It should become spontaneous. Perhaps in our generosity we may give to our sisters or brothers some money, but not to strangers. Generosity should be extended to all. We do not recognise that the whole world has emanated from Isvara. There is so much suffering and you must feel that your body is affected. Then only will you have the Grace of the Lord. All the Siddhis and Riddhis will be at your feet. But unfortunately you have such a constricted heart, a very small heart. You may have a good intellect. You may be a Ph.D., but possess a narrow heart. The spirit of self-sacrifice is completely lacking. Why? Because we do not practise the qualifications prescribed in the Gita. That man is the greatest of the Yogins who does self-sacrifice, recognising all as manifestations of the Lord. Doing charity should become a second nature with you. Keep some change in your pocket wherever you go. Wherever there is distress share what you have and alleviate human suffering wherever it is possible. Thus will you be able to achieve the goal for which you were born, for which God has given you this human body. Many had direct Darshan of the Lord through selfless service and you can also attain the goal.

Do Japa and prayers. Keep some good thoughts of God.

Remember certain Slokas on the evils that will come out of the pursuit of sensual pleasures. Again and again hammer on this mind the evils that would result from the pursuit of sensual pleasures. It requires constant practice. Keep these good thoughts before you go to bed and remember them. You will have to discipline your mind gradually. Side by side the study of religious books is also very important. Study the Upanishads. Study the Yoga Sutras of Patanjali, on Raja Yoga. You can then have theoretical understanding. Books are necessary. These will help you to overcome the obstacles in your way.

How many of you, by now, know by heart the 15th Chapter of the Gita, which you can recite before taking food? Very few. Man is made of food and food is rendered pure and you get strength when you recite these Slokas. Different kinds of food produce different Samskaras and different temperaments arise. Sattvic food develops concentration of mind. When you offer food to the Lord it becomes an act of self-sacrifice. If therefore you remember certain Slokas, it will be useful. So we should know how to regulate our lives.

Let us turn a new leaf, a new chapter in our lives. Even a little Japa, a little Kirtan releases tremendous force. Let us therefore be more sincere in our love for the Lord, and keep the ideal before us. Study the Gita. Time is flying. When you get angry remember the Avanti Brahmin. Amidst all trials and tribulations remember the Lord. You must be able to use sweet words. Gain strength day by day. Have a fixed programme of life. It is difficult to get a human birth. Let us not waste the precious life. Remember the great saints of our land—Ramdas, Shams Tabriez, Sri Ramakrishna Paramahamsa. They had direct realisation. Let us aspire to become Jivanmuktas in this very life. Just listen to the story of Sadasiva Brahman.

Sadasiva Brahman was a Yogin in Karur and lived 150 years ago. His Samadhi is there even today. He has written beautiful books and commentary on Brahma Sutras. He was a learned scholar and was undergoing training under his Guru, when he received a telegram that his wife had attained puberty. He was returning from his teacher's house after the studies. His mother was rejoicing when she heard the news that her son was coming back to the house. She prepared some "Payasam" that day and so many other dishes. So he had to wait till 3 o'clock for his dinner. He was a man of discrimination. He was a

Yogabhrashta. He remembered his previous birth and found out the misery he would be getting by entering the householder's life. He said to himself "Now I got meal at 3 o'clock. When I am fully in the Grihasthasrama, I do not know when I will get the meal. What is the use of the Grihasthasrama?" He at once renounced the world and he was not bound. He had not performed his duties towards his wife and mother. Still he was not bound.

Do not pay exaggerated attention to the sayings "You have not brought forth a progeny to keep the family and so you will incur the curse of your ancestors and so on." Sadasiva Brahman was not bound. He became the greatest Yogi, even though he had not discharged his duties to his mother and wife. Afterwards when he was in Samadhi he got buried underground. Some agriculturists came there and when they were digging, they hit against his head unknowingly. There was bleeding. At once they dug up the place and found him. He was not a bit affected. He then came back from Samadhi. He exhibited various other miracles.

From these it is clear that marriage is a social institution, because many are born with great passion and lustful Samskaras and these Samskaras have to be appeased a little, so that the man can gain some experience and learn discrimination as to how much this world can give him happiness. He gets knocks from people. He gets kicks. His wife and children cease to give him his soul's longing. He becomes discontented with the world and then turns to religion. It is to gain this experience that one enters Grihastha life. But those who are born with spiritual Samskaras get Vairagya very soon even without passing through the experience of a Grihastha. There are so many other instances also of spiritual persons renouncing the world without entering the Grihasthasrama.

Observe strictly the rules of Brahmacharya. We have passed through hundreds of lives before in vain, in not observing the rules of Brahmacharya. The Vasanas are very strong. Remember that as a son is born the wife becomes a mother. Look at the animals as to how they observe the Laws of Nature. It is only man who does not stick to these Laws of Nature, and it is only man who is endowed with reason. He alone has the power of discrimination. That faculty, that power of discrimination is in man alone. So to reach God-head, Brahmacharya is essential. The whole energy must be converted into Ojas Sakti. It will then prove a great asset to man to face the battle of life. He who has conserved his energy can turn out more vital work in the world and earn more. Still more important is this to the spiritual aspirant as he cannot make any progress otherwise. Let me repeat to you that getting up at 4 o'clock is important. But people do not do it. They do not get up before it is 7 o'clock. The world is moving at a terrific speed, and every moment is precious. How long are you going to argue whether God exists or not? Try to do as much Japa as possible.

Through constant service, through charity and spontaneous and unrestricted generosity you will have to remove mental impurity. People who have two crores of rupees may give one lakh to war-fund. There is not much magnanimity in this. But if a poor devotee who has two rupees gives a rupee in charity: it is glorious. These are the utterances from the Upanishads that you cannot hoard even a little bit of wealth. It should be distributed. There are people who earn much and spend it away in public charities and institutions. This is a great help no doubt. But money cannot be earned without incurring sin. He who is able to share what little he has with others is the truest Yogi, not the man who earns four crores and spends 20 lakhs on charities. That man who earns 8 annas but is able to share it with another is more beloved of the Lord.

You have heard of the story of the poor Brahmin and his family. This family had only a few grains of rice left, and when he was about to take meal, Lord Narayana appeared as an Atithi to test the charity of this devotee. The Brahmin and his wife and children fed this Atithi and starved themselves. That is real charity. So charity should be spontaneous, unrestricted and generous. It should be part and parcel of our daily conduct. One's life may pass away at any moment, and it is idle to keep on clinging to one's wealth.

I shall give you an instance. In the Swarga Ashram a rich man built a temple. He had a big contract work and he was able to earn quite a good bit. The Lord was pleased with his work. He built a sugar factory and earned a crore of rupees. Gradually some spirituality dawned on him. He took to Sadhana, but did not get much benefit. Suddenly he developed some symptoms and died one fine morning. He had only greed for money. He had a crore of rupees. No doubt he had opened some hospitals, etc., and had done some other good things, but he was not wise. A wise man would be he who spends away his all on others and relieves suffering. God has given you a guarantee of life at the moment and let that moment not pass by without your doing the maximum good to others. It is a good thing to build hospitals, etc. They are all necessary for the expansion of the heart. But if it is only a poor man who is able to do charity he is dear to the Lord, because he has a heart to give. Those who have money must spend. There is no certainty of the tomorrow. It is for doing good actions that God gives you money. You must use money well as a trustee.

PERSEVERANCE IN SADHANA

Life is the manifestation of Sakti. All life is therefore dynamic. Nothing remains stationary, even for half a moment. The Universal Energy ever works on untiringly and inexhaustibly, operating alike in a tiny speck of dust as in the mighty orb of the sun. Ceaseless progress and growth is the Law of Nature and evolution.

O aspirants! You are also a centre of this cosmic energy. Activity and advancement is the law of your being. You must continuously keep advancing in the spiritual path. Do not remain satisfied in having filled up a resolve form or drawing up daily routine. It is not enough to have a nice meditation room or a deer skin and a Mala. No doubt you have changed your old ways of life. But how far have you advanced along the new?

A great sage once said: "Do not stand still even for a moment for to stand still in the way of holiness and perfection is not to take breath or courage but to fall back and to become weaker than before." Bear this in mind. In the spiritual path it is a case of progress or regress. There is no comfortable 'sitting on the wall' frequently. To rest is to rust. With a flaming aspiration push forward. Every day must show that you have taken one step more upon the path. Progress is not to be counted in number of days that have passed in practice. It lies in how far you have outgrown your former ways of thinking and living. What is the extent of your victory over external environments? Do you maintain a calm and balanced mind? Do you remain unaffected by little annoyances and irritations? Are you more ready to forgive and less ready to offend? Has your aspiration grown stronger? Are you doing increased Sadhana or are you expecting

Divine grace to help you to carry out your resolves and vows? Are you waiting to get blessings or Asirvad from saints and Avataras? Blessings are always there, but unless you prepare to boldly struggle upwards and onwards blessings are just as useful as staff and shoes to a traveller who does not care to march ahead.

There was a saint who took up his abode in a hill-side cave by the side of the jungle road. He was very industrious by nature. He collected boulders from all around the cave, raised a platform and walls, etc. By ceaseless work he soon made the wild dwelling into a perfect miniature rock fort. He cleared all the surrounding space except for one boulder in front of the cave. He came to be called by the name 'Pather Baba' or the stone saint. As he was a great Virakta many people came for his Darshan. When aspirants frequently asked for his blessings he kept quiet. But if anyone pressed him too much for his Asirvad he used to turn towards the little rock ramparts constructed by him and say, "See, this is the result of Mehnat (exertion or industry)." Then he led them to the solitary stone and pointing to it said, "Well, you want my Asirvad. There, look at that stone. It is regularly receiving my Asirvad three times a day. I bless it daily morning, noon and at dusk. I find it however the same as before. This is all Asirvad had done and that (referring to the rock construction) is the product of constant application and effort."

Do not, therefore look always for external aids. Proceed onwards. Help will come from within where necessary. The distance you have to cover is great, time is short, obstacles are many. Days, months and years fly away rapidly. Every minute is precious. Therefore, advance quickly towards the goal.

No doubt the Lord is so very merciful that if you take one step towards Him, He hurries forwards ten steps to meet you. Quite true. But you are required to step forward towards Him first. You perhaps feel that circumstances stand against your progress, that you are everywhere surrounded by unfavourable conditions and forces. Now a man in a valley will never be able to sweep away a mist, but by ascending a little he will altogether rise above it. Therefore, never brood over disadvantages and disabilities. Rise into higher realms of Atmic knowledge through steady Sadhana. It is your folly to sit in gloom and cry 'light, light.' Arise and march forward into sunshine.

Excel in service. Expand in love. Advance in knowledge. Create opportunities to serve. Learn something new every day. Develop greater devotion to the Lord. Increase your Sadhana. Persevere on the path. Let your progress be continuous. Ceaseless perseverance is the certain safeguard against slipping backward. It is the surest way to success. Never stop or slacken. Keep marching forward. May you soon reach the goal.

CONTINUITY IN SADHANA

Do not stop Sadhana when you get a few glimpses of realisation (Alpam). Continue the practice till you are fully established in Bhuma (unconditioned Brahman). This is important. If you stop the practice, and move about in the world, there is every likelihood of a downfall. The reaction will be tremendous. Examples are not lacking. Numerous persons have been ruined. A glimpse cannot give you perfect safety. Do not be carried away by Loka-Eshana (name and fame). You can renounce your wife, children, parents, house, friends and relatives. It is very, very difficult to renounce the intellectual pleasure, the pleasure from name and fame. I seriously warn you. A man who can draw happiness from Atman within will never care a jot for this trivial paltry affair. The world is a mighty big thing for a worldly man. The world is a straw for a knower of Brahman. It is a mustard, a pin's point, a dot, a bubble, an airy nothing for a Brahma Jnani. Be circumspective. Ignore all these trivial things. Be steady with your practice. Never stop the practice till the final beatitude is reached. Never stop Sadhana till you can constantly dwell in full Brahmic consciousness.

FOUR PROGRESSIVE STAGES IN SADHANA

In the first stage of progress in Sadhana, there is achieved the purity of mind; in the second, the power to concentrate is greatly increased; then there intervenes the stage where profound meditation becomes possible and easy of achievement. In the fourth stage, the aspirant gains illumination; thereafter there is the identification of the inner spiritual Self with the all-pervading, omniscient, and omnipotent Divinity; and finally there is the experience of complete absorption in the infinite Being.

CHAPTER THREE
TYPES OF SADHANA

FOURFOLD SADHANA

Fourfold Sadhana of the student in the path of Jnana Yoga consists of Viveka, Vairagya, Shad-sampat or sixfold virtues and Mumukshutva or strong yearning for liberation.

Viveka dawns in a man, through the grace of God, who has done virtuous actions in his previous births as offerings unto the Lord without expectation of fruits and without egoism. Viveka is the discrimination between the real and the unreal, the permanent and the non-permanent, Atman and Anatman.

You must first develop Viveka or discrimination between the real and the unreal and Vairagya or dispassion for the enjoyment of objects herein and hereafter. Then only you will have success in the practice of Sama. Vairagya born of Viveka only will be of a lasting nature. Such a Vairagya only will be helpful to you in your spiritual practices. Karana Vairagya due to the loss of property or death of wife or son will be temporary. It will be of no use to you. It is volatile like ammonia.

Sama is serenity of mind produced by the constant eradication of Vasanas or desires. Whenever desires crop up in your mind do not try to fulfil them. Reject them through discrimination, right enquiry and dispassion. You will get tranquillity of mind and mental strength by constant practice. The mind is thinned out. The mind is checked directly from wandering. Its outgoing tendencies are curbed. If desires are eradicated, the thoughts also will die by themselves. The mind is detached from the manifold sense-objects by continuously observing their defects and is fixed on Brahman. In the practice of Sama, the five Jnana Indriyas or organs of knowledge, viz., ear, skin, eye, tongue and nose are also controlled.

Dama is the control of the external organs, i.e., the organs of action or the five Karma Indriyas, viz., organ of speech, hands, feet, genitals and the anus—the external instruments. The organs are withdrawn and fixed in their respective centres.

The eyes run outside to see a beautiful object. If you at once withdraw the eyes from that object, it is called Dama. You should restrain the other Indriyas also by the practice of Dama.

Some say, "Practice of Dama is not necessary. It is included in Sama. The Indriyas cannot work independently. They can work only in conjunction with the mind. If the mind is checked, the Indriyas will come under control automatically."

The mind will come under control very easily if Dama also is practised. It is a double attack on the enemy from within and without. He is crushed or subdued soon. If the front and the back doors are closed simultaneously, the enemy is caught quite readily. There is no escape for him on any side. By practice of Dama you do not allow either the Indriya or the mind to come in contact with the objects. You do not allow the mind to come through the external instrument, viz., the eye, to assume the form of the object. In neophytes the mind never remains self-centred despite rigorous practice of Sama. It tries to run outside towards external objects. If Dama is also practised, it will be of immense help to curb the mind efficiently. If you tie the hands of a mischievous boy, he tries to do mischief with his feet. If his feet also are tied he keeps quiet. Sama corresponds to the tying of the hands and Dama to the tying of the feet. Therefore the practice of Dama is also necessary.

Dama is the practice of a student of Jnana Yoga. Pratyahara corresponds to the practice of Dama. Pratyahara is the practice of a Raja Yogi. In the former it follows the practice of Sama; in the latter it follows the practice of Pranayama. In the former the Indriyas are withdrawn by calming or restraining the mind; in the latter the Indriyas are withdrawn by restraining the Prana. The Indriyas can be withdrawn more effectively by the process of double withdrawal, by withdrawing the mind and the Prana at the same time. It is the mind that moves the Indriyas. It is the Prana that vivifies or energises or galvanises the Indriyas. Sama and Dama are strictly Raja Yogic practices.

Now we come to the practice of Uparati. Some define Uparati as renunciation of all works and taking up Sannyasa. Uparati follows the practice of Sama and Dama. Uparati is self-withdrawal. It consists in the mind-function ceasing to act by means of external objects. Uparati is extreme abstention. It is the turning of the mind from the objects of enjoyment.

The mind of the student who is established in Uparati will

never be agitated even a bit when he sees a beautiful object. There will be no attraction. He will have the same feeling which he experiences when he sees a woman as when he looks at a tree or a log of wood. When he looks at delicious fruits or palatable dishes, he will not be tempted. He will have no craving for them. He will have no craving for any particular object or dish. He will never say, "I want such and such a preparation for my food." He will be satisfied with anything that is placed before him. This is due to the strength of mind he has developed by the practice of Viveka, Vairagya, Sama and Dama. Further the mind is experiencing a wonderful calmness and transcendental spiritual bliss by the above practices. It does not want these little, illusory pleasures. If you have got sugar-candy, your mind will not run after black sugar. You can wean the mind from the object to which it is attached by training it to taste a superior kind of bliss. If you give cotton-seed extract to a bull or a cow, it will not run towards dry grass or hay. Mind is like a bull.

Those who practise Brahmacharya must be fully conversant with the technique of Sama, Dama and Uparati. Then only they will be established in the practice of celibacy.

Titiksha is the power of endurance. A Titikshu is able to bear pain, insult, heat and cold. He does not care to redress them. He is free from anxiety. He does not lament on this score.

Sraddha is unshakable faith in the existence of Brahman, in the teachings of Guru and scriptures, and faith in one's own self. If any one possesses these qualifications he will get Samadhana or one-pointedness of mind and burning desire for liberation. The mind will move naturally towards the inner self always. The student should now approach a Brahmasrotri, Brahmanishtha Guru, hear the Srutis, reflect and meditate on the significance of the 'TAT TVAM ASI' Mahavakya constantly. He will attain Self-realisation or Atma-Sakshatkara.

If you have Viveka, Vairagya will come by itself. If you possess Viveka and Vairagya, Sama will dawn by itself. If you are endowed with Viveka, Vairagya and Sama, Dama will come by itself. If you have Sama and Dama, Uparati will come by itself. If you have all these qualifications Titiksha, Sraddha and Samadhana or one-pointedness will come by themselves. If you possess Viveka, Vairagya, Sama, Dama, Uparati, Sraddha and Samadhana, Mumukshutva or burning desire for liberation will manifest by itself.

Even in a Jivanmukta or a liberated sage the eyes will move towards the objects through the force of habit. But he can withdraw them completely and make them mere empty sockets if he wills. When he sees a woman, he does not see her outside himself. He sees the whole world within himself. He feels that the woman is his own self. He has no sex-idea. There are no evil thoughts in his mind. He has no sexual attraction for her. Whereas a worldly man sees the woman outside himself; he entertains lustful thoughts. He has no idea of the Self. He is attracted towards her. This is the difference between the vision of a Jnani and a worldly man. There is no harm in looking at a woman but you must not entertain evil thoughts. Feel that women are manifestations of Mother Kali. Feel that the beauty of women is the beauty of the Lord. Feel that all forms are images of the Lord. Your mind will be elevated at once.

Some students ask, "Shall we practise Viveka, Vairagya, etc., in order, one by one after mastering each Anga or shall we practise all the Angas simultaneously? If we practise one by one, perhaps we will not be able to get mastery over one or two Angas in this life. We may require several births for perfect mastery over all Angas. Life is very short. What shall we do?" It depends upon the temperament, taste and capacity of the students. Some like to get perfect mastery over each stage and then proceed to the next step. Some like to practise all the limbs at the same time. For six months concentrate your mind in cultivating Viveka, Vairagya and Sama. For the next six months try to acquire Sraddha, Samadhana and Mumukshutva. Devote more time in developing that virtue which you are seriously lacking. If you are earnest and sincere in your attempt, you can develop the four means and attain Self-realisation in this very birth.

Another Vedantic student says, "Swamiji, there is no necessity for acquiring these four means of salvation—Viveka, Vairagya, etc. It is a long, tedious process. I will not be able to acquire them even in several births. The shortest way is to think of Brahman always. I will acquire all the virtues automatically. Then I will be able to practise deep meditation." He is right. A first-class type of student can adopt this method because he had cultivated the four means in his previous births. A mediocre student will not be able to think of Brahman at the very outset. How can one think of Brahman when the mind is filled with impurities, when the mind is turbulent and the Indriyas are jumping and revolting? Absolutely impossible. He may sit for thinking on the Self. He will be building castles in the air and will be thinking of other objects. He will foolishly imagine that he entered into Nirvikalpa Samadhi. He will mistake deep sleep for Samadhi. Many are deluded in this manner. They do not have any spiritual progress. They can have no idea of Brahman. It is only the mind that is rendered pure by the practice of Viveka, Vairagya, Sama, Dama, etc., that can have definite conception of Brahman. Ideas of Brahman cannot be lodged in a restless, impure mind.

May you all live drowned in the ocean of Brahmic Bliss in an illumined state through the practice of Viveka, Vairagya, Sama, Dama, Uparati, Titiksha, Sraddha and Samadhana!

THE SIMPLE SADHANA

Man is a mixture of three ingredients, viz., human element, brutal instinct and divine ray. He is endowed with finite intellect, a perishable body, a little knowledge and a little power. This makes him distinctly human. Lust, anger, hatred belong to his brutal nature. The reflection of cosmic intelligence is at the back of his intellect. So he is an image of God. When the brutal instincts die, when this ignorance is rent asunder, when he is able to bear insult and injury, he becomes one with the Divine.

A thirsting aspirant is one who practises self-denial. He always tries to feel that the body does not belong to him. If anyone beats him, cuts his hand or throat, he should keep quiet. He must not speak even a single harsh word to him because the body is not his. He starts his Sadhana "I am not the body. I am not the mind. *Chidananda Rupah Sivoham.*"

One harsh or unkind word throws a man out of his balance. A little disrespect upsets him. He feels and feels for days together. How weak he has become despite his boasted intellect, high position in society, degrees and diplomas and titles?

Bear insult. Bear injury. This is the essence of all Sadhana. This is the most important Sadhana. If you succeed in this one Sadhana, you can very easily enter the illimitable domain of eternal bliss. Nirvikalpa Samadhi will come by itself. This is the most difficult Sadhana; but it is easy for those who have burning Vairagya and yearning for liberation.

You must become a block of stone. Only then will you be established in this Sadhana. Nothing can affect you. Abuses, ridicules, mockery, insults, persecutions cannot have any influence on you.

Remember the instructions of Lord Jesus: "If anyone gives you a slap on one cheek, show him the other cheek also. If anyone takes your coat, give him your cap also." How sublime is this teaching. If you follow this you will have great spiritual strength and power of endurance. It will make you divine. It will transform the nature of the offender also at once.

Study the life of the Avanti Brahmin in Bhagavata (IX Skandha). You will draw inspiration and strength. People spat at this Brahmin, threw faecal matter on him and yet he stood adamant. A Mohammedan spat on Saint Ekanath 109 times and yet the saint was not affected even a bit. All saints and prophets had this power of endurance. People pelted stones at Prophet Mohammed and threw the ovary of camel on his head and yet he was cool and serene. The Jews pierced thorns on the body of Lord Jesus. He was ill-treated in a variety of ways. He bore all these calmly and blessed the persecutors. He was nailed on the cross and yet he said, "O Lord! Forgive these people. They do not know what they are doing." Read again and again the Sermon on the Mount by Lord Jesus.

All aspirants will be tested by the Lord and a time will come for everybody to bear worst trials, adversities and persecutions. These trials will make them wonderfully strong. They must be ever prepared to bear all these trials and persecutions.

You will have to develop wonderful patience and endurance. You will have to kill your egoism, pride, *Dehaabhimana* or false identification with the perishable body. Then only you can bear insult and injury.

Try at first to control the physical reactions and the feelings. Do not report. Do not speak vulgar words. Do not revenge. Kill the vindictive spirit or attitude. Check the impulses of speech, thought and action. Gradually you will gain control. Regular Japa, meditation, Kirtana, prayer, enquiry, solitude, Satsanga, selfless service, Mouna, Asana, Pranayama, will pave a long way in developing your will-power and give you immense strength to bear insult and injury.

MOST IMPORTANT SADHANA

Too much salt, too much chillies, too much tamarind, make you impulsive and cause anger. Hence give up these three things entirely or take a very, very small quantity.

Speak a little. Speak always sweetly. So not speak harsh or filthy words. Again and again discipline the organ of speech, keep quiet when another abuses you.

Enquire. An abuse is nothing. It is mere jugglery of words or Sabda Jaalam. He who abuses, wastes his energy and spoils his tongue and character.

Mind exaggerates things. Imagination troubles you; you simply imagine that Mr. X is trying to harm you. In reality Mr. X is innocent. He is your friend and well-wisher. Mind does havoc through exaggeration and false imagination.

The mother-in-law falsely thinks that her daughter-in-law is ill-treating her. The daughter-in-law falsely imagines that her mother-in-law is treating her very badly. So the quarrels are going on daily in every house. The manager falsely imagines that the proprietor is ill-treating him. The clerk falsely imagines that the office superintendent is not treating him properly and so bears ill-will towards his superior. This is Maya's jugglery. This is all the trick of the mind. Beware, learn the ways of the mind and become wise. Learn to discriminate. Learn to do selfless service.

Do not make parties. Do not join parties. Be neutral. Remain alone. Keep company with saints, sages and the Indweller within through prayer, Japa and meditation.

Bless the man that curses you. Pray for that man who tries to harm and persecute you. Serve that man who speaks ill of you. Love that man who wants to injure you. Embrace all. Serve all. Love all. Develop Atma Bhava, Narayana Bhava. The two currents of Raga and Dvesha will perish by themselves.

Give up respect and honour. Treat this as dung or poison. Treat disrespect, dishonour as ornaments. Do not expect high seats and kind words. Do not sit on flowery cushion seats. Sit on the floor. Lord Gouranga sat in the place where shoes were kept. Be humble and do those services which are considered as menial services in the eyes of the worldly-minded people, but which are really worship of the Lord and Yoga activities for the knower and wise man. During the Last Supper, Jesus tied the boot-lace and washed the feet of his disciples. Sri Krishna, the Lord of the three worlds, washed the feet of guests and priests in the Rajasuya Yajna performed by Yudhishthira. Remember those two incidents always. This will make you humble.

Daily watch your mind and feelings. Be on the alert. Develop patience little by little. Grow. Evolve. Expand. Become strong like the Avanti Brahmin, Eknath or Jesus and rest peacefully.

May Lord give you inner spiritual strength to bear insult and injury. May you become a Jivanmukta.

A DYNAMIC SADHANA

It is due the veil of ignorance that you have forgotten your real essential nature, the Sat-Chit-Ananda State. It is not at all necessary for you to renounce the world and run to some Himalayan cave to regain your lost divinity. Here is an easy Sadhana by which you can definitely attain God-consciousness, even while living in the world amidst multifarious activities.

You need not necessarily have a separate meditation room or fix some time for meditation. Close your eyes for a minute or two once in every two hours and think of God and His various Divine qualities such as mercy, love, joy, knowledge, purity, perfection, and so forth during work, and mentally repeat: "Hari Om," or "Sri Ram," or "Ram Ram," or any other Mantra according to your taste.

This should be done even during night whenever you happen to get up from bed to micturate or on any other account. Though you are not in the habit of getting up from sleep, you should do this practice at least occassionally when you slightly change your posture during sleep. This sort of habit will come only by repeated practice.

Feel all along that the body is a moving temple of God, your office or business house is a big temple or Vrindavan, and all activities such as walking, eating, breathing, seeing, hearing, reading, etc., are offerings unto the Lord. Work is worship, Work is meditation, when done in the right spirit.

Work for work's sake without any motive, without the idea of agency (i.e., I am the doer, I am the enjoyer), and without expectation of fruits. Feel that you are an instrument in the hands of God and He works through your organs. Feel also that this world is a manifestation of the Lord or Viswa Vrindavan and your children, wife, father, mother and other relations are the images or children of the Lord. See God in every face and in every object. If you develop this changed angle of vision and Divine Bhava by potracted and constant practice, all actions will become Pooja or worship of the Lord. This is quite sufficient. You will have God-realisation soon. This is a dynamic Yoga. This is an easy Sadhana. Hereafter do not bring your old lame excuse: "Swamiji, I have no time to do spiritual practices." Even if you practise this dynamic Yoga for three months, you will become an entirely changed being altogether. Realise right now your identity and intimate relationship with all beings, with ants and dogs, elephants and tigers, Muslims and Hindus, Jews and Christians. There is only a degree of difference in manifastation or expression. All forms belong to God or Saguna Brahman. When you look at a tree or shrub, a Sikh or a Muslim, endeavour to behold behind the veil of form, the real hidden Consciousness. If you do this for some time, you will feel inexpressible joy. All hatred will cease. You will develop Cosmic love or unity of consciousness. This will be a magnanimous experience.

Write daily for half an hour in a notebook your Ishta Mantra observing Mauna and without turning to this side or that. Write down in bold types on cardboards or paper:

SPEAK THE TRUTH.
OM PURITY.
OM COURAGE.
I MUST REALISE GOD NOW.
TIME IS MOST PRECIOUS.
I WILL BE A TRUE BRAHMACHARI.
BRAHMACHARYA IS DIVINE LIFE.
I AM AN EMBODIMENT OF COURAGE,
 PURITY, MERCY, LOVE AND PATIENCE.

And fix them in bedroom, dining hall, front-room and verandahs. Keep such slips in your pocket and diary also. This is an easy way for developing virtuous divine qualities.

Here are some formulae for effecting ungruding and total self-surrender. Repeat them mentally several times daily with Bhava: "O Lord, I am Thine, All is Thine, Thy Will be done. Thou art everything. Thou doest everything." This practice will remove egoism and mineness and the idea of agency also.

ANTARANGA SADHANA

Nishkamya Karma Yoga or the performance of disinterested works is Bahiranga Sadhana, which leads you to meditation on *Aham Brahma Asmi*. Karma is more external than the four means of salvation, Sadhana Chatushtaya. The four means are more external than Sravana. Sravana is more external than Manana or reflection of what is heard through a teacher or books. Manana is more external than Nididhyasana. Antaranga Sadhana is Nididhyasana or deep meditation on *Aham Brahmasmi* and its meaning. In Ashtanga Yoga of Patanjali Maharshi also you have the Bahiranga and Antaranga Sadhana. Yama, Niyama, Asana, Pranayama and Pratyahara are the Bahiranga Sadhana; while Dharana, Dhyana and Samadhi are Antaranga Sadhana.

ETHICAL SADHANA

Atman or Self is one. There is one common consciousness in all beings. All Jivas are reflections of the one Supreme Soul or Paramatma. Just as one sun is reflected in all pots of water, so also the one Supreme Being is reflected in all human beings. One cannot become many. One appears as many. One is real. Many are illusory. Separateness is illusory. Separateness is temporary. Unity is real. Unity is Eternal. One life vibrates in all beings. Life is common in animals, birds and human beings. Existence is common. This is the emphatic declaration of the Upanishads. This primary truth of Religion is the foundation of ethics or Sadachara. If you hurt another man, you hurt yourself. If you help another man, you help yourself. On account of ignorance one man hurts another man. He thinks that other beings are separate from himself. So he exploits others. So he is selfish, greedy, proud and egoistic. If you are really aware that one Self pervades, permeates all beings, that all beings are threaded on the Supreme Self, as rows of pearls on a string, how can you hurt another man, how can you exploit another man?

Who of us are really anxious to know the truth about God or Divine life? We are more ready to ask ourselves: "How much money you have got in the Imperial Bank? Who said that against me? Do you know who I am? How are your wife and children doing?" and questions of this sort than questions like: "Who am I? What is this Samsara? What is bondage? What is freedom? Whence have I come? Whither shall I go? Who is Isvara? What are the attributes of God? What is our relationship to God? How to attain Moksha? What is the Svarupa of Moksha?"

The beginning of ethics is to reflect upon ourselves, our surroundings and our actions. Before we act we must stop to think. When a man earnestly attends to what he recognises as his duties, he will progress and in consequence thereof his comfort and prosperity will increase. His pleasures will be more refined; his happiness, his enjoyments, and recreations will be better and nobler. Happiness is like a shadow; if pursued it will flee from us; but if a man does not trouble himself about it and strictly attends to his duties, pleasures of the best and noblest kind will crop out everywhere in his path. If he does not anxiously pursue it, happiness will follow him.

The increase or rather refinement of happiness, however, cannot be considered as the ultimate aim of ethics for pain and affliction increase at the same rate because man's irritability, his susceptibility to pain, grows with the growth of his intellectuality. The essence of all existence is evolution or a constant realisation of new ideals. Therefore, the elevation of all human emotions, whether they are painful or happy, the elevation of man's whole existence of his actions and aspirations, is the constant aim of ethics.

The Socratic formula: "Virtue is knowledge" is found to be an adequate explanation of the moral life of man. Knowledge of what is right is not coincident with doing it, for man while knowing the right course is found deliberately choosing the wrong one. Desire tends to run counter to the dictates of reason; and the will perplexed by the difficulty of reconciling two such opposite demands, tends to choose the easier course and follow the inclination rather than endure the pain of refusing desire in obedience to the voice of reason. Hence mere intellectual instruction is not sufficient to ensure right doing. There arises the further need for chastisement or the straightening of crooked will, in order to ensure its cooperation with reason in assenting to what it affirms to be right, and its refusal to give preference to desire or irrational element in man's nature when such desire runs counter to the rational principle.

The pure reason urges a man to do what is best. The Asuric nature of a man fights and struggles against the man. The impulses of man who has not undergone the ethical discipline run counter to his reason. All advice, all rebuke and exhortation, all admonition testify that the irrational part is amenable to reason.

The basis of good manner is self-reliance. For such reasons have the great founders and eminent teachers of all religions repeatedly proclaimed the need for recognising the God-head within and for self-reliance in the last resort rather than any texts and persons and customs. Self-reliance is the basis of behaviour.

Self-control is greatest in the man whose life is dominated by ideals and general principles of conduct. The final end of moral discipline is self-control. The whole nature of man must be disciplined. Each element requires its specific training. Discipline harmonises the opposing elements of his soul. The self-control will enable the aspirant to know the Truth, to desire the good and to win the right and thus to realise the Reality.

Discipline is the training of our faculties through instructions and through exercise, in accordance with some settled principle of authority. You must discipline not only the intellect but also the will and the emotions. A disciplined man will control his actions. He is no longer at the mercy of the moment. He ceases to be a slave of his impulses and Indriyas. Such mastery is not the result of one day's effort. One can acquire the power by protracted practice and daily self-discipline. You must learn to refuse the demands of impulses. A self-controlled man will have to resist the wrong action to which a worldly man is most strongly impelled.

MOUNA SADHANA
A DIDACTIC EXPLANATION OF MOUNA SADHANA

Mouna is the vow of silence. It is absolutely necessary for a spiritual life. Much energy is wasted by idle gossiping and tall talk. All energies must be conserved and transmuted into Ojas Sakti. This will help you in meditation.

If circumstances prevent you to observe Mouna, strictly avoid long talk, big talk, tall talk, all unnecessary talks, all sorts of vain debates and discussions, etc., and withdraw yourself from society as much as possible. If this energy is conserved

TYPES OF SADHANA

by Mouna, it will be transmuted into Ojas Sakti, which will be of immense use in your Sadhana. Speech is Tejomaya according to Chhandogya Upanishad. The gross portion of fire goes to constitute bone, the middle portion to form marrow, and the subtle portion to form speech. So speech is a very powerful energy. Remember this. Remember this always.

Observe Mouna for one year or six months. If you cannot do for six months continuously, observe the vow of silence at least for a day in a week, just as Mahatma Gandhiji did. You must draw the inspiration from Mahatmas.

When the Indriyas are silent, it is termed Indriya Mouna or Karana Mouna. When you keep the body steady, immovable, it is termed Kashtha Mouna. In Sushupti (deep slumber) there is Sushupti Mouna. The real Mouna comes only when there is absence of duality and separation, when all mental modifications cease. This is Maha Mouna. It is Para Brahman.

IMPORTANCE OF MOUNA SADHANA

Five things are indispensably requisite if you want to practise rigorous meditation and attain Samadhi or Self-realisation quickly. They are: Mouna, light diet or a diet of milk and fruits, solitude with charming scenery, personal contact with a teacher and a cool place.

Vak-Indriya is a strong weapon of Maya to delude the Jivas and to distract their minds. Quarrels, disputes, etc., occur through the play or mischief of this turbulent Indriya. If you control this Indriya you have already controlled half the mind.

The Vak-Indriya is very mischievous and troublesome and turbulent and impetuous. It must be steadily and gradually controlled. When you begin to check it, it will try to rebound upon you. You must be bold and courageous.

Do not allow anything to come out from the mind through the Vak-Indriya (organ of speech). Observe Mouna. This will help you. Now you have shut out a big source of disturbance. You will rest now in Peace. Meditate on God or Brahman in right earnest.

The subjugation of the Vak-Indriya or the control of speech is Karana Mouna. The complete cessation of one's physical actions is Kashtha Mouna. In Vak Mouna and Kashtha Mouna the mental modifications are not destroyed. In Kashtha Mouna you should not nod your head. You should not show any signs. You should not write anything on a piece of paper or slate to express your ideas.

Vak Mouna is only a help to the attainment of Maha Mouna wherein the mind rests in Sat-Chit-Ananda Brahman and all thoughts are completely annihilated. Mouna conserves energy, develops will-power and controls the impulses of speech. It is a help to the practice of truthfulness and to control anger.

The Brahmic Bliss without beginning and without the differentiated pains whether enjoyed by one with direct cognition of such a bliss or not is Sushupti Mouna in Jivanmuktas. The expurgation from the mind of all doubts, after realising firmly the illusory character of this world with all its Gunas is Sushupti Mouna. The settled conclusion that the universe is no other than the All-full Brahman is Sushupti Mouna. Equality of vision over all and quiescence of mind with the idea that which are Sat, Asat or Sat-asat are no other than the eternal Chidakasa is Sushupti Mouna.

Even Brahmavadins should practise Vak Mouna in the beginning of their Sadhana. They should not be puffed up with false egoism and pride: "I am a Vedantin. There is no necessity for Vak Mouna." This Vak Mouna is a great help in the beginning even for a Vedantin. You can begin with Vak Mouna if your environments will not permit for Kashtha Mouna.

He who observes Mouna should keep himself perfectly occupied in Japa, meditation, Mantra-writing. He should not mix with others. He should not come out of his room frequently. The energy of speech should be sublimated into spiritual energy and utilised for meditation. Then only you will enjoy serenity, calmness, peace, inner spiritual strength.

You should feel that you will derive much benefit from observing Mouna and experience much peace, inner strength and joy. Then only you will take pleasure in observing Mouna. Then only you will not attempt to speak a word even. Forced Mouna simply to imitate or from compulsion will make you restless and gloomy.

During Mouna you can nicely introspect and practise self-analysis. You can watch the thoughts. You can understand the ways of the mind and its workings. You can notice how the mind runs from one object to another in a moment's time. You will derive immense benefit from the practice of Mouna. Real

Mouna is silence of the mind. Physical Mouna will eventually lead to the silence of the mind.

Mouna develops will-force, checks the force of Sankalpa, curbs the impulse of speech and gives peace of mind. You will get the power of endurance. You will not tell lies. You will have control over speech.

Mouna develops will-power. Mouna checks the impulses of speech. It is a great help for the observance of truth and control of anger. Emotions are controlled and irritability is checked. A Mouni will use measured words and his speech is very impressive. In ordinary persons there is not a bit of control over speech. They speak at random whatever they like. They cannot put a check on the current of speech. A Mouni first thinks whether the word will wound the feelings of others or not, what sort of impression it will produce on the minds of others, etc. He is very careful in his speech. He is very thoughtful and considerate. He weighs every word before it comes out of his mouth. A Mouni can stay even for a long time in seclusion. A worldly talkative man cannot stay even for some hours in solitude. He always wants company. The advantages of Mouna are indescribable. Practise, feel the peace and enjoy the silence yourself.

The study of Sanskrit makes some persons very talkative and forces them to enter into unnecessary discussions with others to show their scholarly erudition. Pedantry or vain display of learning is a special attribute of some Sanskrit scholars. How much energy is wasted in such loose talks; how much benefit can one derive if he conserves the energy and utilises it in Divine contemplation! He can move heaven and earth.

During times of ailment, observance of Mouna will give great peace of mind. It will check mental irritability also. Energy is wasted in idle talking. Mouna conserves the energy and you can turn out more mental and physical work. You can do a lot of meditation. It exercises a marvellous, soothing influence on the brain and nerves. By practice of Mouna the energy of speech is slowly transmuted or sublimated into Ojas Sakti or spiritual energy.

Observe Mouna for your own spiritual growth and not for making the public understand that you are a great Yogi. Always scrutinise your motives in doing any action.

Observe Mouna while taking food. Live alone. Do not mix with others. Do not make gestures and signs and *hu-hu-hu* sounds. This *hu-hu-hu* is tantamount to talking. This is worse than talking. There is more wastage of energy in uttering *hu-hu-hu*.

Busy people should observe Mouna at least for one hour daily. On Sundays observe Mouna for six hours or the whole day. People also will not disturb you at that time when they come to know that you are regularly observing Mouna. Your family members also will not worry you. Utilise this time of Mouna in Japa and meditation. You must observe Mouna at any convenient time in the morning or evening besides the hours of silence that you have during your morning meditation. If you regard the time you spend in morning meditation as the hours of silence, then you can take sleep also as Mouna.

If the place is not suitable to observe Mouna, go to any other solitary place where your friends will not trouble you.

It is better you observe Mouna for some time in seclusion and try to evolve. After perfection you can work wonders in a short space of time.

If you want to do Anushthana for forty days, keep complete Mouna during these forty days. You will have wonderful peace and spiritual progress. Do the Anushthana on the banks of the Ganga at Rishikesh, Haridwar, Prayag. Ladies of the house are more talkative. They always create some kind of trouble in the house. Mothers-in-law and daughters-in-law cannot keep quiet even for a second. Some kind of friction will take place in the house. Whenever you want to observe Anushthana go to a solitary place.

Long Mouna and Kashtha Mouna for a long period is not necessary. Mouna for a protracted period in an unregenerate and undeveloped aspirant does harm. Keep Mouna for a month and then break and then continue. Do not keep Mouna for a long period. Mouna for a few days or a month will be of immense help to the aspirants in the control of the organ of speech and the mind. Immense energy can be conserved. You will feel also immense peace.

You can observe Mouna for a long time; but if you find it difficult and if you do not utilise the time in Japa and meditation, break it at once. Try to become a man of measured words. This is itself Mouna. To talk profusely for six months and to observe Mouna for the rest of six months is of no avail.

The practice of Mouna should be gradual or you will not be able to observe all of a sudden Mouna for 10 or 15 days. Those who are in the habit of observing Mouna daily for 2 or 3 hours or 24 hours on holidays will be able to observe Mouna for a week or fifteen days. You should clearly understand the value of Mouna. Observe Mouna for two hours daily. Gradually increase it to 6 hours, 24 hours, 2 days in a month, and then one week and so on.

When the energy of speech is not controlled and utilised properly in spiritual pursuit viz., Japa and meditation, when it is not perfectly sublimated it runs riot and manifests or bursts out in the form of *hu-hu-hu* sounds, showing various sorts of gestures and producing various sounds. There is more loss of energy by exhibition of these gestures, etc., than by ordinary talking.

During the period of Mouna you should not show any gestures and various other sorts of movements of the hands and should not utter *hu-hu-hu*. This is worse than talking. If anything is absolutely necessary, you can write on a piece of paper. You should try to avoid such slips also.

Take milk without sugar during the period of Mouna, and dhal and vegetable without salt. This is discipline of the tongue. Milk does not need the addition of sugar. There is milk-sugar already in the milk. It is only through the force of habit man adds sugar to satisfy his palate. Natural milk without sugar has got its own sweet intrinsic taste. If the tongue is controlled, all other senses can easily be controlled. The tongue is the most mischievous sense. Control of the tongue is really control of the mind. Every Vasana that is conquered will develop the will-power and give you strength to conquer another Vasana easily.

During the period of Mouna in seclusion try to lead the life of a Sannyasi (mental Sannyasa). If you say: "I am only a householder. I have not yet become a Sannyasi," these thoughts will give a long lease of life to the mind to have its own ways. There is no half-measure in the spiritual path. No leniency for the mind at least for a few days. All weaknesses will die during the period of rigorous Tapas. You will grow rapidly. Mind cannot be checked without vigorous discipline.

During the period of Mouna in a solitary place you should not read newspapers. Reading newspapers will bring out revival of worldly Samskaras, will disturb your peace of mind. Though you live in the Himalayas you will be in the plains throughout the day. You will not be much benefited by observing Mouna. Your meditation will be seriously disturbed.

During Mouna you should not write too many slips or write on a slate or write on the fore-arm with your finger to express your thoughts to your neighbours. You should not laugh. These are all breaks in Mouna. These are all worse than talking.

Reduce your wants. You should previously arrange with those who attend on you for your menu or regimen of diet and the time at which the food must be served. You should not frequently make changes in diet and always think of the different articles of diet. You should yourself attend to the cleansing of your room and other daily ordinary duties such as drawing water, cleansing clothes and lanterns, etc. Do not bother much about your shaving, polishing the shoes and washing Dhoties by washerman. All these will interfere with the continuity of Divine thoughts. Do not think much of body, and beard. Think more of God or Atman.

The mind will be ever waiting to hurl the aspirant down into the deep abyss of ignorance whenever it gets an opportunity. Therefore be very careful and vigilant.

May you attain Peace through silence. May you enter into the stupendous ocean of silence through Mouna. May you become a Maha Mouni or a Jivanmukta through Mouna. May the Lord grant you strength to observe the vow of silence without any break! Om Santi!

BRAHMACHARYA SADHANA

Brahmacharya is purity in thought, word and deed. Brahmacharya includes the control of not only the sex or reproductive Indriya but also of other Indriyas. This is the definition of Brahmacharya in a broad sense. Brahmacharya is of two kinds, viz., physical and mental. Physical is control of body and the mental is control of evil thoughts. In mental Brahmacharya even a lustful thought will never enter the mind. Freedom from all sexual thoughts in waking as well as dreaming states is strict Brahmacharya.

The vital energy, the Virya, which supports your life, is a

great treasure for you. It is the quintessence of blood. Brahmacharya is truly a precious jewel. It is the most effective medicine or nectar which destroys diseases, decay and death. This Atman or immortal soul is verily the nature of Brahmacharya. Atman resides in Brahmacharya.

Virya is the essence of life, thought, intelligence and consciousness. When the Virya is once lost, it can never be recouped in your lifetime by your taking any amount of Badam, nervine tonics, milk, cream, Makaradhwaja, etc. This fluid when preserved carefully, serves as a master-key for you to open the doors of elysian bliss or the realms of God or Atman and for all sorts of higher achievements in life. By Brahmacharya alone, the Rishis of yore have conquered death and attained the immortal Abode of Joy and Bliss.

You cannot have health and spiritual life without Brahmacharya. Brahmacharya is the keynote of success in every walk of life. Brahmacharya serves as a gateway for bliss beyond. It opens the door of Moksha (Emancipation). Siddhis and Riddhis (psychic powers) roll under the feet of a Brahmachari. Who can describe the majesty and glory of a Brahmachari? Brahmacharya or spotless chastity is the best of penances. There is nothing in this world that cannot be attained by a celibate. He can move the whole world.

Sensuality destroys life, lustre, strength, vitality, memory, wealth, fame, holiness and devotion to the Supreme. Death is hastened by letting out the vital energy from the body. Life is saved and prolonged by preserving it. Those who have lost much of their Virya or the vital energy become easily irritable and lazy. They easily succumb to any disease. They meet with premature death.

Persons are physically, mentally and morally debilitated because of the want of Brahmacharya or because of wasting the seminal power. Such persons become easily irritable for little things. They fall a victim to various diseases and premature death.

A well-disciplined life, study of scriptures, Satsanga, Japa, Dhyana, Sattvic diet, daily self-analysis, practice of Sadachara, and the three kinds of Tapas and such other spiritual discipline, pave a long way in the attainment of this end.

The practice of celibacy is not attended with any danger or any disease or any undesirable result, such as the various sorts of 'complexes' which are wrongly attributed by the Western psychologists to it. They have no practical knowledge of the subject on hand. They have a wrong, ill-founded imagination that the ungratified sex-energy assumes the various forms of complexes in disguise, such as touch-phobia, etc. It is a morbid state of mind due to excessive anger, hatred, jealousy, worry and depression brought about by various causes.

Do not look at obscene pictures. Do not speak vulgar words. Do not read novels that excite passion and produce ignoble, undesirable sentiments in the heart. Shun bad company. Do not go to cinemas. Give up onions, garlic, hot curries, chutneys and spiced dishes. Take wholesome bland Sattvic food. Transmute the sex-energy into spiritual energy (Ojas) by sublime thoughts, practice of Japa, Kirtan (singing God's Name), Vichara or Atmic enquiry, Pranayama (restraint of breath), Sirshasana, Sarvangasana, study of the Gita, the Upanishads and other religious books. Have Satsanga—association with Mahatmas, Yogis and Sadhus. You will be established in Brahmacharya. There will be sublimation of sex-energy.

Regarding Brahmacharya Sage Patanjali says: "By the establishment of celibacy, vigour is gained."

If semen is preserved by the observance of Brahmacharya, and transmuted into Ojas Sakti, the spiritual and intellectual power will increase. Semen is intimately connected with brain and intellect, the former being the stuff of human vitality. It has relation to intelligence, morality and spirituality. There can be no success in Yoga without conserving this essential force in one's system. The vigour that the Yogi attains here is not merely physical, but mental, intellectual, moral, occult and spiritual. By this one can impart knowledge to others without their knowledge.

Brahmacharya is the fundamental qualification of an aspirant. It is the most important virtue for Self-realisation. Brahmacharya is purity in thought, word and deed. The very idea of lust should not enter the mind. No Yoga or spiritual progress is possible without continence.

SADHANA OF THE ANTARMUKHA VRITTI

Remember this triplet—*Search, Understand* and *Realise*. Searching is "Sravana" or hearing of Srutis. It is search for the truth. Understanding is "Manana" or reflection of what you have heard from the Holy Masters and sacred lore. Realising is direct, spiritual Anubhuti of Atman (Sakshatkara) by 'Nididhyasana' or profound and continued meditation on one idea, "I am Brahman." There are three means of Self-realisation according to the Vedantic method.

This is another kind of triplet for developing Vairagya (dispassion) and getting rid of Moha (attraction, delusion) for objects. This is the instruction given by Sri Adi Sankara. As soon as you are attracted towards a woman or object, immediately remember this triplet. Analyse the various parts of a woman or an object. Realise the true nature of these objects. Then abandon them (Tyaga). You will derive immense benefit by constant repetition of the above formula. This will induce Vairagya. The mind will not run towards objects. It will shrink from worldly objects. Attraction for objects will gradually vanish. I have derived considerable benefit by this method. The mind having lost all attraction for objects, will move towards the heart, its "Yatha-Sthana" (original home), towards God. This is termed "Antarmukha Vritti."

SADHANA BY CIRCUMSPECTION

The man who can see his own faults as he sees those of others, will soon become a great soul. Have ceaseless devotion to truth and be ready to sacrifice your all for it.

Do not brood over your past mistakes and failures as this will only fill your mind with grief, regret and depression. Do not repeat them in future. Be cautious. Just think of the causes which led to your failures and try to remove them in the future. Be vigilant and circumspect. Strengthen yourself with new vigour and virtues. Develop slowly your will-power.

SADHANA IN SELF-ANALYSIS

Daily self-analysis or self-examination is indispensably requisite. Then alone can you remove your defects and grow rapidly in spirituality. A gardener watches the young plants very carefully. He removes the weeds daily. He puts a strong fence around them. He waters them at the proper time. Then alone they grow beautifully and yield fruits quickly. Even so, you should find out your defects through daily introspection and self-analysis, and then eradicate them through suitable methods. If one method fails, you must adopt a combined method. If prayer fails, you should take recourse to Satsanga or association with the wise, Pranayama, meditation, dietetic regulation, enquiry, etc. You should destroy not only big waves of pride, hypocrisy, lust, anger, etc., that manifest on the surface of the conscious mind, but also their subtle impressions which lurk in the corners of the subconscious mind. Then only you are perfectly safe.

These subtle impressions are very dangerous. They lurk like thieves and attack you when you are napping, when you are not vigilant, when your dispassion wanes, when you slacken a bit your daily spiritual practice, and when you are provoked. If these defects do not manifest even under extreme provocation on several occasions, even when you are not practising daily introspection and self-analysis, you can rest assured the subtle impressions also are obliterated. Now you are safe. The practice of introspection and self-analysis demands patience, perseverance, leech-like tenacity, application, iron will, iron determination, subtle intellect, courage, etc. But you will gain a fruit of incalculable value. That precious fruit is Immortality, Supreme Peace and Infinite Bliss. You will have to pay a heavy price for this. Therefore you should not murmur when you do daily practice. You should apply your full mind, heart, intellect and soul to spiritual practice. Then only rapid success is possible.

Keep a daily spiritual diary and practise self-analysis (self-examination) at night. Note down how many good actions you have done, what mistakes you have committed during the course of the day. In the morning resolve: "I will not yield to anger today. I will practise celibacy today. I will speak truth today."

SADHANA OF PRATIPAKSHA BHAVANA

If evil thoughts enter your mind, don't use your will-force in driving them out. You will lose your energy only. You will tax your will only. You will fatigue yourself. The greater the efforts you make, the more the evil thoughts will return with redoubled force. They will return more quickly also. The thoughts will become more powerful. Be indifferent. Keep quiet. They will pass off soon. Or substitute good counter-thoughts (*Pratipaksha bhavana* method). Or think of the picture of God and the Mantra again and again forcibly. Or pray.

SADHANA OF SPIRITUAL VISION

There are four ways of transforming evil into good. He who practises this useful Sadhana will never have an evil Drishti or the eye of evil vision, and will gain the eye of spiritual vision. He will have a changed angle of vision. He will never complain of bad environments. You must put these into practice daily.

No man is absolutely bad. Everyone has some good trait or other. Try to see the good in everyone. Develop the good-finding nature. This will act as a powerful antidote against the fault-finding habit.

Even a rogue of the first order is a potential saint. He is a saint of the future. Remember this point well. He is not an eternal rogue. Place him in the company of saints. In a moment his pilfering nature will be changed. Hate roguery but not the rogue.

Remember that Lord Narayana Himself is acting the part of a rogue, thief and prostitute in the world's drama. This is His Lila (sporting). The whole vision becomes changed at once. Devotion arises in your heart immediately when you see a rogue.

Have Narayana-Drishti everywhere. See Narayana everywhere. Feel His presence. Whatever you see, feel, touch and taste is nothing but God.

Change the mental attitude. Change the angle of vision. Then only one will have heaven on earth. What is the earthly use of one's reading of the Upanishads and the Vedanta-Sutras when one has an evil eye and foul tongue.

THE DISCIPLINES OF UNIVERSAL LOVE

The only Sara Vastu in this world is Prema or Love. It is eternal, infinite and undecaying. Physical love is passion or Moha or infatuation. Universal love is divine love. Cosmic love, Visva Prema, universal love are synonymous terms. God is love. Love is God. Selfishness, greed, egoism, vanity, pride and hatred, contract the heart and stand in the way of developing universal love.

Develop universal love gradually through selfless service, Satsanga (association with Mahatmas), prayer, recitation of Guru Mantra, etc. When the heart is contracted through selfishness, man loves his wife, children, a few friends and relatives only, in the beginning. As he evolves, he loves the people of his own district, then the people of his own province. Later on, he develops love for men of his own country, eventually, he begins to love other people of different countries. In the long run, he begins to love all. He develops universal love. All the barriers are broken now. The heart expands infinitely.

It is very easy to talk of universal love. But when you want to put it into actual practice, it becomes extremely difficult. Petty-mindedness of all sorts comes in the way. Old, wrong Samskaras (impressions) which you have created by your wrong mode of life in the past, act as stumbling blocks. Through iron determination, strong will-power, patience, perseverance and Vichara (right enquiry), you can conquer all obstacles quite easily. The grace of the Lord will descend on you if you are sincere, my dear friends!

Universal love terminates in Advaitic unity or oneness or Upanishadic consciousness of seers and sages. Pure love is a great leveller. It brings equality. Hafiz, Kabir, Mira, Gouranga, Tukaram, Ramdas, all have tasted this universal love. What others have achieved, you can also attain.

Feel that the whole world is your body, your own home. Melt or destroy all barriers that separate man from man. Idea of superiority is ignorance or delusion. Develop Visvaprema, all-embracing love. Unite with all. Separation is death. Unity is eternal life. Feel that the whole world is Visvabrindavan. Feel that this body is a moving temple of God. Wherever you are, whether at home, office, railway station or market, feel that you are in the temple. Consecrate every act as an offering unto the Lord. Transmute every work into Yoga by offering its fruits to God. Have Akarta, Sakshi Bhava, if you are a student of Vedanta. Have Nimitta Bhava if you are a student of Bhakti Marga. Feel that all beings are images of God. *Isa Vasyam Idam Sarvam*—this world is indwelt by the Lord. Feel that one power or God works through all hands, sees through all eyes, hears through all ears. You will become a changed being. You will enjoy the highest peace and bliss.

CHAPTER FOUR

SADHANA IN THE PRASTHANATRAYI

THE SADHANA OF THE VEDA

According to the Purusha-Sukta of the Veda, the Supreme Purusha is both transcendent and immanent. He is the thousand-headed, the thousand-eyed and the thousand-legged. He envelops all creation inside and outside and rises above it to Infinity. The Purusha is all this. Whatever was, whatever is and whatever shall be, is the Lord of the Immortal. All beings are sustained in Him. He can be designated as neither existence nor non-existence. He is neither in space nor outside it. He is the magnificent indescribable, which is the root of all that is conceivable. Even the gods do not know what He is and where He is. Lo! May we say perhaps that He Himself knows not? Such is His greatness. He has manifested Himself in this universal sacrificial act of creation. He provides, in His own sensible form as the universe, the field for all types of individual sacrifice. The universe is a Yajna and all actions in this universe is a Yajna. The Supreme Being is Yajna, the Transcendent Sacrifice, to be emulated in all individual forms of sacrifice. The essence of sacrifice is to exist for others and to offer one's own existence into the existence of others. This is the key to Immortality. Temporal sacrifices are relative symbol of this sacrifice in the Absolute.

All that is seen is the form of the Purusha. The visible and the conceivable, the high and the low, the good and the bad, the strong and the feeble, the beautiful and the ugly, the useful and the useless, all this is His manifested form. To adore Him, to worship Him one need not move from one's seat. Whatever is here, just in front of my eyes, is He, and He can be worshipped through it, in it, by it and for it. In this Absolute worship and Absolute sacrifice, He is the articles of worship, He is the worshipper, He is the worship and He is the worshipped. He is the mode of worship, He is the sacrifice and its constituents. His existence is His manifestation and His manifestation is His existence. To be is to act and to act is to be. Immortality and death are His shadows. Life and non-life are His modes. This is the grand vision of the Supreme Being, which shall transform human living into Divine Life.

SADHANA IN THE BRAHMA SUTRAS

The third chapter of the Brahma Sutras, entitled Sadhanadhyaya, deals with practical methods for the obtainment of the realisation of Brahman. This chapter determines those methods or Sadhanas which are the means for attaining the highest Reality or the Infinite. In the first and the second Padas of this chapter are taught two things, viz., a strong yearning or burning desire (Mumukshutva) to realise Brahman or the final emancipation and an equally strong disgust (Vairagya) towards all objects other than Brahman; because these are the two fundamental things among all Sadhanas.

In order to induce Vairagya or dispassion the Sutras show in the first Pada the imperfections of all mundane existences and this they base on the Panchagni Vidya or the doctrine of five fires of the Chhandogya Upanishad in which is taught how the soul passes after death from one condition to another.

The first Pada teaches the great doctrine of reincarnation, the departure of the soul from the physical body, its journey to the Chandraloka on the third plane and its coming back to the earth. This is done in order to create Vairagya or indifference to sensual enjoyments herein and hereafter. In the second Pada are described all the glorious attributes of the Supreme Brahman, His Omniscience, Omnipotence, Loveliness, etc., in order to attract the soul towards Him, so that He may be the sole object of quest.

In the third Pada, the author of the Brahma Sutras sets himself the task of ascertaining the end and aim of the Vidyas or Upasanas or Meditations as prescribed in the Srutis.

The Srutis prescribe various kinds of Vidyas or Meditations to enable the aspirant to attain the knowledge of identity. It is extremely difficult or rather impossible for the ordinary man to have a comprehensive understanding of the Infinite, which is transcendent, extremely subtle and beyond the reach of the senses and gross undisciplined intellect. Therefore the Srutis or the sacred scriptures prescribe easy methods of Saguna-Meditation for approaching the Infinite or the Absolute. They present various symbols of Brahman (Pratikas) such as

Vaisvanara or Virat, Sun, Akasa, Food, Prana and mind for the neophyte or the beginner to contemplate on. These symbols are props for the mind to lean upon in the beginning. The gross mind is rendered subtle, sharp and one-pointed by such Saguna forms of meditation.

These different methods of approaching the Impersonal Absolute are known as Vidyas or Upasanas. This section discusses these various Vidyas by means of which the Supreme Soul is attained by the Jiva. The aim of all these Vidyas is the realisation of Brahman. Brahman alone is the living Reality. Brahman alone is Truth. Brahman is Sat or Existence Absolute. One meditation or Upasana or Vidya is as good as another for attaining emancipation.

Sruti teaches us to meditate on Brahman either directly or through the medium of some Pratikas or symbols, such as the sun, Akasa, food, mind, Prana, the Purusha residing in the eye, the empty space (Daharakasa) within the heart, OM or Pranava and the like.

You will have to search Brahman and adore Him in and through the symbols, but these symbols must not usurp His place. You must concentrate and fix the mind on these symbols and think of His attributes such as Omnipotence, Omniscience, Omnipresence, Sat-Chit-Ananda, Purity, Perfection, Freedom, etc.

The Vidyas appear to be different only from the viewpoint of difference in the symbols but the goal everywhere is the same. Remember this point always. Bear this in mind constantly.

Some attributes of Brahman are found common in some of Vidyas. You should not consider yourself as a distinct entity from Brahman. This is a fundamental or vital point.

In all the Vidyas three things are common. The final goal is the attainment of eternal bliss and immortality, through the realisation of Brahman with or without the aid of the symbols or Pratikas. The attributes which are found in common in all the Vidyas such as Blissfulness, Purity, Perfection, Knowledge, Immortality, Absolute Freedom or Kaivalya, Absolute Independence, Eternal Satisfaction and the like must be invariably associated with the conception of Brahman. The meditator must think himself identical with Brahman, must worship Brahman as his Immortal Atman.

The Brahma Sutras deal with the enquiry into the nature of Brahman. Why should you enquire about Brahman? Because the fruits obtained by sacrifices, etc., are ephemeral, whereas the knowledge of Brahman is eternal. Life in this earth and the life in heaven which you will attain on account of your virtuous deeds are transient. If you know Brahman you will enjoy everlasting bliss and immortality. That is the reason why you must start the quest of Brahman or the Truth or the Ultimate Reality.

A time comes when a person becomes indifferent to Karmas. He knows that Karmas cannot give him everlasting unalloyed happiness which is not mixed with pain, sorrow and fear. Therefore naturally a desire arises in him for the knowledge of Brahman or the all-pervading, eternal Soul which is above Karmas, which is the source of eternal happiness.

You must know and realise the eternal Brahman. Then only you will attain eternal bliss, freedom, perfection and immortality. You must have certain preliminary qualifications for your search. The enquirer should be endowed with certain spiritual requisites which are known as the *Sadhana Chatushtaya* or the four means of attaining salvation. They are (1) *Nitya-anitya-vastu-viveka* (discrimination between the Eternal and the non-eternal); (2) *Ihamutrartha-phalabhoga-viraga* (indifference to the enjoyment in this life or in heaven, and of the fruits of one's actions); (3) *Shatsampat* (sixfold virtues viz., *Sama*, control of mind; *Dama*, control of the external senses; *Uparati*, cessation from worldly enjoyments or not thinking of objects of senses or discontinuance of religious ceremonies; *Titiksha*, endurance of pleasure and pain, heat and cold; *Sraddha*, faith in the words of the preceptor and of the Upanishads; and *Samadhana*, deep concentration); and (4) *Mumukshutva* (desire for liberation).

In the ascertainment of Truth or the Ultimate Reality or the first cause the scriptures alone are authoritative because they are infallible, they contain the direct intuitive experiences of Rishis or Seers who attained *Brahma Sakshatkara* or Self-realisation. You cannot depend on intellect or reason because a man of strong intellect can overthrow a man of weak intellect. Brahman is not an object of the senses. It is beyond the reach of the senses and the intellect.

You can attain knowledge of Brahman through reflection on Its attributes. Otherwise it is not possible to have such knowledge. Inference or reasoning is an instrument of right knowledge if it does not contradict the Vedanta texts. You will attain Self-realisation through meditation on Brahman or the truths declared by Vedantic texts and not through mere reasoning. Pure reason (Suddha Buddhi) is a help in Self-realisation. It investigates and reveals the truths of the Scriptures. It has a place also in the means of Self-realisation. But perverted intellect (Viparita Buddhi) is a great hindrance. It keeps one far away from the Truth.

That which is the cause of the world is Brahman. This is *Tatastha Lakshana*. The origin, sustenance and dissolution of the world are characteristics of the world. They do not pertain to the eternal unchanging Brahman. Yet these indicate Brahman which is the cause for this universe. Srutis give another definition of Brahman. This is a description of its true, essential nature *'Satyam Jnanam Anantam Brahma'*—Truth, Knowledge, Infinity is Brahman. This is *Svarupa Lakshana*.

Knowledge of Brahman cannot come through mere reasoning. You can attain this knowledge through intuition or revelation. Intuition is the final result of the enquiry into Brahman. The object of enquiry is an existing substance. You will have to know this only through intuition or direct cognition (*Aparoksha-anubhuti* or *Anubhava*—experience). *Sravana* (hearing of the Srutis), *Manana* (reflection on what you have heard) and *Nididhyasana* (profound meditation) on Brahman lead to intuition. The Brahmakara Vritti is generated from the Sattvic *Antahkarana* which is equipped with the four means of salvation, and the instructions of the Guru, who has understood the real significance of *'Tat Tvam Asi'* Mahavakya. This Brahmakara Vritti destroys the Mula Avidya or primitive ignorance—the root-cause of all bondage, births and deaths. When the ignorance or veil is removed, Brahman which is self-effulgence reveals Itself or shines by Itself in Its pristine glory and ineffable splendour.

When one realises Brahman, he is totally freed from all sorts of miseries and pains. He attains the goal of life or *summum bonum*. The conception of duality as agent, action and the like is destroyed. Self-realisation is not a fruit of action. It is not a result of your willing or doing. It is the result of realising one's identity with Brahman. Scripture aims only at removing the veil of ignorance or Avidya. Then the self-effulgent

Brahman shines by Itself in Its pristine glory. The state of Moksha or the final emancipation is eternal. It is not transient like the fruits attained through action. Action depends upon the will and is independent of the object. Knowledge depends on the nature of the object and is independent of the will of the knower.

A proper understanding of the Vedantic texts leads to the final emancipation of man. It is not necessary for him to exert or do any superhuman feat or action. It is only mere understanding that it is a rope and not a snake that helps to destroy one's fear. Scripture does not speak only of ethical and ceremonial duties. It reveals the soul and helps one to attain Self-realisation. The sage who has learnt by the help of Vedantic texts to remove the erroneous identification with the body will not experience pain. It is only the ignorant worldly-minded man who experiences pain on account of his identification with the body.

The Vedantic texts give a beautiful description of the nature of Brahman. They teach that Brahman is eternal, all-knowing, absolutely self-sufficient, ever pure, free, pure knowledge, absolute bliss, self-luminous and indivisible. One attains final emancipation as the fruit of meditation on Brahman.

A knowledge of the three states, viz., waking, dreaming and deep sleep, is very necessary for the students of Vedanta. It will help them to understand the nature of the fourth state, viz., Turiya or the state of super-consciousness. For a student of Vedanta, the waking state is as much unreal as the dream state. The state of deep sleep intimates that the nature of the Supreme Soul is Bliss and that Brahman is one without a second and that the world is unreal. Vedantins make a study of the four states very carefully. They do not ignore dream and deep sleep state, whereas the scientists draw their conclusions from the experiences of the waking state only. Hence, their knowledge is limited, partial and incorrect.

He who meditates on Brahman as mind as is taught in the Taittiriya Upanishad Bhrigu Valli must collate all the attributes of the mind not only from his own particular Vedic Sakha, but from other Sakhas also where meditation on Brahman in the form of mind is taught. In meditating on Brahman as mind, he must not bring together attributes not belonging to mind such as those of food, though Brahman is taught to be meditated upon as food also. In fact only those attributes are to be supplied from other

Sakhas which are taught about the particular object of meditation, and not any attribute in general.

SADHANA OF THE UPANISHADS

The Upanishads constitute the central basis of Hindu Religion and Philosophy. They are the Vedanta or the end of the Vedas, the culmination of Knowledge. Nothing can be a match to the wondrous suggestiveness of the Upanishads. They have satisfied the greatest thinkers of the world, and they have pacified the greatest spiritual men here. Nothing that went before or after has been able to surpass the Upanishads in the depth of Wisdom and the message of Satisfaction and Peace. Dadhyanch, Uddalaka, Sanatkumara, Sandilya and Yajnavalkya are some of the outstanding philosophers and sages of the Upanishads who have lit up the torch to the path of Perfection. The Upanishads mainly preach Knowledge through philosophising. They are the text-books for the seeker after the Self. They are styled by different names: Brahma Vidya, Adhyatma-Sastra, Vedanta, Jnana. One who practises the teachings of the Upanishads attains to the Supreme. He breaks the knot of the heart, clears all doubts and destroys all sins. He enters into the All. He is liberated from embodiment. He becomes Immortal. He becomes the Self of all. He is an Apta Kama. He is really blessed. He crosses over sorrow. He crosses over sin. He does not return to the mortal coil. He exists as the Absolute.

The Upanishads are a book of Spiritual Knowledge. The Supreme is pervading all that appears here. One should therefore really enjoy by renouncing the sense of worldliness. He has no reason to covet other's property.

Life is not a misery. One should live for a hundred years by performing action without attachment. Life is not a bondage when it is looked with the proper light. Such a man of proper knowledge looks on all beings as his own Self and his Self as all beings. To him everything is his own Self, and he is not affected by grief, delusion or sorrow of any kind.

The Supreme Reality is indescribable. It is beyond the reach of the mind and the senses. It is beyond even the intellect. It is the light of all else, nothing is a light to It. Speech cannot express It. Mind cannot think It. Intellect cannot understand It. Senses cannot perceive It. Such a wonderful being is the

Truth. Brahma-Jnana is not a knowledge of something but becoming Absolute Knowledge Itself. It is the Infinite subject if speech can be permitted to express like that. It is an experience and not a perception. It is Absoluteness and is, therefore, beyond the conception of duality and pairs of opposites. The greatest blessedness is to know That, and he is an unfortunate man who dies without the Knowledge of It.

Mortal things are ephemeral and so are not worth pursuing. Even a whole life of many years is only very slight. It is nothing. There is no use of enjoying objects. Man is not satisfied with wealth. He craves to become Immortal even against his own conscience. Unfortunately he pursues after the pleasant as against the really good. The good is one thing and the pleasant another. The one liberates and the other binds. One should not catch the pleasant though it is tempting for a moment.

The Atman is not born, nor does It die. It has not come from anywhere and It has not become anything. Unborn, constant, eternal, primeval, this One is not slain when the body is slain. This Atman is hidden in the deep core of the heart of beings. It cannot be attained by any amount of reasoning, study or instruction. It comes only through the Supreme Grace. A man of bad conduct, who has not ceased from crookedness, cannot hope to attain the Atman.

The road to the Supreme is clothed with pricking thorns. It is sharp like the edge of a razor, hard to tread, a very difficult path! It can be trodden only with the help of knowledge obtained from men of wisdom. Knowing That, one is liberated from the terrible mouth of death.

The mind and the senses always run outwards. Only the man of self-discipline and perseverance can gaze inward and experience the State of Atman as it really is. The childish ones who have no knowledge of the Truth, run after external pleasures and they fall into the net of widespread Death. Only the wise, knowing the state of Immortality, seek not the Stable Brahman among things which are impermanent here.

One need not be anxious to possess the things of the world. Whatever is here, that is there, whatever is there, that is here. He obtains death after death who perceives diversity in the world. There are not many things here actually. The One

Supreme Substance appears as many things, clothed in different names, forms and actions.

The Atman or the Brahman has no connection with the world of change. As the sun is not sullied by the faults of the eyes, the Antaratman is not sullied by the defects of the world. As one fire has entered the world and becomes corresponding in form to every form, so the One Antaratman, of all things is corresponding in form to every form and yet is outside all these.

The goodness, the light, the pleasure and the beauty of the world is not to be found there even in name. Even the splendour of the Sun and the grandeur of the creator is superseded by the Absolute. That state is experienced when the senses cease to work together with the mind and when the intellect does not move, and when there is mere consciousness. When all desires that are lodged in the heart are liberated, then the mortal becomes Immortal. Herein he attains Brahman.

The state of becoming the Absolute is not a loss of all that we love, but is the perfect fulfilment of all our aspirations. Our finitude is broken, imperfections destroyed and we are installed in the blessed State of Eternal Satisfaction. All our desires are fulfilled at one and the same time. We become the Source of Infinite Joy and Bliss. We experience birthlessness and deathlessness. None is superior to us.

What is that by knowing which everything else becomes known? That is Brahman. That is to be known. Brahman is Truth, Knowledge, Infinity, Bliss. Brahman is Bhuma where one sees nothing else, hears nothing else and understands nothing else. It rests on nothing else. On It everything else rests. One who knows this rejoices in his own Self and rests contented in his own Self.

Sacrifices cannot bring salvation. They are mere temptations which bind one to birth and death. The deluded people think mere sacrifice and charity constitute eternal blessedness. They are mistaken. What is not the effect of action is not attained by any amount of action. Brahman which is not done cannot be attained by what is done. Having scrutinised the nature of the world, a wise man should arrive at indifference and dispassion. He must approach a preceptor and learn Brahma-Vidya from him. Such a fortunate soul rends asunder the knot of ignorance.

There is no other duty for man except meditation on the Self. Dismissing all else, one should establish himself in the Self. There remains nothing to be done or attained, when the Self is experienced. For, that Brahman, the Immortal, is before, behind, to right and to left, stretched forth below and above. Brahman is all this, the great, the widest extent. There is nothing but Brahman. All this is Brahman.

Truth alone triumphs, never untruth. Falsehood and lie, phantom or unreality cannot succeed in its efforts. The real alone is an enduring being. That real is experienced through Meditation coupled with knowledge.

Whatever a man of purified nature makes clear in his mind, and whatever desires he desires, that he gets and that he fulfils. Therefore, one should have pure and perfect resolves. He that desires for objects is born again and again for fulfilling those desires. He whose desire is satisfied, who is perfected, his desires vanish away here itself.

The state of Moksha or final liberation is a very glorious one. Those blessed souls who attain that State enter into everything. They become the All. They are free from passion, are tranquil and perfect in the highest sense. They are liberated beyond death. They become unified with the Supreme, Imperishable. As the flowing rivers in the ocean disappear, leaving name and form, so the wise man being liberated from name and form, reaches the Supreme which is Absolute. One who knows Brahman becomes Brahman. He crosses over sorrow and death. He becomes Immortal.

The Supreme Self is experienced in the fourth state of consciousness. There is neither this nor that, it has no quality in particular. It is everything. It is peaceful, blessed and non-dual. It is the cessation of all phenomena. That is the Atman. That should be known and realised. That is the purpose of life.

The Jivanmukta or the liberated sage experiences that he is everything. He is the tree and the mountain. He is excellent like the sun. He is a shining treasure, wise, immortal and indestructible. He is the food and the eater of food. He is the knower, knowledge and the known in one. He is the whole universe in himself.

Bliss is the Ultimate Nature of the Reality. From Bliss all this comes forth. By Bliss all this lives. Into Bliss all this enters in the end. The Bliss of all the fourteen worlds is nothing when compared to the Bliss of Brahman. All Bliss of the world is only a shadow of Self-Bliss. Self-Bliss is the most Supreme. It is the only Real Bliss. Other sources of bliss are mere fleeting phantoms. Other Bliss is only a feeble apology for the Supreme Self-Bliss. The greatest bliss which one can conceive of either on earth or in heaven is a mere naught in the presence of the Pure Brahmic Bliss or Self-Bliss. One has not got to run to external objects for obtaining Bliss. The Self is the source of all Bliss. The Self is everything, all Knowledge and all Bliss.

All this is guided by Consciousness, and is based on Consciousness. The world has Consciousness for its guidance. Consciousness is Brahman. I am Brahman. That thou art. This Self is Brahman. These are the metaphysical explanations of Brahman. "All this is Brahman" is the ultimate realisation. One who knows this is not reborn on earth. He becomes Immortal.

Just as by one piece of clay, everything made of clay is known; just as by one nugget of gold everything made of gold is known; just as by a single pair of a nail-scissors everything made of iron is known—all modification is merely a distinction of words, a mere name, the reality is just only clay, gold or iron, so is this Supreme Teaching; the world is only Brahman, by knowing Brahman everything else is known.

Existence alone was in the beginning. This was one alone without a second. From that everything else was produced. The modifications of it are only apparent. There is no world except mere names and forms, mysteriously connected with one another. There is no sun or moon except mere colours or fictitious forms. When colours are distinguished, the sun loses its sunhood, the moon loses its moonhood, things lose their thingness. Brahman alone exists.

One who is guided by a preceptor knows the Truth easily. Otherwise he may miss the path in spiritual blindness. The preceptor teaches: "That which is the finest Essence—this whole world has That as its soul. That is the Atman. That thou art."

The Infinite Fullness (Plenum) alone is Bliss. There is no Bliss in the small finite things. Only the Infinite is Bliss. Where one sees nothing else, hears nothing else, understands nothing else—that is the Infinite Fullness. Where one sees something else, hears something else, understands something else—that is the small finite. The Infinite Fullness is the Immortal, and the small finite is mortal. That Infinite Fullness alone is everywhere. It is all this.

In purity of food, there is purity of nature. In purity of nature, there is established memory. In established memory, there results the release from all knots of the heart. One becomes Immortal.

The Self alone is dear. One who loves something other than the Self loses what he loves. The Self is the Absolute. One who knows this becomes indestructible. He is only a beast who considers he and his God are different. Not for the sake of this all this is dear, but for the sake of the Self this all is dear. By knowing that Self, everything else is automatically known, for the Self indeed is all This.

The Self is an Ocean without a shore and a surface. It is mere Existence, Consciousness and Bliss. Where there is duality, as it were, one can speak to the other, see the other and understand the other, but where everything is just one's own Self, then who can speak to whom, who can see whom, who can understand whom? That is the Supreme End. That is the Supreme Blessing. That is the Supreme Bliss. On a part of this Bliss other creatures are living.

He who is without desire, who is freed from desires, whose desire is satisfied, whose desire is the Self—his Pranas do not depart. He being Brahman Itself, becomes Brahman immediately.

The Jivanmukta is like a child. He is the Source of all Knowledge, but he behaves like an idiot. He is a true Brahmin who has known Brahman.

He who dwells in all things, and yet is other than all things know not, in whose body are all things, who controls all things from within—He is the Soul, the Inner Controller, the Immortal. He is the unseen Seer, the unheard Hearer, is the unthought Thinker, the ununderstood Understander. Other than Him there is nothing whatsoever at any time. One who dies without knowing this Supreme has died in vain, he is a wretched man. He is a great man who dies knowing the Supreme, he is a true Brahmin.

Verily, that great, unborn Soul, undecaying, undying, Immortal, fearless is Brahman. Brahman is fearless. One who attains this becomes the fearless Brahman. That is full. This is full. From the Full, the full does proceed. Withdrawing the full from the full, the full alone still remains. This is the gist of the Upanishads in whole.

The Sadhana of the Upanishads is mainly of the type of the analogy of Bhramara-Kita-Nyaya. Meditation on the Truths declared in the Upanishads is Sadhana. They are of a very highly advanced nature, and only advanced students can take up this method of Sadhana. The name of this method of Sadhana is Jnana Yoga. It is an intellectual analysis for the sake of perfection in Intuition. The Jnana Yogi starts his Sadhana directly from the Vijnana or the intellect. He is not guided by emotions, not by the regulation of Prana and the like. He stills all emotions and centres his mind in the Supreme Self. He attains Sadyo-Mukti or Immediate Salvation. He enters into everything and becomes the Self of everything. This is the end of the Ideal of human life.

SADHANA OF THE BHAGAVAD-GITA

The Bhagavad-Gita is a text-book of practical Sadhana for one and all down from the peasant ploughing his fields right up to the philosopher of the Advaita Vedanta. It discards no aspect of man, it takes into consideration the different aspects of action, emotion, will and understanding of which man is an embodiment. It is a Brahmavidya and a Yoga Sastra, a theory as well as its practice. It is Krishna-Arjuna-Samvada, the meeting of the individual and the Supreme. The Gita is not a book of metaphysical theory, but is a guide for the spiritual man in his daily life of conscious self-effort for attaining Perfection. While the path of Pure Knowledge is possible only for the highly cultured man, the method of the Gita is simple, which is within the reach of all, i.e., devotion to God.

The Gita stresses the performance of duty without reluctance. There is no need to desist from an action which one has undertaken. Action does not bind the soul and the soul is not affected by any external modification. For, the self is eternal. Death is only a change of body and one has no occasion to grieve at the loss of such a body. The soul exists in the past, present and future in the same condition. One who knows this does not grieve at anything. None can destroy the soul. It is Immortal and indestructible. The Soul does not kill anybody and it is killed by nobody. Knowledge of the Self is a wonderful achievement.

One should be even-minded in pain and pleasure. Then one does not incur sin. Man's duty is only to perform action, not to desire for its fruit. Through detachment, one is established in the Yoga of action. Only the fool is attached to fruits of actions.

A Sthitaprajna is one who is established in and satisfied with his own Self. He has no love for anything; he hates none; he fears none. The craving for objects vanishes away on seeing the Supreme. The senses are very powerful; they delude even one who ceaselessly strives to control them. But a Sthitaprajna has all senses under his restraint. Objective attraction leads to final destruction of oneself. He attains peace who is egoless, who is established in the state of the Eternal.

None can live even for a second without action. Prakriti drives man to action even against his will. He is a hypocrite who meditates on objects but keeps silent physically. He is a man of true renunciation who is detached in the mind. Life cannot be lived without action. But there is no action for him who is sporting in the Self and is contented with the Self. He has no duty to perform.

If the Supreme Lord does not act, the whole world will dwindle away in no time. The superior man does action so that others may follow him. Even as ignorant men do action with attachment, the same thing the wise one should do without attachment, for the good of the world. The wise man should not create disturbance in the mind of the ignorant. Gunas as senses move among Gunas as sense-objects. Thus knowing, the wise man is not attached. It is difficult to go against nature. Even a Jnani is dragged by force of Prakriti. The greatest enemies of man are Kama and Krodha born of Rajas. They destroy goodness and eat away purity. They are the sources of great sins. Knowledge is enveloped by Kama or desire. Therefore, one should destroy Kama, the mighty enemy of man.

He is a wise man who finds action in inaction and inaction in action. He is known as a wise man who has burnt all his actions through wisdom. He is unperturbed by what happens as the fruit of his actions. To him everything is merely Brahman. His actions have no meaning since he sees Brahman alone in everything. Such a Knowledge of Brahman comes through service, surrender and enquiry. Knowledge destroys even the mightiest of sins and even the greatest sinner can attain

Supreme Wisdom. Knowledge burns away all actions even as fire burns up fuel. Knowledge comes in the passage of time. Knowledge and action are not distinct in as much as they both lead to liberation. Action without attachment is superior to total renunciation of actions. It is hard for one to renounce actions. Brahman is easily attained through action without attachment. He is unattached even while doing all actions. He is like a lotus-leaf in water.

The Supreme Lord does not give either merit or demerit. It is Prakriti that works as such. Knowledge is enveloped by ignorance, hence the creatures are deluded. But to them the Supreme reveals Itself, who have removed ignorance through the Knowledge of the Self. They are ever immersed in and are one with That. They see the same Eternal in everything. They have conquered birth and death even here itself.

The pleasure born of the contact of objects is the womb of future pain. The wise do not rejoice in that. He who is established in the Self, who is rejoicing in the Self, who rests peacefully in the Self, who witnesses the light of the Self, attains the Supreme Brahman.

A real Yogi is one who has renounced thoughts. This Yoga is attained through meditation on the Self. The bliss attained through this meditation is indestructible, unsurpassable, eternal, full of consciousness, beyond the reach of the senses. By attaining this, one does not consider any other gain as worth striving after. Established in that, one is not shaken even by the heaviest sorrow. That is Yoga which destroys all pains. That is to be practised. One is established in Yoga through Abhyasa and Vairagya. Even if one fails to attain the Goal in this life, he takes another suitable birth to continue the practice, under favourable circumstances. He is guided by his previous Samskaras, and thereby he attains to the Highest.

The Supreme Lord is the Source of all the worlds. He is the creator, preserver and the destroyer. He is all-in-all. The three Gunas have deluded the whole world and hence it does not know the Supreme Lord. This Maya cannot be overcome except through surrender to the Lord. Such people are very dear to the Lord. Among them the Jnani is the best devotee. For he has no selfish desires. Only after many a birth, one realises that everything is God. All are deluded by various desires.

They cannot reach the Lord except through many rounds of births and deaths, which are the effects of their desires.

He who meditates on the Lord and chants OM at the time of death attains the Supreme State. By attaining Him, there is no more fear of Samsara. Even Brahma-Loka is a perishable one and from there one has to revert to this mortal world. But after attaining the Supreme Lord, there is no more rebirth.

Heavenly pleasure is not to be striven for. At the end of the merit, the enjoyer falls down from the heaven into this mortal world. But those who are ever thinking of the Lord as their sole Refuge, to them the Lord provides with all that is best. Even those who worship other deities are unconsciously and wrongly worshipping the one Supreme Lord and all such propitiations go to Him only. He is the overlord of all. He accepts even a dry leaf if offered with devotion. His devotee never perishes. Even women and Sudras are eligible for Salvation provided they surrender themselves to the Lord. This world is impermanent and so one should take refuge in the Eternal Lord alone. The Lord pervades the whole world. There is nothing in which He is not. The whole universe is sustained by a part of Himself.

Bhakti is the central method for approaching the Lord. Only a Bhakta or a devotee can have vision of God. Even the gods cannot have vision of the Supreme without selfless love. Such a pure devotee hates none and is balanced in pleasure and pain. He neither rejoices, nor hates, nor grieves, nor desires. He is not afraid of the world and the world is not afraid of him. To him censure and praise are equal. He is the same to foe and friend alike. He has abandoned all undertakings. He has crossed over the Gunas.

The Supreme Brahman is indescribable. It is Light of lights and beyond darkness. It is neither existing nor non-existing. It is pervading everything. It is near and far, subtle and gross. It is seated in the heart of beings as their very self. When one sees that all diversity is rooted in this One, he then becomes fit to become Brahman.

Sattva illumines a person, Rajas distracts and Tamas makes him inert. Man is a mixture of passion and inertia. He seldom experiences the state of Pure Sattva. When one perceives that there is no doer except the Gunas, he transcends these qualities and becomes Immortal.

The Samsara is like a tree with its roots upwards and offshoots downwards. One should cut at the root of this tree with the axe of detachment. Then one attains that State of the Supreme where the sun and the moon do not shine, where fire does not have brightness. The greatest light of the world is only a portion of the Supreme Light. Everything of the world is only a reflection or a feeble apology for the Supreme. It transcends all earthly things. It is above Jiva and Maya. That is Purushottama who is sung in the Veda. One who knows this has fulfilled all his duties. He is the wisest man knowing everything.

Men with demoniacal qualities do not love the Lord. They doubt the existence of God and say that the world is only a passion-product. They are proud and egoistic. They are cruel and full of anger. They are bound by hundreds of desires and they live to enjoy. They assert their pride of wealth and fall down to the deep hell after death. They do not attain to the Supreme. Lust, anger and greed are the three gates to hell.

One who mortifies his body without mental discipline is a downright hypocrite. There should be physical, verbal and mental Tapas or discipline. One should be pure in thought, word and deed. A selfish act is immoral. Selflessness constitutes morality and ethics. Every act should be done with the remembrance of the Supreme Being. Without the consciousness of the Eternal, all actions become worthless.

Sannyasa is renunciation of selfish actions. But one's own duty cannot be renounced. One's own duty is sacred. All actions should be done without the least attachment. One should not renounce an action merely because it is difficult to perform it. Action is not done for the sake of pleasure. Sensual pleasures are sweet in the beginning, but turn to be bitter in the end. They must be renounced. Varnashrama-Dharma is a perfect system and it must be strictly adhered to.

In order to have realisation of Brahman one should resort to seclusion and meditate on the Self. He must detach himself from externality and establish himself in the Supreme Ideal. One must abandon all earthly duties and take refuge in the Eternal. He will thus be liberated from the bondage of sin.

The Gita aims at the perfection of man in order to become the Divine. The life of Krishna Himself is the best example of the Gita Ideal of Life. His life itself is the best and the most satisfactory commentary on the Gita. To be like Krishna is to be a perfect man of the Gita Ideal. To be like this, one has not got to choose to be a devotee, a philosopher, a mystic or a man of action. One has to be all these at once. He may start by becoming any one of them in accordance with his predominant nature, but after sometime he will realise that advancement on any one of the so-called paths needs a parallel advancement along all others. There cannot be a one-sided expansion of the individual. Perfection in order to be real and lasting should be all-round. To realise the Absolute is to become the Absolute which is the All. One has to be Infinite, for which he has to develop the entire being.

Our minds are the arenas, the inner battle-fields of the daily Mahabharata, where at every moment we are in a war-situation, where one set of ideas fights against the other. We all, therefore, need the Light, the wisdom and the advice which Lord Krishna bestowed on Arjuna. The Supreme Lord, while discussing with Arjuna the vital issues of life, went to the very root of the riddle of the universe, and revealed such truths as are of universal application. Krishna spoke to the whole of humanity through Arjuna on the eternal verities of existence. Krishna typifies the Eternal and Arjuna typifies man with his imperfections. The instructions of the Gita are meant for man in general and not to a particular individual.

Be in the world. Serve humanity. Love all equally. But be not attached to it. Be detached. Live in the Self. Rest contented in the Self. Have no binding ambitions in life. Serve, love, give, purify, meditate and realise. Surrender yourself to God. This is the gist of the Gita.

Act with the consciousness that all is the Self, all is God. God is man and woman, and the old man tottering on the road. There is no reason for attachment to objects. All is merely the Self. See your self in every being. Love others as you love your own self. Do not see differences of body. See the common essence inside. Have Akartri-Bhava, Narayana-Bhava when you do actions. Action has to be done so long as you know that you possess a body. It is the very nature of the body to agitate. Mind will compel you to act. Prakriti is powerful. Even intelligent men are Her victims. Surrender to the Lord is the only way to get rid of the bondage of Prakriti or Maya.

Be a witness to all events in life. Do your own prescribed

duty. Serve without expectation of fruits. This is the essence of Karma Yoga.

The Lord is seated in the hearts of all beings. He is the Inner Ruler, the Immortal. Run to Him alone and take shelter in Him. There is no other way for liberation. All your duties will perish, all sins will be burnt and all doubts will be cleared when you have unselfish surrender to the Lord.

Control the fluctuations of the mind. Sit in a secluded place and concentrate on the Self. Wisdom will then dawn and destroy all ignorance. The effect is Immortality. Supreme Bliss without decay is the fruit. Eternal satisfaction is the Goal of all aspirations. This is achieved through the Yoga of Synthesis explained above. This is what the Gita has to say to the human world.

CHAPTER FIVE

SADHANA IN THE SMRITIS, EPICS AND PURANAS

SADHANA IN THE MANUSMRITI

The Veda is the source of Dharma, also the Smritis and the behaviour and the conduct of those who know their import. The conscience of oneself will speak Dharma, when it cannot be ascertained from the Veda, Smriti and the sages. By following of Dharma one attains perfectness both here and hereafter. The Pranava (OM) is the emblem of Reality. Pranayama is the highest Tapas. The Gayatri is the highest Mantra. Truth is the greatest vow.

One should not consider oneself inferior or feel dejected due to one's previous faults. One should always hope for the better and it should never be thought that anything is impossible. There is no failure to those who aspire for the good and who endeavour to attain it.

One is born alone and dies alone. One enjoys the fruits of one's deeds also alone, whether good or bad. Father, mother, wife, children and friends will not come to one's help when one is on the verge of death and is proceeding to the other world. It is Dharma alone that helps one at that time.

One should not court either life or death, but live dispassionately, waiting for the final day, doing one's duty properly. Dharma consists in fortitude, forbearance, sense-control, non-appropriation of others' property, purity in thought, word and deed, control of mind, clarity of understanding, wisdom of reality, adherence to truth and freedom from anger.

One should not imagine that one can do evil secretly without anyone's knowledge, for the very sky, earth, water, the sun, moon, fire and wind, day and night, and one's own heart, will stand witness to one's actions when the time comes. Let not anyone imagine that one is alone, unseen by others. The supreme witness is within, who eternally watches one's deeds.

Of all Dharmas, knowledge of the Atman is supreme. This is one's highest duty, for thereby one attains immortality. By seeing oneself in all and all in oneself, thus having an equanimous vision, one attains supreme independence. Thus one will not commit Adharma, when everything is seen within one's own Self. The whole universe is within, including the gods.

By meditation on Brahman through the process of the recession of the effects into their causes, step by step, Brahman is realised here and now.

SADHANA IN THE RAMAYANA

The Ramayana of Valmiki is a didactic heroic poem which has the avowed purpose of glorifying Dharma and inculcating the truths which open up for man the way to supreme perfection. It is one of the two great epics of India. It represents the true Hindu spirit of unconditional adherence to the law of righteousness and the performance of one's prescribed duty. To assert the greatness of a life of activity based on the righteousness underlying the law of the Divine Being is one of the main aims of the Ramayana. The life of the 'ideal man' described in the Ramayana is an incentive to all men to strive to become embodiments of Dharma. Dharma is the soul of life and a life bereft of Dharma is not worth its name. Sri Rama, the incarnation of God, represents in himself the ideal son, the ideal brother, the ideal husband, the ideal king and the emblem of Divinity on earth. Man is expected to root his virtue in the Divine. Virtue is necessarily grounded in a consciousness of the principle of Divinity; else, it would become a mechanical routine of external acts. The Ramayana sounds the eternal spirit of Bharatavarsha, the spirit of heroically facing the realities of existence, without fighting shy of them, and at the same time blending action with devotion and loyalty with law. Law is eternal, for it is the expression of the system of the universe governed by God. To follow this law is the duty of man. The Ramayana teaches man, by way of example, as to how he can fulfil the demands of law.

The beauty of the Ramayana is really beyond human description, for it is a revelation to a Rishi—not merely an intellectual production of a scholar—whose meaning is 'integral', and no one-sided consideration of it can do full justice to it. The entire extent of the life of an Arya is delineated in the Ramayana. Social life and spiritual life are wonderfully harmonised in it. Love and heroism, Ahimsa and Kshatriyadharma are brought together in it. Bhakti and Yoga, Karma and Jnana are fused into one. Sri Rama is the crowning feature of the Ramayana, whose very name is exalted to the status of a supreme purifier of the mind of man. Rama Nama is a panacea for all diseases, and is as invincible and irresistible as the Rama-Bana.

Life in its entirety, individual, social and divine, is depicted by the poet-seer Valmiki. He commences his poem with a description of the ideal individual. He then gives the description, in his poem, of the ideal society, of ideal administration of country, and the ultimate ideal of life, the attainment of God. What a grand work! Valmiki's epic gives a concrete picture of the mysterious link that connects man and the world with God, the Creator. Social life is emphasised, for man is a member of society, and without society's good his good cannot be achieved. And without God's grace no individual and no society can progress. The supreme value of the universe is in its being a field of experience for its contents, necessary for their evolution towards the Eternal Being. The reality of the universe is God. All attempts and endeavours based on Adharma, on selfishness and individual independence, are doomed to failure at the iron hands of the Divine Law. The Ramayana most excellently portrays the victory of Dharma and the final defeat of Adharma. Rama and Ravana respectively stand for these two forces of the universe.

Sri Rama's Government is a specimen of ideal administration. It is in fact an earthly representation of the divine government of the universe under the Supreme Sovereign, the Almighty. To bestow due attention on Dharma, Artha, Kama and Moksha, on the individual, the society, the nation and their relation to the universe as a whole, is the duty of an ideal monarch. Sri Rama exemplifies in himself such a ruler, the symbol of God on earth justifying the great dictum, "*Navishnuh Prithivipatih*"—There is an element of the Divine in a ruler of men. Sri Rama carries this truth to its consummation and makes his rule eternally sound in the quarters of the world as the famous 'Ramarajya', the joy of the spirit of man.

One of the striking characteristics of the Hindu scriptures is their expert handling of the problems of life in consonance with the Transcendent Being which is the final Goal of life. Right from the Vedas and the Upanishads down to the Epics and the Puranas this important element features the catholicity that is in all the scriptures of the Hindus. Life is not as some people would hold, a mere delirium of spirit, a disease and an error, but an opportunity presented for the moulding and training of the self for Eternity. To live in the immediate present, with the strength of the past and a vision of the future, basing one's actions on the ancient system of the fulfilment of duty, with the transforming touch of the glorious ideal of Self-realisation towards which all beings are consciously or unconsciously moving, is the burden of the immortal song of the Ramayana. God is both transcendent and immanent. To love Him as transcendent alone would be an error, for the universe is His immanent aspect; it is He Himself in Self-revelation, and we are duty-bound to consider the universe as our own Self, as the omnipresent God-head. Nor are we to make the mistake of disregarding the transcendent and dropping into a pantheistic view of considering the visible universe alone as a complete manifestation of Reality. The Ramayana pays due respect to the physical, the vital, the mental, the moral and the spiritual values of life, and teaches a gospel of the integration of these in the Divine Harmony of the Supreme Being. The Ramayana, with the Manusmriti and the Mahabharata, forms the standard delineation of the codes of the eternal Dharma, the Srutis. There is no doubt that the inhabitants of India, when they follow and preach the spirit of these scriptures, will pave the way not only to a 'Greater India', but to a 'Greater World' which would reflect the beauty of Heaven, the glory of creation and the greatness of God.

For the purpose of bringing out the full philosophy of the Ramayana, therefore, one has to closely follow the part played by the figures enumerated below:—

(1) King Dasaratha (2) Manthara—the maid-servant of Kaikeyi (3) Kaikeyi—the youngest of King Dasaratha's consorts (4) Ravana—the demon king of Lanka (5) Hanuman—minister of the monkey chief Sugriva (6) Sita—the beloved wife of Sri Rama, the prince of Ayodhya (7) Lakshmana—brother of Sri Rama (8) Sri Rama—the hero of the great epic.

On the eve of the coronation of Sri Rama as the Crown Prince of Ayodhya the whole scheme was shelved behind through the pressure brought on Dasaratha by his wife Kaikeyi under the instigation of her maid-servant Manthara and the king's submission to the dictates of his wife whereby Prince Rama is exiled to the forest where he was to spend a period of fourteen years.

(i) In this context King Dasaratha is to be compared to the ordinary man of the world placed in an atmosphere of pleasure and plenty falling a victim to the promptings of his vicious mind (Manthara), infatuated by sense-objects (Kaikeyi).

(ii) The ten-headed Rakshasa, Ravana, in the absence of Sri Rama and Lakshmana steals away Sita from their forest dwelling. Here Ravana with his ten heads is to be compared with the ten sense-organs—five organs of knowledge, and five organs of action. Stealing away of Sita is to be compared to the loss of reasoning power of the worldly-minded deluded by Maya. The golden deer Maricha is Maya which deluded both Lakshmana and Rama and they lost their power of discrimination (Sita).

(iii) Hanuman the intellectual giant and a strong celibate is an invincible power which indicates that if one has to achieve success in all his undertakings one has to cultivate truth, simplicity, purity, selfless service, devotion to duty and establish himself in absolute Brahmacharya. Sri Rama and Lakshmana developed these qualities and they were able to redeem Sita from the demon Ravana, meaning they got back their reasoning power by Brahmacharya and Tapas.

(iv) In worldly life whatever might be the spiritual progress one has achieved he will never attain Moksha unless he is detached from all worldly ties. This aspect is fully depicted in the ascetic march of Sri Rama, Lakshmana and Sita to the forest in obedience to the wishes of Kaikeyi. The path which led the regal party to the forest was so narrow that it was not possible for them to have a safe passage.

Hence they had to follow one after the other, so much so, Sri Rama was in front, Sita in the middle and Lakshmana at the back. Everyone knows pretty well the brotherly affection that Lakshmana had towards his brother and it is even said that he could not exist even for a second without seeing Rama. While on their march, because of Sita's presence in the middle, Lakshmana could not see his brother properly and at frequent intervals he used to request his sister-in-law to make room for him to see Rama. In this context Sri Rama is to be compared to Paramatma (in fact Rama was the incarnation of the Supreme

Being) and Lakshmana the individual soul, Jivatma. Jivatma constantly endeavours to attain oneness with the Paramatma but Maya (Sita) stands in the way. With an intense yearning it is possible to get rid of Maya and attain the goal of merging oneself in the Paramatma. The possibility of attaining Godhead by the aspirant through strong devotion to the Supreme Being is also stated in the Bhagavad Gita.

SADHANA IN THE MAHABHARATA

The message of the Mahabharata is the message of Truth and Righteousness. The great epic produces a moral awakening in the readers and exhorts them to tread the path of Satya and Dharma. It urges them strongly to do good deeds, practise Dharma, cultivate dispassion by realising the illusory nature of this universe and its vain glories and sensual pleasures, and attain Eternal Bliss and Immortality. It induces people to do what Yudhishthira did and abandon what Duryodhana did. Stick to Dharma tenaciously. You will attain material and spiritual prosperity. You will attain everlasting happiness and Moksha, the *summum bonum* of life. This is the final purport or central teaching of Mahabharata.

The blind Dhritarashtra represents Avidya or Ignorance; Yudhishthira represents Dharma; Duryodhana Adharma, Draupadi Maya, Bhishma dispassion, Dussasana evil quality, Sakuni jealousy and treachery, Arjuna the individual soul, and Lord Krishna the Supreme Soul. Antahkarana, the inner field of human mind, is the *Kurukshetra* or the field of war.

The noble and heroic grandsire Bhishma, who controlled his death and who was unconquerable in war even by the gods, inspires us with the spirit of self-sacrifice, undaunted courage and purity. Yudhishthira is still a model of justice and righteousness. Remembrance of his very name generates a thrill in our hearts and goads us to lead the path of truth and virtue. Karna lives in our hearts on account of his extreme munificence and liberality. Karna's name has become proverbial. People even now say whenever they come across a very generous man, "He is like Karna in gifts."

Even now, we admire Arjuna as a perfect man and worship Lord Krishna as our Protector and Saviour. Whenever we are in trouble and distress we pray to Him, "O Lord! Save us just as you saved Draupadi and Gajendra in days of yore."

The sufferings of the Pandavas and Draupadi, Nala and Damayanti, Savitri and Satyavan, clearly explain to us the fact or hard truth that the goal of life or perfection, can only be attained through pain and suffering. Pain is the means through which man is moulded, disciplined and strengthened. Just as impure gold is turned into pure gold by melting it in the crucible, so also the impure and imperfect weak man is rendered pure, perfect and strong, by being melted in the crucible of pain and suffering. Therefore, one should not be afraid of pain and suffering. They are blessings in disguise. They are eye-openers. They are silent teachers. They turn the mind towards God and instil mercy in the heart, strengthen the will and develop patience and power of endurance, which are the prerequisites for God-realisation.

The Mahabharata is an epic of human life. It magnificently portrays the drama of human existence and describes most picturesquely the law of Dharma. Life is a journey, and its essence is Dharma. God helps those who are virtuous. Vice gets uprooted ultimately. The things of the earth are perishable, and the glory of man is transient. All accumulation ends in exhaustion. All rising ends in fall. Union ends in separation. Life ends in death. As logs of wood meet one another in the vast ocean and then get separated, so do beings meet one another here.

Desire is never extinguished by its fulfilment; on the other hand it increases thereby like fire over which ghee has been poured. Whatever wheat and rice, gold, cattle and sex there are in this world—all these are not enough to bring satisfaction even to one person; knowing this one should rest in peace.

Thousands of mothers and fathers, and countless wives and children, have been seen by us in Samsara. To whom do they belong and to whom do we belong? Every day people see persons dying and being cremated and thrown away; yet the remaining ones imagine that they will not die; what can be a greater wonder in this world!

For a fool there are thousands of sources of grief and even so many causes of happiness every day; a wise man is not affected by these.

There is nothing higher than Dharma in this world. Dharma brings Artha, Kama and Moksha. But it is a surprise that no one seems to pay any attention to this patent truth. Let not anyone do to others what is contrary to the good of one's own self. Death and immortality are both here itself: to assert 'this is mine' and 'that is mine' is death. To feel 'nothing is mine' is immortality. Thus immortality and death are both in one's own person. They are not in some distant place. Everyone engages himself in action, and fights and endeavours in various ways, on account of the opposition of these forces within. This is the real War of the Mahabharata, which is eternally going on in the body.

For the sake of a family, a person may have to be abandoned. For the good of a village, a family may have to be abandoned. For the good of a country, a village may have to be abandoned. For the sake of the Supreme Self within, the whole world may have to be abandoned.

Wherever there is attunement of oneself to God, there is the manifestation of Dharma, and wherever there is Dharma, there is victory. Wherever human effort and Divine grace stand in unison, there is prosperity, victory, happiness and firm polity.

SADHANA IN THE BHAGAVATA PURANA
THE TWENTY-FOUR TEACHERS OF THE AVADHUTA

Yadu who was versed in religion saw a young Brahmin Sannyasin, full of wisdom, wandering about fearlessly and put him the following questions as Yadu was eager to know Dharma.

Yadu asked, "O Sage! How did you, doing nothing, get this clear wisdom and light by which you were able to give up all attachments and roam like a child fearlessly in perfect bliss?

"Generally in this world people exert themselves for virtue, wealth, desire and enquire about the Atman only with the motive of attaining longevity, fame and wealth. You are able-bodied, full of wisdom and skill, and good-looking. Your speech is sweet and is like nectar, and yet you neither work nor exert in the least. You like nothing. People in this world are scorched by the fire of lust and greed. You are not at all afflicted by the fire. You appear self-satisfied and blissful, just as an elephant immersed in the cool waters of the Ganga does not feel the heat of the forest fire on the bank. Please enlighten me as to the source of your joy or bliss. Tell me how you derive bliss in your self alone, untouched by sense-objects and living a solitary life? You have neither family nor sensual enjoyment. Whence then is your bliss?"

Sri Krishna said, "Being thus asked and honoured by the intelligent Yadu who was devoted to Brahmins, the noble Brahmin spoke to the king who stood bending in reverence."

The Brahmin said, "Many are my preceptors, O King, whom I resorted to through my own understanding; with the wisdom imbibed from them I roam about on this earth free from attachments. Listen who they are.

"The earth, air, sky (Akasa), water, fire, the moon, the sun, the pigeon, the python, the sea, the moth, the bee, the elephant, the honey-gatherer, the deer, the fish, the dancing girl Pingala, the osprey (raven, Kurara), the child, the maiden, the arrow-maker, the serpent, the spider, the beetle (the wasp)—these O King, are my twenty-four Gurus or teachers whom I have resorted to. I have learnt all my lessons from their characteristic traits. I will now narrate what I learnt from each of them.

"A wise man should not swerve from the path of righteousness, though he is oppressed by creatures who are themselves under the direction of providence. This is forbearance I have learnt from the earth. I have learnt from the mountain, which is a part of the earth, that all our actions should be for the good of others, and that our very existence is for the sake of others. I have learnt from the tree, which is also a part of the earth, that I should be at the disposal of others.

"The sage should be content with mere supporting his life. He should never long for what gratifies the senses so that knowledge may not be destroyed and the mind may not be dissipated on worthless objects.

"The Yogi should not be attached to the objects, like the air, although he is placed in the midst of objects with different attributes and though he is placed in the physical body. His mind should remain unaffected by the good and evil consequences of the objects, just as the air remains unaffected by the good or bad odour of objects over which it blows. The soul enters the body and the attributes of the body seem to be its own, but it is not so. The air is charged with odour but the odour is not the attribute of the air. This I have learnt from the outside air.

"I have learnt from the Prana (vital air) that one should eat to live and not live to eat. He should not eat to give strength and nourishment to the senses. The food should be just sufficient to feed the flame of life.

"Atman is all-pervading. It is not affected by the body and the bodily attributes. This I have learnt from Akasa which is all-pervading and is not affected by clouds and other objects. Even though the sage lives in the body, he should contemplate through his identity with Self or Atman which is all-pervading like the sky (Akasa), which runs as a substratum or a thread in the garland of flowers through all movable and immovable objects, which is not subject to any limitation in respect of time and place and which is not touched by anything else.

"Naturally pure, smooth and sweet is water. So is the sage among men. He, like unto holy waters, purifies others by mere sight, touch and the utterance of His name. This I have learnt from water.

"Bright, powerful in knowledge, and glowing with asceticism, with no receptacle for food except the belly and eating everything, the sage, like fire, is not polluted thereby. Sometimes he remains unnoticed. Sometimes he becomes known to those who desire welfare. He eats the food offered to him by pious devotees and burns up their past and future evils or impurities.

"Fire is the same and only one, though it enters fuels of various sorts. Just as fire burns in a triangular, circular, rectangular, or other shapes, according to the shape and size of the wood, so also the Lord of the Universe, who has created the world and entered into all beings, appears different because of the different bodies (Upadhis) in which He resides. He enters this Universe of various objects, high and low, created by His own Maya and appears to be like everyone of those objects, just as fire does in different kinds of fuel. Birth and death are for the body and not for the Atman, and are caused by time, just as the flames are subjected to change but not the fire.

"The waning or waxing conditions of the moon are due, not to any change in the substance or luminosity of the moon, but, to the fact that only part of the sun's rays get reflected by it. I learnt therefore that the birth, growth, decay, death, etc., are states of the body and not of Atman which is illimitable, birthless and deathless. The moon remains as it is; only there is an apparent change over it owing to astronomical motions.

"The sun draws water by its rays and gives it all away in time. The sage takes in order to give but not in order to add to his own possessions. Just as the sun, reflected in various pots of water, appears to the ignorant as many, so also the Atman appears as such in different bodies on account of the Upadhis caused by the reflection through the mind.

"Too much attachment is bad. One should not have too much affection or attachment for anyone. Too much attachment towards anything causes one's own destruction. This I have learnt from a pair of pigeons. In a certain forest, on a certain tree, a pigeon built a nest and with his mate lived there for some years. They were much attached to each other in love. They reared their young ones with great affection. One day they left their young ones in the nest and went about in search of food for them. A hunter came and caught the young ones by spreading a net. The parent birds returned to their nest with food. The mother had too much affection for the young ones. She fell into the net of her own accord. The male pigeon also fell into the net himself. The hunter caught the pigeons with the young ones. He was quite satisfied and went home. Thus the miserable family man who has not controlled his senses, who has not withdrawn his senses and mind from the worldly objects, who finds delight only in the married life and maintains his family with intense attachment, comes to grief with all his relations like the pigeons (Kapota and Kapoti). He who, attaining a human birth which is like an open gateway to Mukti or the final liberation, is merely attached to the householder's life like the bird, is considered as one who has fallen from his status.

"The pleasures obtained through the avenues of the senses, whether in this world or the next, are transient and fleeting. The wise man never hankers after them.

"The huge Ajagara serpent remains where he is and is content with whatever food that comes to him. Like the Ajagara, one should make no effort but only swallow the mouthful that is brought to him by chance, delicious or distasteful, much or little. If no food reaches him, he should lie quiet even for a long time without any food and without any exertion to get it; because, he should, like the Ajagara, subsist on what providence brings to him or destiny decrees. Holding still the body endowed with energy, fortitude and strength, he should lie wide awake and not exert, though he has sound organs.

"The sage should be calm, profound or deep, difficult to fathom, illimitable and immovable or not liable to be perturbed by worldly circumstances like the tranquil ocean. The ocean may receive volumes of water from the rivers at times or may receive no water at other times but it remains the same. Even so, the sage who has set his heart upon the Lord, neither swells with joy when he has an abundance of enjoyable objects, nor shrinks with sorrow when he has none.

"The man of uncontrolled senses, seeing a woman, the God's Maya (enchantment created by the Lord) and being allured by her behaviour and feelings, falls into the blinding darkness and comes to grief, just as the moth falls into the fire. The fool, who with his mind allured by women, gold ornaments, clothes and other things created by Maya, regards them as objects of enjoyment, loses his correct vision and perishes like a moth.

"The sage should wander from house to house, taking handfuls from each house till he gets just enough food for his sustenance, without making any house feel burdened, like the bee which gathers honey from all flowers.

"The intelligent man should extract the essence from all scriptures, great or small, just as the bee does from flowers. The sage should not store food for the evening or the next day; the hands or the stomach should be his vessel; he should not hoard like the bee. He who stores food is destroyed with his store like the bee.

"The Sannyasin should not touch even the wooden figure of a young woman even with his feet. If he does so he would be caught as is the elephant through its attachment for the touch of the she-elephant. The wise man should shun the company of women as if it were death to him; for he would be killed like a weak elephant by other elephants.

"The miser who hoards wealth, neither gives nor enjoys his riches. Whatever he collects with difficulty is carried away by someone else, just as the collector of honey carries away the honey, collected by the bees.

"Like the collector of honey, the Sannyasin first enjoys those good things which householders collect through hard-earned wealth in order to enjoy.

"The ascetic should not listen to sensuous music. He should learn a lesson from the deer which, enamoured by the hunter's music, gets ensnared. The Sage Rishyasringa, born of deer, listened to the sensuous music of women and was easily entrapped by them. He became a toy or a playmate in their hands.

"Just as a fish that is attracted by baits falls an easy victim to the bait by means of the hook, so also the foolish man who allows his sense of taste to overpower him, who is stupefied with the charms of taste and delicacies by the turbulent and greedy tongue, meets with death. Tongue or the love of taste is most difficult to conquer. If the sense of taste is controlled, all other senses are controlled. One cannot become master of his organs until he controls the organ of taste. No man can be said to have conquered his senses unless his organ of taste is completely curbed. Thoughtful men soon subdue their senses by fasting.

"There was formerly in the city of Videha a public woman called Pingala. I learnt something from her. Listen to it, O King! One day she put on beautiful dress and waited at the door of her house in the evening, to receive and bargain customers for the night. She invited some persons but sent them away as she thought some other wealthy man would richly pay her. With this inordinate desire she waited sleepless at the door, now going in, now coming out, till it was midnight. Through this anxious expectation of money, she spent the night in a fever of hope, worry and disappointment. She felt extreme disgust for her life of greed and desire which made her unhappy.

"In her utter disappointment she sang, 'Indifference to worldly objects is like a sword to cut asunder a man's fetters of expectation or cords of desire. One does not wish to get rid of the bondage of the body until he has become disgusted, just as no man without insight into the truth or knowledge could rid himself of the notions of "I" and "Mine" or the clinging to objects.' Pingala said, 'Lo! How deluded am I for want of control over my mind! How foolish am I to seek the satisfaction of desire from such puny creatures as men!'

" 'Discarding Lord Narayana or the Eternal Atman, seated near in my heart, who is a fit lover and can satisfy me, who can give me everlasting bliss and wealth, I am courting a puny man who cannot satisfy my desires and who causes misery, fear, disease, grief and infatuation. I have been indeed very stupid.

" 'Oh! In vain I have afflicted my soul by this most

reproachable mode of living, viz., that of a public woman; I have sought wealth and pleasure from pitiable mortals, who are greedy and slaves of women, by selling my body to them.

" 'Who, other than myself, would betake to this house which is built of bones which are like the beams, rafters and posts of a house, which is covered over with skin, hair, and nails, which is furnished with nine openings for discharging filth and filled with offal and urine?

" 'In this town of Videha, full of wise beings, I am the only woman who has tied her hopes, happiness and desire to the body. I am the only silly being or wicked woman who seeks any other source of enjoyment or object of desire than the Lord who bestows Self-realisation.

" 'He is the true friend, protector, Lord, most beloved one, the master and the very Self or Atman of all embodied beings; winning Him over, by giving up the body to Him, I shall enjoy His company like Lakshmi and find everlasting happiness in Him alone.

" 'What is the use of serving others? The favours of gods and mortals are limited by time, capacity and various other obstacles. What delight can the sense-objects, men or the gods confer on women? All have a beginning and an end.

" 'Surely I must have done something in my previous births to propitiate Vishnu, for it is by His grace alone that this Vairagya (dispassion or disgust) cutting at the root of all unholy desires, has arisen in my mind. Through His grace only, I have attained the way to everlasting happiness and peace.

" 'If the Lord had not been propitious to me, such disappointments, as lead to renunciation and dispassion, would not have arisen, which enable one to abandon all attachments and attain happiness.

" 'I accept, with humble devotion, this gift of the Lord on my head. I now abandon all vain expectations and evil desires and take refuge in the Supreme Lord. Contented, full of faith in the Lord, living on what chance brings to me, I shall enjoy the eternal bliss of the Lord, Paramatman. Who else but the Lord can save this Jiva who has fallen into the deep pit of Samsara (births and deaths), with eyes blinded by the objects, with the vision robbed by the senses, and who is swallowed up by the serpent of Time.

" 'When one realises the evanescence of this universe, when he beholds the universe in the jaws of the serpent of Time, he will surely and firmly scorn the fleeting, doubtful, worthless, illusory pleasures of this world and the next. He will become very cautious, turn himself away from the illusory sense-objects and will seek repose in the eternal bliss of his own Atman. When one becomes disgusted with everything else, Atman is the protector of Atman, the Self alone is the saviour of oneself.' "

The Brahmin said, "Pingala having thus determined in her mind, and fixed her mind on the Lord, gave up all hopes and expectations due to hankering for lovers, sat on her bed with a serene mind. She abandoned all unholy desires that troubled her and became happy. She slept soundly with a tranquil mind. It is hope that gives us trouble. Without hope we are happy. Desires, hopes and expectations are the sources of grief. Abandonment of all expectations and desires is the greatest bliss. It is the happiest state. Vairagya is the source of bliss as can be seen from Pingala who slept happily, casting aside the hankering for lovers.

"The source for affliction and misery is indeed the acquisition of anything whatsoever that men hold as dearest. But that man who knows this truth, gives up all possessions and does not think of any acquisition and attains unlimited happiness.

"An osprey (Kurara—a bird of prey) had a piece of flesh in its mouth. The stronger birds that had no flesh pounced upon it, but the Kurara dropped the piece of flesh and became happy. Renunciation of dear objects is good. It gives peace.

"I do not care for honour or dishonour. I do not think of the house, wife or children. I sport in Atman and take delight in Atman and roam on earth like a child.

"Only two are free from anxieties and immersed in the highest bliss—the child that knows nothing and the man who has realised the Supreme Being, who is beyond the influence of the Gunas.

"In a certain place, a girl herself had to attend to the comforts of those who visited the house to ask her in marriage when her relations had gone out to some other place. As she was husking the paddy for their meal in a solitary place, the conch bangles on her wrists made a great noise. The intelligent girl thought it disgraceful and was very much ashamed of her poverty. She thought that the party might detect her poor condition. She broke the bracelets one by one, leaving only two on each hand. Even those two bracelets produced a sound when she went on husking. So she removed one of these also. No sound was then produced from the remaining one though she continued husking.

"Wandering over the world in search of truth and experiences, I learnt from the girl's experience the following instructions. Where many dwell together there would be quarrel. Even between two people there would be occasion for debate or talk. Therefore, one should live alone like the single bangle on the hand of the girl.

"Having controlled the breath and practised firmness in seat, one should, like an archer taking his aim, fix or centre the mind on the Supreme Self. He should be on the alert to keep the mind steady through renunciation, constant application and systematic practice. Just as the fire exhausts itself when the fuel is consumed, so also the mind firmly checked in its outward wanderings, becomes oblivious of the diversities caused by the Gunas, slowly shakes off the bonds of Karma, abandons gradually the impulsions to work, gets free from Rajas and Tamas through increased Sattva, subsides and attains tranquillity in the absence of the fuel of Gunas and their products and the sense-impressions which feed it. It becomes one with the object of meditation. It becomes entirely absorbed in the object of contemplation. Then having his mind entirely absorbed in the Atman, he does not see anything else at that time, inside or outside, just as the arrow-maker with his mind absorbed in making the arrow, did not see the king passing by his side. I have learnt concentration of mind from the arrow-maker.

"The wise man should wander alone. He should be homeless and be ever alert. He should resort to a cave and should not exhibit his real worth. He should remain without friends. He should indulge in as little speech as possible.

"It is very troublesome and useless for an ascetic to build a house as his body is fleeting and perishable. Just as the serpent enters and makes itself comfortable in any hole dug by others, so also he should make himself comfortable at every chance residence or place that comes in his way. He should have no fixed abode.

"Just as the spider brings the thread out of itself, spreads out of the web, sports in it and devours it itself, so the Lord creates the universe out of Himself through His Maya consisting of three Gunas, sports in it and takes it back again into Himself.

"Whatever form a man constantly thinks of through love, hatred or fear, that he attains in course of time through concentration on the form he thinks about, just as a worm becomes the wasp.

"Thus from the above twenty-four preceptors I have learnt the various instructions. Now listen, O king, to what I have learnt from my own body. My own body is also my Guru. I have learnt from it dispassion, discrimination and non-attachment. It is ever undergoing change and is evanescent. It is born only to die. Constant misery is its lot. It becomes the seat of egoism. One has to toil to satisfy its wants. This brings grief and sorrow. I reflect on Truth with its help. I know the Truth by a discriminative study of the body. I regard it as not mine and so I feel no attachment for it. The body belongs to the dogs and jackals who devour it after death.

"For the sake of the comforts of the body a person maintains a wife, domestic animals, servants, children, home and relations and amasses wealth with great difficulty. This body perishes in the end like a tree, creating the seed of a fresh body for him.

"The tongue drags him to one side and thirst to another; the organ of reproduction to some other; the skin, stomach and ear in some other direction; the sense of smell in one direction; the fickle eye to something else, the tendency for work draws to something else, every other physical organ in a different direction of activity. The senses suck his very life-blood, even as the many wives of one husband.

"The Lord created various bodies such as trees, reptiles, beasts, birds, insects and fish but was not satisfied with these. Then He made the human body, which is endowed with intellect, for realising Brahman and He was extremely delighted.

"The wise man, having obtained after many births this extremely rare human body which though transient and frail is yet conducive to the attainment of high purpose, viz., Moksha or the final emancipation, should quickly endeavour to attain liberation or the highest good before it falls a prey to death; for sense-enjoyment may be had indeed in anybody.

"Thus learning from my body Vairagya, or distaste or aversion towards worldly pleasures and a knowledge of the real bliss of my nature which is essentially divine, I wander over the world without egoism and attachment, with the light of true wisdom as my light.

"Verily, the knowledge derived from one preceptor cannot be very firm and sufficiently full; because this Brahman, though one without a second, is variously sung by Rishis."

Sri Krishna said, "The Brahmin having said so much, took leave of Yadu who paid him all proper reverence and went away. Our ancestor Yadu also took to heart the instructions of the sage, gave up all attachments and attained equanimity of mind and tranquillity."

HOW TO WITHDRAW FROM THE SENSE-OBJECTS

Uddhava said: "O Krishna, generally people know that the objects of the senses lead to misery. How is it that they run after them, like a dog, an ass or a goat?"

The Lord said: "In the heart of an indiscriminating man, the wrong notion of 'I' with regard to the body arises; then the terrible Rajas takes possession of the mind, which by its own origin is Sattvic. Doubts and desires arise in the mind which is filled with Rajas. He thinks, 'I should enjoy such and such a thing in such and such a way and so on.' Then the mind dwells upon the excellent attributes of an object 'Oh, how beautiful! What a nice thing,' and gets a strong liking or an inordinate hankering for it.

"The foolish man is overpowered by desires and cravings. He has no control over his senses. As he is deluded by the strong current of Rajas, he knowingly does acts which are seen to bring miseries or evil fruits.

"The man of discrimination is also distracted by Rajas and Tamas, but as he is conscious of their evils, he sleeplessly controls his mind and practises concentration of mind. He is not attached to them.

"Being alert and diligent one should secure firmness in the seat and control the breath, and having set the mind on Me, slowly practise concentration.

"This is the Yoga as taught by My disciples Sanaka and others, in order to withdraw the mind successfully from everything and fix it on Me.

"Look upon this universe as a delusion, a play of the mind, now seen and the next moment destroyed, like a dream, and extremely inconsistent like the circle described by a firebrand (Alata Chakra). One Consciousness appears as many. The threefold distinction of waking, dream and deep sleep which is caused by the transformation of Gunas is Maya.

"Withdraw your senses from this object world. Abandon all desires. Be calm and remain quiet, immersed in the bliss of your own Self. Be silent and free from action. If ever the universe is experienced, if sometimes this still appears, if at times you will have experience of the object in your daily life for getting the necessities of life, it will not cause delusion in you as you have once thrown them aside as unreal, but will linger as a memory only till the fall of the body."

THE METHOD OF MEDITATION IN THE ELEVENTH SKANDHA

The Lord said: "Sitting on an even seat with his body erect in a comfortable posture, placing the two hands on his lap and fixing the eyes on the tip of his nose, one should cleanse the passage of Prana by means of inhalation (Puraka), retention (Kumbhaka) and exhalation (Rechaka) of the breath and should also practise slowly in the inverse order, keeping the senses under control.

"Om, with the sound of a bell, extends all over from Muladhara upwards. He should by Pranayama push upwards the sacred syllable Om which is uninterrupted like a lotus fibre, through the heart and make it ring like a bell and again add to it the vowel.

"Thus one should practise the Pranayama accompanied by Om ten times, thrice daily. He should mentally repeat Om continuously during inhalation and exhalation. Within a month one shall be able to control the Prana. Within the body there is the lotus of the heart with its stalk above and the flower downwards, facing below, with eight petals and pericarp. It is also closed. Meditate on it as facing upwards and full blown. On the pericarp think of the sun, the moon and the fire one within the other. Meditate on the following form of Mine within the fire which is good and very auspicious for meditation.

"My Form—symmetrical, gracious, gentle, with four long

and beautiful arms, well-developed and beautiful neck, beautiful cheeks and a graceful smile.

"With Makara Kundalas or shining pendants adorning symmetrical ears, clad in a cloth of gold, dark complexioned like a cloud, with the splendid Srivatsa mark and Lakshmi on the chest.

"Adorned with conch, disc, mace, lotus and a garland of wild-flowers (Vanamala) with feet adorned with ringing anklets and the chest resplendent with the effulgence of the Kaustubha gem.

"Decked with a brilliant crown, bracelets and a waistband beautiful in every feature, captivating to the heart, with the face and eyes beaming with graciousness and very tender, one should meditate on this form of the above description keeping the mind steady. He should concentrate the mind on all the features. He should withdraw the senses from their objects with a strong mind; with the help of the charioteer intellect as guide, he should direct the mind to My whole body. Then he should concentrate on one part only, My smiling face. He should not meditate on anything else. Then withdraw the mind from the face and fix it on Akasa or the supreme cause. Give up that also. Rest in Me as the pure Brahman devoid of all attributes. Think of nothing at all. Let the Triputi, viz., meditator, object of meditation and meditation vanish. Let them become one. Forget the triple differences. This is the highest Nirvikalpa Samadhi."

VISHNUPURANA: SADHANA FOR LIBERATION

Ribhu said, "Therefore, O king Nidagha, O thou, conversant with duty, do thou consider thyself as one with all beings, regarding equally friend or foe. As the same sky looks apparently as white or blue, so the Soul, which is in reality one, appears diversified to erroneous vision. That, which exists in the universe, is one which is Achyuta. There is nothing distinct from Him. He is I; He is thou; He is all. This universe is His form. Give up therefore the misconceived notion."

The Brahmin said: "The great goal of life must be considered by wise men as Eternal and it would be transient if it were accomplished through transient things. The spirit which is essentially one in one's own and in all other bodies, is the true wisdom of one who knows the unity and the true principles of things. As air spreading all over the world going through the perforation of a flute is distinguished as the notes of the scale, so the (Truth) nature of the Great Spirit is one though it assumes various forms consequent upon the fruits of actions. When the difference, between the various forms such as that of God and man, is destroyed then the distinction of things ceases."

Kesidhvaja said, "The properties of pain, ignorance and impurity are those of nature and not of soul. O Muni, there is no affinity between fire and water but when the latter is placed over the former in a caldron, it bubbles and boils and exhibits the properties of fire. In the same manner when the soul is associated with Prakriti it is vitiated by egoism and such other self-deluding forces and assumes the qualities of grosser nature although essentially distinct from them. Such is the seed of ignorance as I have explained it to you. There is but one remedy for earthly sorrows, the practice of devotion; no other is known."

"One who is capable of discriminative knowledge must restrain his mind from all objects of senses and therewith meditate upon the Supreme Being, who is identical with the Self within, in order to obtain liberation; for that Supreme Spirit attracts to Itself him who meditates upon It, and who is of the same nature, as the loadstone attracts the iron by the virtue which is common to itself and to its products. Contemplative devotion is the union with Brahman effected by that condition of mind which has attained perfection through those exercises which complete the control of the self; and he, whose contemplative devotion is characterised by the property of such absolute perfection is in truth, expectant of a limited life in the phenomenal world.

"One who would bring his mind into a proper state for the performance of devout contemplation, must be devoid of desire and observe invariably continence, compassion, truth, honesty and disinterestedness; he must fix his mind upon the Supreme Brahman, practising holy study, purification, contentment, penance and self-control. These practices bestow excellent rewards, and when they are not prompted by the desire for anything earthly, anything passing, but inspired by love of liberation, they lead one to the highest Beatitude."

SADHANA IN GARUDA PURANA

The sixteenth Adhyaya of Garuda Purana gives an account of the Law for Liberation. Dispassionately it subjects the field of human life to a thorough examination and narrates the limitations and failings of finite life and insists upon the realisation of the divine Self. As attachment is difficult to be shunned, always one should cultivate the friendship with the noble and the great and the good. There is no Liberation by deluded ceremonials, nor by the mere study of Vedas and the reading of the Sastras; Liberation is obtained by true Knowledge. Two phrases make for bondage and liberation: "mine" and "not-mine." The person saying "mine" is bound; the one saying "not-mine" is released. That is the Karma that does not bind, that is the knowledge that gives release; other Karmas are worrying, other knowledge is mere skilful chiselling. With the sword of detachment, one should cut off the desires connected with the body. One should practise mentally upon the supreme threefold pure Word, Om. With breath controlled, with the mind restrained one should contemplate on Om. With desires overcome, freed from attachment, pride and delusion, with the evils of non-discrimination overcome one should live in the Higher Self. Within tranquil Self, full-visioned, freed from thoughts of the other, one should worship the Divine alone.

THE SADHANA OF THE YOGAVASISHTHA

The practical hints on Sadhana presented in Yogavasishtha are unique. Even the most worldly-minded become dispassionate and attain peace of mind, solace and consolation by study of this book.

Those whose minds are turned from this world, who have become indifferent towards the objects of this world and who are thirsting for liberation will be really benefited by a study of this precious book. They will find in this book a vast mine of knowledge and practical spiritual instructions for guidance in their daily life. Yogavasishtha first enunciates a doctrine in its various aspects and then makes it very lucid through interesting stories. This is a book for constant study. It must be read and re-read and studied or re-studied as many times as possible.

Yogavasishtha deals with the subject of effecting union of the individual soul with the Supreme Soul amidst all the trials and tribulations of life. It prescribes various directions for the union of the Jivatma and Paramatma.

The nature of Brahman or the Sat and the methods to attain Self-realisation are vividly described in this work. This is the most inspiring book. Every student of Vedanta keeps this book for constant study. It is a constant companion for a student in the path of Jnana Yoga. It is not a Prakriya Grantha. It does not deal with the Prakriyas or categories of Vedanta. Advanced students can only take this book for their study. Aspirants should first study 'Atma Bodha', 'Tattva Bodha', 'Atmanatma Viveka' of Sri Sankaracharya and 'Panchikarana' before they take up the study of Yogavasishtha.

Moksha according to Yogavasishtha is the attainment of essence of Bliss of Brahman through knowledge of the Self. Moksha is freedom from birth and death; it is the immaculate and imperishable seat of Brahman wherein there are neither Sankalpas nor Vasanas. The mind attains its quiescence here. The sum total of pleasures of the whole world is a mere drop when compared to the bliss of Moksha. That which is called Moksha is neither in Devaloka nor in Patala nor on earth. When all desires are destroyed, the extinction of the expansive mind alone is Moksha. Moksha has neither space nor time in itself; nor is there in it any state external or internal. If the illusory idea of 'I' or Ahamkara perishes, the end of thought which is Maya is Moksha. Extinction of all Vasanas constitutes Moksha. Sankalpa is only Samsara; its annihilation is Moksha. It is only Sankalpa destroyed beyond resurrection that constitutes the immaculate Brahmic seat or Moksha. Moksha is freedom from all sorts of pains and the attainment of Supreme Bliss (Sarva-duhkha Nivritti and Paramananda Prapti). Duhkha means pain or suffering. Birth and death generate greatest pains. Freedom from births and deaths is freedom from all sorts of pains. Brahma Jnana or knowledge of the Self alone will give Moksha. Through the absence of desires for objects, the quiescence in the mind will produce Moksha.

According to the Yogavasishtha this world of experience with various objects, time, space and laws, is a creation of mind, i.e., idea or Kalpana. Just as objects are created by the mind in the dream, so also, everything is created by the mind in the waking state also. Expansion of the mind is Sankalpa. Sankalpa, through its power of differentiation generates this universe. Time and space are mental creations only. Through the play of the mind in objects, nearness seems to be a great distance and vice versa. Through the force of the mind, a Kalpa is regarded as a moment and *vice versa*. A moment of waking experience may be experienced as years in the dream. The mind can have the experience of miles within a short span and miles can also be experienced as a span only. Mind is not anything different and separate from Brahman. Brahman manifests Itself as mind. Mind is endowed with creative power. Mind is the cause of bondage and liberation.

If the four sentinels that wait at the gates of Moksha (salvation) viz., Santi (peace), Vichara (Atmic enquiry), Santosha (contentment) and Satsanga (association with the wise) be befriended then there will be no obstacle to the attainment of the final emancipation. Even if one of them be befriended, then he will introduce you to the rest of his companions.

If you attain knowledge of the Self or Brahma Jnana, you will be freed from the trammels of birth and death. All doubts will vanish and all Karmas will perish. It is through one's own efforts alone that the immortal, all-blissful Brahmic seat can be obtained.

The slayer of the Atman is the mind. The form of the mind is Sankalpas only. The true nature of the mind consists in the Vasanas. The actions of the mind alone are truly termed Karmas or actions. The universe is nothing but the mind manifesting as such only through the potency of Brahman. The mind contemplating on the body becomes the body itself and then enmeshed in it is afflicted by it.

The mind manifests itself as the external world in the shape of pains or pleasures. The mind subjectively is consciousness. Objectively it is this universe. The mind attains through its enemy of discrimination the quiescent state of Para-Brahman. The real bliss is that one which arises when the mind, divested of all desires through the eternal Jnana, destroys its subtle form. The Sankalpas and the Vasanas (subtle desires) which you generate enmesh you as in a net. The self-light of Para-Brahman alone is appearing as the mind or this universe.

The person without Atmic enquiry will see as real the world which is nothing but of the nature of Sankalpa. The expansion of the mind alone is Sankalpa. Sankalpa through its power of differentiation, generates this universe. Extinction of Sankalpas alone is Moksha.

The enemy of Atman is this impure mind only which is filled with excessive delusion and hosts of worldly thoughts. There is no other vessel on this earth to wade through the ocean of re-birth than the mastery of the antagonistic mind.

The original sprout of the painful Ahamkara with its tender stem of re-births at length ramifies itself everywhere with its long branches of 'mine' and 'thine' and yields its unripe fruits of death, disease, old age, pain and sorrow. This tree can be destroyed to its root by the fire of Jnana only.

All the heterogeneous visibles, perceived through the organs of sense are only unreal, but that which is real is Para-Brahman or the Supreme Soul.

If all objects which have an enchanting appearance become eye-sores and present the very reverse of the former feelings, then the mind is destroyed. All your properties are useless. All wealth lands you in dangers. Non-desires will take you to the eternal blissful abode.

Destroy Vasanas and Sankalpas. Kill Egoism. Annihilate this mind. Equip yourself with the four means. Meditate on the Pure, Immortal, All-pervading Self or Atman. Get knowledge of the Self and attain Immortality, everlasting peace, eternal bliss, freedom and perfection.

The Yogavasishtha describes three types of Sadhana: (1) the control of the Prana by the practice of Pranayama, and the raising of the Kundalini power through the different Chakras in the body, (2) the control of the mind by the practice of self-analysis, eradication of vices, dispassion for mundane things, non-attachment, obliteration of the Vasanas, overcoming of egoism, reflection on the dream-like character of the world, and (3) meditation on Brahman by reflection on the solitary nature of the Atman (Kevalabhava), the immanence of the Atman in the process of perception (Drashtr-darsana-sambandha), and the practice of the presence of Brahman in everything (Brahmabhyasa).

CHAPTER SIX
SADHANA IN THE VARIOUS SCHOOLS

SADHANA IN VEERASAIVISM

Veerasaivism or Lingayatism shows the way to attain the Lakshya or Lord Siva. Lord Siva, Lord Subrahmanya, Rishabha king, Sanata Lingar, Kumara Devi, Sivaprakasa had all expounded lucidly the system of Veerasaiva philosophy. Veeragama is the chief source of this system of thought and this way of life. Sharanas are the saints of the Lingayat faith or cult.

Ordinary Saivites keep the Sivalinga in a box and worship it during the time of Puja. The Lingayatas keep a small Linga in a small silver or golden box and wear it in the body with a chain attached to the box. Wearing the Linga in the body will remind one of the Lord and help His constant remembrance. The Christian also wears the cross in the neck. This also has the same object in view. The followers of Veerasaivism who are called Lingayatas, make the meditation on Siva in the form of Linga the sole means of salvation. The perfection of the practice of deep concentration on Linga results in the intuitive experience of the Divine Siva.

SAKTI YOGA SADHANA

He who worships Sakti, that is, God in the form of Mother, as the supreme Power which creates, sustains and withdraws the universe, is a Sakta. All women are forms of the Divine Mother. A Sakta does Sadhana which helps the union of Siva and Sakti through the awakening of the forces within the body. He becomes a Siddha in the Sadhana when he is able to awaken Kundalini and pierce the six Chakras. This is to be done in a perfect practical way under the guidance of a Guru who has become perfect. The Sakti must be awakened by Dhyana, by Bhava, by Japa and by Mantra Sakti.

The Mother, the embodiment of the fifty letters is present in the various letters in the different Chakras. When the chords of a musical instrument are struck harmoniously, fine music is produced. Even so, when the chords of the letters are struck in their order, the Mother who moves in the six Chakras and who is the very self of the letters awakens Herself. The Sadhaka attains Siddhi easily when she is roused. It is difficult to say when and how She shows Herself and to which Sadhaka.

Sadhana means unfolding, rousing up or awakening of Power or Sakti. Mode of Sadhana depends upon the tendencies and capacities of the Sadhaka.

No one can free himself from the thraldom of mind and matter without Mother's Grace. The fetters of Maya are too hard to break. If you worship Her as the great Mother you can very easily go beyond Prakriti through Her benign grace and blessings. She will remove all obstacles in the path and lead you safely into the illimitable domain of eternal bliss and make you free. When She is pleased and bestows Her blessings on you, then alone you can free yourself from the bondage of this formidable Samsara.

The Sakta enjoys Bhukti (enjoyment in the world) and Mukti (liberation from all bondage). Siva is an embodiment of Bliss and Knowledge. Siva Himself appears in the form of man with a life—mixture of pleasure and pain. If you remember this point always, all dualism, all hatred, jealousy, pride will vanish. You must consider every human function as worship or a religious act. Answering calls of nature, micturation, talking, eating, walking, seeing, hearing become worship of Lord, if you develop the right attitude. It is Siva who works in and through man. Where then is egoism or individuality? All human actions are divine actions. One universal life throbs in the hearts of all, hears in the ears of all. What a magnificent experience it is, if one can feel this by crushing this little 'I'! The old Samskaras, the old Vasanas, the old habits of thinking, stand in the way of your realising this Experience-Whole.

The aspirant thinks that the world is identical with the Divine Mother. He moves about thinking his own form to be the form of the Divine Mother and thus beholds oneness everywhere. He also feels that the Divine Mother is identical with Para Brahman.

Saktism is not mere theory or philosophy. It prescribes systematic Sadhana of Yoga, regular discipline, according to the temperament, capacity and degree of evolution of the Sadhaka. It helps the aspirant to arouse the Kundalini and unite

Her with Lord Siva and enjoy the Supreme Bliss or Nirvikalpa Samadhi. When Kundalini sleeps, man is awake to the world. He has objective consciousness. When She awakes, he sleeps. He loses all consciousness of the world and body and becomes one with the Lord. In Samadhi the body is maintained by the nectar which flows from the union of Siva and Sakti in Sahasrara.

Worship of the Divine Mother with intense faith and perfect devotion and self-surrender will help you to attain Her grace. Through Her grace alone, you can attain Knowledge of the Imperishable.

SADHANA IN SAIVASIDDHANTA

One will develop love and devotion for Lord Siva if he is freed from egoism. Sariyai, Kiriyai, Yoga and Jnana are the four Sadhanas or steps to kill egoism and attain Lord Siva. Erecting temples, cleaning them, making garlands of flowers, singing Lord's praises, burning lamps in the temples, constitute Sariyai. Kiriyai is to perform Puja, Archana, etc. Yoga is restraint of the senses and contemplation on the inner light. Jnana is to understand the true significance of Pati, Pasu, Pasam and to become one with Siva by constant meditation on Him after removing the three Malas, viz., Anavam (egoism), Karma (action) and Maya (illusion).

The worship of the all-pervading, eternal Supreme Being through external forms is called Sariyai. The requisite initiation for this is Samaya Diksha. The worship of the cosmic form of the Eternal Ruler of the universe externally and internally is called Kiriyai. The internal worship of Him as formless is called Yoga. For Kiriyai and Yoga the requisite initiation is called Visesha Diksha. The direct realisation of Lord Siva through Jnana Guru is called Jnanam. The initiation that leads to it is called Nirvana Diksha.

The aspirant should free himself from the three kinds of Mala, viz., Anavam, Karma and Maya. Then only will he become one with Lord Siva and enjoy Sivanandam. He should thoroughly annihilate his egoism, free himself from the bondage of Karma and destroy the Maya which is the basis of all impurities.

Guru or the spiritual preceptor is very essential for attaining the final emancipation. Siva is full of grace. He helps the aspirants. He showers His grace on those who worship Him with faith and devotion and who have childlike trust in Him. Siva Himself is the Guru. The grace of Siva is the road to salvation. Siva lives in the Guru and looks with intense love on the sincere aspirant through the eyes of the Guru. Only if you have love for mankind you can love God.

If the aspirant establishes a relationship between himself and Lord Siva he will grow in devotion quickly. He can have the mental attitude or Bhava—Dasya Bhava or the relationship of Master and servant which Tirunavukkarasar had, or the Vatsalya Bhava wherein Lord Siva is the father and the aspirant is the child of Lord Siva which Tirujnanasambandhar had or the Sakhya Bhava or the relationship of friend, (Lord Siva is regarded as the friend of the aspirant) which Sundarar had or the Sanmarga wherein Lord Siva is the very life of the aspirant which Manickavasagar had, which corresponds to the Madhurya Bhava or Atma Nivedana of the Vaishnavites.

The devotee becomes one with Siva like salt with water, milk with milk when the three Malas or Pasas are destroyed, but he cannot do the five functions of creation, etc. God only can perform the five functions.

The liberated soul is called a Jivanmukta. Though he lives in the body he is one in feeling with the Absolute. He does not perform works which can produce further bodies. As he is free from egoism, works cannot bind him. He does meritorious acts for the solidarity of the world (Loka-sangraha). He lives in the body until his Prarabdha Karma is exhausted. All his present actions are consumed by the grace of the Lord. The Jivanmukta does all actions on account of the impulsion of the Lord within him.

SADHANA IN KASHMIR SAIVISM

The Agamas are the basis of Kashmir Saivism. The central themes of Kashmir Saivism are God, world, soul, bondage and salvation. Bondage is due to ignorance or Ajnana. The soul thinks 'I am finite', 'I am this body'. It forgets that the soul is identical with Siva and that the world is wholly unreal apart from Siva.

Pratyabhijna or recognition of the reality is all that is needed for attaining the final emancipation. When the soul recognises itself as God, it rests in the eternal bliss of oneness with God. The liberated soul is merged in Siva, as water in water or milk in milk when the imagination of duality has disappeared.

Performance of duties in accordance with the injunctions of the Agamas, lessens this human delusion of being finite, and the ignorant self-identification of the human soul with the perishable and passing events and things. When the impurities born of ignorance are lessened and eliminated, then one obtains illumination. By spiritual exertion, one has to experience the essential nature of one's Inner Divine Consciousness. For such a spiritual experience of the infinite, the individual must first obtain the divine Grace of Lord Paramasiva. The four means or Upayas which enable the individual to get rid of impurities and ignorance are Anupaya, Sambhavopaya, Saktopaya and Anavopaya. By strictly exercising oneself in these four Upayas, one rises to the realisation of Supreme Consciousness.

SADHANA IN PASUPATA YOGA

Uniting the self with the true Siva Tattva by the control of the senses is real wearing of the Bhasma, because Lord Siva through his third eye of wisdom burnt passions to ashes. The meditation on Pranava should be done through Japa. One should attain the real Jnana, Yoga and Bhakti by steady practice. In the heart there is a ten-petalled lotus. It has ten Nadis. It is the Jivatma's abode. This Jivatma lives in a subtle form in the mind and it is Chitta or Purusha itself. One should ascend to the moon by cutting open or transcending the Dasagni Nadi by the regular practice of Yoga as instructed by the Guru and practising dispassion, righteousness and equality. The moon then gradually attains fullness, as it gets itself pleased or satisfied with the Sadhaka on account of his regular application in Yoga and purification of Nadis. In this state the Sadhaka overcomes waking and sleeping state and through meditation merges himself in the object meditated upon in this waking state itself.

CHAPTER SEVEN
SADHANA IN SIVANANDA SUTRAS

SADHANA OF SIVANANDA UPADESAMRITAM

Thou art divine. Live up to it. Feel and realise thy divine nature. Thou art the master of your destiny. Do not be discouraged when sorrows, difficulties and tribulations manifest in the daily battle of life. Draw up courage and spiritual strength from within. There is a vast inexhaustible magazine of power and knowledge within. Learn the ways to tap the source. Dive deep within. Sink down. Plunge in the sacred waters of Immortality—the holy Triveni within. You will be quite refreshed, renovated and vivified when you go to the divine source and realise: I AM THE IMMORTAL SELF.

Understand the laws of the universe. Move tactfully in this world. Learn the secrets of nature. Try to know the best ways to control the mind. Conquer this mind. Conquest of mind is really conquest of nature and the world. Conquest of mind will enable you to go to the source of Soul Power and you can then realise: I AM THE IMMORTAL SELF.

Do not murmur. Do not grumble when troubles and sorrows descend upon you. Every difficulty is an opportunity for you to develop your will and to grow strong. Welcome it. Difficulties strengthen your will, augment your power of endurance and turn your mind towards God. Face them with a smile. In your weakness lies your real strength. Thou art invincible. Nothing can harm you. Conquer the difficulties one by one. This is the beginning of a new life, a life of expansion, glory and divine splendour. Aspire and draw. Grow. Expand. Build up all positive virtuous qualities—the Daivi Sampatti, viz., fortitude, patience and courage that are dormant in you. Start a new life. Tread the spiritual path and realise: I AM THE IMMORTAL SELF.

Have a new angle of vision. Arm yourself with discrimination, cheerfulness, discernment, alacrity and understanding spirit. A glorious brilliant future is awaiting you. Let the past be buried. You can work miracles. You can do wonders.

Do not give up hope. You can destroy the harmful effects of unfavourable planets through your will-force. You can command the elements and nature. You can neutralise the effect of evil influences and the antagonistic dark forces that may operate against you. You can change the unfavourable circumstances into best possible ones. You can nullify destiny. Many have done this. You can also do so. Assert. Recognise. Claim thy birthright now. THOU ART THE IMMORTAL SELF.

Determination and self-reliance are very necessary for success in Self-realisation. In Mundaka Upanishad you will find: "This Atman cannot be obtained by one who is destitute of strength or without earnestness or by penance without mark. But if a wise man strives after It by those means, then his self enters into Brahman." Fearlessness is an important qualification for an aspirant. One should be prepared to renounce this life at any moment. Without renunciation of this little sensual life, the eternal spiritual life cannot be attained. 'Abhayam' comes first in Daivi Sampatti or divine qualities that are enumerated in the Gita—Chapter XVI-1. A timid man or a coward dies several times before he actually dies. When you have once decided to take to spiritual practices, stick to it tenaciously at any cost, nay, at the risk of your life. Come what may. Be bold. Stand up. Realise the Truth. Proclaim it everywhere. THOU ART THE IMMORTAL SELF.

Destiny is your own creation. You have created your destiny through thoughts and actions. You can undo the same by right thinking and action. Even if there is an evil or a dark antagonistic force to attack you, you can diminish its force by resolutely denying the existence of evil or resolutely turning your mind away from it. Thus you can disarm destiny. The one thought "I am the Immortal Self" will neutralise all evil forces, the evil influences of all malevolent planets and will infuse in you courage and inner spiritual strength. Wrong thinking is the root-cause of all human sufferings. Cultivate right thinking and right action. Work unselfishly in terms of unity with Atma-Bhava. This is right action. The right thinking is when you think: I AM THE IMMORTAL SELF.

There is no such thing as sin. Sin is only a mistake. Sin is a mental creation. The baby-soul must commit some mistakes during the process of evolution. Mistakes are your best teachers. The idea of sin will be blown up in the air if you think: I AM THE IMMORTAL SELF.

Don't say: "Karma, Karma. My Karma has brought this." Exert. Exert. Do Purushartha. Do Tapas. Concentrate. Purify. Meditate. Don't become a fatalist. Don't yield to inertia. Don't bleat like a lamb. Roar Om Om Om like a lion of Vedanta. See how Markandeya, who was destined to die at his sixteenth year, became a Chiranjeevi—an immortal boy of sixteen years—on account of his Tapas. Also note how, Savitri by her Tapas brought back to life her dead husband; how Benjamin Franklin and the late Sir T. Muthuswami Iyer of the Madras Bench, elevated themselves. Remember, my dear Niranjan, that man is the master of his destiny. Visvamitra Rishi, who was a Kshatriya Raja, became a Brahma Rishi like Vasishtha and even created a third world for Trisanku by his power of Tapas. Rogue Ratnakar became the sage Valmiki through Tapas. Rogues, Jagai and Madhai of Bengal, became highly developed saints. They became the disciples of Gouranga. What others have done, you can also do. There is no doubt of this. You can also do wonders and miracles if you apply yourself to spiritual Sadhana, Tapas and meditation. Read the book: "From Poverty to Power" by James Allen with interest and attention. You will be inspired. Draw up a programme of your life. Follow my "Twenty Important Spiritual Instructions" and "Forty Golden Precepts." Read my book "Sure Ways for Success in Life and God-realisation." Adhere to the spiritual routine. Apply yourself with zeal and enthusiasm to Sadhana. Become a Naishthika Brahmachari. Be steady and systematic in your spiritual practices. Shine in your native, pristine Brahmic glory. Become a Jivanmukta. Remember: THOU ART THE CHILDREN OF IMMORTALITY.

Hey Saumya! Dear Immortal Self! Be bold. Be cheerful though you are down and out, though you have nothing to eat, though you are clad in rags. Thy essential nature is Sat-Chit-Ananda (Existence Absolute, Knowledge Absolute and Bliss Absolute). The outer cloak, this mortal physical sheath, is an illusory Mayaic production. Smile. Whistle. Laugh. Jump. Dance in joy and ecstasy. Sing Om Om Om, Ram Ram Ram, Shyam Shyam Shyam, Sivoham Sivoham Sivoham, Soham Soham Soham. Come out of this cage of flesh. Thou art not this perishable body. Thou art the Immortal

Self. Thou art sexless Atman. Thou art the son of the King of kings, an Emperor of emperors, Brahman of the Upanishads, the Atman who dwells in the chambers of your heart (Hridaya Guha). Act as such. Feel as such. Claim your birthright now from this very second. Feel. Assert. Recognise. Realise, not from tomorrow or the day after, but right now from this very second. "*Tat Tvam Asi*," O Niranjan. THOU ART THE IMMORTAL SELF.

Brother! COURAGE is thy birthright and not fear. PEACE is thy divine heritage, not restlessness. IMMORTALITY but not mortality. STRENGTH but not weakness. HEALTH but not disease. BLISS but not sorrow. KNOWLEDGE but not ignorance.

You are the architect of your own fate and fortune. You are the master of your own destiny. You can do and undo things. You can attain Brahmanhood by right thinking, right feeling and right acting. You can break old morbid habits by the power of WILL. You can destroy wrong Samskaras, unholy desires, wrong imaginations. You can build new habits. You can change your nature. You can build up beautiful character. You can move the whole world by your spiritual force. You can elevate others also to the status of divinity. You can control the force of nature. You can command the elements.

Rely on your own Self. Do not be credulous. Believe not in any dogmas. Hear the inner voice of the Soul or promptings of the pure conscience. Be not a slave. Do not sell your liberty. Thou art the Immortal Soul. Destroy the inferiority complex. Draw power, courage, strength from within. Be free. Have no blind faith. Reason out carefully and then accept anything. Do not be carried away by blind surging emotions. Subdue them. Do not be intolerant. Expand. There is a vast magazine of power and knowledge within you. It needs ignition. Then the whole mystery of the Self will be revealed unto thee. The darkness of ignorance will be dispelled by the light of knowledge of the Self. Constant meditation on the Atman is the master-key to open the realms of knowledge. I have given here the gist of Vedanta in a few lines. Taste the Vedantic nectar and attain IMMORTALITY, ETERNAL BLISS and PERENNIAL JOY. This is the goal of life. This is the end and aim of existence. Karma Yoga and Upasana will prepare you to realise the highest goal.

Try to lead a life of non-attachment; discipline your mind gradually. No one is free from pains, diseases, troubles and difficulties. You will have to rest in your own Svarupa, the blissful ATMAN—the source and support for this life. You will have to remember your own divine nature. Then only you will gain inner strength to face the difficulties of life. Then only you will have balanced mind. You will not be affected by external morbid influences and unpleasant discordant vibrations. Regular meditation in the morning will give you new strength and inner life—perennial joy and unalloyed bliss. Practise this. Feel this, despite your adverse, stormy conditions. Gradually you will grow spiritually. You will attain Self-realisation eventually.

Your present ailment is a Karmic purgation. It has come to make you remember Him more and more, to instil mercy in your heart, to strengthen you and to enable you to develop power of endurance. Kunti prayed to God to give her always adversity so that she could remember Him always. Bhaktas rejoice in suffering more. Disease, pain, scorpion, snake, calamities, etc., are messengers from God. A Bhakta welcomes them with a cheerful countenance. He never grumbles. He says once more: "*I am Thine, My Lord. Thou dost everything for my own good.*"

Where then is the room for lamentation and despair, my dear Niranjan? Thou art dear to the Lord. That is the reason why He gives troubles. If He wants to take anyone to His side, He takes away all money. He removes his dear kith and kin. He destroys all his pleasure-centres, so that his mind may fully rest at His Lotus-Feet. Face everything with a smiling cheerful countenance. Understand His mysterious ways. See God in everything, in every face—out of sight, but not out of mind. We are closer when we live physically at a distance. Let us dwell in our hearts. Krishna suddenly hides Himself, so that Radha and the Gopis might thirst for Him more eagerly. Sing like Radha. Thirst like Gopis for His vision. Krishna's grace is bound to descend. He is thy Immortal Friend. Forget not the Flute-Bearer of Brindavana, thy Solace and the joy of Devaki.

The all-merciful God resides in the chambers of your heart. He is quite close to you. You have forgotten Him. But He still cares for you. Troubles are His blessings in disguise. He wants to mould your body and mind as fit instruments for His unhampered play or Lila. He ministers or attends to your wants in a better manner than you yourself will do. Keep the load down that you are carrying on your shoulder unnecessarily on account of your egoism. Give up your self-created responsibilities and be at perfect ease. Have perfect faith in Him. Do total unreserved self-surrender. Run to Him now. He is waiting with outstretched hands to embrace you. He will do everything for you. Believe me. Take my word for it. Open your heart to Him quite freely like a child. All miseries will come to an end. Say unto Him at least once with Bhava sincerely: "*I am Thine, my Lord. All is Thine. Thy Will be done.*"

The gulf of separation will vanish now. All miseries, troubles, worries and diseases will melt away. You will become one with the Lord!

Feel that the whole world is your body, your own home. Melt or destroy all barriers that separate man from man. Idea of superiority is ignorance or delusion. *Isavasyam idam Sarvam*. Develop Visva-Prem, all-embracing, all-inclusive love. Unite with all. Separation is death. Unity is eternal life. The whole world is Visva Brindavan. Feel that this body is a moving temple of God. Wherever you are, whether at home, office, etc., know you are in the temple of God. Every work is an offering unto the Lord. Feel that all beings are images of God. Transmute every work into Yoga or an offering unto the Lord. Have Akarta, Sakshi Bhava if you are a student of Vedanta. Have Nimitta Bhava if you are an aspirant in the path of Bhakti. Feel that God works through your hands; that One Power works through all hands, sees through all eyes, hears through all ears. You will become a changed being. You will have a new angle of vision. You will enjoy the highest Peace and Bliss!

SIVANANDA MANO-VIJNANA SADHANA SUTRAS

The mind can be controlled by Abhyasa and Vairagya. Abhyasa is constant effort to fix the mind on God. Vairagya is dispassion or non-attachment to sensual objects.

Enquire "Who am I"? Do Vichara. Do mental Japa of Om and meditate on Atman. All thoughts will die by themselves. You will rest in Sat-Chit-Ananda Atman.

Sit alone and watch the Vrittis of the mind. Be indifferent. Remain as a Sakshi. Do not identify yourself with the Vrittis. The mind will come under your control.

Destroy the fuel of desire, the fire of thought will be extinguished. With the annihilation of Sankalpa, the reality of Brahman will shine.

Cultivate divine qualities such as friendliness, mercy, gladness and indifference towards happiness, pain, virtue and vice. You will get peace of mind.

Don't think of the past. Don't plan for the future. Do not allow the mind to build images. Live in the solid present.

Do a thing which the mind does not want to do. Do not do a thing which the mind wants to do.

Don't try to fulfil your desires. Don't hope. Don't expect anything. Destroy the vicious desires through virtuous desires and destroy the virtuous desires also through one strong desire for liberation.

Practice of Pranayama destroys Rajas and Tamas: makes the mind steady.

Study of religious books, Tapas, charity and Satsanga with Mahatmas, Sadhus and Sannyasins overhauls vicious Samskaras and paves a long way in the control of mind.

Japa of any Mantra and Upasana destroys impurities of mind, makes the mind inward, induces Vairagya, helps concentration and eventually leads to control of the mind.

"*Kalau Kesava-Kirtanat.*" In this Kali Yuga the easiest way for controlling the mind and attaining Moksha is Kirtan or singing the Name of the Lord.

Food has influence over mind. Sattvic food (milk, fruits, etc.) calms the mind. Rajasic food (meat, alcohol, etc.) excites the mind. Take Sattvic food. Have Mitahara.

Destroy evil habits by establishing new good habits. Control the lower instinctive mind through the higher Sattvic mind.

Constant selfless service with Atma Bhava is highly efficacious in purifying and controlling the mind.

Don't wrestle or struggle with the mind. Be regular in your concentration and meditation. May Peace, Joy, Bliss and Immortality abide in you for ever!

SIVANANDA HATHA YOGA SADHANA SUTRAS
1. Now then an enquiry into Hatha Yoga.
2. Hatha Yoga concerns with the body and the breath.
3. A Hatha Yogi purifies the Nadis through Pranayama.

4. He purifies the body through Shat-Karmas.
5. He practises Tratak and steadies the gaze.
6. He practises Asanas, Pranayama, Bandhas and Mudras.
7. He unites Prana with Apana.
8. He awakens the Kundalini by such practices.
9. He then takes it to Sahasrara through Shat-Chakras.
10. He concentrates on the Chakras.
11. He unites Kundalini with Sadasiva in Sahasrara.
12. He drinks the nectar, attains Immortality.
13. A Hatha Yogi attains Kaya Siddhi.
14. Raja Yoga begins where Hatha Yoga ends.

SIVANANDA KARMA YOGA SADHANA SUTRAS

1. Now then an enquiry into Karma Yoga Sadhana.
2. Karma Yoga Sadhana purifies the heart.
3. It is an auxiliary to knowledge.
4. No knowledge is possible without Chitta-Suddhi.
5. Karma Yoga Sadhana develops love and mercy.
6. Karma Yoga expands the heart.
7. Give up I-ness and mine-ness.
8. Develop adaptability, tolerance and courage.
9. Have command over temper.
10. Kill selfishness and idea of superiority.
11. Be humble and gentle and sweet.
12. Speak measured words.
13. Be truthful and sincere.
14. Do not expect fruits.
15. Surrender the fruits to the Lord.
16. Be an instrument in the hands of the Lord.
17. Surrender body, mind and wealth to the Lord.
18. Have equal vision and balanced mind.
19. Feel all forms are the forms of the Lord.
20. Feel you are serving the Lord alone.
21. Serve the sick, the poor and the parents.
22. Serve the country.

SIVANANDA BHAKTI YOGA SADHANA SUTRAS

1. Now then an enquiry into Bhakti Sadhana.
2. Bhakti Sadhana is that process by which we attain the Lord.
3. Develop nine modes of Bhakti.
4. Cultivate the five Bhavanas.

5. Serve the saints.
6. Be devoted to your Guru.
7. Have intense unswerving faith.
8. Study the Bhagavata, the Ramayana.
9. Hear the Lord's Lilas and Glory.
10. Feel the Divine Presence everywhere.
11. Do total, ungrudging self-surrender.
12. Recite Lord's Names always.
13. Sing His praises and do Kirtan.
14. The fruit of Bhakti Sadhana is Jnana.
15. Para Bhakti and Jnana are one.

SIVANANDA YOGA SADHANA SUTRAS

1. Now then an enquiry into Yoga Sadhana.
2. Yoga Sadhana results in union with the Lord.
3. Learn Yoga under a Guru.
4. Practise Ahimsa, Satya, Brahmacharya.
5. Cultivate mercy, humility, patience.
6. Have an easy, comfortable steady pose.
7. Regulate the breath, control the Prana.
8. Control the modifications of the mind.
9. Surrender the fruits of your actions to the Lord.
10. Take light diet, milk and fruits.
11. Practise Dharana, Dhyana, Samadhi.
12. Siddhis are obstacles in Yoga. Shun them.
13. Practise first the lower Samadhi.
14. Enter the Asamprajnata Samadhi.

SIVANANDA VEDANTA SADHANA SUTRAS

1. Now then an enquiry into Brahman.
2. Brahman is the material and efficient cause of this world.
3. Brahman is Infinite, Eternal, Unchanging.
4. That which hides the real is Maya.
5. That which veils the Jiva is Avidya.
6. Attainment of eternal Bliss and removal of all pain is Moksha.
7. Knowledge alone can give liberation.
8. The four means are auxiliaries to knowledge.
9. Knowledge comes through Sravana, Manana, Nididhyasana.
10. Brahmakara Vritti annihilates Avidya.

11. Meditate "I am Brahman"—this is Ahamgraha-Upasana.
12. A Jivanmukta is ever blissful and has equal vision.
13. A Jivanmukta must enjoy the Prarabdha.
14. His Pranas are absorbed in Brahman; he does not move.

INTEGRAL YOGA SADHANA
INTEGRAL DEVELOPMENT OF PERSONALITY

The Lord Himself declared in the Gita that there are two paths to Godhead and of the two He Himself holds one as superior to the other. This one is Karma Yoga. Karma Yoga is not entirely different from the Yoga of Wisdom, for wisdom is inherent in the former. The choice then is between abandonment of actions or their due performance in accordance with the principles enunciated by the Lord Himself, i.e., without egoism, attachment and desire.

Activity is the very soul of creation. Manifestation of phenomena is the result of the Primordial Activity in the Unmanifest. The inverse process of evolution into the Unmanifest Godhead has also, therefore, to be through activity; for, activity can drop off of its own accord only when creation is transcended. Forced restraint of the external organs of perception and action will result only in a hypocritical suppression of natural tendencies in man and not in their sublimation into the divine. It is this wisdom that prompted Janaka and other Jnanins to follow the path of action to reach the goal.

The essential prerequisite of Self-realisation being the infinite expansion of individual consciousness the separatist ego which limits the Jiva to the five sheaths has to be annihilated. Whichever be the missile chosen the target is the ego. The utter destruction of the ego is brought about only by the exercise of discrimination. This is taken as the basis for Yoga.

When the fast-binding shackle of ego is broken, the Yogi perceives the Atman ever remaining unmoved and unaffected by external activities, the Eternal Sakshi who neither acts nor enjoys. Actions belong to the realm of Prakriti or the ever-changing principle in nature, not to the Self, the Eternal Purusha. The six states appertain to the Gunas and their combination: not to the transcendental Atman, which ever remains tranquil and equanimous.

Dynamic actions sprout forth from the Yogi, but inwardly he ever remains quiescent! Herculean tasks that he might undertake for the commonweal move him not a hair's breadth from his Abode of Peace! Gigantic endeavours gather not their offspring to cling to the desire-lapel of his soul, for he has burnt it! The ego causeway having been destroyed, the fruits of actions which constitute the noose of Samsara dare not approach him.

Into this Karma-Jnana-synthesis is thrown devotion, too. Emotion forms quite a prominent part in the make-up of man and claims a place equal (at least) to those of his head and his hand. Emotion with its seat in the heart of man encloses within it the seed for rapid expansion of consciousness. According to the Gita, Para and Apara Bhakti both have their place in the unique process of evolution. Apara Bhakti leads to Para Bhakti which is identical with Jnana. A true Bhakta sees the Lord seated in his own heart, in every bit of creation. When the heart expands to limitless consciousness, the ego-covering slowly and gradually thins out and ultimately vanishes. The goal is reached.

Man—his entire being—is thus homogeneously developed into God. There is no stunted growth of any part to mar the beauty or the grandeur of his godly stature. He is no more in danger of becoming the prey of the deadly lioness (ego), for no part of his being is vulnerable. He is no more in danger of exposing an unregenerated corner of himself to the hungry gaze of worldliness, for there is none such in the expanded consciousness.

Nor is the practice of the Yoga of Meditation ignored. It is a fortress built morning and evening by the Yogi around himself, and equipped adequately to protect him from the external forces and the internal enemies. It is the main switch, which when on, sets the dynamo in motion to enable the latter to generate a high voltage of wisdom throughout the day, and electrocute the ego if it chances to come within the circuit.

This is the Yoga of Synthesis.

ALL-ROUND DEVELOPMENT

Man thinks, feels and wills. He must develop his heart, intellect and hand. The three Doshas can be removed by the three Yogas viz., Karma Yoga, Bhakti Yoga and Jnana Yoga. Have one as basic Yoga. Combine other Yogas also. This is Yoga of Synthesis.

Mokshapriya said:

O Gurudev! You very often speak of the Yoga of Synthesis. You lay great stress on this Yoga. You seem to be a great votary of this Yoga. Please enlighten me on this Yoga. I am very anxious to know all about this Yoga.

The Guru said:

Yoga of Synthesis is suitable for the vast majority of persons. It is a unique Yoga.

Man thinks, feels and wills. He is a triune being. He is a tricycle or a three-wheeled chariot. He has abundant emotion and feeling. He reasons and ratiocinates. He wills. He must develop his heart, intellect and hand. Then alone can he attain perfection. Many aspirants have lop-sided development. They do not possess integral development.

The three wheels must be in perfect order. Then alone will the chariot or tricycle move smoothly. Even so this body-chariot will move in harmony if you develop the heart, intellect and hand.

Further, there are three Doshas or defects in the mind viz., Mala (impurity), Vikshepa (tossing of mind) and Avarana (veiling).

Mala should be removed by Nishkama Karma Yoga or selfless service. Vikshepa should be removed by Upasana or worship (Bhakti Yoga). Avarana should be removed by study of Vedantic literature, Vichara or enquiry and Self-realisation.

Hence everyone should have one Yoga as a basic Yoga. He must combine Nishkama Karma Yoga, Hatha Yoga, Raja Yoga, Bhakti Yoga, etc. This is Yoga of Synthesis.

A little practice of Hatha Yoga (Asanas and Pranayamas) will give you good health. Raja Yoga will steady your mind. Upasana and Karma Yoga will purify your heart, and prepare you for the practice of Vedanta. Sankirtan will relax your mind and inspire you.

Such a Yogi has all-round development. The Yoga of Synthesis will help you to attain God-realisation quickly. The Upanishads, the Gita and other scriptures speak of this Yoga. Therefore, O Mokshapriya, practise this unique Yoga of Synthesis, and attain Self-realisation quickly.

CHAPTER EIGHT
SARVA-SADHANA-SANGRAHA

TRIPLETS IN THE FOUR MAIN PATHS OF SADHANA

KARMA YOGA

Grow.	Expand.	Sacrifice.
Serve.	Give.	Purify.

BHAKTI YOGA

Love.	Sing.	Surrender.
Remember.	Weep.	Worship
		(Ram Ram Ram)

RAJA YOGA

Control.	Subdue.	Restrain.

JNANA YOGA

Hear.	Reflect.	Meditate.
Enquire.	Investigate.	Ratiocinate.
Assert.	Know.	Feel.
Search.	Understand.	Realise.
		(Om Om Om)

SVARA SADHANA
EXPLANATION

In the body of a human being, the total number of Nadis or astral tubes which carry energy are 72,000. Of these 24 are the chief. Out of these 24 again 10 are important and of them 3 are the most important. These three Nadis are (1) Ida or Ingala or Chandra, (2) Pingala or Surya and (3) Sushumna.

During the course of one day and night breathing comes in and goes out 21,600 times.

When the breath comes and goes out through the right nostril then Surya or Pingala Nadi is functioning. When the breath comes and goes out through the left nostril, Chandra or Ida is functioning.

The colour of Prithvi Tattva (earth) is yellow; the colour of

Jala Tattva (water) is white; the colour of Agni Tattva (fire) is red; the colour of Vayu Tattva (wind) is green; the colour of Akasa Tattva (ether) is black.

If in the morning Surya Nadi is functioning, then to walk with the right leg placed on the ground first, either in the eastern or northern direction is beneficial. To place the leg first on the floor after rising from the bed corresponding to the Nadi is beneficial. If Chandra Nadi is functioning, then one should walk three steps placing the left leg first on the ground either in the southern or western direction.

If a man asks a question and if, at that time, Surya Nadi is functioning and if the questioner asks a question standing below, behind or to the right, then there will be success. If the Chandra Nadi is operating and the man stands above, in front or to the left, there will be success.

To see the right palm early in the morning after getting up, is auspicious. To touch the face early in the morning with the palm corresponding to the Nadi is highly beneficial. If Surya Nadi is operating, the face should be touched with the right hand.

The three days of Surya Nadi are Sunday, Tuesday and Saturday. The days of Chandra Nadi are Monday, Wednesday, Thursday and Friday. Of these days, in these Nadis, if questions are asked they are fruitful. A question asked when Sushumna flows is not fruitful.

The length of air coming out is 12 fingers; it is 20 fingers at the time of eating, 24 fingers while walking, 30 fingers in sleep, 36 fingers at the time of copulation, and still more while doing exercise.

Each of the Nadis changes in a healthy person at an interval of $2\frac{1}{2}$ Ghatikas or one hour. When Sushumna flows, meditate on God.

In the bright half of any month for the first three days, the functioning of Chandra Nadi is beneficial. Surya Nadi is auspicious on the 4th, 5th and 6th days. Chandra Nadi is fruitful on 7th, 8th and 9th. On the 10th, 11th and 12th, Surya Nadi and on 13th, 14th and 15th, Chandra Nadi is beneficial. In the dark half of the month for the first three days Surya Nadi is beneficial and so on.

Do holy actions when Ida flows. Eat and copulate when Surya Nadi flows. Ida Nadi showers nectar in all limbs.

When Chandra Nadi flows, start a long journey and pilgrimage, do religious ceremony, dig wells and tanks, inaugurate temples, images, take medicines, perform marriage, enter a new house, start agriculture, see a master or friend, worship your preceptor, and start study.

Take exercise when the Surya Nadi is flowing. When you enter or leave a house or a city, place the leg corresponding to the Nadi.

Practise Shanmukhi or Yoni Mudra—close the two ears with the two thumbs, the two nostrils with the middle fingers, the mouth by the last two fingers and the two corners of the eyes with the first fingers. Do a mild Kumbhaka or retention of the breath and concentrate on the space between the two eyebrows.

If the circle seen is yellowish, it is Prithvi Tattva; if it is red, it is Agni Tattva; if it is black, it is Akasa Tattva.

The numbers for Surya Nadi are 3, 5, 7, 9, i.e., odd, while those for Chandra Nadi are even 2, 4, 6, 8, etc. If at the time of Surya Nadi, a question is asked and if the letters of the question are odd, then the question will bear good fruits.

If a question is asked whether a son or daughter will be born, in Surya Nadi a son and in Chandra Nadi a daughter will be born, and in Sushumna, a eunuch. After the menstrual bath on the fifth day, when the husband has Surya Nadi and the wife Chandra Nadi, then copulation at the time gives a son. If the question is asked about the child while standing to the side of the Nadi a son will be born; if from the empty side a daughter; while in Sushumna twins.

TECHNIQUE

By knowing the nature of inspiration and expiration, by having a comprehensive understanding and practice of Svara Sadhana (science of breath), comes into being the knowledge of the past, present and future. This science, the hidden of the hidden, the secret of the secret, the revealer of Satya or Brahman, the bestower of bliss and supreme knowledge is a pearl, a precious gem on the head of the wise. This knowledge is easily understood if faith, interest and attention are sincerely bestowed on the part of aspirants. It excites wonder in the unbelievers. In the Svara are the Vedas and Sastras. The Svara is the reflection of Para Brahman. A knowledge more secret than the science of breath, wealth more useful than the science of breath, has never been seen or heard of. Friends are brought together by the power of breath.

In the body are the Nadis having many forms and extensions. They ought to be known by the wise and the aspirants for the sake of Knowledge. Branching off from the root, Kanda, in the navel, 72,000 Nadis extend in the body. Kundalini Sakti is sleeping like a serpent in the Muladhara Chakra. From here 10 Nadis go upwards and 10 downwards. Of all these, three Nadis, viz., Ida, Pingala and Sushumna are the most important.

Ida is in the left part; Pingala is in the right part and Sushumna is in the middle of the vertebral column. Prana passes through all these Nadis to the different parts of the body. Ida flows through the left nostril. Pingala through the right and Sushumna through both. Ida is the lunar, Moon or the Chandra Nadi, Pingala is the solar, Sun or the Surya Nadi. The Jiva is ever repeating the Soham Mantra. Watch the breath carefully. You will notice that the sound SO is produced during inhalation and HAM during exhalation. Watch very carefully the motion of the Ida and Pingala. Keep the Prana and mind calm. To those men who keep the Sun and Moon in proper order knowledge of the past and future becomes as easy as if they were in their hands.

In Ida, the appearance of the breath is that of Amrita. It is the great nourisher of the world. In the right, the world is always born. In the midst, the Sushumna moves. Do calm acts during the flow of Moon. Do harsh acts during the flow of Sun. Do acts resulting in the attainment of psychic powers, Yoga and Salvation, during the flow of Sushumna.

The Moon and the Sun have duration of five Ghatikas (two hours). They flow in order during the 60 Ghatikas of a day. Then by a Ghatika each, the five Tattvas flow. The days begin with the Pratipada (the first lunar day). When the order is reversed, the effect is reversed. In the bright fortnight, the left is powerful. In the dark fortnight, the right is powerful. If the breath rises by Ida at sunrise and flows throughout the day and Pingala rises at sunset and flows throughout the night, it confers considerable good results.

Let the breath flow through Ida, the left nostril, throughout the whole day from sunrise to sunset, and through Pingala, the right nostril, throughout the night from sunset to sunrise. This is the practice of Svara Sadhana.

He who practises thus is verily a great Yogi. Practise this. Shake off your habitual sloth, indolence, inertia, and all aspects of Tamas. Leave off your idle talks, gossiping and the obnoxious habit of critisising others. Do something useful. Do something practical. Wrong Svara is the cause of a host of ailments. Observance of right Svara as described above confers health and longevity. This will doubtless bestow on you wonderful benefits.

How to change the flow?

The following exercises are for changing the flow of Ida to Pingala. Select anyone of the methods that suits you best. For changing the flow from Pingala to Ida, just do the same exercise on the opposite side:—

(1) Plug the left nostril with a small piece of cotton or fine cloth for a few minutes.

(2) Lie down on the left side for ten minutes.

(3) Sit erect. Draw the left knee up and keep the left heel near the left buttock. Now press the left arm-pit on the knee. In a few seconds the flow will be through Pingala.

(4) Keep the two heels together near the right upper buttock. The right knee will be over the left knee. Keep the left palm on the ground a foot away and let the weight of the trunk rest on the left hand. Turn the head also towards the left side. This is an effective method. Catch hold of the left ankle with the right hand.

(5) The flow of breath can be changed by Nauli Kriya also.

(6) Place the "U" shaped end of the Yoga Danda (wooden stick of about 3 feet long) at the left arm-pit and lean on it by the left side.

(7) The most effective and instantaneous result is produced in changing the flow through Khechari Mudra. The Yogi turns the tongue inside and blocks the passage by the tip of the tongue.

LAYA YOGA SADHANA
METHOD OF LAYA YOGA SADHANA

Dharana is the intense and perfect concentration of the mind upon some internal centre or external object or sounds like Anahata sounds or any abstract idea accompanied by a complete abstraction from everything pertaining to the external universe or the world of senses. Dharana is absolutely necessary in Laya Yoga.

Sit in Padma or Siddha Asana. Practise Yoni Mudra by closing the ears through the thumbs. Hear the internal sound through the right ear. The sound which you hear will make you deaf to all external sounds. Having overcome all obstacles, you will enter the Turiya state within fifteen days by the practice of Laya Yoga. In the beginning of your practice you will hear many loud sounds. They gradually increase in pitch and after steady practice, they are heard more and more subtle. You should try to distinguish sounds that are more subtle. You may change your concentration from the gross sound to the subtle or from the subtle to the gross sound, but you should not allow your mind to be diverted from these to any other object.

The mind, having at first concentrated itself on any one sound, fixes firmly to that and is absorbed in it. The mind becoming insensible to the external impressions, becomes one with the sound as milk with water and then becomes rapidly absorbed in Chidakasa. Being indifferent towards all objects, having controlled the passions, you should by continual practice concentrate your attention upon the sound which destroys the mind. Having abandoned all thoughts and being freed from all actions, you should always concentrate your attention on the sound, and then your Chitta becomes absorbed in it. Just as the bee which is drinking the honey, does not care for the odour; so also the Chitta, which is always absorbed in sound, does not long for sensual objects, as it is bound by the sweet smell of Nada (Anahata sound) and has abandoned its flitting nature. The serpent Chitta, through listening to the Nada, is entirely absorbed in it. The Chitta becomes unconscious of everything and concentrates itself on the sound. The sound serves the purpose of a sharp goad to control the maddened elephant—Chitta which roves in the pleasure-garden of sensual objects. It serves the purpose of a snare for binding the deer—Chitta. It also serves the purpose of a shore to the ocean waves of Chitta.

The sound proceeding from Pranava which is Brahman is of the nature of effulgence. The mind becomes absorbed in it. That is the supreme seat of Vishnu. The mind exists so long as there is sound, but on the cessation of it there is that state termed Turiya. This sound is absorbed in Brahman and the soundless state is the supreme seat. The mind which along with Prana has its Karmic affinities destroyed by the constant concentration upon Nada, is absorbed in Brahman. There is no doubt of it. Being freed from all states and all thoughts, the body will appear like a dead body or like a log of wood and does not feel heat or cold, joy or sorrow. When the spiritual sight becomes fixed without any object to be seen, when the Prana becomes still without any effort, and when the Chitta becomes firm without any support you become Brahman. When Manas is destroyed, when virtues and sins are burnt away, you shine as the effulgent, immaculate, eternal, stainless Suddha Brahman. You are a Mukta now.

EXPERIENCES IN LAYA YOGA SADHANA

Sit in Padmasana or Siddhasana or Sukhasana. Close the ears with the thumbs. This is Shanmukhi Mudra or the Vaishnavi Mudra or Yoni Mudra. Hear the Anahata sound attentively. Occasionally you can hear the sounds through the left ear also. Practise to hear from the right ear only. Why do you hear distinctly through the right ear only? Because of the solar Nadi; Pingala on the right side of the nose. The Anahata sound is also called Omkara Dhvani. It is due to the vibration of the Prana.

Do Japa (Ajapa Japa) of Soham with breath or Japa of any Mantra. Practise Pranayama for one or two months. You will hear the ten Anahata sounds clearly, and enjoy the music of the soul. Abandon all worldly thoughts. Collect the dissipated rays of the mind and concentrate them on the Anahata sound. Practise Yama (self-restraint) or Sadachara (right conduct).

Nada or Anahata that is heard is of ten kinds. The first is *chini* (like the sound of chini); the second is *chini-chini*; the third is the sound of *bell*; the fourth is that of the sound of *conch*; the fifth is that of *tantri* (lute); the sixth is that of the sound of *tala* (cymbals); the seventh is that of *flute*; the eighth is that of *bheri* (drum); the ninth is that of *mridanga* (double drum) and the tenth is that of *thunder*. You can experience the tenth sound without the first nine sounds through the initiation of a Guru. Gradually you will have to change your concentration from the gross sound to the subtle.

Before you set your feet upon the higher rungs of the ladder of Nada Yoga, you should practise to hear the voice of your inner God in seven manners. The first is like the nightingale's sweet voice chanting a song of parting to its mate. The second comes as the sound of a silver cymbal of the Dhyanis, awakening the twinkling stars. The next is as the plaint melodies of the ocean-sprite imprisoned in its shell. And this is followed by the melodious note of Vina. The fifth sound of bamboo-flute shrills in your ear. It changes next into a trumpet-blast. The last vibrates like the dull rumbling of a thunder-cloud. The seventh swallows all the other sounds. They all die, and then you will be able to hear the subtle music of the inner Spirit.

You will get knowledge of hidden things in the seventh. In the later stages you will hear Paravak and develop the divine eye. And lastly you will attain the Para Brahman.

The sound entraps the mind. The mind becomes one with the sound as milk with water. It becomes absorbed in Brahman or the Absolute.

You cannot have any tangible result in the path of Laya Yoga without purification of the heart. You will have to purify your heart first by untiring selfless service, Kirtan, Japa, meditation, cultivation of divine virtues and thereby eradicating the negative qualities. You will have to equip yourself with the four means, and practise the Laya Yoga Sadhana. Then alone you will attain the seat of Eternal Bliss and Immortality.

PRANAVA SADHANA

Pranava (OM) is a ferry-boat for men who have fallen into the never-ending ocean of mundane life. Many have crossed this ocean with the help of this ferry-boat. You can also do so if you meditate constantly on OM and live in the spirit of OM.

OM is the only symbol for that Immortal, All-pervading Self. Think of OM to the exclusion of everything else. Shut out all mundane thoughts. They may, of course, recur again and again. But you will have to generate the thoughts of the pure Self repeatedly. Associate the ideas of purity, perfection, freedom, knowledge, immortality, eternity, infinity, etc., with OM. Repeat OM mentally.

Constantly meditate upon the following thoughts and repeat mentally:—

All-pervading ocean of light	I am, OM OM OM
Light of lights	I am, OM OM OM

Sun of suns	I am, OM OM OM
Infinity	I am, OM OM OM
Pure Chit (Consciousness)	I am, OM OM OM
All-pervading, infinite Light	I am, OM OM OM
Vyapaka paripurna	I am, OM OM OM
Jyotirmaya Brahman	I am, OM OM OM
Omnipotent, omniscient	I am, OM OM OM
All-bliss, all-purity	I am, OM OM OM
All-glory, all-joy	I am, OM OM OM
All-health, all-peace	I am, OM OM OM

Aspirants bold! Remember always the last word of Advaita, "TAT TVAM ASI"—That thou art. Feel as such. Recognise as such. Realise your real identity with the all-blissful Self, right now, in this very moment!

Association with Om is to become one with the thing signified. "*Tat-Japah tadartha bhavanam.*" Try to identify yourself with the all-blissful Self when you think or meditate or chant OM and negate the five Kosas as illusory adjuncts created by Maya. You have to take the symbol OM as Sat-Chit-Ananda Brahman or Atman. This is the meaning. During meditation you should feel that you are all-purity, all-light, all-pervading existence etc. Meditate on the Self daily. Think that you are entirely different from the mind or body. Feel: I am Sat-Chit-Ananda Atman, I am all-pervading consciousness. This is the Vedantic meditation.

Meditation on OM with Bhavana and meaning leads to realisation or Brahma-Jnana. This is the Jnana Yoga. Besides A,U,M and Ardha-matra, there are four other parts of OM, viz., Bindu, Bija, Sakti and Santi. The latter four have to be felt through Bhavana or feeling during meditation. Laya Chintana of OM leads to Advaita Nishtha or Nirvikalpa Samadhi.

(a) Visva gets Laya or dissolution in Virat: Virat in "A".

(b) Taijasa gets Laya in Hiranyagarbha: Hiranyagarbha in "U".

(c) Prajna gets Laya in Isvara: Isvara in "M".

Turiya is common to both Jiva and Isvara. "A" Matra gets Laya in Kutastha—Jiva-Brahmaikyam—oneness of Jiva and Brahman. Thus you will have to realise your identity with Supreme Self through such Pranava Sadhana.

May you all rest in the non-dual Brahman and taste the

nectar of Immortality. May you all reach the fourth state of bliss (Turiya) by analysing the experiences of the waking, dream and deep sleep states. May you all have a comprehensive understanding of Omkara, or Pranava and the "A" Matra. May you all enter the soundless OM by transcending the sounds of A, U and M. May you all meditate on OM and attain the goal of life, the ultimate Reality. May this OM guide you. May this OM be your centre, ideal and goal!

SOHAM SADHANA

Soham means He am I or I am Brahman. Sa means He. Aham means I. This is the greatest of all Mantras. This is an Abheda-bodha-vakya which signifies the identity of Jiva or the individual soul and Brahman or the Supreme Self.

Soham is only OM. Delete the consonants S and H. You get OM. Soham is modified Pranava or OM. Meditation on Soham is the same as meditation on OM. Before you take up Soham Sadhana you must practise the Neti-Neti (not this, not this) doctrine. You must negate or deny the body and the other Kosas by repeating '*Naham Idam Sariram*'—'Ahametat na.' I am not this body, mind or Prana. I am He, He am I—Soham, Soham!

The Jiva or the individual soul is repeating this Mantra unconsciously 21,600 times within 24 hours. Even during sleep the Soham repetition goes on by itself. Watch the breath very carefully and you will know this. When you inhale the sound '*So*' is produced, and when you exhale '*hum*' is produced. This is termed Ajapa Mantra.

Repeat this Mantra mentally. You should feel with all your heart and soul that you are all-pervading, omnipotent, all-blissful soul or the Brahman. Mere mechanical repetition will not help you much. But maximum benefits can only be realised by Anubhuti or feeling. If intellect tries to feel, I am Brahman, I am the omnipotent, but the Chitta tries to feel, I am so and so, I am weak, I am helpless etc., realisation is not possible. You must destroy all wrong Samskaras, all false imaginations, weaknesses, superstitions and fears. You must destroy Avidya or ignorance. It is Avidya, it is the mind that has brought one to this limitation through identification with the perishable body. Pierce the veil of ignorance. Tear the five sheaths. Remove the curtain of Avidya and rest in your own essential Sat-Chit-Ananda Svarupa through the force of

Soham Sadhana. Assert *"Aham Brahmasmi."* Proclaim—*"Tat Tvam Asi."*

Sing:—
I am neither mind nor body; Immortal Self I am,
I am witness of three states; Existence Absolute,
I am witness of three states; Knowledge Absolute,
I am witness of three states; Bliss Absolute,
   Soham Soham, Sivoham Soham,
   Soham Soham, Sivoham Soham,
I am not this body; This body is not mine
I am not this Prana; This Prana is not mine
I am not this mind; This mind is not mine
I am not this Buddhi; This Buddhi is not mine
I am that I am; I am that I am
I am That I am, That I am That, I am That
   (Soham Soham.........)
I am Sat Chit; Ananda Svarupa
I am Nitya Suddha Buddha; Mukta Svabhava,
I am Svayam Prakasa; I am Santi Svarupa
I am Akarta Abhokta; I am Asanga Sakshi
Prajnanam Brahma; Aham Brahma Asmi
Tat Tvam Asi; Ayam Atma Brahma,
Satyam Jnanam; Anantam Brahma,
Ekam Eva Advitiyam; Sarvam Khalvidam
Brahma Neha Nanasti Kinchana.
   (OM OM OM OM, OM OM OM OM.....)

Recognise your own Svarupa by negating the body-idea and identifying yourself with supreme Self. Mentally always repeat the Soham. Meditate on Sat-Chit-Ananda, the non-dual Brahman. Watch the breath with silent Soham repetition while sitting, standing, eating, talking, etc. This is an easy method for concentration. The Soham Bhava must become habitual.

The Soham Sadhana is suitable only for the advanced students in spiritual path, particularly those who are monistically inclined. However one has to pass through the preliminary spiritual practices. He should ascend in the ladder of Yoga step by step. Unless the heart is purified and the dross of mind is cleansed, unless the idea of doership and the little self-assertive ego is completely purged out, one cannot attain any tangible result in the path of Soham Sadhana.

VICHARA SADHANA

I

Very often we run after the shadow, discarding the substance in the background. In the spiritual sense, this theory is the very root of bondage. Instead of seeking God and realising his oneness with Him, man runs after His shadow, the world. This is the cause of all misery on earth.

Even in the case of the meaning of the word "God" itself we more often than not understand the "shadow" rather than the real "Substance" that is God. We concentrate so much on this unreal thing that in course of time we lose consciousness of the tree, we miss the grand spectacle of the wood!

This is true of our understanding of the Scriptures, too. How often have not reformers had to thunder forth to antagonistic millions the true significance of the teaching of the Prophets and Saints and dispel the darkness of wrong notions that had covered up the essence! The origin of most of the religions of the world could be traced out to this sort of renaissance. The source was only one religion. In course of time, people of deluded understanding began to interpret it as tenets variously and started forming parties. They split themselves into opposing camps, each owning to be the sole votaries of the real purport of the ancients' utterances. Then will arise a star who will dive deeper into the ocean of Wisdom and bring out the pearl of Truth. Some will follow him; others will still strike the discordant note. The new seer will get together a band of followers to propagate his teachings; and these will establish a new religion. And, so the game has gone on for ages!

Besides the Scriptural teachings, all religions have had the "Sayings" of their prophets. These are also classed under proverbs, though these include other ideas. Those of the proverbs which have such a spiritual background have as much of deep, secret and mystical meaning as the scriptural utterances themselves. This makes the real idea which they wish to convey to be misconstrued by posterity; and often some nonsensical notes are sounded in a futile attempt to give a true rendering of this sublime music.

Let us take a few examples from the Tamil literature. There is a beautiful (and amusing as it has become nowadays) proverb which means: "When you see (the) dog, there is no stone; when you see (the) stone, there is no dog." This has come to be regarded as a remark made by someone in light vein, or at least not in a very serious mood. The proverb is taken to convey what it literally does. A man is passing along the road in a village. Several dogs stroll about him , "What a pity!" he is made to think. "There are so many dogs all about me. How I wish there was a stone near at hand, so that I could enjoy a throw at them!" During a pilgrimage the same man looks at beautiful, well-polished stones lining the banks of the Ganga, then he thinks: "What a pity, again! Here there are any number of the most lovely stones. But, not a dog to hit them with!" This is the interpretation of the vulgar proverb. Even the serious amongst humanity nowadays will at best interpret it to mean that this proverb merely restates an old idea regarding earthly fortunes. Where money is most needed, it is usually absent; where it is already superfluous, it is found in more and more abundance. Few care to stop to think what the proverb really has to convey.

Before we proceed to examine the underlying sense of this proverb let us divert our attention to "God" vis-a-vis the world. What is this world and what is God? "*Brahma Satyam Jagan Mithya Jivo Brahmaiva Na-aparah,*" roared the ancient seers. God alone is Truth; the world does not exist at all, they said. But, we see it!—posed the uninitiated. Yes, we see it as we see a snake in the rope; as we see water in the mirage; as we see silver in the mother-of-pearl. A man comes home from his office, tired and exhausted and as he steps into his house, he feels that he had trodden a snake. He is not able to examine the thing in the darkness. In that weakened state, his reasoning fails him. His head reels, he is in the grip of fear. He imagines that he has been badly bitten by this snake. He staggers into the house and collapses into the nearest bed. At once a hue and cry! The man has been bitten by the snake. He almost loses consciousness. Crowds of people surround his cot. Weeping and wailing; praying and prattling; pandemonium prevails in the house. A seasoned man with flowing grey hairs of wisdom enters and shouts: "Leave the way, let me examine the patient." He gets nearer the bed, and calmly examines the patient. Unable to detect any signs of snake-bite, he thinks, his hands combing the long beard, "No, this can't be." He is determined! "Let me see," he says: "Where did the snake bite you?" The dying man feebly answers: "Four yards away from the entrance." With a lantern in hand, the old man sets out on his errand. Of course, the snake if it had bitten him would not be stationary, still. Exactly, on the spot mentioned by the patient, there was "the snake." But the flash of light has turned it into an old garland of flowers! Triumphantly, with that garland-snake in hand the old man returns to the death-bed and with a sagacious twitch playing on his lips, he exhibits the snake to the astounded audience. "This is, my dear man, the snake that bit you. It has no poison-fangs. So, wake up. Change your shirt which is wet with perspiration." The dying man is at once electrified and the pain and fear leave him. Brightly he gets up, embraces his saviour and bids good-bye to the crowd!

That is what the world is. It is a superimposition on Brahman. In essence, it is not there; at least, as what it seems to be. So long as you see it in darkness, it appears as the snake. Light the lamp of wisdom and in its effulgence, the world, as such, will disappear and you will perceive the Essence (Brahman) in all Its grandeur. Several Tamil saints have conveyed this idea in the very beautiful, and sublime verses. He who sees God, does not perceive the world made up of the five elements; and he who is engrossed in the play of the elements, is blinded to the vision of God.

To arrive at the real purport of the proverbs, we should know the context in which that proverb took its birth. Only then can we understand the sense which the letters wish to convey.

A sculptor moves around an old temple, with everyone of his senses and the mind absorbed in the beauty of the carvings on the walls of the temple. He feels the tail of a cat. "Ah, how beautiful it is! There, the mouth of that lion with that stone-ball inside!" So, he moves from one carving to another. He takes a turn. "Lo! That huge dog! If only it jumps on me! Look at its sharp teeth; and its blood-thirsty tongue flowing out of its mouth. It is looking directly at me. Oh, my God, what am I to do now?" Perplexed, he closes his eyes. One minute passes, two, three, four. Still the dog is hesitant. "Why, probably it is chained." He throws a small stone at it. It does not move. He goes nearer. Still it stands where it was, staring at him all the time. "Why, it does not even wag its tail? Peculiar dog it must be." He goes yet nearer, and touches its tail. His whole body rocks with laughter at his own idiotic behaviour. It is made of stone! Yet, such was the workmanship, the colouring and the art that it actually looks like a live dog. This is what was meant by the poet who said; "When there is the dog, there is no stone; when there is the stone, there is no dog." When you see the dog there is no idea that it is of stone. When you realise it is made of stone, the idea of dog vanishes. What a travesty of truth it is to superimpose all sorts of ludicrous ideas on this proverb which conveys the highest truth. When you see the diversity, Unity disappears; and vice versa. When you realise God, world disappears; when you lose yourself in the world, you cannot realise God.

This idea is beautifully expressed in many a couplet in Tamil literature. One says; "The elephant screened the wood; and in the wood disappeared the elephant." It sounds mystic! Take an instance. A young child has an elephant made of mango-wood which he got as a present from his fond parent. A carpenter is working on the verandah. It runs to him and shows the elephant to him, "See, how big are his legs. Look at his winnow-like ears. Pooh! The tusks will pierce your chest." It plays with it as if it were an elephant in reality. The carpenter takes the doll in his hand and examines it. "Why child, it is not a good one." "What my elephant?" "Yes it is made of mango-wood. It gets spoiled soon." To the carpenter, it is not an elephant; but a piece of wood. Such is the difference in the attitude towards the world between the worldly man and a saint. The worldly man sees the world as a diversity, as a mixture of pleasure and pain, as a conglomeration of objects; the saint perceives the one Hidden Essence which pervades the whole universe; to him it is an "Abhasa" of That Existence-Knowledge-Bliss Absolute, Brahman.

II

Now, take another proverb. Translated into English it means: "When the 'Ooru,' is split, things were easy for the dancer." This word 'Ooru' is taken to mean "Village." There once lived in a village a big zamindar who owned the entire village itself. A street-dancer used to visit the place once in a day and get rich presents from the zamindar after a performance of his art. The zamindar died and his two sons inherited their father's property. Naturally, it was divided between the two. As happens with most of the South Indian families, they both established their own houses. Now, the street-dancer again visited the village and found the zamindar's household divided between two brothers. He went to one of the brothers and exhibited his feats. He received rich presents from him. He then visited the other brother and gave a performance there also. This brother also gave him rich presents; but found out by and by the value of those given by his brother. Out of sheer vanity, he gave more than his brother did! Thus, whereas the dancer would have got presents only from one zamindar, he was now able to get a lion's share in view of the fact that the family was split into two. This is taken to be the real meaning of the proverb.

A moral is usually drawn from the story that families should ever try to remain united: or else some "Third" party would plunder both parties to his own advantage at the expense of both of them! When we understand the real meaning, however, we would merely *laugh* at such perverted explanations.

An important word in the proverb 'Ooru' is misunderstood to mean 'a village' and a whole parable is woven round it! If we think for a while, we are sure to arrive at the correct meaning of the whole proverb. The word 'Ooru' has been borrowed from Sanskrit where it means "thigh."

You are probably aware of the story of Oorvasi's birth. Sage Narayana was performing severe penance in the Himalayas for innumerable years. Indra, who usually gets upset whenever a saint performs penance, wanted to foil Narayana's attempts. He sent many celestial damsels to tempt Sage Narayana. They approached him with this end in view. They danced, sang and spread their tempting net over the saint absorbed in his Self. He sensed the mischief, opened his eye and saw the damsels straining everyone of their nerves to disturb him. He smiled at their folly. And as they were looking on, struck his right thigh with his palm. To the bewilderment of the celestials, there arose from that thigh a veritable army of the most bewitching female forms. These latter charmed Indra's messengers who fell their victims instantly. They soon forgot all about their mission and remained there itself. Indra waited, and waited. At last, despaired of the return of his missionaries, he sent some of his deputies to find out the cause of their delay. Those Devas, in their turn, were themselves the victims of Sage Narayana's creations. Indra himself came later, found out the facts. But for the sage's grace upon him, Indra would himself have fallen a victim to the lustful looks of these women. Realising his capacity, Indra at once fell prostrate at Narayana's feet and begged his pardon. Afraid that his own celestials would fade into insignificance if the sage's creation were allowed to compete with them, he requested Narayana to withdraw the women that he created. The sage at once recalled all the damsels except one to enter his thigh. This one he sent with Indra. She was Oorvasi—one who lived in the thigh of Narayana.

That is what 'Ooru' means. Now, taking this meaning of the word, let us analyse the proverb again. "Because of the separation of the thigh, it was easy for the dancer." The famous story of the Dance of Siva comes before our mind's eye. Parvati, Lord Siva's consort, challenged her husband to a dance competition. To establish his supremacy over her, the Lord danced for a long time. Parvati was equally adept. She proved His equal in every respect. At last a queer idea struck him. He raised one of his legs up and danced. No decent woman could do that without losing her chastity and proper demeanour. Parvati reflected for a moment and submitted. She acknowledged defeat. The proverb reminds us of this Divine Event; "Was it not because the thighs were separated, that victory was easy for the Dancer?"

III

One more to the point.

There is, what is commonly agreed to be a funny proverb which taken literally means: "The burning ghat can be known only if (one) has died previously." It is absurd on the face of it. It is not necessary for one to have died previously to know where the dead bodies are burnt. One passes by the village burning ghat often enough to know where it is. Further, one who dies does not know where he is being taken! So, it is impossible for a dead man to know the burning ghat.

A proverb cannot be without meaning; and the meaning is often hidden in a mystery. This proverb should have its meaning; it cannot be for mere fun.

Now, let us probe a little deeper. "Burning Ghat" represents destruction, or that which burns. The first part of the proverb literally means, "At the death of 'before' and 'after' only....." We all know that the first thing that asserts itself in man is 'I' the false ego that arrogates to itself the doership of every action.

The next is a natural corollary of the first—the idea of "mineness" which spreads its possessive net over a large field and gets the 'I' itself entangled in its meshes. Everyone of the saints and seers of India has declared emphatically that unless this false ego is annihilated *in toto* a man cannot attain salvation. Whatever path he might follow, this is a condition prerequisite to realisation. All the Tamil Saints of South India have trumpeted this Truth in unmistakable terms; and one has chosen to express it in the form of this proverb. "O fool! Only when the first thing (I) and the later thing (mind) die, can you perceive that Ghat of Knowledge which burns ignorance." What a sublime thought! And, what a tragic mutilation has it suffered by the passage of time and by falling into the hands of unthinking revellers!

May you all understand the real import of the Great Sayings and imbibe it in your everyday life!

OM Santi Santi Santih!

DHYANA YOGA SADHANA
QUALIFICATIONS FOR PRACTISING DHYANA

Before saturating the mind with thoughts of Brahman you will have to assimilate the divine ideas first. Assimilation first and then saturation. Then comes realisation at once without a moment's delay. Remember this "Triplet," always: ASSIMILATION-SATURATION-REALISATION.

Your will should be rendered strong, pure and irresistible by more Atma Chintana, eradication of Vasanas, control of the senses and more inner life. You must utilise every second on Sundays and holidays to your best spiritual advantage.

If you have tasted Rasagulla—a Bengal-sweetmeat—for a month, mental adhesion to Rasagulla comes in the mind. If you are in the company of Sannyasins, if you read books on Yoga, Vedanta, etc., a similar mental adhesion takes place in the mind for attaining God-realisation, God-consciousness. Mere mental adhesion will not help you much. Burning Vairagya, burning Mumukshutva, capacity for spiritual Sadhana, intense and constant application and Nididhyasana (meditation) are needed. Then only Self-knowledge is possible.

Leading a virtuous life is not by itself sufficient for God-realisation. Constant meditation is absolutely necessary. A good virtuous life only prepares the mind as a fit instrument for concentration and meditation. It is concentration and meditation that eventually lead to Self-realisation.

You will find very often these terms in the Gita, "Manmanah, Matparah." These terms connote that you will have to give your full mind, entire 100 per cent mind to God. Then only you will have Self-realisation. Even if one ray of mind runs outside, it is impossible to attain God-consciousness.

Just as you render the turbid water pure by the addition of clearing nut (strychnos potatorum), so also you will have to make the turbid mind filled with Vasanas and false Sankalpas pure by Brahmachintana (thinking and reflecting on the Absolute). Then only there will be true illumination.

You must not be too hasty in longing for the fruits at once, when you take to meditation. A young lady perambulated one Asvattha tree (Ficus Religiosa) 108 times for getting an offspring and then immediately touched her abdomen to see whether there was a child or not. It is simply foolishness. She will have to wait for some months. Even so, if you will meditate for some time regularly, then the mind will be ripened and eventually you will get Atma-Sakshatkara (Self-realisation). Haste makes waste.

It behoves well that advanced Grihastha Yogic students (householders) will have to stop all the worldly activities when they advance in meditation, if they desire to progress further. They themselves will be forced to give up all work, if they are really sincere. Work is hindrance in meditation for advanced students. That is the reason why Lord Krishna says in the Gita "For a sage who is seeking Yoga action is called the means; for the same sage who is enthroned in Yoga (state of Yogarudha) serenity (Sama) is called the means." Then work and meditation become incompatible like acid and alkali or fire and water or light and darkness.

You must daily increase your Vairagya, meditation and Sattvic virtues such as patience, perseverance, mercy, love, forgiveness, purity, etc. Vairagya and good qualities help meditation. Meditation increases the Sattvic qualities.

Have the one all-pervading Brahma Bhavana (feeling). Deny the finite body as a mere appearance. Try to keep up the feeling always.

Why do you close your eyes during the meditation? Open your eyes, and meditate. You must keep your balance of mind even when you are in the bustle of a city. Then only you are perfect. In the beginning when you are a neophyte you can close your eyes to remove the distraction of mind, as you are very weak. But later on you must meditate with eyes open even during the walking. Think strongly that the world is unreal, that there is no world, that there is Atman only. If you can meditate on Atman even when the eyes are open you will be a strong man. You will not be easily disturbed. You can meditate only when the mind is beyond all anxieties.

In meditation and concentration you will have to train the mind in a variety of ways. Then only the gross mind will become subtle (Sukshma).

All Vrittis such as anger, jealousy, hatred etc., assume subtle forms when you practise Japa and meditation. They are thinned out. They should be destroyed *in toto* through Samadhi. Then only you are safe. Latent Vrittis will be waiting for opportunities to assume a grave and expanded form. You should be ever careful and vigilant.

Resist the fatal downward pull caused by the dark, antagonistic forces through regular meditation. Check the aimless wanderings of the mind through clear and orderly thinking. Hear not the false whispers of the lower mind. Turn your inner gaze to the divine centre. Do not be afraid of the severe set-backs that you will encounter in your journey. Be brave. March on boldly, till you finally rest in your centre of eternal bliss.

In a big city there is much bustle and sound at 8 p.m. At 9 o'clock there is not so much bustle and sound. At 10 p.m. it is still reduced, at 11 p.m. it is still much less. At 1 a.m. there is peace everywhere. Even so in the beginning of Yogic practices there are countless Vrittis in the mind. There is much agitation and tossing in the mind. Gradually the thought-waves subside. In the end all mental modifications are controlled. The Yogi enjoys perfect peace.

When you pass through a market of a big city, you will not be able to notice small sounds but when you sit for common meditation with some of your friends in a quiet room in the morning you will be able to detect even a little sneezing or coughing. Even so you are not able to find out the evil thoughts when you are engaged in some work or other, but you are able to detect them when you sit for meditation. Do not be afraid when evil thoughts pass through your mind when you sit for meditation. Do vigorous Japa and meditation. They will pass off soon.

The student of Yoga should not possess much wealth as it will drag him to the worldly temptations. He can keep a little sum to meet the wants of the body. Economical independence will relieve the mind from anxieties and will enable him to continue the Sadhana uninterruptedly.

NECESSITY OF SITTING POSTURE IN MEDITATION

One has to meditate sitting, because it is not possible to meditate standing or lying down. Sitting is necessary for meditation because Dhyana is the continuity of the mental state and such continuity will not exist when one walks or runs, because then the mind will attend to the body and cannot concentrate, or when one lies down because then he will be soon overpowered by sleep.

Upasana being mainly of the nature of concentration should be practised in a sitting posture which is conducive to concentration. Concentration being an unintermittent and uninterrupted current of thought sent towards a particular object, the sitting posture becomes indispensable.

In Upasana one has to concentrate one's mind on a single object. This is not possible if one is standing or lying. The mind of a standing man is directed on maintaining the balance of the body or keeping it in an erect position and therefore incapable of reflection on any subtle matter. A sitting person may easily avoid these several untoward occurrences and is, therefore, in a position to carry on his meditation. The sitting posture contributes that composure of mind which is the *sine qua non* of meditation. Meditation is to be practised in a sitting posture only. In that case only true meditation is possible. Further, such continuity of thoughts, i.e., Dhyana can come only when the limbs are not active and the mind is calm.

The word 'Upasana' also means exactly what meditation means, that is concentrating on a single object with a fixed look, and without any movement of the limbs. This is possible only in sitting posture.

In Karmanga Upasanas there is no question as to whether they should be done sitting or standing as they depend on the particular Karma. In pure realisation or perfect intuition there could be no such question as it depends on the object of such realisation. In other Upasanas sitting is necessary for meditation. Some may argue that as meditation in something mental there can be no restriction as to the attitude of the body. But the above arguments clearly denote the futility of the objection.

The constant remembrance of the Lord or Brahman is fit to be practised always. This can be practised without the sitting pose. But deep meditation is possible only in the sitting posture. This is possible only for him who sits up in wakefulness, but not for him who is lying in bed; overpowered by sleep, or standing or walking; for them distraction would necessarily set in. Meditation is far superior to mere remembrance. This is beyond a doubt. Hence the necessity for the sitting posture in meditation is proved.

Meditation denotes a lengthened carrying on of the same train of ideas. You ascribe thoughtfulness to those whose mind is concentrated on one and the same object while their look is fixed and their limbs do not move. You say that Ramakrishna is thoughtful. Now such thoughtfulness is easy for those who sit. The wife sits and thinks deeply over her husband gone on a distant journey. You, therefore, conclude herefrom also that meditation is the occupation of a sitting person.

Dhyana or meditation is thinking on one subject continuously, without the inrush of ideas incongruous with the subject of thought. Such meditation is possible in a sitting posture only, and not while lying down or stranding etc., because the distraction of the mind is minimised when you meditate in a sitting posture. Therefore, a sitting posture should be adopted both for prayers as well as for meditation.

Meditativeness is attributed to the earth on account of its immobility or steadiness. This also helps us to infer that meditation is possible in one when he is sitting and not while he is standing or walking. Steadiness accompanies meditation. Steadiness of body and mind is possible only while sitting and not while standing or walking.

With reference to the immobility of the earth the scripture fancies the earth as being engaged in concentration, as if it remains fixed in space in the act of pious meditation. It suggests that such a steady application of the mind can be attained by meditating only in a sitting posture.

For the same reason the Yoga Sastra teaches different sitting postures viz., Padmasana, Siddhasana, Sukhasana etc., for meditation.

SAGUNA DHYANA SADHANA

Saguna meditation is meditation on a form or object. This is a concrete form of meditation for the people of devotional temperament. This is meditation with Gunas, or the attributes of God. Select any Murti of God you like best, either Siva, Vishnu, Krishna or Rama according to your inclination or taste. An archer first aims at grosser, bigger objects. Then he takes up medium objects. Finally he shoots at finer and subtle objects. Even so, one should take to Saguna meditation to start with and when the mind is trained and disciplined well, the Nirguna or Nirakara meditation will come by itself.

Sit on either Padma, Siddha or Sukhasana with the head, neck and the trunk in a straight line. Place a picture of your Ishta Devata in front of you; for example, a photo of Lord Hari. Gaze at the picture steadily for some time, then close your eyes and try to visualise the form either in the space between the two eyebrows or within the heart or on the tip of your nose, as you may find it convenient. During visualisation move the mind on the various parts of the deity. Visualise His feet first and then in the following order: His legs, His yellow silk cloth, His golden necklace, studded with gems, on His neck, then the face, the crown on the head, then the disc in the right upper hand, the conch in the left upper hand, the mace in the lower right hand and the lotus in the left lower hand. Then come down to the feet in the same process. Repeat this process again and again. Finally fix the mind either at the feet or the face.

When the form gets faded or shaky, open your eyes and steadily gaze at the picture again. Then visualise the form within. Continue this process till you are able to meditate perfectly without the aid of the picture. While meditating repeat the Ishta Mantra of Lord Hari "Om Namo Narayanaya" mentally. Think of His attributes like omnipresence, omnipotence, omniscience, purity, merciful nature etc. Suppose, if you meditate within the heart, i.e. on Anahata Chakra, think that Lord Hari is seated or standing on the blazing lotus of 16 petals and His entire form is illumined with the lustrous light like that of the sun. Feel that His Divine qualities are spontaneously flowing towards you, you are now purified and purged of all the impurities, you are now the embodiment of all the Divine qualities. This process will quicken your progress.

In a similar way you can also meditate on the form of Lord Siva or Rama or Krishna, as per your taste.

Practise meditation in the early morning between 3 to 6 a.m. This is the best time for the practice of meditation. You can also meditate at the dead of night. The atmosphere is more peaceful and serene. You are not likely to be disturbed. The mind automatically gets the meditative mood. It is like a blank sheet of paper. You can also have another sitting just before retiring to bed.

It is well and good if you can have a separate meditation room. Keep the room always clean and pure. Never allow anybody to enter the room. Burn Ghrita-Pradeepa or candle and incense before the deity. This will make the mind more meditative. You will have good concentration. If possible take a bath or wash at least your face, feet, etc., before you sit for meditation. Keep the mind always pure, serene and calm. Entertain holy, divine thoughts.

When you meditate, disregard the substratum awakenings in the mind that arise out of the senses. Avoid carefully the comparisons with all other cross references and memories. Concentrate the whole energy of the mind on the idea of God. Avoid all other sense-impressions and ideas. Prevent the complications that arise out of the co-related action in the substratum of the mind. Abstract the mind on your object of meditation alone. Shut out all other processes of meditation. Now the whole mind will be filled with one idea alone. Nishtha will ensue. Just as the recurrence or repetition of a thought or action leads to perfection of that thought or action, so also does recurrence of the same process, the same idea leads to the perfection of abstraction, concentration and uninterrupted meditation.

When you meditate, various kinds of thoughts, subtle impressions and past memories will arise in the mind. They will hinder your meditation. Only sustained and patient efforts and practice can control them. Never apply any force. They will retort with redoubled force. When you sit for meditation, relax the mind completely. Be perfectly serene. Watch your thoughts very carefully. Be on the alert. Be a silent witness to your thoughts and their play. Then gradually collect the dissipated rays of the mind one by one and concentrate them on your object. Whenever evil thoughts crop up, immediately turn the mind towards the holy attributes of the Lord, forgetting all the evil impressions completely.

To practise meditation with a mind unprepared by the non-adherence to the moral precepts is like building a house on a rotten frail foundation. Therefore, mental purity through ethical training is of paramount importance if you wish to achieve success in meditation. Be perfectly established in Yama and Niyama. Lead a well-regulated moral life. Practise austerity of speech. Take one meal a day and light fruit and milk diet at night. This will keep the mind more steady. Perfect serenity, cultivation of divine virtues, entertaining holy thoughts, discipline of diet—all these pave a long way to attain success in a spiritual path.

NIRGUNA DHYANA SADHANA: THE SIX METHODS

A strong will and Manana are the two important factors that play a conspicuous part in Nirguna Dhyana Sadhana or the Vedantic Sadhana. Manana is preceded by Sravana or hearing of the Srutis; and ultimately followed by Nididhyasana of a constant nature with zeal and enthusiasm. Nididhyasana is profound meditation. Sakshatkara or Aparoksha realisation is Nididhyasana. Just as a drop of water when dropped on a hot iron is absorbed by the hot iron so also the mind and the Abhasa Chaitanya (reflected consciousness) become absorbed in Brahman. The balance left is Chinmatra Chaitanya or the Consciousness-Absolute. Thus through this process of Sadhana-Chatushtaya, Sravana and Manana one can qualify himself for the practice of Nirguna Dhyana Sadhana.

In Nirguna Dhyana, the mind loses its own consciousness and becomes identified with the all-pervading, formless, nameless, attributeless One Absolute-undivided-unmanifest-Infinite Existence. The meditator and the meditated, the thinker and the thought, Aham and Idam (I and this) become one. This is the final stage of Nirguna Dhyana Sadhana. The world vanishes from the view of the meditator and he rests on the Suddha, Nirguna Brahman.

Generally it is seen that unless and until one is well-advanced in Saguna Dhyana, he cannot achieve any notable result by directly taking up the Nirguna Dhyana Sadhana. It is he who is well-established in the path of Yama, Niyama and Sadhana Chatushtaya, it is he who perceives the all-pervading homogeneous Spirit in all, through intense selfless service and thereby shuffling off the petty feelings of doership and the self-assertive ego, it is he who has attained perfect tranquillity of the mind through discrimination, dispassion and by the practice of Sravana and Manana—can take up this Nirguna Dhyana Sadhana and can attain the Supreme One in a far shorter period than any other means.

This Sadhana is practised in six ways. They are: 1. Neti-Neti method. 2. Sakshi method. 3. Anvaya-Vyatireka method. 4. Bhaga-Tyaga Lakshana method. 5. Laya-Chintana method. 6. Meditation on Om with Tadrupa-Tadartha Bhavana.

Now I shall briefly describe them one by one. You will have to practise them constantly with adamant will and zeal.

1. *Neti-Neti* method—Not this, not this. This is the method of negation. The Upanishads proclaim, this physical body is not the Atman or Brahman, this Prana is not the Atman or Brahman, this mind is not Atman, this Buddhi (intelligence) is not Atman, this Anandamaya Kosa is not the Atman (Neti Neti). Therefore, the balance left after negating or sublating these false, illusory, limiting adjuncts, which are superimposed on Atman, is Suddha, Vyapaka, Sat-Chit-Ananda Atman. You are in reality this Atman. This is the process of explaining by Nishedha.

2. *Sakshi* method—Sakshi means witness. You will have to introspect and watch the Vrittis. You will have to separate yourself from the Vrittis of the mind by not identifying yourself with them. You should remain as a Sakshi without being affected by the Vrittis. Repeat mentally 'Om Sakshi Aham'—'I am Sakshi' at all times. That idea must become deep-rooted by constant repetition and feeling. You will become impersonal eventually. The Jiva-Bhavana will vanish in toto. Even during work you must be a Sakshi for all actions that you do. In reality it is the mind and its senses that do everything. You are the witness only. You must always entertain this idea. Constantly repeat the 8th Sloka of Chap. V in the Gita—"I do not do anything, should think the harmonised one, who knoweth the essence of things, seeing, hearing, touching, smelling, eating, moving, sleeping and breathing." The senses move among the objects of the senses.

3. *Anvaya-Vyatireka method*—Every object has 5 parts viz., Nama, Rupa, Asti, Bhati, Priya—name, form, existence, knowledge and bliss. Names and forms are illusory. They be-

long to Maya. Asti, Bhati, Priya are the Svarupa of Brahman. They are real. Asti, Bhati, Priya means 'Sat-Chit-Ananda.' Names and forms differ, but the Asti, Bhati and Priya are the same in all. They are the attributes of Atman. Names and forms are Vyatireka. Asti, Bhati and Priya are Anvaya. Through Anvaya-Vyatireka Yukti you will have to eliminate the name and form and take out (realise) the Asti, Bhati, Priya Atman that is hidden in all objects. This is, of course, the means to attain the final stage of Nirguna Dhyana Sadhana, where you identify yourself with the attributeless Self. Through constant thinking and force of meditation, the names and forms will vanish. Asti, Bhati, Priya alone will shine everywhere. Practise this always, even while you are at work.

4. *Bhaga-Tyaga-Lakshana method*—This concerns the 'Tat Tvam Asi' Mahavakya. There are two kinds of meanings of Tat and Tvam. The first is literal meaning, i.e., Tat is Isvara, and the second is indicative meaning i.e., Tat is Brahman. The first meaning of Tvam is Jiva, and the second meaning of Tvam is Kutastha, identifying with the Brahman. You will have to eliminate the Upadhi Avidya, its Dharmas and the reflected Chaitanya in Avidya in the case of Jiva and the Upadhi Maya, its Dharmas and the reflected Chaitanya in Maya in the case of Isvara. You will have to take out the common essence for both Jiva and Isvara and show identity with them. This is Bhagatyagalakshana. You will have to cull out the common essence. You can now meditate on the identity of Jiva and Brahman through the above method.

5. *Laya-Chintana* method—Laya means involution of the effect into the cause. There are three kinds of practice. The first is, that you will have to think that the mind is merged in Buddhi, Buddhi in Avyaktam, and Avyaktam in Brahman. The second is, that you should think that the earth gets merged in water, then water in fire, fire in air, air in Akasa (ether) and Akasa in Avyaktam and Avyaktam in Brahman. The third process is, that you should think that Visva (microcosm) gets merged in Virat (macrocosm), Taijasa in Hiranyagarbha, and Prajna in Isvara. The Kutastha becomes one with Brahman. Thus here you see that all the external elements or the attributes gradually get merged in the One common Source i.e., the Brahman. You go back to the original source, the Brahman who is the womb for all minds and Pancha-Bhutas. Finally you rest in the Brahman alone.

6. Meditation on OM with Tadrupa-Tadartha Bhavana—You associate yourself with OM on the ideas of purity, perfection, peace, infinity etc., as it has been described in "Pranava Sadhana."

There are various temperaments and types of the mind. So there are various ways also for the approach of Brahman to suit various individuals.

Anyone can take up any method, that appeals to him most, and then work out his Self-realisation through that particular Sadhana.

JAPA YOGA SADHANA
INTRODUCTORY

Sadhana is purifying and steadying the mind and fixing it on the Lord. Without Sadhana you cannot attain the Sadhya or the object of meditation i.e., the Supreme Being, the abode of Immortality and Bliss.

Japa is an important Sadhana. Make a resolve "I will do ten Malas of Japa today" and do not get up from your Asana or seat till you finish the required number of Malas. This will strengthen your will and enable you to control the mind easily.

Another important point is that there should not be any break in your Sadhana till you finish the required number of Malas. Entry of worldly thoughts, planning etc., constitute break. If there is any break after finishing two Malas of Japa, you should not include the two Malas of Japa. You must again start the Japa and try to finish ten Malas. If there is any break after finishing four Malas, do not include the four Malas. Again try to finish ten Malas. This will be trying discipline indeed. But the fruit of such a Sadhana is immortality or eternal blissful life in the Atman. You will have to practise it if you wish to attain this highest end or supreme Goal.

If a boy commits a mistake, the teacher asks him to catch hold of his ears and do 'Baitaks' ten times continuously as a sort of punishment. If he makes a break after doing four 'Baitaks,' he again asks him to do ten more 'Baitaks' without any break. Similar is the case with this Japa Sadhana. Similar is the punishment you will have to inflict on the mind when you do Japa Sadhana. You should not give leniency to the mind. Spare the rod, you will spoil the child. Be lenient, the mind will jump upon you.

The moment you sit on the Asana in a closed room, feel that you are a mental Sannyasin. You have nothing to do with the world or family members. Forget everything. If anybody taps at your door, do not be perturbed. Do not open the door. Tell your family people not to disturb you on any score till you finish your Sadhana.

When you come out of the room try to keep up the same Sattvic Bhava. Recite the Mantra or Name of the Lord always. If there is any break again keep up the remembrance. Gradually meditation and recitation of Japa will become habitual or Sahaja. The subconscious or the subjective mind will be ever repeating the Name, though the conscious or objective mind may forget it occasionally.

The Samskaras or impressions you have created during your Sadhana period within a closed room will be wiped out if you are not careful or vigilant during the period of activity in the world. You must be careful about the company you keep, about worldly talks, the food you take, the dress you wear, the objects at which you look, the words that you hear etc.

You must not speak vulgar or harsh words. You must take Sattvic food and wear simple dress. You must not visit cinemas. You must make the mind ever dwell on the form of the Lord and put a stamp of it on any form you see. You must not visit clubs. You must not read newspapers and novels. Novels, newspapers, cinemas constitute evil Sanga. They generate worldly thoughts and disturb the peace of mind. You do not gain anything.

There are many obstacles and difficulties in the world. But if you want to attain Immortality you will have to observe the Rules of Yoga. Where there is a will, there is a way. If there is strong aspiration and burning Mumukshutva, strength will come from within and you will be able to observe all the rules even though you remain in the world only. Pandit Madanmohan Malavya, Gandhiji and many others have evolved while remaining in the world. Do not bring lame excuses. The world is not a hindrance in your spiritual path. The world is your Guru. The world is a training school. World is Virat or Isvara.

Spend your holidays and privilege leave in solitary places like Rishikesh and do intense Sadhana. Come alone and lead the life of a Sannyasin during that period.

May you all be freed from the cycle of births and deaths. May you all rejoice in the innermost Atman alone, the ocean of bliss, the fountain of joy, the pool of wisdom, the sea of peace, the spring of eternal satisfaction!

PRACTICAL AIDS TO JAPA SADHANA

You have a thorough knowledge of Japa Yoga and the glory of the Name. Now you can start real Sadhana from this minute. I have given below a number of practical hints of great use for your daily Sadhana. Kindly note and follow them carefully.

1. *Fixed hours:* Most effective time for Japa is early dawn Brahmamuhurta and dusk, when Sattva is predominant. Regularity in Japa is very essential.

2. *Definite place:* It is highly advantageous to sit in the same place every day. Do not change it now and then. When you sit there you will have automatically the mood to do Japa. Just as you have a mood to study books when you enter a library or pray when you enter a temple so also you will get the mood to do Japa when you sit in your usual Asana.

3. *A steady pose:* A comfortable Asana helps to make the mind steady also, controls Rajas and aids concentration. Concentration cannot be acquired by one whose pose is not steady. Keep the Merudand (spine) always erect. If you droop down like an old man while sitting for Japa and meditation your mind will always waver and wander. Have a steady pose all throughout the period of Japa.

4. *Face North or East:* This exercises a subtle influence and enhances the efficacy of Japa. Sages and Rishis of the Himalayas help those who sit facing North for Japa because they come in contact with them by facing North.

5. *A Seat:* Deer skin or Kusa-mat or a rug should be used. The Gita says '*Chailajinakusottaram.*' Have a Kusa mat, a deer-skin over that and a clean white cloth above. This is the seat prescribed by the Gita. Energy is conserved which is otherwise dissipated without a proper seat.

6. *Repeat elevating prayers:* Invoking the aid of the Ishtam with appropriate prayer induces a proper Sattvic Bhava. In all spiritual Sadhana divine help is prerequisite. Without it no spiritual progress can be attained and control of the wandering, mischievous mind becomes impossible.

7. *Clear articulation:* Start the Japa pronouncing the Mantra distinctly and without mistakes. Mantra Sakti is quickly

awakened, mind is easily elevated and made one-pointed if the pronunciation is clear and distinct.

8. *Vigilance and alertness:* This is very important. You will be fresh and alert when you commence. After a time unconsciously the mind becomes weary, begins to wander and drowsiness overpowers you. Avoid this state. Some sleep during Japa and meditation and imagine to have attained spiritual bliss. This is mere hallucination.

9. *Japa Mala:* Using a Mala helps alertness and acts as an incentive to carry on the Japa continuously. Resolve to finish a certain number of Malas before leaving the seat. The mind will deceive you if you do Japa without a Mala. You will imagine that you have done Japa for a long time and that you have done more than the required number.

10. *Variety in Japa:* This is necessary to sustain interest, avoid fatigue and counteract monotony. Repeat aloud for a time, then hum the Mantra and repeat mentally sometimes. When the real bliss or taste for Japa is acquired then Japa becomes habitual and pleasant. There will be no monotony at all. The variety of Japa is for beginners only. Mental Japa is the most powerful. It directly counteracts the evil Vrittis of the mind and makes the mind pure.

11. *Meditation:* Side by side with Japa think of the Lord as present before you and picture His entrancing beautiful form. This practice adds tremendously to the efficacy and power of your Sadhana. The mind is fully engrossed in the form of the Lord by this practice and there is no chance for the mind to get hold of the objects of senses which are like straw or chaff before the bliss of the presence of God.

12. *Concluding prayer and rest:* This is important. After Japa is over do not immediately leave the place, mix with everyone and plunge into worldly activity. Sit very quietly for about 10 minutes at least humming some prayer, remembering the Lord or reflecting upon His infinite love. Then after devout prostration leave the place and commence your work. Spiritual vibrations will be intact. You will find it easy to remember the Lord even while at work. Combine prayer with your daily routine and occasionally remember Him.

GREATNESS OF DIVINE NAME

The glory of the Name of God cannot be established

through reasoning. It can certainly be experienced through faith, devotion and constant repetition. Have reverence and faith for the Name. Do not argue. Every Name is filled with countless powers. Just as fire has the natural property of burning things, so also the Name of God has the power of burning sins and desires. The power of the Name is ineffable. Its Glory is indescribable. The efficacy and inherent Sakti of the Name of God is unfathomable.

O Man! Take refuge in the Name. Nami and Name are inseparable. Sing the Lord's Name incessantly. Remember the Name of the Lord with every incoming and outgoing breath. In this iron age Namasmarana or Japa is the easiest, quickest, safest and surest way to reach God and attain immortality and perennial Joy. Glory to the Lord! Glory to His Name.

Just hear the glory of Ram Nam. Mahatma Gandhiji writes "You might ask me why I tell you to use the word Ram and not one of the many other names of the creator. True, His Names are as many as and more than the leaves on a tree; and I might, for instance ask you to use the word God. But what meaning, what associations would it have for you here. In order to enable you to feel anything when repeating the word God, I should have to teach you some English. I should have to explain to you the foreign people's thoughts and associations.

"But in telling you to repeat the Name of Ram, I am giving you a Name worshipped since countless generations by the people of this land—a Name familiar to the very animals and birds, the very trees and stones of Hindustan through many thousand years. You will learn from Ramayana how a stone by the roadside sprang to life at the touch of Ram's foot as he passed by. You must learn to repeat the blessed Name of Ram with sweetness and such devotion that the birds will pause in their singing to listen to you—that the very trees will bend their branches towards you stirred by the Divine melody of that Name."

Sant Kabirdas sent his son Kamal to Sant Tulasidas. Tulasidas wrote Ram Nam on a Tulasi leaf and sprinkled the juice over 500 lepers. All were cured. Kamal was quite astonished. Then Kabir sent Kamal to blind Sur Das. Sur Das asked Kamal to bring the corpse that was floating in the river. Sur Das repeated Ram only once in one ear of the corpse, and it was brought back to life. Kamal's heart was filled with awe and wonder. Such is the power of God's Name. Kabir says: "If any one utters Ram, Ram even in dream, I would like to make a pair of shoes out of my skin for his daily use."

Who can describe the glory of God's sacred Name? Who can really comprehend the greatness and splendour of the holy names of God? Even Parvati, Lord Siva's consort failed to describe in adequate terms the grandeur and true significance of God's Name. When one sings His Name or hears it sung, he is unconsciously raised to sublime spiritual heights. He looses his body-consciousness. He is immersed in joy. He drinks deep the divine nectar of immortality. He gets divine intoxication. Repetition of God's Name enables the devotee to feel the Divine Presence, the Divine glory, and the Divine consciousness within himself and everywhere also. How sweet is Hari's Name! How powerful is God's Name! How much joy, peace and strength it brings to one who repeats His Name! Blessed indeed are those who repeat God's Name, for they will be free from the wheel of birth and death and will attain immortality!

You may be aware how the Ganika (prostitute) Pingala was mysteriously transformed into a saintly lady by the power of Name (repeating the Name of Sri Rama), through her Guru the parrot, which she obtained as a lovely present from a thief and how she easily obtained salvation. The parrot was trained to utter the Name "Sri Rama, Sri Rama." Pingala knew nothing of Rama-nama. She heard the sound Rama-Rama through the mouth of the parrot. It was very melodious and charming. Pingala was very much attracted. She fixed her mind on Rama Nama uttered by the parrot and mysteriously entered into Bhava Samadhi (union with Rama). Such is the power of Name of the Lord.

GAYATRI SADHANA
PHILOSOPHY OF GAYATRI SADHANA

All power is in the Atman. The nature of the Self is omnipotence. The Atman is possessed of Anantasakti. This power is first manifest as sound, from which proceeds the entire creation. All phenomena are evolved out of sound. The Vedas embody in themselves this sound aspect of the Supreme. Each Mantra in the Vedas is the storehouse of infinite power. Each Mantra is a veritable mine of limitless Sakti. Upon this Mantra

Sakti does the true seeker rely. This is the secret of his power. Of all such Mantras, the Supreme and the most potent power of powers is the great, glorious Gayatri Mantra.

It is the life and the support of every true Hindu, nay, it is the support of every seeker after Truth who believes in its efficacy, power and glory, be he of any caste, creed, clime or sect. It is only one's faith and purity of heart that really count. Indeed, Gayatri is an impregnable, spiritual armour, veritable fortress, that guards and protects its votary, that transforms him into the Divine and blesses him with the brilliant light of the highest spiritual illumination. Whichever your Ishta-devata may be, yet the regular repetition of a few Malas of Gayatri every day will bestow upon you all that is auspicious and benevolent to you, herein and hereafter.

It is wrong to conceive of the notion that it is solely meant for the chosen orthodox Brahmin class. It is universally applicable, for it is nothing but an earnest prayer for Light, addressed to the Almighty Supreme Spirit. It is verily the sole transcendental guide-light to humanity.

The nature of Gayatri is such that you can adore and worship it in any form or name you like. It is generally conceived of by the majority of the devotional class that its deity is an aspect of Sakti, a five-faced Devi. In case, you are a Sakta or a worshipper of the Mother aspect of God, you can adhere to that belief.

But in its true light, the Gayatri never speaks of a mother-aspect at all. You cannot find a single word in the entire Gayatri Mantra which speaks of a mother aspect of God. The mere word Gayatri cannot make its deity a female. It is only the name of its metre and not the deity. Again, some think that the Gayatri is presided over by the sun. In fact, even this idea is to be modified a little. The sun that it speaks of is not this sun, that is shining before our physical eyes, but that 'Tat Savituh' or that Sun, the Great Sun, which this sun or moon does not illumine, and that is the Impersonal Absolute Brahman.

Therefore this is the Greatest of all Mantras and its presiding deity is the Para Brahman Itself. Yet, it is acceptable to all types of aspirants, for it is conceived as worship of Devi, worship of Lord Hari, worship of Aditya or the sun, and also as pure Nirguna worship of Brahman.

The Tejas of the Brahmachari lies in his Gayatri Japa. The support and prosperity of the Grihastha is again the Gayatri, strength and solace of the Vanaprastha is again the Gayatri. Thus from the moment of the young student's Upanayanam (investiture with the sacred thread) upto the moment when he enters the glorious state of Sannyasa, throughout his life the Gayatri Mantra is his constant guide, support and strength. To him the Gayatri Mantra is the *summum bonum* of life.

So great is its importance that the Japa of the Gayatri is laid down as a compulsory daily Sadhana, in the life of every Hindu. No matter, what his Kuladevata (family deity) might be, no matter what his Ishta-devata may be, yet the daily repetition of the Gayatri Mantra and the offering of Arghya, repeating the Gayatri, is enjoined upon every Hindu. Even if you are of a different religion or caste, you can also take to Gayatri Sadhana if you are really sincere, earnest and faithful. Your life will be indeed blessed. Dear aspirants! realise the wondrous potency of the glorious Gayatri. Realise clearly what a precious heritage you have in this Mantra. Neglect not this divine Sakti that the Rishis of yore have bequeathed. This is the only true Sakti before which electricity, radio-active nuclei, and atomic forces appear as mere vulgar, futile trifles. Start regular daily Gayatri Japa and feel for yourself wondrous power that you derive therefrom. Fix a particular time for the Japa and stick to it, permanently. At least one Mala of Japa you must do daily without break. It will guard you from all dangers, give you infinite strength to overcome all obstacles and take you to the very pinnacle of splendour, power, peace and bliss.

PRACTICE OF GAYATRI SADHANA

Brahma milked out, as it were, from the three Vedas the letter A, the letter U and the letter M formed by their coalition three trilateral monosyllable, together with three mysterious words—Bhur, Bhuvah, and Svah or the earth, sky and heaven. From the three Vedas also, the Lord of creatures incomprehensibly exalted, successfully milked out the three measures of that ineffable text, beginning with the word Tat and entitled Savitri or Gayatri. (Manu Smriti, Chap. III.)

Thus came:

OM Bhur Bhuvah Svah; Tat Saviturvarenyam
Bhargo devasya dheemahi; dhiyo yo nah Prachodayat.

"Let us meditate on Isvara and His glory who has created the universe, who is fit to be worshipped, who is the remover of all sins and ignorance. May He enlighten our intellect."

What is that enlightenment? Now you have Deha-atmabuddhi, a Buddhi that makes you to identify with body, to mistake the body for the Soul. Now you are praying to the blessed Mother of the Vedas—the Gayatri; to bestow on you a pure Sattvic intellect which will help you to realise—*"Aham Brahma Asmi"*—I am the Brahman. This is an Advaitic meaning for Gayatri. Advanced students of Yoga may take up this meaning; "I am that supreme Light of all lights, that gives light to the Buddhi or intellect."

The Lord says in the Vedas, *"Samano Mantrah"*—let one Mantra be common to all, and that Mantra is the Gayatri. The secret lore of the Upanishads is the essence of the four Vedas, while the Gayatri with the three Vyahritis is the essence of Upanishads. He is indeed the real Brahmin who knows and understands thus, the Gayatri. Without its knowledge, he is verily a Sudra, even though he may be well-versed in the four Vedas.

Gayatri is the mother of the Vedas and the destroyer of all sins. The monosyllable OM is an emblem of the Supreme. There is nothing more purifying on earth than the Gayatri.

The Japa of Gayatri brings the same fruit as the recitation of all the Vedas with the Angas. This single Mantra repeated sincerely and with clear conscience brings the supreme good.

Gayatri destroys the three kinds of Taapa or pain. Gayatri bestows the four kinds of Purushartha, viz., Dharma, Artha, Kama and Moksha—righteousness, wealth, desired objects and liberation. It destroys the three Granthis or knots of ignorance—Avidya, Kama and Karma. It is a great purifier and bestower of clear conscience. Gayatri eventually gives liberation or emancipation from the wheel of birth and death.

The repetition of Gayatri brings the Darshan of Gayatri eventually, leads to the realisation of the Advaitic Brahman or the unity of consciousness or oneness, and the aspirant who asked for light from Mother Gayatri in the beginning, now sings in exuberant joy: "I am the Light of all lights that gives light to the Buddhi."

MANTRA YOGA SADHANA
PSYCHOLOGY OF MANTRA YOGA SADHANA

Mantra Yoga is an exact science. '*Mananat Trayate Iti Mantrah*—by the Manana (constant thinking or recollection) of which one is released from the round of births and deaths is Mantra.'

Every Mantra has a Rishi who gave it to the world; a Matra, a Devata, the Bija or seed which gives it a special power, the Sakti and the Kilakam or the pillar.

A Mantra is divinity. Mantra and its presiding Devata are one. The Mantra itself is Devata. Mantra is divine power, Daivi Sakti, manifesting in a sound body. Constant repetition of the Mantra with faith, devotion and purity augments the Sakti or power of the aspirant, purifies and awakens the Mantra Chaitanya latent in the Mantra and bestows on the Sadhaka, Mantra Siddhi, illumination, freedom, peace, eternal bliss, immortality.

By constant repetition of the Mantra the Sadhaka imbibes the virtues and powers of the Deity that presides over the Mantra. Repetition of Surya Mantra bestows health, long life, vigour, vitality, Tejas or brilliance. It removes all diseases of the body and the diseases of the eye. No enemy can do any harm. Repetition of Aditya-Hridayam in the early morning is highly beneficial. Lord Rama conquered Ravana through the repetition of Aditya-Hridayam imparted by Agastya Rishi.

Mantras are in the form of praise and appeal to the deities, craving for help and mercy. Some Mantras control and command the evil spirits. Rhythmical vibrations of sounds give rise to forms. Recitation of the Mantras gives rise to the formation of the particular figure of the deity.

Repetition of Sarasvati Mantra 'OM Sri Sarasvatyai Namah' will bestow on you wisdom and good intelligence. You will get inspiration and compose poems. Repetition of 'OM Sri Mahalakshmyai Namah' will confer on you wealth and remove poverty. Ganesa Mantra will remove any obstacle in any undertaking. Maha Mrityunjaya Mantra will remove accidents, incurable diseases and bestow long life and immortality. It is a Moksha Mantra too.

Repetition of Subrahmanya Mantra 'OM Sri Saravanabhavaya Namah' will give you success in any undertaking and make you glorious. It will drive off the evil influences and evil spirits. Repetition of Sri Hanuman Mantra, 'OM Hanumate Namah' will bestow victory and strength. Repetition of Panchadasakshara and Shodasakshara (Sri Vidya) will give you wealth, power, freedom etc. It will give you whatever you want. You must learn this Vidya from a Guru alone.

Repetition of Gayatri or Pranava or OM Namassivaya, OM Namo Narayanaya, OM Namo Bhagavate Vaasudevaya, one and a quarter lakh of times with Bhava, faith and devotion will confer on you Mantra Siddhi.

OM, Soham, Sivoham, Aham Brahmasmi are Moksha Mantras. They will help you to attain Self-realisation. OM Sri Ramaya Namah, OM Namo Bhagavate Vaasudevaya are Saguna Mantras which will enable you to attain Saguna realisation first and then Nirguna realisation in the end.

Mantra for curing scorpion-stings and cobra-bites should be repeated on eclipse days for getting Mantra Siddhi quickly. You should stand in the water and repeat the Mantra. This is more powerful and effective. They can be recited on ordinary days also for attaining Mantra Siddhi.

Mantra Siddhi for curing scorpion-sting, cobra-bite etc., can be attained within 40 days. Repeat the Mantra with faith and devotion regularly. Have a sitting in the early morning after taking bath. Observe Brahmacharya and live on milk and fruits for 40 days. Or take restricted diet.

Chronic diseases can be cured by Mantras. Chanting of Mantras generates potent spiritual waves or divine vibrations. They penetrate the physical and astral bodies of the patients and remove the root-causes of the sufferings. They fill the cells with pure Sattva or divine energy. They destroy the microbes and vivify the cells and tissues. They are the best and most potent antiseptics and germicides. They are more potent than ultra-violet rays or Roentgen rays.

Mantra Siddhi should not be misused for the destruction of others. Those who misuse the Mantra power for destroying others are themselves destroyed in the end.

Those who utilise the Mantra power in curing snake-bites, scorpion-stings and chronic diseases should not accept any kind of presents or money. They must be absolutely unselfish. They should not accept even fruits or clothes. They will lose the power if they utilise the power for selfish purposes. If they are absolutely unselfish, if they serve the humanity with Sarvatma Bhava, their power will increase through the grace of the Lord.

He who has attained Mantra Siddhi, can cure cobra-bite or scorpion-bite or any chronic disease by mere touch on the affected part. When a man is bitten by a cobra a telegram is sent to the Mantra Siddha. The Mantra Siddha recites the Mantra and the man who is bitten by a cobra is cured. Does this not prove the tremendous power of Mantra?

Get the Mantra initiation from your Guru. Or pray to your Ishta Devata and start doing Japa of the particular Mantra, if you find it difficult to get a Guru.

METHOD OF MANTRA PURASCHARANA

The repetition of a Mantra with rigid spiritual observances a fixed number of times to obtain quick spiritual progress is known as Mantra Purascharana. It can be performed for material progress too. The practitioner should observe certain rules and undergo strict dietetic discipline to ensure quick Mantra Siddhi.

During the Purascharana take only fresh vegetables, fruits, milk, roots, barley and Havis-Anna (rice cooked with ghee, sugar, milk). A Sadhaka can live on pure Bhiksha (alms) also. If you can live on milk alone during the period of Purascharana it is highly laudable. You can have Mantra Siddhi even by repeating the Mantra a lakh of times.

Select any holy place of pilgrimage on the banks of sacred Ganga, confluence of rivers, mountain valleys of charming scenery, temples, Tulasi gardens, below Asvattha trees or convert a portion of your house into a temple by keeping the picture of the Lord, burning incense etc., and by suitable decorations. Purascharana done in holy places has a benefit hundred times superior to that done in one's own house.

You can select any Mantra for Purascharana. Your Guru Mantra or Ishta Mantra is the best. Sandhya time, sunrise, sunset, midday are all recommended for Japa. Repeat the Mantra as many lakhs of times as there are letters in the Mantra. You can do half of that number. In no case the number should be less than a lakh.

Sit facing East or North during Japa. Select Siddha, Padma, Svastika or Virasana for Japa. Never sit for Japa with a loaded stomach. Have fixed timings for Japa. Take a bath before you start, if possible, or at least wash hands and feet. Perform Achamana or sipping of Sanctified Mantra water. Deer skin, cloth, blanket, Kusa grass or tiger skin can be used as seats while doing Japa. Spatika, Tulasi, Rudraksha Malas can be used for counting the number of Japa. Have a Mala with 108 beads or half or one-fourth that number.

Abstracting the mind from all worldly objects, merged in the inner meaning of the Mantra, thinking of the Lord, the Mantra should be repeated with a uniform speed. Full concentration of the mind on the meaning and divinity of the Mantra brings quick Mantra Siddhi. Continue Purascharana till you attain Mantra Siddhi. Do not stop with one Purascharana. Due to the Doshas of the mind you may not get Mantra Siddhi at once. Madhusudana Sarasvati did 18 Purascharanas of Gayatri before he attained Siddhi.

Sleeping on coarse bed (strictly avoiding cushions and the like), observing strict celibacy, worshipping the deity three times a day, bathing thrice daily, abandoning oil bath, meat, fish, onion, garlic, tea, coffee, chillies, tamarind, observing silence or restricting the speech to a minimum, observing Ahimsa, speaking Truth, shunning all luxuries, one should perform the Purascharana. You should avoid as far as possible absent-mindedness, laziness, spitting during Japa, relaxation of hands and legs, sleeping during the day, mixing with undesirable persons, contact with women, receiving of gifts, looking at obscene pictures, speaking lies, the company of passionate men, chewing of betels, smoking, drinking etc., too much talk, speaking ill of others, finding fault in others, harming others in thought, word or deed, during the period of Purascharana. You should not dissipate your energy during Japa by looking hither and thither unnecessarily by shaking the body, by laughter etc.

Do the same number of Japa every day without variation. Homa or Havan should be performed after every lakh of Japa or at the end of the Purascharana.

After completing the Purascharana perform Homa $\frac{1}{10}$th the number of Japa, Tarpana (water libations) $\frac{1}{10}$th the number of Homa, Marjana (sprinkling) $\frac{1}{10}$th the number of Tarpana and feeding of Brahmins $\frac{1}{10}$th the number of Tarpana. You can do feeding and charity according to your capacity if you cannot adhere to the above strictly.

THE TABLE FOR JAPA

No.	Mantras	Speed per minute			No. of Japa that can be done in one hour				Time required for completion of one Purascharana, devoting 6 hours daily			
		Low	Med.	High	Low	Med.	High		Months	Days	Hours	Mins.
1.	OM	140	250	400	8400	15000	24000	Low	"	"	11	54
								Med.	"	"	6	40
								High	"	"	4	10
2.	Hari OM or Sri Rama	120	200	300	7200	12000	18000	Low	"	1	3	47
								Med.	"	"	16	40
								High	"	"	11	07
3.	OM Namah Sivaya	80	120	140	4800	7200	9000	Low	"	17	2	10
								Med.	"	11	3	30
								High	"	9	1	35
4.	Om Namo Narayanaya	60	80	120	3600	4800	7200	Low	1	7	0	15
								Med.	"	27	4	45
								High	"	18	3	15
5.	OM Namo Bhagavate Vaasudevaya	40	60	90	2400	3600	5400	Low	2	23	2	0
								Med.	1	25	3	30
								High	1	7	0	15
6.	Gayatri Mantra	6	8	10	360	480	600	Low	36	16	0	45
								Med.	29	18	5	30
								High	19	15	3	35
7.	Maha-Mantra or Hare Rama Mantra	8	10	15	480	600	900	Low	36	16	0	45
								Med.	29	8	5	30
								High	19	17	3	35

Mantra Purascharana has incalculable benefits. Brightness, clearness, or tranquillity of the mind, contentment, dispassion towards worldly enjoyments, Darshan of Ishta Devata, success in all undertakings, attainment of purity of the mind—all these will ensue. Give your best attention and earnestness in the performance of Purascharana.

May you attain Moksha or Immortality through performance of a series of Mantra Purascharanas!

BENEFITS OF MANTRA-WRITING

(An easy, practical and scientific form of Yoga for modern busy people)

Mantra-writing Leads to Meditation

Of the various methods of Japa described in the scriptures Mantra-writing is the most efficacious. It helps the aspirant in concentrating the mind and gradually leads to meditation.

Benefits

1. **Concentration**—Distractions are minimised as the mind, tongue, hands and eyes are all engaged with the Mantra. This increases the power of concentration and efficiency in work.

2. **Control**—The mind is controlled by the power of Mantra and it will work better and quicker for you.

3. **Evolution**—Due to repeated innumerable impacts of the Mantra on the subconscious mind, subtle, spiritual impressions are made, which hasten the Soul's progress in evolution.

4. **Peace**—If you are disturbed due to worries or untoward incidents, the mind will get calm and peaceful.

5. **Force**—A mighty spiritual force is generated in course of time in the atmosphere of the place, where you write Mantras or keep the notebooks. It helps in secular and spiritual progress.

Conclusion—Begin today. Do not procrastinate. Give it a sincere trial. Be a master of your mind, not its slave. Write from one to three pages a day. Follow the rules as far as possible if you want quicker results.

RULES FOR MANTRA-WRITING

1. Select a Mantra, or Name of God, and write it with ink in a notebook daily in any script on 1 to 3 pages.
2. Sit in the same place at the same time daily. If possible, keep it under lock and key.
3. Write after a bath, or after washing hands, feet, face and mouth.
4. Sit in one pose throughout. Don't move till completed.
5. Observe silence, and avoid talks, engagements, or calls.
6. Fix the eyes on the notebook. Don't move till completed.
7. Repeat the Mantra or Name mentally while writing.
8. Fix the mind on the form and attributes of the Lord, while writing the Name or Mantra.
9. Adopt one uniform system of writing, top to bottom or left to right.
10. Write each Mantra or Name completely at a time and not in parts.
11. Don't change Mantra or Name. Select one and stick to it for life.
12. Preserve all completed books near your place of worship.

SANKIRTAN SADHANA

Sankirtan is singing God's Name with feeling (Bhava), love (Prema) and faith (Sraddha). In Sankirtan people join together and sing God's Name collectively in a common place. Sankirtan is one of the nine modes of Bhakti. You can realise God through Kirtan alone. This is the easiest method for attaining God-consciousness in Kali Yuga or the Iron Age *"Kalau Kesava-Kirtanat."*

When several people join together and practise Sankirtan, a huge spiritual current or Mahasakti is generated. This purifies the hearts of the aspirants and elevates them to the sublime heights of divine ecstasy or Samadhi. The powerful vibrations are carried to distant places. They bring elevation of mind, solace, strength to all people and work as a harbinger of peace, harmony and concord. They annihilate hostile forces and quickly bring peace and bliss to the whole world.

Lord Hari says to Narada *"Naham Vasami Vaikunthe Yoginam Hridaye na cha, Madbhakta Yatra Gayanti Tatra Tishtami Narada*—I dwell not in Vaikuntha nor in the hearts of the Yogins, but I dwell where My devotees sing My Name, O Narada."

Kirtan destroys sins, Vasanas and Samskaras, fills the heart with Prema and devotion and brings the devotee face to face with God.

Akhanda Kirtan is very powerful. It purifies the heart. The Mahamantra, "Hare Rama Hare Rama, Rama Rama Hare Hare; Hare Krishna Hare Krishna, Krishna Krishna Hare Hare" or "Om Namah Sivaya" is sung continuously for 3 hours or 24 hours, three days, or a week. You will have to form batches. One will lead and others will follow. Do Akhanda Kirtan on Sundays or holidays. Do Prabhata Pheri Kirtan in the morning around the streets. Kirtan in the early morning is more effective than Kirtan at night.

At night sit before the picture of the Lord with your children and other family members and servants. Do Kirtan for one or two hours. Be regular in the practice. You will derive immense peace and strength.

Sing the Lord's Name from the bottom of your heart. Be wholly and solely devoted to Him. Delay in God-realisation is extremely painful. Merge in Him. Live in Him. Be established in Him.

May peace and prosperity abide in you all.

Lokassamastah Sukhino Bhavantu.

TANTRA YOGA SADHANA

Tantra Sadhana bestows tremendous Siddhis or powers. It should be learnt under a Siddha Tantric Guru. The Tantric student must be endowed with purity, faith, devotion, dedication to Guru, dispassion, humility, courage, cosmic love, truthfulness, non-covetousness and contentment. Absence of these qualities in the practitioner means a gross abuse of Saktism.

Saktism had been one of the potent powers for the spiritual regeneration of the Hindus. When practised by the ignorant, unenlightened and unqualified persons, it has led to certain abuses, and there is no denying that some degraded forms of Saktism have sought nothing but magic, immorality and occult powers. An example of the perverted expression of the truth, a travesty of the original practices, is the theory of the five Makaras—Madya or wine, Mamsa or flesh, Matsya or fish, Mudra or symbolical acts and Maithuna or coitus.

In the Sakti doctrine Siva is the supreme unchanging eternal consciousness and Sakti is His kinetic power. Universe is Power. Universe is a manifestation of Devi's glory. This is the affirmation of the Sakti doctrine, Sakti being the power of God. Sakta is one who possesses Sakti.

Sadhakas are of three kinds, viz., Pasu, Veera and Divya. It is only the Pasu Sadhakas who practise the Pancha Makaras, viz., Matsya, Mamsa, Madya, Mudra and Maithuna. The esoteric meaning of these five Makaras is "kill egoism, control flesh, drink the wine of God-intoxication and have union with Lord Siva." This is the divine practice of Divya Sadhakas who lead the life divine. Give up Pasu Vritti, the tendency of animals and raise the Divya Vritti or the divine nature.

Just as the fruit is hidden in the seed, butter in milk, virility in boyhood, so also various Saktis remain latent in man, veiled by ignorance. If you purify your mind and practise concentration and meditation, all these powers will shine forth.

The highest fruit of meditation or Upasana is the identity or non-distinction with the object meditated upon. The meditator and meditated become one. The devotee of Devi attains realisation of oneness with Devi through intense Upasana or worship.

SAVA SADHANA

The classification of aspirants is made thus: a Sattvic man is a spiritual man. He is endowed with Divya or divine qualities. He has Divya-Bhava. He is calm, pure, dispassionate, wise, passionless, egoless, compassionate, kind, pious, devoted. Sattva Guna predominates in him.

If Tamas predominates in a man, he has Pasu-bhava. He is Pasu or animal. He is endowed with ignorance, error, carelessness, inertia, sloth, etc.

If Rajas predominates in a man, he is a Veera. He has Veera-bhava.

Divya-bhava is the best, Veera the next best and Pasu the lowest. From being a Pasu a man rises in this or some other birth to be a Veera. Divya-bhava or Devata-bhava is awakened through Veera-bhava.

Sava Sadhana comes in the practices of Tantra Sadhana. This is practised by some Veera Sadhakas in the cremation ground. Only the fearless can practise this sort of Sadhana.

A human corpse is laid with its face to the ground. The Sadhaka sits on the back of the body of the dead man. He draws a Yantra on the back and then worships.

If the rite is successful, the head of the corpse turns round and asks the Sadhaka the boon he wants; be it Salvation or some material benefit.

The Devi speaks through the mouth of the dead man.

KRIYA YOGA SADHANA

The six purificatory exercises are Dhauti, Basti, Neti, Nauli, Trataka and Kapalabhati.

DHAUTI

Purification is of two kinds, internal and external. Internal purification can be made in several ways. Here you will find the technique of an important exercise.

Take a fine piece of cloth; 3 inches wide and 15 feet long. The borders should be stitched well and no loose thread should be hanging from the sides. Wash it with soap and keep it always clean. Dip it in tepid water. Squeeze out the water and swallow one end of it little by little. On the first day swallow only one foot length of the cloth and draw it out slowly. After gradual practice you can swallow the whole length by catching one end of it. Keep it in the stomach for a few minutes and then slowly draw it out. Do not be hasty and draw out the cloth forcibly. When the Kriya is over, drink a cup of milk. This is a sort of lubrication, for the throat. Do this when the stomach is empty. Morning time is good. It will be quite sufficient if you practise this once in 4 or 5 days. This is an excellent exercise for those who are of a flabby and phlegmatic constitution. Gradual and steady practice cures gulma, gastritis and dyspepsia and all other diseases of the stomach.

NAULI

Nauli is a powerful exercise for regenerating, invigorating and stimulating the abdominal viscera and the gastro-intestinal or alimentary system. For the practice of Nauli, you should have a good practice of Uddiyana Bandha.

Stand, with legs a foot apart and rest your hands on the thighs with a light curve of the back. Do a strong and forcible expiration through the mouth and keep the lungs completely empty. Contract and forcibly draw the abdominal muscles towards the back. This is Uddiyana Bandha. This is the first stage of Nauli.

Then let loose the centre of the abdomen. You will have all the left and right side of the abdomen. You will have all the muscles in the centre in a vertical line. This is called Madhyama Nauli. Keep it as long as you can retain the position comfortably. Then you can release the muscles and inhale. This is the second stage of Nauli.

After some practice, contract the right side of the abdomen and let loose the left side free. You will now have all the muscles on the left side only. This is called Vama Nauli. Again contract the left side and let loose the right side. This is Dakshina Nauli. By such gradual practice, you will understand how to contract the muscles of the central, left and right side of the abdominal muscles from side to side. Practise like this for a few days.

Then draw the muscles in the centre. Slowly move them to the right side and then to the life side in a circular way. Do this several times from the right to left and then do it in reverse way from the left to right side. You should move the muscles always with a circular motion slowly. When you advance in the practice you can do it quickly. This last stage of Nauli will appear like 'churning' when the abdominal muscles are isolated and rotated from side to side. When Nauli is demonstrated by advanced students, you will be surprised to observe the movements of the abdominal muscles. It will look as if an engine is working in the abdominal factory.

When beginners want to do Dakshina Nauli, they have to slightly bend towards the left side and contract left muscles. When they want to do Vama Nauli, they have to bend a little to the right side. In Madhyama Nauli push the entire muscles forward by contracting the two sides.

Nauli Kriya eradicates chronic constipation, dyspepsia and all other diseases of the gastro-intestinal system. The liver and pancreas are toned. All other abdominal organs will function properly.

TRATAKA

This is steady gazing at a particular point or object without winking. This is mainly intended for developing the power of concentration and mental focus. This is very useful for all.

Sit on Padmasana or Siddhasana. You can sit erect even on a chair. Keep the picture of your Ishta Devata or the picture of OM or a black dot on a piece of white paper. Look at the point or picture very steadily. You can gaze at a bright star or on the flames of a ghee lamp. Gazing at the tip of the nose and at the space between the eyebrows is also Trataka. When you gaze at a particular point or picture, it is Trataka. Close your eyes and form a mental picture of the object. Practise this for 2 minutes and cautiously increase the period.

Trataka improves eye-sight. Diseases of the eyes are removed. Many have thrown away their spectacles after some practice in Trataka. It develops the power of concentration to a great degree.

KAPALABHATI

Kapalabhati is an exercise for cleansing the skull. Kapala means 'skull' and Bhati means 'to shine.' This exercise makes the skull shining.

Sit on Padmasana or Siddhasana. Close the eyes. Perform Rechaka and Puraka rapidly. This should be practised vigorously. One will get perspiration profusely. This is a good exercise for the lungs also. Those who are well-versed in Kapalabhati can do Bhastrika very easily. Rechaka should be done forcibly by contracting the abdominal muscles. Do 20 expulsions for a round and gradually increase the number to 120. In Kapalabhati there is no Kumbhaka. Kapalabhati cleanses the respiratory system and the nasal passages. It removes the spasm in bronchial tubes. Consequently asthma is relieved and also cured in course of time. The apices of the lungs get proper oxygenation. Consumption is cured. Impurities of the blood are thrown out. The circulatory and respiratory systems are toned to a considerable degree.

SANGITA SADHANA

Life in the individual, in its ontological aspect is but a ceaseless striving after non-ending unalloyed bliss, eternal, immortal, perennial Bliss. Scriptures have proved it beyond doubt. Sages and Saints are voicing it forth ever since the dawn of creation that Supreme Bliss can and should be had in one's own Self. Thus Self-realisation, Self-awareness or Self-experience-Whole, Aparokshanubhuti is the *summum bonum* of human existence. That alone will bring to an end all our pains and miseries. But, how best are we to attain that?

Atmachaitanya Samadhi or Aparoksha Jnana is possible only when the mind becomes pure and Sattvic. Purity of mind is had only when the little 'I,' egoism or Ahankara is curbed, annihilated which means that I-ness and Mineness have got to be abandoned. In turn, that involves purity and control of the Indriyas. Unless the mind is cultured and controlled, the Indriyas cannot be controlled. Thus, in a circular way, we come again to the mind. Rightly did the Sages exclaim: *Mana Eva Manushyanaam Karanam Bandha-mokshayoh*—Mind alone is the cause for man's release and bondage.

Practical investigation in that direction has led the Sages to conclude that Prana and Mind are interdependent in their functional abilities. As long as one remains uncontrolled, the other cannot be controlled. If one is under control, the other, too, comes under control of its own accord. It is not enough if they are simply controlled. As long as they are not annihilated Vasanas will not leave us. Unless Vasanas are destroyed Chitta cannot be destroyed. The destruction of Chitta alone can lead to Jnana.

Thus we are left with two courses. Firstly bring the Prana under control through various arduous Yogic processes, and then to control the mind and withdraw it from external objects and fix it on the Self. Secondly we can try to annihilate the mind through effecting Mano-laya by finding such a higher powerful principle towards which mind will naturally run and into which it will merge itself thus entering into a state of Laya. The sages found that Mano-Laya followed by Mano-Nasa was a safer means to attain Self-realisation than the arduous process of controlling the mind and culturing it which is always attended by the danger of the mind jumping into the old grooves of Vasanas at any moment.

In the course of further practical investigation the Sages and Seers found that Sound had the power to attract the mind and absorb it, so to say.

Thus Mano-Laya and Mano-Nasa through Nada Yoga

(union or merger into Sound) was found to be an effective and safe means of Self-realisation.

Nadanusandhanam means meditation on Nada or Sound that is heard at the Anahata Chakra.

The essential prerequisites for this type of Sadhana are the same as those for any other Yoga Sadhana. Ethical and moral preparations are the first important prerequisites. Similarly, proficiency in Hatha Yoga and Pranayama is essential. It is better to have sufficient practice in concentration and meditation. That will make it easy for us to concentrate inwardly and meditate on the Anahata sounds. Ajapa Japa or Japa of 'Soham' with breath will help you in your concentration on the subtle sounds. That by itself will take you to the Anahata sound.

There are two aspects of these sounds, gross and subtle. You should proceed from the gross ones to the subtle ones. If the mind runs only towards the gross sounds, do not get perturbed. Let it get first accustomed to and established in the gross sound. Then it can be led to the subtle sound.

Bear in mind that Mano-Laya is not the goal but that Mano-Nasa and Self-realisation is the goal.

Remember not to take any special fancy or liking for any particular sound but try to lead the mind from the first to the second, from the second to the third, and so on to the tenth. There is another school of Nada Yoga that distinguishes three different stages in the hearing of the sounds.

The first stage is when the Prana and Apana are led near the Brahmarandhra. The second stage comes when they enter the Brahmarandhra and the third when they are well established in it. During the first stage sounds like that of the roaring sea, the beating of drums, etc., are heard. During the second, sounds like those of Mridanga, conch, etc., are heard. In the third stage, sounds like Kinkini, humming of the bee, sound of the flute or the lute, etc., are heard.

Knowledge pertaining to hidden things arise in a person who can hear well the seventh sound (like that of the flute).

Highly interesting and most popular among the forms of Nadopasana, is Sangita (music). It is in Sangita that Sreyas and Preyas, otherwise antagonistic to each other meet. Sreyas is that which leads to the Eternal Good of man, viz., Self-realisation. Preyas is that which is immediately pleasant. It is generally recognised that what is Preyas is not Sreyas and vice versa. But here in Sangita or Sankirtana, Sreyas and Preyas are found together.

Sangita pleases the ear, is a rich treat to the senses and the mind—in fact, so much so that the senses and the mind are tamed and controlled by it; and Sangita ennobles the soul and reveals the Self within. Music is, therefore, regarded as the best form of Nadopasana.

That prince among musicians, the emperor among composers, the crest-jewel among saints, the Bhakta-Siromani who adored the Lord with sweet, soul-stirring and perfect music—Sri Tyagaraja whose inspiring songs in praise of Lord Rama and on the fundamental truths of spiritual life are sung throughout India by every lover of music for inspiration and entertainment, has repeatedly pointed out the divine glory of music. He has again and again stressed the fact that music is not food for the senses alone, but is food for the soul.

Tyagaraja says in the Kriti "*Nadopasana*": "It is through Nadopasana that the Trimurtis, the sage-authors of great scriptures, the Maharshis who have propounded Dharma, the seers who are masters of the arts and sciences those who are devoted to music with its three integral parts of Bhava, Raga and Tala—all these are experts in Nadopasana." It is a great truth worth remembering that all our great scriptures—the Vedas, Smritis, Puranas, etc., are all set to music and are metrical compositions. There is rhythm, metre and melody in them. Sama Veda, especially is unrivalled in its music. That is why Sri Tyagaraja regards all the Maharshis and seers as Nadopasakas.

Tyagaraja says: "The knowledge of the science of music is capable of bestowing on you the State of Sarupya" (in his Kriti *Sangita Sastra Jnanamu*). Why? Because "All Sounds have emanated from Om." In another Kriti on the essence of Pranava, he says that Omkara, which is itself the essence of all Vedas, Agamas, Sastras and Puranas, can remove all your miseries and bestow eternal bliss upon you. He crowns this declaration with the marvellous revelation: "It is this Sangita that has taken form in this world as Rama." That is why he said in another Kriti that he who adores the Lord through Sangita will attain Sarupya Mukti. For, Sangita is identical with God; and in accordance with the truth that you become what you intently meditate upon the Nadopasaka becomes Nadasvarupa or God.

Sangita is not mere nerve titillation. It is a Yoga emphasising this truth. Sri Tyagaraja says in his *"Sri Papriya"*: "Music which is composed of the seven Svaras is a treasure for the great Tapasvins who have cooled the Taapa Traya (Adhyatmika, Adhidaivika and Adhibhoutika Taapas)."

In fact, Tyagaraja would go so far as to declare that Moksha is impossible for one who has no music in him! He says in *"Mokshamugalada"*: "Is there Moksha for those who have no knowledge of music which is based on Bhakti, who do not realise the truth that the Sapta-Svaras have emanated from the Pranava which is born of the union of Prana and Agni, and who have a liking for the mere melody of the Veena, but have not understood the Siva-Tattva?" Thus, whilst music is exalted to the status of a potent Sadhana for Moksha, Tyagaraja does not fail always to point out that the mere utterance of sounds will not bestow Moksha upon the songster and that the realisation of the Source and Goal of Music ought to be sought after.

If one realises this Truth, he attains Jivanmukti. Tyagaraja says in his *"Ragasudharasa"*: "Drink the nectar of Ragam and get enlightened. Whatever Siddhi, the most difficult practices like Yaga, Yoga, etc., can bestow on you, you will easily get through Nadopasana. They are Jivanmuktas who have realised that Music which is nothing but Omkara born of the Self and which has Nada for its body—this Music adorned by the Sapta-Svaras is itself the Form of Sadasiva." Therefore it is that the Sadhaka is exhorted to realise the Siva-Tattva which is the Substratum for Music.

One cannot but be deeply moved at the wonderful tribute that Tyagaraja pays to Music, the Nadopasana, in his song, *"Intakanna-anandamemi"* in which he says: "Singing Thy glorious Names in melodious tunes and dancing in joy with the sole aim of having Thy Darshan—will this not do? Is this not the state for which even sages aspire?" For, Tyagaraja declares, Nadopasana itself bestows Advaitic realisation on the Sadhaka. He says in the same song: "In Thee I perceive the world and I merge myself in Thee, with my intellect clear and illumined."

SADHANA BY PRAYER

Prayer is the effort of man to commune with the Lord. Prayer is a mighty spiritual force. It is as real as the force of gravity or attraction.

Prayer elevates the mind. It fills the mind with purity. It is associated with the praise of God. It keeps the mind in tune with God. Prayer can reach a realm where reason dares not enter—it can take you to the Spiritual Realm or Kingdom of God. It frees the devotee from the fear of death. It brings him nearer to God and makes him feel his essential, immortal and blissful nature.

The power of Prayer is indescribable. Its glory is ineffable. Sincere devotees only realise its usefulness and splendour. It should be done with reverence, faith Nishkamya Bhava (without expectation of fruits) and with a heart wet with devotion. Do not argue about the efficacy of Prayer. You will be deluded. There is no arguing in spiritual matters. Intellect is a finite and frail instrument. Do not trust this intellect. Remove now the darkness of your ignorance through the light of Prayer.

Draupadi prayed fervently; Lord Krishna ran from Dvaraka to relieve her distress. Gajendra prayed ardently; Lord Hari marched with his disc to protect him. It was the Prayer of Prahlada that rendered cool the boiling oil when it was poured over his head. It was the power of Prayer of Mira that converted the bed of nails into a bed of roses; cobra into a flower garland.

When you pray, you are in tune with the Infinite, you link yourself with the inexhaustible cosmic power-house of energy (Hiranyagarbha) and thus draw power, energy, light and strength from Him.

Prayer does not demand high intelligence or eloquence. God wants your heart when you pray. Even a few words from a humble, pure soul—though illiterate—will appeal to the Lord more than the eloquent, flowing words of an orator or a Pundit.

Even when the medical board has pronounced a case to be hopeless, Prayer comes to the rescue and the patient is miraculously cured. There have been many instances of this description. You might know this. Healing by prayer is really miraculous and mysterious.

He who prays regularly has already started the spiritual journey towards the domain of everlasting peace and perennial joy. That man who does not pray lives in vain.

Prayer has tremendous influence. I have many experiences. If the Prayer is sincere and if it proceeds from the bottom of your heart (Antarika) it will at once melt the heart of the Lord.

Do not pray for the attainment of any selfish ends or mundane gifts. Pray for His mercy. Pray for divine light, purity and spiritual guidance. Pray constantly. "*O Lord, let me remember Thee at all times. Let my mind be fixed at Thy lotus-feet. Remove my evil habits.*"

Prayer generates good spiritual currents and produces tranquillity of the mind. If you pray regularly, your life will be gradually changed and moulded. Prayer must become habitual. If Prayer becomes a habit with you, you will feel as if you cannot live without It.

Prayer can move mountains. Prayer can work miracles. Pray even once from the bottom of your heart: "*O Lord, I am Thine. Thy Will be done. Have mercy on me. I am Thy servant. Forgive. Guide. Protect. Enlighten. Trahi Mam. Prachodayat.*" Have a meek, receptive attitude of mind. Cultivate Bhava in your heart. The prayer is at once heard and responded. Do this in the daily battle of life and realise yourself the high efficacy of Prayer. You must have strong Astikya Buddhi (strong conviction in the existence of God).

Do not pray to the Lord with selfish motives. Never pray: "O Lord, let me become rich. Let me have many children, cattle and property. Let my enemies perish. Let me enjoy in heaven for a long time." Never, never pray like this. Never bargain with the Lord. The Lord Himself knows all your needs before you think of asking them. He is the Indweller, Antaryamin. He feeds and clothes the entire universe. Will He ever forget thee?

Christians have different prayers for getting various gifts and bounties from God. Muslims and all other religionists have daily prayers at sunrise, noon, sunset, just before retiring to bed, and just before taking food. Prayer is the beginning of Yoga. Prayer is the first important Anga or limb of Yoga. Preliminary, spiritual Sadhana (Spiritual practice) is Prayer.

A Yogi can actually visualise, through his inner eye, the dynamic and beneficial effects produced on the mind and body by Prayer. Pray to God unselfishly and sincerely. You will get devotion, purity, light and divine knowledge.

Get up in the early morning and repeat some Prayer. Pray in any manner you like. Become as simple as a child. Open freely the chambers of your heart. Discard cunningness or crookedness. You will get everything. Sincere Bhaktas know pretty well about the high efficacy of Prayer. Narada Muni is still praying. Nam Dev prayed and Vittal came out of the image to eat his food. Ekanath prayed and Lord Hari showed His form with four hands. Mira prayed and Lord Krishna served her like a servant. Damaji prayed and Lord Krishna played the part of a menial in paying his dues to Badshah. What more do you want? Pray fervently, right now from this very second.

May you all attain immortality through unselfish and sincere prayers offered to the Lord in the early morning hours! May prayer become part and parcel of your very existence! May the inner eye of intuition be opened in you through prayer!

SADHANA OF THE YOGA OF SYNTHESIS

Logical chopping, clever hair-splitting arguments, intellectual gymnastics and word jugglery will not help you in attaining Self-realisation. You must harmoniously develop your head, heart and hand through the practice of the Yoga of Synthesis. Then only you will attain perfection and integral development.

It is easy to repeat "Aham Brahma Asmi" or "Sivoham," but it is very difficult to feel it and recognise the oneness of all beings. No Samadhi is possible till the impurities of the mind are removed by untiring selfless service, Japa, Kirtan and Upasana. The tossing of the mind can be removed by Japa and Upasana. How can you expect to have Brahma Bhavana when the mind is oscillating and jumping?

It is only people like Dattatreya and Yajnavalkya who are really fit for Vedantic Sadhana and repeating "Sivoham." It is only those who have gone above body-consciousness can really say with emphasis and force "The world is illusory. There is no world. This world is like a mirage or a dream." You are all Rottis and Dhal only. You live in Annamaya Kosha all the twenty-four hours. If there is no sugar in tea, no salt or less in Dhal you are upset. You cannot take your food. It is simply absurd and meaningless if you repeat "Sivoham" or "Aham Brahma Asmi" or "Soham."

You think you are in the state of Turiya, highest Jnana Bhumika or the stage of wisdom. You imagine you have gone above body-consciousness, but you will hopelessly fail when you are put to the practical test, when burning charcoal is applied to your body. Lord Buddha was tested. Mara appeared before him and enticed him. Appar and other saints were all tested. They came out victorious in test.

The superstructure of Vedanta can only be built when the foundation has been laid strongly by the practice of Yama-Niyama, when the heart has been purified thoroughly through untiring selfless service and Upasana or worship of Saguna Brahman. The subtle evil Vrittis that are lurking in the mind can only be destroyed *in toto* only through the grace of the Lord. You cannot eradicate them through individual efforts or Sadhana, even in crores of lives. The Lord chooses that man whom He wishes to take to His feet and makes him perfect and free. This is the emphatic declaration of the Kathopanishad also.

One may deliver a lecture on Advaita Philosophy for several hours. One may interpret a verse in hundred and one ways. One may give a discourse on one verse of the Gita for a week and yet these people may not possess an iota of devotion or practical realisation of Vedantic oneness. It is all dry intellectual exercise. Nothing more than that. Vedanta is a living experience. A Vedanti need not advertise that he is an Advaitin. The sweet divine aroma of Vedantic oneness will be ever emanating from him. Everybody will feel this.

A Vedanti feels himself ashamed to bow or prostrate before an idol in the temple. He feels that his Advaita will evaporate if he prostrates. Study the lives of the reputed Tamil Saints, Appar, Sundarar, Sambandhar etc. They had the highest Advaitic realisation. They saw Lord Siva everywhere and yet they visited all temples of Siva, prostrated before the idol and sang hymns, which are on record now. The sixty-three Nayanar Saints practised Chariyai and Kiriyai only and attained to realisation. They swept the floor of the temple, collected flowers, made garlands for the Lord and put on lights in the temple. They were illiterate, but attained the highest realisation. They were practical Yogins and their hearts were saturated with pure devotion. They were an embodiment of Karma Yoga. All practised the Yoga of Synthesis. The idol in the temple was all Chaitanya or consciousness for them. It was not a mere block of stone.

How difficult it is to remove this tea habit, a habit which you have contracted within these few years only. If you do not take it for a day you complain you get headache, constipation, etc. You are not able to work. How weak you have become! Then how much more difficult will it be to eradicate the evil Vrittis which are deep-rooted in the mind and which have gained great strength through repetition from time immemorial.

It is easy to become a lecturer on Vedanta. If you sit in a library for some years and enrich your vocabulary and phraseology and commit to memory some passages you can deliver good lectures, in two or three years, but it is not so easy to eradicate an evil quality. A real aspirant only who is doing Sadhana will realise his difficulty.

Just close your eyes now and find out how many really virtuous selfless actions you have done during your life-time, which can be really consecrated as offerings unto the Lord, and which can really please the Lord. There may not be any selfless, praiseworthy action at all. The practice of Karma Yoga does not require much wealth. It demands a willing heart to serve humanity. If you find a poor man suffering on the roadside, take him on your back and admit him in the hospital, serve and nurse the poor sick persons who live in your neighbourhood. Go to the hospital and see the sick persons with a loving heart. Pray for their speedy recovery. Study the Gita in their presence. Acts of this description will purify your heart and make you feel and recognise the oneness of all beings. Then you will smile with the rose, converse with the trees, running brooks and mountains. Even if you do one noble act without any tinge of selfishness as an offering unto the Lord, it will purify your heart, turn your mind at once towards the Lord and qualify yourself for the reception of the Divine Light and Divine Grace.

Mere sitting on Padmasana in a closed room with closed eyes without removing the dirt or weeds in your heart will not in any way help you to attain Samadhi or Self-realisation. You may be building castles in the air, Mano-rajya. You may be in the state of Tandri or half-sleepy condition. You may be passing into Tushnimbhoota Avastha or natural state of mind. Ignorant aspirants mistake all these states for Samadhi or realisation. This is a serious blunder. Even if one can meditate seriously and deeply with one-pointedness for half an hour he will be a dynamic Yogi. He will radiate peace, joy, power and strength to thousands who come in contact with him.

A real Vedanti who is feeling oneness with all cannot keep even a cup of milk for himself. He will share everything with others. First he will see if any sick man is really in need of milk. He will run to him with panting breath and give him at once and feel joy in such service. Nowadays retired people live on the banks of the Ganga, study a few books on Vedanta and think that they have attained the state of Jivanmukti. They spend everything for themselves and send the major portion of their pension to their sons. They have not developed their heart. They cannot feel for others. They have not made even an inch of progress in the spiritual path, because they have no Chittavisalata or Udaravritti (expression of heart). They remain in the same state as they were some fifteen years ago. This is indeed a sad state! Let them live on Bhiksha for one year and serve the poor with their whole pension. They will have Self-realisation within this year. They should leave the house for two months without money in winter and roam about in unknown places living on alms. They will become humble, compassionate and more generous. They will develop will-power and endurance. They will understand and realise the mysterious ways of the Lord during their wanderings. They will have more faith in the Lord. They will experience the pangs of hunger and the stinging of cold. They will understand well now how the poor people really suffer. They will distribute blankets to the poor and feed the hungry because they realise now fully their sufferings.

You are wasting your time. You are not practising introspection. You get up in the morning, take tea, put on your suits and hat and go to the office for work. You go to the club, gossip in the evening, play cards, visit cinemas and snore till 8 a.m. Your whole life is wasted like this. You are not doing any Japa or meditation. You do not know which Vritti is troubling you, which Guna is functioning at a particular time. You do not know anything about mind-control. You do not know what is Brahma-Vichara, what is Atma-Chintana, what is Brahma-Nishtha. You have not taken recourse to Satsanga with Mahatmas, Yogins and Bhagavatas. You have no programme of life. Even after retirement you try to enter State Service as you do not know how to spend the time in spiritual pursuits, as you have no inner life of reflection and enquiry and as you have not led a life of spiritual discipline in your younger days. You have lived in vain to fill up your pockets and bellies.

Sankirtan is a great help even for Vedantins. When the mind is tired Sankirtan will fill it with new vigour and energy. Sankirtan will relax the mind, elevate it, and prepare it for another sitting in meditation. When the mind revolts to meditate, Sankirtan will coax it and tame it and bring it back to the Lakshya or the point. Those who are practising meditation only can understand this, can know this truth.

Can you meditate for 24 hours? Certainly not. Then how are you going to spend twenty-four hours? In the name of meditation do not allow yourself to become absolutely Tamasic. When the mind begins to wander, when you find it difficult to focus it, come out of the room at once and do some useful service. Keep up the current of meditation while serving also, or do some mental Japa vigorously. Meditation should make you cheerful, introspective, reflective, strong, peaceful, energetic and dynamic. If you are lacking in these virtues surely there is some error in your meditation. Perhaps you are not fit for continuous Dhyana Yoga. You should combine work with meditation; then only you will evolve quickly.

A bird cannot fly without two wings. Though the bird may have two wings yet it cannot fly without the tail. Tail balances and directs the bird to fly in the right direction and saves it from falling. This tail is Bhakti which balances Karma and Jnana. The two wings represent Karma and Jnana. Karma, Bhakti and Jnana are necessary to make you perfect; and to develop the head, hand and heart, and help you in reaching the goal.

Have you seen the picture of Lord Siva's family? Mother Parvati is in the Centre. She has Ganesa and Subrahmanya on her sides. Ganesa is the Lord of wisdom. Subrahmanya is the Lord of action. He is the General of the Army of Devas. Mother Parvati is Bhakti. You should learn a spiritual lesson from this picture. This picture teaches that you can attain perfection only by the practice of Yoga of Synthesis.

Lord Krishna is an adept in the Yoga of Synthesis. He is a charioteer. He is a Statesman. He is a Master Musician. He is an expert Rasa-lila dancer. He is a dexterous archer. He says "There is nothing in the three worlds that should be done by Me, nor anything unattained." Sri Sankara, Lord Jesus, Lord Buddha were all masters of Yoga of Synthesis. Sri Aurobindo,

Mahatma Gandhi, Sadhu Vaswani, etc., were all practising the Supreme Yoga, the Yoga of Synthesis.

Jnana Yoga is rooted in Sadhana-Chatushtaya (discrimination and self-denial), blossoms as Brahma Jnana and bears the fruit of Moksha or Kaivalya (Absolute Independence), freedom and perfection.

Bhakti is rooted in faith and self-surrender, blossoms as intense Prema and bears the fruit of communion with the Lord (Isvara-prapti) or ecstasy or Bhavasamadhi.

Raja Yoga is rooted in Yama (right conduct) and Niyama, blossoms as Ekagra-Chitta (one-pointedness of mind) and bears the fruit of Asamprajnata or Nirvikalpa Samadhi (Superconscious state).

Karma Yoga is rooted in self-sacrifice, blossoms as Chitta Suddhi (purity of heart) and Chitta-Visalata (expansion of heart) and bears the fruit of Knowledge of the Imperishable.

Kundalini Yoga is rooted in Satya and Brahmacharya, blossoms as the grace of the Divine Mother and bears the fruit of union with Lord Siva.

Hatha Yoga is rooted in Asanas and Pranayama, blossoms as restfulness, and bears fruit of perfect health, long life and awakening of Kundalini.

CHAPTER NINE
IMPORTANCE OF SADHANA

SPIRITUALISATION OF HUMAN NATURE

The petty, obstinate egoism which actuates the human personality is a serious obstacle in meditation or the path of Self-realisation. This little self-arrogating principle supports its surface thoughts and dominates its habitual ways of feeling, character and action. This is Rajasic and Tamasic egoism which conceals or covers the higher, divine, Sattvic nature. It veils the self-luminous Immortal Soul or Atman.

You may have aspiration to the Truth. You may be endowed with devotion. You may possess a will to overcome the obstacles and hostile forces. If the little ego asserts or persists, if the external personality has not consented to change or transformation, you cannot have rapid progress in the spiritual path. It will have its own ways and inclinations.

The lower nature must be thoroughly regenerated. The habitual lower personality of the Sadhaka must be entirely changed. If this is not done any spiritual experience or power is of no value. If this little ego or human personality persists in retaining its petty, limited, selfish, ignoble, false and stupid human consciousness, any amount of Tapas or Sadhana will bear no fruit. This means that you do not really thirst for God-realisation. It is nothing more than idle curiosity. The aspirant says to the preceptor "I want to practise Yoga. I want to enter into Nirvikalpa Samadhi. I want to sit at your feet," but he does not want to change his lower nature and old habits. He wants to have his own ways and old habits, old character, behaviour and conduct.

If the aspirant or Yogic student declines to change his petty, lower nature or if he refuses even to admit the need for any change in his lower, habitual personality, he can never make even an iota of real spiritual advancement. Any partial or temporary elevation, slight occasional inspiration during some exalted moments, any momentary spiritual opening within,

IMPORTANCE OF SADHANA

without any true or radical transformation of the lower nature or habitual little personality, is of no practical value.

This change of the lower nature is not easy. The force of habit is ever strong and inveterate. It demands great strength of will. The aspirant often feels helpless against the force of old habits. He will have to develop his Sattva and will to a considerable degree by regular Japa, Kirtan, meditation, untiring selfless service, Satsanga. He must introspect and find out his own defects and weaknesses. He must live under the guidance of his Guru. The Guru finds out his defects and points out suitable ways to eradicate them. If the lower nature or old personality becomes obstinate, self-assertive or aggressive, and if it is supported and justified by the lower mind and will, then the matter becomes very serious. He becomes incorrigible, turbulent, unruly, arrogant and impertinent. He breaks all the rules and discipline.

Such an aspirant clings to his old self. He has not surrendered himself either to the Lord or to a personal Guru. He is ever ready to revolt against any man for little things. He will never obey. He is not willing to receive any spiritual instruction. He is self-willed, self-satisfied and self-sufficient. He is not ready to accept his weaknesses and defects. He thinks that he is a flawless man of great achievements. He leads a happy-go-lucky life.

The old personality asserts itself with the past forms of lower nature. He asserts and follows his own crude and egoistic ideas, desires, fancies, impulses or conveniences. He claims the right to follow his own inhuman unregenerate Asuric or diabolical nature with all untruthfulness, ignorance, selfishness, rudeness and to express all impure stuff in speech, action and behaviour.

He argues vehemently and defends himself in a variety of ways and paints in special colours. He tries to continue his past habitual ways of thinking. speaking and feeling.

He professes one thing and practises another thing. He tries to force his wrong views and opinions on others. If others are not willing to accept his wrong views, he is ready to fight against them. He at once stands up in revolt. He asserts that his views only are correct and that those who try to oppose his views are unjust, unreasonable, uneducated. He tries to persuade and convince others that his views are very reasonable and that his ways of action are the right ways of action for all and that his ways and views are in full accordance with the science of Yoga. Marvellous people they are!

If he is really frank with himself and straightforward to his Guru, if he really desires to improve himself, he will begin to realise his folly and defects and recognise the source and nature of the resistance. He will soon be on the direct road to correct and change himself. But he prefers to conceal his old Asuric nature, his old diabolical thoughts under some justification or excuse or other shelter.

The self-assertive, arrogant Sadhaka tries to make a figure in society. He wants to maintain a position and prestige in the society. He poses himself that he is a great Yogi and possesses several Yogic powers. He claims the part of a superior Sadhaka or an advanced Yogi with greater knowledge and experience of Nirvikalpa Samadhi. These defects of vanity, arrogance of Rajasic nature are present in most human natures on a smaller scale.

He is unwilling to obey the orders of his Guru and respect elders and superiors. He is ever ready to break discipline. He has got his ideas and impulses. The habit of disobedience and disregard of discipline is ingrained in him. He sometimes promises that he will be obedient to his Guru and elders, but the action done is frequently the very opposite of his promise. Non-observance of discipline is indeed a serious obstacle to the Sadhana. He sets the worst possible example to others.

He who is disobedient, who breaks the discipline, who is not straightforward to his Guru, who cannot open his heart to his preceptor or spiritual guide, cannot be benefited by the help of his Guru. He remains stuck in his own self-creating mire or mud and cannot progress in the divine path. What a great pity! His lot is highly lamentable indeed!

He practises dissimulation. He plays the hypocrite. He pretends falsely. He exaggerates things. He makes a false use of his imagination. He does distortion and falsification of facts. He conceals his thoughts and facts. He denies positively certain facts. He tells terrible, deliberate lies. He does this to cover up his disobedience or wrong course of action, to keep up his position and to have his own ways or indulge in his old habits and desires.

He himself does not know what he is exactly doing as his

intellect is clouded by impurity. He does not know what he means and does not mean what he says.

He never admits his faults and defects. Even if any one points out his defects for correcting him, he feels extremely annoyed. He wages war against him. He has more brute in him.

He has got the most dangerous habit of self-justification. He always tries to justify himself, to stick to his own ideas to maintain his own position or course of action by bringing any kind of foolish, inconsistent arguments, clever tricks or devices. He misuses his intellect to support his own foolish actions. These defects are common, in some in a less, in others in a great degree.

If he feels even a little bit, for his present deplorable condition, if he attempts to show even a slight improvement, if there is a little receptive attitude, he can be corrected. He can have progress in the path of Yoga. If he is obstinate and pig-headed, if he is absolutely self-willed, if he deliberately shuts his eyes or hardens his heart against the truth or Divine light, no one can help him.

The aspirant should give his full consent with all his being (Sarva Bhava) for the change of his lower nature into Divine nature. He must make total, unreserved, ungrudging self-surrender to the Lord or Guru. He must have the true spirit and right abiding attitude. He must make the right persistent endeavours. Then only the real change will come. Mere nodding the head, mere professing, mere saying 'yes' will not serve any purpose. It will not make you a Superman or a Yogi.

Yoga can be practised only by those who are very earnest about it and who are ready to annihilate their little ego and its demands. There is no half-measure in the spiritual path. Rigid discipline of senses and mind, rigorous Tapas and constant meditation are necessary for the attainment of God-realisation. The hostile forces are ever ready to overwhelm you if you are not vigilant, if you give the least sanction or the smallest opening for them. Yoga cannot be practised if you cling to your old little self, old habits, old unregenerate self-assertive lower nature.

You cannot lead a double life at the same time. Pure divine life, life of Yoga, cannot co-exist with mundane life of passion and ignorance. Divine life cannot conform to your own little standards. You must rise above petty human level. You must raise yourself to a higher level of divine consciousness. You cannot claim freedom for your petty mind and little ego if you want to become a Yogi. You should not affirm your own thoughts, judgment, desires, impulses. The lower nature with its retinue, viz., arrogance, ignorance, turbulence stands in the way of descent of the divine light.

Become a true, sincere aspirant in the path of Yoga. Kill this lower nature by developing the higher divine nature. Soar high. Get yourself ready for the descent of the divine light. Purify and become a dynamic Yogi.

LIFE'S SUPREME PURPOSE

Life on earth is a School for Wisdom and Realisation of the Self. God is the unseen teacher who through his Great Sons, through Nature Herself, teaches man the secret and source of attainment of eternal Bliss. Thus Life abounds in lessons. He who heeds them heads towards freedom and light; he who neglects, lives in darkness in which the world today is steeped. The misery and suffering that abound everywhere reveal clearly that you have wantonly rejected the lessons of life. Foolish man! your repeated, wanton neglect to learn the lessons of centuries has wrecked your boasted civilisation upon the rocks of hatred and greed. By arrogantly refusing to heed countless warnings you have brought ruin and misery upon the earth. All along History has, time after time, taught that abuse of power brings endless sufferings; that violence and hatred result in destruction and misery. O deluded one! blinded by selfishness you have not yet learnt to restrain your greed, to control your ambitions, to love thy neighbour and to temper might with mercy, strength with justice. Material advancement has perhaps enabled you to dominate over the weak, the meek "that are the salt of the earth"; but you have yourself become enslaved by the fascination of physical might. You are power mad. Your delusion is pitiable. Stand not as a beggar before the door of science seeking power that kills more than heals. Seek within. All power dwells in you, infinite power for good. In your intoxication you think you have won victories. No. You have lost. It is the beast in you that has won the victory and what victory? It is a victory over the man in you. You imagine you have succeeded very well. You have failed miserably. Humanity has sought to attack hatred with greater hatred. The Lesson of Life has ever been "Hatred is not overcome by Hatred, by Love alone is Hatred conquered." The Great Buddha, has he lived in vain then? Spiritual wealth alone is the True Treasure, the wealth of all earth is but vanity. This Truth, Life taught the world through a jewel of Son Mammon. But today Mammon is enshrined in the temple of Man's heart. "All phenomena are false, strive to attain the supreme Reality" is the bold declaration of Sri Sankara. Yet you have made the material world alone the only solid reality. This treacherous mirage is luring humanity to its destruction.

The perverted turn taken by modern commercial and political doctrines of acquisition, exploitation, domination and oppression is a deep fathomless abyss of Maya into which humanity is plunging headlong. Talks and plans of reconstruction are developing into reconstruction of war weapons for fresh destruction. Stop! Stop this downward plunge. Beware in time. Rise up again! Turn this apparent victory into Real Victory now. Manifest your mastery over Mara's machination. You may build a mansion with beautiful plastering, coloured tiles, glass sky-lights, painted doors and windows but if the foundation is sand and the bricks are straw then the whole structure is doomed to collapse. It is the human being that has built up this structure of modern civilisation. The individual is the brick to this structure and he himself has degenerated into an un-Godly, Adharmic, unscrupulous being characterised by extreme greed and utter self-seeking. Therefore with all its external gloss the rotten structure has fallen to earth before the blast of the winds of hatred and passion.

To every man I say "Regenerate Yourself. Strive to be an Ideal Man and soon a New Civilisation will come to prevail upon earth." The apparent triumph of having learnt to harness the atomic energy is like the boon of Bhasmasura that proved his own undoing and burnt him to ashes. Awake! Let this not happen. Humanity, wake up. Turn Godwards! Turn towards the Divine Light while there is yet time. You can yet mend and make good. However low you may have fallen you can rise yet. The Lord has assured Glory even to the worst being if he but mend his ways.

The cycle of darkness and degeneracy has reached its nadir. Come now. Arise victorious and step up towards the zenith of Perfection that awaits mankind.

THE STRUGGLE FOR PERFECTION

Live with a definite purpose. Do not roam about aimlessly. Walk with a definite aim. Climb the hill of knowledge steadily and reach the summit of the temple of Brahman or the Sweet Abode of Immortality.

In the spiritual path there are constant failures and set-backs. Repeated endeavour, constant vigilance and undaunted perseverance are needed.

When the heart-knots are gradually loosened, when the Vasanas are thinned out, when the bonds of Karma are loosened, when ignorance is loosened, when weakness vanishes, you will become more and more peaceful, strong and serene. You get more and more light from within. You become more and more divine.

Hard enough is it to purify the lower nature. Difficult enough is it to practise concentration and meditation. But vigilance, perseverance, constant practice, steady and persistent efforts, company of sages (Satsanga), resolute will, strong determination will obviate all difficulties and render the path easy, pleasant and attractive.

Fight with the mind bravely. March onwards. Spiritual Hero! Go on fighting with an undaunted heart. Struggle now. Be courageous. At the end of your battle you will attain the illimitable dominion of Eternal Bliss, the Sweet Abode of Immortality, the immaculate, imperishable Self or Brahman.

Strive ceaselessly. Despair not. The light is on the path. Serve all. Love truth. Be serene. Meditate regularly. You will soon attain the life beautiful, the Silence and the Supreme Peace.

Even when you get a glimpse of Truth or the Supreme, your whole life will be changed. You will become a changed Being. You will have a new heart and a new vision. A new thrill of spiritual current will pass through your entire being. A wave of spiritual bliss will sweep over you. The state is indescribable. There are no words to express. There is no language to describe your inner experience.

NEED FOR SADHANA

Time is most precious. You do not realise the value of time. When the patient is on the death-bed you will ask the doctor who is standing by the side of the patient, "O doctor! just do something for the patient. Give a powerful injection. Let the breath continue for some hours at least. My brother is coming from Bombay to see the patient." The doctor can only reply "My dear friend! I cannot do anything. The case is perfectly hopeless. He will pass away within five minutes." Now you will realise the value of time. You will repent for the days, months and years you have wasted in idle gossiping and sensual pleasures.

You may waste two hours in tying your turban. You may waste much time in self-shaving, combing the hair but if a devotee calls you to attend Satsanga, Sankirtan or Bhajan, you will say, "Babaji, I have no time at all. I have to go to the doctor to get medicine. I must go to the market for shopping" and you will give a thousand and one lame excuses.

You keep vigil for cinemas and dramas. You keep vigil all the night if a scorpion stings you. But you cannot keep vigil if there is Akhanda Kirtan during Vaikuntha Ekadasi or Sivaratri. What a pity?

Everybody wants to see God but nobody wants to do any Sadhana. If the Guru says, 'Practise meditation, Pranayama and study scriptures,' the disciple replies 'I have no time for that.' The teacher says, "Repeat the name of Lord Hari." The disciple replies: "I know that already. It is a long, cumbersome and ineffective way. I do not have much faith in Name."

If the Master says, "Then practise Raja Yoga and control the Vrittis gradually. Sit on one Asana for one or two hours," you will say, "I cannot sit for more than 15 minutes. My limbs ache if I sit for a long time." If you are asked to do Upasana, you will say, "There is nothing in Upasana. Idol worship is useless. I cannot concentrate on a picture. A picture is only the imagination of a painter or an artist. I wish to meditate on the all-pervading formless Brahman. Meditation on a picture is a child's play. This does not suit me well." If the teacher says, "Then do Kirtan and Japa for two hours daily," you will say, "There is nothing in Japa or Kirtan. This is suitable only for dull-headed persons. I know science well. I cannot stop to do these things. I am above Japa and Kirtan. I am quite modern." If the priest performs the Havan in the proper prescribed manner you say, "Well, Purohit! What is all this? Hurry up. I am feeling hungry. I want to go to the office at 10." If the priest hurries up, you say, "What is this? The priest said something for a couple of hours and says it is all over now. It is all waste of time, money and energy. I have no faith in Havan. There is no good in it."

If the teacher says, "Then do Pranayama and practise Sirshasana, your Kundalini will be awakened quickly," you will say, "I practised Pranayama for six months. The body became very hot. It did not agree with me. I gave up the practice. I had a fall when doing Sirshasana. I gave it up also."

This is your state of affairs. Anyhow you want spiritual bliss and realisation without doing Sadhana. You want Samadhi in the twinkling of an eye.

You lead a happy-go-lucky life. You do not want to strive hard for attaining God-realisation. If there is any work you will say, 'I will do it tomorrow. I am not quite well today. Doctor has advised me to take perfect rest in bed.' But if there is some sweetmeat—Halva or Rasagulla—you will say, "I am hungry; give it to me now. My health is all right. I can digest it quite easily."

O Man! Lord Buddha strove hard and did Tapas in the Uruvela forest. Lord Jesus did rigorous Sadhana during the missing period. All saints and Yogins have done severe Tapas and meditation. The boy Dhruva did Tapas living on air, water and grass.

The evil Vrittis such as lust, pride, jealousy, Raga-Dvesha are very deep-rooted. Pride and Raga-Dvesha do not leave even Sannyasins and Sadhus. Go to a Mahatma and tell him: "Your lecture was very beautiful and inspiring. You have touched on all points very nicely; but I cannot agree with one or two points." He will at once become angry and jump upon you and say, "O you fool! How can you criticise me? I am a great scholar and practical Yogi." Maya is very powerful. You will have to obtain the grace of the Lord through self-surrender. That is the reason why Lord Krishna says, "This divine illusion of Mine, caused by the qualities is hard to pierce (*Mama Maya Duratyaya*); they who come to Me, cross over this illusion."

The terrible enemy of Immortality is attachment or Moha. It is very difficult to get rid of attachment. The bee can make holes even in wood; but it perishes on account of its attachment to the honey. It sits on the flowers to gather honey. It sits on the lotus in the evening and slowly sucks honey. The lotus closes itself in the evening when the sun sets. The bee does not want to get out of the flower on account of attachment. It foolishly thinks, "I will get out of the flower tomorrow when the sun rises." An elephant comes, crushes the lotus and with it the bee also. This is the case with man also. He can do many wonderful deeds. But he gets attached to the various objects of the world and perishes. The elephant Time consumes him before he can get out of the lotus (of woman and wealth).

The serpent has the frog in its mouth. Only the head of the frog is outside. It will be devoured within a few minutes, yet even in this condition, the wretched frog projects its tongue outside to catch and eat an insect or two. Even so, O ignorant man, you are already in the mouth of Kala or Time. You will be nowhere in a few minutes. Yet you crave for and cling to the sensual objects again and again. You have become a slave of Moha or delusion and attachment.

Death is ever waiting to devour you. Pierce the lotus through dispassion, renunciation and discrimination. Give up attachment. Have faith in Lord's name. Do Japa, meditation and attain Immortality.

Do Sadhana, therefore, when there is yet time; when you are young and the body is healthy. When you are young, when you have abundant energy, you must practise concentration and meditation. You cannot do any spiritual practice during old age.

OUTGOING TENDENCIES OF THE SENSES AND THE NEED FOR SELF-CONTROL

Brahma created the senses with outgoing tendencies. The eyes want to see beautiful forms. The ears want to hear good music. The tongue wants sweet things and so on, all due to outgoing tendencies of the senses or Rajas. Man thinks he can get happiness from external objects. "If I have some money in my pocket I can have good coffee in the morning. I can command most delicious dishes. I can keep myself perfectly healthy. I can have a bungalow like some rich people. I can own a summer house in a hill station. I will furnish the room in this way and that" and so on the mind plans and runs towards the external world to have more money, more comforts. There is no end to one's exertion to possess objects of pleasure. Yet through gratification of the senses, man does not attain peace.

The mind is a mischievous imp. It will often revolt. It will ask you "why should I take Sattvic food? Why should I get up at

4 o' clock?" All of a sudden various kinds of doubts will crop up which will try to bring down the aspirant. Being placed in the world of objects you are liable to be carried away by the currents. You get immersed in the old Samskaras of how to get money, how to get this and that. Maya deludes you every moment. You devote much attention to fashions, in dressing yourself and so on. When you have 4 shirts you want 6 more and so on; wants multiply. These are the thoughts which occupy your mind. You will, therefore, have to tackle this mind carefully. The positive always overcomes the negative. This is the law of nature.

So long as your senses are not subdued or weakened, you will have to practise Tapas or self-restraint, Dama or Pratyahara.

When the electric lamp is covered by many wrappings of cloth, there will be no bright light. When the cloth is removed one by one, the light grows brighter and brighter. Even so, when the self-resplendent Atman which is covered by the five sheaths is stripped off by meditation on the pure Self and the practice of 'Neti-Neti' doctrine, the Self-luminous Atman reveals Itself to the meditator.

Sit down with a composed mind. Assert your mastery over the body and the mind. Plunge deep into the chambers of the heart and enter into the stupendous ocean of silence. Listen to the voice which is soundless.

Purify the heart first and then climb the ladder of Yoga steadily with courage and undaunted spirit. Climb onwards swiftly. Attain Ritambara Prajna and reach the summit of the ladder, the temple of wisdom, where the cloud of virtue or nectar drizzles from Dharmamegha Samadhi.

Build your spiritual life on a sure foundation, on the rock of the divine grace and strength of your character. Take refuge in the Lord and His eternal law. There is no power in the heavens or on this earth that can bar your march now. Success in Self-realisation is certain. Failure exists not for you. There is light on your path. All is brilliant.

QUALIFICATION FOR SADHANA

If you serve God with a fraction of the zeal with which you serve mammon or your wife and children you will certainly realise God within a very short period. Even one moment of intense love for God with burning Viraha, God-intoxication and keen longing will suffice to bring you face to face with God.

Works should be performed without attachment, without the feeling of doing them for one's own personal purity. Perform works merely for God's sake, abandoning even such attachment as this—"May God be pleased." You must be prepared to abandon the work at any time however interesting the work may be, however much you like the work. Whenever the inner voice of the soul commands you to give up the work, you must at once relinquish it. Attachment to any work will bind you. Understand well these subtle secrets of Karma Yoga and march boldly in the path of Karma Yoga.

Maya havocs through imagination of the mind. Woman is not beautiful but the imagination is beautiful. Sugar is not sweet but the imagination is sweet. Food is not palatable but the imagination is palatable. Man is not weak but the imagination is weak. Understand the nature of Maya and mind and become wise. Curb this imagination of the mind by Vichara or right thinking and rest in Brahman wherein there is neither imagination nor Sankalpa, nor thought.

You show your anger towards your servants, inferiors and helpless weak persons only but you do not show it towards your Master or boss or superiors or strong persons. Why? Because you practise some sort of self-restraint on account of fear towards your Master. Can you not practise self-restraint towards your servants also? If you attempt to see the Lord in the servant, you will not become angry towards your servant. Anger will bring about your destruction. Under the influence of anger only you commit crimes, do wrong actions, insult your elders and speak harsh words. Therefore you should control anger by all means.

Develop patience, tolerance, mercy and love. Practise Vichara. Enquire "Who am I?" Serve others with Atma Bhava. Enquire within yourself. "What will I gain by becoming angry? My whole energy is lost when I become angry. The Self is one. The Self is common in all beings. In hurting another I hurt myself. There is nothing but my own Self. There is no anger in Atman. Atman is an embodiment of peace." This evil Vritti will die by itself.

Some people have curiosity for the spiritual line. They have no real thirsting for liberation. They think that they will get certain powers or Siddhis if they do some Yogic practices. When they do not attain the powers they lose patience, give up the practices, abandon the spiritual path and pooh-pooh the Yogis and Yoga. Mere curiosity will not help you to attain any spiritual progress. Curiosity-mongering is more abominable than mischief-mongering. Introspect. Analyse your thoughts and find out whether you have real spiritual hunger or mere curiosity-mongering. Transmute curiosity-mongering into real thirsting for salvation by constant Satsanga, study of good religious books, prayer, Japa and meditation.

Your mind will sometimes shudder when evil thoughts enter your mind. This is a sign of your spiritual progress. You are growing spiritually. You will be much tormented when you think of some of your evil actions committed in the past. This is also a sign of your spiritual upheaval. You will not repeat now the same actions. Your mind will tremble, your body will quiver whenever a wrong Samskara or evil action urges you to do the same act, through force of habit. Continue your meditation with full vigour and earnestness. All memories of evil actions, all evil thoughts, all evil promptings of Satan will die by themselves. You will be established in perfect purity and peace.

Passion is lurking in you. You may ask me the reason why you become frequently angry. Anger is nothing but a modification of passion. When passion is not gratified it assumes the form of anger. The real cause for anger is ungratified passion. It expresses itself in the form of anger, when you deal with the mistakes of your servants. This is an indirect cause or external stimulus for its expression. Raga-Dvesha currents are not thoroughly eradicated. They are only attenuated or thinned out to some extent. The Indriyas or senses are yet turbulent. They are subjugated to a small degree. They are not perfectly curbed, disciplined or subdued. There are still undercurrents of Vasanas and Trishnas. The outgoing tendency of the senses is not totally checked. You are not established in Pratyahara. The Vrittis are still powerful. There is not strong and sustained discrimination or dispassion. The aspiration for the divine has not become intense. Rajas and Tamas are still havocing. There is only a small increase in the quantity of Sattva. Evil Vrittis are not thinned out. They are still powerful. Positive virtues have not been cultivated to a considerable degree. That is the reason why you have not attained perfect concentration. Purify the mind first. Concentration will come by itself.

Saguna Upasakas or those who meditate on the images of the Lord should do Trataka first with open eyes till they can visualise a clear-cut, well-defined picture. Later on they can visualise the picture with closed eyes. The picture must be very pleasing to the mind and the eyes. It should have a good, agreeable background. When you have created a strong mental image of your Lord in the mind by continuous practice of meditation on one form you should not disturb the mental image by changing the picture. Stick to the same picture and strengthen and feel the mental image, through repeated practice of Trataka, visualisation and constant meditation on the form. Through force of habit the same mental image will appear quite easily in your mind. Sometimes you may change even your Mantra or formula when the mind is tired or wants variety but do not change your mental image or Bhava.

Environments are not bad but your mind is bad. Your mind is not disciplined properly. Wage war with this terrible and horrible mind. Do not complain against bad environments but complain first against your own mind. Train your mind first. If you practise concentration amidst unfavourable environments you will grow stronger, you will develop your will-force quickly, you will become a dynamic personality. See good in everything and transmute evil into good. This is real Yoga. This is the real work of a Yogi.

SADHANA—THE MAIN PURPOSE OF LIFE

Sadhana means any spiritual practice that helps the aspirant to realise God. It is a means to attain the goal of human life. Sadhana is steadying the mind and fixing it on the Lord.

Everyone must take to some kind of Sadhana to attain the state of final beatitude.

Sadhana is the real wealth. It is the only thing of real and everlasting value. There is butter in milk, but it can be got only after churning. Similarly if you want to realise God, do Sadhana and worship constantly in right earnest.

Whatever spiritual practice you do, either Japa, practice of Asanas, meditation or Pranayama, do it systematically and regularly every day. You will attain immortality or eternal bliss.

If you persist in your Sadhana vigorously and diligently, if you are regular, systematic and punctual in your Sadhana, you will attain success.

Be contented with whatever you get by chance and apply yourself to Sadhana with a dispassionate mind.

Regularity in Sadhana is of paramount importance. He who meditates regularly gets Samadhi quickly. That man who is irregular and does his actions by fits and starts cannot reap the fruits of his efforts.

Keep your mind always busy in doing Japa, concentration, meditation, study of religious books, Satsanga or in doing something useful to others.

Little acts of virtues, little acts of purity will help you a lot in your Sadhana. Removal of Vrittis and impurities is the most important Sadhana. The wandering mind must be controlled by sticking to one place, one preceptor and one progressive method of Sadhana.

That Sadhaka who has turned the mind inward by the practice of Sama and Dama and who has keen longing for liberation sees the Self in his own Self by constant and deep meditation.

You can move the whole world by your spiritual force.

A spiritual diary is a whip for goading the mind towards righteousness.

Selfishness retards spiritual progress. If anyone can destroy his selfishness, half of his spiritual Sadhana is over.

You must get up at 4 a.m. and start meditation. Have concrete meditation in the beginning. Feel the indwelling presence of God in the form and think of the attributes—purity, perfection, all-pervading intelligence, bliss absolute, omnipotence, etc. When the mind runs again and again bring it to the point. Have another sitting for meditation at night. Be regular in your practice.

Write your Ishta Mantra in a notebook for one hour daily. Discipline the senses. Observe the vow of silence. Develop right thinking, right feeling, right acting and right speaking. Eradicate vicious qualities, such as anger, lust, greed, egoism, hatred, etc. He who regulates his life on the above lines, is sure to attain success in this very birth, nay, in this very second.

BRAHMAMUHURTA: THE BEST TIME FOR SADHANA

Get up at Brahmamuhurta and practise meditation. Do not fail at any cost. Brahmamuhurta is the morning period from 4 to 6 a.m. It is very favourable for meditation. The mind is quite refreshed after good sleep. It is quite calm and serene. There is the preponderance of Sattva or purity in the mind at this time. In the atmosphere also, Sattva predominates at this period.

The mind is like a blank sheet of paper or a clean tablet and comparatively free from worldly Samskaras or impressions at this period. Raga-Dvesha currents have not yet deeply entered the mind. The mind can be moulded very easily at this period in any way you like. You can charge the mind now easily with divine thoughts.

Further all the Yogins, Paramahamsas, Sannyasins, aspirants and the Rishis of the Himalayas start their meditation at this period and send their vibrations throughout the world. You will be immensely benefited by the spiritual currents. Meditation will come by itself, without any effort. It is a terrible spiritual loss for you if you do not utilise the period in divine contemplation and if you snore at this time. Do not become a Kumbhakarna. Become a Yogi like Jnana Deva.

In winter it is not necessary that you should take a cold bath. A mental bath will suffice. Imagine and feel, "I am taking a bath now in the sacred Triveni at Prayag or Manikarnika at Benaras." Remember the pure Atman. Repeat the formula, "I am ever pure soul." This is the most powerful wisdom-bath in Jnana Ganga. This is highly purifying. It burns all sins. Answer the call of nature quickly. Cleanse the teeth quickly. Do not waste much time in cleansing the teeth and taking bath. Be quick. Hurry up. Get ready soon. The Brahmamuhurta will pass quickly. You must utilise this precious time in Japa and meditation.

Wash the face, hands and feet quickly. Dash cold water on the face and on top of the head. This will cool the brain and the eyes. Sit in Siddha, Padma or Sukha Asana. Try to climb the supreme height of Brahman, the peak of divine glory and splendour.

If you are not in the habit of getting up early, have an alarm timepiece. Once the habit is established, there will be no difficulty. The subconscious mind will become your willing and obedient servant to wake you up at the particular time.

If you are a subject of chronic constipation you can drink a tumblerful of cold water or luke-warm water as soon as you get up after cleansing the teeth. This is Ushah-pana treatment in the science of Hatha Yoga. This will give you a good motion. You can drink Triphala water also. Soak two Harads (myrobalan), two Amalaka and two Thandrikkai in a tumblerful of cold water at night. Drink the water in the morning after cleansing the teeth. You can keep a ready-made powder of these drugs and put one or two teaspoonful in the water.

Cultivate the habit of answering the calls of nature as soon as you get up from bed. If you suffer from incurable, old constipation, due to old sins, do meditation as soon as you get up. You can answer the calls after finishing your morning meditation with the help of a cup of hot milk.

As soon as you get up from your bed do Japa and meditation. This is important. After finishing your Japa and meditation you can take to the practice of Asana, Pranayama and study of the Gita and other religious books.

Every Sandhya time, or dusk, is also favourable for meditation. During Brahmamuhurta and dusk, Sushumna Nadi flows readily. You will enter into deep meditation and Samadhi without much effort when Sushumna Nadi flows. That is the reason why Rishis, Yogins and scriptures speak very highly of these two periods of time. When the breath flows through both nostrils, know that the Sushumna is working. Whenever the Sushumna functions sit for meditation and enjoy the inner peace of Atman or Soul.

Repeat some divine Stotras or hymns or Guru Stotras or chant OM twelve times, or do Kirtan for five minutes before you start your Japa and meditation. This will quickly elevate your mind.

A SERMON ON SADHANA

The life of the spiritual aspirant in the world is verily like a fierce struggle and fight with a deadly serpent. Samsara or worldly life is a terrible and deadly serpent. Man must keep constant and alert watchfulness lest the Samsara-sarpa takes you unawares. Keep the twin eyes of Viveka and sharp Vichara wide open. At times the man becomes poisoned in the course of his Vyavahara. He must retire periodically from the worldly atmosphere and take recourse to Satsanga, Sadhana, seclusion and silent meditation. This is the spiritual Sanjivini for you to revive yourself and enter the daily spiritual life again without fear. Satsanga and seclusion are the magic herbs which remove completely all poison of worldliness from you. With their help you will keep yourself safe.

The Supreme Lord of all creations gives to the Jiva this precious human body in which to cultivate all the good things of life. The Jiva listening to the promptings of its lower nature allows the body to get into the possession of innumerable evil Gunas. They dominate the person and make the Jiva helpless. The evil qualities take such strong hold upon him that later on when he tries to acquire virtues and to develop Yama and Niyama, there commences a regular challenge. The old vicious Vrittis and Samskaras do not allow virtues to gain entry. They revolt and push them out, but when the aspirant in this helpless condition prays sincerely to the Lord for strength, then the Grace of the Lord gives him the necessary inner force which enables him to throw out his old viciousness and to obtain the fruits of Sadhana.

Desire is a great obstacle, a great barrier in the path of Self-realisation. Control of mind means really abandoning desires. If one wants to discipline the mind perfectly well, one must give up all desires without reserve, all longings for worldly objects and building castles in the air. The monkey-like mind will always be restless, desiring something or other, Just as the fish taken out of water tries to get into the water by some means or other, so also the mind will always entertain evil thoughts. Killing all the desires ruthlessly, controlling the mind, freeing it from the surging emotions and bubbling thoughts one can attain the one-pointedness of mind. Such a mind will be as calm as a lamp in a windless place. One who attains such a state of mind can meditate for a long time. Meditation will come by itself.

If one allows one's mind to run towards the worldly things as per its own wish and to entertain unholy thoughts and evil desires one will surely meet with destruction in the end.

Therefore give up desire. Have always that one idea to attain that supreme abode, the abode of joy, peace, bliss and immortality. Practise Sadhana. Be regular in your Yogic practices. Strive to attain the Goal. You will rejoice for ever.

CHAPTER TEN
SADHANA FOR THE CONQUEST OF LOWER NATURE

SADHANA FOR MASTERING THE MIND

You take great care of the body. You desire that it should be clean, healthy, beautiful and strong. You take bath with sweet soaps and hot water. You regularly feed it with nourishing food. If there is the least pain or disease medicine is given. Doctor is consulted. But you never give a thought to the much more important thing—MIND. Body is only the outward appearance, a projection of the mind. Mind operates through the senses and the sense-organs. If the mind is well then the body is well. If the mind is sick the body becomes ill. Mind is everything. It controls your whole life. Upon it depends your happiness or misery, success or failure. 'Mana eva Manushyanam Karanam Bandhamokshayoh' thus say the Upanishads. Again, 'Yena Manojitam Jagat Jitam Tena' is the great truth. As you think, so you become. Do you fully realise now the great importance of controlling, training and overcoming the mind? So long you have neglected the care of the mind. Attend to this vital subject from now. Mastery of mind means success in all fields of life. To achieve this mastery you must study the mind. You must understand its nature, habits, tricks and the effective methods of bringing it under restraint.

Mind is a bundle of desires, thoughts, feelings and emotions. It is nothing but a collection of Samskaras, desires arising from contact of the sense-organs with different objects, feeling aroused by worldly botherations, ideas gathered together from various different objects. These desires, feelings and ideas are not steady—they will be constantly changing. Suddenly some will subside and some others will occupy their places like the waves in the seas. Some old ones will depart from the storehouse, the mind and some new ones will replace them at once. It is also a bundle of habits. The bad habits and prejudices, although hidden by one's own nature will come up and occupy the surface of the mind as and when opportunity occurs.

According to the Vedantic school of philosophy mind is of middling size (same size as that of the body), it is atomic (Anu) as per Nyaya school and Patanjali Maharshi says in Raja Yoga that it is Vibhu (all-pervading). Most of the western doctors, who are still groping in utter darkness, say that it is an excretion of the brain, like bile from liver.

Lord Krishna says, "The senses of which the mind is the sixth (*Manah-shashtanindriyani*)"—Gita, Chap. XV-7. Here the five senses are the five Jnana Indriyas, viz., the ear, the skin, the tongue, the nose, the eye; and the mind is termed as the sixth. Mind is the common sensory and an aggregate of the five senses. As all the five senses are mingled with it, the mind is able to see, hear, smell, taste and feel independently of the senses.

Mind assumes the shape of any object instantly it thinks upon it. If it thinks of a mango, it assumes the form of a mango. Then it gets an attachment with the mango. Now a desire arises in the mind to taste it. Then the mind makes a firm determination to eat that mango and satisfy itself. One thought follows another. The thought of the mango invites instantaneously the thought of the mango-fruit seller, the tree, the garden where the tree is and so on and so forth. This is the expansion of thoughts or Sankalpas. The whole world is nothing but the expansion of Sankalpas. This expansion of Sankalpas of mind towards the various objects is called BONDAGE. The present-day people have no right understanding, discriminative power between unreal and real. They are completely deluded by Maya. They are under the firm grip or crocodile catch of Maya. They have fallen prey to worldly desires and enjoyments. Therefore they are victims to this bondage, forgetting totally their divine birthright—liberation from the dire disease of births and deaths and attainment of Immortality, the Life Eternal and final Beatitude!

Mind is a monkey which jumps from one place to another. It is like the air, which is always moving (Chanchala). Just as the quick-silver it scatters its rays over various objects. It can also be compared to a furious elephant, because of its passionate impetuosity. Like the fish out of the water, it will always be thirsting to run after evil habits and entertain bad and vicious thoughts. It is also known as a "Great Bird" because it skips from one object to another just as the bird wanders from one tree to another tree, one twig to another, and one place to another.

The last thought determines the next birth. "Whosoever at the end leaves the body, thinking upon any being, to that being only he goes, O Kaunteya! because of the constant thought of that being"—Gita, Chap. VIII-6. Whatever thought you entertain at the last breath, accordingly you take your next birth. This thought entirely depends upon the constant desires and ideas you entertained throughout your whole life.

Every man has a definite outlook of life; due to the power of the mind he has got a definite thinking, definite craving, desire and hope and definite character, temperament, taste and attitude. For the gratification of the mind these desires, cravings etc., are constantly repeated again and again, and these acts leave definite impressions upon the subconscious mind. The impressions take indelible forms in the subconscious mind.

At the time of death the whole storehouse, the subconscious mind which is full of various thoughts, feelings, ideas etc., is churned out and the strongest and most cherished desire comes to the surface of the subconscious mind or the field of mental consciousness. This churned up butter or cream (cherished desire) arrests his attention for immediate gratification. You will think of this desire only at the time of death. If you are much attached to your pet dog, the thought of the dog will come at the time of death and you will take the form of a dog in the next birth. If you always think of body and identify yourself with the perishable body you will be born again. If you constantly think of Immortal Self during your lifetime, you will entertain the thought of Atman only at the time of death and you will surely attain freedom from births and deaths, Immortality and Everlasting Bliss! For this you must have a well-regulated, perfectly disciplined, correctly moulded, well-controlled and pure and devoted mind. Mark here! the importance of Sadhana, particularly the control of mind which is the central purpose of Sadhana!

Mind is like a mirror. When the mirror is dusty and dirt-laden, you cannot see your face clearly. So also when the mind is dirty, full of impurities, caught in the network of desires, you cannot perceive the Atman or Truth. Just as the eczematous part of the leg and scabiatic hand is always itching, the mind will always be itching for lust. Purify and control the itching mind by uninterrupted, undaunted and regular practice of Sadhana, meditation, devotion, selfless works, by wisdom, Vichara, light Sattvic diet, Japa, study of the Gita, Satsanga, Asanas.

The mind in the vast majority of persons, has been allowed to run wild and follow its sweet will and desires. It is like a spoiled child which is given too much of indulgence by the parents or a badly trained animal. The minds of many of us are like menageries of wild animals each pursuing the bent of its own nature and going on its way. Like the light feather in the wind and a ship in the violent storm, the mind is tossed about among objects of love and hatred. It whirls far and wide like a strolling city-dog vainly among sensual objects.

It whirls at the mere sight of the skeleton covered with flesh and dressed fashionably with coloured silken clothes. It is intoxicated by wealth. It will flit in a moment more swiftly than air from Calcutta to New York. In a second it will be in Paris thinking of the up-to-date fashions. In short, it fluctuates, gets excited and confused. It flits about from object to object forever discontented and never satiated. It rejoices in vain. It weeps in regret. It is humiliated for one moment. And it is again puffed up with pride and filled with Ahankara.

Mind havocs through the power of imagination. Imaginary fears of various sorts, exaggeration, concoction, mental dramatisation, building castles in the air are all due to the power of imagination. Even a perfect healthy man has some imaginary disease or other due to the power of imagination. Much energy is wasted through imaginary fears.

Mind tricks and plays. It always wants to be doing something or other and when it attaches itself with objects, it cherishes, it feels amused and happy. For example, a play at cards has nothing in it, but the attachment and attention give pleasure. Having no idea that these momentary pleasures will result in misery, people take delight and repeat the same act again and again. These evil acts, in due course form as bad habits. Then it becomes very difficult to divert the mind from such evil habits which were practised from infancy.

To make a Bhasma by purifying the Haital (yellow oxide or arsenic orpiment) it takes very long time. The Harital is to be soaked in cow's urine for seven days, in lime water for ten days, and in milk for seven days. Then it is burnt out one hundred and eight times to make it into Bhasma (ash). Even so it will take a very long time to purify the mind and attain the state of Blessedness, but success in this earnest attempt is sure and certain!

Aspire fervently. Be vigilant. Be on the alert. Watch your mind always very carefully. Check the surging emotions and bubbling thoughts. Do not allow the waves of irritability, jealousy, anger, lust and hatred to rise in your mind. Do not allow the current of bad thoughts, evil notions, vicious ideas to pass through your mind.

Mind is generally attracted by brilliant light, beauty, intelligence, varied colours and pleasant sounds. Do not be deceived by these paltry things. Enquire within, "What is the Adhishthana or substratum for all these things? What is the background of all these things?" You will then find that there is one Real Essence behind these names and forms—beyond the objects of this seeming sense-universe. That Real Essence is that All-full, Ever-blissful, All-pervading Atman, immanent in all beings. Identify with that Atman, you will reach the Supreme!

Positive always overpowers negative—this is the natural law. When the sun rises the fog vanishes—this is a daily occurrence. When light is lighted in a dark room the darkness is removed—this is a common incidence. If you substitute divine virtuous qualities, the evil qualities will disappear. If you entertain new sublime thoughts, old vicious thoughts will subside by themselves. Courage overcomes fear. Patience overcomes anger and irritability. Love overcomes hatred. Purity overcomes lust. Take this Pratipaksha Bhavana (meditating on the opposite method). At the early dawn, in the precious Brahmamuhurta meditate on a virtuous quality. Think of its various attributes, benefits and some moral stories relating to the virtue. Feel day by day that you are possessing that virtue. Gradually that virtue will be developed. The vice will be destroyed. The evil qualities will leave their hold one by one. You can check them out one by one with redoubled force at every time. The evil qualities, once you welcomed and entertained and nourished well till now from time immemorial, will all fly away. You will notice a marvellous change. Your mind will be at ease. It will be one-pointed.

You must think of your Hidden Indweller. Remember His Lilas only every moment. Discriminate between the unreal and real. Determine to do Brahma Chintana. Just as you saturate the water with salt or sugar you will have to saturate the mind with thoughts of God or Brahman, with Divine Glory, Divine Presence, with sublime and soul-stirring and awakening spiritual thoughts. Only then the one-pointed mind will be established in the Divine Consciousness always.

To control the Indriyas through introspection, to develop Vairagya for restraining the Indriyas, to give up the objects which one particular Indriya tries to grasp, to destroy the thirsting for objects and sense-enjoyments, to observe Brahmacharya, to fix your mind gradually on your Ishta Devata—is a supreme blessing. This must be your aim in your life.

To give up attending Nautch party, and hearing vulgar music, to give up attending cinemas, to give up looking at ladies with lustful look, to give up using scents, to speak truth at any cost, to live on simple Sattvic food, to fast on Ekadasi days, to talk little and observe Mouna—is a supreme blessing. This must be your daily practice.

VARIOUS METHODS OF MIND-CONTROL

The mind can be controlled by Abhyasa and Vairagya. Abhyasa is constant effort to fix the mind on God or Atman. Vairagya is dispassion or non-attachment to sensual objects.

Enquire "Who am I?" Do Vichara. Do mental Japa of Om and meditate on Atman. All thoughts will die by themselves. You will rest in Sat-Chit-Ananda Atman.

Sit alone and watch the Vrittis (thought-waves) of the mind. Be indifferent. Remain as a Sakshi (witness). Don't identify yourself with the Vrittis. The mind will then be under your control.

Destroy the fuel of desire, and the fire of thought will be extinguished. With the annihilation of Sankalpa, the reality of Brahman will shine. Cultivate divine qualities such as friendliness, mercy, gladness and indifference towards happiness, pain, virtue and vice. You will get peace of mind.

Don't think of the past. Don't plan for the future. Don't allow the mind to build images. Live in the solid present.

Do a thing which the mind does not want to do. Don't do a thing which the mind wants to do.

Don't try to fulfil your desires. Don't hope. Don't expect anything. Destroy the vicious desires through virtuous desires and destroy the virtuous desires also through one strong desire for liberation.

Practice of Pranayama destroys Rajas and Tamas, makes the mind steady and one-pointed.

Study of religious books, Tapas, charity and Satsanga with Mahatmas, Sadhus and Sannyasins overhaul worldly vicious Samskaras (latent impressions) and pave a long way in the control of mind.

Japa of any Mantra and Upasana (worship of God) destroy the impurities of the mind, makes the mind inwards, induce Vairagya, help concentration and eventually lead to control of mind and attainment of God-consciousness.

"*Kalau Kesavakirtanam.*" "In this Kali Yuga the easiest way for controlling the mind and attaining Moksha is Kirtan or singing the Name of the Lord."

Food has influence over the mind. Sattvic food (milk, fruits, etc.) calms the mind. Rajasic food (meat, alcohol, etc.) excites the mind. Take Sattvic food; have Mitahara (moderation in diet).

Destroy evil habits by establishing new good habits. Control the lower instinctive mind through the higher Sattvic mind.

Constant selfless service with Atma-Bhava is highly efficacious in purifying and controlling the mind.

Don't wrestle or struggle with the mind. Be regular in your concentration and meditation.

SADHANA FOR CONTROLLING THE TEN SENSES

Repression or suppression brings vehement reaction and the senses become formidable, turbulent and boisterous. What is wanted is sublimation of the senses through proper and good use but not repression or suppression. The senses must be thinned first through the practice of Pranayama. Vairagya (dispassion), Tyaga (renunciation), meditation, reduction of wants, control of desires help a long way in the control of the senses.

The senses are very strong and impetuous. They should be controlled gradually by intelligent methods, enquiry and discrimination. Violent Tamasic Tapas will not help much in their control. It is not a day's or month's work. It is a patient, continuous struggle. Plod on with patience and perseverance. Satsanga gives strength and helps to control them efficiently.

Above all God's grace is very necessary. Obtain this through surrender, faith and devotion.

JNANA INDRIYAS (ORGANS OF SENSATION)

Control the ears by hearing the glories, the Lilas and Kirtans of the Lord, by hearing the Anahata sounds by the practice of Yoni Mudra.

Control the sense of touch by practice of Brahmacharya, sleeping on a coarse mat and wearing coarse blanket, coarse shirt and coarse clothes.

Practise Trataka daily and control the wandering eyes. Feel that every form is the form of the Lord. Put a stamp of the picture of the Lord in every form mentally. Do Trataka on your Ishta-Devata and visualise the picture with closed eyes.

Give up those articles which the mind likes best for a week or a month. Give up salt on Sundays. Take sugarless milk. Abandon pickles, chutney. Do not ask for extra salt, or sugar for tea or milk. Take very simple, bland food. Eat three things. Fast on Ekadasi, Amavasya, Purnima, Janmashtami, Sivaratri, Vaikuntha Ekadasi and Dassera.

KARMA INDRIYAS (ORGANS OF ACTION)

Observe Mouna for two hours daily and 24 hours on Sundays. Speak measured words. Speak sweetly. Speak the Truth. You can control the organ of speech.

Serve the sick and the poor. Serve your parents. Serve the Sadhus. Practise Ahimsa or non-injury in thought, word and deed. Do Archana or offer flowers to the Lord. Put up light in the temple. Sweep the floor in the temple. Bring water for Abhisheka. Do other services in the temple. Do charity. You can control the hand.

Visit the temple. Visit the holy places of pilgrimage. Perambulate round the temple. Sit on one Asana for 2 or 3 hours. You can control the restlessness of the legs.

Practise Brahmacharya. You can control the organ of generation.

Eat moderately. Fast. You can control the anus.

SADHANA FOR DEVELOPING VAIRAGYA

I

Sensual pleasure is momentary, deceptive, illusory and imaginary. A mustard of pleasure is mixed with mountain of pain. Enjoyment cannot bring about satisfaction of a desire. On the contrary it makes the mind more restless after enjoyment through intense craving. Sensual pleasure is an enemy of Brahma-Jnana. Sensual pleasure is the cause for birth and death. The body is nothing but a mass of flesh, bones and all sorts of filth.

Place before the mind the fruits of Self-realisation or life in the Soul or Brahman or the Eternal, such as Immortality, Eternal Peace, Supreme Bliss, Infinite Knowledge.

If you remember the above points always, the mind will be weaned from the craving for sensual pleasures. Vairagya, Viveka and Mumukshutva (dispassion, discrimination from the real and the unreal, and keen longing for liberation from birth and death) will dawn. You should seriously look into the defects of the sensual life (Dosha-Drishti) and into the unreal nature of worldly life (Mithya-Drishti).

Read this once daily as soon as you get up from bed.

II

During the moments of doubt Satsanga is very helpful. Constant contact with Mahatmas will enable you to develop Vairagya. Again and again study books like Bhartrihari. Vairagya may slacken for various causes and so you will have to strengthen yourself whenever the mind wanders away. Have conversations on religious topics with realised souls and keep up the flame of Vairagya. It must be a Vairagya of a supreme kind. Discrimination under all conditions must be cultivated. When some disease which the body suffers from gets cured or when you are placed in affluent circumstances you forget everything about God or Atman. The work of Maya or the force of Avidya makes you believe that there is nothing beyond this world, makes you believe that your wealth and children can give you all the happiness that you want, makes you believe that your happiness lies in the objects of the world. Therefore, rise above the delusions of Maya by Satsanga with Mahatmas. Serve them and try to win their sympathy.

If, however, one cannot be in the company of sages,

books written by great souls will be of immense help. But the writer should be a realised soul, one who had trodden the path, had done intense Tapascharya and one who is a true Vedantin. Thus, an aspirant, who follows the great works of a Vedantin, if he is not fortunate enough to have a realised Guru to guide him, at least would have very good Samskaras to his credit, which will take him in the end to Brahma Loka and there his hunger will be appeased; he will get initiated into the mysteries of Kaivalya and he will reincarnate on earth as a Sage for the purpose of Loka Sangraha. Even if there is a veil he will be able to remove it and recognise his identity with the Supreme Self.

SADHANA FOR ELIMINATION OF EGOISM

I

Egoism is the self-arrogating principle in man. It is a Vritti or modification that arises in the mind. Patanjali Maharshi calls it by the name, Asmita. The same mind assumes the form of egoism when man begins to self-arrogate. Ahankara manifests first and then comes Mamata or attachment.

This baneful egoism generates actions, desires and pain. It is the source of all evils. It is illusory. It deludes people. Though it is nothing, it is everything for the worldly people. It associates with mineness. It is born of Avidya or ignorance. It springs from the false conceit. Vanity fosters it. It is the greatest enemy of peace. If one renounces this dire Ahankara he will be ever happy. The secret of renunciation is renunciation of egoism.

Ahankara has its seat in the mind. It is under the influence of egoism that man commits evils and wrong actions. It is deep-rooted. Anxieties and troubles proceed from egoism. It is a veritable disease. Pride, lust, anger, delusion, greed, jealousy, love and hatred are the attendants of Ahankara. Ahankara destroys the virtues and peace of mind. It spreads the snare of affection to entrap man in it. He who is free from egoism is ever happy and peaceful. Desires multiply and expand on account of egoism. Man's inveterate enemy of egoism has spread about him the enchantments of his wife, children, friends and relatives, whose spell is hard to break. There is no enemy greater than egoism.

He who neither desires, nor dislikes anything, who preserves the serenity of his mind at all times is not affected by the feeling of egoism.

There are three kinds of egoism. Of these, two kinds of egoism are beneficial and of superior nature, but the third, is of a vile kind and is to be abandoned by all. The first is the supreme and undivided ego which is eternal and which pervades throughout the world. It is the supreme Soul (Paramatman), besides which there is nothing in nature. Meditate on the formula, "*Aham Brahma Asmi*—I am the Brahman." Identify yourself with Brahman. It is Sattvic Ahankara. The knowledge which makes us perceive our own Self to be more subtle than the tail-end of paddy or to be as minute as the hundredth part of a hair and to be ever existent is the second kind of Ahankara. The two kinds of egoism are found in Jivanmuktas or liberated sages. They lead to the liberation of man. They will not cause bondage. Hence, they are of a beneficial and superior nature.

The third kind of Ahankara is the knowledge which identifies the 'I' with the body, composed of five elements, which takes the body for the Atman. This is the worst or the basest form of egoism. This is found in all worldly persons. This is the cause for growth of the poisonous tree of rebirth. Those who possess this kind of egoism can never come to their right senses. Countless persons have been deluded by this form of Ahankara. They have lost their intelligence, power of discrimination and the power of enquiry. This kind of egoism produces baneful results. People come under the influence of all the evils of life. Those who are slaves of this form of Ahankara are troubled by various desires which induce them to do wrong actions. It debases them to the state of a beast. This kind of Ahankara should be destroyed by the other two kinds of Ahankara. The more you thin out this egoism, the more you will get knowledge of Brahman or the light of the Self.

Again there are three sub-forms of Ahankara, viz., Sattvic egoism, Rajasic egoism and Tamasic egoism. Sattvic egoism will not bind a man to Samsara. It will help the aspirant to attain the final emancipation. If you try to assert "I am the servant of the Lord, He is the manifest form in me and I have been given this birth to serve the Lord, manifest in all." Even in the Jivanmukta there is a slight trace of this Sattvic egoism. He does actions through this Sattvic egoism. "I am a king, I know everything. I am very intelligent,"—this is the form of Rajasic egoism. "I am a fool, I do not know anything" and even with this notion if one is impertinent and arrogant—this is the Tamasic egoism.

The literal meaning or Vachya Artha of 'Aham' Pada is the Aham Vritti that arises in the mind, the little 'I' which identifies itself with the physical body. The indicative meaning or Lakshya Artha of 'Aham' Pada is Atman or Brahman or the infinite 'I'. Mere illusion or Maya is the cause of egoism. Knowledge is the cause of egoism. Knowledge is produced through the illusory objects such as, the body, tree, river, mountain, animals, etc. If the objects do not exist, we can neither think of, nor know anything. If there are no objects, we will have no knowledge of objects at all. Then egoism, the seed of Manas will be absorbed.

The idea of 'I' which is the nest, containing all frailties is the seed of the tree of mind. The sprout which at first germinates from the seed of Ahankara is Buddhi or intellect. From this sprout, the ramifying branches called Sankalpas take their origin. Through such a differentiation, the mind, Chitta and Buddhi are but the different names or qualities of the one Ahankara. The branches of Vasanas will naturally produce innumerable crops of Karmas, but if, with the sword of Jnana, you sever them from the heart's core, they will be destroyed. Cut the branches of the dire tree of mind and eventually destroy the tree at its root completely. Cutting the branches is only a secondary thing—the primary being the eradication of the tree at its root. If you through virtuous actions destroy the idea of 'I' at the root of the tree (mind), then it will not spring up. Atma Jnana or knowledge of the Self is the fire which destroys the conception of the Ahankara, the seed of the tree (mind).

There is another classification of egoism viz., gross (Sthula) and subtle (Sukshma). When you identify yourself with the gross physical body, it is gross egoism. When you identify yourself with the mind and the Karana Sarira (seed body), it is subtle egoism. If you destroy pride, selfishness, desires and identification with the body, the gross egoism will perish but the subtle egoism will remain. You must annihilate the subtle egoism also. Subtle egoism is more dangerous and more difficult to eradicate. "I am a rich man, I am a king, I am a Brahmin"—this is gross egoism. "I am a Yogi. I am a Jnani. I am a good Karma Yogi. I am a moral man. I am a good Sadhaka or a Sadhu"—this is subtle egoism. There is also another classification of egoism viz., Samanya Ahankara (ordinary egoism) and Visesha Ahankara (special egoism). Ordinary egoism is present in animals. Visesha egoism is present in human beings.

You say, "This body is mine." The vultures, jackals and fishes also say, "this body is mine." If you peel off the layers of the onion one by one, the onion dwindles into an airy nothing. So is the 'I'. This body, mind, Prana, senses etc., are all combinations of the five elements and Tanmatras. They are all modifications of the Prakriti only. Where is the 'I' then? 'I' is an illusory nothing, fabricated by the juggler, mind. Nothing can be said to exist, which is not produced by some cause. This body which is produced through Karmas is not itself the cause. The knowledge or consciousness that we have of it is itself illusory. Therefore Ahankara and other effects which are produced through the delusion of knowledge are also non-existent. The real 'I' is only the Sat-Chit-Ananda Brahman.

Just as the motion of the train or the boat is transferred to the tree, so also 'I' is transferred through the jugglery of the mind to the body, mind, Prana and the senses. When you say, "I am stout, I am lean," the 'I' is transferred to the senses and you identify with the senses; when you say "I am hungry, I am thirsty," the 'I' is transferred to the Prana; when you say, "I am angry, I am lustful," the 'I' is transferred to the mind. If you identify yourself with the supreme Self, all false identifications will vanish.

If you kill the commander of an army, you can very easily subdue the soldiers. Even so, if you kill this commander-egoism in the Adhyatmic battle, you can very easily subdue the soldiers viz., lust, anger, pride, jealousy, greed, delusion, hypocrisy, who fight for their master—egoism.

Try to attain Brahman by means of the first two kinds of superior egoism. If you are firmly established in that supreme immaculate state wherein even these two kinds of superior egoism are abandoned one by one, then such a state is the imperishable abode of Brahman. Do not identify the 'I' with the physical body. Identify yourself with the supreme Self or the Para Brahman.

You might have reduced or thinned out your egoism to a very great extent, but if you are still susceptible to censure and praise, know that the subtle egoism is still lurking in you.

An aspirant who treads the path of devotion destroys his egoism through self-surrender or Atma-Nivedana to the Lord. He says, "I am Thine my Lord, all is Thine, Thy Will be done." He feels he is an instrument in the hands of the Lord. He dedicates all his actions and the fruits of his actions to the Lord. He feels that there is nothing but the Lord, that everything is done by the Lord, that even an atom cannot move without Him and that all beings live, move and have their very existence in Him.

A Karma Yogin destroys his egoism through self-sacrifice. A Jnana Yogin kills his egoism through self-denial or self-abnegation, through Vichara and the practice of Neti-Neti doctrine—'I am not this body, I am not this Prana. I am not this mind or the senses', and through identification with the supreme Self by meditating on the formula, 'I am the all-pervading Self or the Brahman'.

II

Ego is a steel wall that separates man from the Lord or the Immortal Atman. It is a stinking substance that has brought down man from his highest level of divinity and made him degenerate into a being with base animal instincts and brutal impulses. It is a magical chemical manufactured in the Laboratory of Prakriti or Maya which has made him forget his original, essential, divine nature, and run after shadowy toys of mundane, perishable combination of opium, cannabis indica, alcohol, wine, brandy, gin, rum, essence of grapes, malt, whisky and something else whose composition is unknown to scientists and even to Brahma, the Creator. It is a mysterious gas which evaporates into nothing for an enquirer but appears like a granite rock for a man of indiscrimination and worldliness, which cannot be blown out even by dynamite and potent bombs.

It is highly powerful. Its ways are peculiar. Its nature is ineffable. Its mysterious working is beyond the reach of intellect. It is insidious and treacherous in its invasion and onslaught. It brings down a Yogi or a Sannyasi, who has ascended to a great height in the ladder of Yoga, to a low level in the twinkling of an eye. It assumes various forms, attacks in various ways and deludes a man.

This whole world is a play of ego. Ego, sex and world are inseparable. If you understand the nature of ego, you have understood the whole mystery of creation. Therefore scrutinise.

Study of ego is imperatively necessary. It will help you in the attainment of Eternal Bliss or the Ultimate Reality.

Ego is a modification of Prakriti or Maya. It is the self-arrogating Tattva or principle. It is an effect of Avidya. It is born of ignorance. It has got three forms, viz., Sattvic ego, Rajasic ego and Tamasic ego. Sattvic ego leads to liberation; Rajasic and Tamasic ego binds you to the wheel of births and deaths.

Its favourite abode is the mind of a rich man, a dry Pundit, big officers, ministers, scientists, doctors, atheists, rationalists, agnostics, communists, whose minds are turned away from religion and the pursuit of Truth.

You feel Aham Asmi, 'I exist.' This is Sattvic ego. Vibhishana and Tulasidas said "I will not bow my head to any other God than Sri Rama." This is Sattvic ego. A desire to know one's own self, to attain liberation, to lead a virtuous life, is born of Sattvic ego. A desire to rule others, to possess estates, to have position, power and prestige is born of Rajasic ego. Idleness, procrastination, carelessness, inertia, obstinacy, head-strong nature are born of Tamasic ego.

Ego is a Vritti or modification of the mind. First Aham Vritti manifests and then all other Vrittis cling to this Aham Vritti. From ego is born mind. Reflection of intelligence that is associated with ego is Jiva. It makes the Jiva identify himself with the physical body. Then the notion of 'I' in the body arises. This is the cause for human sufferings and miseries.

Wealth, beauty, physical strength, possession of virtues, erudition, Rajasic diet, fatten or thicken the ego. Satsanga, Japa, meditation, study of religious books, Sattvic diet and Kirtan, thin out the ego.

If the ego is directly killed by Brahma Chintana or enquiry of 'Who am I?' or Jnana Abhyasa, all its modifications will perish by themselves. They have no independent existence. Annihilation of lust, anger, etc., leads to thinning of egoism.

Through repetition of acts, lust, anger and pride are strengthened. They become deep-rooted or inveterate. You must struggle very hard with great patience and indomitable will to eradicate these evil Vrittis.

Pride or vanity is a long-standing associate of the ego. It will not leave even advanced Sannyasins and Yogins. If proper respect is not shown to them, they become offended, even though they may not exhibit violent fits of rage. What is the reason for this? This is due to wounded vanity. The ego still persists. It wants respect and honour for its secret gratification.

If you keep the servant Bhava, even when you are in a high position, vanity will not affect you. You should think also that your exalted position may change at any moment.

If a Sannyasi or a Yogi or a great man is honoured, saluted and garlanded very often by his admirers and disciples, if he occupies always a high seat, he finds it difficult to return the salutations and bend his body or sit down on the floor. After some time gradually vanity creeps in his mind unconsciously and he becomes a slave of respect and honour.

Sometimes a Rajasic man asserts and says, "I will never withdraw my remarks and statements even if I die. I will never yield. I will never talk to him first. I will never salute him first. I will never apologise. I must have the first seat." These are expressions of a man of vanity. If his vanity is wounded, he will try his level best to attack and kill those who have wounded his vanity. If a man corrects his nature and develops a little humility and adaptability, if he can bend a bit and speak sweet words, he can win the hearts of all and can become the real king of the whole world. Man suffers terribly on account of his wounded vanity. He cannot stick to his position in one place, to one superior, to one Guru. He creates troubles, fights and quarrels, loses his conveniences and other advantages and aimlessly wanders from place to place, dragging a cheerless existence. All these are due to his wounded vanity and stiff ego which is harder than steel and granite.

Maya is powerful. She deludes him. He has no time to introspect and look within to find out his defects. He is annoyed even if his defects are pointed out by his best well-wishers. He has not the strength to remove his defects, to eradicate his vanity. These defects lurk in his mind birth after birth. He repeats the same mistakes again and again and leads a miserable life. It is easy to become a M.A., Ph.D., in Universities. It is easy to deliver thrilling lectures and electrify the audience but it is difficult to remove this vanity and stiff ego which is the root-cause for human sufferings.

Ego never spares even a Yogi or a Vedanti. A woman is vain of her physical beauty and gracefulness, a king of his dominions, a Vedanti of his erudition, a Yogi of his Samadhi and Siddhis, a Brahmachari of his purity. It is only a real Bhakta who is free from the evil trait is saved from this dire enemy through the grace of the Lord.

O Man! Know clearly what this mischievous ego is. Study its nature very carefully. Sit calmly with closed eyes daily for a few minutes. Introspect and find out your defects. Be regular in your meditation. Have constant Satsanga. Remove vanity. Annihilate this ego and rest in your original Satchidananda state.

III

The workings of the ego is very mysterious. It is very difficult to detect its various ways of working. It needs a subtle and sharp intellect and keen introspection to find out its operations. If you practise introspection daily and discriminate you will be able to find out its mysterious ways of working.

Wherever there is ego, there are selfishness, likes, dislikes, arrogance, conceit, impertinence, Vasanas, Trishnas or cravings, Vrittis and Sankalpas, clinging to earthly life of hypocrisy and the idea of agency and doership. You must have a very clear understanding if you wish to annihilate this ego. Only patient and sustained efforts can give you success.

This ego likes one's own birth-place, his own province, the people of his province, his mother tongue, his own relations and friends, his own ways of eating, mode of dressing and similar things. He has his own predilections and preferences. He dislikes others' ways of eating, dressing, etc.

This ego wants to exercise power and influence over others. He wants titles, prestige, status, respect, prosperity, house, wife and children. He wants to self-aggrandise. He wishes to dominate and rule over others. If any body points out his defects, his vanity is offended. If any one praises him, he is elated. Thus the ego says, "I know everything. He does not know anything. What I say is quite correct. What he says is quite wrong. He is inferior to me. I am superior to him." He forces others to follow his ways and views. These are the general modifications of the ego.

This ego will lurk like a thief when you start introspection and self-analysis. It will elude your understanding. You must be ever alert and vigilant. If you obtain the grace of the Lord through Japa, Kirtan, prayer and devotion, you can easily kill this ego. Through Lord's grace alone your self-surrender will become perfect. When this ego melts in the cosmic ego, you will attain communion with the Lord through Self-realisation.

Try to know the ways and habits of this Ahankara. It thirsts for self-aggrandisement or self-advancement, power, possession of objects and enjoyment. Kill this Ahankara and selfishness. Be disinterested. Pin your faith to the opposite virtues, spirit of sacrifice and service as the guiding principles of life. At once you will have a rich, expanded spiritual life.

Kindle the powers of resistance. Keep up the positive ideal of active service to humanity and pure love. Generate the positive Sattvic counter current of energy to combat the downward, negative currents of Vasanas. Keep yourself in a positive state. Overcome negative thoughts by entertaining positive divine thoughts. Rise from impurity, impotence and faintness of heart. Be bold, be cheerful always. Cultivate Daivi Sampat as mercy, peace, forgiveness, tolerance, etc. Destroy Asuric Sampat as arrogance, egoism, pride, anger, lust, etc. You are bound to attain the highest bliss and knowledge of the Eternal.

Aspirants bold! take refuge in your own Self, the Immortal Soul. Be steadfast in your resolve. Tread the path of truth and righteousness. Watch your mind very carefully. Be vigilant and diligent. Discipline the turbulent Indriyas. Curb the tongue and the impure desires. You will cross the ocean of Samsara and attain immortality, perennial peace and joy.

SIX SADHANAS FOR ERADICATING JEALOUSY

There are six ways of eradicating this emotion of jealousy:

1. Rajayogic Method.
2. Vedantic Method.
3. Bhakta's Method.
4. Karma Yogin's Method.
5. Method of Vichara of Vivekins.
6. Theosophist's Method.

1. *Rajayogic Method:* A Raja Yogi destroys the Vritti by "*Yogah Chittavritti-nirodhah.*" He destroys all Sankalpas of jealousy by introspection, careful watch and meditation. He adopts another method of "Pratipaksha Bhavana" by cultivating the opposite virtues of jealousy, viz., nobility or magnanimity (Udarata). Jealousy is the result of petty-mindedness. If nobility is supplanted, jealousy will die of itself. Have a meditation

room. Sit on Padma or Siddha or Sukha Asana for half an hour in the morning. Meditate on this virtue, nobility. Think of the advantages in possessing this virtue and the disadvantages you derive from jealousy. Think of those great persons who possess this virtue, magnanimity. Imagine when you move in society that you are in actual possession of this quality. Constantly repeat the watch-words "OM Nobility" mentally during the course of the day. Keep this word-image "Nobility" before the mind's eye. Have this auto-suggestion "I am becoming better and better every day, in every way." You will doubtless develop this virtue within some months. Even if you fail, it does not matter much. *Nil desperandum.* Never despair. Go on with the above Sadhana (practice) systematically and regularly. Eventually this virtuous quality, nobility will become part and parcel of your nature. Jealousy will vanish altogether.

2. *Vedantic Method:* The Vedantin repeats the formulae "I am the All," "I am in all," "All is Self." "There is nothing but my own Self in this whole universe. I see my own Self everywhere. Who is to be jealous of whom?" he says. He tries to identify himself with an enemy, a scavenger, a thief, a drunkard, a murderer, a stone, a snake, a tiger and a scorpion (cosmic identification). Jealousy disappears by this Vedantic Sadhana.

3. *Bhakta's Method:* A Bhakta or devotee sees Narayana, Krishna, everywhere. He says: "*Sarvam Vishnumayam Jagat*"—Everything is Lord Vishnu. By this practice, jealousy dies eventually.

4. *Karma Yogin's Method:* A Karma Yogin reduces his wants and slowly controls the Indriyas. He serves all with pure, cosmic love, with Sama Bhavana (equal vision) as manifestation of the Lord. Jealousy vanishes completely in the long run by constant service.

5. *Method of Vichara of Vivekins:* If your brother is in a high prosperous position you are not jealous. If your thick friend, your chum is in affluent circumstances you don't evince jealousy. Similarly when a Vritti of jealousy arises with reference to other persons, identify yourself with that man as your best amiable friend. Immediately the Vritti of jealousy will die. By constant practice of this kind, you can slowly eradicate jealousy.

6. *Theosophist's Method:* This goes on lines of universal brotherhood. All are equal. All are children of the One

universal Father—Isvara. By constant remembrance of this brotherhood idea, you can get rid of jealousy.

The Sanskrit term for jealousy is Irshya. Matsarya and Asuya are also synonymous terms. But there is a subtle difference. Jealousy is a particular kind of emotion or Vritti that arises in a Rajasic mind wherein the victim looks upon with a grudging eye on the prosperity or success or higher virtuous qualities of others. His heart burns when another man is more prosperous or happy than himself. Hatred and anger are the modifications of jealousy. A man filled with jealousy hates another man if he is in a better position than himself. He gets grief at the sight of another's success. He tries his level best to pull him down to undermine him by various foul means, by back-biting, tale-bearing or vilification. He tries to injure him. He attempts to annihilate him. He creates dissensions, party-spirit amongst his friends. These are the external physical manifestations of a man of jealousy.

A man of Irshya thinks that he should not get any kind of sorrow or discomfort and that those whom he dislikes should be afflicted and should suffer. There can be no worst vile, vicious nature of a man than his jealousy towards others. It is filthy, ignoble and beast-like. The ignorant, deluded souls of a very narrow mind are greatly affected by this deadly cancer. One who gets agitated when another man enjoys his own status is termed as Asuya. A man of Matsarya cannot bear the sight of a man more prosperous and of better qualities than himself. This is the subtle difference between, Irshya, Asuya and Matsarya.

Jealousy is the very root of all evils. This is a great obstacle to all aspirants. It is very common among the Sadhu class also. This is one of the prominent reasons for their degeneration. Even highly educated cultured persons are affected by this. It is due to their mean-mindedness and impure, filthy heart. No one can enjoy an iota of real happiness if his mind is filled with jealousy. How can there be peace of mind when the heart burns with jealousy? It can only augment the uneasiness of the mind.

Every aspirant must be ever on alert. They should not become slaves of name and fame or physical comfort or the appeasement of his palate. If there is jealousy, he is far from God. One should rejoice in the welfare of others. He must purify his heart first through utter self-dedication for the welfare and good of others. Real renunciation is the most effective way to get rid of jealousy. Discrimination and dispassion are the surest means of eradicating jealousy. You must discriminate every moment of your life between the good and evil, between the real and unreal. Then alone you can get rid of this deadly curse. Remember well that all are the children of the same God and are reaping the fruits of their own Karmas, either good or bad. There is no use of getting jealous at others' prosperity. You can also achieve the same status, if you do good actions, if you exert your best and persevere. All faculties and efficiencies are dormant within you. Everything is there. It is only the exertion and perseverance that can expose your latent faculties. It is verily the vilest quality of a coward, timid and weak to get jealous of others.

You must destroy every form of jealousy by introspection, carefully watching the mind, discrimination and meditation. You should have to adopt the method of Pratipaksha Bhavana by cultivating the opposite virtuous qualities of jealousy, viz., nobility and magnanimity. Jealousy is the result of petty-mindedness. If nobility is supplanted, jealousy will die by itself.

SADHANA FOR ANNIHILATION OF ARROGANCE

The Sanskrit word for arrogance is "Darpa." Arrogance is undue assumption of importance. Arrogance is claiming proudly and unduly. It is a mixture of Rajasa-tamasic egoism, insolence, rudeness, overbearing nature and impertinence or impudence. It is a modification of egoism. It is Ahankara itself. It is born of ignorance. Maya keeps her Lila or play through the arrogance of the deluded souls.

A man behaves insolently with an elderly man, treats him with contempt, sneers at him and speaks disrespectful words. This is arrogance.

Another man throws a book or a notebook in front of a person in anger and utters vulgar words. This is arrogance.

Another person says to another man in anger, "Don't you know who I am? I will break your jaw. I will break your skull. I will break your teeth. I will drink your blood." This is arrogance.

Another man says, "I cannot be dictated by anybody. I have my own ways. Nobody can question me anything. I cannot dance before him. Why should I go to him? Why should I follow his instruction? Is he more learned than me? Who is he, after all? Who are you to order me? Who are you to question me?" This is arrogance.

Generally a thoughtless man who is not practising introspection and self-analysis says, "I have no arrogance at all. I am humble, gentle and kind." But when the test comes, he hopelessly and miserably fails a thousand and one times. Such is the force and strength of arrogance.

A Sadhaka is very good. He is very intelligent. He is a learned man. He delivers lectures. He meditates silently in a solitary room for hours together. And yet he is not free from arrogance. When a man goes against his sweet will or wish, when a man speaks ill of him or criticises him, when he is not respected he becomes arrogant and behaves very rudely.

Arrogance assumes various forms. One man may be arrogant on account of his great physical strength. He may say, "I will neck you out now. Get thee gone." Another man may be arrogant on account of his wealth, position and power. Another man may be arrogant on account of his secular learning. Another man may be arrogant owing to his scriptural erudition. Another man may be arrogant owing to his psychic Siddhis, moral virtues, spiritual progress, Sannyasihood, Mahantship, etc.

A man may renounce his wife, children, property, position, wealth etc. He may renounce the world and live in a cave in the Himalayas for several years, practising Yoga and yet he finds it difficult to renounce arrogance. When he becomes impulsive he is overpowered by arrogance. He does not know what he is exactly doing. He repents afterwards. Impulse is a motive force to make one arrogant.

Watch your thoughts, words and actions very carefully. Know the power of words, and use them cautiously. Respect all. Speak sweet measured words. Be kind. Cultivate patience, love, humility. Enquire. Observe Mouna, or the vow of silence. Again and again think, "This world is unreal. What will I gain by being arrogant. Think of the immense benefits of the opposite virtue, HUMILITY.

You may fail hundred times. But again stand up and strengthen your resolves, "I have failed yesterday. I will be humble, kind and patient today." Gradually your will-force will develop and you will conquer arrogance—the enemy of your peace, devotion and wisdom.

With all your care and vigilance, arrogance will hiss and raise its hood several times daily. Raise the rod of Viveka, discrimination and sword of humility and chop its head. Arrogance is a myriad-headed monster, or Asura like the Raktabeeja who fought with Devi. He will again develop more heads. Continue the battle with more vigour, force and strength. Use combined methods, prayer, meditation, enquiry, Brahmacharya, self-restraint, Japa, Kirtan, Pranayama. Take recourse to the Yoga of synthesis. He will be burnt *in toto* and reduced to ashes.

If an arrogant man remains in a cave or in the room, there is no scope for him to eradicate this Vritti. It will lurk in his mind and harass him. An aspirant must mix with persons of different mentality and temperaments and watch his thoughts, when he is ill-treated, disrespected and persecuted. If he is calm, serene and humble even under worst trying conditions, know that he has eradicated this terrible foe.

The more the learning, the more the arrogance. The bigger the position, the greater the arrogance. The more the wealth, the more the arrogance.

May you all be free from this evil trait. May you all conquer this demon through humility, patience, kindness and love, and enjoy eternal bliss and immortality.

SADHANA FOR THE SUBJUGATION OF HATRED

Adveshta Sarvabhutanam Maitrah Karuna Eva Cha
Nirmamo Nirahankarah Samaduhkhasukhah Kshamee

A Bhagavata or devotee who has attained God-realisation has no hatred to anything. He is friendly and compassionate. He is without attachment and egoism. He is balanced in pleasure and pain and forgiving.—Gita, Chap. XII-13.

Hatred can be removed by the cultivation of virtues such as friendliness, compassion, forgiveness and eradication of egoism and mineness. Positive overcomes negative.

An egoistic man is easily upset by trifling things. As his heart is filled with vanity and pride, a little disrespect or harsh word or mild rebuke or censure throws him out of his balance. He hates others on account of his wounded vanity. Hence, removal of pride and egoism will pave a long way towards eradication of hatred.

Hatred is born of egoism. Eradication of egoism which is the root-cause will itself lead to the annihilation of hatred.

If you are attached to a thing you will hate that man who tries to take away from you the thing to which you are attached. If you remove the ideas of possession and mineness and attain the state of Nirmamata, hatred will vanish.

If you are endowed with the quality of forgiveness you will excuse that man who tries to harm you or who has done you any harm, and you will entertain no hatred for anybody.

Cultivation of divine virtues like compassion, love, forgiveness, etc., will only thin out or attenuate hatred. Vision of God or God-realisation or the knowledge of the Supreme Being can completely eradicate or burn hatred.

SADHANA FOR CONTROLLING ANGER

Anger destroys all spiritual merits in a moment. It is all-consuming and all-polluting, a great enemy of peace, and a direct gateway to hell. An aspirant must control this anger if he wishes to progress in spiritual path and attain happiness. One who has controlled anger, is verily a Yogin. That is what Sri Krishna says in the Gita, "He who is able, while still here (in this world) to withstand, before the liberation from the body, the impulse born of desire and anger, is a Yogin, is a happy man" (Chap. V-23).

Develop patience to a considerable extent. People lose their temper when they become impatient. Allow the mind to dwell constantly on the opposite virtue of anger—patience. This is the Pratipaksha-Bhavana method of the Raja Yogins.

Try to control first the small ripple of irritability when it arises in the subconscious mind. Nip it in the bud. Do not allow it to assume the big form of a wave. When you are not able to control anger leave the place at once and take a walk chanting Om. Drink some cold water. Count 1, 2, 3, 4, up to 20. Repeat Om Santi, Om Santi, Om Santi. Do not argue much. Do not retort. Speak sweetly. Speak only measured words. If anyone abuses or insults, keep quiet. Identify yourself with the Atman. Atman is the same in all. It can never be hurt or insulted. Do not give vent to anger. Be regular in your Japa, meditation and Kirtan. This will give you great inner spiritual strength.

Food has a great deal to do with irritability. Take Sattvic diet: milk, fruits, curd, spinach, barley, nuts, buttermilk etc.

Prohibit carrot, onion, garlic, meat, liquor and other stimulating foodstuffs.

Observe Mouna for two hours daily and six hours on Sundays. Occasionally, observe Mouna for a whole day. This will put a check on the impulse of speech. When a man gets excited he speaks anything and everything. He has no control over the organ of speech. Therefore, austerity of speech (Mouna) is very essential to combat irritable impulses.

Prana entwines the mind like a creeper. Prana is the overcoat of the mind. Control of Prana leads to the control of the mind. Practice of Pranayama will put a break on the impulse of speech. It will give you abundant energy to check anger.

A Vedantin denies the body and the mind as illusory sheaths. He does Vichara, enquires "Who am I?" and practises "*Neti-Neti*—not this, not this": "I am not the body, nor am I the mind; *Chidananda-rupah Sivoham*—I am the blissful Siva or Atman." He identifies himself with Brahman or Atman, the Eternal. The world is unreal for him. He chants Om, sings Om, does Japa of Om, meditates on Om and derives soul-power and spiritual strength from the perennial source of Om. If you always entertain the Mithya-Drishti or Dosha-Drishti, if you look into the defects of anger and benefits of patience, you will never become angry.

The combined practice of these methods will enable you to control anger and bestow upon you spiritual strength, peace and happiness.

SADHANA FOR THE CONQUEST OF FEAR

Fear is a very great obstacle in the path of Sadhana. A timid aspirant is absolutely unfit for the spiritual path. One must risk his very life if he wishes to attain immortality. The spiritual wealth cannot be gained without self-sacrifice, self-denial or self-abnegation.

Fear is purely an imaginary non-entity. It is a common instinct in every man. Even the elements of nature, animals, insects and practically every creation on earth are subject to fear. You must conquer this worst malady of mind if you wish to succeed in either material or spiritual path. If one conquers fear, he is on the road to success. Freedom from fear can be achieved by liberation from the objects of fear. Re-educating the mind, bringing forth the power of the inner Spirit, dealing with the practical affairs, diligently putting into practice the knowledge that one possesses are all essential factors to overcome fear. It must be felt that there is no object on earth which is to be afraid of or to be feared at. You must essentially be bold, courageous and chivalrous.

Fear is generally the result of pain, injury and discomfort. There is a hereditary aspect of this instinct which accounts for its universality and its persistence. Factors of environment and training are also significant. The idea of some external superior power over one's self is the chief cause of fear. Relatively the mind adopts an entirely different attitude. Vision changes. Glaring perception fails. The mind is not balanced. There is some abnormality in thoughts and actions. Hysteric and neurasthenic convulsions are all due to one form of fear or other. Impulsion and desire to escape or flee from the dangerous situation are the immediate results.

But how to conquer fear? Whenever a child is afraid of something, you tell him that there is nothing to be feared at, thus denying the object of fear. Denial is the first step in the procedure. Subsequently you explain to the child the actual thing, the Truth. Thus you convince that it was only his fancy which created the sensation of fear in him. You just positively affirm and assert what is true. You must develop constantly the knowledge that there is nothing in the universe to cause fear. The subconscious mind which is first startled by an unusual sight, or incoherent voice should be kept assured that all such things are only false, the truth behind them being well acquainted with the normal sense and knowledge. When fear is completely removed nothing can hurt you.

Mere re-educating the mind will not strengthen the courage. Putting into practice on every occasion is quite essential. Well-developed knowledge coupled with practice alone can relieve men from fear.

Denying fear one can overcome the object of fear itself. You should not have dualism in mind. You must always develop cosmic love and universal brotherhood. When there is love and brotherhood there is no enmity. There is no superiority or inferiority of power. There is no pleasure or pain. Ultimately there is no fear. This is the preliminary stage. The final stage is the feeling of oneness of all. All are the manifest forms of Brahman. All merge in Brahman. You can develop this feeling by giving up all attachment to this perishable body and identifying yourself with the Indweller, the supreme Atman. This process entirely uproots fear and brings one into eternal peace. Fear does not emanate from one's self. It is the knowledge of the Self, the eternal Truth that totally annihilates fear.

As regards the Sadhaka of devotional temperament, he should under all circumstances lay his fullest faith in God, take refuge in Him and fully believe that He alone is his sole refuge. You must be very practical. You should first face boldly those which you are afraid of.

You should meditate upon the various statements of Truth, that are contained in the scriptures; then your eye of wisdom will open, you will be gifted with right understanding and you will know the truth. This is worship of God. This is adoration to the Lord. It is this which liberates you from all evils.

Working mentally and practising physically and at all times dwelling spiritually upon the divine thoughts, remaining in a higher stratum of mind, you not only overcome fear, but merge in the Brahman Itself.

CHAPTER ELEVEN
SADHANAS FOR VARIOUS SIDDHIS

FOUR SADHANAS FOR GOD-REALISATION

Allow the waves of love to arise constantly in your heart. Feel the warmth of Divine Love. Bask in the sunshine of Divine Love. Do not murmur when you encounter difficulties, troubles, diseases and sorrows. Cultivate serenity of mind. Educate your will. You will possess tremendous inner spiritual strength and have rapid spiritual progress.

Lead a life of intense activity. Keep always a calm mind. Mentally repeat your "Mantra." Mix with all. Serve all with the feeling that all are forms of God. See God in them.

Do not be guided and influenced by other people's opinions. March boldly and cheerfully on the path of Truth, consulting your conscience and hearing the inner, small, sweet voice of the Soul. Keep company with the Sattvic or pure and enlightened persons.

Associate the ideas of purity, infinity, eternity, immortality when you think of God. Do mental "Puja" also. If your surrender to the Divine Being is total and sincere, there is free flow of Divine Grace. Control the thoughts and desires. Watch your thoughts carefully. Do not allow any evil thought to enter the gates of the mental factory. Develop great love for God-realisation. You will attain the goal of life.

SADHANA FOR DEVELOPING WILL-POWER

Attention, power of endurance, overcoming aversion, dislikes and irritations, fortitude in suffering, Tapas (austerities such as standing on one foot, sitting in the hot sun) or Panchagni Tapas before five fires, standing in cold water in piercing winter, raising the hands above and keeping in the same position for an hour, fasting, patience, command of temper, forbearance, clemency, mental power of resistance or attack, Satyagraha, keeping up daily diary—all pave a long way in developing the will. One should patiently hear the words of others even though they are not interesting and charming. He should not fret and fume. Patient hearing develops will and wins the hearts of others. One should do actions or tasks that are interesting. This also develops the will-power. The actions that are not interesting will become interesting after some time.

Never complain against bad environments. Create your own mental world wherever you remain and wherever you go. There are some difficulties and disadvantages wherever you go. If the mind deludes you, at every moment and at every step, try to overcome the obstacles and difficulties by suitable means. Do not try to run away from bad, unfavourable environments. God had placed you there to make you grow quickly.

If you get all sorts of comforts in a place you will not grow strong. Your mind will be puzzled in a new place when you cannot get these comforts. Therefore, make the best use of all places. Never complain against surroundings and environments. Live in your own mental world. Nothing can upset your mind. You will find Raga-Dvesha even in the eternal snowy regions of the Himalayas, near Gangotri. You cannot get an ideal place and ideal surroundings in any part of the world. Kashmir is very cool, the scenery is very enchanting but Pissus (small insects like fleas) trouble you at night: you cannot sleep. Varanasi is a centre of Sanskrit learning but it is famous for hot winds in summer. Uttarakasi in the Himalayas is beautiful but you cannot get vegetables or fruits there; the cold is so very biting in winter. This world is a relative plane of good and evil. Remember this point at all times. Try to live happily in any place, under any condition. You will become strong and dynamic and unlock the Elysian regions, the spiritual realms and the immortal abode. You can get sanguine success in any undertaking. You can conquer any difficulty.

The practice of concentration is of great help to strengthen the will. You must have an intelligent understanding of the habits of the mind; how it wanders and how it operates. You must know suitable means and effective methods to control the wandering of the mind. The practice of thought-culture, the practice of concentration, the practice of memory-culture, are all allied subjects. All these are of immense help in the practice of will-culture. You cannot draw a line of demarcation to denote where the practice of concentration or memory-culture ends and the practice of will-culture begins. There is no hard and fast rule. For further particulars on the practice of concentration, please see my book "Concentration and Meditation."

Mr. Gladstone and Mr. Balfour could go to sleep the moment they went to bed through mere willing. They had such a strong will. Even Mahatma Gandhi had this practice. They could get up in the morning at any time they wanted, to the very minute. The subconscious mind was their obedient servant. It would wake them up at the very second. Everyone of you should develop this habit through will and become a Gandhi, a Gladstone or a Balfour. Generally, the vast majority of persons simply roll in their beds for hours together and do not get sound sleep even for half an hour. It is the quality of sleep and not the quantity that gives refreshment. Sound sleep for even an hour is quite sufficient to refresh the body and revitalise the mind. The moment you go to bed, simply relax the mind, give the suggestion "I will have good sleep now." Do not think of anything. Napoleon had this habit. Even when the bugle was blowing and the drums were beating on the battle-field, he would be snoring. His subconscious mind would wake him up at the very second he wanted to get up. With a cool mind Napoleon would appear like a lion on the battle-field. One should train himself to sleep in running cars, trains and when moving in aeroplanes even in a sitting posture. This practice is of immense help for busy medical practitioners, advocates and businessmen, who have to do immense work daily and a good deal of travelling. Life has become so very complex nowadays that busy people do not find time to get enough sleep. Whenever they find some leisure, even for five minutes, they should close their eyes in any place and go to sleep for a short time. This would give great rest. They can continue their further activities. This kind of practice is a blessing to busy people. Their nerves are under great tension and pressure. By relaxing them every now and then, they could refresh themselves and keep quite fit for further activities. One should be able to sleep on the platforms of Howrah or Bombay railway stations when trains are moving at all times. This is a wonderful practice that gives immense strength. Dr. Annie Besant used to write editorial columns, when moving in cars. There are some busy doctors who read newspapers, even when they are in the water closet. They keep their minds fully occupied. The practice of keeping the mind fully occupied is the best of all practices for keeping up physical and mental Brahmacharya. Those who want to become magnetic and dynamic personalities or prodigies should utilise every second to the best possible advantage and should try to grow mentally, morally and spiritually every second. Idle gossiping should be given up entirely. Every one of us should realise the value of time. The will is bound to become dynamic if one utilises his time very profitably. Application and tenacity, interest and attention, patience and perseverance, faith and self-reliance, can make a man a wonderful world-figure.

SADHANA FOR SENSE-CONTROL

I

Of all the organs the sense of touch (Tvagindriya) is the most difficult to be controlled. You always like to be in contact with soft things which are pleasant and agreeable to touch.

You do not want a coarse bedding. You want soft bedding, nice quilts, silken pillows, fine soft coverings etc. You do not want to touch hot or very cold objects. You do not want to walk bare-footed. You want a shoe to protect you from stones and thorns. You do not want to wear rough Khadi but you prefer '1901 Glasgow Mulmul' or Dacca muslin. You want soft cemented floor with cushion seat to sit on. You want a back rest also. You can not sit on bare ground or underneath a tree and carry on your work.

You do not like to eat hard bread or half boiled potatoes. You want well-boiled rice, *Malpua* or very soft butter-like *Dosai* to eat.

You do not want to live in hill stations in winter. You run away from the plains in summer. You bathe in hot water in winter and the cold waters of the Ganga in summer. You can not take cold dips in winter nor hot baths in summer.

You do not want to hear harsh words. You like sweet music. You do not want to see disarranged topsy-turvy objects. You like to see everything arranged artistically and nicely.

Pleasure is connected with touch. In fact every pleasure is connected with touch. Touch is the master-key of all senses. If you are able to effectively control the whimsical cravings of the organ of touch and exercise full power over it, you can easily become a Jitendriya. Touch is the essence of all senses. It is the pre-eminent of all organs. Therefore control the organ of touch and all its different ramifications.

The wind or Vayu is the presiding deity of the organ of touch. Propitiate wind-God and his son Hanuman. You can easily control the Tvagindriya. It is intimately connected with the mind. It is as unsteady as the wind.

II

Many aspirants fail to enter into Samadhi or Brahmic Bliss on account of restlessness of anyone of the Indriyas (senses). Control of Indriyas is an indispensable requisite for spiritual practice.

Develop Vairagya. Without Vairagya and restraint of Indriyas no meditation or Samadhi is possible. Energy will leak out if Vairagya wanes. Vairagya is non-attachment to sensual objects. It is a mental state.

Control the Indriyas. Through introspection find out which Indriya is troubling you and curb it ruthlessly. Give up the objects which the particular Indriya tries to grasp. Destroy the thirst for objects and sense-enjoyments. Then you will be established in Samadhi or Supreme Peace.

Discipline the Indriyas. Speak the truth. Talk little. Observe Mouna for two hours daily. Speak sweet, loving, soft words. Do not utter harsh words. Do not abuse anybody. This is the discipline of the tongue, the organ of speech.

Do not go to cinema. Do not look at ladies with lustful eyes. When you move in the streets look at the big toe and walk. Do not look hither and thither. This is the discipline of the eye, the organ of sight.

Do not attend dance parties and do not hear vulgar music. Give up musical entertainments. Do not hear worldly topics. This is the discipline of the ear, the organ of hearing.

Do not use scents. This is the discipline of the nose, the organ of smell.

Give up chillies, tamarind, tea, coffee, onions, sweetmeats, etc. Give up salt and sugar for a week. Live on simple food. Fast on Ekadasi days or live on milk. This is the discipline of the tongue, the organ of taste.

Observe Brahmacharya. This is the discipline of the reproductive organ.

Sleep on a hard mat. Walk bare-footed. Do not use an umbrella. This is the discipline of the skin, the organ of touch.

Fix the mind on your Ishta Devata (tutelary Deity). Bring it back again and again when it wanders and fix it on the image. This is the Sadhana for checking the wandering mind and developing concentration. By constant, regular practice, you can fix the mind steadily on God.

You may think or falsely conjecture that senses are under your control. You may be duped. All of a sudden you will become a victim or a slave to them. You must have not only control of one Indriya but also supreme control (Parama Vasyam) of all the Indriyas. *The senses may become turbulent at any time. Reaction may set in.* Beware!

SADHANA FOR CONQUEST OF RAGA-DVESHA

I

Raga is like, attraction, attachment, love. Dvesha is dislike, repulsion, hatred. Raga and Dvesha are two Vrittis that arise from the mind. They are both born of ignorance or nescience. They are products of Avidya. This mysterious Samsara is kept up by Raga-Dvesha. Raga and Dvesha are the two strong weapons of Maya. The individual soul is tied to this world by this strong rope of Raga-Dvesha.

Raga-Dvesha has four Avasthas or states, viz., Udaravastha or expanded state, Vichhinna Avastha or hidden state, Tanu Avastha or attenuated state and Dagdha Avastha or burnt up state. The Udaravastha and Vichhinna Avastha are present in worldly-minded persons. Raga-Dvesha has its full vigour and virility in the expanded state in worldly persons. It does great harm. It overwhelms the person completely. Man becomes a mere victim or prey to Raga-Dvesha. He has not the least control over Raga-Dvesha. In Vichhinna Avastha Raga-Dvesha is hidden. When you quarrel with your wife your affection or Raga is temporarily hidden. She smiles and laughs. Again Raga manifests. Aspirants do Sadhana. They develop Vairagya and cosmic love, gradually. In them Raga-Dvesha get thinned out. They cannot do any havoc. They may raise their head slowly when they come in contact with pleasant objects, but they are beaten down by the strong rod of Viveka or discrimination and sword of Vichara or Atmic enquiry. In a

Jivanmukta or fully developed Yogi, Raga and Dvesha are burnt *in toto* through knowledge or Samadhi.

Go anywhere in the world, you will find Raga-Dvesha. Even on Mount Everest or Gangotri, Himalayas there will be Raga-Dvesha, because man carries his Vasanas with him wherever he goes. Human nature is the same in all places. But, if you want to evolve in the spiritual path, you will have to ignore these and create your atmosphere around you.

There is intimate connection between Raga-Dvesha, Vasanas and Gunas. Raga and Dvesha themselves are impure Vasanas that emanate from the bed of Samskaras of Rajo-Guna and Tamo-Guna. Vasanas, Samskaras, Gunas and Raga-Dvesha are products of Maya's jugglery. One thing will assume various forms. One thing will change its colour like a chameleon. One thing will change its form like a ghost. Raga will become a Vasana, a Vasana will become a Samskara and a Samskara will become a Guna. The play is very mysterious. It is very difficult, nay, well-nigh impossible, to detect the workings of Maya. The Lord only, the Indweller, the Inner Ruler, knows the ways of Maya—His inscrutable Sakti. If you destroy ignorance, all the links of the chain of Avidya will be broken at once, at one stroke.

The worldly man thinks of the objects of the senses and develops an attachment to these. From attachment arise desires, from desire anger, from anger delusion, from delusion confused memory, from confused memory destruction of reason, from destruction of reason he perishes. But the disciplined Self or the Sage moving among sense-objects with senses free from attraction and repulsion, mastered by the Self, attains everlasting Peace.

Wherever there is Dvesha there is anger. Anger is a long-standing associate of Dvesha. Fear is another friend of Raga. Wherever there is Raga, there is fear. Man is afraid of losing his objects of possession, as he is intensely attached to them. Wherever there is pleasure there is Raga. Wherever there is pain, there is hatred. You love your wife because you derive pleasure through her and so you are attached to her blindly. You love sweetmeats or mangoes because you derive pleasure from them and so you are attached to them. You hate a scorpion because it gives you pain.

You will find the play of the two currents, viz., Raga-Dvesha, attraction and repulsion, even among the lower creatures, elements, plants and planets. There is repulsion between Sun and Saturn, Sun and Uranus. The friendship or attraction or affinity between Sun and Mars is very strong. There is strong sympathy between Saturn and Venus. Venus and Saturn are inimical towards their master Sun.

Like attracts like. A songster joins with other songsters. A poet joins with other poets. A doctor with other doctors, a rogue with other rogues, a statesman with other statesmen, a saint with other saints. Raga-Dvesha is real Karma. Trees, rivers and other objects do not constitute the world. Raga-Dvesha is the real world. There is no world for that sage who has neither Raga nor Dvesha. The mind runs into the same grooves cut by Raga-Dvesha. As soon as you get up from bed, the Raga-Dvesha begins to play. You take tea, put on your suit and hat and begin to do the same actions of eating, etc., again and again. You are a mere toy in the hands of Raga-Dvesha. But those who do self-analysis, introspection and meditation, go above Raga-Dvesha and attain eternal bliss and immortality. Through Raga you love a man or woman, you favour some; through Dvesha you hate a man or woman and injure others. Now the Samsara has started. Through Raga-Dvesha you do virtuous and vicious actions. You reap a harvest of pleasure for good actions and pain for wicked deeds. You are caught up in the wheel of births and deaths. The six-spoked wheel of Raga-Dvesha, virtue and vice, pleasure and pain is revolving from eternity. A Yogi or a sage or a Bhagavata only stops this wheel through meditation and worship.

The tree of Raga-Dvesha is deep-rooted. It ramifies in all directions. It branches out on all sides. The mind clings tenaciously to objects. Mark how a monkey is attached to its baby. It carries a dead body even for a month. If you go near a baby monkey all the monkeys attack you violently. Repetition of acts intensify Raga and Dvesha. If you have Raga for some one, all your family members like him. If you dislike the same for some reason or other, all family members dislike a man without any cause or reason whatsoever. There is hatred among family members, among clans, among nations, among people of different schools of philosophy. You may be attached to a man or a woman, a cat or a dog, a stick or a cloth, a house or a town.

Raga-Dvesha, affection and aversion for the objects of the senses abide in the senses. They are obstructions in the path of truth or spirituality. Do not come under the domination of these two. Crush them or powder them through the method of Pratipaksha Bhavana of Raja Yogins. Develop the opposite virtues, viz., Vairagya and cosmic love. Vairagya will crush Raga; cosmic love will crush Dvesha. If you have inner spiritual strength and strong will, extract them altogether through knowledge of Brahman just as you extract the tooth with the forceps.

Egoism or Ahankara is the commander. Raga-Dvesha, pride, anger, hypocrisy are his constant attendants or soldiers. If you kill egoism, the commander, the soldiers will at once make ungrudging, unconditional surrender.

From Avidya is born Aviveka or non-discrimination; from Aviveka is born egoism; from egoism Raga-Dvesha; from Raga-Dvesha, Kama; from Kama, body; from body, pain and death. If you destroy Avidya, the root-cause of Samsara and all evils through knowledge of Atman, then egoism and Raga-Dvesha will die by themselves. Reduction or thinning of egoism will only thin out or attenuate Raga-Dvesha. The Atmic bomb or knowledge of Brahman will destroy Avidya and Raga-Dvesha to the very root.

May you all be free from the clutches of Raga-Dvesha, your real foes on this earth, your real enemies of peace, devotion and knowledge. May you all annihilate these enemies through the sword of knowledge. May you all shine as Jivanmuktas or liberated sages in this very life itself.

II

Raga-Dvesha (likes and dislikes) only constitutes this Samsara or this world of phenomena. It can be totally destroyed by the knowledge of Brahman.

Raga-Dvesha is a Vasana. It has four states. Raga-Dvesha, Vasanas, Samskaras and Gunas are intertwined. They co-exist. The seat of Raga-Dvesha is the mind and the senses. Destruction of one will lead to the destruction of others. But the destruction of the source, Avidya or Ajnana, the seed of Samsara through Brahma-Jnana will destroy everything to the very root.

The cultivation of virtues like Maitri (friendship), Karuna (mercy), Mudita (complacency) and Upeksha (indifference) can only thin out or attenuate Raga-Dvesha. This is the Pratipaksha-Bhavana method or cultivation of the opposite positive qualities of the Raja Yogins.

Destruction of Avidya will lead to the destruction of Raga-Dvesha. Raga and Dvesha are the modifications or the effects of Avidya or ignorance.

The fire of devotion also can burn Raga-Dvesha *in toto*. The practice of Nishkamya Karma Yoga or disinterested selfless service can thin out Raga-Dvesha to a very great extent.

Kill Raga (attachment) by the sword of Vairagya (non-attachment or dispassion or indifference to sensual objects) and Dvesha by developing cosmic love.

Raga-Dvesha assumes various forms. You like certain foods and dislike certain other foods. You like certain clothing and dislike certain other clothing. You like certain sounds and dislike certain other sounds. You like certain colours and dislike certain other colours. You like soft things and dislike hard things. You like praise, respect, honour and dislike censure, disregard, dishonour. You like a religion, view, opinion and dislike other religions, views and opinions. You like comforts, pleasures and dislike discomforts and pains. Thus there is no peace of mind for you as the mind is ever restless and agitated. The waves of Raga-Dvesha are ever disturbing the mind. One wave of Raga-Dvesha arises in the mind and subsides after some time. Again another wave rises and so on. There is no balance of mind. There is no peace. He who has destroyed Raga-Dvesha will be ever happy, peaceful, joyful, strong and healthy. Only he who is free from Raga-Dvesha will have long life. Raga-Dvesha is the real cause for all diseases (Adhi).

Wherever there is pleasure, there is Raga, wherever there is pain there is Dvesha. Man wants to remain in close contact with those objects which give him pleasure. He shuns those objects which give him pain.

Though the objects that give pain are far away from you, the memory of the objects will give you pain. It is the removal of the Dvesha currents only that will give you happiness. It is the Vritti or thought-wave that gives pain, but not the objects. Hence try to destroy the Dvesha currents by developing cosmic love and Brahmabhavana or Isvarabhavana in all objects.

Then the whole world will appear to you as the Lord in manifestation. The world or the worldly objects are neither good nor bad, but it is your lower, instinctive mind that makes them good or bad. Remember this point well, always. Do not find fault with the world or objects. Find fault with your own mind.

Destruction of Raga-Dvesha means destruction of ignorance or mind and the idea of the world.

No meditation, no peace, no Samadhi is possible in a man who has not removed those currents, true foes of peace, knowledge and devotion. He who says "I enter into deep meditation. I have attained Self-realisation and Samadhi. I can help you to enter into Samadhi" is a confirmed hypocrite. If you find in him Raga-Dvesha, attachment, hatred, prejudice, intolerance, anger, irritability, know him to be a Mithyachari. Shun his company. Remain at a respectable distance from him, because you will also catch the infection or contagion. Beware! Beware! Be cautious, friends!

SADHANA FOR FREEDOM FROM ACCIDENTS

MAHA-MRITYUNJAYA MANTRA

॥ महामृत्युञ्जयमन्त्रः ॥

ॐ त्र्यंबकं यजामहे सुगन्धिं पुष्टिवर्धनम् ।
उर्वारुकमिव बन्धनान्मृत्योर्मुक्षीय माऽमृतात् ॥

*Om Tryambakam Yajamahe Sugandhim Pushtivardhanam;
Urvarukamiva Bandhanaat Mrityormuksheeya Maamritaat.*

MEANING

We worship the three-eyed One (Lord Siva) who is fragrant and who nourishes well all beings; may He liberate us from death for the sake of Immortality even as the cucumber is severed from its bondage (to the creeper).

BENEFITS

1. This Maha-Mrityunjaya Mantra is a life-giving Mantra. In these days, when life is very complex and accidents are an everyday affair, this Mantra wards off deaths by snake-bite, lightning, motor-accidents, fire-accidents, cycle-accidents, water-accidents, air-accidents and accidents of all descriptions.

Besides, it has a great curative effect. Again, diseases pronounced incurable by doctors are cured by this Mantra, when chanted with sincerity, faith and devotion. It is a weapon against diseases. It is a Mantra to conquer death.

2. It is also a Moksha Mantra. It is Lord Siva's Mantra. It bestows long life (Deergha Ayush), peace (Santi), wealth (Aisvarya), prosperity (Pushti), satisfaction (Tushti) and Immortality (Moksha).

3. On your birthday, repeat one lakh of this Mantra or at least 50,000; perform Havan and feed Sadhus, the poor and the sick. This will bestow on you long life, peace and prosperity.

SADHANA FOR SUCCESS, PROSPERITY AND ENLIGHTENMENT

MANTRA FOR SUCCESS

कृष्ण कृष्ण महायोगिन् भक्तानामभयंकर।
गोविन्द परमानन्द सर्वं मे वशमानय॥

Krishna Krishna Mahayogin Bhaktanam-abyayankara;
Govinda Paramananda Sarvam Me Vasamanaya.

O Krishna! O Krishna! Thou art the Yogi of Yogins. Thou bestoweth fearlessness on Thy devotees. O Govinda! Thou art the giver of Supreme Bliss. Bring everything in my favour.

MANTRA FOR PROSPERITY

आयुर्देहि धनं देहि विद्यां देहि महेश्वरि।
समस्तमखिलां देहि देहि मे परमेश्वरि॥

Ayurdehi Dhanam Dehi Vidyam Dehi Maheswari;
Samastam-akhilaam Dehi Dehi Me Parameswari.

Give me long life, give me wealth, give me knowledge, O Mahesvari—the consort of Mahesvara, Siva. O Paramesvari, give me also everything else that I desire.

MANTRA FOR ENLIGHTENMENT

ॐ भूर्भुवःस्वः॥
तत्सवितुर्वरेण्यं भर्गो देवस्य धीमहि॥
धियो यो नः प्रचोदयात्॥

SADHANAS FOR VARIOUS SIDDHIS

OM Bhur Bhuvah Svah; Tat Saviturvarenyam
Bhargo Devasya Dheemahi; Dhiyo Yo Nah Prachodayat.

Let us meditate on Isvara and His glory, who has created this universe, who is fit to be worshipped, who is the remover of all sins and ignorance. May He enlighten our intellect!

THE NINETEEN FACTORS OF SADHANA FOR PEACE

The aids to peace are: (1) Solitude. (2) Live alone; do not mix. (3) Keep 4 clothes, 1 blanket, 1 lota. (4) Eat 2 or 3 things only—Dhall-Rottie or Dhall, rice and vegetables. (5) Observe Mouna. (6) Asana Pranayama. (7) Japa and Meditation. (8) Study of the Yoga-Vasishtha, the Gita, the Upanishads, the Avadhuta Gita and the Viveka Chudamani. (9) Satsanga. (10) Santosha or Sattvic contentment. (11) Do not plan. (12) Do not hope or expect. (13) Destroy desires—Nishkama state. (14) Destroy anger—Akrodha state. (15) Destroy hatred—Nirvaira state. (16) Have equal vision—Samata state. (17) Have constant Vichara. (18) Develop strong patience. (19) Have Kshama, Titiksha, tolerance, Daya, Karuna, Udarata, benevolence, universal love.

You will find Mouna, solitude and non-mixing as great helpers in the achievement of peace. Development of virtues like Daya, Love, Karuna will remove the cruel nature of the heart. Pranayama, meditation and Vichara will check restless nature, will destroy emotions and passions. You will rest in peace. What is wanted is steady Abhyasa. You must not be hasty. Peace comes gradually, slowly, stage by stage, step by step. Wait patiently.

"Whosoever forsaketh all desires and goeth onwards free from yearnings, selfless and without egoism—he goeth to Peace."—Gita, II-71.

"The man who is full of faith obtaineth wisdom, and he also who hath mastery over his senses; and having obtained wisdom he goeth swiftly to the supreme Peace."—Gita, IV-39.

"The Yogi ever united thus with the self, with the mind controlled, goeth to Peace, to the Supreme Bliss, that abideth in Me."—Gita, VI-15.

Contentment is real wealth. Contentment is natural wealth, because it gives peace of mind. Contentment is a sentinel on the domain of Moksha. If you keep company with him, if you befriend him he will introduce you to his friends, the other three sentinels viz., Satsanga, Atma-Vichara and Santi. You can then very easily enter the illimitable kingdom of Moksha.

If you are earning one hundred rupees per month, do not compare yourself with a man who is earning five hundred rupees per month. If you compare you will get discontentment. This will disturb the peace of mind. Compare yourself with a man who is earning twenty-five only per month. Thank God for having given you this present state. There is no end for your desires. Contentment alone can calm your restless mind. There is no wealth greater than contentment. Worldly ambitions are useless. Aim high. Aim at attaining Brahman. Have this highest spiritual ambition. Worldly ambitions will land you in pain, sorrow and disappointment.

If you earn money by the sweat of your brow you can never grow rich. Wealth cannot be acquired without committing sin. It will not be of any use to you after your death. Artha (wealth) is Anartha (evil). To earn money is painful. If it decreases it is also painful. To preserve it is more painful. To lose it is still more painful. Wealth is the source for all sorts of pains.

Insure your life with God. Depend upon Him alone. All other insurance companies will fail, but this divine company will not fail. You need not pay any premium to this divine company. You will have to love God only. You will have to give Him your heart only.

This physical body comes, stays and goes. It is a combination of five elements. It is insentient. It has a beginning and an end. This pure Atman or the Self neither comes nor goes. Why do you then mourn for it? My child, thou art pure intelligence itself.

Understand the true nature of Atman or the Highest Self. He is untouched by Karmas, pains, afflictions and sins. He is one, eternal, bodiless, all-pervading, independent, unchanging, self-luminous, self-existent, self-contained.

Atman has no connection with Karma. He is not Anga of Karma. Atman is not an effect or product of modification. He is neither a thing to be attained nor a thing to be befriended. He is neither a doer nor an enjoyer. He is always the silent witness or Sakshi.

Self-realisation will remove Avidya or ignorance, the root-cause of human sufferings and produce in you the knowledge of oneness of the Self which is the means for eradicating grief, delusion, the dire malady of birth and death, the concomitants of Samsara or world's process.

Give the delusion of agency, ownership of objects and the differentiation of that or this man, 'I,' 'You' and 'He'. You will soon attain Jnana. Desires arise through non-discrimination (Aviveka). Desires will become extinct with the dawn of discrimination. Learn to discriminate between the real and the unreal. May you journey on quickly in the domain of eternal bliss of Moksha.

Stand firm on the rock of Truth or Brahman. Have a firm grip of your reality, the self-luminous, immortal Atman or Soul. Look upon the universe as your all-full form. Only when knowledge of the Self dawns in your heart, you can free yourself from rebirths and become identical with the supreme Self. Equip yourself with the four means. Hear the Srutis, reflect, meditate and realise. May you become a sage.

Within you is a vast magazine of power. Within you is the fountain of bliss. All faculties are latent in you. The inner man is the immortal soul. Thou art identical with the Supreme Self. Realise this and be free. Unfold your latent faculties through meditation. Tap the source. Dive deep within and bring out the Atmic pearl. Be bold. Be cheerful.

The performance of rituals cannot remove Avidya or ignorance which is the root-cause of Samsara; but it can purify the heart when done with Nishkama Bhava. Knowledge of Atman alone is the means of uprooting ignorance and its effects.

Knowledge of the Self can be attained only by the grace of the Guru or the spiritual preceptor. The knowledge is transmitted from the preceptor to the disciple.

The knower of Brahman becomes Brahman Itself. Having become Brahman while yet alive he is freed from the round of births and deaths. Knowledge of Brahman alone is the means of emancipation or Moksha.

The destruction of Vasanas (Vasanakshaya) produces destruction of the mind (Manonasa). When the mind is annihilated all residual impressions (Samskaras) are also destroyed. Then one attains Jivanmukti or the final release.

Great Rishis and sages of yore like Yajnavalkya, Uddalaka acquired the knowledge of the Self which is a means to secure the highest consummation through deep and intense meditation. So Self-realisation does not come by arguing or studying many books. Sit alone and peep within. Sit quietly and look within. You will attain Self-realisation.

Bhakti culminates in Jnana. Para Bhakti and Jnana are one. Bhakti begins with two and ends in one. Bhakti Yoga only is most suitable for the vast majority of persons. Cultivate this Bhakti through Japa, Kirtan, Satsanga, service of Bhaktas. There is no name greater than Ram-Nam. Take refuge in this name, obtain the grace of Rama and enjoy the eternal bliss.

Moksha is freedom from births and deaths. It is the attainment of eternal bliss. It has neither space nor time in itself; nor is there in it any state external or internal. You are bound to attain Moksha or final emancipation. Moksha is your goal. Kill this little 'I' or egoism through enquiry of 'who am I?' You will attain Moksha and shine as an emperor of this world.

SADHANA FOR SAMADHI IN SIX MONTHS

Samadhi is union with God or Brahman. If you are an Uttama Adhikari, first-class aspirant, equipped with the four means or qualifications and endowed with Teevra Vairagya and an intense longing for liberation and if you have a Brahmasrotri-Brahmanishtha, like Sri Sankara or Lord Krishna to back you up, you will realise the Self in the twinkling of an eye. Within the time taken to squeeze a flower with your fingers, you can realise the Self. Within the time taken for a grain of gram to roll when placed on the outer surface of a pot, you can have "Atma-Darshan." There is no difficulty at all. The aspirant should be like Hastamalaka or Padmapada of Sri Sankara or Arjuna of Lord Krishna. He should have intense devotion towards his Guru. Sraddha is a great qualification in the path of Jnana Yoga. It is rational faith here, while in Bhakti Yoga it is blind faith. If the ground of Antahkarana is not well-prepared, if there is no "Chitta-Suddhi" (purity of heart), even Isvara, even thousand Sankaras or Krishnas cannot do anything in this matter. Be rest assured of this. Though Ashtavakra and Raja Janaka realised within the twinkling of an eye, Arjuna had Self-realisation in the battle-field within an hour and a half.

Mukunda Rai of Maharashtra put a Badshah on Samadhi in a second, when he was on horse-back. There are so many instances. I need not relate them here.

In this Kaliyuga, you need not do much Tapas as people did in days of yore. People used to stand on one leg for several years, before. They did many austerities. This you will find in Mahabharata and other religious books. Isvara has shown His mercy on people of this age owing to the poor physique and short duration of life. By Tapas and meditation one can realise very quickly if he is earnest, sincere and vigilant in this age. When you want to catch a train at four a.m., how vigilant, cautious and nimble you are! You prepare the bundles at night. You prepare at night some sweets or eatables for the morning "chota-hazri." You adjust the alarm in the time-piece to get up at 3 a.m. So many other things you do. If you show even a tenth part of this vigilance, sincerity, dexterity in the spiritual line also, you can have Samadhi in six months. No one on earth or heaven can prevent you from getting at it.

SADHANA FOR AWAKENING KUNDALINI

Kundalini, the serpent power or mystic fire is that primordial energy or Sakti that lies dormant in the basal Muladhara Chakra. It is an electric occult or kinetic power, the great pristine force which underlies all organic and inorganic matter. Chakras are centres of spiritual energy situated in the Linga Sarira, astral body. They have corresponding centres in the Sthula Sarira, physical body also, just as Buddhi, understanding, intelligence, etc., which are really in the Linga Sarira, have corresponding centres in the brain also.

Kundalini can be awakened through concentration and control of Vrittis by Raja Yogins, through the grace of the Guru and devotion by Bhaktas, through the analytical will by the Jnana Yogins, and through Mantras by Mantra Yogins.

As soon as it is awakened, it pierces the Muladhara Chakra. It should be taken up to the Sahasrara Chakra through various Chakras. When the Kundalini is awakened, the Yogi sees mentally a huge mass of golden light, enveloping his body as if to consume him. He should not at all be afraid. The Yogi experiences different grades of Ananda and Siddhis at different Chakras. Supreme fearlessness, astral visions, mental visions, Vijnana visions, Siddhis and spiritual Ananda are the signs to denote the awakening of the Kundalini. The Sadhana for this Kundalini Yoga should be done carefully and the space in this book will not permit me to deal with this subject in detail giving the descriptions of the various Nadis and Chakras. Readers are requested to refer to my book "Kundalini Yoga."

SADHANA FOR REALISATION OF ONENESS

The realisation of oneness in all existences, manifested and unmanifested, is the goal of human life. This unity already exists. We have forgotten it through ignorance. The removal of this veil of ignorance, the idea that we are confined within the mind and the body is our chief effort in Sadhana. It logically follows that to realise unity, we must give up diversity. We must constantly keep up the idea that we are all-pervading, all-powerful, etc. There is no room here for desire because in unity there is no emotional attraction, but steady, persistent, calm, eternal bliss. Desire for liberation is terminological inexactitude. Liberation means attainment of the state of infinity. It already exists. It is our real nature. There can be no desire for a thing which is your very nature. All desires for progeny, wealth, for happiness in this world or in the next and lastly even the desire for liberation should be completely annihilated and all actions guided by pure and disinterested will towards the goal.

This Sadhana—the constant attempt to feel that you are the all—can be practised or rather ought to be practised in the midst of intense activity. That is the central teaching of the Gita. It stands to reason also. Because God is both Saguna and Nirguna, with form and without form. Let the mind and the body work. Feel that you are above them, their controlling witness. Do not identify yourself with the Adhara (Adhara means support for mind and body), even when you are employed in activity. Of course meditation in the beginning has to be resorted to. Only an exceptionally strong-willed man can dispense with it. For ordinary human beings, it is an indispensable necessity. In meditation, the Adhara is steady. So the Sadhana, the effort to feel Unity is comparatively easy. In the midst of activities, this effort is difficult. Karma Yoga is more difficult than pure Jnana Yoga. We must, however, keep up the practice at all times. That is absolutely essential; otherwise the progress is slow; because, a few hours' meditation on the idea that you are the all and identification with mind and body for a greater portion of the day do not bring about rapid or substantial advance.

It is much better to associate some word-symbol, OM with the idea. From time immemorial, this symbol has been used for expressing the idea of unity. So the best method is to repeat this word OM and meditate on its meaning at all times. But we must set apart some hours for meditation in the morning and evening.

CHAPTER TWELVE
OBSTACLES TO PROGRESS IN SADHANA

THE MIND OF THE ASPIRANT:
A PSYCHOLOGICAL STUDY

One who seriously takes to the spiritual path and begins to do systematic Sadhana finds himself face to face with certain peculiar difficulties and disappointing experiences that at first tend to dismay and discourage the beginner. These problems and obstacles are common to the generality of aspirants and therefore it is important to know about them and to have a proper understanding of the methods of overcoming them.

The first is this. The Sadhaka or an aspirant starts upon his spiritual life with certain definite self-formed ideas about Sadhana, realisation, Guru, Upadesa and the like. Such cherished conceptions unconsciously get crystallised into firmly rooted bias. But actually true spiritual life is quite different from what individual imagination fondly pictures it to be. Very many things are found to be quite at variance with his mental picture of them. Realities turn out to be not merely contrary but at times absolutely contradictory to his old ideas that he had so fondly hugged to himself. All his preconceived notions receive a rude shock. What happens? More often than not the neophyte is unable to reconcile himself to these unexpected eye-openers and usually retraces his steps to land once again into the former deluded sensual life. This is the greatest blunder he would be committing. A peerless gem is grasped in the hand and then foolishly thrown away. A priceless opportunity is lost. The mind will once again pursue with vigour the same sensual grooves. What takes place is that the aspirant does not wish to let go off the long-cherished conceptions. His ego clings to them. He has for instance a certain idea of what constitutes Sadhana. He imagines that the one whom he accepts as his Guru would prescribe such Sadhana to him as will fit in with his idea. If not dissatisfaction makes its appearance. He thinks that a Guru should behave in such and such a manner. If the latter does not, then his loyalty wanes. To surrender to the feet of the Guru and then begin to doubt or dislike his conduct is the most awful and colossal error that an aspirant can ever commit. By this he lays a knife at the very root of Sadhana and spiritual life. And again the Sadhaka enters the path with a particular estimation of his own spiritual progress and the stage he has reached. But in fact God alone really knows where exactly he stands. Yet he will act according to his previous notion. When later events prove that he is wrong then he becomes disappointed and loses all enthusiasm. All this is totally harmful. To be preyed upon by a series of disillusionments and disappointments at the very start of spiritual life is a terrible handicap. It will cripple your capacity and urge for Sadhana. You will lose heart and be disgusted with spiritual life. Sadhana should be based and backed upon keen enthusiasm and joy.

Take up the life of Sadhana with an open mind. Be free of cramping preconceived notions formed out of your own egoism. Approach things spiritual with a sincere receptive attitude, with the idea to learn. Be prepared to sanely adapt yourself to them instead of foolishly wishing them to adjust themselves to suit your own mental pattern. Else disharmony will mark the very beginning of your Sadhana life. You will fall into dejection very hard to come out from. This will colour the entire course of subsequent Sadhana and valuable years will be wasted. This is the experience of countless aspirants of today. Tyaga of pet notions and peculiar ways of thinking is quite necessary if you wish to enter and proceed on the path smoothly. Then as you proceed you yourself will understand things gradually. They will become clear to you one by one.

The second thing that invariably vexes the beginner is the miscellaneous thoughts and ideas of duty. Curiously enough it will be found that as long as you are not doing any Sadhana or thinking of pursuing the spiritual path no such ideas of duty, etc., ever bother you. Most likely you will be indifferent and even negligent towards your duties or your kith and kin. Your parents may be daily urging you to find out some job and contribute to the upkeep of the family. You will be turning a deaf ear and enjoying cinemas and restaurants. Perhaps even if you get into a job then you will begin wearing tweed suits and silk neck-ties. But you would not mind your mother and sister washing and wearing the same pair of old sarees on alternate days. For, is not the mother's maintenance the father's responsibility? The sister, well she will soon be cared for by her future husband. So you will argue. But when the question of Sadhana and spiritual life comes then the mind will begin to say you have duties towards your family. You will fail in your duty to mother, brother, sister, etc. All these ideas occur only now, when you take to the path of Sadhana. You begin to waver, hesitate and weaken. Added to this there will be the dissuasion of friends and opposition of your own people to all things spiritual. "What is all this Japa, Dhyana and the wearing of Mala etc.? Such things have got their own proper time. You may attend to them when the time comes. Do your immediate duty first." They will say. This will snuff out the little spiritual aspiration with which you start. This is a typical deception of the mind. Mind is Maya. Its function is to somehow or other prevent man from getting a glimpse of the Reality. It is that which ever seeks to veil up the Truth. You have therefore to be alert and continuously counter its moves at every step. Just when you seek to enter the Path the mind will create all these ideas of duty, responsibility, important undertaking etc., which never troubled you before. Be fully aware of this. You have different duties at different times. But to do Sadhana for Self-realisation is the most important and urgent duty that is present throughout your life right up to the last moment. You cannot afford to, nay, you should not postpone or delay it even for one single moment. *Let this idea firmly sink into your mind.* Do not waver. Start regular and systematic spiritual Sadhana from the second you read this line. Now put a bookmark in this page, close the book and sit silent, relaxed and straight with closed eyes. Think about the lofty purpose of life, how it is meant solely for spiritual Sadhana. Repeat the Lord's Name for ten minutes. You have made a good beginning now. Enter the Path, proceed undauntedly. Push on with determination and vigour. Fix your mind once for all firmly upon the ideal to be attained. You will reach the Goal in this very life.

Once you actually make up your mind and start regular Sadhana you will perhaps be assailed by a host of difficulties and problems that you did not have before. You may find yourself beset at the start with obstacles on every side. You will begin to think that it is commencing Sadhana that started all the trouble and you were better off before. Do not be dismayed. There is a reason for it. Sadhana implies imposing certain restrictions upon yourself. Up to this time you had always followed the course of the senses. You never therefore came up against any opposition from them. Now you enter upon a path that is primarily one of discipline both external and internal. This means coming into conflict with the unruly, self-willed sense-propensities. When you thus come into conflict you begin to feel their force whereas formerly they seemed to be comparatively quiescent *to all appearances*. When you are merrily cycling down the hillside everything seems to be wonderfully pleasant and smooth sailing. It is when you turn right about and try to climb upwards you begin to feel what a heart-breaking job it is. The calf and thigh muscles seem to crack under the strain. This is what happens when you take up Sadhana in right earnest. Sadhana is an up-hill task. It is a regular battling up-stream against the entire current of age-long Samsaric tendencies. It means the regaining of the height that you have lost in your unchecked downward descent into the abyss of gross worldliness. And in the beginning the neophyte is quite unused to this struggle, effort and strain. Such concerted onrush of troubles and difficulties confuses and unnerves him for a time. This is but natural. Do not be perturbed. Bear up with fortitude. These initial difficulties will soon vanish. You will gain strength day by day. If you just think about what a lot of troubles, trials and risks you ordinarily bear up with when it is a worldly matter of a little monetary gain, some business deal, an examination or a law-suit then you will readily put up with all the early difficulties you are faced with upon entering the Path bearing in mind the infinite, immeasurable and imperishable Atmic treasure you will attain ultimately. On the spiritual Path a little pain will bestow limitless gain. Success is sure to him who does a little sacrifice. Up till now the Sadhaka was moving in a petty circle, sacrificing some time and energy and getting some glittering metal, silky cloth and dainty dishes. He was merely sacrificing a portion of the finite to get another portion of the same perishable finite. Now entering upon the straight and glorious Path the Sadhaka, sacrificing the transitory finite things endeavours to obtain THAT which is Eternal and Infinite.

Enter now upon the Sadhana Marga with an open mind free of all prejudices, be fully aware of the onerous and indispensable duty of doing spiritual Sadhana and bear up calmly and cheerfully with all the initial trials and tests. You will inherit Eternal Life, Everlasting Splendour, Peace and Bliss!

SADHANA AND THE VAGARIES OF THE PRACTITIONER

The aspirant is very enthusiastic in his Sadhana in the beginning. He is full of zeal. He takes a great deal of interest. He expects to get some results or Siddhis. When he does not get these results, he gets discouraged. He loses his interest in his Abhyasa and slackens his efforts. He gives up his Sadhana completely. He loses his faith in the efficacy of the Sadhana. Sometimes the mind gets disgusted with one particular kind of Sadhana. It wants some new kind of Sadhana. Just as the mind wants some variety in food and other things, so also it wants variety in the mode of Sadhana also. It rebels against monotonous practice. The aspirant should know how to coax the mind on such occasions and to extract work from it by a little relaxation of mind. The cessation of Sadhana is a grave mistake. Spiritual practice should never be given up under any circumstance. Evil thoughts will be ever waiting to enter the gates of the mental factory. If the aspirant stops his Sadhana, his mind will be Satan's workshop. Do not expect anything. Be sincere and regular in your daily routine, Tapas and meditation. The Sadhana will take care of itself.

Mind your own daily business. The fruit will come by itself. Let me repeat here the words of Lord Krishna: "Thy business is with the action (Tapas, Sadhana and meditation) only, never with its fruits; so let not the fruits of action be thy motive, nor be thou to inaction attached." Your efforts will be crowned with sanguine success by the Lord. It takes a long time for purification of the mind and getting one-pointed mind. Be cool and patient. Continue your Sadhana regularly.

Be careful in the selection of your companions. Undesirable persons easily shake your faith and belief. Have full faith in your spiritual preceptor and the Sadhana which you are pursuing. Never allow your own convictions to be changed. Continue your Sadhana with zeal and enthusiasm. You will have quick spiritual progress and you will ascend the spiritual ladder step by step and reach the goal ultimately.

TEMPTATIONS IN SADHANA

Temptations will assail even a very advanced aspirant. When you are assailed by temptations, during meditation, your guiding Deity will form a protective circle round you. Therefore, fear not; be bold and march on heroically. If you are patient, persevering and plodding on, you will easily cross the vast void and region of darkness during meditation, and reach the radiant light through the grace of the Lord.

You will be attacked from within through the projection of dark thoughts from your subconscious mind. Dark thoughts will take various terrible hideous forms. They will frighten you. Lower astral entities will terrify you. But they will perish through the Grace of God and the power of your meditation. You will be tested whether you are free from fear, ambition and passion. Even the superior celestial forces will tempt you. Do not yield to them. Beautiful celestial damsels will appear before you. They will sing, dance and smile. They will try to seduce you. Beware!

THE DIFFICULTY OF PROGRESS IN SADHANA

The workings of Maya are very extremely subtle, so very difficult to overcome and human nature is fundamentally so Asuric and unregenerate that real spiritual development and progress in Sadhana are indeed very hard to obtain. To achieve success in any measure in the spiritual life is the most difficult and an up-hill task that truly it is Divine Grace alone that can raise the aspirant from darkness to Light. So vehement, self-assertive and rebellious is the egoistic self of man that it refuses to be changed from its vicious state to a state of virtue, goodness and saintliness. It is a great blunder to think that the mere act of renunciation is sufficient achievement in spiritual life. If renunciation makes you feel that you have at once become quite superior to the rest of mankind and has bestowed on you the right to preach and to dictate to others, then the very purpose of renunciation gets blasted. You destroy the very foundation of spiritual life by this egoistic assumption. The eradication of egoism in all its numerous aggressive forms comprises the very core of spirituality and all spiritual Sadhana.

Right from the very beginning of your spiritual life, you must understand clearly that in true humility, sincere desire to root out gradually pride, egoism and jealousy, earnest and unceasing introspection to find out one's own defects and improve oneself lies your hope of progress. Without this basis, any Sadhana becomes a delusion and waste. It makes the aspirant puffed up, more proud and egoistic. When this happens, all good advices and instructions fall flat upon him. Higher influences cease to have any effect as the aspirant becomes deliberately and obstinately non-respective to them.

Eternal vigilance should be exercised by every aspirant if he is to avoid falling into this dangerous state. Spiritual life is not a light matter. To grow in Yoga is not an easy joke. Sadhakas must take to the path sincerely. Always feel that you are just a beginner and strive diligently to acquire the primary virtues of kindness, charitability, patience, forbearance. With boldness, manliness and self-reliance, combine humility, softness of speech and behaviour and self-denial. Be ready to serve others and put up with provocation and abuse without retaliation. Remove all harshness and rudeness from your nature. Courtesy and politeness must become part of your very nature. Then alone the hardened heart gets softened and good sentiments and spiritual emotions arise in it.

Concentration, meditation and Samadhi are still far from him who has not purified himself and got rid of his evil traits. Sinning and evil has become so much a habit with man that he never feels that he is committing them even though day and night he is doing so constantly. And the greatest harm is done by the fact that even while in this unregenerate state, the aspirant becomes deluded by Maya into thinking that he has already progressed considerably in spirituality. He deceives himself with the thought that as far as he is concerned he is pretty advanced in Sadhana. He thinks he has acquired that Nirlipta (unattached) attitude where he can commit any sort of act and yet remain unaffected by it. This self-deception puts a bar to all progress. Under this grave delusion he allows himself to be unrestrained and runs wild, intolerant of criticism, resentful of the least opposition, utterly disregardful of others feelings and absolutely unamenable to advice and correction. All senses of discrimination, sane judgment and introspection vanish from him. Even the common courtesy and culture possessed by an ordinary worldly man take leave of the aspirant on account of his presumption of spiritual advancement and growth of wisdom. He becomes disposed to attack even venerable and elderly persons and spiritually superior souls.

O aspirants! Beware of these dangers in your spiritual life. Be vigilant always. Always regard yourself as a beginner just commencing Sadhana. Never underestimate the importance of Yama, Niyama, of ethical culture and Sadhana-Chatushtaya.

They are everything. Japa, Kirtan, Svadhyaya, Upasana should all be done side by side with this ethical training and character-building. Without the latter, Sadhana becomes fruitless as filling a vessel which is full of holes in the bottom. Without the eager and earnest desire to obey the Guru and improve oneself, without service, humility, sincerity, simplicity and eagerness to learn and improve oneself, Sadhana is useless like rowing a boat which is firmly anchored to the river-bed or like sowing seeds upon the rock.

Spirituality means growing into the form of the Divine Ideal. It is the transformation of your nature from the human to the Divine. You can hope to achieve perfection only when you effect this transformation. It is purification and change of heart alone that makes Dharana and Dhyana possible. To grow in Sattva, you must entirely destroy the Asuric side of your nature. Never imagine for a moment that you are anywhere near the Goal unless and until you strive with earnestness and diligence to rid yourself of evil tendencies, get established in a pure Sattvic ethical character.

Remember this point clearly. Constantly reflect upon this. Meditate upon this. Know what true spirituality is. Fully realise the importance of becoming a changed man ethically and morally, before you can claim to be a Sadhaka. Carefully avoid the dangers of self-deception by constant vigilance and introspection. Do Sadhana regularly and pray for His grace. Imagine not that you have scaled the heights of spirituality. Patiently wait for the result. When your nature is changed, purified and prepared, Grace will flow down of itself, illumination will flash by itself, in the firmament of your pure heart. Bliss and Ananda will spontaneously flow in and fill you when you have emptied yourself of all harshness, egoism, pride and passion. Perfection and Immortality will be yours. Where there is kindness, humility and purity, there spirituality springs up, saintliness shines, divinity descends and perfection manifests itself.

MAIN IMPEDIMENTS TO SADHANA

The spiritual path is thorny, rugged, precipitous, steep and slippery. But it is nothing for a man who has virtuous qualities and a Brahma Nishtha Guru to guide him.

The spiritual path is doubtless beset with various difficulties. It is the razor path. You will fall down several times. But you will have to rise up quickly and walk again with more zeal, boldness and cheerfulness. Every stumbling block will become a stepping-stone to success or ascent in the hill of spiritual knowledge.

Every aspirant will have to face various sorts of difficulties in the spiritual path. You need not be discouraged. Muster all your strength and courage and march afresh on the path with redoubled vigour and energy.

If you can give up idle talks and gossiping and idle curiosity to hear rumours and news of others and if you do not meddle with the affairs of others, you will be free from all sorts of obstacles that crop up in your way.

If worldly thoughts try to enter the mind, reject them. Have steady devotion to the spiritual path.

Know things in their proper light. Emotion is mistaken for devotion; violent jumping in the air during Sankirtan for divine ecstasy; falling down in swoon on account of exhaustion from too much jumping for Bhava Samadhi; Rajasic restlessness and motion for divine activities and Karma; a Tamasic man for a Sattvic man; movement of air in rheumatism in the back for ascent of Kundalini; Tandri and deep sleep for Samadhi; Manorajya or building castles in the air for meditation; physical nudity for Jivanmukti state. These are the obstacles in the spiritual path. A Sadhaka should discard them ruthlessly and march forward.

Depression, doubt and fear are some of the main obstacles even for an advanced student in the spiritual path. They should be removed by right enquiry and good association.

Sometimes depression will come and trouble you. The mind will revolt. The senses will pull your legs. The undercurrent of Vasanas will gush to the surface of the mind and torment you. Sensuous thoughts will agitate the mind and try to overwhelm you. Be bold. Stand adamant. Face these passing obstacles. Do not identify yourself with these obstacles. Increase your period of Japa. All these obstacles will pass away.

Doubt or uncertainty is a great obstacle in the path of Self-realisation. It bars the spiritual progress. This must be removed by good company, study of religious books, right thinking and right reasoning. It should be killed beyond resurrection by certainty of conviction and firm unshakable faith based on reasoning.

The Vasanas are very powerful. The senses and the mind are very turbulent and impetuous. Again and again the battle must be fought and won. That is the reason why the spiritual path is called the razor path. There is no difficulty for a man of strong determination and iron will even in the razor path.

Passion is lurking in you. It is the deadliest enemy of a spiritual aspirant. From passion proceed anger and other evil qualities, which destroy the spiritual wealth of an aspirant.

Leakage of energy, hidden under-current of Vasanas, lack of sense-control, slackness in Sadhana, waning of dispassion, lack of intense aspiration, irregularity in Sadhana are the various obstacles in the path of Self-realisation.

Overloading the stomach, work that produces fatigue or exhaustion, too much talking, taking heavy food at night, too much mixing with people are obstacles for a spiritual aspirant.

Give up arguing. Become silent. Do not indulge in sundry talks and miscellaneous thoughts just to ease the mind. Be serious. Think and talk of God and God alone.

Power, name, fame and wealth stiffen the ego. They strengthen the personality. Hence renounce them if you want success in spiritual path.

Desire for powers will act like puffs of air which may blow out the lamp of spirituality that is being carefully tended. Any slackness in feeding it due to carelessness or selfish desires for Siddhis will blow out the little spiritual light that the Yogi has kindled after so much struggle and will hurl the student down into the deep abyss of ignorance. Temptations are simply waiting to overwhelm the unwary student. Temptations of the astral, mental and Gandharva worlds are more powerful than the earthly temptations.

Various psychic Siddhis and other powers come to the Yogin who has controlled his senses, Prana and mind. But these are all hindrances to Self-realisation. They are stumbling blocks.

Stop the Vrittis. Still the mind. Overcome the Vrittis that rise up from the bed of impressions. Face all the obstacles boldly and come out victoriously with the crown of success, i.e., Self-realisation.

CHAPTER THIRTEEN
KARMA YOGA SADHANA

SERVICE IS ESSENTIAL

You must completely engross and saturate yourself in service. It is no use sitting in a closed room or on the bank of the Ganga and meditating for hours together. How long can you meditate? Ask yourself. Say, for half an hour or an hour at the most. Then your mind will begin to wander, innumerable thoughts will crop up, you will begin to imagine so many useless things and start building castles in the air. You will not be able to control your thoughts or concentrate on your object of meditation. What is the reason for this? Because of your bad Samskaras, because you have no serenity and the mind is always ruffled by worldly thoughts, and because you have not purified your heart by selfless service. You can purge out your bad Samskaras only through intense selfless service. Then peace and serenity will come and you will have perfect, vigorous meditation.

I have heard of so many aspirants complaining that they are not able to do sufficient Japa, meditation, etc., because they are always engaged in service. Well, I would ask them to go to some solitary place or shut themselves in a room for a day or two and just see how long they can meditate. It is impossible for a neophyte to meditate twenty four hours a day. The mind wants something to be engaged with. Have you seen any person meditating on the Ganga bank? Watch him for some time. He will perhaps be able to meditate quietly for an hour at the most, then you will see him playing with the pebbles or engaged with similar silly things. That is why I say that service is very essential in the beginning. Because the mind wants variety. You should engage it with some noble, benevolent work for the good of others. Service alone will bestow upon you everything. Through service alone you can have Realisation. Side by side you must also carry on your Japa, meditation and other preliminary Sadhanas. A synthetic practice alone can give you perfection.

Truly speaking, this is the best ground for spiritual practices to all aspirants. Because, here you have a beautiful blend of all Sadhanas, very attractive, practicable and suitable even to the most modern mind. You may say that such selfless service is not needed for the advanced class. But how many are they? Indeed, very few. It is only very highly evolved souls who can absorb themselves in meditation day and night. But what about the general class? This synthetic Sadhana alone is best suited for them.

Most of the persons renounce their hearth and home in search of peace and some serene atmosphere, and perhaps, a very few renounce for the sake of their quick spiritual evolution. They come to places like Rishikesh and Uttarkashi. But what do they find? The same world wherever they go. Why? It is because they carry their same mind along with them. The mind is saturated with all sorts of impurities. It wants society and its favourite objects. It can never remain peacefully in solitude without any work. That is why Karma Yoga is most suitable for such types of aspirants.

One ought to adjust himself with all sorts of circumstances. Suppose, you are capable of doing vigorous meditation; suppose you are a peace-loving, solitude-seeking Sadhaka and you can avoid getting stagnated in repose; then you may, of course, go to Uttarkashi or such other solitary places. But after five years when you come down to the plains, you will not be able to tolerate the secular circumstances, your mind will be very easily disturbed, you will never be able to meditate amidst noise and bustle, and you will be very easily perturbed by secular influence; in short, you will be just like a fish out of water. You will always require a cave or a solitary place for your Sadhana. Is this the result of your five years' Sadhana? Of what use then is your rigorous meditation, when you have no mastery over your mind, when you get easily upset by a few unpleasant words, when you are unable to bear insult, injury, censure and persecution? Of what use is your remaining in solitude for so long a time, when you are so easily carried away by the petty temptations of creature comfort, when you are unable to withstand the secular atmosphere? You must rigorously train your mind to remain unshaken, unperturbed and peaceful amidst distraction and dissipation. You must be able to move amicably with others and be adaptable, tolerant, sociable and serviceable. You must be able to adjust yourself with all types of people and make yourself useful to others; you should adore, serve and worship the same Lord manifest in the poor, the sick and the suffering, just as you adore and worship Him in the temple of your heart. Therein indeed lies the success of your Sadhana.

Suppose, if you go on observing Mouna for five years, afterwards you will begin to stammer, you will not be able to talk properly to others. Is this all you are to gain during your Sadhana? Be wise. Discriminate. Analyse and scrutinise your thoughts. Boldly proclaim, "I would devote my entire life in the service of others, no matter, whether I get salvation or not, that is not my concern; my duty is to serve my Lord in all, to untiringly serve the poor and the sick, to saturate my entire being in the service of others." This indeed should be the bold proclamation of every Sadhaka. You must go on hammering this to each and everyone with whom you come in contact.

If you are a real, sincere Sadhaka, you must be able to enter into Samadhi by merely once repeating "Tat Tvam Asi"—Thou art That—like the great king Janaka. Svetaketu had realised only by repeating "Tat Tvam Asi" nine times. And why not you? Your heart must melt the very moment you utter "Tat Tvam Asi." Your feeling should be intense. Otherwise, if you go on stammering "Soham", "Sivoham" and "Aham Brahma Asmi" even five thousand times, what is the use if you do not actually feel their grave, infinite significance? You would be only wasting your time.

I have seen some persons rolling beads inside their Chaddar during the night class. This Brindavan method is of no use. Obviously, he will not be able to fully concentrate his mind on Japa when the class is going on. On the other hand, he would not also follow what is being read in the class. Thus he is not benefited in any way. So many useful things are being read in the class. If he follows them, he will have so many good ideas, it will be a good food for the mind and he will be highly benefited. But he thinks that he would be doing more good by mere rolling the beads without any concentration. Then what is the use of his coming to class? Be sincere. Spiritual life is not an easy joke. Be serious, practical and earnest. Wash away the impurities of your heart through intense selfless service, colour it with unswerving, ungrudging, unconditional self-surrender to the Lord and polish it with Vichara and Viveka. Then alone you will be able to behold the Almighty Lord with all His glory in your heart.

I would suggest you a nice method, so that you can practise a beautiful blend of synthetic Sadhana even while you are at work. Vigorously work for an hour or two. Now your mind is completely saturated in work. You are unconscious of the outside world. You are fully engrossed. Now stop all your work. Close your eyes and withdraw the mind slowly. Forget all about the work. Concentrate your thoughts gradually and converge them upon your Ishta-Devata or upon some lofty, divine ideas. Be calm, peaceful and serene. Relax yourself completely. Your thoughts should gently, naturally and spontaneously dwell upon your object of meditation. After ten minutes or so come down to your normal state and start your work. You will get fresh energy, you will be revitalised and will be able to do your work wonderfully.

Another method: If you are unable to meditate due to disturbances, take your Mantra notebook and write your Ishta-Mantra for ten minutes. Concentrate your thoughts upon Likhita-Japa. Or even this if you are not inclined to do, you may read some book and dwell upon the ideas contained therein. Analyse and reflect upon the ideas. Or, repeat a few Slokas from the Gita and meditate upon their ideas, or start doing mental Japa. In this way you may utilise five to ten minutes. Then again do your work for another two hours and repeat this process simultaneously. The mind will have variety, you will be able to work more efficiently and side by side you will be also doing your Sadhana.

In the same way you can also practise meditation. You may be able to do intense meditation for half an hour and then the mind will begin to wander, you will be thinking on so many useless, and even sometimes on some evil topics. Have you carefully watched what a variety of thoughts crop up during meditation? Your attention is drifted from your Lakshya and you are not aware of it at that particular moment. Now you will begin to think on so many peculiar ideas, events and topics. Your thoughts are concentrated upon them. You must now withdraw the dissipated rays of the mind again and again and concentrate them upon your Lakshya. When you find it difficult to do this, you should stop your meditation and start doing Kirtan or hum some elevating Slokas for sometime. You may also read some books, or write your Ishta-Mantra or have a little stroll outside your room. The mind will be energised and you will be able to meditate again with intensity. You will have to repeat this method whenever you find that meditation is becoming strenuous, monotonous or tiresome.

I would suggest you another method. When you feel disgusting or monotonous while working at a stretch, take a holiday for a day or two, go to some nearby place and have complete relaxation. Take ample rest. Do not think of your work you have left behind. Take long walks in solitary places or loiter in the forest. You will be energised. Now you can join your work with a fresh mind. In this way, you will be able to turn out more solid work than working continuously at a stretch in spite of monotony and disgust. Always use your common sense. Discriminate and persevere in Sadhana.

You will find even educated persons often indulge in meaningless guffaw, giggle and such other frivolous acts. They think that they have very eloquently expressed their joy. But it is not so. It is very silly and uncourteous. By a mere sweet smile one's joy can be expressed very well. It will elevate others, soothe the distressed and give solace to the afflicted. This is courteous and mannerly. A Sadhaka must not indulge in violent laughter. He must be always gentle, polite, peaceful and serene. The real joy of intuitive experience can never be expressed by loud laughter or gusto. His serene countenance itself will radiate his inner joy and make others also experience his intuitive bliss. It is only worldly persons who indulge in such silly guffaw. As a Sadhaka you must be the embodiment of sweetness, politeness and mannerliness.

KARMA CAN BE TRANSFORMED INTO YOGA

Keep the goal of Self-realisation before you ALL THE TIME. No doubt, you are Eternal; no doubt you have eternity before you. You are deathless. You are beyond the bounds of time. It is true; but let this not slacken your efforts to realise the Self in this birth. You do not know when you will get this human birth again. You cannot realise in a subhuman or in a superhuman birth—either as an animal or as a god. In both of these series of births, the soul only enjoys or suffers according to the fruits of the Karma that he performs in his human birth. After this momentum is over, he will have to take a human birth again with another chance of realising the Self. This will enable you to realise how very important it is that we should strive our utmost to realise the Self here and now. Not a moment of this precious life is to be wasted. Every day you must introspect and find out if you are progressing. This is very, very essential. Otherwise, you are in the gravest danger of being led away from the path. INTROSPECT! Find out Maya is ever ready to delude you and lead you astray. Take care. She has ever so many forms. Pride of service, arrogance of position, conceit of achievement, attachment to accomplishments, desire for comforts, greed for power, anger at those who obstruct your seizure of power, and an innate craving to override, oppress and misbehave towards others on account of an inborn superiority-complex—these are some of the heavenly damsels that always surround you to tempt you away from your high goal. BEWARE!

You must be able to turn every act into a brick to construct a canal through which will flow freely and continuously the thought of God. The Bhava that "Work is worship" must be kept up. This will effectively counteract the allurements of Maya and nullify her temptations. Know that you are in essence the Atman, the Akarta and Abhokta. God works through you for His own inscrutable purposes. How, then can you claim any merit or suffer a demerit? The One Atman that is in you—nay, that You Are—is everywhere. Nought else is there in the entire universe. Everything is dear to you only because everything is your own Self. Who, then can be your friend; who, your foe? Who, then, can be your superior; who, your inferior? Who can cheat you; and whom can you cheat? Who can do you any harm; and how can you do any harm to others? Love! Love! Love! For everything is your own Self. Will you wantonly cut your own throat? That is what you are doing when you injure another—in thought, word or deed. Again, supposing your finger hurts your eye by mistake, will you cut it off? Similarly, you should not retaliate when your brother hurts you by mistake. You should accept whatever comes—applause and criticism, praise and condemnation, love and hatred, gain and loss—as God's kindly gifts. Take everyone who comes in contact with you as a manifestation of God Himself. Bow to everyone; prostrate even before asses. Develop humility to the maximum extent. "To become humbler than the blade of grass" should be your ideal. If you feel everybody is but a manifestation of God, you will not only tolerate, but positively love criticisms. When another man criticises you, at once think he is right—for he is God. You should analyse the ideas contained in the criticism only afterwards and arrive at a mature judgment. By this method you would very easily conquer the temptation to offer a rebuff. You will develop patience, understanding; and you will have goodwill on all sides from everyone. You should introspect in silence and solitude and analyse the points of criticism. Solitude will calm your emotions and the conclusion you arrive at will be sound. Karma Yogins should never let emotions and excitement get the better part of themselves. By following these instructions, any action—sacred or secular, even if it is service of the family—may be converted into an act of worship, leading to the most sublime goal of Self-realisation! May you all become perfect Karma Yogins!

RESULTS OF KARMA YOGA SADHANA

The practice of Karma Yoga alone leads to the Advaitic realisation of oneness. Without it there is no hope of Vedantic realisation of unity of Self. "Janaka attained perfection by action."—Gita, Chap. III, Sloka 20.

Ordinary man of the world has a very small constricted heart on account of selfishness, jealousy, prejudice, hatred and pride. Selfishness, jealousy etc., leave their deposits on the mind and act as a veil or thick crust, and so he separates himself from others.

The practice of Karma Yoga breaks the veil, removes the crust and causes expansion of heart. It purifies the heart. A Karma Yogin feels for others and serves them in a variety of ways. He shares what he has with others. He brings water from the river for the aged pilgrims, medicine for the sick persons, supplies fuel and gets vegetables from the bazaar. All these little acts of kindness render the heart soft and instil compassion in the heart. He develops various virtues like tolerance, patience, humility which are necessary for the dawn of knowledge. He experiences peculiar, indescribable joy and inner spiritual strength. The love current is strengthened in him gradually. He is also loved by others. Those who are served by him bless him and he attains longevity, through the power of their Sankalpas and blessings.

Karma Yoga is more difficult than Vedanta or Bhakti Yoga. Karma Yoga is not mere mechanical action. The Vedantic Bhava or Bhakti Bhava should be kept up during action or service.

A Karma Yoga practitioner soon obtains Virat Darshan as he is constantly serving the Virat, or the manifested Brahman.

A Karma Yogi never is in want of anything. Even when he goes to an unknown place, people give him all his bodily wants without asking. Invitations for dinner come from various quarters. A sweet, divine aroma emanates from the Karma Yogi which stirs people to serve the Karma Yogi and serve him intensely. The whole nature is ever ready to serve a Karma Yogi. All divine Aisvaryas belong to him.

The truths of the Upanishads are revealed unto him without study of the Srutis on account of purity of heart and grace of the Lord. Knowledge of the Self dawns in him without Manana (reflection) and Nididhyasana (meditation), as he becomes the chosen devotee of the Lord, for the descent of His grace:-

"This Atman cannot be obtained by study of the Vedas, nor by intelligence, nor by much hearing. He whom the Self chooses by him the self can be gained. To him this Atman reveals Its true nature."—Katha Upanishad, Ch. I, Valli II, Sloka 23.

"Children, not the wise, speak of Sankhya (knowledge) and Yoga (Yoga of action or performance of action) as distinct; he who is truly established in one obtains the fruits of both."—Gita, Chap. V, Sloka 4.

"That place which is reached by the Sankhyas (Jnanins) is reached by the Yogins (Karma Yogins). He sees, who sees Sankhya and Yoga are one."—Gita, Chap. V, Sloka 5.

There is no hope of salvation even in crores of births for the dry Vedantic student who has taken to the study of Upanishads and Brahma Sutras and practice of Vedanta without purifying his heart through the protracted practice of Karma Yoga. He is like the frog which makes much noise and disturbance in the rainy season. A frog disturbs the people only in the rainy season, but the dry Vedantic frog, the mere book-worm without purification of heart, disturbs the world throughout the year by unnecessary arguments, quarrels and useless discussions. A real Vedantin is a blessing to the world. He preaches through the language of silence or the language of the heart. He always serves with Atma-Bhava.

May you all realise the Eternal one through purity of heart attained by the practice of Karma Yoga!

CHAPTER FOURTEEN
BHAKTI YOGA SADHANA

OUTLINES OF BHAKTI YOGA SADHANA

What is Bhakti? Bhakti or devotion is supreme Love directed towards God.

There are two kinds of Bhakti: Kamya and Nishkamya.

The two kinds of Nishkamya Bhakti are: 1. Vaidhi or external Puja and Japa etc. and 2. Ragatmika or Prema (internal) due to extreme Prema or intense Love.

Four kinds of Bhaktas (Gita, VII-16): 1. Aarta (the sufferers as Draupadi and Gajendra etc.); 2. Jijnasu (the seeker as Uddhava); 3. Artharthi (he who has the desire to obtain some object. Dhruva is an example) and 4. Jnani (the Wise as Sukdeva etc.)

Five kinds of Muktis: 1. Salokya (residence in the same abode as the Lord): 2. Sameepya (to abide near God); 3. Sarupya (similarity of form with the Lord); 4. Sayujya (complete identity with the Lord) and 5. Sarishti (enjoyment of Divine Powers).

Nine modes of Bhakti (Bhagavatam: 7-5-23): 1. Sravanam (hearing of Lord's Lilas, Kathas etc.); 2. Kirtanam (musical chanting of his name and Lilas, Kathas etc.); 3. Smaranam (remembrance of the Lord); 4. Padasevanam (service of His feet and service of Guru, parents, country and humanity); 5. Archanam (offering of flowers, sacred leaves etc.); 6. Vandanam (prostrations before Lord and mental prostrations to every being); 7. Dasyam (servant and Master Bhava); 8. Sakhyam (friendship-attitude) and 9. Atma-Nivedanam (self-surrender, literally offering oneself up).

Five kinds of Bhavas: 1. Santa (peaceful, self-controlled and serene as Bhishma); 2. Dasya (servant and master Bhava, as Hanuman); 3. Sakhya (friendship as Arjuna); 4. Vatsalya (parental affection as Kausalya, Yasoda) and 5. Madhurya (wife and husband, or lover and beloved, like Gopis, Gauranga).

Six means of developing Bhakti: 1. Service of Bhagavatas, Sadhus, Sannyasins etc.; 2. Repetition of God's

Name, Japa, Smarana etc.; 3. Satsanga; 4. Hari Kirtan (Loud repetition of Lord's Name); 5. Study of religious books as the Gita, the Ramayana, the Bhagavata etc., and 6. Pilgrimage and stay in Holy Places like Brindavan, Ayodhya, Pandarpur, Chitrakuta, etc.

Eight signs of Bhakti: 1. Asrupaata (tears), 2. Pulaka (horripilation), 3. Kampana (tremor), 4. Rodana (crying or weeping), 5. Haasya (laughing), 6. Sveda (perspiration or sweating), 7. Murchha (fainting) and 8. Svarabhanga (inability to speak).

Four qualifications of a Bhakta: 1. Humble as a blade of grass, 2. Forbearance like a tree, 3. Not to desire praise or respect for himself but to praise and respect others, and 4. Always repeating Lord's Name.

Five thorns in the path of Bhakti: Pride of 1. Caste, 2. Learning, 3. Position, 4. Beauty and 5. Youth.

Two inner enemies in the path of Sadhana: 1. Lust and 2. Anger.

Ten vices that follow lust: 1. Love of hunting, 2. Gambling, 3. Sleeping in day time, 4. Slandering (abusing), 5. Company with bad women, 6. Drinking, 7. Singing love songs, 8. Dancing, 9. Music of vulgar nature and 10. Aimlessly wandering.

Eight vices that follow Anger: 1. Injustice, 2. Rashness, 3. Persecution, 4. Jealousy, 5. Captiousness (Fault-finding nature), 6. Cheating, 7. Harsh words and 8. Cruelty.

Three Eshanas: 1. Desire for wealth, 2. Desire for wife and children, and 3. Desire for name, fame and heaven etc.

Three great dangers in Bhakti: Association with 1. Women, 2. Wealth and 3. Atheists.

Requisites in Bhakti: 1. Nishkamya (without any desire for fruits), 2. Ananya (undivided love towards God only), 3. Avyabhicharini (intense love towards the chosen Deity or Ishta-Devata), 4. Akhanda (Taila Dharavat, unbroken, continuous love), 5. Sadachara Sahita (with noble qualities and character) and 6. Deeply earnest and serious i.e. real and not for show.

Seven forms of Prema: 1. Sneha (Melting of heart by love or Prema); 2. Mana (that sentiment which interferes with the enjoyment of a couple who are at heart desperately in love with each other notwithstanding their being together for enjoyment); 3. Pranaya, (love which makes the lover think himself at one with the beloved, it is the thorough unification of the one with the other); 4. Raga-Sneha (when it makes its object feel happiness even when put to misery for the sake of the beloved one is called Raga); 5. Anuraga (Raga, when it discovers ever new sweetness in the beloved one is Anuraga-Raga); 6. Bhava (Bhava is the name of that emotional state the essence of which is likened unto the rays of the rising sun, i.e. it ushers in Prema just as the rays usher in the rising sun. It melts the heart by unquenchable desire for attainment of Sri Krishna); and 7. Maha-Bhava (the highest pitch or consummation of Bhava)

Twenty-Four Avataras: 1. Matsya Avatara brought the Vedas from the waters of Pralaya; 2. Kurma Avatara supported Mandara Mountain in the ocean churning; 3. Varaha Avatara to raise the earth from water after destroying Hiranyaksha; 4. Nrisimha from the Pillar destroyed Hiranyakasipu and gave Darshan to Prahlad; 5. Vamana Avatara put down the might of king Bali; 6. Parasurama destroyed 21 times Kshatriya Kings and gave land to Brahmins; 7. Rama destroyed Ravana; 8. Krishna destroyed Kamsa, and taught Brahma-Vidya to Arjuna and Uddhava; 9. Buddha preached Ahimsa to Asuras; 10. Kalki will appear in the end of Kaliyuga; 11. Yajna was born of Ruchi and Akuti. (The Suyama Devas were born of Yajna. He removed the fear of Triloki); 12. Kapila was born of Kardama Prajapati and Devahuti (Founder of Sankhya system of Philosophy. He taught Brahma-Vidya to his mother); 13. Dattatreya, the Avatara of Tri-Murtis (Brahma-Vishnu-Siva) born of Atri Muni and Anasuya Devi; 14. The Four Kumaras i.e. Sanaka, Sanandana, Sanatana and Sanatkumara—mental sons of Brahma always about six years of age—Brahma-Vidya Gurus; 15. Nara-Narayana were born of Dharma and Murti and did Tapas in Badrikashrama; 16. Sri Hari gave Darshan to Dhruva (son of Uttanapada and Suneeti); 17. Prithu took out riches and eatables from earth; 18. Rishabha, (Paramahamsa) a great Brahma-varishta born of Nabhi and Sudevi, or Meru Devi; 19. Hayagreeva (the horse-headed Avatara) appeared in Vedic Yajna and promulgated the Vedas; 20. Hari saved Gajendra from Makara; 21. Hamsa narrated Bhakti Yoga, Jnana and Bhagavata Purana to Rishi Narada; 22. The Presiding Deity of each Manvantara; 23. Dhanvantari disseminated the science of Medicine (Ayurveda); and 24. Vyasa who compiled and edited the four Vedas and wrote eighteen Puranas.

Five forms of Vishnu: 1. Narayana, 2. Vaasudeva, 3. Sankarshana, 4. Pradyumna and 5. Aniruddha.

Two kinds of Puja: 1. External and 2. Internal (Manasika).

Four kinds of Bhava in Puja: 1. Brahma-Bhava (Paramatma and Jivatma are one); 2. Dhyana-Bhava (constant meditation with Yoga process); 3. Stuti-Bhava (Japa and Hymns of worship) and 4. Bahya-Bhava (external worship).

Sixteen limbs of Puja: 1. Asana (offering of seat to the Deity or Image); 2. Svagata (welcoming the Lord or Devata); 3. Padya (water for washing the feet); 4. Arghya (water offering made in a vessel); 5. Achamana (water for sipping); 6. Madhuparka (honey, ghee, milk and curd); 7. Snanam (water for bathing); 8. Vastra (cloth or garments); 9. Bhushana (ornaments and jewels); 10. Gandha (perfume); 11. Pushpa (flowers offering); 12. Dhupa (incense); 13. Deepa (light); 14. Naivedya (food); 15. Tambulam (betel nuts, etc.) and 16. Vandana or Namaskara (prostrations and prayers).

Four kinds of sound: 1. Para (manifestation in Prana); 2. Pasyanti (manifestation in mind); 3. Madhyama (manifestation in Indriyas) and 4. Vaikhari (manifestation in articulate expression). The first three remain deep and unfathomable like an ocean.

Three kinds of Japa: 1. Vaikhari (by tongue with audible sound); 2. Upamsu (by tongue without sound—semi-verbal) and 3. Manasic (by mind—internal).

Three kinds of Kirtan: 1. Ekanta (alone); 2. Sankirtan (many persons together) and 3. Akhanda-Kirtan (continuous without break).

Ten offences against Divine Name: 1. Vilification of saints and devotees; 2. Differentiation among Divine Names; 3. Irreverence towards preceptor; 4. Speaking slightly of scriptures; 5. Treating the Glory of Name as nothing but exaggerated praise; 6. Commission of sins under the cover of Name; 7. Ranking the Name with other virtues, and practising fasting, charity, sacrifices etc., without Name; 8. Recommending practice of Name to irreverent and ungodly persons who are not prepared to hear such advice; 9. Want of love for Name, even after hearing its Glory and 10. Emphasis on 'I' and 'mine,' attachment to objects of enjoyment.

Five acts of Isvara: 1. Creation, 2. Preservation, 3. Destruction, 4. Veiling and 5. Showering of Grace.

Six qualities of Bhagavan: 1. Aisvarya (Divine powers); 2. Dharma (righteousness); 3. Sri (wealth of all kinds); 4. Yasas (honour, praise, glory, etc.); 5. Jnana (knowledge) and 6. Vairagya (renunciation).

Three kinds of Karma: 1. Sanchita (accumulated actions done in innumerable previous births); 2. Prarabdha (that portion of Sanchita Karma which is to be enjoyed in this birth) and 3. Kriyamana or Agami (the action we do in this birth which will bear fruit in this or next birth).

Five kinds of Kriyamana or Agami Karmas: 1. Nitya (of obligatory nature); 2. Naimittika (incidental on certain occasions); 3. Kamya (proceeding from desire for wealth, wife, son, etc., or removal of illness); 4. Nishiddha (prohibited as stealing, untruth, eating meat and drinking etc.) and 5. Prayaschitta (expiatory or done for removal of sins etc.)

Nine stages in Bhakti: 1. Satsanga, Svadhyaya (study of devotional books); 2. Admiration; 3. Sraddha (faith in God); 4. Devotion (Sadhana, Bhakti or Japa, Kirtan, Smaran etc.); 5. Nishtha (Devoutness); 6. Ruchi (taste for hearing and chanting the names and glories of the Lord); 7. Rati (intense attachment); 8. Sthayee Bhava (steadiness or permanent Bhava of Bhakti Rasa) and 9. Maha Bhava—Premamaya (In this stage the devotee is dead to the world and its attractions. He becomes a Jivanmukta).

Four kinds of Purushartha are: 1. Dharma (fulfilment of Dharmic duties); 2. Artha (attaining wealth etc.); 3. Kama (satisfaction of desires) and 4. Moksha (liberation from birth and death).

A FEW FACETS OF BHAKTI YOGA SADHANA

1. Bhakti is the slender silken thread of Prem or Love that binds the heart of a devotee to the Lotus Feet of the Lord. Bhakti is intense devotion and supreme attachment to God. It is the spontaneous outpouring of love towards God. It is pure, unselfish, Divine Love or Suddha Prem. Bhakti is the sacred, higher emotion of sublime sentiments that unites the devotee with the Lord. It has to be experienced by the Bhaktas.

2. Human love is hollow. It is mere animal attraction. It is passion. It is carnal love. It is selfish love. It is ever changing. It is all hypocrisy and mere show. The wife does not care for her husband when he is in the role of unemployment. She frowns at

him. The husband dislikes his wife when she loses her beauty on account of some chronic disease. You can find real, lasting love in God alone. His love knows no change.

3. Bhakti is the basis of all religious life. Bhakti destroys Vasanas and egoism. A life without Bhakti, faith, love and devotion is a dreary waste. Bhakti softens the heart and removes jealousy, hatred, lust, anger, egoism, pride and arrogance. It infuses Joy, Divine Ecstasy, Bliss, Peace and Knowledge. All cares, worries, anxieties, fears, mental torments and tribulations entirely vanish. The devotee is freed from the Samsaric wheel of births and deaths. He attains the Immortal Abode of everlasting Peace, Bliss and Knowledge.

4. Sakamya Bhakti is one where the Bhakta worships God for getting riches, son or for removal of sufferings from diseases. Vyabhicharini Bhakti is one in which the devotee worships or loves God for some time and then his wife, children and property for some time. To love God and God alone for ever and ever is Avyabhicharini Bhakti. Prahlada in the advanced stage of devotion meditated on his own self as Lord Hari. This is Abheda Bhakti.

5. The Bhakta remains in the Loka where Lord Vishnu resides, like an inhabitant of a state. This is Salokya Mukti. In Sameepya Mukti, the Bhakta remains in close proximity with the Lord, like the attendant of a king. In Sarupya Mukti he gets the same form like that of the Lord, like the brother of a king. In Sayujya Mukti, he becomes one with the Lord, like salt and water. Thus there are four kinds of Mukti for the Bhaktas.

6. Out of love, the formless Brahman assumes the form of Lord Hari to please His devotees. God is an embodiment of mercy. The Lord runs after His devotees with food and water in His hands to the forests. He becomes a slave of His devotees. Lord Vishnu says to Prahlada: "Dear, you are too tender of age and too delicate of body to stand the terrible tortures inflicted on you by your hot-headed father. A parallel of his atrocious deeds I have never seen before. Pray, therefore, excuse me if I was late in coming to your rescue." Again Lord Krishna says: "I am not in My control. I am under the complete control of My Bhaktas. They have taken entire possession of My heart. How can I leave them when they have taken entire possession of My heart? How can I leave them when they have renounced

everything for My sake? He who seeks Me in all things and all things in Me, to Him I am never lost, nor is he lost to Me."

7. Study the Gita, the Ramayana, the Bhagavata. Have Satsanga. Visit holy places (Yatra). Do Japa. Meditate. Sing His Name. You can develop Bhakti and have His Darshan.

8. Do you really want God? Do you really thirst for His Darshan? Have you got spiritual hunger? You may deliver thrilling lectures on Bhakti. You may write several volumes on Bhakti, and yet you may not possess even a grain of true devotion. He who thirsts for Darshan of God will develop Bhakti. If there is sincere demand for God, then the supply will come. By regular steady Sadhana, may you attain Peace, Bliss, Knowledge, Perfection and God-realisation!

9. The Name of God chanted in any way, correctly or incorrectly, knowingly or unknowingly, carefully or carelessly is sure to give the desired result. The glory of the Name of God cannot be established through reasoning and intellect. It can be certainly experienced or realised through devotion, faith and constant repetition of the Name. Every Name is filled with countless potencies or Saktis. The power of the Name is ineffable. Its glory is indescribable. The efficacy and inherent Sakti of the Name of God is unfathomable.

10. Just as fire has the natural property of burning inflammable things, so also the Name of God has the power of burning sins, Samskaras and Vasanas and of bestowing eternal Bliss and everlasting Peace on those who repeat the Name of the Lord. Just as the burning quality is natural and inherent in fire, so also is the power of destroying sins with their very root and branch and of bringing the aspirant into blissful union with the Lord through Bhava Samadhi, natural and inherent in the Name of God.

11. O Man! Take refuge in the Name. Nami and Nama are inseparable. Sing the Lord's Name incessantly. Remember the Name of the Lord with every incoming and outgoing breath. In this iron age Nama Smarana or Japa is the easiest, quickest, safest and surest way to reach God and to attain Immortality and perennial Joy. Glory to the Lord. Glory to His Name. Sing Hari Om, Sri Ram, Radheyshyam or '*Hare Rama Hare Rama, Rama Rama Hare Hare; Hare Krishna Hare Krishna, Krishna Krishna Hare Hare.*'

FAITH, ASPIRATION AND SELF-SURRENDER

Faith is Sraddha. Faith is the greatest thing in the world. Even the highest rationality has faith as its background. One cannot ratiocinate on things in which he has no faith. Even the greatest philosopher has faith as his stronghold. No intellectualism can prove good if it is not supported by faith. The whole world stands on faith and is guided by faith. Religion has faith as its root. One cannot prove God if he has no faith in God. God is only a matter of faith. This faith is the outcome of previous Samskaras. Certain men are born-philosophers and certain others do not grasp the fundamentals of religion even at the age of seventy. This is all due to past Samskaras or impressions. Faith is guided by impressions of actions done in the previous births and the present faith is nearer or farther from the Truth in accordance with the advancement made in spiritual evolution.

Blind faith should be turned into rational faith. Faith without understanding is blind faith. Bhakti is the development of faith. Jnana is the development of Bhakti. Faith leads to Final Experience. Whatever a person strongly believes in, that he experiences, and that he becomes. The whole world is a product of faithful imagination. If you have no faith in the world the world does not exist. If you have no faith in sensual objects, they will not give you pleasure. If you have no faith in God, you never reach perfection. Wrong faith turns even existence into non-existence. "One who thinks that Brahman does not exist, himself becomes non-existent" says the Taittiriyopanishad. Faith is the fundamental necessity for spiritual Sadhana.

Aspiration is a development of faith. It is one step ahead of faith. The flame of faith burns as the conflagration of spiritual aspiration for Moksha. The aspirant yearns to have divine experience. It is no more mere faith but strong feeling which cannot be easily shaken by external events. The devotee longs to have union with the Beloved. He has no sleep, no rest. He always contemplates on how to attain the object of his love. He prays, sings, and gets mad of his Lord. Divine madness overtakes the devotee and he completely loses personality in the aspiration for attaining God. This is called self-surrender.

Self-surrender is the end of Bhakti Yoga. The self or the ego is surrendered or parted with for ever as an offering to the Lord. The devotee is lost in the consciousness of God. He has plunged into the ocean of bliss. He has taken a bath in the sea of nectar. He has drunk deep the essence of Immortality. He has become an Apta-Kama, for he has attained God, the root of the universe.

NINE MODES OF BHAKTI YOGA SADHANA

In the Srimad Bhagavata and the Vishnu Purana it is told that the nine forms of Bhakti are Sravana (hearing of God's Lilas and stories), Kirtana (singing of His glories), Smarana (remembrance of His Name and presence), Padasevana (service of His feet), Archana (worship of God), Vandana (prostration to the Lord), Dasya (cultivating the Bhava of a servant with God), Sakhya (cultivation of the friend-Bhava) and Atmanivedana (complete surrender of the self).

A devotee can practise any method of Bhakti which suits him best. Through that he will attain Divine illumination.

श्रवणं कीर्तनं विष्णोः स्मरणं पादसेवनम् ।
अर्चनं वन्दनं दास्यं सख्यमात्मनिवेदनम् ॥

Sravanam Kirtanam Vishnoh Smaranam Pada-sevanam;
Archanam Vandanam Dasyam Sakhyam Atma-nivedanam.

1. SRAVANA

Sravana is hearing of Lord's Lilas. Sravana includes hearing of God's virtues, glories, sports and stories connected with His divine Name and Form. The devotee gets absorbed in the hearing of divine stories and his mind merges in the thought of Divinity, it cannot think of undivine things. The mind loses, as it were, its charm for the world. The devotee remembers God only, even in dream.

Sri Sankaracharya says:

क्षणमपि सज्जनसङ्गतिरेका भवति भवार्णवतरणे नौका ।

Kshanam-api Sajjana-sangatireka
Bhavati Bhavarnava-tarane Nauka

"The company of the wise, even for a moment, becomes the boat to cross across the ocean of Samsara." Without Satsanga, Sadhana does not become perfect and strong. The fort of Sadhana should be built on the foundation of Satsanga. Mere austerities are not the end of Sadhana. Satsanga illumines the devotee and removes his impurities. It is only then that subtle truths are grasped well by the devotee. Lord Krishna says to Uddhava that nothing but Satsanga alone can put an end to all worldly attachments. In the Bhagavata Mahatmya it is told that the best Dharma in this world is to hear Lord's glories. For, thereby, one attains to the Divine Abode.

2. KIRTANA

Kirtana is singing of Lord's glories. The devotee is thrilled with Divine Emotion. He loses himself in the love of God. He gets horripilation in the body due to extreme love for God. He weeps in the middle when thinking of the glory of God. His voice becomes choked, and he flies into a state of divine Bhava. The devotee is ever engaged in Japa of the Lord's Name and describing His glories to one and all. Wherever he goes he begins to sing the praise of God. He requests all to join his Kirtana. He sings and dances in ecstasy. He makes others also dance.

Such practices should be the outcome of a pure heart, and they should not be merely a show. God knows the inner secret of all and none can cheat Him. There should be perfect straightforwardness and all his actions should be the natural outpouring from his heart. This is the easiest of all modes of approach to God. In the Kali Yuga, iron age, Kirtana alone is the best Yoga—'*Kalau Kesavakirtanam.*' This is the prescribed method of devotion for this age. The mind is ever intent upon singing Lord's Names and glories and it has no occasion to take interest in things of the world. Day and night the devotee feels the presence of God and thins out his ego. He becomes Sattvic and pure at heart.

3. SMARANA

Smarana is remembrance of the Lord at all times. This is unbroken memory of the Name and Form of the Lord. The mind does not think of any object of the world, but is ever engrossed in thinking of the glorious Lord alone. The mind meditates on what is heard about the glories of God and His virtues, Names, etc., and forgets even the body and contents itself in the remembrance of God, just as Dhruva or Prahlada did. Even Japa is only remembrance of God and comes under this category of Bhakti. Remembrance also includes hearing of stories pertaining to God at all times, talking of God, teaching to others what pertains to God, meditation on the attributes of God, etc. Remembrance has no particular time. God is to be remembered at all times, without break, so long as one has got his consciousness intact. Right up from his getting up from sleep in the morning, until he is completely overpowered by sleep in the night, a person is to remember God. He has no other duty in this world except remembrance of God. Remembrance of God alone can destroy all worldly Samskaras. Remembrance of God alone can turn away the mind from sense-objects. Generally the mind runs extrovert. But remembrance of God makes it introvert and does not allow it to run to particular objects of the world. Remembrance of God is a very difficult method of Sadhana. It is not possible to remember God at all times. The mind will cheat the person. He will think that he is meditating on God, but actually he will be dreaming of some object of the world or something connected with name and fame. Remembrance is equal to concentration or meditation. All the qualities which a Raja Yogin prescribes for the practice of meditation should be acquired by a Bhakta who wants to practise Smarana-Bhakti. Smarana is swimming against the forceful current of the river of Maya. Smarana leads to exclusive meditation on God, as is done in Raja Yoga.

4. PADASEVANA

Padasevana is serving the Lord's feet. Actually this can be done only by Lakshmi or Parvati. No mortal being has got the fortune to practise this method of Bhakti for the Lord is not visible to the physical eyes. But it is possible to serve the image of God in idols and better still, taking the whole humanity as God. This is Padasevana. Padasevana is service of the sick. Padasevana is service of the poor. Padasevana is service of the whole humanity at large. The whole universe is only Virat-Svarupa. Service of the world is service of the Lord.

Service of the Lord's feet can be done through formal worship to Murtis or idols in temples or to a mental image of God.

5. ARCHANA

Archana is worship of the Lord. "Those who perform the worship of Vishnu in this world, attain the immortal and blissful state of Moksha." Thus says the Vishnu-Rahasya. Worship can be done either through an image or a picture or even a mental form. The image should be one appealing to the mind of the worshipper.

Worship can be done either with external materials or merely through an internal Bhava or strong feeling. The latter one is an advanced form of worship which only men of purified intellect can do. Worship should be done according to the rules laid down in the Varnashrama-Dharma or in the case of advanced devotees worship can be done in any manner they like. The purpose of worship is to please the Lord, to purify the heart through surrender of the ego and love of God.

Serving the poor people and worshipping saints is also worship of the Virat-Svarupa of the Lord. The Lord appears in all forms. He is everything. The scriptures declare that the Lord alone appears as the sentient and the insentient beings. The devotee should have Narayana-Bhava or Isvara-Bhava in all beings. He should consider all creatures, down even to the worm as merely God. This is the highest form of Worship.

6. VANDANA

Vandana is prayer and prostration. Humble prostration touching the earth with the eight limbs of the body (Sashtanga-Namaskara), with faith and reverence, before a form of God, or prostration to all beings knowing them to be the forms of the One God, and getting absorbed in the Divine Love of the Lord is termed prostration to God. The Bhagavata says: "The sky, air, fire, water, earth, stars, planets, the cardinal points (directions), trees, rivers, seas and all living beings constitute the body of Sri Hari. The devotee should bow before everything in absolute devotion, thinking that he is bowing before God Himself." Lord Krishna says to Uddhava: "Giving no attention to those who laugh in ridicule, forgetting the body and insensible to shame, one should prostrate and bow down to all beings, even to the dog, the ass, the Chandala and the cow. All is Myself, and nothing is but Myself."

The ego or Ahankara is effaced out completely through devout prayer and prostration to God. The Divine Grace descends upon the devotee and man becomes God.

7. DASYA

Dasya-Bhakti is the love of God through servant-sentiment. To serve God and carry out His wishes, realising His virtues, nature, mystery and glory, considering oneself as a slave of God, the Supreme Master is Dasya-Bhakti.

Serving and worshipping the Murtis in temples, sweeping the temples, meditating on God, and mentally serving Him like a slave, serving the saints and the sages, serving the devotees of God, serving the poor and the sick people who are forms of God, is also included in Dasya-Bhakti.

To follow the words of the scriptures, to act according to the injunctions of the Vedas, considering them to be direct words of God, is Dasya-Bhakti. Association with and service of love-intoxicated devotees and service of those who have knowledge of God is Dasya-Bhakti. The purpose behind Dasya-Bhakti is to be ever with God in order to offer services to Him and win His Divine Grace and attain thereby Immortality.

8. SAKHYA

Sakhya-Bhava is cultivation of friend-sentiment with God. The inmates of the family of Nandagopa cultivated this Bhakti. Arjuna cultivated this kind of Bhakti. The Bhagavata says: "Oh, how wonderful is the fortune of the people of Vraja, of cowherd Nanda whose dear friend is the perfect, eternal Brahman of Absolute Bliss!"

To be always with the Lord, to treat Him as one's own relative or a friend, belonging to one's own family, to be in His company at all times, to love Him as one's own Self, is Sakhya-Bhava of Bhakti-Marga. The devotee of Sakhya-Bhava takes up with eagerness any work of the Lord leaving aside even the most important and urgent and pressing work, assuming an attitude of neglect towards personal work, and totally concerning himself with the love of the Lord. How do friends, real friends love in this world? What an amount of love they possess between one another? Such a love is developed towards God instead of towards man. Physical love is turned into spiritual love. There is a transformation of the mundane into the Eternal.

9. ATMA-NIVEDANA

Atma-Nivedana is self-surrender. In the Vishnu-Sahasranama it is said: "The heart of one who has taken refuge in Vasudeva, who is wholly devoted to Vasudeva, gets entirely purified, and he attains Brahman, the Eternal."

The devotee offers everything to God, including his body, mind and soul. He keeps nothing for himself. He loses even his own self. He has no personal and independent existence. He has given his self for God. He has become part and parcel of God. God takes care of him and God treats him as Himself. Grief and sorrow, pleasure and pain, the devotee treats as gifts sent by God and does not attach himself to them. He considers himself as a puppet of God and an instrument in the hands of God. He does not feel egoistic, for he has no ego. His ego has gone over to God. It is not his duty to take care of his wife, children, etc., for he himself has no independent existence apart from God. God will take care of all. He knows how to lead the world in the right path. One need not think that he is born to lead the world. God is there who will look to everything which man cannot even dream of. He has no sensual craving, for he has no body as it is offered to God. He does not adore or love his body for it is God's business to see to it. He only feels the presence of God and nothing else. He is fearless, for God is helping him at all times. He has no enemy for he has given himself up to God who has no enemies or friends. He has no anxiety for he has attained everything by attaining the grace of God. He has not even the thought of salvation; rather he does not want salvation even; he merely wants God and nothing but God. He is satisfied with the love of God for by that there is nothing that is not attained. What is there to be attained, when God has sent His grace upon the devotee? The devotee does not want to become sugar but taste sugar. There is pleasure in tasting sugar, but not in becoming sugar itself. So the devotee feels that there is supreme joy more in loving God than becoming God. God shall take complete care of the devotee. "I am Thine," says the devotee.

ESSENTIALS IN BHAKTI YOGA SADHANA

There are different types of mind. People have different tastes, tendencies, temperaments, inclinations and capacities for Sadhana. So various paths are necessary although the goal to be reached, i.e., Self-realisation is always the same. The path of Bhakti Yoga is open to all and is the easiest path for God-realisation in this Iron Age. Anybody can become a devotee. No distinction of caste, colour or sex finds a place in the realm of Bhakti. Devotion has nothing to do with age, caste, position or rank in life. The desire for liberation alone makes one a fit person for developing devotion and taking up the path of Bhakti Yoga. Merits acquired in the previous births generate devotion in the heart of a man in the following birth. Liberation comes to him who is devoted to the Lord.

Bhakti is supreme devotion and intense attachment to the Lord. Faith in the existence of God is the foundation of Bhakti. Service of Bhagavatas, Sadhus and Sannyasins, repetition of God's name, Satsanga, Hari-kirtan, study of the Bhagavata or the Ramayana, stay in Brindavan, Pandharpur, Chitrakuta or Ayodhya—these are the six means of cultivating and developing Bhakti. Navavidha Bhakti or nine modes of devotion should be practised by all aspirants in the path of Bhakti Yoga. They are: *Sravanam* hearing the Lilas of the Lord, *Kirtanam* singing His praises, *Smaranam* remembering God, *Padasevanam* worshipping the lotus feet of God (service of humanity, country and poor people), *Archanam* offering of flowers, *Vandanam* prostration, *Dasyam* service, *Sakhyam* friendship and *Atmanivedanam* complete self-surrender.

Bhakti should be of a Nishkamya type. It should be Avyabhicharini also. It should be continuous like the flow of oil. The aspirant should observe Sadachara or right conduct. He should be very very serious and earnest in his devotional practices. These are the five indispensable requisites in the Bhakti Yoga. Then only realisation of God will come quickly.

Know that caste, learning, position, beauty and youth are the five thorns in the path of devotion. Beware of the two inner enemies, viz., lust and anger that stand in the way of developing Bhakti. Know that ten kinds of vices follow lust and eight kinds of vices accompany anger. Lajja or shyness for the utterance of the names of the Lord is also a great obstacle for the beginners in the path of devotion. Trishna or internal craving for sensual objects is quite detrimental to the growth of Bhakti.

Have true, perfect, living, unswerving faith in God, in His grace and in the power of His name. Faith can work wonders. Faith can move mountains. Faith can take you to the inner Chambers of the Lord. Faith can make you Divine. Faith can give you peace, inner spiritual strength, joy, freedom, immortality and bliss. Therefore have genuine and living faith in the existence of God, in the scriptures, in the words of your Guru and in your own self.

God tries His devotees in various ways in the beginning.

He puts them to severe trials and tests. Eventually He becomes a slave of the Bhaktas. Lord Krishna says, "I am not in My control. I am under the complete control of My Bhaktas. They have taken entire possession of My heart. How can I leave them when they have renounced everything for My sake only?" God is full of mercy, compassion and love. He has been described as the ocean of mercy. His mercy flows like the streams of the Ganga and the Yamuna. He willingly suffers endless pain in the eyes of the world in order to alleviate the sufferings of His devotees. He ran with His Chakra to kill the Asura who was in the form of a crocodile, when He heard the cry from Gajendra, the lord of the elephants and gave him salvation. He posed as Inspector of Schools and signed in the register when Roop Kalaji of Ayodhya was very busy in his worship of Lord Rama and forgot all about his inspection work. Lord Rama took the form of a sepoy and did sentinel duty when His sepoy Bhakta in Punjab left his duty and attended a Sankirtan party.

Stand up dear friends! Life is short and time is fleeting. Time is more precious. Remember the goal and the purpose for which you have taken this physical body. Struggle hard. Do intense Sadhana. Annihilate egoism, selfishness, pride and hatred. Consecrate everything at the lotus feet of the Lord. Strive in right earnest after the achievement of that great end of human life, the true essence of all religions—Devotion to God's Divine Prem or Bhakti, which alone can free us from the Samsaric wheel of births and deaths and give us highest knowledge, infinite bliss, supreme peace and Immortality. May you all tread the path of devotion and ever rest in the state of divine ecstasy and unalloyed bliss of joy and happiness.

THE ROLE OF FAITH IN BHAKTI SADHANA

Arm yourself with faith in God. Vain argumentation is a sign of ignorance. Faith leads to peace and harmony. Argument produces restlessness. However much you argue you cannot understand the nature of God; even as, however much you try you cannot see your own eye-balls, except in a mirror. That mirror is faith. Faith reflects God; intellect veils Him. God is the Hand that holds the torch of your intellect; it is useless trying to apply your intellect to the Truth of His Existence. What is required is faith. Faith in the Existence of God, faith in the words of saints and sages, will lead to inward peace and joy; and in that stillness you will discover God. You will shine as an embodiment of peace, love and unity. From you will spring forth thoughts, words and actions that will flood the entire world with peace, plenty and prosperity. May you all shine as saints, Yogins, sages and Jivanmuktas! May there be peace in the world and love in the heart of man! May His Divine Power triumph in this universe, now and for ever! May God bless you all with health, long life, peace, prosperity and Eternal Bliss!

IMPORTANT SADHANA IN BHAKTI YOGA

Self-surrender is complete surrendering of the self to God. Self-surrender makes the devotee feel the reality of divine grace and Lord's readiness to bestow on him help at all times. The divine influence streams into his being and moulds it to make it a fit medium for divine realisation and divine instrumentality.

Surrender and grace are interrelated. Surrender draws down grace and grace makes surrender complete. Surrender starts the purification of the heart. Grace completes it. Without grace the complete unification is not possible. Grace divinises your being in order that the constant inflow and inspiration can be received and retained. It is through divine grace alone that his whole being is galvanised, rejuvenated.

You can realise the Absolute or the Impersonal by surrender to the Divine. Surrender is not a thing that is done in a week or a month. You cannot make total surrender from the very beginning of your Sadhana.

The self-arrogating little ego persists and resists again and again. It clings leech-like to its old habits, cravings and desires. It wages guerilla war. It resists surrender. It demands certain objects for its secret gratification. The whole being should be surrendered. That is the reason why Lord Krishna says, "*Tameva Saranam Gaccha Sarvabhavena Bharata*—Flee unto Him for shelter with all thy being, O Bharata." The Chitta, the ego, the mind, the intellect and the soul should be placed at the feet of the Lord. Mira did this and so she obtained Lord Krishna's grace and became one with Him.

The vulgar, stiff, obstinate ego is harder than diamond, reinforced concrete or steel. It is very difficult to melt it. Constant vigilance and ceaseless effort is necessary to slay this dire enemy of peace and wisdom. It keeps subtle desires for its own silent appeasement. Introspect and find out the subtle desires that lurk in the corners of your heart through the search-light of concentration and discrimination and kill them ruthlessly through regular, silent meditation.

Do not bother about taking care of your body. God will save it if He needs it for further service in this body. Surrender it at His feet and rest in peace. He will take care of it. A real devotee says, "Let me take millions of births. It does not matter. But let me be attached to the lotus feet of Lord Hari. Let me have spontaneous devotion to the Lord. Let me be endowed with purity, spiritual strength, spirit of selfless service and divine virtues."

If you simply say without real inner feeling "I am Thine, O Lord", this will not constitute real integral self-surrender. It should come from the core of your heart. You must be prepared for a radical change. You should not stick to your old habits, ways and motives. You should not expect that everything should happen in the way you want. You should live to carry out the divine purpose. You should not think of those ambitions which the mind likes to gratify. You should not think of using even the divine grace or the divine force for your own purpose. The irrepressible ego will assert in various ways and refuse to give up its old habits and ways. It will try to get everything from the Divine. It will totally decline to give itself to the Divine. That is the reason why aspirants do not make any substantial progress in the spiritual path even after doing Sadhana for several years.

There is no loss in self-surrender. You get from the Lord everything. You enjoy all divine Aisvarya of the Lord. The whole wealth of the Lord belongs to you. Siddhis and Riddhis will roll under your feet. You become one with the Lord. You are freed from all wants and desires and cravings. The spiritually hungry and real thirsty aspirant who yearns for the vision of the Lord turns towards the Divine and is quite willing, eager and happy to consecrate his body, life, mind and soul at the feet of the Lord.

The first stage of self-surrender is only a firm resolve to surrender oneself to God or the Preceptor. A Sadhaka who has dedicated his life for the service of his teacher or the service of humanity or for attaining Self-realisation is not at all bound by the actions he performs, subsequent to his self-surrender. Self-surrender becomes perfect only after God-realisation.

Renunciation of the family life is the beginning of self-surrender. He who is endowed with burning Vairagya and discrimination and is really earnest for his spiritual rejuvenation can also do complete self-surrender even though he is in the world. In and through the world he realises the Lord by complete surrender of his entire being to Him. But it is only a very few who are capable of doing this. Because, the worldly life is beset with innumerable obstacles and temptations and the aspirant finds it very difficult to attain complete dispassion in the midst of so many dissipations and distractions. Therefore, renunciation of family life makes his path easier and smoother. The seed is now sown. Then the aspirant goes to his preceptor and falls at his feet. Now the seed germinates. He starts the service of his Guru. As he advances in his devotion and sincere service, his surrender becomes more and more perfect and complete. His heart becomes purer and purer and gradually the light of knowledge dawns in him and he cognises the Supreme Atman, which pervades all and everywhere.

The actions performed by the Sadhaka after renunciation do not bind him, as he offers all his actions as offerings unto his preceptor or Lord. He does not do any action, which can be considered as selfish. Thus through service of one's preceptor with utter self-dedication, his heart becomes purified, and ultimately the Lord becomes his preceptor. Now he has completely surrendered himself to the Lord and he attains the highest intuition.

In the beginning individual effort is very necessary. When surrender has been complete, the divine Grace dawns in him and the divine Power itself does the Sadhana for the Sadhaka. The descent of divine grace and power take complete possession of his mind, will, life and body. The Sadhana goes on with tremendous speed.

Through self-surrender, the devotee becomes one with the Personal God or Saguna Brahman, just as through self-denial the Vedantic student or aspirant in the path of Jnana Yoga, becomes one with the Impersonal Absolute. The divine grace destroys the Satan and his kingdom.

The aspirant must not do any action which he is ashamed to tell in public. If he does any action, this will retard his spiritual progress. This physical body and the mind are offered at the altar of the service of Lord, who is the manifest form of every being. Ultimately his mind merges in the soul within. The Sadhaka becomes a Jivanmukta or a liberated sage.

Sadhakas bold! The Lord loves you even when you turn away from Him. How much more shall He love you, if you turn to Him again sincerely with faith and devotion! Very great is His Love, greater than the greatest mountains; very deep is His affection, deeper than the fathomless depth of the ocean!

THE GIST OF BHAKTI YOGA SADHANA

Select an Ishta Devata either Siva, Krishna, Rama, Vishnu, Dattatreya, Gayatri or Sakti according to the advice of your Guru, or your own inclination or on consultation with a good astrologer who will name the Deity according to your planetary influence. Get the proper Mantra also OM Namah Sivaya, or OM Namo Bhagavate Vasudevaya, OM Sri Ram Jaya Ram Jaya Jaya Ram, or OM Namo Narayanaya. Keep a photo of your Ishtam in front of you in the meditation room. For 6 months, do Trataka on the picture. See the picture carefully with concentration for half an hour without winking till tears flow profusely.

Study constantly the Bhagavata, the Ramayana, Narada Bhakti Sutras and Sandilya Sutras. Live for one year in Ayodhya, Mathura, Pandharpur or Nadia, Bengal. Pass through the course of Nava Vidha Bhakti, Sravana, Smarana, Kirtana, Vandana, Archana, Pada Sevana, Sakhya, Dasya, Atmanivedana. Repeat your Guru Mantra constantly, all throughout the 24 hours. Have sleep for 3 hours. Select a Bhava suitable for you, either Madhurya, Sakhya, Dasya or Vatsalya. Make ungrudging, unreserved, true, perfect self-surrender to God. Do Antarika prayer from the bottom of your heart. Prayer can move mountains. Prayer can reach a realm wherein reason can hardly enter.

Have Eka Nishtha, devotion to one ideal. The Bhakti must be Ananya, Avyabhicharini (unwavering, one-pointed, single-minded devotion). Develop slowly Anurag, Prem, Preeti, Viraha (pain of separation from God), Bhava, Maha Bhava. In Maha Bhava, the devotee is unconscious of his body and the world and is absolutely merged in God. From Apara or lower Bhakti, the devotee passes on to Para or Abheda Bhakti. A devotee gets Krama Mukti or progressive emancipation after passing through Salokya, Sameepya, Sarupya and Sayujya Mukti.

"Dadami Buddhiyogam Tam Yena Mam Upayanti Te: I give the Yoga of discrimination by which they come unto Me."—Gita, X, 10.

After enjoying the lower Mukti, a devotee finally attains Kaivalya Moksha, the same state as that of a Jnani. An earnest Sadhaka with Utsaha (perseverance) can realise within 2 or 3 years. I assure you emphatically. I assure you sincerely and boldly. Make a sincere effort, and watch the results.

Follow Lord Krishna's instructions in the Gita, as described in the terms 'MACCHITTA', 'YUKTA', 'MATPARA'.

CHAPTER FIFTEEN
YOGA SADHANA

YOGA SADHANA: INTRODUCTORY

The earliest Seers who realised the Truth have explained the cosmic process as the work of Maya, the inscrutable power of the Supreme Spirit. By the mysterious operation of this veiling power, the undivided Absolute Blissful One is made to reflect Itself in an infinite multiplicity of names and forms. As described in verse 6, Chap. IV of the Gita, Maya brings about this phenomenal existence with its duality and diversity. Each centre of consciousness thus evolved from the Infinite has therefore to transcend Maya to realise its essential identity with the Supreme Being.

Now Maya is the eternal negation as distinguished from the Ultimate Reality that shines as the Eternal 'I am', the Eternal 'SAT'. Maya is used to denote the *sum total* of the forces of negativity. Nescience, oscillation, delusion, attachment, egoism, disharmony, discord and sensuality are some of the prominent forms in which it finds expression upon the human plane. Yoga then concerns itself in enabling the individuals to effectively deal with and overcome the above factors that keep him pinned down to the phenomenal existence. A state of knowledge through a constant discrimination between the real and the unreal, combined with a ceaseless assertion of an identification with the ideas of omniscience and perfection, a state of unshakable equilibrium and one-pointedness, non-attachment to everything mundane coupled with an intense unabated attachment to some particular aspect of the divine, a complete self-effacement and active selflessness, constitute, therefore, the major means of obtaining a victory over Maya. A determined development along any one or more of these lines broadly go to form the paths of knowledge, occult meditation, devotion or divine love and selfless action.

The process of Yoga embodies an ascent into purity, into that absolute perfection, which is the original state of man. It implies therefore the removal of the enveloping impurities, the stilling of the discordant vibratory tempo of the lower Kosas and the establishment of a state of perfect balance and harmony.

Now all the above-mentioned factors that bind down the Jiva may be seen to be operating upon a larger scale through humanity as a whole. The present age is enmeshed in ignorance, characterised by restlessness, a blind clinging to earthly existence; perverted individualism and voluptuous abandonment to pleasures of the flesh and violence, strife and discord in all walks of life.

Modern age is the machine age. As such, it is power-ridden. Discovery of newer ways of generating power, exploiting fresh aspects of known forces, inventing machine to make machine is the present craze under man's control but man himself does not have his senses and mind under his control. This has resulted in the misuse and abuse of the fruits of civilisation and science, because all power corrupts. The adoption of the Yogic way of life is the release from and the guarantee against such abuse of power and the resultant disaster. Training in Yoga brings to man several supernormal powers that no machine can ever generate. Yet the discipline laid down on the path ensures against their abuse.

All methods of Yoga have ethical training and moral perfection as their basis. The eradication of vices, the development of certain virtues forms the first step in the ladder of Yoga. Disciplining of your nature and the formation of a steady and pure character through a set of right habits and regular daily observances is the next step. This is Yama-Niyama in Raja Yoga. The acquiring of Sadhana-Chatushtaya by the neophyte on the path of knowledge and the insistence upon Sraddha, Sadachara and self-consecration, desirelessness, sacrifice for the devotee and the Karma Yogi respectively have as their aim the development of character and ethical perfection. Thus the ringing in of a new world order of love and sacrifice, of cooperation and brotherhood and the realisation of the ideals of universal perfection can be effected by a willing unreserved allegiance to even the initial stages of Yoga. Upon this firm foundation of a well-established and virtuous moral character is built the further structure of Yoga.

The inherent restlessness of the mind constitutes the greatest problem to the follower of Yoga. By its very nature, mind is ever outgoing. Also it is always unsteady. The resolute turning away from earthly attachment, the determined effacement of the ego, deliberate stoppage of all inharmonious mental processes and the constant dwelling upon a single idea, all these methods require a firm control of the mind and the conscious direction of its powers towards the desired end.

The greatest external manifestation of the mental impulses is physical action. Actions when repeated crystallise into habits. In course of time, habits through indulgence get incorporated as definite traits in the individual's personality. The plan of Yoga Science, in obtaining mastery over the mind proceeds step by step most systematically, regulating and controlling first the grosser and then the subtler manifestation. Yama overcomes all vice and implants virtue. It weakens out all evil traits and implants godly qualities. Niyama regulates the habits and aims at giving the Sadhaka mastery over his behaviour. Instead of being a slave to habits the aspirant now controls his conduct and develops certain habits by determined will. Next the inherent urge to activity is checked through Asanology. By a practice of a system of steady postures, the tendency to unrestrained and aimless movements is curbed and overcome. Character developed, ennobling traits acquired, old habits overcome and replaced by new ones, activity regulated and checked, now the vagaries of the mind are next restrained by a control of its counterpart, namely the breath. This stage is Pranayama. Though thoughts are checked, the mind yet continues to agitate in the form of desires and cravings. Thus fifth limb of Yoga is the withdrawal of all the centripetal senseward movements of the desire element in the mind, turning away from the external world and withdrawing the senses from the objects. Pratyahara paves the way for the sixth rung in the Yogic ladder, Dharana or concentration of the mind at a single point. The indrawn mind is made to fix upon any one given idea or image technically referred to as the Lakshya or object of meditation. Dharana deepened and made lengthened becomes meditation. When Dhyana (meditation) is intensified and made continuous Samadhi results. A state of blissful union with the Infinite Spirit, the Oversoul, frees him from the thraldom of birth and death. This transcendental experience makes him transformed into a being endowed with the cosmic vision beholding everywhere a Divine unity behind apparent diversity. Henceforth his entire life becomes a spontaneous expression of the unhindered flow of the Supreme Energy through every act. He lives and acts purely for the welfare of all Humanity, carrying on the Divine Plan to its glorious consummation.

YOGA SADHANA EXPLAINED

Study carefully Yoga Darsana of Patanjali Maharshi. I shall give here the gist of Sadhana in a terse or a laconic manner. Practise Yama and Niyama first. Observe physical and mental Brahmacharya. Speak the truth always at any cost. Do not hurt anyone in thought, word and deed. Give up greed and covetousness. Do not steal. This is the practice of Yama. Be contented. Observe purity of the body and mind. Practise the austerities of the body, mind and speech as described in the Gita in chapter XVII, 14, 15 and 16. Observe occasional fasts. Regularly fast on Ekadasi days. Study scriptures. Surrender the fruits of your actions to the Lord. This is practice of Niyama. Try to sit on Padma, Siddha or Svastika Asana continuously for 3 hours at one stretch from morning 4 a.m. to 7 a.m. Face East or North. Keep the head neck and trunk in one straight line. Have a meditation room separately for yourself. Do not allow anybody to enter. Reduce your wants. Eat simple food. Wear simple clothing. Do charity. Serve the Sadhus and the wise. Have Satsanga. Serve the poor and sick persons. Do simple Pranayama for 2 years as described in my books "Raja Yoga" and "Practice of Yoga." Control the Indriyas. Destroy all vain desires and material ambitions. When desires crop up, do not try to fulfil them. This is a great secret.

Destroy all thoughts, desires, fancies, whims, caprice, appetites, emotions, wrong Samskaras, superstitions, moods and impulses. Have an Ishta Devata. Lord Krishna and Lord Siva are the Lords of Yoga. Be under the guidance of a Yogic Guru for 3 years. Watch the mind and its Vrittis carefully all the 24 hours. Sit on one Asana. Pray to Sri Ganesa. Do mental Puja.

Practise non-attachment. Make the mind blank. Do not allow any thoughts to crop up. Drive them immediately. Do not think of anything. When there is no thought, there is no desire. Desire is the product of evil Samskaras, produced from contact. Desire is the outcome of thoughts when they associate with objects; when thoughts will cease to exist, desire will also cease to exist. Thoughts and desires co-exist. By constant, intense and protracted practice you are bound to succeed in controlling all thoughts. Change all Vrittis into a Vritti. This is Savikalpa Samadhi. If you give up this one Vritti also, you will enter into Nirvikalpa Samadhi, a state of the highest knowledge and bliss.

"By restraint of even this (impressions which obstruct all other impressions) all being restrained, comes the seedless Samadhi" (Patanjali Yoga Sutras, I, 51).

You can definitely become a Raja Yogi within 2 or 3 years, if you do earnest, constant and intense Sadhana with zeal, interest and enthusiasm. I solemnly make this bold assertion.

YOGA SADHANA: ITS EIGHT FUNDAMENTALS

The eight fundamentals or accessories of Raja Yoga, as it has been described by Maharshi Patanjali, are Yama, Niyama, Asana, Pranayama, Pratyahara, Dharana, Dhyana and Samadhi. These eight accessories are like the eight rungs in the ladder of Raja Yoga. They all should be practised in the order given. Through the practice of these eight accessories, the impurities of the mind are destroyed and the light of wisdom, the discriminative knowledge illumines the life of the practitioner. Then he attains Kaivalya or the Supreme Perfection.

Now, Yama is the practice of Ahimsa (abstinence from injury or non-violence), Satya (truthfulness), Brahmacharya (continence), Asteya (abstinence from theft or earning through illegal methods) and Aparigraha (abstinence from avariciousness or greed).

The other restraints that follow have their origin in Ahimsa. Practice of Ahimsa culminates eventually in realisation of unity or oneness of life, of cosmic love and universal brotherhood and ultimately the Advaitic consciousness. The second aspect of Yama, viz., Satyam or truthfulness is the most important qualification of a Sadhaka. Truth is the symbol of God and He can be realised only through unflinching adherence to truth. The fourth aspect i.e., Asteya means complete annihilation of one's pilfering nature. The Sadhaka has to be contented with whatever he gets through honest means. He must completely abstain himself from illegal appropriation or confistication of others' property and other illegal ways of maintaining his livelihood. Brahmacharya, the third aspect, means purity in thought, word and deed. No Yoga or spiritual evolution is possible without the observance of rigid celibacy. The fifth and the last aspect of Yama i.e., Aparigraha means freedom from greed or covetousness. The aspirant should live on the barest necessities of life, abstaining from receiving any gift or presentation from others. He must live independently without the support of others.

The second accessory of Raja Yoga viz., Niyama is the observance of the five canons: Saucha (internal and external cleanliness), Santosha (contentment), Tapas (austerity or mortification), Svadhyaya (study of scriptures) and Isvarapranidhana (worship of God or self-surrender).

The first aspect of Niyama, Saucha or purification is of two kinds: internal (mental) and external (physical). Cleanliness is next to godliness. Just as you need soap, water etc., for washing the body, so also you need Japa, Kirtan, prayer, meditation and selfless service for washing your mind. Keep the body always neat and clean and the mind always pure and healthy, free from evil thoughts, evil desires or cravings. The second aspect Santosha or contentment brings a fullness of life, happiness and peace. If there is no contentment, the mind is always restless and ruffled, and naturally the Sadhana becomes impossible. The third aspect—Tapas is austerity of the mind and the body. You should be able to bear heat and cold, physical discomfort and fatigue, as well as insult, injury, persecution and any sort of humiliation or crucifixion. You should keep your body and the senses ever pure and carefully guarded. The fourth aspect—Svadhyaya or the study of scriptures and religious books, elevates and inspires the mind. It gives you an idea of your goal and the necessary practices that are necessary for its accomplishment. Practical application of what you read that are amicable to your temperament and applicable to your mode of life, is very necessary if you wish to derive any permanent, substantial benefit out of your study. The fifth and the last aspect of Niyama—Isvarapranidhana is worship of God and ultimate self-surrender. Worship Him with a pure heart and stainless mind, surrender your ego at His feet, and annihilate the idea of doership or separateness from the Lord. You will realise the Advaitic Oneness of the Self.

Asana is the third Anga of Raja Yoga. Physical fitness, a diseaseless healthy body is essential for spiritual practices. Without good health you cannot fight against the turbulent senses and the boisterous mind. Regular practice of Asanas will keep the body fit and the mind calm, and will give you abundant energy, vigour, strength and nerve-power. You will be able to do intense Sadhana without physical discomfort.

Padmasana, Siddhasana and Sukhasana are prescribed for meditation. For all-round physical and internal development, Sirshasana, Sarvangasana, Matsyasana, Paschimottanasana, Ardha-Matsyendrasana, Bhujangasana, Dhanurasana, Salabhasana, Trikonasana, Padahastasana, Halasana and Mayurasana are the important ones. Bandhas and Mudras are auxiliaries to Asanas.

The fourth Anga or accessory—Pranayama is regulation and control of breath. Literally it means the process by which you can know the secret of Prana and its control. The mind can be made to transcend ordinary experience and exist on a plane higher than that of reason known as superconscious state of concentration and also beyond the limit of concentration. The Yogi comes face to face with facts which ordinary consciousness cannot comprehend. This is achieved by proper training and manipulation of the subtle forces of the body so as to cause them to give, as it were, an upward push to the mind into the higher planes. When the mind is so raised into the superconscious state of perception, it begins to act from there and experiences higher facts and higher knowledge. Such is the ultimate object of Pranayama which is achieved through the control of the vibratory Prana.

That which moves through the nerves of the physical body is gross Prana. That which moves in subtle tubes of Yoga Nadis of the astral body is subtle Prana or psychic Prana. Breath is an external effect or manifestation of the gross Prana. There is intimate connection with the gross Prana and the subtle Prana. The control of the external breath leads to the control of the gross and subtle Prana of the body and mind. Hence Pranayama-exercises are practised. When the Prana and the mind are controlled, then all the mental modifications cease to arise. Then you become the master of your mind and body. Then dawn the intuitive knowledge of the Self, and you realise your essential nature—the supreme Reality.

The important Pranayamas practised are: Sukha Purvaka (Puraka, Kumbhaka and Rechaka), Bhastrika, Ujjai, Sitali,

Sitkari, Kapala Bhati, Plavani, Brahmananda Murcha and Surya Bheda.

Now about the fifth accessory—Pratyahara is abstraction. It is the withdrawal of the senses from the objects. The senses are assimilated in the mind which is rendered pure through the practice of Yama, Niyama, Asana and Pranayama. The mind becomes more calm now. The nature of the senses is to have always connection with the objects. Where the vision is turned outward, the rush of fleeting events engages the mind. The outgoing energies of the mind begin to play. When they are obstructed by the practice of Pratyahara, the other course for them is to mix with the mind, to be absorbed in the mind. The mind will not assume any form of any object. It will be ultimately merged in the Self within.

Pratyahara itself is termed as Yoga, as it is the most important Anga in Yoga Sadhana. The first four rungs deal with ethical training and purification of the body, mind and Nadis. Now with Pratyahara proper Yoga begins, which eventually culminates in Dharana, Dhyana and finally in Samadhi.

Dharana or concentration is fixing the mind on something, internal or external. Having controlled the Prana through Pranayama and the senses through Pratyahara, you should now try to fix your mind on the Self within. The beginners should practise Dharana or concentration on some external object or on the form of their tutelary Deity. Thus when the mind gets trained, turn the gaze inward and it will naturally merge in the Self within.

Concentration is practised on the tip of the nose, or on the Ajna-Chakra (the space between the two eyebrows), or on Sahasrara (particularly for those who are inclined to Jnana Yoga Sadhana), or on the Anahata Chakra (for those who are of devotional temperament) or upon any of the six Chakras. Concentration is also practised externally on the idol or picture of the Lord or upon any particular spot or mark.

Prolonged Dharana is termed as meditation. It is a continuous, unhampered flow of one thought of God or the Self. Meditation is of two kinds, viz., Saguna and Nirguna. In Saguna or concrete meditation, the student of Yoga meditates on the form of his tutelary Deity; and in Nirguna or abstract meditation he meditates on his own Self or Atma. Nirguna meditation follows Saguna meditation.

The same Dhyana is Samadhi when it shines with object alone, as it were, devoid of itself. The thinker and the thought, the meditator and the meditated become one. The mind assumes Divya-rupa. The separate notions, contemplation, contemplated and contemplator vanish. In the state of Samadhi the aspirant is not conscious of any external or internal objects. With the destruction of the wandering mind, and with the increase of the one-pointed nature of the mind, the mind assumes the state of Samadhi. The bliss that is derived from that state of superconsciousness is inexpressible. It is beyond words. It is beyond apprehension of the finite mind. You will have to experience this by yourself only. There are different stages of Samadhi which ultimately lead to Nirvikalpa Samadhi. Here all Sadhana ends, and the Yogi becomes one with the Immortal Lord, one with the cosmic spirit. He is immanent and yet transcendent.

MENTAL PURIFICATION: AN ESSENTIAL CONDITION

In the Upanishads the Atman is described as beyond the mind and speech. In another place you will find that the Atman can be known through the pure mind—the Buddhi. There are two kinds of minds—pure mind and impure mind. What we possess is impure mind. We have to remove all the gross impurities through Tapas, Yoga, Austerities and Pranayama and then acquire the four means of Viveka, Vairagya, Shad-Sampat and Mumukshutva. Then you approach a Guru and study the Upanishads, practise Sravana, Manana and Nididhyasana. The Atma is beyond the reach of the mind. It is beyond the reach of the impure mind. But it can be reached. It should be reached by a man who is a Viveki, who has performed Tapascharya, who has Vairagya and Shad-Sampat, who has practised concentration and Nididhyasana. So there is no contradiction in the Upanishadic utterances, if only we can take the trouble to find out what the Rishis told us. Though Atman is beyond the reach of impure mind, it is attainable through the pure mind.

NEED FOR YOGA SADHANA

Why should you prolong your bondage unnecessarily? Why should you not claim your divine birthright right now? Why should you not break your bondage now? Delay means prolongation of your sufferings. You can break it at any moment. This is in your power. Do it now. Stand up. Gird up your loins. Do rigorous and vigorous Sadhana and attain freedom, which is immortality or eternal bliss.

Make the lower nature the servant of the higher through discipline, Tapas, self-restraint and meditation. This is the beginning of your freedom.

The divine within you is stronger than anything that is without you. Therefore be not afraid of anything. Rely on your own Inner Self, the Divinity within you. Tap the source through looking within.

Without renunciation you can never be happy. Without renunciation you can never be successful in gaining the highest good i.e., Moksha. Without renunciation you can never be at your ease. Therefore renounce everything. Make happiness your own. Hold renunciation as the foremost of things.

Improve yourself. Build your character. Purify the heart. Develop divine virtues. Eradicate evil traits. Conquer all that is base in you. Endeavour to attain all that is worthy and noble.

Only when you have purified the heart, silenced the mind, stilled the thoughts and surging emotions, withdrawn the outgoing senses, thinned out the Vasanas, you can behold the glorious Atman during deep meditation.

There are five means by which perfect tranquillity or emancipation can be attained. These form the highest happiness. They are Satsanga or association with the wise, discrimination between the real and the unreal, dispassion, enquiry of 'Who am I?' and meditation. These are called Heaven. These are religion. These form the highest happiness.

Become a good man first. Then control the senses. Then subdue the lower mind by the higher mind. Then the divine light will descend. Only then the vessel will be able to receive and hold the divine light.

Practise meditation persistently and calmly without haste. You will soon attain Samadhi or the Nirvikalpa state.

Spiritual life is toilsome and laborious. It demands constant vigilance and long perseverance before substantial progress is made.

You have yourself built the walls of your prison-house through ignorance. You can demolish the walls through discrimination and enquiry of "Who am I?"

Sufferings purify the soul. They burn up the gross material

sins and impurities. The Divinity becomes more and more manifest. They give inner spiritual strength and develop the will force, the power of endurance. Hence sufferings are blessings in disguise.

Even a ray of inner light during meditation will lighten your path. It will give you a great deal of encouragement and inner strength. It will goad you to do more Sadhana. You will experience this ray of light when the meditation becomes deeper and when you rise above body-consciousness.

Meditation and worship are the means of evolving your potentialities and seeking a higher level of consciousness or existence.

Life is the unfolding of the latent capacities of the soul. Lead the divine life. Generate sublime divine thoughts in your mind through meditation, Japa, Kirtan and study of sacred scriptures.

Bathe in the river of life everlasting. Plunge in it. Take a dip in it. Swim in it. Float in it. Rejoice.

Bask the body in the physical sunlight. Bask the soul in the sunlight of the Eternal. You will have good health and everlasting life.

Worship is the unfolding of the bud of the flower of the soul. Worship is life. Worship bestows life eternal.

You may conquer millions of persons in battle, but you will become the greatest conqueror only if you can conquer your own lower self or mind.

So long as your senses are not subdued or weakened, you will have to practise Tapas or self-restraint, Dama or Pratyahara.

Sit down with a composed mind. Assert your mastery over the body and mind. Plunge deep into the chambers of the heart, and enter into the stupendous ocean of Silence. Listen to the voice which is soundless.

Build your spiritual life on a sure foundation, on the rock of divine grace and strength of character. Take refuge in the Lord and His eternal law. There is no power in heaven or on earth that can bar your march now. Success in Self-realisation is certain. Failure exists not for you. There is light on your path. All is brilliant.

STRUCTURE OF YOGA SADHANA

Ethical discipline is incumbent for success in Yoga. Ethical discipline is the practice of right conduct in life. The two moral pivots of Yoga are Yama and Niyama, which the aspirant must practise in his daily life. These correspond broadly to the ten commandments of the Bible or to the noble eightfold path of Lord Buddha. Non-injuring (Ahimsa), truthfulness (Satya), continence (Brahmacharya), non-stealing (Asteya) and non-covetousness (Aparigraha) are the component parts of Yama. Internal and external purification (Saucha), contentment (Santosha), austerity (Tapas), study of religious and philosophical books (Svadhyaya) and self-surrender to the Lord (Isvarapranidhana) come under Niyama. Practice of Yama and Niyama will eradicate all the impurities of the mind. In fact, Yama and Niyama form the corner-stones of Yoga Philosophy.

Pre-eminence is given to abstention from injuring any living creature (Ahimsa) amongst all other virtues. There must be non-injuring in thought, word and deed. Non-injuring is placed first because it is the source of the following nine. The practice of universal love or brotherhood is nothing but the practice of non-injuring. He who practises non-injuring will get quick success in Yoga. The practitioner must abandon even harsh words and unkind looks. He must show goodwill and friendliness to one and all. He must respect life. He must always remember that one common Self dwells in the hearts of all beings.

Truthfulness (Satya) comes next in order. Thought must agree with word, and word with action. This is truthfulness. These virtues are attainable only by the unselfish. Truth can hardly arise unless there is pure motive behind all actions. The word of a Yogi must be a blessing to others.

Then comes non-stealing (Asteya). You must be satisfied with what you get by honest means. The law of Karma is inexorable. You will have to suffer for every wrong action of yours. Action and reaction are equal and opposite. Amassing wealth is really theft. The whole wealth of all the three worlds belongs to the Lord. You are only a care-taker of this wealth. You must willingly share what you have with all and spend it in charity.

The third virtue is the practice of celibacy.

Brahmacharya is the substratum for a life in the Atman. It is a potent weapon for waging a relentless war against the internal monsters—passion, greed, anger, miserliness, hypocrisy, etc. It contributes to perennial joy and uninterrupted, undecaying bliss. It gives tremendous energy, clear brain, gigantic will-power, bold understanding, retentive memory and good power of enquiry (Vichara-Sakti).

What is wanted is deep inner life. Silence the bubbling thoughts. Keep the mind cool and calm. Open yourself to higher spiritual consciousness. Feel the Divine Presence and Divine Guidance. Fix your mind at the lotus-feet of the Lord. Become like a child. Speak to Him freely. Become absolutely candid. Do not hide your thoughts. You cannot do so because He is the Inner Ruler (Antaryami). He watches all your thoughts. Pray for mercy, light, purity, strength, peace and knowledge. You will surely get them.

A Yogic student should abstain from greed. He should not receive luxurious presents from anybody. Gifts affect the mind of the receiver. These five virtues must be practised in thought, word and deed, for they are not merely restraints but change the character of the practitioner, implying inward purity and strength.

Two things are necessary for attaining success in mind-control, viz., practice (Abhyasa) and dispassion (Vairagya).

You must try your level best to be free from any desire for any pleasure, seen or unseen, and this dispassion can be attained through constant perception of evil in them. Dispassion is renunciation of attainment. It is aversion to sensual enjoyments herein and hereafter. The detachment or dispassion is of two kinds, the lower and the higher. Vijnana Bhikshu distinguishes the superior and the inferior types of Vairagya in the following way: "The former is a distaste for the good things of life, here or hereafter due to the experience that they cannot be acquired or preserved without trouble, while their loss causes pain and that the quest is never free from egoistic feelings. The latter, however is based on a clear perception of the difference between intelligence and the objects that appear in its light."

There are various stages in dispassion. The determination to refrain from enjoying all sorts of sensual objects is the first stage. In the second stage certain objects lose their charm for the spiritual aspirant and he attempts to destroy the attraction for others also. In the third stage the senses are controlled, but a vague longing for the sensual enjoyment remains in the mind. In the fourth the aspirant loses completely all interest whatsoever in the external objects. The final stage is a state of highest desirelessness. It is this kind of dispassion that bestows Absolute Independence on the Yogi. In this stage the Yogi renounces all kinds of psychic powers even as Omniscience, etc.

It is by practice and dispassion that the passage of thought towards external objects can be checked. Mere indifference will not serve the purpose. Practice is also necessary. Remembering God always is also practice. Lord Krishna says to Arjuna with reference to this practice of controlling the mind: "Abandoning without reserve all desires born of the imagination by the mind, curbing in the aggregate of the senses on every side, little by little let him gain tranquillity by means of reason controlled by steadiness; having made the mind abide in the Self, let him not think of anything. As often as the wavering and unsteady mind goeth forth, so often reining it in, let him bring it under control of the Self." (Bhagavad Gita, Ch. VI-24, 25, 26)

Mind is drawn towards external objects by the force of desire. By convincing oneself of the illusoriness of sense-objects through an investigation into their nature and by cultivating indifference to worldly objects, the mind can be restrained and brought back to the Self to abide finally. In virtue of this practice of Yoga, the Yogi's mind attains peace in the Self. Practice consists in constantly repeating the same idea or thought regarding any one object. By constant reflection and exercise of will-power, suggestions should be given to the subconscious mind not to look for enjoyment in the changing world without, but in the changeless within. You should exercise great vigilance to get hold of opportunities, when the mind dwells on sense-objects and suggest to it new meanings and interpretations and make it change its attitude towards them with a view to its ultimate withdrawal therefrom. This is called practice.

The chief characteristic of the mind in the waking state is to have some object before it to dwell upon. It can never remain blank. It can concentrate on one object at a time. It constantly changes its objects and so it is restless. It is impetuous, strong and difficult to bend. It is as hard to curb as the wind. That is the reason why Patanjali Maharshi says, that the practice must be steady and continuous and it must stretch over a considerable period and be undertaken with a perfect faith in its regenerating and uplifting powers. You must not show any slackening symptoms at any stage of practice.

Restraint does not come in a day, but by long and continued practice with zeal and enthusiasm. The progress in Yoga can only be gradual. Many people give up practice of concentration after some time, when they do not see any tangible prospect of getting psychic powers. They become impatient. They do little and expect much. This is bad. Doing any kind of practice by fits and starts will not bring the desired fruit. Direct experience is the goal of life. Though the effort or practice is painful in the beginning, yet it brings Supreme Joy in the end. Lord Krishna says to Arjuna: "Supreme Joy is for the Yogi, whose mind is peaceful, whose passionate nature is controlled, who is sinless, and of the nature of the eternal!"—Bhagavad Gita, Ch. VI-27.

"Mind alone is to man the cause of bondage or liberation; lost in enjoyment it leads to bondage, freed from the objective, it leads to liberation. As mind freed from the objective leads to liberation, one desirous of liberation or success in the path of Yoga must always try to wipe off the objective from the plane of his mind. When the mind, severed from all connection with sensual objects and confined to the light of the heart, finds itself in ecstasy, it is said to have reached its culminating point. The mind should be prevented from functioning, till its dissolution is attained in the heart; this is Gnosis, this is concentration, the rest is all mere logomachy."

Desire may be described as the hankering for things which gains such mastery over the mind as to preclude even enquiring into their antecedents and consequences. Man at once becomes that which he identifies himself with, by force of strong and deep attachment and loses memory of everything else in the act. The man thus subdued by desire, fixing his eye on everything and anything, is deluded into believing it as the real thing. Due to loss of control man perceives everything with beclouded eyes in this deluded fashion, like one under the influence of a strong intoxicant.

Desire is born of ignorance (Avidya). Attachment, longing and preference are the constituents of desire. Do not endeavour to fulfil desires. Try to reduce your desires as best as you can. Withdraw the fuel of gratification. Then the fire of desire will get extinguished by itself. Just as a gheeless lamp dies out when the ghee is withdrawn, even so the fire of desire dies when the fuel of gratification is withdrawn. If attachment is eradicated, then longing and preference for objects will die by themselves.

Man commits various sorts of sins and injures others, when he exerts to get the desired objects. He has to reap the fruits of his actions; hence he is brought again and again in this round of births and deaths. If you increase one object in the list of your possessions or wants, the desire also increases ten times. The more worldly objects you possess, the more distant you are from God. Your mind will always be thinking and planning as to how to get and guard the objects, how to earn tons of money and keep them safe. If the acquired objects are lost, your mind is completely upset. Cares, worries, anxieties and all sorts of mental torments increase with the objects.

Free yourself from the tyranny of the mind. It has tormented you mercilessly for so long a time. You have allowed it to indulge in sensual pleasures and have its own ways. Now is the time to curb it, just as you would curb a wild horse. Be patient and persevering. Practise daily 'thoughtlessness' or inhibition of thoughts. The task may be difficult in the beginning. It will be indeed disgusting and tiring but the reward is great. You will reap Immortality, Supreme Joy, Eternal Peace and Infinite Bliss. Therefore practise diligently in right earnest. It is worth doing. Be on the alert. If you are sincere in your wish and strong in your resolve, nothing is impossible under the sun to accomplish. Nothing can stand in your way.

From the condition of your mind, from your feelings and conduct, you can very well understand the nature of your actions in your previous lives and can nullify or counteract the effects of evil actions by doing good actions, Tapas, discipline and meditation. Try to lead a life of non-attachment. Discipline your mind carefully. No one is free from pains, diseases, troubles, difficulties. You will have to rest in your divine nature. Then alone you will draw strength to face the difficulties of life. Then only you will have a balanced mind. Then only you will not be affected by external morbid influences and discordant vibrations. Regular meditation in the morning will give you new strength and inner life of joy and bliss. Practise meditation. Feel this joy and bliss despite unhelpful conditions and adverse circumstances. Gradually you will grow spiritually. You will attain Self-realisation.

PRACTICE OF YOGA SADHANA

Meditate regularly on your ideal. Strive to live in it.

Weed out the vices. Scrutinise your character. Enlarge your capacities. Cultivate mental and moral qualities.

Close the doors of the senses. Make the mind steady and calm by silencing the thoughts, subduing the surging emotions and crushing all desires and cravings. Meditate. You will behold now the majesty and the glory of the Supreme Self, the Indweller.

Forgive those who slander or speak ill of you. Do not harm anyone who injures you. If anybody from aversion speaks disparagingly of you, greet him courteously without caring for those disagreeable words.

Steadily resist the promptings of the lower nature. Gradually it will lose its power over you. You will gain strength. Even if you fail, it is one step nearer to victory or the goal. You will develop your will-power. The will-force will penetrate into the subconscious mind and eradicate all wrong impressions, vicious habits and evil traits.

You will encounter various difficulties in the beginning of your Sadhana. You are not conscious of any spiritual progress, but you are only conscious of your failures in your attempts, in meditation, the resistance you meet and your defects and weaknesses.

If you persist in your Sadhana vigorously and diligently, if you are regular in your Sadhana you will attain success. Meditation will come without effort. Meditation will become habitual. All resistance will vanish. You will develop strong will-power. You will have triumph at every step. Failure and despair will be unknown to you. Sadhana will go on in great strides.

Evil thoughts perish when divine thoughts are entertained. Evil thoughts die when good thoughts are cherished. Evil thoughts and evil desires perish merely from want of nourishment.

Abstention from gratification of a desire will cause starvation of desire and then its death.

The desire will fade away if you do not indulge in the objects of desire.

Do not talk of Samadhi and awakening of Kundalini. The greater things you can begin to do afterwards. Do the smaller things first. Practise, Yama, Niyama first. Be good, do good. Attain ethical perfection first. Eradicate evil traits and develop divine qualities first. Control the senses and purify the heart first. What is the use of talking of Samadhi and awakening of Kundalini when the first steps are not yet taken up and practised?

Be abstemious in everything. Abandon fear, anger, cupidity and errors of judgment. Stick to your vows at any cost, even at the risk of your life. Then only you are fit to attain immortality.

Sticking to the vows will contribute to your true happiness. Observe the vow with your passions under control, with a pure heart.

If you like mangoes very much, if you are longing intensely to eat them, if they are actually in front of you and if you are quite ready to eat them do not eat them. Control the desire through discrimination. Practise this again and again in respect of those things which you like best. Gradually you will be able to control the tongue.

Each failure sows the seed of your future success or triumph. Stand up. Do not be afraid of your failures. March forward boldly with undaunted spirit and redoubled energy.

If you do a wrong action, when you do not wish to do it, your weak will has been overpowered by the strong force of past habit. Do more virtuous actions daily. You will develop a strong will. Then you will not repeat wrong actions.

Strong will-power consists in overcoming desires, irritability, anger, impurities, evil emotions and in possessing serenity, self-possession, presence of mind, balanced mind in success and failure, censure and praise, honour and dishonour, gain and loss.

PRACTICAL YOGIC INSTRUCTIONS

Control your senses. Calm your mind. Still the bubbling thoughts. Fix the mind on the lotus of the heart. Concentrate. Meditate. Realise Him intuitively this very second and enjoy the Bliss of the Self.

Have firm and unshakable faith in the existence of God,

the supreme, undying, intelligent Principle or Essence or Substance who exists in the three periods of time—past, present and future. He has neither beginning, middle nor end. He is Sat-Chit-Ananda (Existence Absolute, Knowledge Absolute and Bliss Absolute).

O ignorant man! Why do you vainly search for happiness in the perishable external objects of the world conditioned in time, space and causation? You have no peace of mind. Your desires are never fully gratified. You may amass boundless wealth, beget beautiful babies, earn titles, honours, name, fame, power, publicity, and all you want, and yet your mind is restless. You have no real, abiding happiness. You feel you still want something. You have no feeling of fullness. Never, therefore, forget from this moment onwards that this feeling of fullness or eternal satisfaction can be obtained only in God by realising Him through constant practice of self-control, purity, concentration, meditation and practice of Yoga.

There is restlessness everywhere. Selfishness, greed, jealousy and lust are playing unimaginable havoc in every heart. Fights, skirmishes and petty quarrels are polluting the atmosphere of the world and creating discord, disharmony and unrest. The bugle is blown and the armies march to the battle-field to destroy their enemies. One nation wages war against another nation for acquiring more dominions and power. Side by side with these bloody wars, peace movement is also working for bringing harmony and peace, for eradicating dire ignorance, the root-cause of all human sufferings and for disseminating Divine Knowledge.

The greatest need of the world today is the message of Love. Kindle the light of love in your own heart first. Love all. Include all creatures in the warm embrace of your love. Nations can be united by pure love only. World-wars can be put an end to by pure love only. The United Nations cannot do much. Love is a mysterious divine glue that unites the hearts of all. It is a magical healing balm of very high potency. Charge every action with pure love. Kill cunningness, greed, crookedness and selfishness. It is extremely cruel to take away the lives of others by using poisonous gas. This is a capital crime. The scientist who manufactures the gas in the laboratory cannot escape without being punished for this crime by the great Lord. Forget not the Day of Judgment. What will you say unto the Lord, O ye mortals, who run after power, dominions and wealth? Have a clean conscience and pure love. You will verily enter into the Kingdom of God.

Ah, how mysterious is the universe! How mysterious are the silent workings of the unseen Power, who prompts passionate people to wage wars on the one side and pious people to disseminate Divine Knowledge on the other and bring peace and happiness to the suffering humanity at large!

As you think, so you become. Think you are a High Court Judge, High Court Judge you will become. Think you are the monarch of the whole world, monarch of the whole world you will become. Think you are a great teacher, teacher you will become. Think you are poor and weak, poor and weak you will become. Think you are a multi-millionaire, multi-millionaire you will become. Think you are a saint of spotless character, saint of spotless character you will become. Think you are God or Atman or Brahman, God or Atman or Brahman you will become. The whole universe is governed by this wonderful Law of Nature.

Always think rightly and act rightly. Never try to seize the possessions of others. Never envy your neighbours. Entertain noble and sublime thoughts. Have supreme self-confidence and courage. Whatever you do, do it with a will to succeed. You will by all means succeed in all your endeavours. Success is yours. You will know no failures. This is the Sovereign Secret. Meditate upon this Secret daily in the morning for some time and enjoy the Bliss of the Self.

In the Vishnupurana you will find: "If the deluded fool loves the body, a mere collection of flesh, blood, pus, faeces, urine, muscles, fat and bones, he will verily love hell itself! To him who is not disgusted with the nasty smell from his own body, what other argument need be adduced for detachment?"

It is a well-known fact that enjoyment cannot bring you satisfaction of desire. On the contrary, it aggravates desire and makes man more restless. The root-cause of all human sufferings and miseries is the craving for worldly enjoyments. The more you hanker after these sensual enjoyments, the more unhappy do you become. The desires also grow, when they are not fulfilled. You can never be happy as long as the craving for enjoyments exists.

It is painful to earn money. It is more painful to keep the

money that is earned. It is still more painful, if the money gets reduced. And it is extremely painful, if the whole money is lost. Money is the abode of all sorts of pain. That is the reason why in India a Sadhu or a Sannyasin does not possess anything. In his grand vision, he does not possess his body also. He constantly asserts: "The body is not mine; I am not body." A real Sannyasin is one who feels: "I am bodiless." These Sannyasins lead a life of perfect dispassion and ruthless renunciation. Renunciation brings in its train supreme Peace.

It is very difficult to become absolutely desireless. A liberated sage or a full-blown Yogi alone is entirely free from the taint of desires, for he has completely annihilated his mind and is enjoying the Supreme Bliss of the Self within. How can desires arise in him who is plunged in the ocean of Divine Bliss?

A neophyte in the spiritual path should entertain noble desires. He should do virtuous actions. He should develop intense longing for liberation. In order to achieve this end, he should study the Holy Scriptures regularly and systematically. He should betake himself to the company of the wise. He should practise right conduct, right thinking, right speaking and right acting. He should practise regular meditation. By and by all old vicious desires, sensual cravings and evil propensities will vanish. Hey Saumya! Lead a life of perfect contentment. Contentment is the bliss of life. The cold ambrosial waters of contentment will quickly extinguish the fire of desires. Contentment is the chief sentinel who keeps watch over the domain of Peace or the Kingdom of God.

The old subdued desires recur, persist and resist. They assert: "O ungrateful man! You gave me shelter in your mind all along. You enjoyed various objects of the world through me only. If there is no desire for food and drink how can you enjoy food and drink? Why are you so cruel towards me now? I have every right to dwell in this abode of your mind. Do whatever you like." But you should not be discouraged even a bit by these threats. All desires will be thinned out gradually by meditation and Yoga. They will eventually perish in toto beyond resurrection.

A strong mind has influence over a weak mind. Mind has influence over the physical body. Mind acts upon matter. Mind brings bondage. Mind gives you liberation. Mind is the devil. Mind is your best friend. Mind is your Guru (Spiritual Preceptor). You will have to tame your mind. You will have to discipline your mind. You will have to control your mind. This is all you have to do.

Study your feelings and emotions. Analyse them. Dissect them. Do not identify yourself with these feelings and emotions. Separate yourself from these feelings and emotions. Stand as a silent witness. Identification with these feelings and emotions is the cause of bondage and misery.

Anger is a modification of desire in the mind. There is no modification in the Self or the real "I" or Atman. A worldly man identifies himself with anger and so he becomes miserable. This is ignorance only. The body and the mind are your instruments for growth and evolution. Identify yourself with the big, infinite "I" by utilising these two instruments and become a master of your mind and body. You are the driver of this engine—body and mind. Assert your birthright and become free, my child. Understand the trick of this mischievous mind. It has played with you long enough. Attain complete mastery over it. You can do this easily by the practice of Yoga.

Watch and chop and clip the thoughts as soon as they arise from the mind. Kill them dead on the spot. If you find it difficult to do this, become indifferent. Do not mind them. Allow them to take their own shape. They will soon die by themselves. Or, sometimes you can chop the thoughts and when you get tired of doing so, you can adopt the method of remaining indifferent. The latter method is more easy. If you tie a monkey to a post, it becomes more turbulent; if you allow it to move about at its own will and pleasure, it is not so very turbulent. Even so, when you try to fix the mind at a point, it becomes more turbulent. Therefore various kinds of evil thoughts enter into the minds of neophytes at the time of concentration. But they need not be unnecessarily alarmed. If you find it difficult to focus the mind at one point, allow it to jump awhile like a monkey. Do not wrestle with the mind. It will soon get exhausted, and will then be waiting to obey your behests. Now you can tackle it easily.

Free yourself from the tyranny of the mind. It has tormented you mercilessly for so long a time. You have allowed it to indulge in sensual pleasures and have its own ways. Now is the time to curb it just as you would curb a wild horse. Be patient and persevering. Practise daily thoughtlessness or inhibition of thoughts. The task may be difficult in the beginning. It will be indeed disgusting and tiring, but the reward is great. You will reap Immortality, Supreme Joy, Eternal Peace and Infinite Bliss. Therefore practise diligently in right earnest. It is worth doing. Be on the alert. If you are sincere in your wish and strong in your resolve, nothing is impossible under the sun to accomplish. Nothing can stand in your way. If you fail in your attempt, do not be discouraged. Remember the thrilling story of the dreadful fight between Hercules and the prodigious giant. In the course of his journey in quest of adventures, Hercules encountered a monster, who was so wonderfully contrived by nature that every time he touched the earth, he became ten times as strong as ever he had been before! By remembering this incident you will get inner strength and courage. You are bound to succeed.

Realise that you are neither body nor mind, that you were never born nor will you ever die, that you are invincible, that nothing in this world can hurt you, that you are the Sun round whom the whole universe revolves. The whole knowledge is treasured up within the chambers of your heart. Procure the key and unlock the doors of Knowledge. Yoga is the key. You will attain unruffled peace, marvellous self-control and tremendous will-power.

Behold! There on the banks of the holy Ganga at Rishikesh, Himalayas, a Sage, a Paramahamsa Sannyasin of eighty summers, with lustrous eyes, serene face, magnetic personality, bright complexion, sits with a loin cloth only. There is a small grass-hut besides him underneath a tree. Inside the hut you will find a small wooden bowl (Kamandalu) for keeping water and an ordinary stick. This is all his personal effects. He is always sitting there in a contemplative mood. He never talks, nor laughs, but occasionally nods his round-shapely head and smiles gently. He never stirs from the place. He is unaffected by the heat of the summer sun or the biting cold of the winter. He never uses blankets, no, not even in winter. What a wonderful power of endurance! He lives on some milk and fruits only. His heart is filled with purity, mercy, compassion, sympathy and love!

People from various parts of the country flock to him in hundreds and thousands in season and out of season with flowers and fruits in their hands, prostrate at his holy feet, worship him with their offerings and leave the place with his ready blessings. He never talks, but all doubts are cleared in his mere presence. People forget the world, their families, their children. They bathe in his magnetic aura. Such is the benign influence of a liberated sage who is verily a beacon-light to the world at large.

Now here is a man living in the busiest part of a metropolis. He earns a fat salary. He spends half of his earnings in gambling and in drinking. The other half goes to cinema and prostitutes. He eats fish, meat and smokes heavily. He runs into debts every month and finds it hard to make both ends meet. He dislikes sages and saints. He has no faith in God or in scriptures. He is very cruel-hearted. He attends ball-rooms and theatres, goes to bed at 2 a.m. and gets up at 9 a.m. He wears a careworn face even though he appears in costly silken finery. He is always gloomy and depressed. His heart is filled with lust, anger, greed, vanity, hypocrisy and egoism. Compare for a moment the life of this man with that magnanimous Sage of the Himalayas! They are poles asunder. The one is a God-man, the other is a brute-man. But if the brute-man seeks the company of the God-man, he will surely give up his old dirty habits. Just as iron is transmuted into gold by the touch of the philosopher's stone, so also the brute-man will be radically changed into a veritable saint by and by through constant contact with a developed Yogi.

Good friend! Slay this serpent of ignorance mercilessly. Get Knowledge of Self. This will give you Freedom or Liberation. Ignorance is your deadliest enemy. He has plundered the Jewel of Wisdom for long ages. Rise above temptations of this little world. This world is a show for five minutes directed by the juggler, Maya or mind. Beware. Do not get yourself entrapped. Money, woman, power, name, fame—these are the five tempting baits of Maya. Those who have not fallen victims to these illusory baits will surely reach the other shore of immortality and fearlessness—the shore beyond darkness, where there is perennial joy and eternal sunshine. Reach this shore through indefatigable struggle, rigid discipline and rigorous practice of Yoga.

From the condition of your mind, from your feelings and conduct, you can very well understand the nature of your actions in your previous lives and can nullify or counteract the effects of evil actions by doing good actions, Tapas, discipline and meditation. Try to lead a life of non-attachment. Discipline your mind carefully. No one is free from pains, diseases, troubles, difficulties. You will have to rest in your divine nature. Then alone you will draw strength to face the difficulties of life. Then only you will have a balanced mind. Then only you will not be affected by external morbid influences and discordant vibrations. Regular meditation in the morning will give you new strength and inner life of joy and bliss. Practise meditation. Feel this joy and bliss despite your stormy conditions and adverse circumstances. Gradually you will grow spiritually. You will attain Self-realisation.

Abandon this eat-drink-and-be-merry policy. Look always upwards and onwards. Have an ideal before you. Live up to it at any cost. You can become as great as any one else. Give up this inferiority-complex. Give up the superiority-complex also. The idea of inferiority and superiority is born of ignorance. Inferiority-complex will cause worry. Superiority-complex will generate pride and vanity. Put on the switch of the eternal Light in the innermost chambers of your heart. Keep the Divine Flame burning steadily. Feed it regularly. Throw your whole heart and soul in spiritual practices. Waste not even a single moment. Be persistent and methodical in your Sadhana. Marshal up all your forces properly and powerfully even as the Lieutenant-General in the army marshals up the armies on the battle-field. All miseries will melt away soon. You will shine as a glorious Jivanmukta with the highest realisation. All sense of separateness, distinction, duality, difference will vanish out of sight. You will feel oneness and unity everywhere. You will feel that there is nothing but Brahman or God. What a magnanimous vision you are blessed with! What an exalted state, what a sublime soul-stirring and stupendous experience will be yours! You will get dumbfounded. This state is indescribable. You must experience it by direct intuitive perception.

Introspect daily in the morning and examine the various nooks and corners of your heart. The mind is very diplomatic and cunning. The ego will keep several desires for secret gratification. Many desires will be lurking in your mind. It is very hard to detect their presence. Aspirants who are puffed up with their scholarly erudition and some powers (Siddhis) cannot trace the existence of these undercurrents of desires in their minds.

They pose themselves as great Yogins, deliver lectures in various parts of the world, build Ashrams and make lady-disciples. Nevertheless, it should be admitted, their speeches do not produce any deep impression in the minds of the hearers. These speeches are like empty bullets. The secret desires attack the student of Yoga mercilessly, whenever a suitable opportunity presents itself and destroys all his noble qualities and sublime ideas. They pounce upon the student of Yoga with a vengeance and redoubled vigour and bring a hopeless downfall that has no parallel. Those who have a pure, subtle intellect, who remember God always, who thirst for communion with Him, who practise daily introspection, self-analysis and meditation will be able to detect the presence of lurking desires, not others. He who has abandoned all desires, who is free from all yearnings, attains everlasting Peace. He enjoys the supreme happiness. The fewer the desires, the greater the happiness. That desireless Yogi who roams about in the world with a loin-cloth and a blanket only is the most happy man in all the three worlds.

Selfishness is a negative attribute of the lower mind. It is a modification of desire that arises in a mind filled with passion. It is the first-born child of ignorance or indiscrimination. It is the greatest obstacle to the practice of Yoga. It is the bane of life. It contracts the heart *ad infinitum* and intensifies the idea of separateness from others. Selfishness goes hand in hand with egoism, hypocrisy, vanity, miserliness, cunningness, dishonesty and pride.

How to eradicate this selfishness? The answer is simple enough. Selfless service in some form or another, cultivation of the opposite virtuous qualities, viz., nobility, magnanimity, disinterestedness, integrity, generosity, charitable nature, mercy and universal love—all these will pave a long way in the eradication of this dire malady, the deadly foe of peace and Yoga. Positive overpowers the negative. This is an infallible *dictum* in Yoga.

To sum up the fundamental requisites for the practice of Yoga: you should have absolute fearlessness, regard for every creature that breathes, respect for truth, continence, absence of greed, a life of contentment, austerity, absence of anger and hypocrisy. Moral excellence is not the final goal of life but is only the means to that end. When the Yogi is established in these virtues, he gets some powers such as effectiveness of speech, arrival of unsought wealth, vigour of body and mind, clear and lucid understanding of life's events, clarity of thoughts, steadiness of attention, control of the senses, immense joy and intuition.

Beloved Immortal Self! Observe vow of silence. Keep the mind fully occupied. Sit on your favourite Asana and do regular meditation. Sing the Name of the Lord. Twirl the beads. Study the scriptures. Practise celibacy. Take almonds and sugarcandy every morning (*Soak 10 or 12 almond seeds overnight in cold water. Peel off the skin the next morning and eat them with sugar-candy*). Do not consult doctors. Do not think of your disease. Divert the mind from the body. Be cheerful always. Smile, whistle, laugh, dance in joy and ecstasy. Think of God and meditate upon Him with true devotion and feeling and merge in Him. This is the goal of Life. You have attained it after a long and continued struggle for some years with zeal and enthusiasm. You have now become a Jivanmukta (living liberated soul). Hail, hail to thee, a thousand hails, my child!

INNER YOGIC DISCIPLINE

I

Yoga is the discipline of the mind, senses and the physical body. Yoga helps in the coordination and control of the subtle forces within the body. Yoga brings in Perfection, Peace and everlasting Happiness. Yoga can help you in your business and in your daily life. You can have calmness of mind at all times by the practice of Yoga. You can have restful sleep. You can have increased energy, vigour, vitality, longevity and a high standard of health. You can turn out efficient work within a short space of time. You can have success in every walk of life. Yoga will infuse in you new strength, confidence and self-reliance. Through Yoga you can have complete mastery over the mind, passions, emotions, impulses, temper, tongue, and so forth. The body and mind will be ever at your beck and call.

God-consciousness or communion with the Lord is the acme of the ethico-religious discipline of Yoga. This is attended by a remarkable sense of freedom and moral elevation on account of the crumbling down of the false, illusory, little 'I'. The Yogi is in possession of all Divine Powers now. He enjoys unalloyed eternal Bliss.

Power of endurance is a virtue to be possessed by a Yogi, a Jnani and a Bhakta. Many hardships and privations have to be faced by the aspirant in the successful performance of Yoga. Titiksha develops will-power. That is the reason why Lord Krishna says to Arjuna: "The contacts of matter, O son of Kunti! giving cold and heat, pleasure and pain, they come and go, impermanent, endure them bravely, O Bharata! The man whom these torment not, O chief of men, balanced in pain and pleasure, steadfast, he is fit for immortality."—Bhagavad-Gita: Ch. II-14, 15.

Moral excellence or ethical perfection is not, however, the final goal of the Yogi. It is only a means to the attainment of the end of life. Ethical development is more difficult than the attainment of intellectual eminence, because the truth can only be grasped by the Yogi who possesses a pure or untainted heart.

The essentials of moral life are straightforwardness, honesty, mercy, humility, respect for life or tender regard for every creature that breathes, absolute unselfishness, truthfulness, celibacy, non-covetousness, absence of vanity and hypocrisy, and cosmic love.

The student of Yoga should be abstemious in his diet. He should avoid laziness, ease, habitual languor and excess of sleep. He should observe silence and occasional mild fasts to ensure a good tone to his constitution. He should develop correct habits. He should check all sorts of ambitions and counter-currents of worldly desires by enquiry, thinking and discrimination. He should say unto the deceiving mind: "O mind! I know your tricks. I have got dispassion and discrimination now. Do not wag your tail now. I will snip it off ruthlessly. I have learnt many lessons. It is only ignorance that makes man prefer a transient gain to permanent benefits. I do not want again these sensual enjoyments. They are like vomited matter for me. I have resolved to attain the free, everlasting fruits of Yoga viz., EVERLASTING PEACE, INFINITE BLISS AND SUPREME JOY."

Yoga advocates complete detachment from secular interests for the sake of practising uninterrupted meditation. It recommends meditation on the inner Light of the heart or anything that is pleasing to you. It prescribes that one should withdraw oneself from the ordinary affairs of life for the purpose of practising constant meditation. Yoga can also be practised at home by having well-regulated life.

A Yogi claims that he can attain extraordinary powers and knowledge by subduing the passions and appetites and by practising Yama, Niyama and Samyama (or the practice of concentration, meditation and Samadhi at one and the same time). Patanjali Maharshi, the author of 'Yoga-Sutras', clearly warns the students that they should not be carried away by the temptations of powers. The gods themselves tempt the unwary Yogi by offering him a position similar to theirs. Students seek more after Siddhis than after Truth and spiritual attainment despite the clear note of warning.

Desire for power acts like puffs of air which may blow out the lamp of Yoga that is being carefully tended. Any slackness in feeding it due to carelessness or selfishness for Siddhis will blow out the little spiritual light that the Yogi has kindled after so much struggle and will hurl him down into the deep abyss of ignorance. He cannot rise up again to the original height to which he had ascended in the Hill of Yoga. Temptations are simply waiting like vultures to overwhelm the unwary student. Temptations of the astral, mental and Gandharva worlds are more powerful than the earthly temptations.

Success in Yoga is possible only if the aspirant practises profound and constant meditation. He must practise self-restraint at all times, because all of a sudden the senses may become turbulent. That is the reason why Lord Krishna advises Arjuna: "O son of Kunti! The excited senses of even a wise man, though he be striving impetuously, carry away his mind. For the mind, which follows in the wake of the wandering senses, carries away his discrimination, as the wind (carries away) a boat on the waters."—Bhagavad-Gita: Ch. II-60, 67.

Very often various sorts of obstacles come in the way of the Yogi. Disappointment, despair, sickness, depression, doubt, indecision, lack of physical and mental energy, slothfulness, unsteadiness, craving for sensual objects, blunder, act as stumbling blocks. He should not be discouraged. Patanjali Maharshi prescribes *Eka-Tattva-Abhyasa* i.e., practice of concentration on one subject to overcome them. This will give him steadiness and strength. He further advocates the practice of friendship between equals, mercy towards inferiors, complacency towards superiors and indifference towards wicked people. This practice will generate peace of mind or composure and will destroy hatred, jealousy, etc. A new life will dawn in him when he practises these virtues. What is needed is perseverance. It is the key-note of Yoga. The Yogi is amply rewarded, when he gets full control over the mind. He enjoys the highest bliss of Asamprajnata Samadhi.

II

Keep your balance of mind always. This is a very important practice. This is, doubtless, a difficult practice, but you will have to do it at any cost. Then alone you can be really happy. Then and then alone you can enjoy real peace of mind. Keeping up the balance of mind in pleasure and in pain, in heat and in cold, in gain and in loss, in success and in failure, in praise and in censure, in respect and in disrespect is wisdom. This practice is a trying discipline indeed, but it gives inner spiritual strength. He who is able to keep a balanced mind at all times, in all conditions, even under extreme provocation, is a mighty potentate on earth. He must be adored. He is the most wealthy man, though he is clad in rags, though he has nothing to eat. He is the strongest man even if he has a dilapidated physical frame. Worldly people lose their balance of mind even for trifling things. They get irritated and lose their temper soon. Energy is wasted when one loses his temper. An irritable man is a very weak man though he possesses immense physical strength and a fine muscular, well-developed body. Those who want to practise balance of mind should develop discrimination and practise celibacy and meditation. Those who have wasted their semen much, get irritated very frequently.

Irritability manifests itself as an outburst of temper when any opportunity offers itself. You will have to be very careful. You will have to nip the irritability in its bud. Do not allow it to assume the form of a big wave of anger. Every time you become a victim to a passion of any kind, you make it a little more difficult to resist its next attack; on the contrary, if you succeed in your attempt in subduing it, it will be very easy for you in getting triumph over it next time. This is the immutable Law of Nature.

The fit of anger passes away but it leaves a definite impression in the astral body. The man is more and more susceptible to further attacks of irritability. Each outburst of temper augments the capacity for anger and the possibility of being irritated quickly. The astral body responds more readily than before to these unpleasant fits of rage. Man completely loses the power of self-control. In a moment he may do any kind of atrocious crime. He may commit murder or any other atrocious cruelty. He is polluting the thought-world and is injuring all those around him by his vicious vibrations. It behoves, therefore, that every man should surely take great care to avoid these outbursts of anger. He must be careful when he moves and talks with others.

The senses are your enemies. They draw you out and disturb your peace of mind. Do not keep company with them. Subdue them. Restrain them. Curb them just as you curb the restive horse. Discipline of the senses gives spiritual strength and peace of mind. The discipline of the senses is not a day's work. It demands continuous and patient practice for a very long time. Control of the senses is really control of the mind. All the ten Indriyas must be controlled. Starve them to death. Do not give them what they want. They will then be slowly thinned out. They will obey your orders implicitly. Worldly-minded persons are mere slaves of their Indriyas, though they are educated, though they possess immense wealth and judicial or executive powers. If you are a slave of meat-eating, you will begin to exercise control over the tongue if you give up meat-eating for six months. You will consciously feel that you have gained a little supremacy over this troublesome Indriya which was of a revolting nature sometime ago.

Be cautious, vigilant and circumspect. Watch your mind and Vrittis. Lord Jesus says: "Watch and pray." Watching the mind is introspection. One in a million does this beneficial, soul-elevating practice or discipline. People are immersed in worldliness. They run after money and women. They have no time to think of the Soul or higher spiritual things. The sun dawns, the mind runs in its old, usual, sensual grooves of eating, drinking, amusing and sleeping. The day has passed. In this way the whole life passes away. There is neither moral development nor spiritual progress. The so-called educated, cultured people also have no idea of introspection. They simply develop their intellect, earn some money, hold some rank and position, get some vain and empty titles and honours and pass away from the scene without attaining the Knowledge of the Self or the Goal of life. Is this not really sad? Is this not highly lamentable? He who does introspection daily can find out his own defects and can remove them by suitable methods and have perfect control over the mind. He cannot allow the intruders—lust, anger, greed, delusion and pride—to enter the mental factory. He can cultivate various divine virtues such as mercy, forbearance, purity, courage, etc.

Daily self-analysis and self-examination are indispensably requisite. Then only the Yogic student can obviate his defects and can grow rapidly in spirituality. What does a gardener do? He watches the young plants very carefully. He removes the weeds daily. He puts a nice strong fence round them. He waters them daily at the proper time. Then alone they grow beautifully and yield fruits quickly. Even so, the Yogic student should find out his defects through daily self-analysis and then eradicate them through suitable means. If one method fails, he must take recourse to a combined method. If prayer fails, he should take recourse to Satsanga, Pranayama, meditation, dietetic regulation, enquiry, and so on. He should destroy not only the big waves of pride, hypocrisy, lust, anger, etc., that manifest on the surface of the conscious mind, but also their subtle impressions that lurk in the corners of the subconscious mind. Then only he is perfectly safe. These subtle impressions are very dangerous. They lurk themselves like thieves and attack the aspirant, when he is a bit careless, when he slackens a bit his daily spiritual practices, and when he is provoked. If these defects did not manifest even under extreme provocation on several occasions, even when you are not practising daily introspection and self-analysis, you can be rest assured that the subtle impressions also are obliterated. Now you are safe. The practice of introspection and self-analysis demands patience, perseverance, leech-like tenacity, application, iron will, iron determination, subtle intellect, courage, etc. But you will get a fruit of incalculable value. That fruit is Immortality, Supreme Peace and Infinite Bliss. You will have to pay a heavy price for this. Therefore do not grumble when you do daily practice. You should apply your full mind, heart, intellect and soul. Then only rapid success is possible.

Every aspirant in the path of Yoga should try to possess a serene mind. An aspirant with a restless mind cannot make an iota of progress in Yoga. The first prerequisite for a Yogic student is serenity of mind. Silent meditation in the morning, renunciation of desires, Sattvic diet, discipline of the senses, observance of Mouna (silence) daily for one hour will pave a long way in the attainment of a settled peace of mind. All vain, habitual thoughts, feelings, cares, anxieties, confused ideas, all sorts of imaginary fears, must be eradicated. Then only you will have a peaceful mind. The foundation of Yoga can be well and truly laid only if the aspirant possesses serenity of mind to a maximum degree. A calm mind only can grasp the truth. A silent mind only can receive the Divine Light. A peaceful mind only will be a proper vessel to hold the spiritual light. The spiritual experiences will be permanent if one possesses a quiet mind. Otherwise they will come and go.

As soon as you get up from bed in the morning, do some prayer, Japa and meditation from 4 to 6. Then make a firm determination: "I will observe celibacy today. I will speak the truth today. I will not hurt others' feelings today. I will not lose my temper today." Watch the mind. Have an iron will. Be resolute. You will surely succeed that day. Then you can continue the vow for the whole week. You will gain strength gradually. Your will-force will develop. Then continue the vow for the whole month. Even if you commit some mistakes in the beginning you need not be unnecessarily alarmed. Mistakes are your best teachers. You will not commit the same mistakes again. If you are sincere and earnest, the Divine Grace will descend upon your head. The Lord will give you strength to face difficulties and troubles.

He who has controlled his mind is really happy and free. Physical freedom is no freedom at all. If a man is easily carried away by his emotions and impulses, if he is under the grip of moods, cravings and passions, how can he be really happy? He is like a rudderless boat. He is tossed about hither and thither like a piece of straw in a river. He laughs for five minutes and weeps for five hours. What can wife, son, friends, money, fame, titles, powers, do for him when he is swayed by the impulses of the mind? A true hero is he who has controlled his mind. There is a proverb: "He who has controlled his mind has controlled the world." True victory is victory over the mind. Then only one can enjoy real freedom. Through rigorous discipline and self-imposed restrictions, you will have to eradicate all your desires, thoughts, impulses, cravings, etc. Then only you can free yourself from the thraldom of the mind. You should not give leniency to the mind. The mind is a mischievous imp. You should curb it by drastic measures. Then only you can become a perfect Yogi. Money cannot give you freedom. Freedom is not a commodity that can be purchased in the Crawford Market! It is a rare hidden treasure guarded by a five-hooded serpent. Unless you kill the serpent, you cannot get the treasure. That treasure is the Spiritual Wealth. The serpent is the mind. The five hoods are the five senses through which the mind hisses.

Rajasic mind always wants new things. It wants variety. It gets disgusted with monotony. It wants change of place, change of food, and change of everything, in short. But a Yogic student should train the mind to stick to one thing. He should not be afraid of monotony. He should have asinine patience, adamantine will and untiring perseverance. Then only he can succeed in Yoga. He who wants something new always, is unfit for Yoga. You should stick to one place, one teacher, one method, one system of Yoga. Then only rapid progress is possible. You should have real thirst for God-realisation. Then all obstacles will be obviated. Then only you can stick to the path of Yoga. Mere emotional bubbling for the time being out of sheer curiosity or for getting powers and Siddhis cannot bring any tangible results.

When you have made some progress in meditation, you cannot be carried away by surging emotions. Occasional irritability and undesirable cravings of various sorts may manifest, but you will have strength to control or repress them. You will not yield to them. Gradually these cravings will be completely burnt by the fire of meditation.

If you are careless, if you are irregular in your Yogic practices, if your dispassion wanes, if you give up your Sadhana for some days on account of laziness, the adverse forces will take you away from the true path of Yoga. You will be stranded. It will be very difficult for you to rise up again to the original pinnacle. Therefore be very regular in your practices.

The restless mind must be rendered quiet by reducing your wants, by destroying useless earthly desires. Have one strong desire for liberation. Then you can open your mind to the higher spiritual influences. The Divine Light will slowly descend. You can actually feel the inner change and spiritual uplift. Gradually the personal consciousness will merge itself into the Cosmic Consciousness, the individual will will merge into the Divine Will or Cosmic Will. This is the state of Samadhi or Superconscious state. Man has become transmuted into God now. After many ages he has gone back to his original home or abode of Immortality and eternal Bliss.

You will have to squeeze out all Rajas from the mind. Rajas is passion. All worldly ambitions are the products of Rajas. Ambition renders the mind restless. If the ambition is not realised, the mind is filled with depression and anxieties. The ambitious man has no peace of mind. He worries himself: "Will I succeed in my attempt? Even if I succeed, will I be able to have the same influence and power which Mr. So and so possesses?" Ambition is a great obstacle in Yoga. You must try to get peace of mind first. Then only the superstructure of Yoga can be built up quickly. The Divine Light can only descend in a peaceful mind. If you have a peaceful mind, you will get flashes of higher vision.

A gloomy man radiates unpleasant and morbid vibrations all around. There is nothing more infectious than depression. Never come out of your room, if you are depressed, because you will spread the contagion to your friends and neighbours. Depression eats the very core of your being. It havocs like a canker. It is a deadly plague. It may be due to some disappointment or failure, severe dyspepsia or heated debates, wrong thinking or wrong feeling, etc. Separate yourself from this negative feeling and identify yourself with the Supreme Purusha. Have an inner life. No external influences can affect you. You will be invulnerable. You will be proof against depression or any dark antagonistic force. Drive the feeling of depression at once by enquiry, singing the Name of the Lord, prayer, chanting of OM, Pranayama, a brisk walk in the open air, thinking of the opposite viz., the feeling of joy. Try to be happy in all states and radiate joy to all around you.

This world is nothing but the materialisation of the thought-forms of Hiranyagarbha or God. You have got the waves of heat and light and electricity in science. There are also thought-waves in Yoga. Thought has tremendous power. Everybody is exercising the power of thought unconsciously to some extent. If you have a comprehensive understanding of the working of the thought-vibrations, if you know the technique of controlling thoughts, if you know the method of transmitting beneficial thoughts to others at a distance by forming clear-cut, well-defined, powerful thought-images, you can use this thought-power a thousandfold more effectively. Thought moves. Thought works wonders. Thought heals. Thought has weight, shape, size and colour. A wrong thought binds; a right thought liberates. Therefore think rightly and attain freedom.

It is not thought alone that determines an action. There are some intelligent people who think nicely on the pros and cons of a thing but when the time comes they are led astray by temptations. They do wrong actions and repent bitterly. It is the feeling that really goads a man to do action. Some psychologists lay much stress on imagination and say that it is imagination that really determines an action. They bring the following illustrations in support of their statements:— Suppose a long plank 1 foot broad is placed on two turrets each 20 feet high. If you begin to walk over this plank you imagine that you will fall down and so you actually fall down; whereas you are able to walk nicely on the same plank when it is placed on the ground. Again, suppose you go on a bicycle along a narrow lane. There is a big stone on the way. You imagine that you will hit the cycle against the stone and so you actually run the cycle against the stone on account of your false imagination. Some other psychologists say that it is the will that determines an action and that will can do everything. To them will is Soul-force. Vedantins also are of this opinion.

Man is a complex social animal with a multiplicity of interests. He is a biological organism and so he is definitely characterised by the possession of certain physiological functions such as circulation of blood, digestion, respiration, excretion, etc. He is also definitely characterised by the possession of certain psychological functions such as thinking, perception, memory, imagination, etc. He sees, thinks, tastes, smells and feels. Philosophically speaking he is the image of God, nay, he is Brahman Himself. He lost his divine glory by tasting the fruit of the "Forbidden Tree." He can regain his lost divinity by mental discipline and the practice of Yoga.

Why do you weep, my child? Take away the bandage from your eyes and see. Lift up the veil of Maya. You are surrounded by Truth and Truth alone. Open your eyes and see clearly now. Wherever you see, there is the All-Full Light and Bliss only. The cataract of ignorance has blurred your vision. Have the cataract extracted immediately. Put on a new pair of glasses by developing the inner eye of wisdom through regular meditation.

LIGHT ON YOGA SADHANA

Question: In "Practical Lessons on Yoga" it is stated that Bandha Traya can be practised during Pranayama, concentration and meditation, with much advantage. But is not Bandha Traya a strenuous exercise by itself? Will not the combination distract the attention from the Lakshya?

Answer: While practising Bandha Traya, the mind should be engaged in meditation. This will help Kumbhaka to be prolonged during Pranayama, concentration and meditation. If the mind is allowed to wander about, Kumbhaka will last for a very short period only. Bandha Traya should be practised at the primary stages of meditation for success in Kevala Kumbhaka. In the advanced stages the combination is not necessary.

Q.: Should one do Kumbhaka after inhaling the breath when one does simple Bandha Traya, i.e., without combining it with Pranayama? How many times this Kriya should be performed, especially for the purpose of Brahmacharya?

A.: Bandha Traya (particularly Jalandhara Bandha) is a necessity for Kumbhaka only, soon after inhalation. It is just to arrest the involuntary impulse to exhale. Even ten times Bandha Traya during Pranayama practice in the morning and evening will give success in observing Brahmacharya. Much depends, however, on diet and changing the angle of vision towards spiritual values.

Q.: I read in a book that a Yogi once gave some magnetised water to a patient. When the boy was asked to take the water, the Yogi touched the glass with his fingers, and the water began to boil. How is it?

A.: I have seen many 'Yogins' creating water from empty pots, making water boil, and preparing rice in it. This is not associated with Yoga. It is pure jugglery. Healing power can be increased only by spiritual power through purity and intensity of concentration. Yoga confers this power. But no ostentation is resorted to for attracting attention for personal fame or gain or even for creating belief. By mere Sankalpa wonders can be effected by a man of unbroken truthfulness, celibacy and ethical virtues. Even the proper practice of Satya, Ahimsa and Brahmacharya by an ordinary man, irrespective of his past records, can work miracles.

Q.: Some one has written that by mastery over Yoni Mudra, Kutastha can be seen. How can the Absolute Consciousness (Kutastha) be seen thus?

A.: Yoni Mudra is meant only for developing deep concentration through the avoidance of external distractions. Kutastha or other points relating to the Sukshma Sarira or beyond cannot be seen by the physical eyes. One has to develop the internal divine vision or intuition to perceive the hidden truths of Yoga.

Q.: Is Kundalini awakened only through particular Yoga, e.g. the method of Rishi Patanjali? Is it essential for acquiring Siddhis?

A.: Raja Yogins awaken Kundalini through Samyama, Hatha Yogins through various Yogic Kriyas, Jnana Yogins through Pure Will, and the Bhaktas through immaculate devotion. Awakening Kundalini through any of these methods will bestow Siddhis. When Kundalini passes through various Chakras, the aspirant attains their respective Siddhis. Intelligent Yogins never demonstrate Siddhis, as in most cases they cause downfall. The ultimate goal is Self-realisation, for which Siddhis are absolutely useless. Misused Siddhis lose their effectiveness and cause untold suffering.

MAIN OBSTACLES IN YOGA SADHANA

Real aspirants who thirst for Self-realisation should be absolutely honest in every dealing. Honesty should not be the policy for them but it should be their strict rule of daily conduct.

Steya or the pilfering habit is very dangerous. It may develop into a serious crime under suitable conditions and favourable circumstances. He who commits even small thefts will have neither moral strength nor peace of mind. If the aspirant is not established in perfect Asteya or non-stealing, he cannot hope to get an iota of progress in the spiritual path. He may retain his breath for five hours, he may do Trataka in the mid-day sun, he may get himself buried underneath the ground for three months or he may show many other dexterous Yogic feats. These are of no value if he has the pilfering habit. He may be respected and adored for a week or a month. People will treat him with contempt when he starts pilfering.

Do not be deceived by external appearances. Just hear this remarkable incidence. A Pundit of vast erudition was a guest of a high personage. The Pundit could recite by heart the whole of the Vedas and the Upanishads and he had done great Tapasya. He was very abstemious in his diet and took only a very small quantity of food. He would never waste unnecessarily a single minute of the day and was always absorbed in the study of religious books, Puja, Japa and meditation. His host held him in very high esteem. This learned Pundit stole one day some articles from his host's house. They were not valuable at all. In the beginning he totally denied the theft. Later on he admitted it and apologised. Would anybody take such a learned Pundit of severe austerities for a petty thief? The subtle Vritti of pilfering was hidden in the Pundit's mind; he had not destroyed it through self-analysis and drastic purificatory Sadhana. He had not developed the virtues of nobility and integrity. He had only controlled his tongue to a small extent and crammed some sacred books.

The habit of telling lies co-exists with the habit of pilfering. Some aspirants tell lies even for trifling things. We can excuse householders but we cannot excuse aspirants. If the preceptor asks the disciple, "O Ram, have you taken quinine mixture this morning?" he replies, "Swamiji, yes, I have taken already." Ram tells a lie for this trifling thing and on further strict investigation he is found out to be a liar.

Many aspirants pose as great Yogins when they know only a few Asanas and Mudras and pose as great Vedantins when they have read only Vichara Sagara and Panchadasi. This is also another great obstacle in the path.

Religious hypocrisy of an aspirant is more dangerous than the hypocrisy of worldly-minded persons. This is an evil quality born of a mixture of Rajas and Tamas. Religious hypocrisy is a great bar to the descent of Divine Light and knowledge. It is very difficult to eradicate religious hypocrisy. What is this religious hypocrisy then? It is pretending to be what one is not. When the aspirant pretends to be a realised soul or a Jivanmukta when he is really otherwise, it is a pure type of religious hypocrisy. A religious hypocrite can never reach the goal of life and will soon be detected by the public though he may hide his face like an ostrich.

No Yoga or no union with Atma or Samadhi is possible if one is a victim of hypocrisy. He who says "I am a realised soul" when he is a slave of evil Vrittis is a confirmed hypocrite. Let no such man be trusted.

Self-sufficiency is another evil Vritti in the mind-lake. This is also born of a mixture of Rajas and Tamas. It acts as a stumbling block in the spiritual path. The student who is a victim to this evil trait thinks foolishly that he knows everything. He is quite contented with his little knowledge and achievements. He stops his Sadhana. He never attempts for further acquisition of knowledge. He never endeavours to attain the highest knowledge of Bhuma (highest Self). He does not know that there is a vast realm of knowledge beyond. He is like the toad in the well which has no knowledge of the ocean, which thinks that the well is the only illimitable expanse of water.

A self-sufficient man foolishly thinks and imagines "I know everything. There is nothing more to be known by me." Maya spreads a thick veil in his mind. The self-sufficient man has a turbid mind, clouded understanding and a perverted intellect.

Self-sufficiency is a strong weapon of Maya with which she deludes people and puts a strong break in the Sadhana of an aspirant. She does not allow him to proceed further or look beyond the veil as he is carried away by false contentment through self-sufficiency.

The self-sufficient scientist who has knowledge of the electrons and laws of the physical aspect of nature thinks that there is nothing beyond this. The moralist who has developed some ethical virtues thinks that there is nothing beyond this. The self-sufficient Yogic student who experiences Anahata sounds and flashes of lights thinks that there is nothing beyond this. The self-sufficient Sannyasin who knows the Gita and the Upanishads by heart thinks that there is nothing beyond this. The self-sufficient Yogi or Vedantin who gets experiences of the lower Samadhi thinks that there is nothing beyond this. All are groping in the dark. They know not what perfection is.

Maya tests the students in every step, at every stage and appears before the student in various forms or colours like an Asura or a chameleon. It is very difficult to detect Her presence. But he who has obtained the grace of the Mother will experience no difficulty in his onward march. She Herself lifts him up and carries him with Her hands to the destination to introduce him to Her Lord—Lord Siva—and to get him established in unshaken Nirvikalpa Samadhi.

The aspirant should always think, "What I know is very little. It is only a handful of knowledge. What is still to be learnt by me is oceanful." Then only he will have intense thirst and intense aspiration or yearning for further knowledge.

Self-justification is a very dangerous habit. It is an abominable evil quality born of Rajas. The aspirant does wrong actions and tries to stick to his own ideas, his own course of action, his own position. He brings various sorts of foolish arguments and gives wrong interpretations of scriptures to support himself. He will never admit his mistakes and faults. He tries to keep up his self-esteem. His mind is rendered turbid, crooked. He cannot perceive things in their true light. No one can help this man. He cannot make any progress in the path of Yoga as he will not listen to the instructions of elders or sages. Self-sufficiency, arrogance, vanity, self-assertions and self-will are the constant companions of self-justification. When these companions join with self-justification, he will be as turbulent as a monkey which drank a glass of liquor and was bitten by a scorpion also. He is entirely shut out from the Divine Light. Mark how Maya influences the deluded people! Self-justification is one of Her subtle forms (of lower nature).

Self-assertive nature is a great obstacle in the spiritual path. This is an evil quality born of Rajas. This is accompanied by vanity and arrogance. The aspirant who is a slave of the self-assertive nature wants to cut an important figure. He poses to be a great Yogi with many Siddhis. He says: "I am much advanced in Yoga. I can influence many people. No one is equal to me in the field of Yoga. I possess tremendous psychic powers." He expects others to pay respects to him and do prostrations. He gets easily annoyed with people if they do not honour him and do not make prostrations. He tries to keep up his position and prestige. The self-assertive aspirant does not pay attention to the instructions of his Guru. He has his own ways. He pretends to be obedient to his Guru. At every step his little ego asserts. He is disobedient and breaks discipline. He creates party spirit, revolt, chaos and disorder. He forms parties. He criticises Mahatmas, Sannyasins, Yogins and Bhaktas. He has no faith in the scriptures and the words of sages. He insults his own Guru even. He conceals facts and tells deliberate lies to keep up his position or to cover up his wrong actions. He tells several lies to cover up one lie. He twists and tortures real facts.

Pig-headedness is Tamasic obstinacy or stubbornness. This is born of Tamo-Guna or darkness. The pig-headed man sticks tenaciously to his own foolish ideas. I gave instructions to an young aspirant: "Do not climb up the hill with a plate in both hands and with shoes on; you will slip and break your bones." I also gave him an example of an European lady who died instantaneously near Badri Hills from a fall from the summit of a mountain when she was making a vigorous attempt to get Himalayan herbs. I further cited to him another example of a Professor of Geology, an M.Sc. of the Lucknow University, who also died from a fall from the top of the mountain in Lakshman Jhula, Rishikesh, when he was attempting to find out the nature of the rock. The young aspirant did not listen to my words. He was very obstinate. Despite my clear instructions, he climbed the Tehri hills with his shoes on and a plate in both his hands. This is a clear case of pig-headedness. Pig-headed students cannot make any definite progress in the spiritual path. You should eradicate this evil modification of the mind. You should be ever eager to get good instructions from any source or from any sage. You should be ever ready to grasp the truth, no matter from whatever corner it comes.

Man is not only a citizen of this world but also of many worlds. He has to face dangers and temptations not only in this world but also in the other worlds. The plane of the Gandharvas is full of temptations. That is the reason why it is said in the Yoga Sastras that the aspirant should purify himself first, should control his senses, should eradicate his desires, and should be established in Yama before he attempts to awaken his Kundalini, the sleeping potential Sakti, that lies dormant in the basal Muladhara Chakra. If Kundalini is awakened before the attainment of purity by means of Asanas, Bandhas, Mudras and Pranayama, the Yogi will come across the temptations of the other planes; he will have no strength of will to resist these temptations and will have a hopeless downfall. It will be very difficult for him to climb up again to the original height to which he climbed in the ladder of Yoga. Therefore the aspirant should try to purify himself first. If perfect purity is attained through Japa, Kirtan and constant selfless service, Kundalini will awaken by itself and move towards Sahasrara at the crown of the head to meet Her Lord—Lord Siva the trident-bearer of Mount Kailasa, the store-house of wisdom, bliss and peace.

Many aspirants climb up a certain height in the ladder of Yoga. They are irresistibly swept away by the temptations of the higher planes (Svarga, Gandharva plane etc.). They lose their power of discrimination and right understanding and thereby lose themselves in heavenly enjoyments. The citizens of the higher planes, the shining ones, tempt the aspirants in a variety of ways. They say unto the aspirants: "O Yogi! we are very much pleased with your Tapas, dispassion, spiritual practices and divine qualities. This is the plane for your final resting which you have earned through your merit and Tapas. We are all your servants to obey your orders and carry out your commands or behests. Here is the celestial car for you. You can move about anywhere you like. Here are the celestial damsels to attend on you. They will please you with their celestial music. Here is the Kalpa Vriksha which will give you whatever you want. Here is the celestial nectar Soma Rasa in the golden cup which will make you immortal. Here is the celestial lake of supreme joy. You can swim freely in this lake." The uncautious Yogi is easily carried away by the invitations and sweet flowery speeches of the Devas. He gets false Tushti or contentment. He thinks that he has reached the highest goal of Yoga. He yields to the temptations, and his energy is dissipated in various directions. As soon as his merits are exhausted he comes down to this earth plane. He will have to start once more his upward climb in the spiritual ladder. But that dispassionate Yogi who is endowed with strong discrimination rejects ruthlessly these invitations from the Devas, marches boldly in the spiritual path and stops not till he attains the highest rung in the ladder of Yoga or the highest summit in the hill of knowledge or the Nirvikalpa Samadhi. He is fully conscious that the enjoyments of Svarga or heaven are as much illusory, transient, monotonous and hollow and therefore worthless as those of this illusory world. The pleasures of the heaven are very subtle, exceedingly intense and highly intoxicating. That is the reason why the uncautious, non-vigilant, slightly dispassionate aspirant yields easily to the temptations of the higher planes. Even in this physical plane, in the West and in America where there is abundance of wealth, plenty of dollars and sovereigns, people enjoy subtle and intense sensual pleasures. Every day scientists bring out new inventions, new forms of sensual pleasures, for the gratification of the mischievous and revolting senses. Even an abstemious man of plain living and simple habits of

India becomes a changed man when he lives in America or Europe for some time. He yields to the temptations. Such is the power of Maya. Such is the influence of temptation. Such is the strength of the impetuous senses. That man who is endowed with strong discrimination, sustained dispassion, good Vichara Sakti, burning yearning for liberation can reach the highest goal of life, the final beatitude or the sublime vision of the Infinite. He alone can resist temptation and can be really happy.

CHAPTER SIXTEEN
VEDANTIC SADHANA

VEDANTIC SADHANA: INTRODUCTORY

Whatever has beginning or end is unreal. That which exists in the past, present and future is real. Brahman only exists in the three periods of time. Hence Brahman alone is real. A real thing only can be eternal, unchanging, beginningless, endless. Anything which is nothing in the beginning and in the end, necessarily does not exist in the middle also.

The reality underlying all names and forms, the primal one from which everything originates is Brahman or the Absolute. Brahman is the ultimate source of all joy and bliss.

Brahman is the inner reality or essence. The five sheaths are the outer husk. The body, the senses, the mind and the intellect are merely the outer covers which conceal the inner permanent Reality. These sheaths are the manifestations of Brahman. They are grounded in Brahman.

Brahman or the Eternal transcends the phenomena. Production and destruction are only phenomena. They are the jugglery of Maya or mind. In reality there is nothing produced or destroyed.

Brahman is infinity. Brahman is eternal. Brahman is Immortality. Infinity must be one. There cannot be two infinities. That which is unchanging, indivisible, non-dual, beginningless, endless, timeless, spaceless, causeless can be infinite. If there are parts in Brahman there will be plurality. There cannot be differences or distinctions in Brahman. Brahman is self-luminous, self-existent, self-contained, self-established, self-revealed. Brahman is birthless and deathless, because He is infinite, bodiless and timeless. Brahman is not a negative blank such as you have in deep dreamless, sound sleep, because He is pure consciousness, knowledge absolute. In Brahman you have perfect awareness, pure intelligence. Brahman or Absolute is *Satyasya Satyam*. It is the Self of all selves.

The objects seen in the waking state are as real as the objects seen in the dreaming state. All objects are unreal. The witnessing subject only is real and eternal. Life is a waking dream. How can a thing which changes be eternal and real?

The individual souls and the world are all unreal. Nothing save Brahman or the Absolute is eternal.

The mental world is as much objective or unreal as the material. The only reality is Brahman or the Atman. The world vanishes in sleep. The objects of the dream vanish as soon as you wake up. Hence the world of experience and the dream world are unreal. Beyond the three states is the Atman or Brahman. This Brahman is the basis of the three states. It is the silent witness or Sakshi. Brahman alone is Turiya or the fourth state.

Moksha is the Life Eternal. Realisation of the oneness of Self is the high water mark of Perfection. Realise this Brahman through hearing of Srutis (Sravana), reflection (Manana) and constant meditation (Nididhyasana) and attain freedom or the final beatitude.

Realisation of Brahman is regarded as the highest of all knowledge. A strong and wise man who is endowed with the four means only can attain Self-realisation. Rebirth can be stopped only through the realisation of Brahman. He who truly realises his unity with Brahman realises immortality.

Withdraw the senses, look within and search your heart. Dive deep into the deepest recess of your heart through deep meditation on the innermost Self. You will doubtless realise your identity with Brahman and get to the heart of the Infinite joy and bliss.

ASPECTS OF JNANA SADHANA

A Sadhaka should reflect and meditate. Sravana is hearing of Srutis, Manana is thinking and reflecting, Nididhyasana is constant and profound meditation. Then comes Atma-Sakshatkara or direct realisation.

This is also known as Brahmanubhava or Aparoksh-anubhuti. Then all doubts and delusions melt away. The knot of ignorance (Hridaya Granthi) is cut asunder. All Karmas (Sanchita and Prarabdha) are destroyed. The Jnani attains Sat-Chit-Ananda state. He is freed from the wheel of Samsara, from births and deaths with its concomitant evils.

The student in the path of Jnana Yoga repeats Om or Soham or Sivoham or Aham Brahma Asmi or Om Tat Sat and associates the ideas of Purity, Perfection, Infinity, Eternity, Immortality, Sat-Chit-Ananda along with the repetition of the above formulae.

ASSERTIONS FOR NIDIDHYASANA

I am the Sun of suns, Light of lights	OM OM OM
All Purity I am	OM OM OM
All Bliss I am	OM OM OM
All-pervading Consciousness I am	OM OM OM
Satchidananda-Svarupoham	OM OM OM
Akhanda Ekarasa Chinmatroham	OM OM OM
Bhumananda-Svarupoham	OM OM OM
Aham Sakshi (I am witness)	OM OM OM
Nirvisesha-Chinmatroham	OM OM OM
Asangoham (I am Unattached)	OM OM OM

LIVE IN OM

Live within. Live in the Spirit. Meditate on Atman, the Reality (Svarupa Dhyana). Make Mano-Japa of Om—Pranava (Manasika Japa). Chant Om. Sing Om. Feel Om. Eat Om. Walk Om. Breathe Om. Sleep Om. Befriend Om.

The uninterrupted practice of meditation 'I am Brahman' destroys the Vikshepa of Avidya (tossing or distraction caused by ignorance), just as the elixir of life (Rasayana) cures all diseases.

Sitting in a solitary place, free from all passions, curbing the Indriyas (senses), one should meditate on that one infinite Atman, without thinking of anything else.

A wise man should by his intelligence submerge in the Atman all that is seen and should always meditate on the One Atman that is like the pure, infinite ether.

THE SEVEN STAGES OF JNANA
(SAPTA-JNANA-BHUMIKAS)

There are seven stages of Jnana or the seven Jnana Bhumikas. First, Jnana should be developed through a deep study of Atma Jnana Sastras and association with the wise and the performance of virtuous actions without any expectation of fruits. This Subheccha or good desire forms the first Bhumika or stage of Jnana. This will irrigate the mind with the waters of discrimination and protect it. There will be non-attraction or indifference to sensual objects in this stage. The first stage is the substratum of the other stages. From it the next two stages, viz., Vicharana and Tanumanasi will be reached. Constant Atma Vichara (Atmic enquiry) forms the second stage. The third stage is Tanumanasi. This is attained through the cultivation of special indifference to objects. The mind becomes thin like a thread. Hence the name Tanumanasi. Tanu means thread—thread-like state of mind. The third stage is also known by the name Asanga Bhavana. In the third stage, the aspirant is free from all attractions. If anyone dies in the third stage, he will remain in heaven for a long time and will reincarnate on earth again as a Jnani. The above three stages can be included under the Jagrat state. The fourth stage is Sattvapatti. This stage will destroy all Vasanas to the root. This can be included under the Svapna state. The world appears like a dream. Those who have reached the fourth stage will look upon all things of the universe with an equal eye. The fifth stage is Asamsakti. There is perfect non-attachment to the objects of the world. There is no Upadhi or waking or sleeping in this stage. This is the Jivanmukti stage in which there is the experience of Ananda Svarupa (the Eternal Bliss of Brahman) replete with spotless Jnana. This will come under Sushupti. The sixth stage is Padartha Bhavana. There is knowledge of Truth. The seventh stage is Turiya or the state of superconsciousness. This is Moksha. This is also known by the name Turiyatita. There are no Sankalpas. All the Gunas disappear. This is above the reach of mind and speech. Disembodied salvation (Videhamukti) is attained in the seventh stage.

    Remaining in the certitude of Atman, without desires, and with an equal vision over all, having completely eradicated all complications of differentiations of 'I' or 'he,' existence or non-existence, is Turiya.

    That which is of the nature of bliss with intelligence is called Turiya. The sage in this stage is completely divested of all Vasanas. He is free from all ideas of difference and non-difference, 'I' and 'not-I,' being and non-being.

    The exalted stage of the seventh is the isolation or Moksha which is partless, equal in all, immaculate, beneficent, quiescent and the pure Turiya. The seventh stage, free from all objects and replete with bliss, is stated by some to be Turiyatita seat of Moksha, which is Chit itself. The seventh stage is above the reach of the mind, self-shining and of the nature of Sat. In the seventh stage, the disembodied salvation is attained. It is homogeneous. It is indescribable; it is beyond the power of speech.

METHODS OF VEDANTIC SADHANA

Sravana, Manana and Nididhyasana are the three stages of Vedantic Sadhana.

Sravana is hearing of the truth. The Abheda-Bodha-Vakya should be heard from the Brahmanishta-Guru. Then Vedantic scriptures and treatises have to be carefully studied for the purpose of properly grasping the meaning of the great Mahavakyas.

Vedantic Granthas are of two kinds: the Pramana-granthas and the Prameya-granthas. One should always study standard works on Vedanta. A complete and exhaustive treatise on the subject has to be studied with the greatest care. Then only the full knowledge of Vedanta will dawn. Works like the Advaitasiddhi, Chitsukhi, Khandanakhanda-khadya, Brahmasutras, etc., are Pramana-granthas, for they refute other theories and establish the Advaitatattva through logic and argumentation. Works like the Upanishads, the Bhagavad-Gita and the Yogavasishtha are Prameya-granthas, for they merely state the Absolute Truth with authority and do not indulge in reasoning for refuting or establishing anything. They are intuitional works, whereas the former are intellectual.

The mind should be pure and tranquil before starting Vedantic Sadhana. Keeping the Vasana in the mind is keeping a black cobra within and feeding it with milk. Your life is ever in danger. Kill these Vasanas through Vichara, Vairagya and meditation on the Atman.

The Sruti texts that deal with creation, such as "from the Atman sprang Akasa, from Akasa Vayu, from Vayu Agni," etc., are only intended for giving preliminary instructions to the neophytes or young aspirants for they cannot grasp at once the Ajativada or the theory of non-evolution. When you read the passages which treat of creation, always remember that all this is only Adhyaropa or superimposition. Never forget this. Never think even for a second that the world is real. Only through

Apavadayukti or refutation of superimposition can you establish the Kevala-Advaita-Siddhanta. If the world is real, if duality is real, you cannot have experience of Advaitic Realisation.

If the impurity of egoism or Ahankara-Mala is destroyed, the other two impurities, viz., Kama-Mala (impurity of desires) and Karma-Mala (impurity of action) will be destroyed by themselves. How, then, can there be Prarabdha for a Jivanmukta or the liberated sage? He is one with the Supreme Absolute.

OBSTACLES IN VEDANTIC SADHANA

Ahankara is the greatest obstacle to Self-realisation. "I know everything. My view or opinion alone is correct. What I do is right. That man does not know anything. Everybody should follow what I say. Everybody should obey me. I am free from any kind of fault. I am full of auspicious qualities. I am very intelligent. That man is very stupid. That man is wretched. That man has got many defects. I am wise. I am beautiful." Thus says the egoistic man. This is the nature of Rajasic Ahankara. He hides his own faults. He exaggerates and advertises his own abilities and qualities. He belittles others. He condemns others. He superimposes faults on others which they have not got. He sees not good but evil in others. He superimposes on himself several good qualities which he does not possess. That man cannot practise Vedantic Sadhana. He is unfit for the path of Jnana.

Raga and Dvesha constitute the great Samsara of the Jiva. They have to be destroyed through the knowledge of the Supreme Brahman. Either through proper understanding and discrimination or through Pratipaksha-Bhavana these currents should be destroyed. Liberation is attained by simplicity, by carefulness, by purity, by controlling the passions and by following the footprints of saints and sages.

Through Vedantic Sadhana the Brahmakara-Vritti is generated. The bamboo strikes against the other bamboos and fire is generated. The whole forest is burnt. There is a huge conflagration. Then the fire subsides by itself. Even so, the Brahmakara-Vritti that is generated in the Sattvika-Manas through meditation on Brahman or the significance of the 'Tat Tvam Asi' Mahavakya destroys Avidya or ignorance and its effects and leads to the attainment of Brahma-Jnana, and finally dies by itself when the Supreme Brahman is realised.

The paste of *strychnos potatorum* (Nirmal seeds)

removes all dirt in the water and helps it to settle at the bottom of the vessel. Along with the dirt the paste also disappears. Even so, the Brahmakara-Vritti destroys all worldly (Vishayakara) Vrittis and finally perishes by itself after the dawn of the knowledge of the Imperishable.

THE NATURE OF THE JNANI

The Jnana Yogi practises neither Pratyahara nor Chittavritti-Nirodha like the Raja Yogi. He tries to behold the One Undivided Essence of Satchidananda in all names and forms. He stands as a witness or Sakshi of all the Vrittis. All Vrittis gradually die by themselves. The Jnani's method is positive (Samyagdarsana), whereas a Raja Yogi's method is negative (Nirodha).

There is no body from the Drishti or view of the sage. How can there be Prarabdha then, for a Jnani? The Jnani is one with the Absolute and hence no change takes place in his being. He is Santam, Sivam and Advaitam. He is a Jivanmukta. He is liberated in this very life itself. His body is like a burnt cloth or a sword that is changed into gold through the touch of the philosopher's stone. His ego is burnt by the fire of Supreme Wisdom.

HINTS ON VEDANTIC SADHANA
THE NATURE OF TRUTH OR BRAHMAN

1. Truth is simple; it is made to appear complex by the distractive intellect. The sublimest things are always the most simple.

2. Truth alone triumphs; not falsehood.

3. Truth can never be defeated by untruth. Truth shall always win victory over untruth. When the path of Truth is trodden, everything else also is done. When the root is watered, all the branches are automatically watered.

4. The path of Truth is a precipitous one. It is slippery and all that is disagreeable. Hard it is to tread that, difficult a path it is. Giants among spiritual men walk over it to the city of Perfection.

5. The Absolute is All. Truth is Absolute. You are That. This is the essence of spiritual teaching.

6. Truth is utterly public. It cannot be hidden even if one would try to do so. Truth persists and is expressed even in the extreme of untruth. The extreme of Truth is the Absolute.

Untruth is a shadow of Truth. The world is untruth and the Absolute is Truth. The world is represented by sex and ego; the Absolute is represented by the Noumenal Gnostic Being.

7. His head shall break who acts against Truth and practises untruth. Truth is Being. Untruth is non-being, a mere naught.

8. Truth is not expressed even by Existence-Consciousness-Joy! It is only the nearest relative of Truth. But Truth is even greater, grander, mightier, truer!

9. All is well with him whose heart is turned towards the Truth. No disease, physical or mental, can assault him.

10. The mover towards the Truth is mighty, lives long, knows everything and is ever delighted, for he is nearing the Almighty Existence-Consciousness-Bliss.

11. Even to talk of Truth and think of Truth raises one to the height of immense satisfaction. What could be the experience of Its Realisation!

12. Truth is; untruth is not; hence it is wrong even to say that Truth is One, for Truth is Existence Itself and is neither one nor not-one. Truth is Absoluteness.

13. The Absolute baffles the mind of even the greatest scholar. It eludes the grasp of even the mightiest intellect. It is experienced as Pure Consciousness, where intellect dies, scholarship perishes and the entire being itself is completely lost in it. All is lost, and all is found.

14. Air rushes into where there is vacuum. The Absolute rushes into where there is no ego.

15. No time is necessary for the Absolute to reveal Itself. In the flash of a moment, like a stroke of lightning, the world will merge into Pure Being.

16. When will the Absolute-Experience take place cannot be said. It may be just immediately now or millions of births afterwards. Hence one should be always eagerly waiting for its arrival. It will come unexpected at any time.

17. Truth is immense; Truth cannot be spoken; Truth can only be experienced.

18. Truth is beyond speech. Truth is changeless and speech is change. Everything that changes itself is untruth. Hence Truth is Infinite. Truth alone endures, while everything else perishes. Everyone, right from Brahma down to a blade of grass, moves towards Truth, some consciously, some uncon-

sciously. They differ only in the degree of consciousness or the extent of mental purification or subtlety of condition. Every leaf that flies in the air, every breath that flows from us, in other words, every act of universal life, is a step taken nearer the Truth, for, Truth is the eternal Home of all beings. Into It they all enter and find permanent satisfaction and peace. It is the ego-sense that shuts us off from Infinite Life, and hence, the realisation of Truth is the dissolution of individual consciousness in Absolute Existence-Knowledge-Bliss.

19. The Absolute is perfectly scientific, logical, symmetrical, balanced, systematic, reasonable, rational. It is not irregular and haphazard. It is not a supra-natural mystery but the natural fact of life. The Infinite and Indivisible nature of existence is not a wonder; it is the actual condition of being even as brilliance is of fire, liquidity of water, weight of lead. It is the Highest Perfection of Eternal, Immortal Real Life.

20. The Highest Reality is Sat-Chit-Ananda where there is not even the slightest tinge of activity. That is why those who go near It become inactive.

21. Reality is the Perfected Embodiment of Existence, Knowledge, Power and Bliss. These four are only the aspects of the One Being which is Indivisible and changeless. These different aspects of Existence cannot be separated even as the Sun's flames, heat and luminosity cannot be distinguished.

22. Truth is Eternity, Infinity, Absoluteness, Intelligence, Consciousness, wisdom, beauty, love and joy. Sringararasa, Madhura-Bhava, or the erotic taste of the world is a shadow of the Supreme Reality of loving beauty and bliss. Aesthetic enjoyment is a reflection of Brahmananda or Absolute Bliss.

23. Infinity, Eternity, Immortality and Absoluteness are the characteristics of the Limitless Existence-Knowledge-Bliss.

24. All that appears here as the extensive manifold world is the One Uniform Reality existing in this form. As the bright light of the Sun appears as tantalising mirages, so does the One Light of Consciousness appear as many. To appear like this is the very nature of the Reality. These mountains, these rivers, this earth, this vast ether—all these are nothing but the One Pure Undying Spirit. Just as an uneven mirror presents an ugly and corrugated reflection of the face, so does this One Mass of Eternal Existence appear as many due to wrong imagination. All the things of this world are really the One

Whole Indivisible Being. The One Ether of Consciousness appears as the concrete many! All this is One, Partless, Divisionless, Beginningless, Endless, Absolute Brahman. The origin, the growth, the enjoyment and the involution of the world are an entire illusion. The network of the worlds is Brahman! The ten directions are Brahman! Time, space, things, activities, cause, effect, actor, birth, death, existence, all are Brahman Itself appearing in Brahman by the power of Brahman! The world is the dazzling of Consciousness! All that is seen below, here, upwards or crosswords, all that exists in the many creatures or within a straw, is Brahman only! There is nothing but That!

25. The Supreme Truth is Oneness! Separateness is for devotion. Manifoldness is not true. There is only One Infinite, Eternal, Nameless and Formless Essence or Principle, in reality which is Existence-Knowledge-Bliss, and That I am!

26. The essence of the Truth or Existence is Beauty, Love and Bliss.

WHAT IS JNANA YOGA?

27. Jnana Yoga is cessation from thinking of particulars, annihilation of the feeling of separateness or individuality, existing as One and united with All.

28. Yoga is the dissolution of thought in Eternal Awareness, Pure Consciousness without objectification, knowing without thinking, merging finitude in Infinity.

29. Yoga is the transformation of the ego-sense consisting of thinking, feeling, willing, understanding, determining and arrogating, into Infinite Consciousness.

30. Yoga is union or identification with the Essence of Absolute Existence.

31. Yoga is intense affirmation of or profound Meditation on the Absolute Being.

32. Yoga is of four types: (i) Service and self-sacrifice, (ii) devotion and self-surrender, (iii) concentration and meditation and (iv) discrimination and wisdom.

THE PATH OF THE VEDANTIC ASPIRANT

33. Do not imitate the Jivanmuktas; you are still a Sadhaka. Vasishtha had a wife, but he was a born Siddha. Janaka ruled the kingdom after severe Tapas and realisation of Truth. Krishna lived a princely life but He was One with the

Infiite. You are not expected to behave like them. You must do Sadhana.

34. Do not think that you are very wise and that you have understood everything; you know nothing, my friend; you are deceived. There is an ocean yet, and you have not tasted even a full drop.

35. Every breath of yours flows towards untruth; you live in the mire of falsehood and repeat "Truth alone triumphs!" Can you deceive Reality? Therefore, be true to yourself.

36. O crooked heart! You think one thing, speak another thing and do a third thing. Do you want God? O, how bold you are to claim the Seat of Bliss! Do not cheat yourself; be straightforward.

37. The so-called active spiritual people of the world who work for material gains and carnal pleasures are the most deluded creatures. They have forgotten their Real Self. Sages pity these people who are engaged in the external play of life.

38. Those who think that they are doing injustice to the world through their Self-realisation, have not yet gone above the credulity of childhood. For, they do not know that the Self which is Absolute includes the whole universe, and is far beyond that.

39. The world can be saved only by those who have already saved themselves. A prisoner cannot liberate other prisoners. Therefore perfect yourself; save yourself.

40. If He begins to give with His Infinite Hands, how much will you be able to receive with your two hands? And if He begins to take away with His Infinite Hands, how much will you hide away from Him with your two hands?

41. If the aspirant takes one step nearer to It, It will come in a hundred leaps and bounds nearer to him. Such is the nature of the Eternal Being. For every bit of action that is done for Its sake, you receive a millionfold in return! This fact is beautifully illustrated in the workings of Bhagavan Sri Krishna for the good of His devotees.

42. Sadhana is practised in order to attain the Goal, the Object or the Ideal. The object is sought because it allays misery and showers peace and bliss. The Absolute or the Brahman, the Infinite Light, the One Goal of all, is Itself Eternal Peace and Immortal Bliss. That is why It is the True Ideal that is to be realised by each and every being. There is nothing else to

be achieved either in this life or the other. If That is gained, everything is gained; if That is lost, everything is lost. That Supreme Being is Truth, God, Infinite, and everything that you may conceive of. That is what exists and That merely Is.

43. Sadhana is a conscious effort exercised for the achievement of an unattained goal or object. Spiritual Sadhana is a conscious mental effort directed towards the realisation and experience of the Absolute Reality. Such a spiritual effort is called "Yoga" in Sanskrit.

44. How clean you keep your house when you invite the ruler of your State! How much more clean and pure should your heart be, O man, if you wish the Immortal Lord to enter into you!

45. It is not necessary that a spiritual giant should have a muscular body. The greatest Jnani may also be a tubercular patient. There is no contradiction between the two.

46. Gold has to pass through fire before becoming brilliant and lustrous. An aspirant has to pass through untold suffering before becoming the absolutely Great.

47. One has to tend the cow with care by dirtying his body with mud and the refuses of the cow, in order to taste the sweet milk. The aspirant has to undergo extreme pains in order to realise the joy of the Spirit.

48. Fear is non-existent in Being. The spiritual aspirant is bolder than a soldier, bolder than a lion, bolder than a giant! In truth, he is the source of all courage and strength.

49. The spiritual aspirant is never helpless. The entire existence is supporting him in his arduous struggle, for he is searching for something which is true to all. One may dislike a certain thing of the world, but Truth can be hated by none.

50. If all the fourteen worlds were to face him in battle, the spiritual aspirant would count them for a straw. For he is the Immortal Spirit, the ruler of the heaven and earth, and the universes at large.

51. The road to the excellent Bliss is clothed with piercing thorns. The road passes through a lonely dense forest haunted by terrific tigers. It is protected by impregnable forts, and guarded by multihooded diabolic cobras. The road is hard to tread; the Bliss is difficult to attain. The sincere spiritual aspirant is one who has become immune to afflictions and terrors. No weapon that is cast against him shall prosper. No thought directed against him shall ever fare well.

52. The Guru's contradictory statements and insultive words are a challenge and a test for the disciple. The Guru sees whether the disciple is tempted and upset. The intelligent disciple should know how to act under such circumstances.

53. Never try to hide the bitter truth with a sweet lie. Be straightforward even if a sword is to pass through your heart. Cling to the naked Truth. If you try to save your 'little' self by hiding a fact, the 'highest' Self will never be reached. Even if your throat is about to be cut, remember that this sweet world of name and fame is only a shadow, and that Truth is Brahman, and nothing else.

54. Maya will sit in your brain and intellect itself. Beware of her snares. Do not try to protect your ego. For the sake of Truth, you must be prepared even to cast off this body at any time. For what purpose are you here on this earth, if not for drowning yourself in the flood of the Infinite Existence? You must get yourself buried in God. Then only you shall live. You gain by losing. You live by dying.

55. All these fourteen worlds with all their inhabitants and riches, beauty and grandeur, joy and happiness, cannot be an adequate price for the Jewel of Self-realisation.

56. The aspirant has to cast off the sheaths, tear the veils and pierce illusion in order to enter the Absolute. The realisation of the Absolute is the fine delicious fruit existing at the top of a terribly thorny tree.

57. A person who has once tasted even a little of the Bliss of spiritual meditation cannot give it up even for the sake of all heaven and earth put together.

58. O man full of craving! When you intensely desire for anything, try your best to desire for everything and not merely one thing. Do not exclude anything from your object of love. Let All be yours. For yours is this All.

59. "When the mind grapples with a great and intricate problem, it makes it advance, it secures its position step by step, with but little realisation of the gains it has made, until suddenly, with an effect of abrupt illumination, it realises its victory." So is the case with spiritual experience in the practice of Yoga.

60. A dense cave darkened by the thick gloom of ages of sunless nights does not require any time to be lighted up when the sun pierces its innermost parts. It is

instantaneously brightened to the fullest extent immediately when the sun's rays enter it in spite of its being dark for ages together. The terrible delusion and the vilest ignorance of man is erased out *in toto* by a flash of Supreme Intelligence attended with Bliss.

61. Sire! Do you, in your meditation, read others' minds? What do you mean? When we enter into the very root of life and existence, where is the question of reading different minds? In deep profound meditation you exist as the Absolute Essence Itself. Do you think that this foolish mind will persist even there? You go beyond the mental state and live in the Glorious Truth.

62. A thing is only a force whirling in a particular direction. One being is separated from the other due to the difference in the method of whirling of the Universal Force. Man is different from a tree because the two are different processes of the movement of the Eternal Force or Energy. This energy is imperishable, eternal. When two beings have a slightly similar movement of these forces or electrons or atoms, they become friends; when they are identical in movement they merge into one another and form One Being. The whole universe is only a diverse movement of the One Energy. When the whirling of this force behaves in a common way then the whole world collapses into Eternal Existence.

63. The whole universe is a gradual, systematic and progressive process of the Self-realisation of the Absolute. This is one view. The whole universe is a dreamy and illusory misrepresentation of the Indivisible Homogeneous Absolute. This is another view. The former view leads to the more advanced latter view. The former is an intellectual judgment, the latter is the intuitional experience. The first view is the beginning of knowledge, the second one is the end of wisdom.

64. "The whole universe is the Para Brahman"—this is the heart of the Advaita metaphysics. The world itself is not an illusion, for the world is Brahman; but the diverse conception of the world is an illusion, for diversity is not ultimate.

65. The world is the appearance of Sat or Truth. The world itself is Truth misrepresented.

66. Ignorance makes Existence appear as non-existence (death), Consciousness as unconsciousness (nescience) and Bliss as misery (pain). It makes a phantom appear as the reality, foolishness as knowledge and pain as joy.

67. We better love a scientific explanation than a dogmatic assertion of facts. The former is like feeding a person with the necessary daily dishes and allowing him to grow stronger and wiser; the latter would be like stuffing his belly with tons of foodstuffs at once in order to give him energy. For example, "Everything is Brahman" is a dogmatic assertion and is not intelligible, or, we may say, is even dangerous. A scientific explanation of it will help in divinising humanity and the world.

68. Idealism is of three kinds: Subjective, Objective and Absolute. The first one says that the whole universe is an imagination of the individual mind and subjective consciousness. The second one says that the universe is an imagination of the Cosmic Mind or God, the objective reality. The third one says that the universe is an appearance of the Absolute which includes as well as transcends the subject and the object. Naturally the first theory necessitates self-effort of the individual, the second, grace of God and the third mere automatism or wisdom, which is neither self-effort of the individual nor grace of God. The Karma Yogins will like the first theory, the Bhaktas the second and the Jnanis the third. The third is the view of the extreme Advaita Vedanta.

69. The world is ruled by ideas. Thought is the beginning of practice. Thought begets action.

70. The individual entities of the universe are steps in the ladder of progress towards Brahman-realisation.

71. Rigorous discipline of the mind through Abhyasa and Vairagya constitutes the method of attaining freedom and happiness. Real freedom which man so much hankers after is not derived from the ego-sense. Man's present conception of freedom is a total misconception and an utter wrong. He simply knows that he should be free, but he does not know where lies freedom. He wants to be happy but he does not know where happiness lies. He wants to live for ever, but he does not know how to do so. He wants to know everything but he does not know how to get knowledge. This is the reflection of Existence-Knowledge-Bliss, that man wants to live, wants to know, and wants to be happy. Who does not want this? All striving of the world is to live, know and enjoy. But the source of this great gain is life, consciousness and joy. Man is essentially Satchidananda. He impotently struggles to get this without knowing it. His present state is a pitiable fall from the glory of

Existence-Knowledge-Bliss. If we want to do anything in this world, it is because we cannot live without being the Absolute. We all, nay, even the unconscious beings—are ignorantly striving to attain the Immortal State of Satchidananda, whether we know it or not. Even a dry leaf flies only towards this Infinite. Every breath that flows, every thought that is projected, every word spoken, and even every action done, is towards the installation of ourselves in the state of Existence-Knowledge-Bliss, for we are That only in reality. This is achieved through spiritual discipline, which is action against the ordinary current of the world, against pleasure and enjoyment, against indulgence and sleep, against attraction for the multifarious, against everything that gives us pleasure here.

72. Do you think that death is an evil? Why do you say that blessed people only escaped death? On the other hand the blessed men would have reached the Eternal quickly, while the deluded mortals are still clinging to their bodies. Death is only a change of Consciousness. It is neither good nor bad. It is a stage in the process of evolution towards Eternity.

73. None can tread the higher path without fulfilling the requirements of the lower. The grosser manifestations have to be complied with their demands before reaching the metaphysical Being.

74. Each higher degree of truth is more concrete and inclusive than the lower one, and therefore Bliss which is Absolute is the most inclusive of all.

75. The head and the heart of man represent the aspects of the eternal realities of Knowledge and Bliss. Knowledge includes Power; wherever Knowledge is, there Power also must be.

76. Male, Purusha, Atman, Brahman, Siva, signify Knowledge. Female, Prakriti, Manas, Maya, Sakti, signify Power. When Knowledge and Power combine together and merge into one another there is the manifestation of Bliss. Power is only the other half and an appearance of Knowledge and as long as these two separate themselves, there is imperfection and pain.

77. Power is a relative necessity. It is not absolute. Hence it is excluded from the conception of the Absolute which is mere Being-Consciousness-Joy.

ANNIHILATION OF THE EGO

78. Negate your ego; deny your separateness; efface yourself; suffer pains and sacrifice pleasures.

79. Deny the wants of thyself; it asks for many a cup of poison. It is a moth that falls into fire thinking it is pleasant. It is a child that walks into the well.

80. Humble thyself, annihilate thyself, if you wish to LIVE.

81. Shame upon the man of mere dry intellect! He cannot avoid crookedness and cunningness. He is a self-deceiver and a husband of everlasting misery. He is far away from the Real. He has married sin.

82. Throw away your learning, O basket of vanity. Give away everything that is dear and behold the Light within.

83. The ego bursts into infinity or sinks into nothingness. These are the two paths by which the ego loses itself *in toto*.

84. Realisation of the Supreme State can come only if one is sincere and earnest in practical Sadhana. The lesser the connection with the ego and the greater the detachment from objective consciousness, the quicker the Realisation of the Absolute.

85. The more the ego-sense is pressed down, the nearer we are to the Eternal. The annihilated ego is taken place of by the revelation of the Absolute Reality.

INTERNAL SADHANA

86. The more you give up the world, the fuller you become and the nearer you are to absolute freedom.

87. The Self alone is dear. If anything else is dear, it shall quickly perish without doubt.

88. If you wish to see everything, pluck out the eyes of consciousness. If you wish to move everywhere, breaks the legs of consciousness. If you want to seize everything, cut off the hands of consciousness. If you wish to become everything, kill the consciousness. If you wish to become Immortal, murder the consciousness, with the axe of wisdom. When you get the whole, you do not cling to the part.

89. Cling passionately to the Infinite Being; you will be in want of nothing; you shall be filled up to the brim.

90. Shut all the doors of the senses; sit in the room of the heart; meditate on the Glorious Truth. Drown yourself and dissolve yourself in the Ocean of that Truth.

91. The nearer we approach the Truth the happier we become, for the Essential Nature of Truth is Positive, Absolute Bliss.

92. Love for the particular has to be set aside and love for the Infinite Whole has to be cherished. The Joy of the Completeness of Being cannot be partaken of in a semblance of it appearing to reflect in a point of space. Attachment for the particular makes us men bereft of intelligence; love for the Absolute makes us drink the Immortal Essence, after which there is no more sorrow, no more crying.

93. The child will not stop wailing and shedding tears until it sucks its mother's breast. So also, O Joy of my Soul! I cannot stop shedding tears of sorrow in this desert of burning sands, until I taste Thy milk of Immortal Sweetness.

94. Victory is won not by might and prowess but by truth, compassion, piety and righteousness.

95. Sattva is light and purity; Rajas is activity and passion; Tamas is darkness and inertia.

96. An exhibition of one's abilities brings physical comforts through objective contact, thickens the ego and strengthens the sense of individuality. These comforts act as a powerful hindrance for the higher aspirations of the soul. Therefore, one should use the wisdom he possesses for the purpose of inner meditation and spiritual attainments and never for external pursuits in the world. Fie upon that wisdom which is used for bringing pleasures to the ego! That is true wisdom which opens the door of Immortal Life!

97. Our ability, our greatness, our name and fame, our different desires and ambitions are to be spread in the world of the Eternal Absolute, not in this world of mortals, not even in the world of gods! Such temptations are to be checked and transformed into a force that reveals the Inner Essence of Life!

98. It is pity to see those people who, before entering into the depths of the Spirit, think that they are born to help the world. They think that they can bring heaven to earth before raising the consciousness to higher states. They have no yearning for Wisdom. They have gone astray.

99. Service that is "self-less" brings men nearer to Unity and the greatest service is the truly "selfless" but "Selfful" unification of the soul into the One Mass of Consciousness.

100. One body can be served by another body. One mind

can serve another mind. But one Atman cannot serve another Atman, for Atman is One. If the Atman realises the common Being of all with its Self, that is the greatest service an individual would do. If this soul melts into the universal Soul that is the greatest service this person would do to the world. Self-realisation is service, prayer, worship and all that is good. Nothing else.

101. One has to wear the armour of wisdom while walking through the battle-field of life. He has to protect himself with the shield of discrimination and cut the enemy of ignorance with the sword of experience.

102. The head and the heart must meet together before the Realisation of the Absolute Truth. The whole man has to be transformed, not merely an aspect of him.

103. The greatest insult received before respectable gentlemen is the beginning of perfection. The greatest pain, sorrow and grief is the beginning of saintliness.

104. One must try to get more insults. Even if people think that he is a good man, he should try to make them feel that he is a rogue, and thus get rid of their love for him. The whole world should oppose him. Then only he will prosper. The whole world should desert him and kick him aside. No earthly happiness can bring true Realisation. All should hate him. Then only his soul will be disciplined. There should be no help from the world of the mortals.

105. Let people pour shame upon one's face! But one should stick to the ideal. One should stick to the Highest Vedantic Ideal even on the edge of the doom.

106. The length of time taken by an individual to possess a desired object is proportional to the intensity of the individual's feeling of identification with the Infinite Absolute. The individual which feels that three-fourth of the entire existence is its own self and that one-fourth is not its being realises an object quicker than the individual that feels that only half of the entire existence is its self. People who feel that their own individual bodies are their self and that everything else of the universe is different from them can never live a happy life. The happiest person, thus, is the one who has lost his personality in the realisation of the fact that the entire existence is his own being and that there is nothing second to him. He is the Immortal, the Powerful, the Blissful, the Ocean of True Wisdom.

107. Brahmabhavana is the individual effort on the part of the subjective ego in order to realise the State of Brahmanubhava or Absolute Experience, the dissolution of the self in the Eternal, the Pure, the Perfect, the Omniscient, the Free, the All-knowing, the All-pervading, the All-powerful, the Peaceful, the Blessed, the Non-dual, the Mass of the One Undivided Essence of Existence-Knowledge-Bliss, the Absolute which is this All; there is nothing diverse here.

108. Stop, O mind, thy plannings! Enough, enough of thy cravings for the body and for the intellect. Make good of every minute that is at thy disposal. Time is a rat that slowly cuts the thread of life. It may break at any moment. Believe not that you will be living to enjoy the objects of life. Death may lay its icy hands on this body and may shatter it at any time. Cherish not objects of the world. Wish not for glory in life. Plan not to immortalise thy name in the world, lest thou wilt be immortalising it in vacuum. Speak not to people, lest thou wilt be speaking to the skies. Beat not space thinking it is a drum. Stop imagining. Stop scheming.

109. Finite pleasure and Infinite Satisfaction cannot be had at one and the same time. Where one is, the other is not. The mortal and the Immortal are utter contradictions.

110. To say "I am the Infinite" is not Abhimana. To feel "I am the Eternal" is not ego. Such an Abhimana or egoism is necessary for the Highest Realisation.

111. Sire! Can you tell me how to attain Perfect Peace? Shut all the doors and windows and sleep in the innermost chamber!

112. The true philosopher's mind is like a shining crystal. It is able to grasp at once the nature of the Reality. The moment such a person sits for meditation, his mind will fly into the depths of being. He will not experience any tossing of mind or any disturbing factor, for, his mind has been already purified by the fire of philosophical thinking.

113. One should have either a sharp intellect to grasp the metaphysical truths, or intense faith and devotion for the One Reality. If both of these qualities are lacking in a person, he cannot tread the spiritual path.

114. In Jnana-Sadhana (Vedanta or Advaita) there is no such thing as "meditation on an object." There is only intellectual analysis, introspection and positive understanding which

has its object in the destruction of the ego and annihilation of the intellect itself. It starts with the intellect and ends with the destruction of the same, which gives way to Experience, immediate and direct, transcending the subject-object-relation. Where there is no such thing as Omkara or anything of the sort in Jnana-Sadhana or Metaphysical Practice, there is no manipulation of word or sound in actual Advaitism. There is only grappling with the Essence of Existence through reason or ratiocination.

115. The pronunciation of the word "OM" includes all the processes of sound-production and word-formation. Hence this word-symbol is said to be the highest form of expression of Sound and is the basis of all speech, even the Vedas! All words and all languages are, thus, produced from the eternal "OM."

116. The highest freedom has its greatest tax, the fullest experience demands the costliest price for it. The dearest and the most beautiful of the world has to be surrendered and the sweetest abandoned for the sake of the joy of the Soul.

117. The most precious object of our love turns to be the price demanded by the Immortal Shop-keeper for our buying the bliss of Eternity and Infinity. Our very self, our very separate existence has to be parted with for obtaining the Joy of the Immortal Spirit!

118. Love is spoiled when it is directed towards an object that is defined by space. Love only the Limitless or the Infinite.

119. Let there be that terrible yearning for Self-Integration, that blazing fire of love for the Bhuma! Then only you are saved!

OBSTACLES IN THE PATH

120. Even a slight tinge of earthliness makes one unfit for the Realisation of the Absolute. No doubt the earth itself is the Absolute, but our attitude towards the earth is not of the nature of the Absolute.

121. Name, power, wealth and sex are the four doors to the fort of self-degeneration and imprisonment. These four are to be carefully abandoned.

122. Passion is the instinctive urge for externalisation through self-preservation and self-multiplication. It is the diversifying power which is directly opposite to the force that moves towards the Integration of Being.

123. There is a sudden revolt of the natural physical consciousness against all endeavour to reach the Absolute Reality. The rebellion is so uncontrollable that realisation seems to be well neigh impossible, for a weak aspirant.

124. People complain of disturbances and failures in meditation due to the impurity and grossness of their minds. A thorough study and understanding of the natural laws and truths of life is absolutely necessary before venturing to start meditation on the Real Essence of Existence. Without such necessary equipments, one is liable to be lost in the dark dungeon of ignorance.

WISDOM AND REALISATION

125. There is but One Immortal bottomless and limitless, surfaceless and shoreless Ocean of Indivisible Consciousness-Bliss-Mass, laughing with the joyous eternal waters of dazzling, brilliant, luminous Light and divine nectarine Sweetness, roaring with the Infinite thundering sound of never-ending Omkara-Nada, ever calm, peaceful, silent, blessed and dashing within Itself with mountain-like waves of unbounded Delight in the majestic grandeur of the Essence of Absolute Existence! There is nothing but That! Thus is the Meditation!

126. Absolute Experience is a state of Self-absorption and not self-expression, for the latter necessitates change and action, which is self-limitation.

127. None is excluded from Absolute-Realisation. One realises today, one tomorrow. But all must realise That one day or other. There is no selection for Liberation. All are the Absolute eternally.

128. There are many wiseacres, but few are wise. He is a man of wisdom who is ever in a state of half-sleep, having drunk deep the wine of the essence of life. Glory be to him! We are his servants.

129. A man of knowledge cannot express all that he knows at one and the same time. He expresses only that part of it which is excited by the contact of an external agent.

130. Many times Jivanmuktas put on a nasty appearance and act like men gone out of their brain. They sometimes behave in a very unpleasant manner which will annoy any man on earth. They will live like fools just to get rid of the love which the

world may develop towards them. They hide their real nature and move like intoxicated drunkards. These are the great men of the earth, not those who are clever in social manners and live like kings and emperors. He who is gone to the Truth cannot behave in a manner which is favourable to the fashions of the ignorant world! Such really great men are many on earth, but the world knows them not due to delusion, and considers only those as great who show a few juggler's tricks before its blinded eyes. The real is ever hidden and unseen. Only the unreal appears before us, and alas! we are cheated by it!

131. You cannot judge a Sage by his words or actions. He will be an ordinary loafer outside but a Jadabharata or a Suka-Maharshi inside.

132. For the sage everything is a play! But he never feels anything at heart except that Everything is One!

133. A person of Absolute Consciousness unconsciously attracts that part of Existence where lies his objects of desire. At once, like a flash of lightning, the things needed by him flow to him like rivers into the ocean, for he is their very Self. The man of wisdom does without acting, enjoys without wishing. He need not command anybody, for, he already is the Self of the one whom he may wish to command. He cannot instruct, order, perceive or even be conscious of anything else, for he is the essential being of everything that he may try to deal with. Even the gods cannot obstruct him from doing anything, for, he is the inner reality of even the gods. The mountains should shake and the earth should crumble into thousand fragments if he so wishes, for he is the self of even the mountain and the earth. If he shuts his eyes, the sun will become dark. If he breathes, all beings will live. If he so desires, the whole universe will become non-existent. If he so wills, the rivers shall flow, the fire burns and the trees blossom with flowers. If he so desires the entire universe shall now experience the State of the Eternal and the Immortal. Such is the glory of an embodiment of Wisdom of the Truth.

134. The might of thought and the strength of feeling melt into the glory of Experience-Whole. The finite is dead and the Infinite is born the very same moment. The birth of Day and the death of Night are simultaneous.

135. The greatest men are those who are lost in Self-Consciousness. Such men are too near to God to be able to do any action. Therefore they are unknown to the world.

136. The vision of God is the awareness of the essence of one's own being. God is the essence of even the Satan. He is the source of even the worst evil. He fills Himself inside and outside and there is nothing which He is not.

137. The devotee of the Eternal is lost in the Consciousness of God. He plunges into the Ocean of Bliss. He takes a bath in the sea of Nectar. He drinks deep the essence of Immortality. He attains the Source, the Root of the Universe!

138. O beloved of my heart! Immortal Joy! Where art Thou? How can I live without Thee? It is very long since I left Thee. Come, come! I am very restless without Thee!

139. "I am all"; this is the beginning of Truth-experience. Silent Be-ness is its highest flight.

140. There is no paper on which to write the Nature of Truth. There is no pen which can dare to write It. There is no person living who can express It. It merely is everything that is, and there ends the matter. Every effort to express It's Nature is trying to kill Its Greatness. I am that Great Being! I am here, I am there; Oh! I am this, I am that! I am the Greatest, the Best, and again the Greatest! My glory knows no bounds! I am the most Blessed, the Immortal, the Great!

VEDANTIC APHORISMS

THE NATURE OF THE INNER SELF

1. Self-consciousness is the ultimate category of existence.

2. The Ultimate Reality is the Mind of the mind, the Eye of the eye and the Ear of the ear.

3. The Atman is unspeakable and unthinkable.

4. The Absolute is the origin of life and the end of all things.

5. Brahman or the Atman is the Ultimate Reality. This world is a mere appearance.

6. The Inner Self governs all external existence.

7. Brahman alone is real; everything else is a modification.

8. God is the subtle essence underlying all things.

9. God is the salt of life.
10. The Atman is the highest object of desire and love.
11. Fear proceeds only from a 'second'.
12. Brahman and the real infinite "I" are identical.
13. God is the Verity of verities.
14. Everything is dear for the sake of Atman.
15. Grasp the Atman, you grasp all things; because all things abide in the Atman.
16. All things spring like sparks from the Supreme Self.
17. The Atman is the Ultimate Seer, Hearer and Thinker.
18. Nirakara, Nirguna, Nirvisesha, Nishkriya, are the negative attributes of Brahman.
19. The Seer sees and yet does not see.
20. The Soul is the mover of the body-chariot.
21. The parts of man are centred in the Lord as spokes in the navel of a wheel.
22. God is the Time of time. He is the Lord of Yama. He is Death unto death itself.
23. The body is the slough of the Soul.
24. The Atman is beyond the known and beyond the Unknown.
25. Matter, life, mind, intellect and Bliss are forms of Brahman.
26. Brahman is the Devourer of the devourer.
27. God is both immanent and transcendent.
28. Atman is subtler than the subtle and greater than the great.
29. Atman moves in a sitting posture.
30. Atman is far off and near. It is far off to worldly persons and near to men of discrimination and dispassion.
31. Hiranyagarbha is the first-born of God.
32. The Atman is always the subject of knowledge and never the object.
33. The Supreme Soul lives apart from Prakriti, while the individual soul is caught in the meshes of Her love.
34. God is the magician and Prakriti is His magic power.

PREREQUISITES FOR SELF-REALISATION

35. Not to destroy or hurt life, not to lie, not to misuse others' property, purity, reduction of personal needs, daily worship and charity are aids to God-realisation.

36. Purity of food and body, one-pointedness, practice of the Presence of God, selfless service—all these lead to the quick attainment of God-realisation.

37. Five virtues that lead to supreme blessedness are truth, integrity, kindness, generosity and gentleness.

38. The ingredients of character are purity, non-violence, truthfulness, courage, humility, forbearance, serenity and simplicity.

39. The Atman cannot be attained by a life of weakness and error.

40. Cessation from sin and introversion are needed for Self-realisation.

41. Dispassion or disgust for the world and humility are necessary for Self-realisation.

42. Truth, penance, insight, aspiration and renunciation are indispensable for Self-realisation.

43. A man without desire attains Brahman and becomes immortal.

44. You should have contempt for wealth, progeny and fame in the interest of spiritual realisation.

45. Knowledge is incomplete without eschatological knowledge.

46. Purity of mind depends upon the purity of food.

PROCESS OF SELF-REALISATION

47. Meditation on OM removes the slough of sin.

48. OM is the representative of the various states of consciousness and the various aspects of the soul.

49. Spiritual fire is churned out of the two sticks of the body and the Pranava.

50. OM is the bow; the Soul is the arrow; Brahman is the mark or the target.

51. Meditate on Atman as Immortality.

52. The message of the Gita is Tyaga or renunciation; the

message of the Mahabharata is Dharma or righteousness; the message of the Upanishads is the identity of the individual soul and the Supreme Soul.

53. If you lack wisdom ask God sincerely. He will give you. Go straight to wisdom

54. In quietness and confidence shall be your strength.

55. Walk towards the Light Divine. It is the way to immediate inner peace.

56. *Tat Tvam Asi* (Thou art That) is an ultimate definition of culture according to Indian philosophy.

57. Self-control means the control of the lower self by the higher Self for the realisation of the Self.

58. The aspiring Yogi experiences Eternal Day and Eternal Sunshine.

59. Meditate on Brahman as resplendence.

60. Meditate on Brahman as support, greatness, wisdom, bliss and existence.

61. If the worshipper of the Deity thinks that he is separate from the Deity he is a beast of the gods.

62. It is not possible to know the Knower, but you can realise the Knower (Atman) through Samadhi or intuition.

63. The spiritual life is a life of childlike simplicity.

64. Immortality means the union of the individual soul with the Supreme Soul.

65. When you are very thirsty you do not get books about thirst or water, you do not attend lectures or take courses of study. You go where there is water and drink. Even so a spiritually thirsty aspirant should ignore all theological controversies. He should take to meditation and realise God.

66. The spiritual fire should be generated day after day.

BEYOND GOOD AND EVIL

67. The Atman grows neither great by good actions, nor small by evil actions.

68. The wise sage grows neither great by good actions, nor small by evil actions.

69. Sin does not touch a sage.

70. The saint is an impenetrable rock.

THE WEB OF MAYA

71. Maya is of two kinds, viz., Avidya Maya and Vidya Maya. Avidya Maya takes you down the path of bondage and is characterised by lust, anger, greed, pride, hatred, etc.

72. The Vidya Maya takes you on the path of liberation and is characterised by discrimination, dispassion, devotion.

73. The Prakriti is made of red, white and dark colours.

74. Maya is an appearance. It is a semblance. It is the illusory power of God.

75. Man is a conglomeration of desire, will and action.

76. The elements welcome the soul and give him the experiences of this world of sensual objects and eventually give him a send-off when he attains perfection and freedom.

THE PHILOSOPHY OF SLEEP

77. Sleep occurs when the mind settles down on breath.

78. In sleep man is united with the Real or the Supreme Soul.

FAITH AND INTELLECT

79. The intellect is filled with devices and plans. It is the heart that can be filled with love, tranquillity, affection and kindness.

80. Faith in the love and goodness of God will comfort you and will give you solace and peace.

RESULTS OF SELF-REALISATION

81. Fear disappears after Self-realisation.

82. Resting in the fearless Brahman confers fearlessness.

83. There is no infatuation and grief for the man of Self-realisation.

84. There is an ignition point of the Soul. Man is transformed. His life is turned from its former worldly way into a new divine life. He is awakened spiritually.

ESSENCE OF VEDANTIC SADHANA

Vedantic Sadhana is otherwise known by the names Nirguna Dhyana, meditation on OM, Pranava Upasana or Brahma Upasana. Purify the Chitta by doing Nishkamya Karma for one year. The effect of Chitta Suddhi is the attainment of Viveka and Vairagya. Acquire the 4 qualifications or Sadhana Chatushtaya: Viveka, Vairagya, Shad-Sampat and Mumukshutva. Then approach a Sat Guru. Have Sravana, Manana and Nididhyasana. Study carefully and constantly 12 classical Upanishads and the Yoga Vasishtha. Have a comprehensive and thorough understanding of the Lakshyartha or indicative (real) meaning of the Maha Vakya "Tat Tvam Asi." Then, constantly reflect over this real meaning throughout 24 hours. This is Brahma Chintana or Brahma Vichara. Do not allow any worldly thoughts to enter the mind. Vedantic realisation comes, not through reasoning but through constant Nididhyasana, like the analogy of Bhramarakeeta Nyaya (caterpillar and wasp). You get Tadakara, Tadrupa, Tanmaya, Tadaikyata, Talleenata (Oneness, identity).

No Asana is necessary for Vedantic Sadhana. You can meditate while talking, standing, sitting, lying in an easy chair, half reclining posture, walking and eating.

Generate the Brahmakara Vritti from your Sattvic Antahkarana, through the influence of reflection of the real meaning of the Maha Vakyas "Aham Brahma Asmi," or "Tat Tvam Asi." When you try to feel that you are Infinity, this Brahmakara Vritti is produced. This Vritti destroys Avidya, induces Brahma Jnana and dies by itself eventually like the analogy of Nirmal seed or *strychnos potatorum* which removes sediment in the water and itself settles down along with the mud and other dirty matter.

MEDITATE ON OM

Retire into the meditation chamber. Sit on Padma, Siddha, Svastika or Sukha Asana. Relax the muscles. Close the eyes. Concentrate the gaze on Trikuti, the space between two eyebrows. Repeat OM mentally with Brahma Bhavana. This Bhavana is a *sine qua non*, very, very important. Silence the conscious mind.

REPEAT MENTALLY

Constantly feel . . . . OM OM OM
All-pervading, ocean of light I am . . . . OM OM OM
Infinity I am. . . . . OM OM OM
All-pervading, Infinite light I am . . . . OM OM OM

Vyapaka, Paripurna, Jyotirmaya Brahman I am . OM OM OM
Omnipotent I am . . . . OM OM OM
Omniscient I am . . . . OM OM OM
All Bliss I am . . . . OM OM OM
Sat-Chit-Ananda I am . . . . OM OM OM
All Purity I am . . . . OM OM OM
All Glory I am. OM OM OM

All Upadhis will be sublated. All Granthis (heart-knot, ignorance) will be cut asunder. The thin veil, Avarana will be pierced. The Pancha Kosa Adhyasa (superimposition) will be removed. You will rest doubtless in Sat-Chit-Ananda state. You will get highest Knowledge, highest Bliss, highest Realisation, and highest End of life. "The knower of Brahman, becomes Brahman Itself," "Brahmavid Brahmaiva Bhavati." You will become Suddha Sat-Chit-Ananda-Vyapaka-Paripurna Brahman. "Nasti Atra Samsayah." There is no doubt of that, here.

There is no difficulty at all in Atma-Darshan. You can have this within the twinkling of an eye as Raja Janaka had, before you can squeeze a flower with the fingers, within the time taken for a grain to fall when rolled over a pot. You must do earnest, constant and intense practice. You are bound to succeed in 2 or 3 years.

Nowadays there are plenty of "talking Brahmans." No flowery talk or verbosity can make a man Brahman. It is constant, intense, earnest Sadhana and Sadhana alone that can give a man direct Aparoksha Brahmic Realisation (Svanubhava or Sakshatkara) wherein he sees the solid Brahman, just as you see this solid white wall in front of you, and feels the Brahman just as you feel this table behind you.

Note:—Study carefully Mandukya Upanishad with Gaudapada's Karika.

CHAPTER SEVENTEEN
COURSES OF PRACTICAL SADHANA

TWELVE ASPECTS OF SAGUNA DHYANA SADHANA
(The Continued Act of Meditation on the Divine Form with Attributes)

TWELVE FORMULAE

1. God is one.
2. God exists.
3. God is Love. He is All-merciful.
4. He is Omniscient (Sarvajna).
5. He is Omnipotent (Sarva Saktiman).
6. He is Omnipresent (Sarva Vyapaka).
7. He is Sarva Antaryamin.
8. He is the support for everything.
9. He is endless (Ananta).
10. He is imperishable (Avinasi).
11. He is indivisible (Akhanda).
12. He is Light of lights (Jyotih-Svarupa).

He gives light to the Sun, moon, stars, lightning, fire and the intellect etc.

Fix the mind on the image of your Ishta-Devata. Keep the image in the heart, in the space between the two eye brows by closing the eyes or in front of you. Meditate on the above ideas. Repeat mentally Om, or your Ishta-Mantra or select any formula you like best. If the mind runs, bring it back to the image and rotate the mind from one formula to another and finally fix it on one formula. Keep the image of your Ishta also before your mind. After some practice the mind will get concentrated. Meditation and Samadhi will result eventually. You will have eternal infinite peace and bliss and Immortality.

A PROGRAMME OF SADHANA

You must have a definite programme of life. Ask an ordinary man, "what is your programme of life?," he will tell you, "I want to retire as a Dewan in a state." Another will aspire to retire as an Engineer in a state. They cannot think further. Why? Because they have not got an introspecting or disciplined mind. He does not know how to spend his time. He does not know the benefits of getting up at 4 o'clock, Brahma Muhurta. He will waste his energy in playing cards. He has education and knowledge, but he does not know how to spend his time. So if he had trained himself when he remained in the world he would have been able to spend time usefully. He will be able to concentrate and devote himself to higher pursuits. If laziness stands in your way, you will at once come to know from the books that Pranayama will help you. Do some Sirshasana. Various other obstacles may come in through lack of a Guru by your side. It is only an earnest Sadhaka who will experience these obstacles. Ordinary people will not come across such obstacles. As soon as they practise Sadhana obstacles come up. You must avoid too much conversation. You must adjust yourself nicely. All these things are necessary. Too much of work, too much of talking—all these are obstacles and must be removed. A combined method seems to be suitable to the majority of Sadhakas. Attack the enemy from within and without. Do Pranayama and introspect, do Japa, study. By all these methods try to destroy the mental Vrittis. In these ways you will be able to control the mind easily.

All these accessories are necessary. He who is interested in the well-being of the world, he who has equal vision, he who has controlled his Indriyas, only that man can become a fit *Arhat* and through him only Atmic light can shine. Only such a man can do real service, since he will be able to realise that all are manifestations of the Lord.

Have you experienced anyone suffering from some disease? Could you remember if you had experience of anyone suffering great pain from lumbago or continuous fever? What sort of feeling was in you then? Just put yourself in the position of the sufferer and imagine the situation. You must be able to feel with the person suffering. You must feel that the suffering body is your body. You must distribute rice particles to those who are hungry. Why all these methods are prescribed is that you must feel that you are one with all Universe. It is to make yourself feel that way that all these are prescribed. A Rajasic man will feel himself proudly separate from others. A Tamasic man will never feel at all for others. It is the duty of the aspirants—those who are endowed with the blessings of the Lord to remove suffering, wherever it exists, as much as possible. You can do your little bit even if it is charity of a pie. You can go to the hospital, try to comfort patients and let them have some comforts. Then only you can feel that you are one with the whole universe. How else can we do it, if we have no mercy? People are merciless and that is the reason why they make no spiritual progress. You must cultivate the virtues of Maitri, Karuna and Mudita. Leave away the negative qualities of jealousy, hatred and cultivate love.

Today the world needs your services. It needs men like Nachiketas. He was educated by Lord Yama Himself. Nachiketas asked Lord Yama "Let me have knowledge of the soul." Lord Yama told him "You will have thousands of cows, wife, children, all the riches of the world. You will be an emperor and so on." But Nachiketas had no attraction for these. He wanted the ultimate Truth. He said, "Teach me, O Lord, what is it which is beyond cause and effect, which exists in the past, present and future. Let me have knowledge of the Supreme Being." We want men like Nachiketas, with discrimination between the Real and the unreal. The world is in need of persons of the type of Nachiketas. Try to imbibe from the inexhaustible spiritual wealth.

So, to attain this, there is the path of knowledge. There is the path of devotion. Devotion is in no way inferior to knowledge. Devotion is concentrated knowledge and service to the Lord. Let us therefore be firm, if we want Supreme Bliss and strength. Atman or God alone can give this. We should try our level best to attain the Goal.

Try to get up at 4 o' clock during Brahmamuhurta and meditate. Meditation is the seventh Anga in the Ashtanga Yoga. But we should do the preliminaries, so that we can be established in meditation. Getting up at 4 o' clock is extremely important. This habit should be firmly impressed in the mind even when one gets old. Start your prayers with a few Slokas and Sat Guru Strotras. Sing CHIDANANDA, CHIDANANDA. The Devatas will be pleased. You will get inspired. Inspiration will come to you as a flash. Try to picture to yourself "What have I to do today?" In the beginning sit for 15 minutes, gradually increase the time by half an hour to two hours. Do not allow distractions to disturb you. Do not spend much time in brushing the teeth and such other things. Those who are old can use an easy-chair. What is wanted is steady and comfortable posture.

Try to gather the dissipated rays of the mind. The mind will begin to wander away. But try to get it again and again to the picture of the Lord if you are meditating on His form. Try to cultivate your will-power by sticking to your resolves. You will day by day gain strength. Keep away $1/10$th of your pay every month towards charity. Keep a spiritual diary and note down how many times you got angry. You can eradicate the evil effects by additional Malas of Japa and fasting. Do not always run after money. Let it come to you by itself. Do not lose your temper. Even if a man abuses you, try to be patient and try to talk to him. Even if you are in the right, tell him "Please excuse me." Keep up your Sadachara and cultivate virtues. They should become part and parcel of your daily conduct. Think well and grow. May all be happy.

PRACTICAL SADHANA: A DISCUSSION

I

What is divine living? What are Yoga and Vedanta? Yoga and Vedanta are the concern of divine life. Divine Life is a life based upon Yoga, and pervaded by the spirit of Vedanta. It is made up of selflessness, service, spiritual practices, and Self-realisation. Yoga and Vedanta form the very fabric of divine life. The more we know about it and the more we are reminded about its important aspects, the better equipped we will be to tread our chosen path, because the most important thing about divine life is in the living of it, not so much in the knowing of it. But the importance of knowing it lies in the plain fact that if you have to live it you must know something of it, so that with a comprehensive knowledge you will be able to live it more effectively.

So knowledge of divine life is important, since in living a life of Yoga, of practical Vedanta, we come across several hurdles, and we are faced many times with situations which we have to manage with intelligence, with knowledge, and therefore, discussion of these matters and getting to know more about the intricacies, the inner subtleties of these things will put us in a very good position so as to be able to deal with these situations effectively.

WHERE YOGA IS TO BE SOUGHT

What are the things we have to understand? Plainly, we

have to understand about Yoga, we have to understand about Vedanta, because these are the ways through which we have to lead the divine life, and approach Divinity and attain bliss. What are Yoga and Vedanta? Are they only in the books or are they in particular places in the Himalayas, or Banaras, or anywhere else? If they are there, are they only there? Are they nowhere else, or what is more important, is it necessary for us to find their location elsewhere also?

They are in the books in one aspect and in some aspect they are in places like Rishikesh, Banaras, and so on. There is a meaning in going to such sacred places, because the people who had lived there lived their lives practically, and they have left the stamp of their life in the very ether of those places. The whole atmosphere is pervaded by the spirit of Yoga and Vedanta, and therefore, when you live there, it evokes in you the similar spirit. But the most important place where divine life, or Yoga, or Vedanta is to be sought and practised, one has to know. Where is that place where you have to work out your practical life? It is Dharmakshetra. Dharmakshetra is the place where all Yoga and Vedanta are practised. It is the mind and heart of man. Yoga and Vedanta have to be achieved here, and if they have not been found here, they will not come out of anywhere else. Everything proceeds from within oneself. Vedanta and Yoga have to come from the heart and mind.

UNDERSTANDING OF ONESELF

How are you to demonstrate your Jnana, Bhakti, selfless service and Yoga? You have to manifest them through the thoughts that you think, through the words that you utter and through the actions you do. If there is Bhakti in the *Narada Bhakti Sutras*, it will not affect you, but if Bhakti comes to you, it is through Kirtan, prayer, meditation and service of saints. Bhakti manifests once it has started generating in the heart. All the scriptures of the world will be of no avail unless you have started to create it here. Sadhana, Vedanta, Yoga, all have to be lived in the heart. To do so, one must understand oneself. One must first of all understand this mysterious Dharmakshetra, the heart or mind of man, where all these things have to be worked out.

Why is it very important? Wherever you are, you cannot run away from yourself. If you think that family bondage is a great obstacle for living a life of Nivritti, you can shake off your family. You can run away from your home or city. All right. If you think that some things with which you are associated stand in the way, you can become an Avadhut. Take off pant and coat, and wear only a Kaupin. If you think that the company of some people is not congenial you can renounce their company. All right; you go away from your family, from your belongings and from company of people, but the peculiar thing is that you cannot run away from yourself. And what does it mean? You have to take your stomach, you have to take all the senses with you, and together with your senses, you have to take the habits to which the senses are addicted. You have to take the body with you, its habits and idiosyncrasies and your mind with its Raga-Dvesha, love and hatred, egoism and frustration.

DISCIPLINE OF MIND

There were two Avadhuts. They were Maha Viraktas (great ascetics). They used to wear only Kaupin. In winter they used to put straw mattress on the ground and sleep, and both of them had straw mattresses. It is difficult to get sunlight in Uttarkashi, and whenever the sun came out, they took the grass beds and put them in the sun, so that they may get a little warm. One Avadhut was drying his grass bed one day and the other Avadhut who was returning from Kshetra happened to tread upon that grass bed inadvertently. Immediately the first Avadhut got wild and shouted, "Can you not see my straw mat put out for drying?" What is the harm if the straw mat is trodden upon by another person? He called it as "my straw mat." The 'mineness' was there. They began to abuse each other. It is not a mere piece of imagination, Kalpana, but it is an actual incident which took place in Uttarkashi. That is why you have to shave the Vasanas, not merely the head. The Avadhut had taken his own mind and Vasanas. He had the sense of 'mineness.' This feeling itself is the jugglery of the mind.

Hinduism says *Sarvam Khalvidam Brahma*—everything is Brahman Himself. There is no separate devil. In all other religions there is God and there is devil. Satan is there in Christianity, Ahriman is there in Zoroastrianism, but in Hinduism, everything is Brahman. Then where is the devil? It is in the mind only. Therefore, whether you live in Uttarkashi or in Bombay, always you have to take along with you your senses and the mind, and as long as you do not know how to deal with them, how to manage them, they will try to manage you and deal with you in a summary manner. And what will happen? Your Virakti (dispassion) and all spirituality will go away. Unless one delves within and tries to understand the inner machinery one cannot practise Sadhana successfully. The inner machinery will follow you everywhere you go.

The mind is a blessing of God. Because without mind you cannot think of God, without it you cannot concentrate and meditate. Without mind and emotions, thoughts and feelings, you cannot have Bhava and Bhakti. Therefore, the mind is a necessary instrument, and at the same time if it is not properly understood and managed, it becomes your own undoer. Therefore it is a necessary evil, which has to be turned into an aid. To turn the impure mind into pure mind is no less a part of Yoga than Kirtan, Japa and the like. Every aspirant has to use his intelligence and manage the important task of ruling the senses and the mind. You can manage an unruly thing, only if you understand it. Unless he who drives the horse, knows its habits, he cannot manage it. Therefore, this is a very important part of Sadhana.

WHAT IS MIND?

The vast number of people know only that the mind is thought or it is something with which we think. It is not so simple as that. Even if you do not want to think, the mind will simply think. It thinks of objects. The mind thinks its own thoughts every minute. As long as the mind is producing thoughts, the mind cannot concentrate. You cannot canalize it and divert it to God easily. You have to divert it to God. But how to do it? Why does the mind wander about? All these an aspirant has to understand. A Karma Yogi has to understand it, a Jnana Yogi has to understand it, a Bhakti Yogi has to understand it.

You have to understand your mind whether you are in seclusion or amidst people. On the other hand when you are alone, mind gets an opportunity to have its full play. What is this mysterious thing which is such a problem for the Sadhaka, and yet without which he cannot do Sadhana, but which if not managed properly pulls him down? How does the mind work? If we have a basic knowledge of its nature, some method we can devise in order to get some control over it.

A BED OF IMPRESSIONS

The mind works in various mysterious ways, and we analyse some important broad aspects of this mind process. What is the mind of a person? What is it made up of? First of all let us take two analogies. You see a gramophone plate. What is it made up of? Ordinarily, you see a plate and you see it is made up of grooves, full of lines. For an ordinary, illiterate person it will mean nothing more than this. A little more intelligent and educated person will say that it contains minutely wavy lines and these lines are sound impressions in silent form. A still more intelligent person will say something more. It is the nature of an effect. This sound is identical with the sound that caused it. A more intelligent man will say that under what particular circumstances, it will produce sound.

Another analogy: Take a seed. A child will say it is a very tiny thing, but a more thinking mind, a poet, will say "In your hands lies a towering oak, which can shelter thousand people." And a still more discerning person will say, "This seed can produce an oak and produce the same type of oak out of which it came, and not only that, if that tree can produce further seeds, it means it has got in it the capacity to restart and fully manifest once again the whole process, which was at the back of it, and, therefore, it is a living thing. It contains in itself the whole city."

Similarly, the mind of each person at a given time contains within it words within words. It is identical to the grooves on a gramophone plate, or the seed. What is this seed? What are these grooves that are in the mind? The mind is a product of experience, previous experience. Just in exactly what way is it a product of experience? We shall take one instance, and we can multiply it *ad infinitum*. There is an experience. The experience may be in the form of a perception. You smell something, touch something, taste something or experience something—a combination of so many things may happen, and immediately just as a groove is created out of a sound in a gramophone plate, immediately an impression is made in the mind. This impression is called Samskara, an impression got out of a perceptional experience in the mind.

WORKING OF THE MIND

What is the nature of Samskaras? Is it like a furrow made on the ground or the grooves in the gramophone record? No. It is dynamic, and a number of such experiences making grooves upon the human mind make that impression a vital impression. It becomes active, it begins to be a dynamic factor in the man's life, i.e., it becomes a dynamic tendency in the person's character, and when it comes to this stage, the repeated taking in of a particular impression, makes it take the form of a vital or living force in the person's character. It becomes a Vasana, and a sum-total of Vasanas always keep the mind in a state of agitation, and they always go on starting ripples in the mind-lake, and these constant ripples create Vrittis.

In ordinary mind, so many Vrittis are rising and sinking. When the Vrittis arise in the mind, the individual starts a series of Kalpanas or imaginations. If the Kalpana is not there, Vrittis do not trouble the mind. When the Vrittis are supported by creating imagination it makes the Vritti take the form of a desire, Ichcha. And what is the nature of this desire, which formed through the force of imagination or Kalpana? It is of the same variety as the experience that formed the Samskara which is the cause for the rise of the Vritti. Even at this stage of desire, Ichcha, there is not great harm. But when the play of ego, the 'I,' in each one of us, identifies itself with that desire, there starts all the trouble. Instead of 'want,' it is 'I want.' Now the individual is in the grip of the mind.

INNER BATTLE

Whether you reside in a cave or in a city when 'I' and Kalpana join together, you feel, "I want to have a cigarette," or this or that. You may be doing meditation, but when you get Ichcha for a particular object, then meditation becomes secondary. But, then, the mind has got two aspects. When a desire comes, it thinks: "Should I fulfil this desire? Or should I continue my meditation? Should I go and take Iddli and waste time?" Now, then, there is Vichara. If the Suddha Manas (pure mind) gets the upper hand, it says 'No' and it pushes off the desire and continues meditation. If, on the other hand, the mind gives way to Asuddha Manas (impure mind), the desire gets the upper hand. Then the Ichcha becomes a Trishna, a strong impelling urge. The person immediately strives to fulfil the desire, and he falls from Yoga.

Yoga is not only in Nirvikalpa Samadhi. It should function every moment. If an impure thought comes, and if you are not able to put it down, you have failed in Yoga. In every thought, in every action, you have to assert your mastery over your Vrittis. Then Yoga is fulfilled; divine life is lived. And what is the time taken for this process? Within a split second a decision is made and the long process of the Samskara which crystallised the impulse is subdued, the higher mind achieving over the lower mind a resounding victory.

From experience you get Samskara, from Samskara you get Vasana, from Vasana you get Vritti. Then imagination makes the Vritti into a desire. Then ego attaches itself to the desire and it becomes then an urge, a Trishna. Then you are forced to do Cheshta or to fulfil the desire. This process of the mind is going on.

The scientists are trying to find a perpetual motion machinery, a machinery that never stops, but is always in motion. If you have to find a perpetual motion machinery, now, it is in you, the mind. You have to deal with the mind. All the Vasanas, Samskaras, which you have formed are already there; you cannot help it. But you can at least do one thing. You can prevent the formation of new Samskaras and stop past Samskaras to get further strengthened by fresh ones. How is it possible?

PREVENTION OF NEW SAMSKARAS

Daily you get new experiences, daily you perceive so many things with your five organs of senses. Then how can you prevent these experiences making impressions upon the mind? Is there any technique? How did these objects get into the mind and form into Samskaras? Take an object. You perceive it, through any one of your senses. First there is contact between the sense and the object. That is the first thing. So far only the outer fringe of man's personality has become touched. Supposing you are very deeply absorbed in some task, and your brother or sister comes and lays his or her hands on you, you are not aware, because though the object has contacted the sense, the sense has not conveyed it to the mind, the sense of 'I' being not associated with the touch-sense.

So, if the ego is not there, the object does not go deep into the mind. If the ego is engaged in some other thought, a particular impression brought by the senses will not produce any effect. But if the 'I' is there, the object goes and impinges upon your awareness, and if this 'I' is in a state of heedlessness, is not vigilant, is in a state of Aviveka or in a state of worldliness or Rajas, it will easily take these perceptions and create in you a desire, for the objects.

FIRE OF ASPIRATION

There is only one fire to burn all desires. Nachiketas had

that fire. So many attractive and alluring things were offered to him by Yama; he was offered money, beauty, strength, power, kingdoms, all Vidyas and alluring objects for the senses but Nachiketas reduced all such impressions into ashes, because he had that one fire, and that was Mumukshutva, spiritual aspiration. Aspiration is a positive fire in which all desires, cravings, are reduced to ashes. This is the fire that should characterise all Sadhakas, Yogins, Vedantins, those who lead the divine life. The disciple should have a furnace of aspiration. Only then is he a real disciple.

If you want to lead the divine life, you inner heart should be a place of aspiration, a fire of Yoga should burn in you always. This blaze should be maintained. You cannot completely change the outward mode of life, but inwardly there should be aspiration. This fire should burn day and night, when you are awake, when your are sleeping, when you are alone, when you are among men, when you are meditating, when you are engaged in work. This fire should not be put out. This aspiration should always form an integral part of your being. Then you are living the divine life. If this fire is there, you need not worry what work you are doing, in which place you are living. Because, you will be leading the divine life. Then you cannot be a victim of sense-pleasures. But you must at any time know if, in spite of your vigilance, the impression of sense-object goes to the inner consciousness, how to burn it through aspiration. If before it enters the outer threshold you have to burn it, what are the techniques?

WITHDRAWAL AND INDIFFERENCE

There are two techniques. They have several aspects according to the Sadhana you do. One technique is, always keep the mind indrawn. Never allow the mind to be completely extrovert, so that even apparently when you are moving amidst objects, the senses are not outgoing, the senses are turned inward. This is a very difficult technique, but this has to be practised. This Pratyahara is very essential. The ideal of the aspirant should always be to acquire this important qualification, Pratyahara.

The other technique is to be indifferent. What does it mean to you? If a non-vegetarian goes into the bazaar where they sell meat dishes, his mouth may water, but supposing one is a pure vegetarian and sees these things, they will not mean anything at all, because there is the absence of interest. Even so, we will have to create an attitude within ourselves by constant reflection; constant Svadhyaya of scriptures which show the vanity of the world, the worthlessness of earthly objects, and the perishable nature of the entire creation. By constantly imbibing such thoughts, an attitude of mind is created when all things cease to have any attraction for you, and then, even when these things come, there is no response from within, and this state is called Udasinata. You are simply not interested, and when there is a thing which you do not like, you are not interested in it.

This is the experience of the people in respect of the things they do not like. When they see a thing they do not like, they are not interested in it. But this feeling should become universalised in respect of sense-objects and other worldly values. An aspirant should hold an attitude of indifference when he is in the midst of objects. This has to be cultivated. This is not a technical thing like Pratyahara, but this attitude of mind can gradually be cultivated and the degree of its intensity can also be increased.

Thus in this way by Pratyahara and Udasinata, we can effectively burn away the impressions of the objects at their initial stage. If you have to live amidst distracting objects, you can cut away contact with them by these two processes. But, if, in spite of that, the sense-perception goes right into your inner chambers, then reject it, burn it, through the fire of aspiration. This way the Sadhaka will have to move in the world. You should have this equipment.

DIVINE REMEMBRANCE

There is also a positive way. You have to live in the world. You cannot get away from it wherever you go. A saint has said, that if you want to go through a forest full of thorns, you cannot cover the forest with a carpet so that you can walk. Instead of that a wise man will wear a pair of slippers or shoes. It is as effective as covering the entire forest with a carpet, because wherever he goes, this protection will be there. Similarly, we can protect ourselves in a such a way that we are not affected by the contact with the sense-objects.

If you have to go through a place which emits a foul smell, you cannot sprinkle the whole place with some fragrant element. But if you keep a bit of musk near your nose, you will always experience the smell of the musk and you will not feel the bad smell. Similarly, one could always do mental repetition of God's name and be engaged in constant remembrance of Him, or of some great ideal. Vedantins will think all is Brahman, Satchidananda. Bhaktas will think all is Rama or all is Krishna. Along with this there should be constant repetition of Mahavakyas or Ishta Mantra. These things form a positive hold to which the mind may cling. Thus the tendency of the mind to move towards other objects is lessened, because it is given a centre which it can catch hold of.

CONTROL OF DESIRE

I

These are the common-sense methods which a man who wants to live a life of Yoga and Vedanta, should have as his equipment. As I told you, we cannot run away from our senses and mind, we have therefore to understand the working of the mind. When a Vritti arises, do not think about it, divert your attention, let it sink back. Do not spin your imagination. It is imagination that strengthens the Vritti. Do not identify yourself with the desire, and if the worse comes to the worst, if the desire is strong, be stubborn, do not submit to it; divert your attention. I have always said, "Try always to nip the desire in the bud." When the desire comes in the form of a ripple, try to liquidate it then and there itself. But if due to lack of your vigilance it takes the form of an impulse, see that it is not fulfilled. Do not make Cheshta outwardly. If a desire comes, "I should go and gossip," say "No. I will not allow the body to move." If the body does not move, the mind cannot fulfil its desire, and ultimately the reverse process will happen, and the desire will sink back into the mind, and there will be calmness.

In the beginning of Sadhana, more and more desires will have to be controlled at the physical level, but as we go on acquiring mastery over ourselves, even when a Vritti comes, it is liquidated by Vichara and Viveka, which are a great help to the Sadhaka. As soon as a Vritti comes, it is put back, and ultimately all these have to be completely destroyed by repeating the Lord's Name, by Satsanga, Svadhyaya, meditation, prayer, performance of Purascharana, etc. All these are powerful, positive methods to deal with the Vrittis and Samskaras which are countless and deep-rooted but which have an end.

The more we understand the machinery of the mind, the more will we be able to deal with it, with all its subtle tricks and undercurrents, and we will be able to make use of the mind as an effective instrument of Sadhana instead of being a constant obstacle. All the most ideal conditions may be given to a Sadhaka. He may have ideal surroundings, ideal company, all sacred books, and yet if he does not do this important task of trying to understand the mysterious nature of the workings of the mind and try to lessen his Vasanas and strengthen his will, he cannot make use of anything. He cannot make use of his Guru. He cannot make use of his seclusion. Because they have to be made use of only through the mind and if the mind is not controlled, cultivated, he cannot make use of any of these. But once that is done, he can make use of all that God has given. Even a sentence from a scripture is enough to raise a flood of spiritual consciousness within him. But until that is done, Yoga will be useless.

Therefore, understand the mind, study the mind and know this machinery well, and know also how to manage it. This is an important part of Yoga, an important part of Vedanta, an important part of Sadhana, or divine life. In the beginning of one's practice all these are important. When one has practised all these, God-realisation is easy. They say that God-realisation is so easy that it can be attained "within the time taken to squeeze a flower," once you are completely rid of all impurities. For that you have to patiently keep on striving, and the more we devote our time with humility, sincerity and earnestness to a study of our own being and especially of this machinery which is inside us, and try to make the best use of it, as an instrument of Yoga, the more will we be able to succeed in the path of Yoga and Vedanta or in leading the divine life.

II

We have examined that how the whole of the living of the divine life, the whole of the process of Yoga and practical Vedanta, takes place primarily within the mind. Outwardly these processes that take place inside, have their expression; they manifest themselves in the form of certain behaviour of the person and his reactions to external influences, in the form of certain actions that he indulges in, but primarily they take place in the inner Kurukshetra, the mind.

An eternal tussle is going on in the mind between the

lower instinctive urges and the higher spiritual aspirations, between that part of the mind which is drawing the senses outward, which is filled with Rajas and Tamas, and the Sattvic portion of the mind, the Vivekayukta Buddhi, the Vicharayukta Manas, or that part of the mind where discrimination has begun to manifest, where the selective power of the human intelligence has begun to function. It begins to select which is proper, which is improper, which ought to be done, which ought not to be done, which is conducive to one's progress, which is detrimental to one's evolution.

When this discriminative faculty begins to operate, man begins to think of the why and the wherefore of things. This discrimination arises due to Satsanga, or due to hard experiences, knocks and blows of life, or flowering of Purva Samskaras, or any of the innumerable factors that go to awaken the discriminative mind. The instinctive mind, filled with desires for objects, tries to pull one down, whereas the higher mind pulls one up. Ultimately it is the spiritual part of man that establishes its own supremacy over the lower instinctive, sensual part of his being, and fully establishes him in Atmic consciousness, which is the ultimate stage of Yoga.

FULFILMENT STRENGTHENS DESIRE

In this process, we have discussed before how the mind works, how it tries again and again to catch the individual in its vicious circle of experience, Samskara, Vasana, Kalpana, Ahankara, Ichcha, Kamana and Cheshta. When you do Cheshta, you again repeat the experience, and a Samskara is formed; from Samskara Vasana originates; Vasana becomes a Vritti, which, taking the help of imagination, becomes an Ichcha; Ichcha takes the help of egoism and becomes a Kamana; Kamana, intensified, becomes Trishna or strong desire; and Cheshta or actual fulfilment of the desire follows Trishna; and enjoyment again strengthens the Samskara. Thus the whole process is repeated again and again.

Therefore, if a desire comes and if you fulfil it, that Samskara which caused that desire, gets more strengthened. The implication is that by fulfilling a desire, the desire never ends. You can never put an end to desires by fulfilling them. Just as the hungry flames will not subside by any amount of ghee poured in it, similarly the desire gets strengthened by fulfilment.

Non-cooperate with the mind. Do not fulfil desires, when they arise in the mind. It is the nature of the mind to desire. Mind and desire are synonymous. Non-fulfilment of desire is the only way of attaining mastery over the mind. Countless desires may arise; be silent. Do not say, "Come along, I will fulfil it." It is only when you make the mistake of saying, "I am the mind," "I am desiring," you commit a blunder.

MASTERY OVER MIND

Only when the mind is purified, it becomes your guide. Till then non-cooperate with it. Then the mind will cease to be the mover of man, and man will become the mover of the mind. You should be the independent mover of the mind. Then you become Manojit or Indriyajit. That is what an aspirant has to become. The law is, desires never perish by fulfilling them.

The desires that come on the surface of the mind have their roots in the subconscious, and in as much as the roots are hidden, you will have to do daily the digging of the mind, and delving to the root of these desires. Set apart a time when there is no external distraction, sit in a secluded place and feel that you are the witness of the mind. Just allow the mind to wander for a while and see how it behaves and try to delve within.

All our time we are engaged in drawing the mind outward. Now make the mind go inward and try to see within yourself what is going on. It requires regular practice, or else we will be thinking we are looking into the mind, but in the processes, we would be drifting with the mind. You should delve inward and introspect. You must do twofold process. One is diverting the mind's rays inward, and when you go inward, focus keenly on a certain part of your mind and analyse it, dissect it.

STUDY OF MIND

If you cannot see an object which is in darkness, you direct the beam of a flash-light upon it. Similarly, focus the rays of the mind inward and examine its characteristics. Supposing a thing is very minute, you are not able to see it. You squint through a microscope. Similarly, you should analyse the part of the mind which is not visible, more minutely; you should analyse it in detail, separately, like looking through a microscope. Then you will come to know more of your mind, what kind of Vrittis are there, whether they are Sattvic, Rajasic or Tamasic.

You have to analyse intelligently. Here, we require a little bit of Viveka. We have to be careful of two things. One is that we should not go inward with partiality. If you are studying the mind, be impartial, because this introspection is done with the purpose of ejecting out all that is undesirable and supplying all that is required. Therefore, you should humbly go about this work.

If after studying the mind, you are full of self-satisfaction, if you are satisfied with whatever is there in the mind, such introspection and self-analysis will serve no purpose. You should have a critical attitude. Just as you find out the defects of other persons, with the same critical mind, you should find out your own defects. Otherwise, the benefit of introspection and self-analysis will be lost.

ERADICATION OF DEFECTS

If as a result of your introspection, you find in your mind certain traits which are not desirable, you should find out the means of removing those defects. Self-justification, self-approbation, are not what is meant by introspection. Once you find out your defects, be practical. Have some effective device to remove the defects.

You should find out how to make the best capital out of what you have discovered in your moments of self-introspection and Sadhana. This is the practical aspect of Kriya Yoga. Thorough purification can only come, if there is detailed, impartial introspection, followed by practical measures to remove the defects. This introspection should be done daily. Daily you should throw out some rubbish from within the mind. This is the process of purification.

IMPORTANCE OF DETAILS

There are two more important steps that one has to take in living the divine life. Each Sadhaka should bear in mind that divine life is to be lived in small details. If you are divine in small details, you can be divine in big things. You cannot afford to be undivine in small actions and expect to be divine fundamentally. If your Yoga becomes practical in little things, then great achievements will come as a matter of course.

Some Sadhakas think that details do not matter much. They think that it does not matter if they use harsh words occasionally. The Sadhaka thinks, "There is no harm in uttering a harsh word. I am quite calm inwardly. God wants only the heart." But a calm heart cannot come unless every word of yours is full of love and compassion. The heart is made up of only the sum-total of all little actions and words. It is not possible to have a wonderful heart inside, and indulge in every type of actions and words.

Every action goes to form one's character even as every drop goes to form the ocean. Day-to-day movements of man constitute the very essence of divine living, the very essence of Yoga and Vedanta. One should not commit the mistake of being content with the idea that by merely having a great idealism, it will manifest itself as perfect goodness in one's actions, words and thoughts. Unless you are careful in your day-to-day life and mould your life in accordance with your idealism, it cannot bear fruit. If you are careful that the broad principles of divine living are observed, the edifice will come by itself.

SELF-RESTRAINT

What are those broad principles? Truthfulness, compassion, purity—these have to cover your entire life down to the minutest details. Your whole life, at least in the beginning, should be characterised by restraint. You should restrain your tongue. Do not think that you can eat anything and say anything and meditate well. If you think so, you are deceiving yourself. Yoga is not a toy, which you can easily take and play with. It is like an iron-fort, lodging well-equipped soldiers.

Every action should be done with proper examination. The quality of food that you take, its quantity, and the time you take food, all are important. A little immoderate food, or improper time of taking food may affect your system and render meditation difficult. So, too, with the thoughts you entertain and actions you are engaged in. The whole body and mind should be restrained. You should live a life of moderation.

When I sing the song of "Eat a little, drink a little," you have to understand it in its proper sense. There are two parts of this song. "Eat a little, drink a little; talk a little, sleep a little." When I say these things I mean moderation. These things should not be indulged in. The instinctive life of eating, drinking, talking, etc., should be kept to the minimum requirement. The other portion of the song, wherein it is said, "Do Japa a little, do Asana a little, do Kirtan a little" also indicates that everyone of these items is essential, that all these items should find a place in your daily programme.

CONCLUSION

All gross things that merely pertain to the body should be kept to the minimum and all the higher aspects of Sadhana should be given proper place in your daily programme. This is the broad, general outline of divine life. Control the mind. Do not fulfil desires when they arise. Nip the Vritti in the bud. Daily have self-introspection and self-analysis, and in doing that be unsparing to yourself. Do not justify what you discover in the mind and give a reason for it, but rather, try to devise suitable methods for overcoming what you find undesirable. Lead a life of self-restraint, and back up the whole process by positive Sadhana like meditation, Japa, Asana, Pranayama.

The underlying secret of overcoming the Vikshepa of the mind is Vairagya. Raga is at the root of Vikshepa. Raga comes through Avichara. You imagine that the objects of the world will give you happiness. This is Avichara. You should do Vichara, discrimination, you should find out the defects of worldly pleasures and develop Vairagya for all kinds of earthly pleasures. So there should be Vichara and Vairagya, and, combined with these, if you practise the things already mentioned, you will be able to progress on the path of Yoga and Vedanta, on the path of divine living.

SADHANA FOR TEN DAYS

You can do this during Christmas holidays or Puja holidays or summer vacation. Shut yourself up in an airy room. Do not talk to anybody. Do not see anybody. Do not hear anything. Get up at 4 a.m. Start Japa of the Mantra of your Ishta Devata or your Guru Mantra and finish it at sunset. Then take some milk and fruits or Kheer (milk and rice boiled with sugar). Take rest for one or two hours but continue the Japa. Then again start Japa seriously. Retire to bed at 11 in the night. You can combine meditation along with Japa. Make all arrangements for bath, food, etc, inside the room. Have two rooms if you can manage, one for bath and the other for meditation. Repeat this four times in a year. This practice can be kept up even for 40 days. You will have wonderful results and various experiences. You will enter into Samadhi. You will have Darshan of your Ishtam. I assure you.

SADHANA FOR FORTY DAYS

You will have to do Japa of Rama Mantra one lakh and twenty-five thousand times in the following manner for 40 days, at the rate of 3,000 daily. During the last five days do 4,000 daily. Get up at 4.00 a.m. Write down in a thin paper Rama Nama 3,000 times. Then cut the paper into small pieces. Each piece will contain one Rama Nama. Then roll it with a small ball of Atta (wheat flour paste). Writing will take two or three hours according to your strength and capacity. Then you will have to cut one by one. You will have to do the whole process by sitting on one Asana. If you will find it difficult to sit on one Asana you can have change of Asana. But you should not leave your seat. Some use a special ink made up of saffron, musk, camphor, etc., and a special writing pen made up of sharp pointed thin Tulasi stick. You can use ordinary ink and pen if you cannot get the above special ink and special pen. You will have to do Anushthana on the bank of the Ganga, Yamuna, Godavari, Kaveri or Narmada, at Rishikesh, Varanasi, Haridwar or Prayag. You can do it at home, if you find it difficult to come to these places. Take milk and fruit or Phalahar during these days. Throw the ball in the Ganga or any river for fishes. You will develop wonderful patience. You will get divine grace.

Study the whole Ramayana 108 times with purity and concentration. This can be done in three years if you can devote three hours daily. You can go through the whole book three times in a month. You will acquire Siddhis. You will have Darshan of Lord Rama.

DAILY ROUTINE

(a) FOR STUDENTS

	From	To
Asana, Pranayama	4.00	4.25 a.m.
Trataka, Japa, Meditation	4.25	5.00 a.m.
Study of school lessons	5.00	6.30 a.m.
Physical exercises and breakfast	6.30	7.00 a.m.
Mantra Writing	7.00	7.15 a.m.
Study of Gita	7.15	7.30 a.m.
Preparation for class lessons	7.30	9.00 a.m.
Bath, meals	9.00	10.00 a.m.
School hours	10.00	5.00 p.m.

COURSES OF PRACTICAL SADHANA

	From	To
Games, walking, Nishkamya Karma	5.00	5.45 p.m.
Japa and Dhyana	5.45	6.45 p.m.
Study of school lessons	6.45	8.15 p.m.
Meals	8.15	8.30 p.m.
Svadhyaya, study of religious books	8.30	9.00 p.m.
Kirtan, Prayers	9.00	9.15 p.m.
Self analysis, introspection, spiritual diary	9.15	9.30 p.m.
Sleep	9.30	4.00 a.m.

Note:—Giving free tuition to poor students or serving the sick persons during intervals will constitute Nishkamya Karma.

(b) FOR BUSY PEOPLE

	From	To
Asana, Pranayama	4.00	4.30 a.m.
Trataka, Japa, Meditation	4.30	6.00 a.m.
Physical exercises and breakfast	6.00	6.45 a.m.
Mantra Writing	6.45	7.00 a.m.
Study of Gita	7.00	7.15 a.m.
Study of spiritual books	7.15	8.00 a.m.
Nishkamya Karma and household duties	8.00	9.00 a.m.
Bath, meals, going to office	9.00	10.00 a.m.
Office hours	10.00	5.00 p.m.
Evening walk, Nishkamya Karma	5.00	6.30 p.m.
Japa and Dhyana	6.30	7.45 p.m.
Meals	7.45	8.15 p.m.
Kirtan, Bhajan, Prayers	8.15	8.30 p.m.
Study of spiritual books	8.30	9.15 p.m.
Atma Vichar, self-analysis, introspection, spiritual diary	9.15	10.00 p.m.
Sleep	10.00	4.00 a.m.

(c) FOR RETIRED PEOPLE

	From	To
Trataka, Japa and Dhyana	3.45	5.45 a.m.
Asana, Pranayama	5.45	6.30 a.m.
Walking, rest, breakfast	6.30	7.30 a.m.
Mantra Writing	7.30	7.45 a.m.
Study of Gita, Bhagavata, Ramayana	7.45	9.00 a.m.
Nishkamya Karma	9.00	10.00 a.m.
Japa, worship	10.00	11.00 a.m.

Meals and rest	11.00	1.30 p.m.
Study of spiritual books, writing	1.30	3.30 p.m.
Satsanga, Sravana	3.30	5.00 p.m.
Evening walk and exercise	5.00	6.00 p.m.
Japa and Dhyana	6.00	7.30 p.m.
Meals and rest	7.30	8.15 p.m.
Bhajan, Kirtan	8.15	8.45 p.m.
Atma Vichar, self-analysis, introspection, spiritual diary	8.45	10.00 p.m.
Sleep	10.00	3.30 a.m.

(d) FOR WHOLE-TIME ASPIRANTS

	From	To
Japa and Dhyana	3.30	6.30 a.m.
Asana, Pranayama	6.30	7.45 a.m.
Svadhyaya	7.45	8.45 a.m.
Nishkamya Karma	8.45	10.30 a.m.
Japa, worship	10.30	11.45 a.m.
Meals and rest	11.45	2.00 p.m.
Mantra writing	2.00	3.00 p.m.
Svadhyaya	3.00	4.00 p.m.
Nishkamya Karma	4.00	5.00 p.m.
Physical exercise or walking	5.00	6.00 p.m.
Japa and Dhyana	6.00	8.00 p.m.
Bhajan, Kirtan	8.00	9.00 p.m.
Atma Vichar, self-analysis, introspection, spiritual diary	9.00	9.30 p.m.
Sleep	9.30	3.30 a.m.

Note:—Spiritual Diary must be kept by all spiritual aspirants irrespective of age, caste, position in life.

Every member should observe Mouna daily at least for one hour between 7.00 a.m. and 7.00 p.m.

A similar routine must be prepared by all spiritual aspirants according to time, temperament and inclination.

On all holidays more time must be given for Japa, Dhyana, concentration, Nishkamya Karma Yoga, Mouna, etc.

If Spiritual Diaries are sent to the President, Divine Life Society, Rishikesh, with appropriate stamps for posting the reply, further lessons will be given.

(e) FOR NIGHT-DUTY PEOPLE

Kirtan, prayer and 1 Mala of Japa	0.30 mts. (afer duty is over)
Sleep	6.00 to 7.30 hrs.
Silent Japa	0.30 mts. after getting up from bed
Asana, Pranayama	0.20 mts.
Rest, bath and food	1.30 hrs.
Study of Gita and Mantra writing	0.30 mts.
Tratak, Japa and Dhyana	1.30 hrs.
Household duties	1.15 hrs.
Svadhyaya of religious books	1.10 hrs.
Self analysis, introspection and spiritual diary	0.30 mts.
Food, dressing and going to office	0.45 mts.
Office duty	8.00 hrs.

Note:—If there be leisure during office hours silent mental Japa or study of spiritual books can be done.

(f) FOR VISITORS TO THE ASHRAM

	Hrs Mts	From	To
Japa and meditation	1.00	5.00	6.00 a.m.
Morning walk	0.30	6.00	6.30 a.m.
Asanas and Pranayama	0.30	6.30	7.00 a.m.
Rest	0.15	7.00	7.15 a.m.
Mouna	0.15	7.15	7.30 a.m.
Bath and breakfast	0.30	7.30	8.00 a.m.
Mantra writing	0.15	8.00	8.15 a.m.
Study of Gita	0.45	8.15	9.00 a.m.
Rest	0.15	9.00	9.15 a.m.
Study of religious books, Upasana or Puja & Kirtan	3.00	9.15	12.15 noon
Food and rest	1.15	12.15	1.30 p.m.
Nishkamya Seva	3.00	1.30	4.30 p.m.
Pranayama	0.10	4.30	4.40 p.m.
Physical exercises	0.20	4.40	5.00 p.m.
Rest	0.15	5.00	5.15 p.m.
Evening walk	1.00	5.15	6.15 p.m.
Bath etc.	0.30	6.15	6.45 p.m.
Japa and meditation	1.00	6.45	7.45 p.m.
Mantra writing	0.15	7.45	8.00 p.m.

Food and rest	1.00	8.00	9.00 p.m.
Kirtan	1.00	9.00	10.00 p.m.
Sleep	7.00	10.00	5.00 p.m.

(g) AN IDEAL TIME-TABLE OF AN ASPIRANT

	H. M.		H. M.
Sleep	7 00	Asana and exercises	0 50
Walk	1 30	Pranayama	0 10
Mouna	0 15	Japa and meditation	2 00
Study of Gita and		Food and rest	3 45
other scriptures	4 00	Nishkamya Seva	3 00
Bath etc.	1 00	Mantra writing	0 30
	13 45		24 00

Note:—A model daily routine is given here. It was observed by a certain young aspirant, who spent his leave in the Ashram. It is an ideal time-table, as it includes all aspects of Sadhana, giving at the same time items of health and recreation like daily walk, physical exercises, etc. It will suit even persons of delicate health, having adequate time for sleep at night and rest during daytime. Though the actual time allotted for Japa and meditation is only two hours, yet you should remember the Lord constantly throughout the day and carry mental Japa during all hours.

(h) SADHANA FOR ADVANCED STUDENTS

This is highly useful for getting quick, solid progress in the spiritual path. Get up at 4 a.m. Start your Japa on any Asana you have mastered. Do not take any food or drink for 14 hours. Do not get up from the Asana. Do not change the Asana if you can manage. Finish the Japa at sunset. Take milk and fruits after sunset. Householders can practise this during holidays. Practise this once in a month or once weekly.

TEN MINUTES SADHANA ON TWELVE VIRTUES

Meditate on these 12 virtues for 10 minutes:
1. Humility in January.
2. Arjava (frankness) in February.
3. Courage in March.
4. Patience in April.
5. Karuna (mercy) in May.
6. Magnanimity in June.

7. Sincerity in July.
8. Pure Love in August.
9. Generosity in September.
10. Kshama (forgiveness) in October.
11. Samata (balance) in November.
12. Contentment in December.

Also Purity, Perseverance, Diligence and Cheerfulness.

Imagine that you are in actual possession of these virtues. Say unto yourself, "I am patient. I will not get irritated from today. I will manifest this virtue in my daily life. I am improving." Think of the advantages in possessing this virtue, patience, and the disadvantages of irritability. In this way you can develop all virtues.

TWENTY IMPORTANT SPIRITUAL INSTRUCTIONS

These twenty instructions contain the very essence of all Yoga Sadhana. Karma, Bhakti, Jnana and Yoga all will come to one who follows them whole-heartedly. They are the KEY to quick development and culture of the physical, mental, moral and spiritual self of man.

1. Hari OM! Get up at 4 a.m. daily. This is Brahmamuhurta which is extremely favourable for Sadhana. Do all your morning spiritual Sadhana during this period from 4 a.m. to 6.30 or 7 a.m. Such Sadhana gives quick and maximum progress.

2. ASANA: Sit on Padma, Siddha or Sukha Asana for Japa and meditation for half an hour, facing the East or the North. Increase the period gradually to three hours. Do Sirshasana and Sarvangasana for keeping up Brahmacharya and health. Take light physical exercises as walking, etc., regularly. Do twenty rounds of easy, comfortable Pranayama.

3. JAPA: Repeat any Mantra as pure Om or Om Namo Narayanaya, Om Namah Sivaya, Om Namo Bhagavate Vaasudevaya, Om Sri Saravanabhavaya Namah, Sita Ram, Sri Ram, Hari Om or Gayatri, according to your taste or inclination, from 108 to 21,600 times daily (200 Malas X 108 = 21,600). Devotees of Christ may repeat the name Jesus or Hail Mary, Mother of Jesus. Parsis, Sikhs and Mohammadans should select a name or Mantra from the Zend Avesta, Granth Sahib or Koran respectively.

4. DIETETIC DISCIPLINE: Take Sattvic food. Give up chillies, tamarind, garlic, onion, sour articles, oil, mustard,

asafoetida. Observe moderation in diet (Mitahara). Do not overload the stomach. Give up those things which the mind likes best forthright once or twice in a year. Eat simple food. Milk and fruits help concentration. Take food as medicine to keep the life going. Eating for enjoyment is sin. Give up salt and sugar for a week or a fortnight. You must be able to live on rice, Dhal and bread without any pickle. Do not ask for extra salt for Dhal and sugar for tea, coffee or milk. People taking non-vegetarian diet should try their best to gradually give up flesh-eating as completely as possible. They will be immensely benefited.

5. Have a separate meditation-room under lock and key. If this is not possible then a corner of the room should be set apart with a small cloth screen or curtain drawn across.

6. CHARITY: Do charity regularly, every month or even daily according to your means or 10 paisas per rupee. Never fail in this item. If necessary forego some personal wants but keep up this charity regularly.

7. SVADHYAYA: Study systematically the Gita, the Ramayana, the Bhagavata, the Vishnu-Sahasranama, the Lalita-Sahasranama, the Aditya Hridaya, the Upanishads, the Yoga Vasishtha, the Bible, the Imitation of Christ, the Koran, the Zend Avesta, the Gathas, the Tripitaka, the Granth Sahib and other religious books from half an hour to one hour daily and have Suddha Vichara (pure thoughts).

8. BRAHMACHARYA: Preserve the vital force (Virya) very, very carefully. Virya is God (in motion or manifestation)—Vibhuti. Virya is all power. Virya is all money. Virya is the essence of life, thought and intelligence. This instruction is not for bachelors only. Householders also must follow this, as far as possible.

9. Get by heart some prayer-Slokas, Stotras and repeat them as soon as you sit on the Asana before starting Japa or meditation. This will elevate the mind quickly.

10. Have constant Satsanga. Give up bad company, smoking, meat and alcoholic liquors entirely. Do not develop any evil habit. Deliberately exert to develop positive virtuous qualities.

11. Fast on Ekadasi or live on milk and fruits only. Christians must fast on alternate Sundays, Muslims on alternate Fridays and Parsis on a suitable day, every fortnight.

12. Have a Japa Mala (rosary) round your neck or in your pocket or underneath your pillow at night.

13. Observe Mouna (vow of silence) for a couple of hours daily. Do not make gestures and inarticulate noises during the silence period.

14. DISCIPLINE OF SPEECH: Speak the truth at any cost. Speak little. Speak sweetly. (Madhurabhashana). Always utter encouraging words. Never condemn or discourage. Do not raise your voice and shout at little children or subordinates.

15. Reduce your wants. If you have four shirts, reduce the number to three or two. Lead a happy, contented life. Avoid unnecessary worry. Be mentally detached. Have simple living and high thinking. Think of those people who do not have even one tenth of what you have. Share what you have with others.

16. Never hurt anybody (*Ahimsa Paramo Dharmah*). Control anger by love, Kshama (forgiveness) and Daya (compassion).

17. Do not depend upon servants. Self-reliance is the highest of all virtues.

18. Think of the mistakes you have committed during the course of the day, just before retiring to bed (self-analysis). Keep daily spiritual diary and self-correction register as Benjamin Franklin did. Do not brood over past mistakes. Maintain daily routine and resolve form. (*Diary and resolve forms can be had from the Secretary, D.L.S. Hqtrs.*)

19. Remember that death is awaiting you at every moment. Never fail to fulfil your duties. Have pure conduct (Sadachara).

20. Think of God as soon as you wake up and just before you go to sleep. Surrender yourself completely to God (Saranagati).

This is the essence of all spiritual Sadhanas. This will lead you to Moksha. All these Niyamas or spiritual canons must be rigidly observed. You must not give leniency to the mind.

THE SCIENCE OF SEVEN CULTURES

[SADHANA TATTVA]

Introduction:—(a) An ounce of practice is better than tons of theory. Practise Yoga, religion and philosophy in daily life and attain Self-realisation. (b) These 32 instructions give the essence of the Eternal Religion (Sanatana Dharma) in its purest form. They are suitable for modern busy householders with fixed hours of work. Modify them to suit your convenience and increase the period gradually. (c) Make a few practicable resolves only in the beginning, which form a small but definite advance over your present habits and character. In case of ill-health, pressure of work or unavoidable engagements, replace your active Sadhana by frequent remembrance of God.

(i) HEALTH CULTURE

1. Eat moderately. Take light and simple food. Offer it to God before you eat. Have a balanced diet.

2. Avoid chillies, garlic, onions, tamarind, etc., as far as possible. Give up tea, coffee, smoking, betels, meat and wine entirely.

3. Fast on Ekadasi days. Take milk, fruits or roots only.

4. Practise Yoga Asanas or physical exercises for 15 to 30 minutes every day. Take a long walk or play some vigorous games daily.

(ii) ENERGY CULTURE

5. Observe silence (Mouna) for two hours daily and four to eight hours on Sundays.

6. Observe celibacy according to your age and circumstances. Restrict the indulgence to once a month. Decrease it gradually to once a year. Finally take a vow of abstinence for whole life.

(iii) ETHICAL CULTURE

7. Speak the Truth. Speak little. Speak kindly. Speak sweetly.

8. Do not injure anyone in thought, word or deed. Be kind to all.

9. Be sincere, straightforward and open-hearted in your talks and dealings.

10. Be honest. Earn by the sweat of your brow. Do not accept any money, thing or favour unless earned lawfully. Develop nobility and integrity.

11. Control fits of anger by serenity, patience, love, mercy and tolerance. Forget and forgive. Adapt yourself to men and events.

(iv) WILL CULTURE

12. Live without sugar for a week or a month. Give up salt on Sundays.

13. Give up cards, novels, cinemas and clubs. Fly from evil company. Avoid discussions with materialists. Do not mix with persons who have no faith in God or who criticise your Sadhana.

14. Curtail your wants. Reduce your possessions. Have plain living and high thinking.

(v) HEART CULTURE

15. Doing good to others is the highest religion. Do some selfless service for a few hours every week, without egoism or expectation of reward. Do your worldly duties in the same spirit. Work is worship. Dedicate it to God.

16. Give two to ten per cent of your income in charity every month. Share what you have with others. Let the world be your family. Remove selfishness.

17. Be humble and prostrate yourself to all beings mentally. Feel the Divine Presence everywhere. Give up vanity, pride and hypocrisy.

18. Have unwavering faith in God, the Gita and your Guru. Make a total self-surrender to God and pray: "Thy Will be done; I want nothing." Submit to the Divine Will in all events with equanimity.

19. See God in all beings and love them as your own Self. Do not hate anyone.

20. Remember God at all times or, at least, on rising from bed, during a pause in work and before going to bed. Keep a Mala in your pocket.

(vi) PSYCHIC CULTURE

21. Study one chapter or 10 to 25 verses of the Gita with meaning daily. Learn Sanskrit, at least sufficient to understand the Gita in the original.

22. Memorise the whole of the Gita, gradually. Keep it always in your pocket.

23. Read the Ramayana, the Bhagavata, the Upanishads, the Yoga-vasishtha or other religious books daily.

24. Attend religious meetings, Kirtans and Satsanga of saints at every opportunity. Organise such functions on Sundays or holidays.

25. Visit a temple or place of worship at least once a week and arrange to hold Kirtans or discourses there.

26. Spend holidays and leave-periods in the company of saints; or practise Sadhana at holy places in seclusion.

(vii) SPIRITUAL CULTURE

27. Go to bed early. Get up at four a.m. Answer calls of nature, clean your mouth and take a bath.

28. Recite some prayers and Kirtan Dhvanis. Practise Pranayama, Japa and meditation from 5 to 6 a.m. Sit in Padma, Siddha or Sukha Asana throughout, without movement, by gradual practice.

29. Perform your daily Sandhya, Gayatri-Japa, Nityakarma and worship, if any.

30. Write your favourite Mantra or Name of God in a note-book for 10 to 30 minutes, daily.

31. Sing the Names of God (Kirtan), prayers, hymns etc., for half to one hour at night, with family and friends.

32. Make annual resolves on the above lines. Regularity, tenacity and fixity are essential. Record your Sadhana in a spiritual diary daily. Review it every month and correct your failures.

EVERYDAY GUIDE TO SADHAKAS

1. Reduce your wants to the utmost minimum.
2. Adapt yourself to circumstances.
3. Never be attached to anything or anybody.
4. Share what you have with others.
5. Be ever ready to serve. Lose no opportunity. Serve with Atma Bhava.
6. Entertain Akarta and Sakshi Bhava.
7. Speak measured and sweet words.
8. Have a burning thirst for God-realisation.
9. Renounce all your belongings and surrender yourself unto God.
10. Spiritual path is a sharp-edged razor path. A Guru is absolutely necessary.

11. Have great patience and perseverance.
12. Never leave the Abhyasa even for a day.
13. The Guru will only guide you. You should yourself tread the path.
14. Life is short. Time of death is uncertain. Apply yourself seriously to Yogic Sadhana.
15. Maintain daily spiritual diary and record correctly your progress and failures. Stick to resolves.
16. Do not complain that there is no time for Sadhana. Reduce sleep and tall talks. Stick to Brahmamuhurta.
17. Let the thought of God (Reality) keep away the thought of the world.
18. Forget the feeling that you are so and so—a male or a female—by vigorous Brahma Chintana.
19. Never postpone a thing for tomorrow if it is possible for you to do it today.
20. Do not boast or make a show of your abilities. Be simple and humble.
21. Be cheerful always. Give up worries.
22. Be indifferent to things that do not concern you.
23. Fly away from company and discussion.
24. Be alone for a few hours daily.
25. Give up greediness, jealousy and hoarding.
26. Control your emotions by discrimination and Vairagya.
27. Maintain equilibrium of mind always.
28. Think twice before you speak and thrice before you act.
29. Give up back-biting, criticising and fault-finding. Beware of reaction.
30. Find out your own faults and weaknesses. See only good in others. Praise the virtues of others.
31. Forgive and forget the harm done by others. Do good to those who hate you.
32. Shun lust, anger, egoism, Moha and Lobha like a venomous cobra.
33. Be prepared to suffer any amount of pain.
34. Have a set of maxims always with you to induce Vairagya.

35. Treat sensual enjoyment as poison, vomited food, Vishta or urine. They cannot give you satisfaction.

36. Preserve your Virya carefully. Sleep always separately.

37. Revere ladies as Mother Divine. Root out the sex idea. Prostrate before all.

38. See God in every face, in everything.

39. Take to Sankirtan, Satsanga, prayer, when the mind is overpowered by lower instincts.

40. Face obstacles coolly and boldly.

41. Care not for criticism when you are in the right path. Yield not to flattery.

42. Respect rogues and scoundrels. Serve them.

43. Admit your faults plainly.

44. Take care of your health. Do not neglect daily Asanas and exercises.

45. Be active and nimble always.

46. Develop your heart by giving. Be extraordinarily charitable. Give more than one's expectations.

47. Desires multiply misery. Develop contentment.

48. Control the senses one by one.

49. Develop Brahmakara Vritti by repeated thinking.

50. Have a check over all your thoughts. Keep them pure and sublime.

51. Do not lose temper when anybody insults, taunts or rebukes you. It is a mere play of words and a variety of sounds.

52. Rest your mind in God and live in Truth.

53. Be up and doing in the path of perfection.

54. Have a definite aim in your life and proceed cautiously.

55. Benefits of Mouna are incalculable. Never give up this practice.

56. Four important means for passion to enter the mind are sound, touch, sight and thoughts. Be vigilant!

57. Have intimate connection with none but God. Mix little with others.

58. Be moderate in everything. Extremes are always dangerous.

59. Every day have self-analysis and introspection. Know the amount of your growth.

60. Give up curiosities in spiritual path. Conserve your

energy and concentrate. Think little of food, body and relatives. Think more of Atman. You must realise in this very birth itself!

IMPORTANCE OF SPIRITUAL DIARY

The keeping up of a daily spiritual diary is an indispensable requisite. It is certainly of paramount importance. Those who are already in the habit of keeping it know its incalculable advantages. A diary is a whip for goading the mind towards righteousness and God. The diary is your teacher and guide. It is the eye-opener. It will help you to destroy all your evil qualities and to be regular in your spiritual practices. It shows the way to freedom and Eternal Bliss. Those who wish to evolve rapidly must keep a daily record of their actions. If you regularly maintain a diary, you will get solace, peace of mind and quick progress in the spiritual path. Maintain daily diary and realise the marvellous results!

Mahatma Gandhi always advised his students to keep a daily diary. I am always keen on this point. My students keep five different kinds of notebooks. They write their Ishta Mantra in a notebook for one hour daily observing the vow of silence. There is a great deal of concentration in writing a Mantra in a notebook. It forms Japa also at the same time. They keep daily record of their actions. They keep a notebook for synonyms. Whenever they come across difficult words, they write down in the notebook those words with their synonyms. They at once refer to the dictionary. This gives a fund of knowledge. They will have a rich vocabulary of words. They can have good command of the language. Every week they go through their notebooks very carefully. They keep another notebook wherein they take down important points of what they read daily. They note down in another notebook my practical instructions which I give them casually. This develops their Manana Sakti or power of reflection. He who regulates his life on the above lines is sure to become a great man in a short time. There is no doubt of this. Do it practically and see how you grow.

All great men of the world keep diaries. The life of Benjamin Franklin is known to you all. He kept a daily diary. He noted down the number of untruths and wrong actions for which he was responsible during the course of the day. In course of time he became a perfect man. He had perfect control over his mind.

You will have to record in your diary the time you get up from the bed in the morning and retire to bed, the hours of sleep, the study of religious books, the number of Malas of Japa, how many hours you meditate daily, the nature of mistake you committed and the self-punishment you have given to rectify yourself in the form of fasting or increase in the number of Malas of Japa, etc., the lies you have uttered in the course of the day, how many times you became angry and how long it lasted, how many hours you spent in selfless service, how many times passion troubled you and how long it lasted, and the methods you adopted in checking it, the number of Pranayamas you did daily, how long you have practised Asanas and how many hours you have wasted in useless company and talk, etc.

You can add also how many hours did you observe Mouna daily. Did you keep vigils on Sivaratri, Sri Krishna Janmashtami or any other days? How many days did you fast? How many times you failed in the control of evil habits? Prepare a similar diary as shown elsewhere in this book and verify whether you are really progressing. Please send a copy of the diary to me every month. Just keep the diary for six months and then watch the results. If you want quick spiritual attainments, you should never neglect to record everything in your diary. To change the worldly nature it needs rigorous Sadhana. You should not hide your weaknesses and defects while making out daily diaries. It is only to correct and mould oneself, to purge out all weaknesses, defects and errors, to develop the divine nature and to attain Self-realisation that this diary is maintained. If the aspirant is sincere in his jottings the diary itself will become his silent master which will open his eyes and direct him Godward. All people keep Dhobi's diary and milk diary, but alas, they have neglected to keep up the most important diary i.e., Spiritual Diary which will help to correct one's mistakes and to attain quickly Self-realisation or the final beatitude of life.

A big thief is hiding himself in your brain. He has snatched away your Atmic pearl. He is giving you immense worries and troubles. He is deluding you. The thief is your mind. You must not be lenient towards him. You must crush him. You must kill

COURSES OF PRACTICAL SADHANA

him ruthlessly. There is no other sword sharper than this diary to kill him. It checks his happy-go-lucky ways and destroys him eventually. All your daily mistakes will be corrected if you maintain daily spiritual diary. A good time will come when you will be entirely free from anger, untruth, lust, etc. You will become a perfect man.

Your father and mother gave you this body. They gave you food and clothing. But this diary is superior to your parents. It shows the way to freedom and eternal bliss. It is your Guru. Turn the pages of your diary once a week. If you can record your actions every hour, your growth will be very rapid. Happy is the man who keeps a daily diary because he is very near to God. He has a strong will and is free from defects and mistakes.

By keeping daily diary you can then and there rectify your mistakes. You can do more Sadhana and evolve quickly. There is no other better friend and more faithful teacher or Guru than your diary. It will teach you the value of time. At the end of every month calculate the total number of hours you have spent in Japa, study of religious books, Pranayama, Asanas, sleep, etc. Then you will be able to know how much time you are spending for religious purposes. You have got every chance to increase the period of Japa, meditation, etc., gradually. If you maintain a daily diary properly without any fault in any of the items you will not like to waste even a single minute unnecessarily. Then alone you will understand the value of time and how it slips away.

INSTRUCTIONS ON MAINTAINING DIARY

Company with worldly-minded people is useless company. Find out your evil habits and remove them. Thou art the best judge in this direction.

Try to minimise the time spent in useless company. To avoid it altogether while remaining in the world is rather an impossibility. Cut short the conversation. Be on the alert. Speak little. Have the time between 4 and 5 p.m. for interview.

Do everything as Isvararpana. Duty for duty's sake, work for work's sake, should be your ideal. By and by when you grow purer and purer, you will understand the spirit of Nishkamya

Karma. When the mind is saturated with selfishness and desires, it is very difficult to understand what Nishkamya Karma is.

Night vigil is to keep waking the whole night as at the time of Sivaratri and Janmashtami. This will lead to conquest of sleep and reduction of sleep. Smoking, tea, betel, coffee, tobacco, sleeping in daytime, novel-reading, cinema, using vulgar words, too much talking, gambling, playing cards, drinking, reading newspaper, scandal-mongering, back-biting, drug-habit such as cocaine habit, opium habit, etc., are all the most important constituents of evil habits.

Annoyance is the ripple of agitation in the mind-lake. It is a mild form of anger. Bragging and exaggeration are modifications of untruth.

Bad dreams, evil looks, unholy lustful thrills, attraction or fascination for the other sex are all breaks in the observance of Brahmacharya. The aspirant should carefully avoid these. He should be ever vigilant and circumspective.

Service of sick persons, service of society or country in any form with Atma Bhava or Narayana Bhava will constitute Nishkamya Karma Yoga in the broad sense of the term.

Do not be ashamed of mentioning your mistakes, vices and failures. You should not utter any falsehood anywhere. You are keeping it only for your own benefit.

This is meant for your own progress. It is the diary of the religious aspirant who is treading the path of Truth to realise Truth. Accept your faults openly and endeavour to rectify them in future. You should not neglect to record everything in your diary. It is better you compare the progress of your work of the present week with that of the previous week. If you are not able to do so every week, you must at any cost compare it once in every month. Then you will be able to make various adjustments in various items, increase the period of Japa and meditation and decrease the time of sleep. Blessed is he who keeps daily diary and compares the work of this week with that of the last week, for he will realise God quickly.

Do not waste precious hours. It is enough that you have wasted so many years in idle gossiping. Yes, enough, enough of all that. Do not say "From tomorrow I will be regular." That "Tomorrow" will never come. Be sincere, and start your

THE SPIRITUAL DIARY
(WEEKLY)

The Spiritual Diary is a whip for goading the mind towards righteousness and God. If you regularly maintain this diary, you will get solace, peace of mind and make quick progress in the spiritual path. Maintain a daily diary and realise the marvellous results.

No	Questions	Month............							Total
		1	2	3	4	5	6	7	
1	When did you get up from bed?								
2	How many hours did you sleep?								
3	How many Maalas of Japa?								
4	How long in Kirtan?								
5	How many Pranayamas?								
6	How long did you perform Asanas?								
7	How long did you meditate in one Asana?								
8	How many Gita Slokas did you read or get by heart?								
9	How long in company of the wise (Satsanga)?								
10	How many hours did you observe Mouna?								
11	How long in disinterested selfless service?								
12	How much did you give in charity?								
13	How many Mantras you wrote?								
14	How long did you practise physical exercise?								
15	How many lies did you tell and with what self-punishment?								
16	How many times and how long of anger and with what self-punishment?								
17	How many hours you spent in useless company?								
18	How many times you failed in Brahmacharya?								
19	How long in study of religious books?								
20	How many times you failed in the control of evil habits and with what self-punishment?								
21	How long you concentrated on your Ishta Devata (Saguna or Nirguna Dhyana)?								
22	How many days did you observe fast and vigil?								
23	Were you regular in your meditation?								
24	What virtues are you developing?								
25	What evil quality are you trying to eradicate?								
26	Which Indriya is troubling you most?								
27	When did you go to bed?								

Name ....

Address ....   *Signature*

Sadhana from this very moment. If you are truly sincere He is ever ready to help you, to give you a push in your spiritual march. Take out a copy of this diary and send it on to your Guru who will guide you, remove all your obstacles and give you further instructions.

RESOLVES FOR QUICK SPIRITUAL PROGRESS

1. Maintain a Daily Spiritual Diary and at the end of every month send a copy of it to your spiritual guide who will give you further lessons for your progress.

2. Keep a daily Mantra notebook and regularly write a page or two of your Ishta Mantra or Guru Mantra in ink.

3. Chalk out a routine for daily practice and stick to it at any cost. Distractions and obstacles are many. Be ever careful and vigilant.

4. Make a few resolves for practice during the New Year as shown below. Any of the resolves may be crossed out, added to or altered, to suit the individual temperament, convenience or stage of development.

5. Do not abruptly change your nature or mode of living. You can grow and evolve quickly in the spiritual path, develop your will-power and control the mind and the senses by sticking to the resolves.

6. If you fail in any of the resolves through lack of self-control, unknowingly or by force of circumstances, you should perform some Malas of Japa or give up one meal to remind yourself of the resolve and to impress upon the mind the importance of these resolves (self-punishment).

7. The resolves form should be prepared in duplicate and one copy signed and sent to your Guru so that you may not be tempted to relax your efforts or ignore the resolves or break any resolve under the slightest pretext or lame excuse.

8. Request all your friends to maintain such resolves, Daily Spiritual Diary and Mantra notebook. Thus you can elevate many from the quagmire of Samsara.

THE RESOLVE FORM

1. I will perform Asanas and Pranayamas for.......minutes daily.

2. I will take milk and fruits only in lieu of night meals once a week/fortnight/month.

3. I will observe fast on Ekadasi days or once a month.

4. I will give up.............. (one of my cherished objects of enjoyment) once every...... days/months or for.... days/months.

5. I will not indulge in any of the following more than once every...........days/months or for............months. (A) Smoking. (B) Cards. (C) Cinemas. (D) Novels.

6. I will observe Mouna (complete silence) for....... minutes/hours daily and............ minutes/hours on Sundays/holidays and utilise the time in concentration, meditation, Japa, introspection.

7. I will observe Brahmacharya (celibacy) for........ weeks/months at a time.

8. I will not utter angry, harsh or vulgar words towards anyone during this year.

9. I will speak truth at all costs during this year.

10. I will not entertain hatred or evil thoughts towards anyone.

11. I will give away..............P. per Rupee of my income in charity.

12. I will perform selfless service (Nishkamya Karma Yoga) for...........hours daily/weekly.

13. I will do......Malas of Japa daily (Mala of 108 beads).

14. I will write my Ishta Mantra/Guru Mantra in a notebook daily for...........minutes or...........pages.

15. I will study...........Slokas of the Gita daily with meaning.

16. I will maintain a daily Spiritual Diary and send a copy of it every month to my Guruji for getting further lessons.

17. I will get up at........a.m. daily and spend......... minutes/hours in Japa, concentration, meditation, prayers, etc.

18. I will conduct Sankirtan with family members and friends daily for.........minutes/hours at night.

Signature..
Name & Address...
....
....

Date..............20.....

SECRET OF SUCCESS IN SADHANA

Sincerity and regularity in Sadhana are the secrets of success in the spiritual path. Even the least or the slightest trace of sensuality ought not to taint the nature of the aspirant. There must be the burning desire to be spotlessly pure. The aspirant who carelessly neglects the all-important Yama or self-restraint, never progresses in the spiritual life. He who is sincere, patient, persevering and earnest will make great progress in the spiritual path. The door of Immortality is open to that man who is endowed with dispassion, discrimination, devotion and who meditates regularly and constantly.

Centre yourself constantly in the spiritual Consciousness; always think of the immortal, all-blissful Self. You will reach the goal quickly. Combine ceaseless aspiration with single-minded devotion to the Lord. The habit of meditation overcomes all temptations and defilement from sensual objects and environments. Possess a most dispassionate heart that is resolutely determined to realise the Divine in this very life.

AN IDEAL GRIHASTHA SADHAKA

Even in the busy world there are very good Sadhakas who do more rigorous Sadhana than the whole-timed Sannyasins of Rishikesh or Uttarkashi or Varanasi. Here is one man "Sri Y....."

Sri 'Y' is a big officer in the Military. He is a Hindusthani. He was born in Uttar Pradesh. He had his military education in England. He is pious and religious-minded. Not only this. He practises regular and serious meditation. He practises Asanas.

He visited this Ashram and stayed for some days. He himself carried his bedding on his shoulders up the hill. He refused to accept the services of the inmates or the servants. See how self-reliant and humble he is!

He puts on a very simple dress. He wears a Khaddar shirt woven by his wife. Anyone will take him for an ordinary soldier only. He freely moves with all. He has not the feeling of any superiority complex. He is simple and humble. We sent food to his Kutir. He declined to accept it. He came down and sat in the dining-hall with others and ate ordinary food. He said, "I am a Sadhaka. I have come here to learn and discipline myself. I do not want even a bit of any special treatment or any special seat." He himself carried his pot of water on his shoulders up the hill.

He gets up at Brahmamuhurta 4 a.m. and practises meditation. He is able to enter into deep meditation. He gets himself absorbed in contemplation. No external sounds can disturb him. In the evening he sits on the banks of the Ganga and meditates. He never wastes even a single minute. Meditation is the food for him.

In the society he does not mix much with people. He never goes to the club. He sticks to his daily spiritual routine tenaciously. He has outgrown some of the society rules and conventions. This should be. He is not afraid of public opinion.

On one occasion there was a scavenger strike. He himself cleansed the latrine. His wife also assisted him. He is a man of self-reliance, high ideas and noble principles.

He is very fond of serving the poor. He opened a free school in his native place. He opened a charitable dispensary also.

People of the world generally complain, "We have no time to practise any meditation. We are very busy. Household affairs and office-work take away all our time. We get tired when we come to our house. We cannot do any Japa." This is only lame excuse. Here is a very busy man with very responsible work. He is the President of some Selection Board. He has multifarious works and yet how regular and keen he is in his spiritual practices! Friends! follow his example and tread the path of Yoga in right earnest. Where there is a will there is a way. God is a question of supply and demand. Do you want God? Are you thirsty for His Darshan? If there is a demand, the supply will soon come. Rise above petty things of this evanescent world. Have faith and aspiration. You will be able to do rigorous Sadhana. You will soon attain God-realisation.

SOME HINTS ON SADHANA

1. No meditation on Truth with a fickle, tainted mind can be of much use.

2. Steadfastness is essential in spiritual life. The aspirant never leaves his efforts in the path of salvation, even though he comes across many stumbling blocks, obstacles, temptations. This is steadfastness or firmness.

3. No meditation is possible when the senses are out of control and thoughts are impure. Therefore, purify and steady

the mind by Karma Yoga and Vichara (discrimination, ratiocination).

4. Self-control is control of the body, mind and the senses.

5. The senses and the body, which naturally run externally towards sensual objects, are checked and directed in the path of salvation by the initial steps indicated in Raja Yoga. This is self-control (Atmavinigraha).

6. A thirsty aspirant does not like even to talk about the objects of the senses.

7. The senses of a wise man do not turn to sensual objects. Therefore practise Vichara.

8. The Vritti or idea that arises in the mind—"I am superior to all"—is egoism or Ahankara. This should be given up.

9. Absence of this Vritti paves the way to enlightenment.

10. Humility is an antidote to egoism, but it should not be obsequious or ostentatious.

11. When a man thinks "This object is mine," the idea of 'mine-ness' enters his mind. He develops Abhimana. Then he begins to love the object. Then he clings to the object and gets attached to it. Feel that all objects belong to the Lord, that you are a temporary pilgrim on this earth.

12. Constant even-mindedness or equanimity should be the ideal of a Sadhaka (aspirant).

13. Non-attachment, absence of Moha or infatuation and equanimity are conducive to the attainment of wisdom and peace.

14. The man of wisdom is neither elated when he gets desirable or pleasant objects, nor grieves when he attains the undesirable or painful objects. That is the goal of Sadhana, equanimity.

15. A Bhakta or devotee has unflinching devotion to the Lord, without thought for other objects.

16. The mind of a devotee merges or enters into union with the Lord.

17. Just as a river, when it merges itself into the ocean becomes completely one with it, so also the mind of the devotee merges with the Lord and becomes one with Him.

18. Satsanga or association with the wise is a means for the attainment of the Knowledge of the Self, or Atman.

19. Purification of mind is achieved by repetition of the Lord's Name, and selfless service.

20. Evil is ignorance; sin is ignorance. Avoid both.

21. Conquer sloth by Asana and Pranayama.

22. Self-knowledge alone is permanent and all other learning relating to this world is subsidiary.

23. The Knowledge which leads to the realisation of Truth dawns when the heart becomes absolutely pure.

24. Study, reflective ratiocination, practice of equanimity, regeneration of the lower nature are essential requirements in the spiritual path.

25. So also are Japa and deep meditation.

26. Lust, anger, greed, pride, hypocrisy, hatred, attachment, are the products of Avidya that binds man to the Samsara or the world. These should be overcome by steady effort.

27. If you wish to attain the Knowledge of Atman, you will have to eradicate these evil traits which stand as stumbling blocks in the path of salvation.

28. If you cultivate the virtues opposite to the evil Vrittis, they will die by themselves.

29. It is difficult to eradicate the evil traits by fighting against them.

30. He who is sweet, cheerful, amiable, sincere and benelovent, will progress more quickly.

31. Be discreet in your speech. This is more than eloquence. You will enjoy peace.

32. Answers for your problems are within you. Enquire. Meditate. Pray. You shall know.

33. Heaven is within you. Why do you seek happiness outside?

34. Learn to live without the least inconvenience to others.

35. Learn to discriminate between the true and the false.

36. Learn to give, with a pure, unstinted, warm heart.

37. Learn to look within, and try to improve yourself first.

38. Learn to introspect, and eradicate the evil Vrittis in you.

39. All actions will be transmuted into Yoga when done with right feeling and right mental attitude—detachment and dedication.

40. Learn to control the mind and the senses by rational auto-suggestions, prayer, meditation and Japa.

41. Learn to fix the mind on God in any aspect He is most appealing to you.

42. Selflessness is the first qualification that a Sadhaka should possess.

43. Do not have any dogmatic, puritanical, differentiative and monomaniac notions about religion or spirituality.

44. Avoid a paranoiac cast in your aspirations.

45. Keep your mind always open to all the good influences in this world.

46. Sadhana should be steady, gradual, full of sincerity, common-sense and perseverance.

47. There are various grades of consciousness. Sadhana, in other words, means the process of the evolution of consciousness.

48. The body, mind and the senses put on the semblance of Chaitanya or consciousness, just as the iron-piece puts on the semblance of a magnet when it is in the presence of a magnet.

49. All life is linked by Cosmic Consciousness, which is the only reality.

50. Means and ends are necessarily identical. One cannot employ a wrong means for achieving a right end. The motive of the objective is judged by the character of the method employed for its attainment. One cannot obviously be a rogue outside and a saint inside. Therefore, be always watchful about the hidden impulse motivating your manners and actions. Do not delude yourself about the appropriateness of a wrong means for securing a right objective. Take not upon yourself the self-righteous duty of improving others in an obstreperous manner, but let your own example be a silent inspiration to transform all those around you.

KABIR'S METHOD OF SADHANA

1. *Detach—Attach*
2. *Pump out—Pump in*
3. *Remember—Forget*

1. Somebody asked Kabir, "O Sant Kabir, what are you doing?" Kabir replied "I am detaching and then attaching, as is done in the Railway junction. Coaches are detached from one train on one line and then attached to the other train on the other line. Even so, I detach the mind from sensual objects and attach it to the Atman or Brahman, the all-pervading Sat-Chit-Ananda Paramatma." Follow Kabir's method, *Detach* and *Attach*. This same process is mentioned by Lord Krishna.

"As often as the wavering and unsteady mind goeth, so often reining it, let him bring it under the control of the self." Repeat the words, *Detach—Attach* mentally several times. Then the process of fixing on the Atman will become automatic and habitual.

2. *Pump out objects, pump in Atman.* (Vairagya and Abhyasa) the two Sadhanas of Lord Krishna.

"Without doubt, O mighty-armed, the mind is hard to curb and restless; but it may be curbed by constant practice and dispassion." You will find an echo of this thought in Patanjali Yoga Sutras also.

"Mind's control is by practice and non-attachment," Chapt. I, 12. "Continuous struggle to keep the Vrittis perfectly restrained is practice." "Practice becomes firmly grounded when observed for a long time with constant and intense zeal (to attain the end)." This is a *sine qua non.*

3. Why have you forgotten your essential nature, Brahman? Because, you are remembering always your body, wife, children, world, objects, etc. Now make an attempt to forget the body, wife, children, to forget the surroundings, to forget the past, to forget what you have learnt. Then you will remember only Atman, Brahman. Forgetting is an important Sadhana.

CHAPTER EIGHTEEN

QUESTIONS AND ANSWERS ON SADHANA

RELIGION, SAINT AND YOGI

Q. What is the purpose of religion?

A. To help one attain purity of heart and God-realisation, to live harmoniously with others, to have spiritual culture and to bring about unity.

Q. Without suffering is there no spiritual growth?

A. No. Suffering moulds the man. It instils mercy in the heart, develops the will and power of endurance.

Q. You are advocating repetition of Lord's Name 'Ram'. How to repeat it?

A. Ram means Purity, Truth, Peace, Bliss, Existence Absolute, Consciousness Absolute. When you repeat the name, meditate on these attributes.

Q. Will you explain creation and how it has come about?

A. This world is a projection through the illusory power of the Lord, Prakriti or Sakti, to help the individual souls to reap the fruits of their past actions.

Q. Is not jealousy the greatest evil?

A. Yes. It is the chief cause of miseries and sufferings of man.

Q. How is it that people with riches are happy in spite of their bad deeds?

A. They are not happy. They are in a miserable condition. Their minds are full of worries and fears. They suffer from various sorts of incurable diseases.

Q. What is the difference between a saint and a Yogi?

A. A saint is a devotee of God. A Yogi is one who has practised the Ashtanga Yoga or Raja Yoga.

Q. What is the benefit of practising Pranayama?

A. It gives concentration of mind and good health.

Q. What is the difference between pleasure and Bliss?

A. Pleasure is derived from contact with sensual

objects. It is changing, fleeting and illusory. But Bliss is eternal. It is attained through realisation of Self or Atman.

Q. Suppose there is a death in one family. What would be the attitude of a person who has attained equilibrium?

A. He will remain calm and peaceful. He will not be affected by sorrow. He knows that soul is immortal and death is only a change.

Q. Love and hate existed ever since the world began. Hence are they not both eternal?

A. No. Hate is not eternal. It has an end when love develops to the fullest extent. Hate is an evil Vritti. It is an enemy of peace.

Q. What brings forth hate?

A. Ignorance.

PREREQUISITES FOR REALISATION

Q. Is love eternal?

A. Yes. Pure divine love or Prema is certainly eternal. Pure love is God and God is pure love.

Q. What things are necessary for realising oneself?

A. Faith, devotion, dispassion, discrimination, mercy, humility, purity, serenity, self-restraint, enquiry, spirit of selfless service.

Q. Suppose a man works selflessly, what will happen to his family?

A. God will take care of his family. His friends will provide everything to this selfless worker. The families of those selfless Congress workers in those days of Satyagraha were taken care by the rich businessmen.

THE SCIENCE OF MANTRA REPETITION

Q. What is the difference between Japa and Dhyana?

A. Japa is the repetition of the Mantra of a Devata. Dhyana is meditation on His or Her form and attributes. It is keeping up of a continuous flow of one idea of God.

Q. What is Japa-Sahita-Dhyana and Japa-Rahita-Dhyana?

A. The spiritual aspirant is repeating the Mantra and at the same time he is meditating on the form of his Ishta-Devata. A Krishna-Bhakta repeats the Mantra, "Om Namo Bhagavate Vaasudevaya," and at the same time he visualises the picture of the Lord Sri Krishna. This is Japa-Sahita-Dhyana. In Japa-Rahita-Dhyana the devotee continues his Japa for some time along with the meditation and afterwards the Japa drops by itself and he is established in meditation only.

Q. Can Japa alone give Moksha?

A. Yes. There is a mysterious power in the Mantra, and this Mantra-Sakti brings meditation and Samadhi and brings the devotee face to face with God.

Q. Should an advanced aspirant use a rosary?

A. It is not necessary for an advanced aspirant. But when sleep overpowers him he can take to rolling of the beads, and when the mind is tired of Japa, by way of relaxation he can take to rolling of the beads.

Q. What is the use of repeating the Mantra again and again?

A. It gives force. It intensifies the spiritual Samskaras.

Q. Can I repeat two or three Mantras?

A. It is better to stick to one Mantra alone. If you are a devotee of Lord Sri Krishna try to see Him alone in Rama, Siva, Durga, Gayatri, etc., also. All are forms of the one God or Isvara. Worship of Krishna is worship of Rama and Devi also, and vice versa.

Q. How to use the rosary?

A. You must not use the index finger while rolling the beads. You must use the thumb and the middle or the third finger. When counting of one Mala is over revert it and come back again. Do not cross the Meru. Cover your hand with a towel, so that the Mala may not be visible.

Q. Can I do Japa while walking?

A. Yes; you can do it mentally. There is no restriction for Japa when it is done with Nishkama-Bhava, i.e., for the sake of realising God alone.

Q. What should be the Bhava while repeating the Mantra?

A. You can take your Ishta-Devata as your Master or Guru or Father or Friend or Beloved. You can have any Bhava which suits you best.

Q. After how many Purascharanas can I realise God?

A. It is not the number of Japa, but purity, concentration, Bhava or feeling and one-pointedness of mind that help the aspirant in the attainment of God-consciousness. You should not do the Japa in a hurried manner, as a contractor tries to finish off work in a hurried way. You must do it with Bhava, purity, one-pointedness of mind and single-minded devotion.

Q. How does Japa burn the old vicious Samskaras?

A. Just as fire has got the property of burning, so also the Names of the Lord have got the property of burning the sins and the old vicious Samskaras.

Q. Can we control the Indriyas by Japa?

A. Yes, Japa fills the mind with Sattva. It destroys the Rajas and the outgoing tendencies of the mind and the Indriyas. Gradually the Indriyas are withdrawn and controlled.

Q. Can a Grihastha do the Japa of Suddha-Pranava?

A. Yes, if he is equipped with the fourfold discipline or Sadhana-Chatushtaya, if he is free from Mala and Vikshepa, and if he has got a strong inclination to Jnana-Yoga-Sadhana, he can repeat Om.

Q. While doing Japa of Om, does it mean that I should become one with that sound, by its constant repetition?

A. When you meditate on Om or repeat Om mentally you should entertain the Bhava or feeling: "I am the all-pervading, pure, Sat-Chit-Ananda Atman." You need not be one with sound. What is wanted is feeling with the meaning "I am Brahman."

Q. What is the meaning of the Mantra "Om Namo Bhagavate Vaasudevaya?"

A. The meaning is "prostration to the Lord Krishna." Vaasudeva means also "All-pervading Intelligence."

Q. How to dwell on the form of the Lord Krishna as well as on the Divine attributes?

A. First practise with open eyes Trataka on the picture. Place it in front of you. Then close the eyes and visualise the picture. Then meditate on the attributes of the Lord such as Omnipotence, Omniscience, Omnipresence, Purity, Perfection, etc.

Q. I am not able to repeat the Mantra mentally. I have to open the lips. Mental repetition of the Mantra takes for me much time and even the letters are not clearly repeated. Kindly tell me what is this due to. While doing Japa and meditation at a time, I am not able to fix or concentrate the mind on the Lord. If I fix the mind on the Lord I forget to repeat the Mantra and roll the beads, when I turn my mind to roll the beads I cannot concentrate on the Lord.

A. You will have to first start with loud repetition of the Mantra and then practise Upamsu-Japa (in a whisper). Only after practice of Upamsu-Japa, for at least three months, you will be in a position to do mental Japa. Mental Japa is more difficult. Only when all other thoughts subside there will be pleasure in mental Japa. Otherwise your mind will be brooding over sensual objects only and you will not be able to do mental Japa.

You cannot do mental Japa and mental visualisation of the Lord's form side by side. You will have to gaze at the picture of the Lord and mentally repeat the Mantra. Rolling the beads is only an auxiliary to concentration for beginners. The Mala also goads the mind to God. It reminds you to do Japa. When you are well established in mental Japa, rolling the beads is not necessary. Till that time you will have to roll the beads and concentrate on the picture of the Lord. You need not mentally visualise them.

Mental Japa prepares the mind for meditation on the Lord. When you are able to meditate on the form of the Lord, without fear of interruption by other thoughts, you can do so as long as you can. But the moment you are assailed by other worldly thoughts once again take to mental Japa. Meditation comes only as a result of long and sustained rigorous practice for a number of years. Much patience is needed. Beginners get disheartened if they are not able to meditate after a few days' practice.

Q. If we do Japa of a Mantra without understanding its meaning, or in a hurry, will it have any bad reaction on the person who does?

A. It cannot have any bad reaction but the spiritual progress will be slow when the Mantra is repeated in a hurry-burry without Bhava or faith. Even when any Mantra is repeated unconsciously or hurriedly without Bhava, without understanding its meaning, it undoubtedly produces beneficial results, just as fire burns inflammable objects when they are brought near.

Q. What are the signs that indicate that the Mantra is really benefiting the Sadhaka?

A. The Sadhaka who practises Mantra-Yoga will feel the presence of the Lord at all times. He will feel the Divine Ecstasy and holy thrill in the heart. He will possess all Divine qualities.

He will have a pure mind and a pure heart. He will feel horripilation. He will shed tears of Prema. He will have holy communion with the Lord.

Q. May I know if mental Japa is more powerful than the practice of chanting of a Mantra loudly?

A. Mental Japa is indeed more powerful. When mental Japa is successfully practised all worldly extraneous thoughts drop off quickly. In Vaikhari and Upamsu-Japa, there is scope for the mind to have its own ways. The tongue may be repeating the Mantra but the mind may be busy with other thoughts. Mental Japa closes the avenues, though worldly thoughts may try to enter the mind. In other words, the trap-door through which thoughts enter the mental factory is closed when the Mantra is being repeated. The mind is filled with the power of the Mantra. But you should be vigilant and prevent sleep from overpowering the mind. Desires, sleep and various sensual thoughts obstruct the successful performance of mental Japa. Regular practice, sincere attempt, sleepless vigilance and earnestness can bring complete success in mental Japa.

Q. Do I hold enough capacity to be enlightened by a Mantra?

A. Yes. Have perfect unshakable faith in the efficacy of a Mantra. A Mantra is filled with countless divine potencies. Repeat it constantly. You will be endowed with capacity, inner spiritual strength and will-power. The Mantra-Chaitanya will be awakened by constant repetition. You will get illumination.

Q. What is the meaning of feeling (Bhava) when one does Japa of a Mantra?

A. He who repeats a Mantra should entertain either the Dasya-Bhava (attitude of a servant) or Sishya-Bhava (attitude of a disciple) or Putra-Bhava (attitude of a son) while doing Japa. He can also have the feeling of a friend, an offspring or of a husband in regard to the Lord.

He should have also the feeling or mental attitude that the Lord is seated in his heart, that Sattva or purity is flowing to him from the Lord, that the Mantra purifies his heart, destroys desires, cravings and evil thoughts, when he does Japa.

Q. May I practise selfless service alone or Japa and service combined?

A. The combined method is more potent. Combine service, Japa, meditation, study of religious books, Satsanga and enquiry. Keep daily spiritual diary. All defects will be quickly eradicated. You can get Chitta Suddhi quickly.

Q. Which is better, whether doing more Japa or more of study?

A. Japa is more important than study. You have studied enough, yet if there is time you can study some elevating, congenial books. Study is highly beneficial. It helps concentration and expansion of intellect, relaxation, elevation. It inspires and adds to the fund of knowledge.

JAPA YOGA

Q. Shall I do Japa of Om Narayana instead of Om in order to make it both Nirguna and Saguna? The Japa of Narayana keeps the Chaturbhuja Murti of the Lord before my mental eyes. I however have been accustomed to meditate on the Murti of Lord Krishna (Banke Bihari) and am in search of a Chaturbhuja Murti of Lord Krishna with Arjuna at His feet. Please let me know how I should go on in future..

A. You have already created a clear mental image, momentum and force by meditating on Lord Krishna. It is not good to change the form now. Even if you change it, it will come before the mind through the force of the habit. Therefore have the same image only. Do not go in for Lord Krishna with four hands. 'Om Narayana' is not the proper Mantra. The proper Mantra is 'Om Namo Narayanaya'.

Om is both Saguna and Nirguna. If you study Prasnopanishad and Mandukyopanishad, you will understand this point well.

If at all you wish to change the Mantra, you can revert to 'Om Namo Bhagavate Vaasudevaya'. You can repeat this for some time.

PROBLEMS OF SADHANA

Q. What is the difference between Vichara and Nididhyasana?

A. Vichara is enquiry into the nature of Atman by sublating the illusory Upadhis or vehicles Prana, mind, intellect and the Anandamaya Kosa. Nididhyasana is intense and profound meditation on Brahman.

Q. How to practise introspection and self-analysis?

A. Get up at 4.00 a.m. Sit quietly with closed eyes in

Padmasana or Siddhasana. Look within. Watch your mind and Vrittis. Be a silent witness or Sakshi. Do not identify yourself with them. Note which Guna or Vritti is operating. Watch the mental menagerie carefully. Sometimes there will be a fight between evil thoughts and good thoughts, evil Vasanas and good Vasanas, old evil Samskaras and new religious Samskaras, Sattva Guna and Rajo Guna. Sometimes Tamo Guna will try to enter. You will be overpowered by sleep. Sometimes lust, anger, hatred will manifest on the mind-lake like ripples or waves. They will subside soon. Divine thoughts will manifest sometimes. Try to raise good, sublime thoughts. Generate the Sattvic currents of light, harmony, peace and knowledge. Old evil thoughts and Vrittis will die by themselves by practice of regular introspection and meditation. You will develop a sharp subtle intellect and purity of mind or Chitta Suddhi and soon enter into deep meditation and Samadhi.

Q. What are the Karmas of those souls who come to this world for the first time?

A. The world is Anadi or beginningless. Karma is also Anadi. The path of Karma is mysterious. Get knowledge of the Self. The mystery of Karma will be revealed unto you.

Q. If the evolution of the Jivas other than that of the human kingdom is progressive and if the law of Karma is not applicable to them, then why one Jiva, say a cow, enjoys a comfortable life in the rich man's stable while the other goes without food and dies uncared for?

A. It is erroneous to assume that evolution in the subhuman kingdom is outside the pale of Karmic law. The very progressive evolution of subhuman soul groups works under the law of Karma. The cow that enjoys a comfortable life is a good human being temporarily thrown into a lower womb to work out some wrong Karma. The other cow is a very vicious soul once again working its way up towards human birth. Whereas the soul arriving at a cow's stage through natural evolution is likely to have a neutral sort of life not touching either extremes of comfort or suffering.

Q. What is the use of trying to do this or that thing and wasting our energies if we are completely bound by our past actions?

A. You are not bound. You have got free-will. You cannot change the experiences, the result of Prarabdha, but you can change your future by right thinking and right action and thus make your will pure and irresistible. You can attain Self-realisation with the help of this dynamic will.

Q. It is said that birth, marriage and death are predestined. Can we not change our destiny of marriage and lead a single life and escape from the bondage of the same?

A. You can change your destiny by strong will-power, by leading a purely spiritual life.

Q. Leaving aside Mahatmas and Saints, to what extent an ordinary man like myself can change his present destiny by his limited self-effort?

A. You can also change your destiny like Mahatmas and Saints. But you should be under the guidance of a Guru for some years.

Q. What is hard fate?

A. Hard fate is the name given to that unseen force which brings unpleasant experiences and tests one's patience, and in which the man concerned is inclined to believe that he deserved a much better fate than that he has obtained. There is no such thing as accident or chance or fate or luck in life except only the results of one's own previous actions that have all these appellations.

WHAT SHOULD BE OUR GOAL?

Q. Should our aim be for Self-realisation and attaining Nirvana; or to take birth again and serve humanity?

A. One should try for Self-realisation and Nirvana alone. We should constantly try to ensure that we do not take birth in this Samsara again.

But, since we have taken birth, we should serve all selflessly. If we take birth again, we should continue to do selfless service. But this does not mean that we should pray for rebirth. Self-realisation should be our goal.

The yearning to realise the Self should not be regarded as selfishness. No. When standing on the peak of Self-realisation you perceive Unity and see nothing but the Self, there is no room for selfishness at all.

But it is true that some great saints have said: "I do not want Nirvana; I wish to be born again and again to sing Kirtan. I do not want to attain union with the Self; I shall take birth again and again in order to serve humanity." We should accept the utterances of great Mahatmas, after examining them! There is a time-honoured method called Arthavada, which great ones have resorted to in order to inspire people. They often emphasise some aspect of Sadhana as superior to all else, in order to draw the attention of the aspirant to its importance.

Whole-souled devotion is necessary if we wish to achieve anything. Half-hearted efforts will bear no fruits. We should not desire anything other than the ideal we wish to reach. For instance, in the Prema Marga, the distinguishing mark is, "love for love's sake." So long as we feel that Prema is a means for Mukti we will not get that complete self-surrender, that is essential in the Prema-Marga. In order to bring about that complete self-surrender, saints place before the devotees this ideal and make them feel "We want only Bhakti, we do not want to have anything else, even Mukti." The highest of the four Purusharthas is Mukti. The saints say that Prema is greater than even Moksha in order to make the devotee realise that Prema is the highest thing to be sought after for only then will he have perfect Nishtha or cultivating the highest Prema, or Para Bhakti. Once that Prema is attained, Moksha also is automatically attained!

METHODS OF MENTAL PURIFICATION

Q. What is Chitta Suddhi?
A. Chitta Suddhi is purity of the whole mind and heart.
Q. What is the fruit of Chitta Suddhi?
A. The Divine Light will descend. Just as you can see your face clearly in a clean mirror, so also you will behold the Atman or God clearly in the pure mirror of mind.
Q. What are the ways to attain Chitta Suddhi?
A. Selfless service of humanity with Atma Bhava, Japa, Sankirtan, Pranayama, Sattvic food, Satsanga, study of religious books, practice of physical, verbal and mental Tapas that is prescribed in the Gita Chapter XVII, Slokas 14, 15 and 16, practice of Yama, Niyama and the Kriya Yoga that are prescribed in the Raja Yoga of Patanjali Maharshi, service of Guru and Mahatmas, regular meditation, Vichara or enquiry of 'Who am I?', living in solitary places, with practice of Anushthana, Agnihotra and Pancha Maha Yajnas, introspection and self-analysis all will pave the way for the attainment of Chitta Suddhi.

Q. Why do I not get success in meditation even though I am practising it for the last six years?

A. You have no Chitta Suddhi.

Q. How can I find out that I have got Chitta Suddhi or not?

A. Sexual thoughts, worldly desires, unholy ideas, sexual Vasanas, anger, vanity, hypocrisy, egoism, greed, jealousy, etc., will not arise in your mind if you have Chitta Suddhi. You will have no attraction for sensual objects. You will have sustained and lasting Vairagya. Even in dreams you will not entertain evil thoughts. You will possess all virtuous divine qualities such as mercy, cosmic love, forgiveness, harmony and balance of mind. These are the signs to indicate that you have attained Chitta Suddhi.

Q. How long will it take for a man to have Chitta Suddhi?

A. It depends upon the state of evolution of the man and the degree of Sadhana. He can have purity of mind within six months if he is a first-class type of student. If he is a mediocre student it may take for him six years.

PROBLEMS OF SELF-REALISATION

Q. Can reading of scriptures give Self-realisation?

A. No. That cannot give one Self-realisation. Indeed they can help one a great deal in progressing towards the attainment of the goal by bestowing intellectual realisation of the Absolute provided one has a robust intellect to choose between the rational and the irrational, the probable and the improbable, the vivid and the vague, the real and the unreal. But Self-realisation is more than intellectual enlightenment. It is innate experience of the Reality, effected through a complete transformation of one's nature. Study of scriptures is an effective auxiliary in this direction.

Q. What is Self-realisation and what is the practical method to attain it?

A. Self-realisation is the consummation of the knowledge of one's true, essential nature. It is the attainment of the consciousness of the ultimate Reality. In other words, it is the fusion of the individual consciousness in the Cosmic Consciousness. Realisation of the Absolute is regarded as the highest of all knowledge. That absolute is birthless and deathless, underlying all names and forms, and yet unaffected by the changing phenomena. The body, the senses, the mind and the intellect are merely the outer covers which conceal the inner, permanent Reality, which is called variously by different people as God, Allah or Brahman.

The practical method of realising one's divine nature is the complete transformation of the base animal nature, transcending the human nature, and awakening fully the dormant spiritual traits within. This is done through perfect ethical evolution, self-restraint, self-analysis, self-purification, concentration, meditation, practice of selfless love and service unto all, and systematic inner culture through right speech and right conduct which is the pathway to Yoga and inner unfoldment.

HATHA YOGA

Q. What is Hatha Yoga?

A. It is the Yoga by which the body is rendered strong and healthy by the practice of Asanas and Mudras and the Prana is united with Apana through the Sushumna to the Sahasrara Chakra at the crown of the head.

Q. Is the practice of Hatha Yoga necessary before the commencement of Raja Yoga?

A. Yes. Asana and Pranayama are the two Angas or limbs of Ashtanga Yoga (Raja Yoga). How can you practise Raja Yoga unless you possess a strong and healthy body? How can you practise meditation if you have no Asana-jaya or control over the pose? You must be able to sit on Padma, Siddha or Sukha Asana steadily for 3 hours at a stretch. Then you will be able to meditate nicely. If the body is unsteady the mind also will be unsteady. There is intimate relation between the body and the mind.

Q. Will the practice of Hatha Yoga lead to Raja Yoga?

A. Yes. Hatha Yoga and Raja Yoga are inseparable. Where Hatha Yoga ends, Raja Yoga begins. Hatha Yoga aims at bodily perfection and a sound healthy body helps a Raja Yogic student in his practice of Yama, Niyama, Dharana, Dhyana and Samadhi.

Q. Will the practice of Pranayama alone awaken the sleeping Kundalini Sakti?

A. No. Asanas, Bandhas, Mudras, Pranayama, Japa, meditation, strong and pure irresistible analytical will, the grace of a Guru, devotion—all these will awaken the Kundalini Sakti.

Q. Is it right to say that Pranayama is unnecessary in the practice of Raja Yoga?

A. No. Pranayama forms one of the eight limbs of Raja Yoga.

Q. Is it dangerous to practise Pranayama without the assistance of a Guru (Teacher)?

A. People are unnecessarily alarmed. You can practise ordinary Pranayama exercises without the help of a Guru. A Guru is necessary if you want to practise Kumbhaka or retention of breath for a long time and unite Apana with Prana. The books written by realised Yogins can guide you if you are not able to get a Guru. But it is better to have a Guru by your side or you can get the lessons from him and practise them at home. You can keep regular correspondence with him. You can retain the breath from $\frac{1}{2}$ to 1 or 2 minutes without any difficulty or danger. If you cannot get a realised Yogi, you can approach senior students of Yoga. They can help you.

Q. What are the effects of the practice of Khechari Mudra?

A. It will help the student to stop the breath. He can have nice concentration and meditation. He will be free from hunger and thirst. He can change the breath from one nostril to another quite easily. He can have Kevala Kumbhaka also very easily.

Q. What should I do if I cannot get a realised Guru?

A. You can take an advanced student of Yoga as your Guru. He will guide you. If you are really ready, if you are able to enter the hall of wisdom, you will find your Sat-Guru or the Supreme Teacher at your very threshold.

Q. Why do great souls also exhibit anger sometimes?

A. Their anger is Abhasa-Matra. It will last for a second only. It will be like the impression produced by striking the water of a lake with a stick. They exhibit anger only to correct and educate the aspirant. They are always cool from within.

Q. Can I not get Samadhi without having Chitta Suddhi?

A. No. Just as a superstructure cannot be built without proper foundation, so also Samadhi cannot be built without the foundation of Chitta Suddhi. Just as the building that is built on a rotten foundation will fall down, so also the Sadhaka who is trying to attain Samadhi without Chitta Suddhi will fall down. Purity of heart is the first prerequisite in the spiritual path, be it Raja Yoga, Bhakti Yoga or Jnana Yoga.

Q. What are the experiences in Samadhi?

A. Experiences in Samadhi are beyond description. Words are imperfect. Language is imperfect. Just as the man who has eaten sugar-candy cannot describe its taste to others, so also the Yogi cannot express his experience to others. Samadhi is an experience that can be felt intuitively by the Yogi. In Samadhi, the Yogi experiences Infinite Bliss and attains Supreme Knowledge.

Q. Step by step what do we see or experience in Samadhi?

A. Steps in Samadhi differ according to the kind of Yoga. A Bhakta gets Bhava Samadhi and Maha Bhava Samadhi through purified mind and devotion. Sraddha, Bhakti, Nishtha, Ruchi, Rati, Sthayee-Bhava and Maha Bhava (Premamaya) are the stages through which a devotee passes. A Raja Yogi gets Savichara, Nirvichara, Savitarka, Nirvitarka, Saasmita, Saananda and then Asamprajnata Samadhi through suppression of thoughts and Samyama. He gets Ritambhara, Prajna, Madhubhumika, Dharmamegha and Prasankhya etc. A Jnani or Vedanti experiences ecstasy, insight, intuition, revelation, illumination and Paramananda. He passes through the stages of Moha, darkness, void stage of infinite space, stage wherein there is neither perception nor non-perception, stage of infinite consciousness and infinite bliss. Subheccha, Suvichara, Tanumanasi, Sattvapatti, Asamsakti, Padartha-Bhavana, Turiya are the seven stages through which the Vedanti passes. A Jnana Yogi is always in Samadhi. There is no in Samadhi and out of Samadhi for him.

Q. When will the mind become universal?

A. When Rajo-Guna is destroyed by the development of Sattvic virtues as Brahmacharya, Kshama, Cosmic Love, Daya, Karuna, Aparigraha, Satya and Santosha, when lower instinctive mind (Kama-manas or desire mind) is annihilated, when you possess the pure Suddha Manas, your mind will become universal. Rajas in the mind splits, divides and separates. Rajas is impurity. Sattva is purity.

THE NEED FOR A SPIRITUAL GUIDE

Q. Is a Guru necessary for Self-realisation?

A. Undoubtedly. A spiritual preceptor is absolutely necessary for everyone. In the initial stages an aspirant will have to face many difficulties and doubts in his path. He must have somebody who is much more acquainted with the subject of his quest than himself and to whom he can approach to get his doubts cleared. Even ordinary secular sciences have to be learnt from a teacher. A primary student would not fare well in his examination if he reads his lessons all by himself without the aid of a private teacher or without having to go to school. To learn the science of Self-knowledge one must have a reliable guide. He should study well the very best of the literature available on the subject, so as to effect a necessary moulding of his ideas and intellectual conviction, together with the advice of his teacher, through faith, devotion, perseverance and practical application to the pursuit of his quest, as well as through observation and company of holy men. It is only the Guru who will find out your defects. The nature of egoism is such that you will not be able to find out your own defects or be convinced of their pernicious effect. In the case of a very few emotionally matured, intellectually precise, decisive and enlightened, and spiritually exalted souls, they themselves can be their guide, and the purity of their heart will enable them to decide the voice of God from within and guide them accordingly.

Q. Is it essential to learn Yoga from a Guru, who has himself done Yoga-Sadhana and has achieved success in it?

A. Yes, one needs the guidance of a Guru. But he can do a lot at home itself and gradually evolve. The world is a great teacher. You can learn ever so many valuable lessons from it. While leading a householder's life you can develop many virtues. Self-control should be practised while living in the world of temptations. You can do Japa, Asanas, Pranayama and meditation at home. Lead a simple and austere life. Be honest and charitable. Induce your wife too to read religious books like the Ramayana, the Gita, etc. Thus you can prepare yourself gradually for the rigid life of a Sannyasin. Maintain a spiritual diary and send it to me for review. Come here for your holidays and undergo the necessary training and discipline. If you suddenly desert your family you shall be giving a shock to them. Let it be gradual; in the course of some years all bonds will be broken, when you can completely devote yourself to Sadhana.

Q. What are the qualifications and essential qualities of a real Guru, teacher or a true guide? Is it possible for an ordinary human being to select a real guide? If so, how?

A. Real Guru is a Srotriya, Brahmanishtha, one who is learned in the scriptures and established in Brahman. He who is wise, desireless and sinless can be a true teacher and guide. The Guru, by virtue of his wisdom and capacity, draws towards himself the souls fit to be guided by him. When one feels that he is thus spontaneously drawn to a Mahapurusha whom he cannot help loving, admiring and serving, who is an embodiment of unruffled tranquillity, mercy and spiritual experience, such a great one can be taken as the Guru. A Guru will be free from lust, anger, greed, egoism, hatred, jealousy, selfishness. He will have self-restraint, peace, perfect knowledge of the technique of all practices of Yoga, balanced mind, equal vision, generosity, tolerance, forgiveness, patience. He will be able to remove the doubts of the aspirants. In his presence all doubts will vanish by themselves. He will be in possession of divine knowledge through Nirvikalpa Samadhi. In his presence you will enjoy peace; you will be inspired and elevated. In his presence you will have a peculiar thrill of joy, peace and upheaval. A Guru is one in whom the disciple can find no defect and who serves as the ideal to be reached by the disciple. In short, the Guru is God in manifested form and when Divinity is seen in a person he can be chosen as the Guru. The relation between the Guru and the Sishya (disciple) is genuine and unbreakable, even as that between God and man is. It is a natural law that when a certain event has to take place in the universe the conditions necessary for the same are brought about exactly at the proper time. When the disciple is ready to receive the higher light, he is brought into contact with a suitable Guru by the Supreme Dispensation.

DEFINITION OF FAITH AND DEVELOPMENT OF DEVOTION

Q. Is not faith that which enables man to read the will of the Maker?

A. Faith does not read the will of the Maker, but enables a person to restrict and annihilate mental distraction and when carried to its ultimate absolute form, makes him attune himself with his Maker and realise Him.

Q. What is the difference between faith and devotion?

A. Faith is belief in the existence of God, the teachings of the sacred scriptures and the words of the Guru or preceptor.

Devotion is love of God. Without having faith in the existence of God, one cannot have devotion to Him.

Q. When one has neither faith nor devotion, how will repetition of God's Name help?

A. It will help. There is a mysterious inscrutable power in the Names of God; they will instil both faith and devotion in the heart.

Q. Can anyone who has no faith and no devotion get enlightenment?

A. No, not until he endeavours and obtains both faith and devotion.

Q. How can one develop pure devotion?

A. By meditation, Love, Japa, Kirtan, Satsanga and intense study of devotional books.

QUESTIONS ON BHAKTI YOGA

Q. What is Bhakti Yoga?

A. It is the path of devotion in which there is attachment to God, the partner of the Soul to man which brings cessation of wants, desires and miseries of mundane life. It is the path of Prema which unites the Jiva with the Lord.

Q. What is that thing which is superior to Rama even?

A. Rama-Nama.

Q. How?

A. Sri Hanuman told Sri Rama, "O my Lord, there is something superior to Thee." Sri Rama was quite astonished. He asked Hanuman, "What is that thing O Hanuman, which is superior to Me?" Hanuman replied, "Hey Prabho, Thou hadst crossed the river with the help of a boat. But I crossed the ocean with the help of, and the power and strength of Thy Name only. The stones floated in Thy Name only. Therefore Thy Name is indeed superior to Thee."

Q. What is the Mahamantra which gives freedom easily in this Iron Age?

A. *Hare Rama Hare Rama,*
Rama Rama Hare Hare;
Hare Krishna Hare Krishna,
Krishna Krishna Hare Hare.

Q. What is Bhakti?

A. It is supreme devotion and intense attachment to the Lord.

Q. What are the six means of developing or cultivating Bhakti?

A. Service of Bhagavatas, Sadhus and Sannyasins, repetition of God's Name, Satsanga, Hari-Kirtan, study of the Bhagavata or the Ramayana, stay in Brindavan, Pandharpur, Chitrakut or Ayodhya—these are the six means of cultivating Bhakti.

Q. Who can sing the Name of Hari?

A. *"Trinadapi suneechena tarorapi sahishnunaa,
Amaninaa manadena kirtaneeyah sada Harih."*

"He who is humbler than a blade of grass, who has the power of endurance like the tree, who cares not for honour and yet honours all, is fit for singing the Name of Hari all the time."

Q. Where is Divine Nectar?

A. Learned people say: That the nectar can be found in the ocean, in the moon, in the world of serpents (Nagaloka), in the heaven. If this be true, how can there be saltishness in the ocean, decrease in the moon, poison in the mouths of serpents, death of Indra (or dethronement)? Therefore the true nectar can be found in the neck (sayings or teachings) of Bhagavatas (devotees of the Lord).

Q. How are Bhaktas to be known?

A. Bhaktas do not care for anything. Their hearts are fixed at the lotus-feet of the Lord. They are very humble. They have equal vision. They have no attachment towards anybody or anything. They are without mineness or I-ness. They have no distinction between sorrow and happiness. They do not take anything from others. They can bear heat, cold or pain. They have love for all living beings. They have no enemies. They are serene. They possess exemplary character. Name of the Lord Hari is always on their lips. They are very pious. They see Hari in all beings and objects. They never hurt the feelings of others. They are friendly towards all. They are free from anger, hatred and pride.

Q. What are the two inner enemies that stand in the way of Bhakti?

A. Lust and anger.

Q. What are the ten vices that follow lust?

A. Love of hunting, gambling, sleeping in day-time, slandering, company with bad women, drinking, singing love songs, dancing, music of a vulgar nature and aimless wandering about.

Q. What are the eight kinds of vices that accompany anger?

A. Injustice, rashness, persecution, jealousy, captiousness, cheating (taking possession of others' property), harsh words and cruelty.

Q. What are the eight signs of Bhakti?

A. Asrupata (tears), Pulaka (horripilation), Kampana (twitching of the muscles), crying, laughing, sweating, Moorcha (fainting) and Svara Bhanga (inability to speak).

Q. How did the Lord help His Bhaktas?

A. Lord Krishna Himself conducted the marriage ceremony of Narsi Mehta's daughter. He brought ghee for the Sraaddha of Narsi's mother. He guided the blind Vilvamangala to Brindavan by holding the stick in His hands. He massaged the feet of the Raja during the days of absence of His barber Bhakta.

Q. What are the five indispensable requisites in the Bhakti Marga?

A. Bhakti should be of a Nishkamya type. It should be Avyabhicharini also. It should be continuous like the flow of oil. The aspirant should observe Sadachara or right conduct. He should be very, very serious and earnest in his devotional practices. Only then realisation of God will come very quickly.

Q. How to do Anushthana for 40 days?

A. Do Japa of Rama Nama one lakh and twenty-five thousand times at the rate of 3,000 daily. Get up at 4 a.m. Do the Japa. Do the Anushthana at Rishikesh, Haridwar, Prayag, Nasik, Varanasi, Brindavan, Ayodhya or Chitrakut. If not do it at your own house. During the last five days do 4,000 Japas. You can do one lakh of Japa also daily by sitting in one Asana alone. On the last day do Havan and feed some Brahmins, Sadhus and Sannyasins.

Q. How can Nirakara become Sakara?

A. Just as water can exist in two states, viz., Nirakara (formless) in the form of vapour and Sakara (with form) in the form of ice, so also Brahman is both Nirakara and Sakara. Nirakara Brahman takes form just for the sake of pious meditation of His Bhaktas. Just as air is formless and takes form as cyclone so also the formless Brahman assumes form.

Q. Are Bhakti and Jnana incompatibles like acid and alkali?

A. No. Jnana intensifies Bhakti. The fruit of Bhakti is Jnana. Para Bhakti and Jnana are one. Sri Sankara, a Kevala Advaita Jnani, was a great Bhakta of Lord Hari, Hara and Devi. Sri Ramakrishna Paramahamsa worshipped Kaali and got Jnana through Swami Totapuri, his Advaita Guru. Appayya Dikshitar, a famous Jnani of South India, was a devout Bhakta of Lord Siva.

Q. How can we practise both Jnana Yoga and Bhakti Yoga? Is it not better to resort to Bhakti Yoga alone and check the craving by thinking of the attributes of the Lord?

A. Yes, you can take to the practice of Bhakti Yoga only. You can think of the lotus-feet of the Lord. All cravings and desires will be eradicated.

Q. What are the two kinds of Bhakti?

A. Apara Bhakti or lower devotion and Para Bhakti or higher devotion.

Q. What is Apara Bhakti?

A. The Bhakta has his chosen idol. He has ritualistic worship and ceremonies. He does Puja of idols.

Q. What is Para Bhakti?

A. The Bhakta of this type sees Hari everywhere and in all objects. His mind is ever fixed at the lotus-feet of the Lord like the flow of oil (continuous). He has all-embracing, all-inclusive, universal love. He has not got the least hatred for any being. He sees the whole world as Visva Brindavan.

Q. What is Sakama Bhakti?

A. The devotee worships God to get money, son or success in an undertaking or to free himself from a disease.

Q. What is Nishkama Bhakti?

A. The devotee has no expectation of fruits. He wants God and God alone. It is love for love's sake.

Q. What is Vyabhicharini Bhakti?

A. To love God for two hours and to love wife, son and property for the remaining time.

Q. What are the nine modes of Bhakti?

A. Sravanam, hearing the Lilas of the Lord; Kirtanam, singing his praises; Smaranam remembering God; Padasevanam, worshipping the lotus-feet of God (service of humanity, country, poor people); Archanam, offering of flowers; Vandanam, prostrations; Dasyam, service; Sakhyam, friendship; Atmanivedanam, complete self-surrender.

Q. What is the difference between Sneha, Prema, Sraddha and Bhakti?

A. The love that is shown to inferiors as children is Sneha. Prema is love towards equals such as wife, friends. Sraddha is love towards superiors such as parents, teachers and others in like position. Bhakti is devotion to God.

Q. What are the five kinds of worship?

A. Santa Bhava (quietude), Dasya Bhava (servitude), Sakhya Bhava (friendship), Vatsalya Bhava (paternity) and Madhurya Bhava (conjugality).

Q. What are the five classes of worship?

A. Worship of elements and departed spirits; worship of Rishis, Devas and Pitrus; worship of Avataras; worship of Saguna Brahman; worship of Nirguna Brahman.

Q. What are the four degrees of Bhakti?

A. Tender emotion, warm affection, glowing love and a burning passion. Another classification is admiration, attraction, attachment and supreme love.

Q. What are the four kinds of Mukti?

A. The Bhakta remains in the Loka wherein Lord Vishnu resides like the inhabitant of a State. This is Salokya Mukti. He remains in close proximity with the Lord like the attendant of a king. This is Sameepya Mukti. He gets the same form of the Lord like the brother of a Raja or Yuvaraja. This is Saroopya Mukti. He becomes one with the Lord like salt or sugar in water. This is Sayujya Mukti.

Q. How to practise Bhakti Yoga?

A. Five Bhavas or attitudes towards the Lord have been prescribed by our Bhakti-Acharyas. They are sublimated inner transformations of the normal human expressions of Love. Vatsalya Bhava (the attitude of treating God as your child); Sakhya Bhava (treating God as your friend); Dasya Bhava (treating yourself as His servant); Madhurya Bhava (treating God as your lover) and Santa Bhava (meditating on Him as the Indweller of your heart, as your own Self, in peace). You can adopt that attitude which comes naturally to you. Find out towards whom, in your daily life, you have the greatest love—a child, a friend, a master, a lover, or none in particular. Worship God in His corresponding aspect.

Feel that you live only to realise Him. Feel every moment that you serve Him and Him alone through His infinite manifestations. See God and God alone in every face. Mentally prostrate to one and all—even to animals "O My Lord! I see you and you alone in all these beings." And, meditate on this Formula morning and evening and at frequent intervals during your daily work: "I am Thine, all is Thine, my Lord! Thy Will be done." You will soon develop intense devotion to Him. He will Himself guide you from within. Repeat His Name with every breath; be regular in your Japa, Kirtan and meditation, morning and evening.

Q. What are the essential qualities of a Bhakta? And how to acquire them?

A. Ethical perfection is the fragrance that emanates from a Bhakta. When the Lord is enthroned in the Bhakta's heart, Dharma takes its abode in him. Righteousness becomes his very nature. As darkness cannot abide alongside light, evil cannot exist where He dwells.

Through rigorous self-analysis find out the evil traits, latent and patent; meditate on the opposite virtue. When you do Japa and Dhyana feel that the Lord who is the very Source and Perfection of that virtue ever dwells in your heart, radiating this virtue and filling your whole being with that virtue. During Vyavahara assert again and again that the vicious quality has left you. You will grow in divine qualities.

Q. What is the easiest way to Realisation?

A. The easiest way to Self-realisation is to do Japa always, to let the Name of the Lord form part and parcel of yourself, to see Him and Him alone in all names and forms, to annihilate egoism and to root out Raga-dvesha. The spiritual path is a razor path to one who has no Sraddha; it is a rosy path to one who has faith and devotion and who has totally surrendered himself at the lotus-feet of the Lord.

Q. How to do Dhyana of Hari?

A. Mentally fix your mind at His Lotus-Feet. Then rotate the mind on His silk cloth (Pitambara), Srivatsa, Koustubha gem on His chest, bracelets on His arms, earrings, crown on the head, then conch, discus, mace, lotus in the hands and then come to His feet. Repeat the process again and again.

QUESTIONS IN VEDANTA

Q. What is Infinite?

A. Where one does not see anything, does not hear anything, it is Infinite. Where there is neither yesterday nor tomorrow, where there is neither colour nor sound, where there is neither East nor West, where there is neither light nor darkness, neither pleasure nor pain, neither hunger nor thirst, neither space nor time, it is Infinite.

Q. Why has this veil of ignorance covered us when we are Brahman?

A. This is a transcendental question (Ati-prasna). The finite intellect that is conditioned in time, space and causation cannot solve this problem. Do not rack your brain on this point. Do not put the cart before the horse. Remove your ignorance first. Get Self-realisation. Then only will you know the nature and origin of Maya or Avidya.

Q. What is the real nature of the Atman? How to realise it?

A. The real nature of the Atman is beyond description, though for the purpose of our guidance Sages have given provisional definitions. Sat (Existence Absolute), Chit (Knowledge Absolute), Ananda (Bliss Absolute), Santam (Peace), Sivam (Auspicious), Advaitam (One without a second; the Transcendental One that remains when all names and forms have been negated)—these are some guiding hints. Your innermost Self which is awake while you are asleep, which is beyond your mind, body and senses—that is the Atman.

First purify through the practice of Nishkama Karma Yoga. Side by side, do Japa, Kirtan, Pranayama, to steady your mind.

Enquire "Who am I?" Persevere in this Sadhana till you realise the Self.

Q. The mind is attracted by brilliant lights, beauty, pleasant colours, sounds, etc. How can we bring it back to steadiness?

A. If you follow the path of Vedanta, through discrimination you can clearly understand that what you see is mere appearance and unreal and that the Self, the substratum for the world is eternal and real. Now the mind will not run towards external objects. It will move towards its source, the Atman within. If you think that the external objects are the mere manifestations of your own Self and so exist in you, then also the mind will not run towards the sensual objects. If you follow the path of devotion try to fix your mind on the Lotus-Feet of your Ishta Devata whenever the mind runs outside. Gradually the mind can be controlled.

QUESTIONS IN RAJA YOGA

Q. What is the easiest way for concentration?

A. Again Japa of the Name of the Lord. And a very important point to bear in mind in this connection is that perfect concentration is just not achieved in a day; you should never despair and give up your efforts. Be calm. Be patient. Do not worry yourself if the mind wanders. Be regular in your Japa; stick to the meditation-hour. Slowly the mind will automatically turn God-ward. And, once it tastes the bliss of the Lord nothing will be able to shake it.

Q. What is Soucha? How many kinds?

A. Saucha is purity. It is of two kinds, viz., external and internal. External Saucha is done with mud and water and bath. Internal Saucha is done by Japa, Pranayama, Vichara or enquiry of "Who am I?" Svadhyaya, Kirtan, meditation, practice of Ahimsa, Satyam, Brahmacharya or Sadachara, cultivation of virtuous qualities such as Maitri, Karuna, Mudita (friendship, mercy, complacency). Internal Saucha is more important.

Q. What are the advantages gained by a Sadhaka, by meditating in Brahmamuhurta?

A. In Brahmamuhurta the mind is calm and serene. It is free from worldly thoughts, worries and anxieties. The mind is like a blank sheet of paper and comparatively free from worldly

Samskaras. It can be very easily moulded at this time before worldly distractions enter the mind. Further the atmosphere also is charged with more Sattva at this particular time. There is no bustle and much noise outside.

Q. When I sit for meditation, I am assailed by different worldly thoughts. When will the agitation subside?

A. In a big city there is much bustle and sound at 8.00 p.m. At 9.00 p.m. there is not so much bustle and sound. At 10.00 p.m. it is still reduced and at 11.00 p.m. it is much less. At 1.00 a.m. there is peace everywhere. Even so in the beginning of Yogic practice there are countless Vrittis in the mind. There is much agitation and tossing in the mind. Gradually the thought-waves will subside. In the end all mental modifications are controlled. The Yogi enjoys perfect peace.

Q. How to enter Samadhi quickly?

A. Cut off all connections with friends, relatives, etc. Do not write letters to anybody. Observe Akhanda Mouna (vow of continued silence). Live alone. Walk alone. Take very little but nutritious food, live on milk alone if you can afford. Plunge in deep meditation. Dive deep. Have constant practice. You will be immersed in Samadhi. Be cautious. Use your common-sense. Do not make violent struggle with the mind. Relax. Allow the Divine thoughts to flow gently in the mind.

Q. Where to concentrate the mind?

A. In the lotus of the heart (Anahata Chakra) or the space between the two eyebrows (Trikuti) according to your taste and predilection.

YOGA AND THE LIFE DIVINE

Q. What is Yoga?

A. Yoga means "union"—union of the individual soul with the Cosmic Soul, fusing of the limited consciousness in the Supreme Consciousness. Balance of mind is Yoga. Freedom from attachment, egoism and imperfections is Yoga.

Q. Can Yoga solve all the problems of this world? How to develop faith in it?

A. Yes; in fact, Yoga is the only solution to the problems of the world. Meditate on the transient, impermanent and unreal nature of the world. Do Vichara. Understand that all the pleasures of the world are only so many wombs of pain. Know that even if you get the sovereignty of the three worlds you cannot enjoy Supreme Unalloyed and Perennial peace which you can have in Yoga (the Union of the Individual soul with the Supreme Soul) alone. When, through constant Vichara done along these lines, Viveka dawns in your heart, then you will have an unshakable faith in Yoga.

Q. What are the principles of Divine Life?

A. Ahimsa, Satya, Brahmacharya, detachment and yearning for Self-realisation are the principles of divine life. Divine life is life in God. You can lead a divine life even while leading an active life, performing your duties but what is wanted is renunciation of egoism, attachment, cravings etc. Give the hands to work and the mind to God.

Q. Which is better, the Dvaita or the Advaita philosophy?

A. Both are ideals for different temperaments. Emotional and devotional type of aspirants practise Bhakti (Dvaita). The strong-willed and the intellectual type practise Jnana (Advaita). The Dvaitin feels that he is the servant of the Lord. The Advaitin feels that he is one with the Lord. Both lead to the same goal, union with the Divine, fusing of the individual consciousness with the Divine Consciousness.

Q. What is the meaning of Dehadhyasa? Sri Sankaracharya had said to the untouchable "I did not want your body nor the soul to get aside but the Dehadhyasa, etc."

A. Dehadhyasa is identification of the soul due to delusion with the physical body.

Q. Who is the Adhikari (qualified person) to tread the path of Vedanta?

A. He who has removed Mala, sin and impurity, by Nishkama Karma Yoga, Vikshepa, tossing of the mind or oscillation, by Upasana or worship of Saguna Murti, and who has Sadhana Chatushtaya or four qualifications such as Viveka, Vairagya, Shat-Sampat and Mumukshutva, is alone fit to take up the Vedantic practice.

WORLD AND RENUNCIATION

Q. When should I renounce the world?

A. Renounce the world on that very day when you get perfect Vairagya. This is the emphatic declaration of the Srutis (Jabala Upanishad). That Vairagya must be the outcome of pure Viveka. Otherwise you cannot stand. You cannot stick to the path of renunciation.

Q. Is this world unreal?
A. This world is unreal because from the absolute point of view, it is seen to be self-contradictory, transitory, and totally dependent on the passing modes or phases of consciousness which cognise it. It has no independent value or existence, and it gets negated in Self-realisation.

CHAPTER NINETEEN
INTIMATE ADVICE TO ASPIRANTS

ASPIRANTS—A DISTINCT CLASS BY THEMSELVES

The spiritual aspirant class is verily a merest microscopic minority in the sum-totality of world humanity. How very distinctive and special, therefore, should be its conduct and mode of reaction to externals in comparison to that of the generality of the secular world? How very different must his motives be? It is wrong for him to continue to judge either his own or others' actions with the same old standard as of the worldly life. What is perfectly correct there will be preposterously impossible here in the spiritual line. What is quite natural and right there will be unthinkable here.

Take the case of the soldiers drafted into the Army. Just consider what a lot of severe restrictions they are subject to and have to put up with. Their entire life is ordered upon exceptional lines. Special rules govern their movements at every step. Numerous places are strictly 'out of bounds' to the troops. Whether they like it or not the members of the fighting forces must move about in their distinctive uniforms; they must be within 'barracks' before 'lights out' time. Any breach of these numerous Army Regulations will at once bring the M.Ps. swooping down upon him and he will find himself in the military 'lock up'. Why all this? Just because he happens to belong to a select class particularly picked out from among millions for achieving a special purpose, i.e., to fight and to win the war.

When such is the case for a group engaged in working for a mere earthly attainment as a military victory, you can imagine how very great then is the need for a thoroughly distinct and exceptional conduct for the spiritual aspirant set upon achieving something infinitely more difficult and more complicated than earthly victory over visible physical forces? Yet, what do we see among spiritual aspirants today? Is there a change of nature? Or mode of conduct, alteration of attitudes, reorientation of ideals and the substitution of a subtler sense of values in place of the gross selfish ones of a pre-novitiate days? Rather, he has hidden in him his own measuring rod and balance to assess and to estimate the quality and works of men and things, events and actions that he used before. He has brought with him as luggage all his old possessions, his old cloak, coloured spectacles, special seat, etc. His mental equipment is the identical one as of the pre-Sadhaka days. What to say it has not even received as much as a polish or a brush-up even.

Nay, in too many cases, it seems as though the bestial part of the aspirant, the 'Pasu' as they call it, or the 'Papa Purusha' assumes a decidedly aggressive form with an access of virulence hitherto absent in its nature. This may be traced to the very fact that he has become a seeker. For, this fact puffs him up with a feeling that he is exceptional, privileged, something superior to the vast common majority. This sense directly supports and abets the super-arrogation of the lower ego-principle in him. Thus spiritual life, the very beginning of it is vitiated by a deliberate alliance with a wanton allegiance to the sworn enemy of spirituality. When spiritual life is thus sought to be founded upon attitudes and emotions that are the very direct antithesis of higher life and of divine culture, then one may well imagine its dire consequences. The result is the most awful, the most poignant of all tragedies in the universe. In all creation there cannot be a more fearsome or terrible occurrence than this.

Of course, from the standpoint of transcendent Vedanta this is a mere nothing. For nothing has happened at all. Nothing ever took place in reality. For neither has there been any manifestation nor creation, etc. (vide Goudapada's famous Ajata-Vada theory). But to the lesser one with a somewhat lower vision this is none-the-less a truly heart-breaking eye-opener. It is to say the least, most deeply regrettable. One stands aghast, stunned, and cruelly wounded to the core, for, the heart says, "True indeed it is that only One, the Supreme Unmanifest alone exists. There is no universe. But yet, the Supreme is Sarva as well as Sunya. Even this tragedy, therefore, is but truth. One trembles at the fate of such Sadhakas. The ladder which is to take the struggler up and higher up into heaven is kept pointing downwards and its very ascending rungs are used as descending steps to go down into the regions of Eternal Darkness.

This last reason is precisely why the whole matter becomes such a great tragedy. For, the phenomenon of an essential earthly person working himself to perdition does not evoke the same shudder as a spiritual aspirant going to ruin. The worldly man proposes to do nothing else. He knows what he is about. And, he cares a hoot for the consequences. "Eat, drink and be merry, for tomorrow you may die"—is his aggressive philosophy. Then again "Each man for himself and the devil take the hindmost" is openly his conception of the best policy. But, the aspirant starts to escape this state and sets to work to become superhuman and indeed divine. All his life's effort is therefore considered to be directed at this goal by becoming free of the state the worldling has got into. And if by identifying himself with the demoniacal side in him he starts plunging headlong into a condition, infinitely worse than that of the sinner and worldling, what then can be a more staggering sight. What then can be a more shocking revelation? Is there no help for this state of things? What is the safeguard against this? What is the antidote for this? What is the curative remedy for such a state of being?

To all this, the answer is more or less the same. It is the acquiring and the active application of One Fundamental Virtue, in its different aspects. Just as today, the variations of the self-same Sulfa Drug is administered to fight different infections, even so antidote, safeguard, the curative remedy may be all summed up in the one, sublime, grand and the supreme word—HUMILITY—Yes. True spontaneous, genuine HUMILITY.

Let him be humble. He will be saved from pride and egoism. Let him strive to become humble. Arrogance will lose its footing in his nature. Let him repent truly and with genuine humility pray for forgiveness to the Lord. He shall be healed of the fell disease of Asurism and aggressive self-assertion and heartlessness that has assailed him.

Have you noted the shape of an axe-head? Thin, pointed, fine-edged in the beginning and broader at the back. The shape of the needle is similar—fine and pointed at the tip and thickening as it goes. You have all read of the spear-head of the shock troop and the now world famous Panzer divisions of the most modern mechanised army of Europe. A narrow, fast-moving unit denting and breaking through the strongest defence with a lightning stroke and then the pouring in into the breach of the formidable bulk of the main army. HUMILITY is the fine point in the Sadhaka's arms. This and this alone will take him through the most difficult starting period when the entire strength of the undivine forces are ranged against him en masse. This and this alone will save him from a terrible downfall from the deluded heights of Asuric egotism. This is as the fine and thin edge of the axe which helps it to enter and to split its way through the heaviest, the toughest and the hugest of timber. Had it been a big, broad and blunt front, it would fail miserably to make any headway whatsoever. Oh! Beloved Aspirants! Learn life's lesson from this. Save yourself from a dire and terrible fate. A whole precious life will be irretrievably lost otherwise.

O dear Sadhakas! Become humble. Change your nature. Develop compassion. A true Vedantin will drip with Compassion and Love with every breath of his body. GOD is LOVE. He is KRIPASAGARA. And if the Vedantin identifies himself with this Infinite Being, then he must needs become a veritable ocean of love and mercy. His very presence, nay his memory even, should at once flood the driest of hearts with an overflow of the waters of Prema and Kripa. Do not be merely Vidya-Sagara. Remain for ever a true Daya-Sagara, too. Vidya may be like unto a pure transparent glass through which one may look, perceive and get to know all things of the universe, but it is Daya that indeed, like the dazzling coating of mercury in the glass makes it spring into life as a mirror to catch and reflect the Divinity that is immanent in the Universe.

May the loving Lord shower His divine compassion upon such misguided seekers! May He bless them with the faculty of and the desire for self-analysis and deep introspection! May they perceive their grave defects and great errors; and strive to make amends and to correct themselves! May they attain true happiness through right knowledge, love and compassion.

ADVICE TO SADHAKAS

The cardinal defect that which has been always standing in the way and is now isolated in an extreme prominence is seated or concentrated in the lower vital being. I mean that part of the vital physical nature with its petty and obstinate egoism which actuates the external human personality, that which supports its surface thoughts and dominated its habitual ways of feeling, character and action. When the lower vital rises, the higher mind, (the psychic self) or the higher and larger vital nature are pushed into the background, if not covered over for the time by this lower vital being and this external personality. Hear the teachings of Lord Krishna in the Gita to corroborate this idea.

"*Rajas tamaschabhibhuya sattvam bhavati bharata,
Rajah sattvam tamas chaiva tamah sattvam rajas tatha.*"

"Now harmony prevaileth, having overpowered passion and inertia, O Bharata; now passion, having overpowered harmony and inertia and now inertia, having overpowered harmony and passion."—Gita, XIV, 10.

Whatever here may be the Higher parts, as aspiration to the Truth, devotion or Will to conquer the obstacles and the hostile forces, it cannot become integral, so long as the lower vital and the external personality have not accepted light and consented to change.

It is inevitable that in the course of the Sadhana these inferior parts of the nature should be brought forward in order that like the rest of the being they may make the crucial choice and either accept or refuse transformation. The physical Consciousness and the material life cannot change if this does not change. Nothing that may have been done before, no inner illumination, experience, power of Ananda is of any eventual value, if this is not done. If this little external personality is to persist in retaining its obscure and limited, its petty and ignoble, its selfish, false and stupid human consciousness, this amounts to a flat negation of the work and the Sadhana. I have no intention of giving any sanction to a partial and transient spiritual opening within with no true and radical change in the law of the external nature. If, then, any Sadhaka refuses in practice to admit this change or if he refuses even to admit the necessity for any change of his lower vital being and his habitual external personality, I am quite sure that he can never make even an iota of real spiritual advancement.

I am well aware that this change is not easy, the dynamic Will towards it does not come at once and is difficult to fix, and even afterwards, the Sadhaka often feels helpless against the force of habit. Knowing this, I have shown sufficient patience in giving time for the true spirit to come up and form and act effectively in the external being of those around me. But if in any one of this part not only becomes obstinate, self-assertive or aggressive, but is supported and justified by the mind and Will and tries to spread itself in the atmosphere, then it is a different and very serious matter.

The difficulty in the lower vital being is that it is still wedded to its old self (little "I") and in revolt against the Light, it has not only not surrendered either to a greater Truth nor to a personal Guru, but it has up to now no such will and hardly any idea even of what true surrender is. Many emotional, self-willed and obstinate boys from Punjab, Deccan, Gujarat, Madras and particularly from Bengal are spoiled wholesale nowadays by their leading a happy-go-lucky life and by their not living for some years under the direct supervision and instruction of a spiritual guide. When the lower vital assumes this attitude, it takes its stand upon a constant affirmation of the old personality and the past forms of the lower nature. Every time they are discouraged, it supports and brings them back and asserts its right to freedom; the freedom to affirm and follow its own crude and egoistic ideas, desires, fancies, impulses or conveniences whenever it chooses. It claims secretly, or in so many words the right to follow its nature, its human unregenerate nature; the right to be itself, its natural original unchanged self, with all the falsehood, ignorance and incoherence proper to this part of the being.

And it claims or, if it does not claim in theory, it asserts in practice the right to express all this impure and inferior stuff in speech and act and behaviour. It defends, glosses over, paints in specious colours and tries to prolong indefinitely the past habitual ways of thinking, speaking and feeling and to eternize what is distorted and misfound in the character. This it does sometimes by open self-assertion and revolt, branding all that is done or said against it as error or oppression or injustice, sometimes behind a cover of self-deception or a mask of dissimulation, professing one thing and practising another. Often it tries to persuade itself and convince others that these things are the only right reason and right way of acting for itself or for all or even that they are part of the true movement of the Yoga.

When this lower vital being is allowed to the action, as happens when the Sadhaka in anyway endorses its suggestions, its attitude, whether masked to himself or coming to the surface, dictates a considerable part of his speech and action and against it he makes no serious obstacle. If he is frank with himself and straightforward to the Guru he will begin to recognise the source and nature of the resistance and will soon be on the direct road to correct and change it. But this, when under the adverse influence, he persistently refuses to be, he prefers to hide up these movements under any kind of concealment, denial, justification or excuse or other shelter.

In the nature the resistance takes certain characteristic forms which add to the confusion and to the difficulty of transformation. It is necessary to outline some of these forms, because they are sufficiently common, in some in a less, in others in a greater degree, to demand a strong and clear exposure.

DISOBEDIENCE AND INDISCIPLINE

This lower part of the being is always random, wayward, self-assertive and unwilling to accept the imposition on it of any order and discipline other than its own idea or impulse. Its defects, even from the beginning stand in the way of efforts of the higher vital to impose on the nature a truly regenerating Tapasya. This habit of disobedience and disregard of discipline is so strong that it does not always need to be immediate, irresistible and instinctive. Thus, obedience to the Guru is repeatedly promised or professed but the action done or the course followed is frequently the very opposite of the profession or promise. This constant indiscipline is a radical obstacle to the Sadhana and the worst possible example to others.

DISSIMULATION AND FALSITY OF SPEECH

This is exceedingly an injurious habit of the lower nature. Those who are not straightforward cannot profit by the Guru's help, for they themselves turn it away. Unless they change they cannot hope for the descent of the Brahmic Light and Truth into the lower vital and physical nature; they remain stuck in their own self-created mud and cannot progress. Often it is not mere exaggeration or a false use of the imagination embroidering on the actual truth that is marked in the Sadhaka, but also a positive denial and distortion as well as a falsifying concealment of facts. This he does sometimes to cover up his disobedience or wrong or doubtful course of action, sometimes to keep up his position, at others to get his own way or indulge his preferred habits and desires. Very often, when one has this kind of vital habit, he clouds his own consciousness and does not altogether realise the falsity of what he is saying or doing; but in such that he says and does, it is quite impossible to extend to him even this inadequate excuse.

A DANGEROUS HABIT OF CONSTANT SELF-JUSTIFICATION

When this becomes strong in the Sadhaka, it is impossible to turn him in this part of his being to the right consciousness and action because at each step his whole preoccupation is to justify himself. His mind rushes at once to maintain his own ideas, his own position or his own course of action. This he is ready to do by any kind of argument, sometimes the most clumsy and foolish or inconsistent with what he has been protesting the moment before, by any kind or mis-statement or any kind of device. This is a common misuse, none-the-less misuse of the thinking mind; but it takes in him exaggerated proportions and so long as he keeps to it, it will be impossible for him to see or like the truth.

Whatever the difficulties of the natures, however long and painful the process of dealing with them, they cannot stand to the end against the Truth, if there is or if there comes in these parts the true spirit, attitude and endeavour. But if a Sadhaka continues out of self-esteem and self-will or out of Tamasic inertia to shun his eyes or harden his heart against the Light, so long as he does that, no one can help him. The consent of all the being is necessary for the divine change, and it is the completeness and fullness of the consent that constitutes the integral surrender. But the consent of the lower vital must not be only a mental profession or a passing emotional adhesion; it must translate itself into an abiding attitude and persistent and consistent action.

Yoga can only be done to the end by those who are in total earnest about it and ready to abolish their little human ego and its demands in order to find themselves in the Divine. It cannot be done in a spirit of levity or laxity; the work is too high and difficult, the adverse powers in the lower nature too ready to take advantage of the least sanction or the smallest opening, the aspiration and Tapasya needed too constant and intense. It cannot be done if there is a petulant self-assertion of the ideas of the human mind or wilful indulgence of the demands and instincts and pretensions of the lowest part of the being commonly justified under the name of human nature. It cannot be done if you insist on identifying these lowest things of the ignorance with the Divine Truth or even the lesser truth permissible on the way. It cannot be done if you cling to your past self and its old mental, vital and physical formations and habits; one has continually to leave behind his past selves and to see, act and live from always a higher and higher conscious level. It cannot be done if you insist on "freedom" for your human mind and vital ego. All the parts of the human being are entitled to express and satisfy themselves in their own way at their own risk and peril, if he so chooses, as long as he leads the ordinary life. But to enter into a path of Yoga, whose whole object is to substitute for these human things the law and power of a greater Truth and the whole heart of whose method is a surrender to the Divine Sakti, and yet to go on claiming this so-called freedom, which is no more than a subjection to certain ignorant cosmic forces is to indulge in a blind contradiction and to claim the right to lead a double life.

Last of all, Yoga can be done if those who profess to be its Sadhakas, continue always to make themselves centres, instruments or spokesmen of the forces of ignorance which oppose, deny and ridicule its very principle and object. On one side there is the Brahmic realisation, the overshadowing and descending power of the supramental Divine, the light and force of a far greater Truth than any yet realised on the earth, something therefore beyond what the little human mind and its logic regard as the only permanent realities, something whose nature and way and process of development here it cannot conceive and perceive by its own inadequate instrument or judge by its puerile standards. On the other side if this lower vital nature with all its pretensions, arrogance, ignorance, obscurity, dullness, turbulence, standing for its own prolongation, standing against the descent—refusing to believe in any real reality or real possibility of a supramental or superhuman consciousness and creation, or still more absurd, demanding, if it exists at all, that it should conform to its own little standards, seizing greedily upon everything that seems to disprove it, denying the presence of the Divine.

For this opposition, this sterile obstruction and blockade against its descent of the Divine Truth cannot blast for ever; everyone must come down finally on one side or the other, on the side of the Truth or against it. The Brahmic realisation cannot co-exist with the persistence of the lower ignorance; it is incompatible with continued satisfaction in a double nature.

INSTRUCTIONS TO SANNYASINS

I

A true, spiritually hungry and thirsty aspirant with true, lasting, sustained and burning dispassion and burning yearning for Liberation, who is already treading the path of renunciation, can really understand the true import and the true spirit of these instructions. These are the quintessence of the Narada-Parivrajaka-Upanishad and scriptures which treat of Vairagya, Tyaga, Divine Life, right conduct and rules for Yatis or Sannyasins.

Lord Krishna says: "O Son of Kunti! the excited senses of even a wise man, though he be striving, impetuously carry away his mind." Hence all instructions should be rigidly observed to the very letter. Any leniency will lead to disastrous consequences and downfall of the aspirants. Beware! Beware! Be vigilant! Be on the alert!

Do not try to imitate the Siddhas in certain respects, whose ways are sometimes mysterious, but really educative and instructive. Do not think you are also a Siddha when you have only entered the path and when you are not even a third-class aspirant.

Many have been deceived by the voice of the lower mind which is taken for "Adesha" from the Lord and by vile imitation, leniency given to the mind and relaxing the rigour of the instructions, have had a hopeless downfall.

Some unwise modern people may bring a charge that there is much orthodoxy here. But such orthodoxy or discipline only can help one to attain Self-realisation. Comfortable Sannyasa will not take one to the Goal.

1. Do not keep money. Do not even touch it. This will bring bondage. This will give rise to pride and lead to downfall. You will lose sight of the Ideal.

2. Maintain a spotless character. Do not give any cause for even the slightest suspicion.

3. Live on mere Bhiksha. This will make you quite independent.

INTIMATE ADVICE TO ASPIRANTS

4. Do not enter the house of a householder. Do not take meals in his house.

5. Take only one meal at noon. Take the minimum quantity necessary.

6. Do not visit your native village, town or district, at least for a period of full twelve years after taking Sannyasa.

7. Do not write letters to anybody. Do not keep connections with any man of the world.

8. Always keep only one blanket and two clothes for your use, and not more than that.

9. Live always singly and independently in Uttarakhand.

10. Do not sleep in other's bed. Do not sleep during daytime. Reduce the sleep to the barest minimum.

11. Do not make friends and do not keep company with anybody; even with aspirants. Do not be intimate with anybody, particularly with ladies.

12. Do not accept any position or job even if it is honorary.

13. Do not raise your hand for defence even if you are assaulted. Bear insult, bear injury. You have no right to defend yourself.

14. Do not talk of people connected to this body in the previous Ashram (i.e. the old family life).

15. Stick to your holy garb even if your throat is about to be cut. Do not change the cloth under any condition throughout the life.

16. Do not do any action such as meat-eating, drinking and smoking which would bring disgrace on yourself or the holy order.

17. Do not talk vulgar words. Let your speech be majestic and be blooming with Spiritual Force.

18. Do not sit on the same carpet or mat or bench in which a woman is sitting. A woman also should observe the same precaution.

19. Do not sit alone with a woman in a room.

20. Do not earn money by doing business for maintaining yourself. Do not practise astrology, palmistry, etc., for the purpose of money and food.

21. Do not write to householders to send you money-order when you are sick. Rely on the Supreme Lord.

22. Do not love, fondle or play with children.

23. Be an embodiment of humility at all times. Have the Bhava that you are a servant of humanity. Be ready to help and serve others.

24. Do not expect reverence and respect and exceptional treatment as a privilege of the order. Your only privilege is to serve and to meditate on the Supreme Ideal.

25. Offer salutation to others first. Do not wait for the others to salute you in the beginning.

26. Do not sing or dance. Do not practise any of the fine arts.

27. Do not be influenced by the false changing fashions of the world.

28. Do not care for public opinion and do not try to become a centre of attraction and reverence for all.

29. Do not mix with social, political and such secular organisations.

30. Do not make any lady disciple even if she is a great devotee.

31. Do not allow anybody to shampoo your legs and feet. Do not keep any servant.

32. Do not injure any being either in thought, word or deed. Do not trample over insects. Walk looking on the ground.

33. Do not undergo medical treatment except in unavoidable and extreme conditions. Ordinary ailments should be borne with fortitude.

34. Do not keep such pots or vessels like those made of silver, brass, copper, etc., as may bring about attachment.

35. As far as possible try to take Bhiksha only with hands. Do not use utensils.

36. If you note that a person is unwilling to give Bhiksha or is himself not in good circumstances, do not visit that house once again.

37. Be contented with whatever that comes as food, clothing or shelter.

38. Whenever you take Bhiksha, mentally bless that person to have Spiritual enlightenment and Liberation.

39. Never hoard anything for tomorrow. Forget the past. Live always in the immediate present.

40. Do not use oil, scent, sandal-paste, flowers for the body.

41. Do not be a permanent dependent upon certain devotees or admirers.

42. Do not cut jokes with anybody. Do not laugh vehemently like a worldly man. Be always calm, serene and deep.

43. Do not read newspapers. You have nothing to do with this world or its business of life.

44. Do not open your mouth except during taking Bhiksha or giving Upadesa on Spiritual Realisation. During Bhiksha say only "Narayana Hari!"

45. Have a clean shaving of the head. Do not have scissors-cuttings or stylish machine-cuttings.

46. Do not use clothes of colours other than orange (Gerua). Do not use multi-coloured clothing.

47. Lead the life of a Parivrajaka for sometime in the beginning. Then stick to one place for Sadhana.

48. Always walk on foot. Do not use any vehicle.

49. Do not be tempted by Siddhis. Do not try to get them. Do not exhibit your spiritual powers.

50. Shun honour, praise, worship and respect. Be indifferent to censure and criticism.

51. Treat every object of the world as a worthless piece of straw.

52. Do not keep yourself wantonly dirty. Be neat and clean, in thought, word and deed.

53. Do not build an Ashram and do not make disciples.

54. Do not try to become famous. Do not advertise yourself as a Mahatma. Cut at the very root of all ambitions. Your only ambition should be for Self-realisation.

55. Do not allow yourself to be photographed or pictured or filmed.

56. Do not play any kind of games. Do not give way for the thought of pleasurable recreation.

57. Do not run like a busy man. Do not shout at the top of your voice.

58. Be simple like a child. Cut off all dealings with others.

59. When you are firmly established in the path, initiate at least one fit person into Sannyasa.

60. You have no other duty to perform in this world except Meditation on the Supreme Self or Brahman.

61. Be always saturated in the continuous thought of peace, knowledge and bliss without decay.

62. You are not the body. Do not love it. Do not caress it.

63. Be always true and loyal to the doctrines of Advaita-Vedanta.

64. The Eternal Brahman alone exists everywhere. There is nothing else but That. Therefore be silent and wise.

65. Do not forget that whatever you see, hear, smell, taste, touch, or feel is nothing but Brahman in reality.

66. Do not talk unless somebody questions you. If anybody speaks without proper decorum, be silent and indifferent. Knowing the nature of the world, be always silent and indifferent.

67. Cleverness of action and powers of oratory do not make a real Sannyasin. Fame and respect, erudite learning and marvellous feats do not make a real Sannyasin. Dispassion and Wisdom of the Self make one a real Sannyasin.

68. Study without fail the Upanishads and the Brahma-sutras, especially during the period of Chaturmasya.

69. Be always meditating on OM and its meaning, and on the significance of the Mahavakyas.

70. Remember that you are the Immortal Atman, and that the whole world is but Brahman only.

II

1. Do not sail or fly to foreign countries.

2. Do not tie turban or wear a cap on the head.

3. As far as possible, try to dispense with the use of shoes and umbrellas.

4. Do not sleep on cushions and do not use soft pillows.

5. Do not observe the calendar of the year. Do not wish to know the date, the day, the Tithi, Nakshatra, like Ekadasi, Amavasya, Purnima, Jayanti, New-year-day, etc. Your concern should be only with day and night.

6. Regard your body and the mind of the previous Ashrama as completely dead and that you have started a new life both in body and mind after taking Sannyasa.

7. Cast off any waist-chain, earring, or any other ornament from the body.

8. Destroy the feeling of difference between one thing and the other. Try to see oneness everywhere.

9. Do not practise gymnastics or any body-building exercises.

10. Do not write anything. Dispense with that habit. Do not read books unless they are directly concerned with Self-realisation, viz., the Upanishads, the Yogavasishtha, etc.

11. Do not have self-shaving. Depend upon the barber if available. Otherwise grow hair until a barber comes.

12. Do not have any curiosity to know things of the world. Nip all curiosity in its bud.

13. Do not wait near a house for long if you do not get Bhiksha quickly. Move on to another place.

14. Do not have ill-feeling against one who does not give you Bhiksha.

15. Do not be attached to your new name or garb. It may increase your pride.

16. Do not have lock and key if at any time you happen to live in a Kutir.

17. Do not live in the company of many Sannyasins. Live singly.

18. As far as possible, when you are well established in the Path, try to avoid going to Bhiksha from house to house or even to Kshetra. Sit at a place and take whatever that comes there.

19. Do not keep your titles or degrees after taking Sannyasa.

20. Do not praise or try to please a person for the sake of getting Bhiksha from him.

21. Do not use light at night. Live in the dark and meditate.

22. Do not use seats or Asanas or Japamalas which may cause attachment. You may become sorry if you lose them.

23. Do not ride on animals. Do not wish to be carried by persons.

24. Do not preach or give Upadesa unless you are approached or compelled to do so.

25. Do not apply Vibhuti, Kumkum or Chandan to the body.

26. Along with the steadiness of the mind in the constant contemplation upon the Self, try to keep the body also as steady and activeless as possible.

27. Do not take Bhiksha from more than seven houses. The total collected should not exceed the minimum quantity necessary.

28. Never feel sorry or depressed or grieved if you witness a pitiable sight, like a suffering man or a dead man.

29. Never wander at night. Stick to a place after sun-set.

30. Do not love cows, dogs or cats, etc. Do not keep pet animals. Look upon a snake, a scorpion, a cow, a tiger, a deer with equal vision.

31. Do not swim, jump, skip, clap or whistle.

32. When taking Bhiksha, do not touch the hand of the person who gives Bhiksha.

33. Do not file suits against anybody. Do not go to courts.

34. If anybody takes away your articles, like Kamandalu, cloth, etc., allow him to take it away. Do not quarrel with him.

35. If you are forcibly chained or taken to the jail or prison, do not grudge. Go with an undisturbed state of mind.

36. Do not cook your food. Do not touch fire. Be satisfied with whatever kind of food you get, whether raw or cooked.

37. Do not wear spectacles even if you have no good sight.

38. Never think of death. Remember you have no death. You are the Eternal Homogeneous Essence of Satchidananda.

GUIDING LIGHTS

1. Man is only a brute if he has no Manushyatva, if he does not possess mercy, love, kindness, self-control, good behaviour, courtesy, politeness, etc.

2. A kind, sympathetic, pure, loving and merciful heart is the garden. Virtuous Samskaras are the seeds. Sublime, divine thoughts are the roots. Sattvic qualities are the sprouts. Kind, loving, truthful words are the leaves. Virtuous actions are the blossoms. Moksha is the fruit. Therefore develop mercy. Entertain sublime thoughts. Speak truth. Do virtuous actions. Eat the divine fruit.

3. Do not fight against evil thoughts, evil qualities, defects, weaknesses and bad habits. If you fight against them, they will

become stronger and stronger, and it will be difficult for you to overcome them, by fighting against them. Cultivate sublime, divine thoughts. Develop virtuous qualities. Build up good habits. Do Japa. Meditate regularly. Try to live in God. All defects, all evil thoughts, all weaknesses will vanish *in toto*.

4. Righteousness, frankness, amiable disposition, kindness, benevolence, service and mercy will protect you from the acts of certain self-interested persons of undesirable character. Gradually cultivate these positive, Sattvic qualities one by one. You can win the hearts of all.

5. Have the wisdom of Vidura, the virtues of Yudhishthira, the purity of Bhishma, the liberality of Karna, the gallantry of Arjuna and the strength of Bhima. You will attain greatness and immortality.

6. To begin with, drink the Prema Mixture twice daily at 4 a.m. and 8 p.m. Mix a teaspoonful of Sraddha with 3 teaspoonfuls of Prema and half a teaspoonful of Bhava. Add to this mixture 2 teaspoonfuls of Hari Kirtan and one ounce of Japa. Gradually increase the quantities in the mixture. This will form an infallible specific or panacea for attaining immortality and destroying the disease of births and deaths.

7. Eat three things. Wear three things. Practise three things, viz., Ahimsa, Satya, Brahmacharya. Remember three things: death, pains of Samsara and God. Renounce three things, viz., egoism, desire and attachment. Cultivate three things: humility, fearlessness and love. Eradicate three things: lust, anger and greed.

8. Action is the source of all virtue, wealth and desire. He who has no activity, has no energy or valour. The end of virtue and wealth is the attainment of salvation. He who does not practise virtue commits sin. The fruits of righteous acts and of wealth occur either in this world or in the next.

9. Overcome anger by love, lust by purity, greed by liberality, pride by humility, egoism by self-surrender to the Lord. Thou wilt become Divine.

10. Earnestness is the path of blessedness. Thoughtlessness is the royal road to births and deaths. Evince more earnestness and enthusiasm in your Sadhana. You will soon attain the Immortal.

11. Sit less. Serve more. Hate none. Love all. Clothe less. Bathe more. Take less. Give more. Talk less. Think more. Eat

less. Masticate more. Preach less, practise more. Worry less, laugh more. Indulge less, restrain more. Rest less, work more. Sleep less, meditate more. You will enjoy wonderful health and inner peace of the Soul.

12. Do not become a victim of your emotions. Govern them. Control them. Do not allow yourself to be governed by them. That man who has controlled his emotions has a serene mind. He is really a strong man.

13. Give up hate and strife and greed for power, position and gold. Wear the crown of humility. Become pure and bright. Build your faith in God. Be steadfast in Japa and meditation. Attain love and light.

14. If you take a vow, you will have to stick to it even at the cost of your life, even if your throat is cut, even if you are burnt alive, even under any sort of persecution.

15. If you fail in keeping your resolves, make fresh resolves. Just as a child falls many a time when it tries to walk without the help of the wall, just as the new cyclist falls from the cycle a number of times before he learns to sit steadily on the seat, so also the new aspirant will fall a number of times in his resolves. He has to make repeated attempts. Ultimately he will come out victoriously.

16. If you leave the public service simply because some jealous persons attempted to vilify and injure you, simply because you will have to face various sorts of bitter experiences, it is a great loss for you. Your spiritual growth will be terribly retarded. You must have moral strength and moral courage to face public criticism, harsh remarks and persecution. Your suffering is nothing when compared with the persecutions underwent by Sri Rama and the five Pandavas. Show your manliness, moral courage and spiritual strength now. The inner strength that you have obtained by meditation, is tested now. Had you really done good meditation, you ought to have abundant strength now to face these difficulties with a smile. If you have no strength it shows that there had been some error in meditation. Real meditation gives immense inner strength.

17. Serve and love. Give and relinquish. Tolerate and endure. Restrain and subdue. Forget and forgive. Adjust and adapt. Persevere and plod. Aspire and purify. Reflect and enquire. Meditate and realise. May you attain Kaivalya!

SWEETNESS IN SADHAKAS

Really sweet people are rarely found in this universe. Though sweetness is a feminine virtue, yet it is not found in the females too. Most of the females are harsh and gall hearted though their speech appears to be sweet for the time being. A business man, a lawyer, a doctor and a sister of ill-fame are all apparently sweet till they get money from their clients. This is not natural, lasting, beneficent, elevating sweetness. It is false glittering. It is commercial or mercenary.

A really sweet man is divine. He does not expect anything from others. His very nature is sweet. He brings joy to others by his innate sweetness.

Sweetness is born of Sattva. It is the sweet potent divine golden residuum after Rajas and Tamas have been squeezed out through protracted Yoga Sadhana. It is the concentrated quintessence of Sattva. It is the sweet aroma that is wafted from the blossoming of the rare sweet flower of a perfected Soul—Siddha Purusha, adept or Arhat through long and intense Tapas, discipline, Yoga practice and communion through mind-melting in silence.

Sweetness must be an essential attribute of a spiritual propagandist and public worker. Without possessing this virtue, no propagandist can turn out efficient and solid work. He who wants to establish a Mutt or Ashram or spiritual institution must possess this ennobling virtue. All public workers and Ashramites must equip themselves with this divine quality.

The Rajasic ego should melt in the crucible of Yoga fire. Then this golden sweetness will shine in its glory. Rajas must be churned out. Then the butter of sweetness will float on the surface of the Sattvic mind.

Be sweet in speech. Be sweet in behaviour. Be sweet in manners. Be sweet in singing Kirtan. Be sweet in lecturing. Be sweet in serving others. Be soft, gentle, cautious and polite too. This increases your sweetness.

Develop this sweetness through service, self-restraint, Mouna, prayer, Pranayama, meditation, introspection, self-analysis, control of anger.

Sweetness is Radha Tattva. Sweetness is the stuff out of which the heart of Radha is fashioned. Truthfulness, Prema, sincerity, cosmic love, shyness, are all modifications of sweetness. Sweetness is a rare, divine blend of all these Sattvic attributes. It is millennium potency.

An argumentative, intolerant, impatient, proud, irritable, fault-finding man cannot cultivate sweetness.

Glory to Brahman, the Sweetness of sweetness.

SPIRITUAL GUIDANCE FOR ASPIRANTS

The spirit of universality is the first step towards Self-realisation. It is not the attitude of automatism, or mechanical subservience to a particular universalised doctrine. It does not imply antagonism to the genius of individuality; it does not prevent the individual to grow according to the law of his own growth. It implies transcending over sectarian loyalties, bigoted animosities and self-centred vanities. It means the denial of the bane influences of individuality.

Material objects are best offered to God by placing them at the disposal of those who really need them. We offer material objects to God, not that He is in want of these, but to deny our sense of possession and to evolve ourselves into a state of complete self-surrender.

Forgetfulness of the spiritual consciousness that is inherent in every human being is ignorance. Ignorance is rooted in the selfish love for one's own self. Wisdom lies in effacing this ego-ridden selfishness through dedication, service, thoughtfulness, compassion, piety and devotion to God.

People's minds are saturated with hatred and retribution. But even this will pass away. Hatred cannot be requited by hatred. If hatred is sought to be avenged by hatred, then it will be perpetuated to endlessness. If the heart is not pure enough to forgive, then the only judicious course is dissociation. Time is a great healing factor; time is also a forerunner to forgiveness.

It is not the life of devotions, rituals and pilgrimages that matters, but the spirit which pervades one's thought, speech and action. Be not ego-centric. Be humane, kind and sincere. Reflect and restrain. Adapt and adjust. Let the spiritual awareness in you grow profounder by every day.

You must awaken the dormant powers and faculties within you by the practice of Yoga. You have within you tremendous latent powers and capacities. Generally, ninety nine per cent of the potentials are left untapped in most human beings. Develop your will-power through controlling and sublimating the sense-urges. Practise concentration. Contemplate on the divine virtues that are a part of your essential nature. Raise the consciousness from the lower to the higher planes. As you evolve, you will unfold new powers, new faculties, new qualities. Conquest over oneself erases all fears. Then you become an embodiment of courage and strength. Then you are in a position to change your environment, transform the life of another, and heal the sick.

Practise introspection and self-analysis. Watch from the reactions of others as to what is undesirable in you. Sometimes you may not yourself be able to judge your own negative qualities. You have to take the clue from other people's reactions and mould your nature accordingly. It is true that you cannot fit in according to the measurement of each and everyone, but wisdom lies in taking the ruling from general public opinion.

Do not be injudiciously free with your opinion. Do not bother to express your views unless asked for. Even then you have to be careful in not to rub another on the wrong side. Control yourself from contradicting others, while not assenting in a hypocritical manner. Restrain yourself from speaking out directly the undesirable traits that might be conspicuous in your friend.

Life without lust, egoism, greed, anger and pride is itself divine life. Try to live a life of purity and spiritual contemplation with a spirit of self-dedication. You must have unswerving faith in God during trials, disappointments and under dismal circumstances.

To be introvert and contemplative, to cherish seclusion and to keep withdrawn from external environments, are no doubt, most desirable ideals in the spiritual path. But these have their own drawbacks, and one has to be extremely careful in not to succumb to their negative effects. Most people who are apparently introvert and who try to shield themselves from the world are by nature highly selfish, conceited, hostile and arrogant. It is very difficult to find in them even a slight trace of charity and selflessness. Their real spiritual worth is very doubtful. Their religious exterior is a mantle of neurosis. One has, therefore, to be cautious and judicious in weeding out the evil qualities from one's nature through humility, service, ready acceptance of the goodness in others, introspection and self-culture.

The spiritual aspirant has to continuously fight back the ill effects of despondence. In him depressing thoughts should find no place. Everything has a purpose behind. Setbacks and difficulties come only to awaken one to the purpose of one's life. He who learns by others' examples does not have to suffer himself much. Mistakes and failures have to be accepted as they are. To allow them to weigh upon oneself is by itself a mistake. To chaff them to be mere nothing is to perpetuate their ill-effects in the subconscious. Mistakes should make one wiser and infuse new determination and strength of will to overcome them.

The senses are not meant for revelling in delusive pleasure-experiences, and the mind is not meant to create a barrier between one thing and another. They are all aids to the realisation of the Absolute, and if these instruments are misused in life, the person responsible has to pay the penalty in the form of suffering.

There are three elements which obstruct the spiritual consciousness to find expression in oneself. They are Mala or impurity, Vikshepa or oscillation, and Avarana or the veil of ignorance. Impurity should be removed by study of holy books, repetition of the divine Name and selfless service. Oscillation of mind should be encountered by the practice of concentration, Asana and Pranayama. And the veil of ignorance should be rent asunder by profound meditation on the Atman.

Without right exertion nothing in the world is achieved. Without right resolution no Sadhana can begin. Therefore, resolve to follow the path of truth, purity and compassion. Aspire to be progressive in your thought and action, and be intent on growing in virtue, goodness and holiness through every waking moment.

NEED FOR GREAT VIGILANCE

Society plays a very prominent part in the moulding of a man's character. He is highly influenced by the customs and manners as are adopted by his surroundings. One's own determination, will-power and discrimination to discharge the normal duties are often crippled by his environments. He may be virtuous in his thoughts, faithful in putting them into practice and faultless in their execution; but imposition of attributes, depiction of certain wrong ideals and involuntary bondage pull him

INTIMATE ADVICE TO ASPIRANTS

down from the heights of virtue. He tumbles down. He is lost in the deep abyss of materialism.

Many Sadhakas and aspirants readily take themselves to have surpassed all the obstacles in the spiritual path even at the commencement of their Sadhana. This is nothing but foolishness. After undergoing training for a few months or days even under a perfected and realised soul, they conclude that they are on the peaks of unapproachable spiritual heights. They re-enter the world, pose themselves as realised souls. Bread becomes the foremost problem for them. They seek the protection of some householders for a pretty long time hopping from house to house; and during this period instead of inspiring, advising and turning the host round to idealistic life, begin to dominate over them without thinking for a moment their unauthorised intervention. Worst of all, due to want of proper training, they fail ingloriously to stand the slightest test from the aspiring householder and are forced to retreat to the broad streets, grave and glum. Still worse are those who are chameleons drowned in chaos and confusion saying nothing but 'yes' to whatever opinion their host may hold. Aspirants! Are you real in your Sadhana? Do you remember what made you discard the society? Then know that the path is perilous to the end. Do not be carried away by trivials. Do not be proud of your achievements if you have really achieved any. First and foremost, never dream to re-enter the society as long as the organs of senses still dominate over you. Not to speak of the power of lust that lurks in most of the people till the body is entirely consummated. Not only this. Till the sex is felt in you by others.

A worm may die as a worm if left alone. But if stung by a wasp continuously it turns a wasp itself. You might have curbed the sex-idea in you. You might have turned completely sexless. But those whom you might mingle with do not readily take you to be so. They find sex in you. Some think that you are one among them and take undue advantage thereof in nursing you even. Some others shrink and repel recognising you as belonging to the opposite. More than the former the behaviour of the latter strongly rouses the sex-consciousness that you are persistently endeavouring to efface. The sex-idea is reinstalled in you. You are once for all lost.

Equip yourself suitably. Do not run among here and there. Stand at your post. Be where you are. Restrict your movements. Stand still. Attain the Great stillness of mind. Emit spiritual vibrations as from a wireless broadcasting station. May you become a dynamic Yogi!

THE VOICE OF SPIRITUAL AID

You are a precious gem. You are unsmelt flower. Safeguard, preserve your pure fragrance. Offer it to the Lord, in all its unsoiled grandeur. Your foremost duty is to do spiritual Sadhana. All other things are pitfalls only. Beware of the deception of the lower nature. Maya even catches hold of man in the apparently elevating form of spirituality.

I am telling you for your good, for your happiness. I wish to see you succeed. I wish to see you as a spiritual superman. Kick aside all these petty delusions. Draw strength from the Supreme Divine Guru. Resolutely turn your face towards the real Destination—the supreme Goal of your life. Proceed onward in the spiritual path. Do not wander and be caught in the midst of the alluring mazes. Shatter the bonds and get yourself free from the lower forces.

Whenever you get anger, try to keep silence and think for yourself in your leisure moments how absurd and totally useless the anger is. It benefits none, gives pain to all, spreads hostility. Think again and again. Laugh at the absolute folly of the anger.

You are meant to achieve a great purpose in this life. Your ideal is different. Never have weak sentiment. Always discriminate. This alone will save you from all the pitfalls and temptations. At each step, at every moment, discriminate between the real and the unreal, right and wrong, proper and improper, pure and impure, good and bad. You will be quite safe. This will keep you alert and strengthen your aspiration. You will be perfectly safe.

During concentration, you must see that there is absolutely no strain, tension or effort in Trataka. While concentrating you must keep yourself completely relaxed and be calm and cool. If you strain, instead of attaining steadiness, there will be the opposite effect. Nerves will be irritated.

The chief cause of all mistaken notions, false conclusions and misunderstanding is thinking that there is some crooked motive behind what another person does. As a matter of fact, even if a man does actually a thing with inner motive, the

spiritual aspirant should not notice it, but should judge it with liberal mind (Udara Buddhi) and tolerant attitude. A cheerful patience is the hall-mark of the expanded heart. Santosha and Sahanaseelata, these two distinguish the Sadhaka.

To counteract falsehood I would suggest this method. Though due to long previous habits, lies are sometimes suddenly uttered unconsciously, yet after a short time, you go to the person to whom you have uttered falsehood and tell him, "What I told you a little while ago is not truth. Please excuse me." Persist in this practice.

Mind is the great tormentor, whenever the mind tries to take you in its circle; you must then think of the saints, who lived before and how they have had to struggle with the tricks of the mind. This will suggest some easy methods of dealing with it at that moment. The most important way of calming the mind is mental Japa. Mental Japa is the sheet-anchor of the aspirant's struggle. It will enable him to tide over any trial of whatever magnitude it may be.

Whatever particular Sadhana you do, try to do as quietly as possible. Never indulge in talk about it. Sadhana should never be known to anyone. Special worship, Japa, Purascharana and meditation are better unadvertised. The inner Sadhana of an aspirant is not known.

It is far better to believe a hundred times and be deceived a hundred times than to make the heart completely devoid of all trust and belief in human nature. Lack of belief turns a man into a cynic in the end.

A Karma Yogi is expected to be very sociable, readily pleasing, cheerful, adaptable and of pleasant speech. He must know to mix with all, anticipate one's wants and serve on, day and night. This is all right. But could this same free attitude be assumed, when moving with members of the opposite sex. This answer is self-evident. Beware of women.

You are a selfless server. You are to cultivate sociable nature. But there is also the most important aspect. You are an aspirant. You are a Brahmacharin. Your ideal is of the Sannyasin. This should be borne in the mind always and the strictest and the most unrelaxing vigilance be exercised when moving with and serving ladies. An aspirant should have absolutely nothing to do with women. He should have perforce to serve them, then personal contact should be barest minimum.

You must know that the woman is the Achintya Maya Sakti, meant specially to ensnare and to delude. Gold or money deludes man after he comes in their contact. But woman powerfully draws and pulls down even one who vigilantly remains aloof. No doubt, they are Devis and Mothers. That is for the one who has acquired that vision, not for you. From a distance you can warm yourself in the heat of the fire. But go near, you are destroyed. It will reduce you to ashes. Remember and beware.

Of course, all things are Divine and some Divinity is specially manifest but when the Lord said, "*Sarasaamasmi Sagarah*", He did not mean you to jump into the ocean and be drowned. Therefore the instructions of sages, even one's Guru should be followed with discrimination and wisdom. The Guru wants the disciple to be wise and not a fool. He gives his general instructions to suit all. He says, "Love all, embrace all." But he also says, "Brahmacharin should not think of a woman even in dream."

The strange fascination exercised by woman is something altogether inexpressible and dangerous. However wise or strong-minded a person may be in other matters, here he succumbs and falls miserably. Do not have any idea of service in connection with woman. This way, you cannot attain salvation. The chances are rather of perdition. Be a Karma Yogi, but remain always as a Sadhaka or as a Brahmacharin, that you are and emulate the Sannyasin, you are to be.

Take my advice seriously. You will not regret it. Tread with infinite care where the ground is treacherous and slippery. May all happiness be thine! May you become calm and quiet under all circumstances and attain the supreme state of perfect silence! May you realise the all-pervading nature of the supreme Lord!

SADHANA AND SAMADHI

Keep your footstep on the spiritual path. Never fear. Just plod on. There is absolutely no room at all for despair on the spiritual path. Progress may be slow, but you will surely achieve the goal. You are meant to achieve it. Success is sure. Not even a moment's effort goes in vain. Remember the bold assurance of the blessed Lord: "*Kaunteya pratijaneehi na me bhaktah pranasyati,*" and again "*Na hi kalyanakrit kaschit durgatim tata gachchati.*"

Calmly carry on the practices regularly. Keep Abhyasa (practice) and Vairagya (dispassion) as your guiding watchwords. They will confer illumination and realisation. Put thy firm trust upon Him, thy Indweller.

Train yourself to become incapable of seeing evil in anything. In this world everywhere there is nothing else but imperfection. Faults fill every nook and corner of the universe. But beneath it all there is only Divinity and Divinity alone. This is the only reality that exists. Become completely oblivious to the faults of others. Try to correct your faults first. Always think, "Oh, he is a good man. I may not like his action. But really he is doing good only, what he thinks to be good. Anyhow I am sure that the motive is good only." Thus thinking you should ascribe only a virtuous motive to another's action.

Though you may not remember your fault, yet it is your duty to admit, because you yourself do not know, about the sudden mischief of the subconscious mind. It plays all errors, but very tactfully. You do not know anything about it. Even if you may know it, it takes you in its circle so nicely and skilfully that you think yourself as a master of the mind. Never think like this. Never get annoyed, even if anybody points out your mistake. Try to annihilate this form of ego.

Cultivate the quality of respecting all creatures, whatever it may be, even the lowest. "Hate the sin and not the sinner"—is practising the habit of giving respect to all and honouring everyone and everything without expectation. Then only this Bhava of reverence becomes natural to your Svabhava. By respecting others we will acquire dignity. We will be benefited in a most marvellous manner. If you try this, you will verily realise its effects.

However busily engaged you are, somehow you must find time to carry on your study also. If you wait to get some special leisure for doing it, you will never be able to study at all. Because such separate time one can never get as there is always fresh work creeping up. One wishing to take bath in the sea should not wait for the waves to subside in order to take a dip.

Be regular in the practice of Yoga Asanas and Pranayamas. Do not neglect your health. Never torture the body with intense and austere Tapas to the extent of making it unfit for the Jiva to dwell. Otherwise the body, which is your helpmate to tread the path of God-realisation, will become emaciated and weak. Incurable diseases will take refuge in your body. Understand that renunciation is an internal state and not an outward show. Do not think that if you attend to bodily comforts, you can never remove the body-idea. Indulgence in objects alone creates attachment but not enjoyment of the legitimate requirements of the body.

Sadhana or spiritual practice should make you ever cheerful, more concentrated, joyful, balanced, peaceful, contented, blissful, dispassionate, fearless, compassionate, discriminative, reflective, courageous, unattached, angerless, I-less, desireless, mineless. Sadhana should give you rich inner life, introspective inner vision and unruffled state of mind, under all conditions of life. These are signs of your spiritual growth. Seeing of visions, lights, hearing of Anahata-sounds, Divya-Gandha or super-sensuous fragrance, feeling of the movement of currents upwards or downwards do not have much spiritual value although they indicate, you have attained the first degree of concentration.

Aspirants think that they have attained Savikalpa Samadhi when they see some lights, hear Anahata sounds and experience some extraordinary smell and that what remains to be realised is only Nirvikalpa Samadhi. This is a sad mistake. Samadhi is not an easy thing. It is not a cheap bazaar commodity. Samadhi demands perfect regeneration and purification of the Adhara, vigorous and protracted Sadhana and intense Tapas. When they are put to the test they will hopelessly fail in all directions. Some pretend to be Samadhists and some are 420 and 840 even in this line also. One in a million may attain Samadhi through the grace of the Lord. Even if you become a good aspirant with good character, moral virtues, knowledge of the scriptures, Vairagya and discrimination, you can thrill and purify the whole world.

Beloved Child! Strive to make yourself fully worthy of His abundant Kindness! Be thou always happy. May He bless you with the highest happiness! May the glory of the thorough knowledge of the Self be to you! May the effulgence of spirituality be to you! May you understand the mysteries of the mind, which has retarded your spiritual progress to a great extent! May you always keep your body, which is the divine temple of God, in perfectly sound condition and become a Vedantin of the highest order so that you may become the fittest instrument of God in relieving the pains of the vast human mass! May you understand the secret of spiritual Sadhana and attain the ultimate Truth—the One Ultimate Effort of human aspiration! May you all be established in Samadhi and enjoy the supreme Bliss!

SOME SPIRITUAL DON'TS

Don't forget God.
Don't covet others' wealth.
Don't blame or speak ill of others.
Don't depend upon servants.
Don't follow the dictates of the mind and senses.
Don't indulge in sensual thoughts.
Don't attend cinemas.
Don't read novels and newspapers.
Don't use bad words.
Don't smoke or drink.
Don't utter falsehood.
Don't talk too much.
Don't waste even a minute.
Don't overload your stomach.
Don't displease others.
Don't waste Veerya (semen).
Don't make mountains of little things.
Don't plan for the future.
Don't revenge.

SADHANA AND THE GUIDE

I

The importance of sticking to one mode of Sadhana, and to one Guru cannot be overemphasised. Now please listen to the story of Gautama, the Brahmin and Satyakama Jabala.

A real Brahmin is he who has thirst for God-realisation, who speaks the Truth, whose thought agrees with his speech, and his speech with his action. Generally you will find today in the world complete disharmony. Men think in one way, speak in another way and act in a third way. Thought, speech and action should agree with one another, and then only one can be said to have entered the path of spirituality.

Gautama was a true Brahmin of great austerities. He had a disciple named Satyakama Jabala, who was a thirsty aspirant for God-realisation. Satyakama approached his Guru for knowledge. What did Gautama do? He gave four hundred cows to Satyakama and told him, "Go to the forest. You can only return with these four hundred cows multiplied into a thousand." Satyakama strictly followed the instructions of his Guru.

What do we find these days? A student approaches a Teacher, does Sadhana for some time, immediately changes his Guru and changes the method of Sadhana also. He is impatient. He has not the patience to follow the instructions of his Guru. He does some Kirtan and a little Japa and immediately he wants Siddhi!

Let me sound a note of warning that he who thirsts for Siddhis is far from the goal of Self-realisation. The spiritual path is a razor-edged path, and Siddhis are bound to prove serious obstacles in the long run and bring about the downfall of the aspirant. The young aspirant may misuse these occult powers and that is the reason why great caution is prescribed in the beginning. He who is established in Yoga firmly can never misuse these powers.

Satyakama was extremely patient. He remained in the forest till the four hundred cows multiplied into a thousand. He strictly followed the instructions of his Guru and never wanted to return home. As a reward he had initiation from Mother Nature Herself. All the Devatas of the forest came to his help. He had Brahmic realisation in the forest itself. When he returned to his Guru, his Guru was astonished. He told him, "I behold Brahma Varchas in your face." See how extremely patient Satyakama was! Patience is a *sine qua non* for God-realisation. A real aspirant should shun Siddhis like poison. He must tell himself, "It is my duty to do the job allotted to me completely. It is my duty to follow the instructions of my Guru completely." He must wait patiently.

You will see in the same Upanishad the story of how Vajara (Indra) approached Prajapati for initiation. The teacher at a glance knew the stage of growth of the aspirant and found out at once that Vajara was not fit enough for initiation. Through deep insight, he found out the stage of growth of Vajara. The true teacher found out the many lurking Vasanas in the various corners of the mind of the student and prescribed to him various exercises for purification.

As aspirant attains purity very quickly by service to the

Guru. In these days nobody wants to serve the Guru. They simply listen to him for the time being, and never care for what the Teacher is saying or doing. They do not want to work in harmony with the Teacher. Reverence is seriously lacking nowadays.

II

The subtle points, the secrets and the true nature of Sadhana, Yogabhyasa and spiritual life one has to learn from a person who has already traversed this path and progressed considerably upon it. But if you should wish to learn these things, you must first become awakened to the urgent necessity of such knowledge; or else, you will never have the urge or the hankering for such spiritual knowledge. In your deep sleep of ignorance and sensuality you are entirely oblivious of the lofty purpose of life and the meaning and importance of spiritual Sadhana. Therefore you have first to be aroused to this forgotten fact. Once awakened, you are to be taught all the knowledge of the intricacies of the Path. The Guru is the one that awakens and teaches.

What part does the Guru play in the evolution of the individual? What should be one's attitude if this ancient and time-honoured institution of the spiritual preceptor is to be of real practical benefit to you? The Guru, as has been pointed out above, awakens you when you have temporarily fallen off from the awareness of the Ideal and the means and methods for its attainment.

Essentially, man is said to be the ever-awakened, ever-shining, luminous spirit. But he has forgotten his nature and the Guru as conceived of by the genius of India is the one that does the awakening work. Awakening and teaching also mean a reciprocal willingness to learn on the part of the one who is in need of the Guru. Also it suggests another idea that if one would but keep himself ever ready to receive any such awakening impulse will he find such awakening impulses abound in nature.

God has so constituted creation as to make it an ever-ready teacher. Nature Herself, the whole of creation, is a grand Guru, is a great teacher of mankind, ever imparting precious lessons, if man would but put himself in the proper receptive attitude. There is the energising, vitalising power, electricity. But the non-conducting wood fails to benefit by a charge of electricity if brought into contact with it in spite of the latter's power. The wood remains wood. But a piece of copper or iron at once acquires the power, the force and the properties of electricity. Not only that, but itself in its turn is able to communicate the electricity to other objects which are of a similar nature. I shall give you another example that practically demonstrates this truth. Millions of different surfaces receive the impressions from outside from the rays of the sun. They do not absorb the picture. It is only the sensitised plate of the camera, the film that is able to absorb those impressions that it receives and in itself reflects the picture. Thus, you have to learn from the non-conducting piece of wood and the good conductor iron and copper, the necessity of such receptivity; you have to learn from the sensitised surface of films and other blank surfaces, the necessity of such receptivity. Like this, everywhere you turn, you will be able to learn many things.

You see the example of the Avadhoota in the eleventh Skandha of the Bhagavata who learnt many spiritual lessons from various things in nature. You have to admit that you are in no way better or superior or more highly evolved than the Avadhoota and you should always be readily capable of putting yourself in this receptive mood. It is the lack of this that makes even the presence of such educators futile. Your duty is to learn, yet you play truant to this great school, called Life. Christ gave His lofty message and in the end he has said, "He that hath ears let him hear; he that hath eyes to see, let him see," because the message is there, the listeners are there; but supposing a man is in a dark room and he wants light; a kind neighbour gets him the light, immediately this man closes his eyes—what is the use of the illumination that has been brought into the room? Even so, you may have teachers; but the moment the teaching is given you close your doors against it and you are in the same condition as before.

Why spiritual lessons and great ethical teachings fail to make any impression upon man? Supposing a very fine garden of health-giving juicy fruits is opened up to a set of four or five people. Perhaps there is a man with spiritual bent of mind, Sattvic Samskaras or tendencies. He may partake of the fruit daily and have good meditation, do some Upasana and Japa and the fruit that he has thus eaten, he will convert into Sattvic force to illumine himself and help in illuminating others. Another is an athlete. He partakes of the same fruit and then he does exercise. He indulges in athletics, develops a fine physique and he runs, jumps and swims. Probably the third is a glutton. He eats the same fruit and gets Tamasic, sleeps, becomes useless to himself and others. Perhaps there is another who is a dyspeptic. He eats the fruit and is not able to digest it. It is the same fruit-garden; with one it is Sattvic, another Rajasic, another Tamasic; and yet to another it gives pain.

Just reflect deeply over another instance. Many people assemble at sacred shrines during holy festival-days. The atmosphere is solemn and elevating. The true devotee will be lost in worship and ecstasy. But the professional swindler in the crowd is looking out only for a gull. The pick-pocket has eyes only for a bulging coat pocket and the amorous youth scans but the faces of the fair sex. So it does not happen that all of you receive the same benefit out of the Satsanga and spirituality, pervading such sacred and auspicious occasions. People attend religious discourses; some imbibe the teachings, others the funny points, still another mimics the manners of the speaker, his gestures, etc., while a fourth section seek to condemn everything that is uttered at the discourse. You give milk to the snake, you have poison. You prepare food out of grain and give it to man; it turns into faecal matter.

You have got that colourful splashes of floral glory abounding in parks, gardens and house-balconies. It is earth, it is sunlight, it is water—common elements which abound in nature—out of a combination of these three you have got these. These floral plants receive water with which we clean our feet; and there, it is the fragrant, cooling, joy-giving flowers adorning the Lord in church altars and temple sanctorums. Different natures receive the same thing differently and react differently.

Thus, it is not all that are able to be benefited by a Guru. Living Sat-Gurus, the grand Guru Nature and the silent Gurus, they have a message but they silently give out this message. He that has ears can listen; he that has eyes can see. There are also, say, some who look but do not see; some who listen but do not hear. Thus it is that there are Gurus abounding in various shapes of the grand phenomenon of nature, silent but effective teachers of mankind.

Every copy of a spiritual book, each little booklet, leaflet or placard is a silent, yet readily elevating teacher. Yet man remains unaffected. Why? It is because of the tendency of the mind. It always moves downwards. It would rather revel in the darkness and multiply and die there, than come and live for a short time in the sunshine, like flowers. Man's mind is something like the housefly. Of course, sometimes, if some sweet-smelling object is kept, it may perch upon it for a moment. But the next moment it would prefer to alight upon a dung-heap. Its nature is there. So, perhaps a nice tune might attract your attention for a while, but the next moment if something is given to which it is accustomed always, this house-fly of the human mind at once goes and sits upon that. It is used to frivolities. It is used to mere flippancies. It is used to taunt and give torment to others. When a very delicious dish is put before it, it forgets the spiritual path and alights upon it.

Another little lesson is that in spite of man's boasted, strong body, in spite of culture, in spite of having moved in high society, the external refinement, he is at heart the coward. How you have taken resolves—lofty resolves of Ahimsa, Satya and Brahmacharya, how Kama, Krodha and Lobha are the terrible gates to hell—you have all taken a resolve, you have all known that societies like the Divine Life Society stand for Ahimsa, Satya and Brahmacharya. Man will think of himself as a hero. But Ahimsa is not in him. If a mosquito sits on your hand, you will heroically smash it with a smart slap. It is so simple. But should a scorpion approach you this courage does not come! There essentially man is a coward and it is not easy for a man to boast of his strength. Let him be humble; let him learn from little things. Let him thus keep himself open and try to benefit by the lessons that are ever abounding before his eyes and ears. In conclusion, I say let us be not like the house-fly; but like the bee that even though it has the option of sitting anywhere it likes, chooses to sit upon the flower and draw honey.

GUIDANCE FROM THE SCRIPTURES

Nowadays everyone knows that the sacred scriptures of all religions, the ancient sacred books are storehouses of the secrets of life. They hold hidden wisdom behind their apparent word. Thus, in the overwhelming generosity of heart, the modern man is sporting enough to tolerate them to exist. In stately neglect the sacred texts have continued to be. The most unfortunate among this family are the Puranas. The very word Purana has by kind convention come to take on the meaning of a long-winded rigmarole. Any boring recital is usually cut short with a "All right Bhai-Sab, I don't want to hear this Purana" which means 'Dry up brother. Shut your shop'. Such is the bathos.

Is this attitude in keeping with man's claim to rationality? Have you done justice by merely accepting that the Puranas are valuable allegories symbolising great spiritual truths? If man does not tap the wisdom and utilise it, does it not amount to neglecting the Puranas? They were and are not meant merely to be ornaments but are as greatly utilitarian as any modern scientific invention. They are allegories. They are documents in cipher. By neglecting them man neglects his own welfare. We all know how in the period of war no scrap of paper, however trifling it may seem, is let to pass without the strictest and closest scrutiny. Even the most seemingly inconsequential narrative or letter receives the most careful attention. They do not simply see the writing but look at it with care. Even more, they not only look at it but look for what may at first not be visible on the surface. More often than not it was sure to contain valuable information and guidance that would perhaps help to win the war. It might mean all the difference between victory and defeat. This ought to be our attitude towards the scriptures if we accept that they contain esoteric import, which in fact they do. Such is the perception we need.

Let us take a typical example. There is the story of the ten incarnations or Avataras of the Lord. A little thoughtful research will bring to light the startling fact that more than the recital of the Lord's Lilas, they actually summarise the process of the seeker's spiritual progress affording a clear view of the pattern of the Sadhaka's inner development.

The opening act of this wonderful revelation is the Matsyavatara rescuing and bringing up the Vedas concealed in the ocean waters. Vedas give man the knowledge of the true purpose of life and open his eyes to the lofty mission of human beings on earth. This knowledge is fully covered over by the waters of ignorance. It has to be brought up. This is the first step in the life of the Sadhaka. This awareness comes to the surface. This is man's first awakening, the glimmering of his spiritual dawn. The consciousness of life's purpose is brought up from the depth of ignorance. Matsyavatara is thus enacted.

What happens next. The forces of darkness will not allow the newly awakened one to arise and march on. There commences the inner struggle, the struggle between the forces of good and evil, each trying to get the upper hand over the other. A regular tug-of-war, a vigorous churning takes place inside. This is the fight between the Devas and the Asuras, the celestials and the demons depicted on the eve of the Kurma-Avatara. This process of churning (the Amrita-Mathan of the Puranas) is absolutely necessary before the Sadhaka can enter the next stage. One or two points are to be noted in this period. Doubtless the churning brings up the Amrita or the Nectar of realisation ultimately but during the process things like the Kalakuta, the disastrous venom concealed inside, rise up to the surface; they too have to be reckoned with. Spiritual purification is akin to the opening of the Pandora's Box of Grecian Mythology.

Now, so far we dealt with the poisons that rise to the surface. These at least are visible and can be fought with face to face. But certain aspects of man's lower nature instead of coming to the surface dive deeper into the unfathomable subconscious and defy all attempts of the Sadhaka to get at them. But, no, he must get at them. There is no other go. He must reach down and annihilate them. These aspects are depicted in the Puranas as the Asura Hiranyaksha. The drama of the great Varaha-Avatara tells you how you have to dig deep down into the very bowels of the dark earth and give battle to the demon in his own element. Hiranyaksha is to be slain. This symbolises the deep self-analysis the Sadhaka has to do probing into the innermost recesses of his subconscious self, relentlessly pursuing and tracking down the hidden Vasanas like lust, anger, greed, etc., and destroying them.

When this is done, when the Sadhaka takes this resolute step then starts the greater inner war. The Asuric part of man rises in revolt against this divine force and swears vengeance for the injury done to it. It becomes the Hiranyakashipu. Now a significant fact. Why does all the vengeful hatred of this Asura take the form of a terrible persecution of a little child? Why is the divine side depicted as the "little" Prahlada? Because this is the struggle in the beginning stages of the Sadhaka's spiritual life when he is but a mere infant upon the spiritual path. Here the deep advanced knowledge or Jnana element is absent in the picture. It is all faith, love and outpouring in incessant prayer. The Lord comes to the rescue. But here again is a very significant point. The Lord comes in a dual form. Not entirely divine, but yet four-armed divinity coupled with an earthly aspect too. And this earthly part is that of Lion. Why Lion? Now in spiritual parlance the human being is conceived of as Pasu and the Lord, the only Purusha as the Pati. The human-cum-divine being who comes to the rescue of the seeker at this stage is the Guru-God. Among the Pasus i.e. mankind, the Guru is verily lion among men. And he is divine too. *'Hey Guro Dayabdhe Nrikesari'* in such terms does a Marathi saint address his Guru. This Guru, the Nrisimhavatara hastens to the rescue of the Sadhaka. He emerges victorious.

Vice is vanquished. Virtues develop in him. This paves the way for the enactment of the drama of the fifth Avatara namely the Vamanavatara. The aspirant grows into the Paragon of power and virtue, into Emperor Bali, having domain over illimitable wealth. Pride creeps in. This sudden access of power and plenty brings undreamt of fame and renown. The Sadhaka's head is turned. The Lord perceives that it is high time a lesson is taught for his (the Sadhaka's) own good. But before pride, the forces of good seem powerless to operate with success. Arrogance is a formidable factor in the life of Sadhana. The counteracting agent has to come in disguise, in a tiny diminutive form. The mysterious force called humility alone is an equal match to spiritual pride. It operates subtly and gradually; coming as a humble suppliant in the beginning. One aspect of the Sadhaka's ego-sense tries to obstruct this good work. But it is a divine force and in the end drives pride down to the earth. The next battle is won. Sukrachrya's tactics, fail, Bali is vanquished.

Spiritual life now takes a decisive turn. Major obstacles and tests are surmounted, passed. The zero hour arrives that is the crux of spiritual life. It is the crucial moment of the Sadhaka being transformed into the saint. The final adieu is to be bidden to the minutest traces of *earthly nature*. He has to get free of the body-sense, nay even the human consciousness and make a complete break with Prakriti and all She stands for. This is the slaying of the Mother by Parasurama. An absolute surrender to the Purusha (obedience to Jamadagni) is made so that the full grace of the Divine flows into him. The tremendous incident throbbing with a wealth of human emotion, the drama of

Parasurama's implicit obedience to Jamadagni's command and the determined slaying of his own mother with the ruthless axe is this death of the Prakriti consciousness of the saint by the complete taking over of the Purushakara Vritti, Parasurama. Now symbolising as it does the crucial stage of the threshold of enlightenment the subsequent actions of the Lord as Parasurama elaborate the inner processes that are implied by this transformation. Parasurama exterminates the entire Kshatriya race root and branch demonstrating thereby the law that the very moment realisation dawns upon the evolving soul then the entire host of 'Agami' and 'Sanchita' Karmas are wiped out at one stroke. You know how the Kshatriya is the most vigorous, active and aggressive race. It is as a class embodiment of Rajas. The Karmas partake of such Rajas, being dynamic seed-sources of countless further actions one behind the other, ever moving up into the front line of their inevitable fruition. They form a restless ever-moving chain and constitute as it were the motive force that keeps the terrible wheel of birth and death constantly rotating. Their formidable legion gets annihilated in a trice upon the dawn of transcendental experience. But wait—two lone remnants—survive the family of Dasaratha and Janaka's too. And these are the Prarabdha Karma concretised as the body—Dasaratha (with its ten Indriyas) wedded to the play of the three Gunas (three wives) and the four Antahkaranas (four sons) and secondly the motiveless, absolutely unattached activities that the enlightened sage carries on without the idea of agency, Lokasangraha, the grand Raja-Karya of Janaka with the spirit '*Mithilayam pradeeptayam na me dahati kaschana*':

Hence onward it is all joy and victory. All the divine forces now swear allegiance to him. The entire Deva hosts, the Kapi-sena of Ramavatara is on his side. Only one thing remains that is to cross the final barrier of duality, of Savikalpa and reach that region wherein awaits *Rama*: the Prize of Ultimate realisation. The Drama of Ramavatara does bridge this *Krishna*: gulf and win the supreme prize. Rama Rajya follows and the next Avatara Krishna, reveals the perfect Jivanmukta stage, where it is all Lila. He is the chief vendor in the mart of bliss. It is all bliss. Divine play. Sahaja Samadhi—all activities in continuous unbroken consciousness of this essential Nature.

Buddha: Buddha Avatara. It is the solemn consummation

of a glorious grand life. It is the final sunset, withdrawing all the brilliant rays in the evening of his saintly life, getting self-absorbed, the Buddha under the Bodhi Vriksha. The sage now plunges into Nirvana under the tree of supreme transcendental wisdom and attains oneness with the Infinite, returning to his primal source. With paeans of joy and the hail and hosanna of victory the curtain gracefully swings down to silvery notes of divine joy bells.

Well, we are now confronted with the Kalki Avatara. What is this anti-climax? No. It is the logical fruition of the Life Triumphant. Just as the Sun that has burst forth at last from the enshrouding mass of dense dark clouds forthwith radiates its throbbing, vital brilliance in streams of potent dazzling light, even so a life perfected becomes a source-point of positive Power for Good. It becomes a divine force crusading forth into the universe breaking a heroic lance for Dharma and sweeping down as an avenging terror upon Adharma. Such is the symbol of the Kalki Avatara-to-be sounding the death knell to all unrighteousness and establishing the Kingdom of God on earth.

Thus from the dramatic incident of the Matsyavatara to the grand climax Kalki, the Dasa-Avatara depicts with wonderful vividness and marvellous insight the process of the human Monad struggling and successfully attaining to the Universal Consciousness. And also the ultimate nature of the impact of such realisation upon the destiny and history of Humankind.

This is but one example I have taken. The scriptures teem with a wealth of such marvellous, esoteric and philosophical allegory. The typical example I took, I have but treated in mere general outline. There are details there in plenty and deeply interesting too. Approached with the right perspective every scripture worth the name will reveal veritable mines of wisdom. Let not Puranas mean so many antiquated scrap-books merely tolerated to exist. They hold within their neglected covers a valuable spiritual heritage for our edification. They are precious documents worth their weight in gold. With them it is indeed a case of Seek and you shall find. May the great sacred texts of all religions continue to guide, inspire and illumine Mankind on the march towards realisation and perfection.

SADHANA PANCHAKAM OF SRI SANKARACHARYA

1. Study the Vedas daily. Do properly the actions that are enjoined therein. Offer the fruits of actions as Isvararpana and do worship of Isvara through Karmanushthana. Remove the desire for Sakama actions. Be away from sinful actions. Think of the Doshas of sensual pleasures of this Samsara. Be firm in the desire for Self-realisation. Leave the house of Samsara forthwith.

2. Have the company of the wise. Develop firm devotion towards the Lord. Cultivate firmly virtues like Santi, etc. Remove Sakama actions at once. Go to the best teacher. Serve his lotus-feet daily. Try to get the knowledge of the one-syllable Brahman. Hear the great sentences, Mahavakyas of the Upanishads, Vedanta.

3. Enquire into the significance of the Mahavakyas or great sentences. Take refuge in Vedanta. Save yourself from unnecessary vain discussions. Investigate with the help of arguments that are in agreement with the Srutis. Enquire day and night that "I am Brahman." Remove egoism. Remove the idea of self (Aham Buddhi) in the body. Do not argue unnecessarily with spiritual teachers.

4. Treat the disease hunger. Eat food (Bhiksha) as medicine. Never ask for palatable food. Be contented with what you get by Prarabdha. Endure heat and cold. Give up idle talk. Live to be an Udaseena. Give up mercy and harshness for the people of the world.

5. Sit comfortably in solitude. Fix the mind on the Supreme Self. Realise the All-full Brahman. The world will vanish when the Self is realised.

6. Dissolve the Sanchita Karmas in the Self by the force of Jnana. Do not have any connection with the current actions. Enjoy in this life the Prarabdha. When the enjoyment of Prarabdha is over, get established in Brahman.

7. The burning fire of Samsara and the terrible Tapa are freed through the grace of Brahman.

CHAPTER TWENTY
INSPIRING SVADHYAYA FOR ASPIRANTS

PHYSICAL BODY AND LIFE DIVINE

This body is a bubble. It is like lightning. This world is a play for two days. It lasts today. It continues tomorrow. No more. No more. Awake. Awake. Seek the Eternal. Rest in thy Satchidananda Atman.

Divine life is perfect life led according to the laws of truth. Divine life is life immortal in which ideal state of perfection and expansion of self in infinity and eternity is attained. It is a means to attain the true ideal of all beings, namely God-realisation. Divine life aims at harmony, peace, concord.

REPETITION OF DIVINE NAME

Silent repetition of the Lord's Name is a tremendous tonic and potent specific for all diseases. It should never be stopped even for a single day under any circumstances. It is like food. It is spiritual food for the hungry soul.

MAN AND HIS STEPPING STONES

Man is more than what he thinks to be. He is eternal and Immortal. He is perfect knowledge and joy without decay. He is in want of nothing, he is Apta Kama. He is Supreme Bliss. This is the highest truth.

Every failure is a stepping-stone to success. Every difficulty or disappointment is a trial of your faith. Every disease is a Karmic purgation. Every unpleasant incident is a test of your trust in God. Every temptation is a test of your spiritual strength.

PEACE, SALT OF LIFE AND SANKIRTAN

The salt of life is selfless service. The bread of life is universal love. The water of life is purity. The sweetness of life is devotion. The fragrance of life is generosity. The pivot of life is meditation. The goal of life is Self-realisation.

There is no softening agent more efficacious than Sankirtan. Sankirtan is melting the sin-hardened stony hearts of sceptical scoffers, non-believers and all sorts of sinners.

Peace is a divine attribute. It is a quality of the soul. It cannot remain with greedy persons. It fills the pure heart. It deserts the lustful. It runs away from the selfish. Look within the chambers of your heart. When you are established in the Highest Self within, you will not be shaken even by heavy sorrow, loss or failure. Marvellous is this Peace.

THE SAGE, HAPPINESS AND POWER

Just as the Himalaya stands unmoved by storms, so also the Sage stands unmoved by praise and censure, respect and disrespect, gain and loss, victory and defeat.

Happy is the man who is under the care and protection of a Guru. Happy is the man who serves the Guru and meditates by his side. He who serves the Guru knows the way. The way cannot be found without the Grace of a Guru.

The path of communion by love, devotion and self-surrender to God is the easiest of all paths and intense earnestness is the only power that takes you to the Goal of life.

The Power of powers who gives power to the mind, the Light of lights who sheds light on the mind, the Seer of seers who witnesses the motives and movements of the mind, the Support of supports on which the mind rests in sleep is God.

LIFE, THE MELTING HEART AND DIVINE GRACE

Cultivate a melting heart, the giving hand, kindly speech, life of service, equal vision and impartial attitude. Keep your mind calm and cool at all times and in all conditions of trials.

God is the silent and unseen listener of surgings of your mind. God is your unseen Guest at every meal. God is the head of your house. God sees and hears everything that you do. Have utter Trust in God and do the right.

Life is a valuable asset; utilise it for attaining God-realisation. Life without worthy ideals is like a rudderless boat. Life without aspiration is like vegetable existence. Live for God and attain God-realisation.

Divine life teaches control of mind by concentrating all attention on the inner Self. Right conduct, self-conquest, compassion, benevolence, pursuit of truth, service of humanity, meditation, self-inquiry—this is good living, this is divine life.

HUMANITY, LOVE AND GOODNESS

There is only one caste—the caste of humanity. There is only one religion—the religion of love or religion of Vedanta. There is only one Dharma—the Dharma of truthfulness. There is only one Law—the law of cause and effect. There is only one language—the language of heart or the language of silence.

To be childlike is good; to be childish is not good. To be devotional is good; to be emotional is not good. To have strong will is good; to be self-willed is not good. To stick to one's ideal is good; to be obstinate is not good. To be courageous is good; to expose another's faults is not good.

Love is divine. Love is nectar. Love is the greatest power on this earth. Love alone can transform the world. Love alone can bring peace on this earth. Love alone can conquer the hearts of others.

PURITY, ASPIRATION, REALISATION

As a small bulb cannot withstand excessive electric voltage, so the nerves and the heart are not ready to receive the cosmic current when the mind is not thoroughly purified. Wait patiently. Carry on purifying process vigorously.

There is no boat safer than Satsanga to take us to the other shore of Samsara, the shore of absolute fearlessness and immortality.

Realisation is not the monopoly of cave-dwellers and mountaineering nomads. External conditions may at times be helpful; but the essential thing is inner attitude—and even external circumstances are conditioned by this attitude. You create your own world of worries and troubles. No one forces it on you.

The heart lit up with the flame of spiritual aspiration and perfumed with the scent of devotion is the rarest acquisition of man. Therefore, endeavour hard to purify the lower self and attain supreme success.

SADHANA AND SAKTI

God is the fountain-source of life, health, strength and power. Meditation on God is the panacea for all ills. To develop your muscular power is not your goal. To be disease free, to be free to carry on your Sadhana is your aim.

Eternal happiness is the only ideal that is worthy of human endeavour. He who is purified through wisdom, who is serene, self-controlled without egoism and mineness is freed from all sins.

Sakti is the path to Siva. The Divine Mother is the promise and the possibility of the attainment by the human being of the highest end of existence, the Supreme Purushartha—Dharma, Artha, Kama and Moksha. Look to Her for grace. Your prosperity here and beatitude hereafter are assured.

ANGER, MIND AND SELF-CONQUEST

Anger is un-Atmic. Anger wastes energy and clouds the mind. Conquest of anger makes one a spiritual hero, commanding success in life, getting happiness from every moment of existence on earth.

Victory over the mind is certainly victory over death. The inner war with the mind is more terrible than the outer war with machine-guns. Conquest of mind is more difficult than the conquest of the world by force of arms.

To attain ethical purity, concentration and meditation, you must understand the mind, destroy its evil properties, battle with it and gain victory.

Love, truth and purity form the foundation of the edifice of divine life. The Temple of divine life has four pillars—meditation, purity, love and righteousness. Lead the divine life and become divine.

COMPASSION, SATSANGA AND DISCRIMINATION

Discrimination and dispassion are the two wings of the Soul which will take you to the eternal abode of Bliss. He who dies to the lower self, rises to Immortality.

Divine Light radiates through the pure heart. God's Grace floods the prayerful heart. Compassionate heart is the abode of God.

Just as a single match-stick burns huge bales of cotton in a few seconds, so also the company of saints burns all ignorance within a short time. That is the reason why Sankara and others have spoken so highly of Satsanga in all their books.

Life in this physical plane is a mere preparation for the Eternal Life of everlasting bliss which is to come when one gets the knowledge of the Self. The great problem of human life is the freedom of the soul from the coil of mortality.

Like one iron shaping another iron, the pure mind should correct and mould the impure mind.

If the mind which flits from one object to another is slain with the sword of discrimination, then the self-shining Brahman will be realised.

TRUTH, VEDANTA AND HUMAN IMAGINATION

Truth alone triumphs, never untruth. Falsehood and lie, phantom or unreality cannot succeed in its efforts. The real alone is an enduring being. That real is experienced through Meditation coupled with Knowledge.

Vedanta wants everybody to destroy Moha or selfish love and passion for the body, and to develop pure, disinterested cosmic love or the magnanimous divine Prema. It never preaches pessimism, but it preaches the pinnacle of optimism.

Feel the majesty of your Self. Then nature will obey you, and you will command all the elements. All the eight Siddhis and the nine Riddhis will roll under your feet. They will stand with folded hands to carry out your behests. This is the sublime teaching of Vedanta.

Just as a dog that sucks a dry bone in the street imagines foolishly that blood is oozing out of the dry bone, whereas blood is really oozing from its own palate, so also worldly-minded people imagine that the happiness they enjoy in everyday life comes from objects only. You can find Eternal, Infinite, supreme peace and bliss only in your Atman, which shines in all its splendour and glory in the chambers of your heart.

INNER HAPPINESS AND OMNIPRESENCE OF THE LORD

Waves originate in water, depend on water and dissolve in water. The only support for the whole world is the Lord. Realising thus and feeling the Omnipresence of the Lord, the wise worship Him with devotion and affection in all places. The Supreme is the same in all countries and at all times.

The necklace contains many beads of various forms but there is one single thread that connects them. The thread is their very support and being. Even so in the diverse Jivas and worlds that exist, there is one common Life-principle, the Supreme Brahman as it is called, that unifies the entirety of Existence.

Happiness is only within. Fix your gaze on the divine flame within, which is the essence of the Universal Light, which only shines and spreads peace. Find more time for meditation, for sitting alone and seeking and gazing at the flame within.

He who will learn to swim must attempt swimming for some days. None can venture to swim in the sea after a single day's practice. So if you want to swim in the sea of Brahman, you must make many ineffectual attempts at first before you can successfully swim therein at last.

Within you is the hidden God. Within you is the Immortal soul. Within you is the inexhaustible spiritual treasure. Within you is the ocean of bliss. Look within for the happiness, which you have sought in vain in the perishable sensual objects. Rest peacefully in your Atman.

Flowers bloom and then fade. There is no need to praise the former and condemn the latter. We must receive whatever comes without excitement, pain or revolt.

If a woman is pure, she can save and purify man. Woman can purify the race. Woman can make the home a sacred temple.

Happiness is not to be found in external objects alone, in wealth and children, in power and position, in going from shop to shop, or by receiving present after present, but real happiness is to be found in one's own immortal blissful Atman alone by practising purity, dispassion and meditation.

GOD AND HIS NAME

God is. God exists. Give up idle controversies, theological dissension. Be pure in heart. Serve humanity. Love God. Treat all creatures with love.

This physical body in the phenomenal world is only a passing shadow. Be intensely conscious of the ever-present, supreme, eternal Soul that is immanent in all beings and pervades everywhere.

The regular practice of constant Japa with Bhava and concentration will ultimately remove all fickleness of mind and make it steady and calm.

The mind may run about a little in the beginning due to

previous habit, but the repetition of the Divine Name is the magic wand to subdue the turbulent and irregular mind.

THE BODY AND THE BLESSING OF HUMAN BIRTH

This body is a source of infinite miseries. It is full of impurities. It brings disrespect, censure, pain, etc. It is like froth or bubble or mirage. It remains like a useless log of wood on the ground when the Pranas depart from the body.

This body is certainly not meant for the satisfaction of petty ends. It is for rigorous penance here and infinite happiness hereafter. It is an instrument for achieving the goal of human life i.e. the attainment of Brahma Jnana. This serves the purpose of a boat to cross this ocean of Samsara to the other side.

There is no hope of immortality by means of riches. Such indeed is the emphatic and irrefutable declaration of the Upanishads "Neither by rituals, nor by progeny nor by riches but by renunciation alone can one attain immortality."

For all beings a human birth is very difficult to attain, more so with a male body. It is said, that there are three things which are rare indeed and are due to the grace of God, viz., a human birth, the longing for liberation and the protecting care of a perfected sage.

THE MAIN SUPPORTS IN SADHANA

There is nothing which is irrevocable. With courage, determination and application, there is no obstacle or impediment that cannot be surmounted. It is the faculty of reason, the spirit of restraint and renunciation that differentiates man from animal.

The lotus of Self-realisation does not bloom so long as the sunlight of the Absolute Vision remains hidden by the cloud of ego.

The light of Atman, the Light of the Spirit, the Wisdom of the Soul, is hidden from man, but is revealed to those who are humble, faithful, devoted, dispassionate, bold and are endowed with the four means of salvation.

The essentials of moral life are straightforwardness, honesty, mercy, humility, respect for a life or tender regard for every creature that breathes, absolute unselfishness, truthfulness, celibacy, non-covetousness, absence of vanity, hypocrisy and cosmic love.

THE DEMANDS OF YOGA AND THE WORLDLY-MINDED

Yoga advocates complete detachment from secular interests for the sake of practising uninterrupted meditation. It recommends meditation on the inner light of the heart or anything that is pleasing to you.

Just as a nail cannot enter into a stone, however hard you may try to drive it in with a hammer so also religious ideals, talks of God, cannot enter the minds of the worldly minded, however lucidly you may explain them with stories, analogies, similes and parables.

DIFFICULTIES IN LIFE AND THE MESSAGES OF THE SAINT

The ploughman should plough on without weeping over the famine and all of a sudden when rain comes he will have a rich harvest; so also one must be up and doing. All difficulties and unfavourable circumstances will pass away like a rent autumnal cloud. You will have a rich spiritual harvest of Eternal peace and Perennial Joy.

The Ultimate Reality can best be described only in terms of contradictions: "Smaller than the smallest, greater than the greatest, is the Atman or the Supreme Self. Seated Himself He travels far; static He goes in all directions."

The messages of the Saints are essentially the same. They have always been a call to man to discover the wisdom of the Self or Atman.

One must have intense childlike faith and a keen longing that a child feels to see its mother. You will attain God-realisation if you are endowed with such a burning yearning or aspiration.

By love, selfless service, by sacrifice and renunciation and meditation the soul is roused, exalted, elevated and transformed into Divinity.

GOD-CONSCIOUSNESS AND SAT-CHIT-ANANDA

God-consciousness or communion with the Lord is the acme of the ethico-religious discipline of Yoga. This is attended by a remarkable sense of freedom and moral elevation on account of the crumbling down of the false, illusory, little 'I'.

Just as people attribute blue colour to the sky, so also they attribute on account of indiscrimination the qualities and activities of the body and the organs to the pure, Satchidananda-Atman.

The Atman alone illumines the intellect, senses, etc., just as a light illumines the pot and other objects; but the Atman is not illumined by these which are insentient (intellect, mind, senses, etc.)

One should sing of Hari with the submissive spirit of a blade of grass and the endurance of a tree. One should not hope for honour but should give it to others.

What outshines all, reducing the whole world into mere nothingness before it, is the all-conscious, all-blissful and the all-pure Name of Hari and Hari alone.

Cultivate peace of mind in the garden of your heart by removing weeds, viz., hatred, greed, selfishness, jealousy. Then only can you manifest it externally.

Just as the child falls many a time when he tries to walk without the help of the wall, just as the new cyclist falls from the cycle a number of times before he learns to sit steadily on the seat, so also the new aspirant will fall a number of times in his resolves. He has to make repeated attempts but ultimately he will come out victoriously.

PATIENCE, CONTENTMENT AND DIVINE LIGHT

Human birth, longing for liberation and contact of a great Mahatma—all are obtained by the grace of God. He verily commits suicide who, having obtained all these means, does not exert for liberation.

Contentment is real wealth as it gives peace of mind. It is a sentinel on the domain of Moksha. If you keep company with him, he will introduce you to his friends, the other sentinels, viz., Satsanga, Santosha, Vichara and Santi.

Just as fruit is hidden in the seed, butter in milk, virility in boyhood, so also various Saktis remain latent in man. If you purify your mind and practise concentration and meditation, all these powers will shine forth.

Truth alone triumphs but not falsehood. Dharma is rooted in Truth. Sages reach the Immortal abode where the supreme seat of Truth is situated.

The Divine Light descends through Sadhana into the pure mind. The pure, higher mind grasps easily and readily the light that descends.

The Divine Light filters into the denser regions of the emotions, desires and vital dynamism. Finally it gets into the entire body.

LOVE AND SECRET OF GOD-REALISATION

Build the shrine of devotion in your heart. Enter the silence. Enjoy the life transcendent.

In purity is the secret of God-realisation, in self-restraint is the strength of character, and in dispassion is the spiritual progress. Purity is freedom from desire. Meditation and contentment are the secrets of good health and long life.

Just as you can cultivate good flowers and fruits in a garden by ploughing, manuring the land, removing the weeds and thorns and watering the plants and trees, so also you can cultivate the power of devotion in the garden of your mind by removing the impurities of the mind such as lust, anger, greed, pride, etc., and watering it with Divine thoughts.

Love conquers, with its soothing touch, more things. Love is the balm which heals all wounds of the heart. Love changes the feeling. The whole being is shaped by love. Love cannot be overcome by any other force. Love is unifying. It works in the realm of harmony, equality, oneness, peace and joy. Love can win ultimate victory over all things.

When the lamp is wrapped with many layers of cloth, there will be no bright light. When the cloth is removed one by one the light grows brighter and brighter. Even so, when the self-resplendent Atman which is covered by the five sheaths, is stripped of by meditating on the pure Self and through the practice of "Neti-neti" doctrine the self-luminous Atman reveals Itself to the meditator.

Just as a king acts the part of a beggar, out of his own free-will, on the stage in a drama, so also the Sat-Chit-Ananda Brahman acts the part of a Jiva in this drama of the world out of His own free-will for sport.

Have tremendous self-confidence and devotion to the

Lord and Guru. You can uproot the Himalayas and swallow the ocean.

There is infinite Sakti in Lord's Names. Lord's Name is the solution for all the troubles that have beset mankind of this Atomic Bomb Age. Atomic Bomb can annihilate only a City. But Lord's Name can annihilate the whole world. Such is the glory of Lord's Name.

There is a mysterious Buti or celestial herb, the herb that immortalises and transforms man into Divinity; a beverage made out of this Buti is most delicious and invigorating. It is the "Hari Nam Buti." It is the Name of the Lord.

Name is the most powerful food. Name is the food of all foods. Name is the most well-balanced diet. The food Name is available at all times; this is the most potent, cheapest and best, this Name immortalised Prahlada and Dhruva.

If you move one foot to meet the Lord, He will run a mile to receive you! He is very kind and compassionate. There is at your back His hand to protect you at all times. Place thy trust in Him for support, feel His hidden hand working through all sources. Surrender your ego at His Feet; and be at ease for ever!

WISDOM AND PERFECTION

Just as the moon appears to be running when the clouds move, so also the Atman seems to be active to the non-discriminating, while in truth, the organs alone are working.

Wisdom is the sharpest weapon. It surely saves you from evil. It is the strongest, invulnerable citadel. It cannot be destroyed by atom bombs. One can live within this citadel safely.

Perfection is the attainment of Immortal Life and Pure consciousness. This is not the acquisition of something new, it is the discovery of the forgotten treasure already within.

Intellect gives the Knowledge of the external objects. Intellect is struggle. Intellect guesses, believes. Intellect is a product of Prakriti.

The Lord and His Sakti are inseparably blended like flower and fragrance, sun and ray, life and body. Sakti is the Mother aspect of the Lord. She is the energy aspect of Isvara. Sakti is Sat-Chit-Ananda Rupini, Chinmaya Rupini, Anandamaya Rupini. Obtain the grace of the Mother.

This body is a temple of God; the Lord is the Proprietor of this temple. He is the Indweller. It is an instrument for God-realisation, therefore it should be kept healthy and strong. Ever think of Him and Him alone for guidance and help.

The Infinite Brahman is the centre in your heart. Tear this veil of ignorance. Powder this ego. Melt this mind. Become one with Brahman.

Just as a musk-deer roams fast to enjoy the fragrance of the musk, so also men are befooled by the notion that the Eternal being is away from them.

Just as one light does not require the help of another light to make itself known, since it illuminates itself, so also the Atman, whose very nature is knowledge Itself, does not depend for a knowledge of itself on any other knowledge.

There is no life in education if it is destitute of the religious consciousness, for religion is the very meaning of life's purposes, the one aim of the struggle for existence. If religion is rejected, there is nothing left in the mortal except a heap of bones and a mass of flesh.

He who is wise, modest and forgiving, who believes in God, and is humble, and who remembers the Lord at all times, goes to the region of everlasting peace.

THE LORD, HIS FORM AND HIS PRESENCE

The Lord is everywhere. Feel His Presence everywhere. His eyes behold everything; His hands protect all. Trust in Him. Take refuge in His sweet Name. You need not despair. You need not be afraid of anything.

The greatest men are those who are lost in Self-consciousness. Such men are too near to God to be able to do any action. Therefore they are unknown to the world.

A saint is really a King of kings. He is a great hero. He has annihilated all desires, aversion and anger. He is ever peaceful. He radiates joy and peace. He has inner and outer control. He moves about in the world to enlighten the ignorant worldlings. He beholds God everywhere.

A fire is concealed by ashes, sword by the scabbard, Sun by the clouds, foetus by amnion, rubies by the earth, mattresses by the bed-sheet, so also Brahman is concealed by flesh and bones.

God is formless and yet He is the form of all forms. Pain

and pleasure cannot touch the Soul or Atman, because Atman is spirit. In essence you are the Atman. Realise this and be free. *Tat Tvam Asi.* Thou Art That.

Just as the scent of Jasmine or sandalwood pervades a room, so also the perfume of a virtuous man pervades everywhere.

As by watering of a tree at the root all its trunk, branches and twigs get enlivened, and as the senses are gratified by the feeding of the Prana with food, so also the worship of Lord Hari gratifies all the gods.

People go here and there in search of flowers in thick forests, summit of hills, lakes and gardens for offering to the Lord, and yet fail to attain the bliss Supreme. They can easily get eternal bliss if they can offer to the Lord the single, stainless flower of their heart.

He who is endowed with perfect serenity will always and everywhere be happy. Even the wealth of the whole world cannot make a man so happy as the possession of serenity.

Just as the river Ganga flows to the East, slopes to the East, inclines to the East, so also, the Yogi who practises meditation flows to Samadhi, slopes to Samadhi and inclines to Samadhi.

He who is fearless, desireless, 'I'less, mineless, humble, faithful, truthful, will soon attain knowledge of the imperishable. Perfect knowledge, perfect peace, eternal bliss are the fruit of Self-realisation.

ANALOGIES AND SOME FORMS OF BLESSING

Just as a bird that is chased by a hawk goes inside a house and comes out immediately for want of a suitable resting place, so also the mind comes outside to wander about in the sensual objects as it finds it difficult to rest in the very, very subtle Atman.

Contentment is the bliss of life. The cold ambrosial waters of Contentment will quickly extinguish the fire of desires. Contentment is the chief sentinel who keeps watch over the domain of Peace or the Kingdom of God.

Just as iron is transmuted into gold by the touch of the Philosopher's stone, so also the brute man will be radically changed into a veritable saint by and through constant contact with a developed Yogi.

This world came out of Love, it exists in Love and it will ultimately dissolve in Love. A heart without love is a desert without water. God is an ocean of Love.

A virtuous life is the greatest blessing; service of Guru is the greatest purifier; contentment is the greatest wealth; Nirvikalpa Samadhi is the greatest bliss.

Sickness is a blessing. It is a messenger from God. It is an act of mercy calculated to turn your mind inward, to direct your mind towards Him.

The chanting of the Lord's Name brightens the mirror of mind, burns the forest of desires and bathes the whole being in a flood of joy.

LIFE ON EARTH AND THE LIBERATED SAGE

A liberated sage is an ocean of mercy. He is a great spiritual hero. He has no identification with the body and senses. He has no idea, "I am the doer."

Life of man on earth is nothing but a life of temptation and tribulations. Those who have real and intense Vairagya and strong Viveka can hardly be tempted by worldly objects, by Mara and Satan.

He who has slain the stork of desire with the sword of supreme or mature dispassion crosses the Ocean of Samsara without obstacles.

There is no penance higher than truth-speaking. There is no virtue higher than mercy. There is no bliss higher than the bliss of the soul. There is no wealth greater than spiritual wealth.

For a man of contentment, sovereignty of the whole world is no better than a bit of rotten straw. He is indeed miserable and poor, who is discontented.

The bliss of Self-realisation cannot be described in words. It is like the experiencing of joy which a dumb man has when he tastes a delicious sweet-meat or sugarcandy.

SELF-CONTROL AND BRAHMA JNANA

A life of self-control is the first requisite for the attainment of God-realisation. Therefore, practise self-control daily by cultivating forbearance, patience, forgiveness, endurance, angerlessness, etc.

To be in the company of a Satguru is the greatest blessing;

to do Japa on the banks of the Ganga is the greatest spiritual wealth; to possess good health is the greatest boon; to taste the bliss of Samadhi is the supreme blessing.

Brahma Jnana dawns by itself on one who has serene mind. Serenity is a very important virtue which an aspirant should possess. It is the harbinger of peace and emancipation.

The enemy of Atman is the fluctuating mind only. The mind through its power of fluctuation generates countless Vasanas and Sankalpas. Destroy this fluctuating power of the mind through constant Brahmavichara.

Just as the mirror is dimmed by dirt, so Brahman is veiled by Avidya. Therefore human beings are deluded by this Avidya. When one gets knowledge of the Self, this Avidya vanishes.

VIRTUES AND BHAKTI

True love is as boundless as the ocean, as wide as the sky, as firm as the Himalayas. Pure love ennobles the personality, purifies the heart and sanctifies the existence.

Where there are kindness, humility and purity, there spirituality springs up, saintliness shines, divinity descends and perfection manifests itself.

A devotee of Hari is always meek and humble. The Name of God is always on his lips. He sheds profuse tears when he is alone. He is very pious. He is friendly towards all. He has equal vision. He does good always. He never hurts the feeling of others. He sees Hari in all beings.

Bhakti can be acquired and cultivated. Constant Satsanga with devotees and Bhagavatas, repetition of His Name, constant remembrance of Lord, prayer, study of religious books, Hari Kirtan, service of Bhaktas, etc., can infuse Bhakti in the heart of a devotee.

The worshipping of the Name of Rama never goes in vain, just as the practice of swimming in one's boyhood is of great help at some future time. If anyone remembers Rama in his pleasant mood, or unpleasant mood, it is sure to give its good effect, just as the seeds in the fields thrown either rightly or wrongly give good results.

REWARDS OF JAPA AND UPANISHADIC STUDY

Every man is filled with countless powers. Just as fire has the natural property of burning things, so also the Name of God has the power of burning sins and desires.

Practice of Japa removes the impurities of the mind, destroys sins and brings the devotee face to face with God. Japa must become habitual. Japa is the easiest and surest way for God-realisation. Constant study of Upanishads will elevate your mind and help you to reach the first stage of Jnana. Meditation on OM with meaning and feeling will enable you to attain Self-realisation.

VAIRAGYA, ABHYASA AND MEDITATION

Just as pure gold which has been treated in the crucible with borax, etc. and rendered pure, shines brilliantly so also the Yogi, whose mind is rendered pure by the agents of Vairagya and Abhyasa, becomes a lustrous person.

A seed which has remained in fire for a second will not sprout into leaves even though sown in a fertile soil. Even so a mind that does meditation for sometime but runs towards sensual objects on account of unsteadiness will not bring in the full fruits of Yoga.

The Self is hidden in all beings like butter in milk. It is seen by subtle seers who are endowed with pure, sharp and subtle intellect and who practise constant deep meditation regularly.

The noble aspirant, who has a serene mind, who thinks and acts rightly, who is endowed with right conduct, who has subdued all his senses, who is composed and tranquil, can obtain Brahman by constant and protracted meditations.

He who practises the religion of renunciation, who eats sparingly and who has his senses under his complete control, can attain Brahman which is immutable, eternal and self-luminous, and which is above nature.

Viveka and Vairagya are the master-weapons to kill this dire enemy of peace. Cravings take to their heels whenever they hear of Viveka and Vairagya. Just as darkness cannot exist in the presence of the sun, so also desires cannot show their faces before Viveka and Vairagya.

As a mass of salt has neither inside nor outside, but is entirely a mass of taste, thus indeed has that Self neither inside nor outside but is altogether a mass of knowledge. The sage cognises one illimitable homogeneous mass of consciousness only.

There is no difficulty for a man of strong determination and iron-will even on the razor path. Strength comes from within at every step. Extreme asceticism and self-torture are not necessary for the attainment of the knowledge of the Self.

Life is dearer than the senses. If the king orders to take away the life of a criminal, the criminal rather prefers to have one of his limbs removed than give up his life. Atman is dearer than life because it is an embodiment of bliss.

Repetition of Mantra raises vibrations. Vibrations give rise to definite forms. Repetition of Om Namah Sivaya gives rise to the form of Lord Siva in the mind, repetition of Om Namo Narayanaya gives rise to the form of Lord Hari.

The glory of the Name of God cannot be established through reasoning and intellect. It can certainly be experienced or realised, only through devotion, faith and constant repetition.

IGNORANCE AND THE CORRODING HUMAN PASSION

Loss of judgment springs from ignorance and sinfulness of habits. When the victim whom this fault attacks begins to remain in the company of a wise man, it immediately vanishes.

Intense passion, hatred, long-standing bitter jealousy, corroding anxiety, fits of hot temper actually destroy the cells of the body and induce diseases of the heart, liver, kidneys, spleen and stomach.

Envy of others takes its origin from anger and covetousness. It disappears through mercy and knowledge of the Self and disregard for all worldly objects. It also originates from seeing the weakness of other people. But in intelligent men it quickly vanishes through true knowledge.

In the garden of your heart, plant the lily of love, the rose of purity, the Champaka of courage, the Mandara of humility and lady-of-the-night of compassion.

Just as the sweater keeps the body warm when there is cold and gives you happiness, so also the knowledge of Atman or the Self protects you from all external draughts of worries, anxieties, sufferings, etc. and blesses you with eternal Peace, infinite Joy and immortal Bliss.

REPRESENTATIVES OF THE DIVINE BEAUTY

The beautiful flower reminds us of the Unseen, the Beauty of the beauties. It is a symbol of God. Be fragrant like the flower and radiate joy and peace.

All the phenomena of nature are governed by one important Law, the law of causation, the law of Karma. It is that law that keeps up the inner harmony and logical order of the universe. No phenomena can escape from the operation of this mighty law.

All hopes of happiness in this world terminate in pain, despair and sorrow. Pleasures are mixed with pain, beauty with ugliness; kindness is mixed with anger and harsh words. There is no real prop in this world to lean upon. Money and power fill the mind with vanity.

PATHWAY TO PURITY

Vices are the destroyers of ethical life. They are the poisonous weeds that rapidly grow and choke up the fragrant flower of virtue that blossoms in the fair garden of ethical life. Unless vices are eradicated through resolute effort and self-purification the moral well-being of anyone is not safe. It is in constant danger.

The insentient engine of a railway train cannot move without the intelligent driver. Even so, this insentient body-engine cannot move without the intelligent driver God or Isvara. From the existence of the body, one can infer the existence of the hidden driver of the body-engine.

Life is a journey from impurity to purity, from hatred to cosmic love, from death to immortality, from imperfection to perfection, from slavery to freedom, from diversity to unity, from ignorance to eternal wisdom, from pain to eternal bliss, from weakness to strength.

Meditation is a mysterious ladder which reaches from earth to heaven (Vaikuntha or Kailasa or Brahman) from error to truth, from darkness to light, from pain to Bliss, from restlessness to abiding Peace, from ignorance to Knowledge, from mortality to Immortality.

Even Indra, the Lord of the Devas who is rolling in abundant wealth, cannot enjoy that bliss which comes to a sage who has a self-centred mind free from desires, who is resting in his own Svarupa and who has equal vision for all.

Just as one renders the turbid water pure by the addition of clearing-nut (*strychnos potatorum*) so also one will have to make the turbid mind filled with Vasanas and false Sankalpas pure by Brahmachintana (thinking and reflecting on the Absolute). Then only there will be true illumination.

THE SAGE AND EQUAL VISION

A saint or a sage is a spiritual washerman. He applies the soap of illumination, beats his clothes on the rock of serenity and washes them in the river of wisdom.

Equal vision is the touchstone of knowledge. Unselfishness is the touchstone of virtue. Celibacy is the touchstone of ethics. Oneness is the touchstone of Self-realisation. Humility is the touchstone of devotion.

The scenery is the same, but in that the layman sees trees and bushes, the artist is enchanted by nature's beauty, and the saint sees His Beloved Lord in and through the beauty of His creation! Everything depends on training the vision.

To aspire is to rise or reach upward. To aspire is to have an earnest desire, wish or longing as for something high and good, not yet attained, usually accompanied by endeavour to attain it. God is the one true aim of all right human aspirations.

THOUGHTFULNESS AND SWEET DISPOSITION

A man of amiability is of sweet disposition. He radiates so much of mental sunshine, love and joy that he is reflected in all appreciative hearts. He is kind-hearted, gracious, genial. He is free from irritation.

A thoughtless man who has not controlled his organ of speech speaks at random without any consideration and weeps for his foolishness in the end. He is put to shame and disgrace. Therefore, be considerate at all times, on all occasions.

A contented mind is the greatest blessing a man can enjoy in this world. It has a beneficial influence on the soul of man. It destroys all inordinate ambitions, all murmuring, repining, and makes one serene, happy and rich. It is a pearl of inestimable value.

CHEERFULNESS AND THE ONENESS WITH THE DIVINE

Wonderful is the strength of cheerfulness. Cheerfulness is a power. A cheerful man has great power of endurance. He will do more in the same time, will do it better, will persevere in it longer than a cheerless man. What sunshine is to flowers, cheerful and happy smiles are to humanity.

Meditation is a balloon or a parachute or the aeroplane that helps the aspirant to soar high into the realms of eternal bliss, everlasting peace and undying joy. Meditation kills all pains, sufferings and sorrows and gives the vision of unity.

Contentment is a gift of God which you get through faith in the Lord and self-surrender. Daily reading of elevating spiritual literature should form an essential part of your daily Sadhana. Mental peace is obtained only by complete self-surrender to the Lord, who is our Father, Friend, Philosopher and Guide. In times of stress, His Will comes unfailingly to our aid.

Just as the water in the pot that is placed in the ocean becomes one with the waters of the ocean, when the pot is broken, so also when the body-pot is broken by meditation on the Atman, the individual soul becomes identical with the Supreme Self.

Brahmacharya is the bright light that shines in the house of human body. It is the fully blossomed flower of life around which bees of strength, patience, knowledge, purity and Dhriti wander about humming hither and thither. In other words he who observes Brahmacharya will be endowed with the above qualities.

Just as coloured water penetrates freely and nicely over a piece of pure white cloth, so also the instructions of a sage can penetrate and settle down in the hearts of aspirants only when their minds are calm, when there are no desires for enjoyments and when the impurities of their minds are destroyed.

MAN, THE ARCHITECT OF CIRCUMSTANCES

Man is not a creature of circumstances. He is really the architect of circumstances. A man of character builds an existence out of circumstances. He steadily preserves and plods. He does not look back, but marches forward bravely without being afraid of obstacles.

Once you learn to look upon the world as His playground, all your miseries will vanish; you will enjoy peace and bliss.

Desires for external objects dissipate the rays of the mind, weaken the will and weaken the body, too; they waste away precious life. Centre all your desires in Him. You will get everything besides.

Out of the keenest longing comes fulfilment of the object. Every moment of your life should be spent in yearning for the Lord. If you have the same desire for God as one immersed in water has for a breath of air, you will have Him this very moment.

YOGA, THE EPITOME OF RELIGIOUS EXPERIENCE

Yoga is the epitome of all religious experiences. Through practice of Yoga the Yogi can display wonders which defy science. The goal of Yoga is to calm the mind so that it may mirror without distortion the Atman that is behind the mind. Yoga offers a clear, definite path for the realisation of the Highest End of Life.

Clear-sightedness, tranquillity, self-restraint, fortitude, faith, collectedness of mind, indifference to the world and yearning for liberation are the prerequisites of meditation.

THE ORIGIN OF DESIRE AND BRAHMIC REALISATION

Desire arises from a sense of imperfection or limitation, by identifying with the finite body, mind and ego. Desire is the seed from which sprout ceaseless births. Desire is born of ignorance. The fundamental desire is the urge for a mate. Destruction of desire, is destruction of ignorance.

The carrier of a load on a hot day throws his load down and attains rest. Even so, the intellect which carries the Samsaric rich load, gives up the load and attains the Peace of the Eternal through meditation. An hour's meditation is better than ten years' study.

He who has realised Brahman becomes silent. Discussions and argumentations exist so long as the realisation of the Infinite is not attained.

Absolute Ananda is the Supreme Reality. Rise step by step from the sensuous place of experience to the transcendental spiritual experience wherein all names and forms vanish, self-delight alone exists.

For him who sees the all-pervading, tranquil, secondless, blissful Atman, here remains nothing to be attained or known. Know this perfect Atman and obtain perennial joy.

GOOD CONDUCT AND OBSTACLES ON THE PATH

Good conduct, pure and truthful dealings, good character, ethical perfection, cultivation of divine virtues form the very heart and soul of all religions of the world. True Dharma does not oppose any other religion.

A sage is the torch-bearer of wisdom. He is the beacon light or light-house that guides humanity in the dark ocean of Samsara. A sage or a saint is the ultimate source of knowledge of the soul.

Disturbing elements on your path towards Self-realisation and bliss are like examination papers. Do not avoid them. Answer them to your best knowledge and in a harmonious way and do not care for the results. Always keep your mind clear and strong.

THE PERVASIVE BRAHMAN, THE ASTRAL BODY

The astral body made up of desires, together with the organs of perception and action, the Prana, the intellect and the mind, constitutes the subtle adjunct of the Atman.

A king played the part of a beggar for his own sporting; a sage played the part of a fool for his own sporting. Even so, this world is a sport or Leela of Brahman or the Absolute.

Just as sugar-cane juice pervades the sugar-cane, just as salt pervades the water when a lump of salt is dissolved in it, just as butter pervades milk, so also Brahman pervades all the objects, animate or inanimate.

A mighty banyan tree has come out from the subtle essence of a seed; so also this world has come out from the subtle essence of Reality.

The process of practising and realising the unity of existence consists in seeing cause and effect as one and the same, in seeing the whole universe as an expression of God.

The Divine Grace is life's greatest treasure. If there is self-surrender there is inflow of grace. Lord's grace will descend in proportion to the degree of surrender; the more the surrender the more the grace.

VEDANTA, THE PATH OF WISDOM

In Vedanta, Truth is aimed at through the power of intellect; in Bhakti the realisation of God is aimed at through the power of emotion and love.

Jnana and Vairagya are the two wings and are indispensable for the soul to soar to its eternal home of freedom, peace and immortal bliss.

All spiritual practices are to enable man to tear this veil of ignorance, to love the neighbour as oneself. With the dawn of the sun of Jnana in the heart, Ajnana or ignorance will take to its heels.

Ignorance lasts as long as one has egoism. There can be no emancipation so long as there is egoism. Egoism is the great perversion.

FAITH AND THE LOVE OF GOD

Love and service are two keys to Divine Life. Religion and life are not two but one. Lead the Life Divine always. Study, serve, meditate, worship the Divine in and through man.

The deeper a man's love of God is, the greater is his spiritual knowledge, in due proportion to his capacity and depth of love. The final consummation of the love of God is union with God. Love of God is inborn in man by virtue of his spiritual evolution.

God is the source of all happiness. All beings abide in Him. He is an embodiment of peace, wisdom, and bliss. He is Truth, Love, Beauty and Goodness. All beings abide in Him.

God is one. God and His law are one. God is Love and Law. God is pure spirit. God is the path and the goal. God alone is your real father, mother, friend and Guru.

Faith heals, faith creates, faith works wonders, faith moves mountains. Faith is the searchlight for finding God. Faith makes the weak strong and the timid brave. Faith makes the impossible possible.

Consider that God is always with you, within you and around you. You will derive immense strength, inward peace and happiness. You will be a changed man.

THE INNER LIGHT AND THE TRULY WISE

Within you is the key to every problem, the wisdom to guide you in every situation and the strength to rise to magnanimous heights of divine splendour and glory.

When Sattva Guna works in the mental sheath, there is wonderful calmness. The tossing of the mind stops and the power of concentration develops. When the Sattva Guna powerfully vibrates in the Vijnanamaya Kosa, there is wonderful knowledge, powerful memory, and a profound understanding of complex problems.

A man is not an 'elder' because his hair is grey. Mere old age is called empty old age. He is called 'elder' in whom dwells truth, virtue, love, harmlessness, self-control, moderation, who is free from impurity and is wise.

Just as bees come and perch as soon as flowers blossom, so also people of lesser minds are attracted to men of strong personality, of their own accord.

DEFINITION OF RELIGION AND A LIFE IN THE LORD

Religion is faith for knowing and worshipping God. It is not a matter for discussion on a club-table. It is the perception and realisation of the True Self. It is the fulfilment of the deepest craving in man. Live every moment of your life for its realisation. Life without religion is real death.

Just as one sows, so does one reap. Virtuous actions cause good effects; evil actions cause negative results. The Law of Karma alone can account for the differences and inequalities in the world.

Solitude is painful to young persons with great ambition, but is very soothing and peaceful for those who are dispassionate and contemplative.

By service of humanity with Atma-Bhava, discrimination into the nature of cause and effect, dispassion, serenity, self-restraint, concentration, faith, purity and selflessness, one attains the highest wisdom.

Those pious souls alone who are free from egoism and attachment, who have fully controlled the senses and who remain absorbed in meditation are able to attain that realm of immortal bliss and eternal peace from where there is no return to any bondage or limitation.

Neither art, nor science, nor erudition is necessary to approach God or realise Him. What is wanted is a pure heart with love and devotion to God, a heart resolutely determined to apply itself to Him alone, for His sake alone and to love Him alone.

OBSTACLES TO SPIRITUAL PROGRESS AND THE VALUE OF SUFFERING

Live for the Lord. Ceaselessly aspire for God-vision. Practise Dharma. Through selflessness and service, devotion and worship, reflection and meditation attain God-realisation.

Likes and dislikes are a network of attraction and repulsion which hinder the soul's progress towards infinite Existence. These knots must be cut and the sense of high and low broken, before the portal of Eternity is stepped into.

Just as a greedy man is very careful in the accumulation of wealth and does not waste even a single pie and considers it as his very blood, so also, aspirants and those who want to rise up in the world as men, in the real sense of the word, should conserve even a minute quantity of energy and utilise it for good purposes.

The fruit that is allowed to ripen in the tree itself will be very sweet. But this takes a long time. That tree which grows slowly for a number of years will become very strong and be useful for various purposes. Even so, that aspirant who does rigorous Sadhana for a long time with patience will become a dynamic and perfect Yogi. Nowadays students are very impatient. They want to become Yogins within two or three years by doing a little Pranayama, Sirshasana and some Japa.

Suffering turns the mind towards God. Suffering infuses mercy in the heart and softens it. Suffering strengthens. Suffering produces dispassion. Just like you get the scent by squeezing the leaves of a walnut or a verbena tree, you get the essence out of people when they are suffering or in trouble. Therefore suffering is a blessing in disguise. It is the only best thing in this world.

Concentration brings supreme joy, spiritual inner strength, unalloyed felicity and infinite eternal peace. Concentration brings profound knowledge and deep inner sight, intuition and communion with God. It is a wonderful science.

Just as the child enjoys full security and peace when he is in the lap of his mother, just as a baron experiences full security when he has surrendered himself in the hands of a mighty potentate, so also, the aspirant can enjoy abiding peace and can have complete mastery over his senses only when he has totally surrendered himself at the feet of the Lord.

WORLD, MIND AND PRAYER

The world is a mere reflection in the mind, like the image in the mirror. The mind is the mirror. When the mirror is removed, the image becomes merged in the object. So also when the mind is merged in the Self, the world ceases to exist as a separate entity. The whole world is nothing but Brahman. It is the existence of this mind which is the cause for miseries, troubles and tribulations.

The feeling of pleasure is an internal feeling. There is no pleasure in physical objects, though they excite pleasure in man. Sensual pleasure is only a reflection of the Bliss of the Atman. When a desire is gratified the mind moves towards the Atman and rests in Atman for a very short time and the man experiences pleasure. Atman or Brahman only is the embodiment of Bliss.

A king is no king without a treasury, subjects and an army. A flower is no flower without fragrance. A river is no river without water. Even so, a man is no man without the virtue of celibacy. Hunger, passion, fear and sleep are common to man and animal. That which differentiates man from animal is Jnana and Vichara. So, such of those in whom the sex-idea is deep-rooted can never dream of understanding Vedanta and realising Brahman even after one hundred crores of births.

Prayer is the effort of man to commune with the Lord. It is as real as the force of gravity or attraction. The power of prayer is indescribable. It should be done with reverence and with a heart wet with faith and devotion.

He who has no liking for what is agreeable and no dislike for what is disagreeable, who practises self-restraint, who regards pleasure and pain as same and who injures no creature is considered as good and virtuous.

Universal love is the very foundation of righteousness. Selfless service is the corner-stone. Dispassion, discrimination, cultivation of virtues and a strong yearning for liberation are the pillars. The superstructure is eternal happiness, peace, prosperity and immortality. In this temple is the Supreme Lord enshrined. Adore Him there.

Empty prayer is like sounding brass or tinkling cymbal. Heart-felt prayer clearly shows the devotee, the next step. Prayer is the trustworthy companion along the weary path.

ATTRIBUTES OF THE DIVINE CONSCIOUSNESS

Peaceful, auspicious and beautiful, radiant, ever-pure and immortal is the nature of the inner consciousness, the Atman that pervades all creation. To realise this inner consciousness is the essence of spiritual life. Eliminate all that is negative and that is sublime and good.

Every religion is only a new statement of the eternal truth, which was once proclaimed but has perished in the world by lapse of time. Hence the need for Saints and prophets.

Annadana purifies the heart of the giver. One who does charity of food and delights in feeding others, develops cosmic love or universal brotherhood. He feels that the Lord is seated in the hearts of all and feeds the hungry. This pious mental attitude that he is feeding the Lord, helps to purify his mind very quickly.

Though the thief may take the help of moonlight for the purpose of stealing, the moon is not in anyway to be held responsible for the thief's act or its result. Even so, God is not affected by the egoistic actions of man, though He gives light to the ego.

If a thorn gets stuck to the leg, it is carefully removed with the help of another thorn. But after the work is over, both the thorns are thrown away and one becomes happy. Even so, the evil qualities and ignorance born of Avidya should be removed by virtuous qualities and knowledge and after attaining Peace one has to discard them both and transcend all differences.

Nobility is that elevation of soul which comprehends bravery, generosity, magnanimity, intrepidity, and contempt of everything that dishonours character. Nobility is the state or quality of being noble in character as distinguished from selfishness, cowardice and meanness. It is dignity, grace of character, greatness of mind, magnanimity, excellence. The true standard of quality is in the mind. He who thinks nobly is really noble. Nobility is the finer portion of the mind and heart, linked to divinity.

INDISCRIMINATION, ANGER AND THE LANGUAGE OF THE HEART

Improper action, thoughtless action without discrimination gives rise to all miseries. To get freedom from misery, the noble path of virtue, Sadachara is the royal way. Let purity pervade your inner motives and outer conduct. Be loving and charitable in your opinion of men and things and also in all your dealings with others.

Anger is the greatest enemy. Contentment is the Nandana garden (the heavenly bower of Indra) and peace is the Kamadhenu (the heavenly cow). Therefore, take to forgiveness. Atman is different from the body, the Indriyas, Prana and the intellect. It is self-effulgent, unchangeable, pure and formless.

Languages are many but the language of the heart and the mental pictures are one. Cows have many colours but the colour of milk is one. Prophets are many but the essentials of their teachings are the same. Schools of philosophy are many but the goal is one. Opinions and methods of worship are many but Brahman or God is one.

SAINTLINESS AND THE TENDER IN HEART

The beginning of saintliness is killing of egoism. The end of saintliness is Eternal life. The key to saintliness is Brahmacharya. The light of saintliness is universal love. The garb of saintliness is virtue. The mark of saintliness is equal vision. The road to saintliness is regular meditation. The foundation of saintliness is Yama and Niyama.

Love is the immediate way to Truth or Kingdom of God or the vast domain of perennial peace and joy. It is the life-principle of creation. It was the driving force behind Mira, Tukaram, Gauranga. Therefore, develop pure unselfish love. Pure love is a rare commodity. Cultivate it gradually. All your negative qualities like dislike, prejudice, will be eradicated. Love is a great purifier of the mind.

When a person is lighted up by wisdom, his intellect becomes a part of Brahman Itself; and he, the sage, burns the bondage of Karma with the fire of the Knowledge of Brahman.

Cows are of different colours, but milk is of the same

colour. Similarly wisdom is of the same nature though bodies are of different natures like the variegated cows.

The bull of Jiva sleeps its long sleep under the large shadows of Moha in the forest of Samsara, weltering in the mire of sinful actions, goaded by the goad of Ajnana and lashed by the whip of sensual enjoyments, while it is bound by the strong cords of desire and is ever and anon needled by the flea-bites of rare diseases.

A Sage's power lies in lifting through unintermittent efforts this bull which is groaning under the heavy load of pains and, being quite lacerated through ceaseless motions backward and forward, has fallen into the deep pool of numberless births and deaths.

Apart from the knowledge of scriptures and erudition one should develop a tender heart. Austerity devoid of compassion, charity devoid of faith, spiritual Sadhana devoid of purity, a heart devoid of fellow-feeling, a life without prayer are all as fruitless as the waters of sandy deserts.

Love, compassion or mercy, purity, truth, non-injury are the stepping-stones to success in the path of God-realisation. Satsanga, contentment, dispassion and patience are the different steps that lead to the portals of the Kingdom of God.

ART, LIFE AND BHAKTI

Art is a gift of the Lord Himself and an artist is an Amsa of the Lord Himself. By devoting his art to the glorification of the Lord, the artist expands this Amsa and makes it pervade his entire being. He grows more and more into the Lord. Thus can an artist make the best use of his art and use it as his bridge to cross the ocean of Samsara.

The aim of life is to avoid misery and attain Eternal Bliss. Birth in this world is inseparably connected with misery. If you wish to avoid misery, pain and sorrow, you must avoid rebirth. Knowledge of Brahman is the only means of avoiding rebirth.

Real life is nothing else but the Divine, because nothing exists but God and God is love. Welcome Divine Life. Man is eternally in search of infinite Bliss and complete extinction of misery and pain. When he fails to get happiness from worldly life, he turns his mind towards God, the Ocean of Eternal Bliss.

Balanced mind is the touchstone of wisdom. Purity is the touchstone of virtue. Dedication is the touchstone of devotion.

Non-violence is the touchstone of ethics. Brahma Jnana is the touchstone of Self-realisation.

The heart of the scriptures is not the fleshy heart. It is a mysterious divine substance which is sentient, which feels, which is filled with sublime sentiments and higher emotions and which is the seat of the Lord.

Name purifies the heart. Name destroys Vasanas. Name gives you Moksha. Name burns all sins. Name confers prosperity. Name removes troubles. Name is an asset for you. Name is real wealth for you. If you repeat the Name one lakh times, you will have immense spiritual wealth, in the spiritual Bank of the Lord. Name of the Lord gives immense bliss. All great sins vanish in a moment. Untie the bundle of your sins.

He who finds taste and relish in the Names of the Lord, who sheds tears of joy, whose hairs on body stand on their ends, who is kind and merciful to all beings, who knows that his wife, sons, wealth and property and everything else belong to the Lord—is a great devotee.

A RATIONAL KNOWLEDGE OF THE DIVINE

God is the source and Essence. He is the Light of lights. He is Knowledge. He is Bliss. He is Peace. He is approached by discipline, devotion and meditation. A rational understanding of God is the first step towards God-realisation. You must have a living faith in the existence of God, a faith that makes you feel and see the unseen hand of God at all times, a faith that carries conviction with it.

The foremost requisites to communion with God are ethical culture and purification of heart. God's light can be well reflected only over a good mind and a pure heart.

Those pious souls alone who are free from egoism and attachment, who have fully controlled the senses and who remain absorbed in meditation, are able to attain that realm of immortal bliss and eternal peace from where there is no return to any bondage or limitation.

Just as one finds out lost cattle by their footprints, so also one finds this All by the footprints of spiritual values.

One has to cross the wide ocean of illusion through investigation, discrimination, dispassion and meditation and reach the sorrowless shore of immortality.

God is the jewel and lustre, the germ and life, the bud and

flower, the path and destination. He is the same soul in the ant, elephant and man. God appears to His devotees who pray to Him sincerely in whichever form they think of Him.

THE SEARCH FOR IMMORTALITY

The life of power, pleasure and fame, politics and luxury, erudition, wealth and soulless learning cannot give everlasting peace and immortality.

Life is a great mystery. Life is a voyage in the infinite ocean of time where every object is perpetually changing. Life is a tremendous battle with ignorance. Life is a terrible warfare with the mind and the senses.

Man longs for immortality, wisdom, eternal bliss and peace. He can attain these through purity, devotion, discrimination, dispassion and meditation.

In this transient world, in the heart of every individual there is strong latent desire to obtain perfect eternal happiness. In every man, in every living being there is a strong aversion to pain and sorrow. It is the first universal feature of life.

The man who is blind from birth does not know what is day and what is night. Even so, the man who has no doubts, does not know what is truth, what is falsehood, what is proper, what is improper, what is beneficial and what is harmful.

In the midst of darkness, light persists. In the midst of materialistic life, Divine Life stands aloft to lead man towards Godhead and Bliss Eternal.

Under pressure of Yoga and meditation various sorts of dirt in the mind come out just as the dirt of a room that is shut up for six months comes out when we carefully sweep. Aspirants should introspect and watch their mind. They should remove them one by one by applying suitable effective methods.

GAURANGA AND THE MIRACLES OF NAME

One Sachi rocked the cradle of her son with the Dhvani of Hari's Name: "Hari Hari Bol, Bol Hari Bol, Mukunda Madhava Govinda Bol," infused in him the honey of devotion and brought forth to the world a Gauranga who changed the mentality of the people of Bengal. So also the Name of Hari if uttered with Bhava will work miracles.

Just as a turbulent horse carries away the rider along with him, so also the emotion of anger carries away the little Jiva. Just as a capable rider controls the horses and reaches the destination fully so also the emotion of self-restraint controls the emotion of anger, enjoys peace and reaches the goal of life.

In the field of religion there is no Asian, African, Australian, European or American but they are only children of one God. Worship Him in the grand Temple of the universe, and realise the true aim of religion.

Practical religion is truthfulness, non-violence, purity, selflessness, love for all living creatures, self-restraint, magnanimity, toleration and implicit adherence to ethics.

Ethics is an enquiry into the nature of good, and is concerned with an analysis of the concepts of good and bad, virtue and vice, right and wrong. Ethical discipline is a necessary prerequisite for philosophical enquiry.

ETHICAL LIFE AND CONTROL OF EMOTIONS

Right conduct, self-conquest, compassion, benevolence, pursuit of truth, service of humanity, meditation and self-enquiry: this is good living; this is Divine Life.

Happiness is only within. Fix your gaze on the divine flame within, which is the essence of the Universal Light, which only shines and spreads peace. Find more time for meditation, for sitting alone and seeking and gazing of the flame within.

Every death is a reminder. Every bell that rings says "the end is near." Every day robs off from you one part of your precious life. Therefore you should be very earnest in plunging yourself in constant Sadhana.

When the mind is still, when the senses are quiet, when the intellect ceases functioning, you enter the Silence, wherein dwells the unfathomable Peace of the Eternal.

By controlling the surging emotions, by subduing the tossing of likes and dislikes, love and hate, pleasure and pain, elation and depression, peace can be realised.

IDEALS IN NATURE

Be like Hanuman or Bhima in your strength; be broad-minded like the sky; be deep like the ocean; be firm and steady like the Himalayas; be fragrant like the Jasmine.

By service of humanity with Atma-Bhava, discrimination

into the nature of cause and effect, dispassion, serenity, self-restraint, concentration, faith, purity and selflessness, one attains the highest Wisdom.

Just as fire has the natural property of burning inflammable things, so also the Name of Lord Siva has the power of burning sins, Samskaras and Vasanas and bestowing eternal bliss and everlasting peace on those who repeat the Name of the Lord.

Ram is everywhere present. Sat is Ram. Chit is Ram. Ananda is Ram. The fragrance of the rose is Ram. The greenness of the leaves is Ram. The brilliance of the sun is Ram. In the music of the southern breeze is melodiously blended the sweet Name of the Lord. Feel His Presence everywhere. Behold Him in all beings.

Just as a man who does not know the place of a hidden treasure is not able to find it, even though he passes over it several times daily, so also you are not able to find Brahman or the Immortal Self, though you daily enter into Him in deep sleep. If the ignorance is destroyed through knowledge you will have direct cognition of the Supreme Tattva.

Just as lotus-flower and swans depend upon a lake of water for the keeping up their very lives, so also the devotee depends upon Lord Krishna for the maintenance of his very life. He feels that Lord Krishna is His Prananatha (Lord of Prana) or Pranavallabha.

Just as the one flame of a lamp can pass over into several flames (lighted at the original flame), because it possesses the power of modifying itself, thus the soul of a Bhagavata, although one only, multiplying itself through its lordly power, enters into all those bodies.

IMPORTANCE OF VIRTUE AND PREM

Virtue abides where there is truth, vice abides where there is greed and Lord abides where there is devotion.

There is no religion higher than virtue and virtue brings peace. Virtue is greater than life and prosperity. Virtue is the gateway to Bliss.

In Prem the heart is softened more markedly. Prem is the abode of all bliss. It is the one thing needed. It is the culmination of Bhakti to the Lord.

The lane of Prem is extremely narrow indeed. It cannot contain two. Where there is 'I' the Lord is not, where there is the Lord, this 'I' ceases to be.

Hear the divine whisper in silence. Realise the power of faith. Feel God's sustaining grace. Know the way of escape.

Just as heat is inseparable from fire, just as coolness is inseparable from ice, just as shadow is inseparable form man, so is Radha inseparable from Lord Krishna. Worship of Radha is really worship of Lord Krishna and worship of Lord Krishna really includes worship of Radha. Radha is an embodiment of Prem (love) and Bhakti (devotion).

The Truth speaks inwardly without noise of words. It is the language of silence. It is the voice of God. A clear conscience gives joy. There are no pin-pricks.

SILENCE, ITS MEANING AND ITS PLACE

Where is silence? Is it in the forest, or is it in the caves? It is in the heart.

What is silence? Silence is Consciousness, silence is Bliss, silence is Peace.

How to attain silence? Silence the thoughts, silence the emotions and rest in silence.

THE MIDDLE PATH

The spiritual path is a subtle path. It leads you straight to God. Swerve not from this; stray not into the extremes.

Be moderate in eating, sleeping, working and playing. Neglect none and overdo none, either.

Extreme indulgence wears you out; extreme austerity makes you a fanatic and leads to reaction. Overeating produces diseases; and starvation weakens your system. Too much activity tires you; laziness makes you a walking corpse.

Therefore stick to the Path of the Golden Mean. That is the path through which men have become Supermen and Supermen have become God.

STEPS OF ASPIRATION

To grow a little wiser every day,
To teach our mind and body to obey,
To keep our inner lives both clean and strong,
To free our lives from sex, our hands from wrong,

To shut the door on hate and scorn and pride,
To open it to Love, the window wide,
To meet with cheerful hearts what comes to us,
To change life's discords into harmony,
To share some weary worker's heavy load,
To guide some straying comrade to the road,
To know that what we have is not our own,
To feel that we are never quite alone,
This shall we pray from day to day.
For then we know this life would grow.

BYWAYS OF BLESSEDNESS

Attain truth through speaking truth and practising truth in all your daily action and behaviour towards others.

Keep up love for a life of righteousness.

If you control the tongue, you have controlled all the senses.

Sacrifice is truly the sacrifice of egoism.

Learn to realise that sensual pleasure is never complete and full.

In whatever situation God places you, it is only for your betterment. Kindly do not be discouraged.

Do not worry about obstacles. They will pass away.

Adapt yourself to your surroundings and environments. You will enjoy peace and strength.

You can pursue Yoga even while remaining where you are.

Be honest. Be sincere. Be truthful. Be alert. Be diligent. Be vigilant. Be bold. Be of good character. Success and glory will be yours.

Develop a correct value of life here. It is not full. It is not perfect. There is always a sense of want.

Promise not what you cannot fulfil. If you promise, carry it out at any cost.

Never worry about what other people say or think. Do the right. Have a clear conscience and roam about happily.

Persevere and be tenacious. You will get success in everything.

Blessed is he who is tired of this tormenting, degenerating materialistic life and who longs to lead a divine life; twice blessed is he who has dispassion and discrimination, who goes to Mahatmas to have Satsanga, and gets advice and tries to lead a Divine Life; thrice blessed is he who lives in God always, who feels the Divine presence everywhere in every face, in every motion, in every feeling, in every sentiment and in every atom or electron.

MANASIC PUJA SLOKA
BY SRI SANKARACHARYA

Atma tvam girija matih sahacharah pranah
                         sareeram griham,
Puja te vishayopabhogarachana nidra samadhisthitih,
Sancharah padayoh pradakshinavidhih stotrani
                         sarva giro,
Yadyat karma karomi tat-tad-akhilam sambho
                         tava-aradhanam.

Repeat this Sloka before starting meditation.

EXCELLENT SLOKAS FROM AVADHUTA GITA FOR MEDITATION

1. *Janmamrityur na te chittam bandhamokshou*
                         subhasubhou,
   Katham rodishi re vatsa namarupam na te na me.
2. *Ahameva avyayonantah shuddhavijnanavigrahah,*
   Sukhaduhkham na janami katham kasyapi vartate.
3. *Vedantasara sarvasvam jnana vijnanameva cha.*
   Aham atma nirakarah sarvavyapee svabhavatah.
4. *Na manasam karma subhasubham me*
   Na kayikam karma subhasubham me
   Na vachikam karma subhasubham me
   Jnanamritam shuddham ateendriyoham.
5. *Mahadadi jagat sarvam na kinchit pratibhati me,*
   Brahmaiva kevalam sarvam katham varnashramasthitih.

THE LIFE TRIUMPHANT

Live wisely. Live happily. Live to serve others. Live to elevate others. Live to disseminate knowledge. Develop an understanding heart. Help your younger brothers in the spiritual path. Throw light in their path. Do not expect perfection from them. Be kind to them. They are doing their best as you are yourself doing yours. You will grow by helping them.

Penetrate more deeply into the kingdom of Truth. Aspire to realise the Truth. Sacrifice your all for Truth. Die for Truth. Speak the Truth. Truth is life and power. Truth is existence. Truth is knowledge. Truth is bliss. Truth is silence. Truth is peace. Truth is Light. Truth is love. Live to know the Truth. Live to realise Truth. Live to penetrate more deeply into the realms of eternal sunshine and perennial joy. May that Truth guide you in all your actions. May that Truth be your centre, ideal and goal, O lover of Truth!

THE TREE OF SELF, SADHANA AND SAMADHI

The Self is the seed.

Ahimsa, Brahmacharya and Truth are air, water and light.

Dharma is the root, dissemination of spiritual knowledge and disinterested service are trunk and branches.

His (God's) Names are the tender leaves.

A dip in meditation is the bud.

Nirvikalpa Samadhi is the flower.

Absolute Bliss in Brahman is the fruit.

Sadhana is only Self-realisation.

A seed realising the fruit, its nativity.

CHAPTER TWENTY-ONE
SONGS OF SADHANA

Sitaram Sitaram Sitaram Bol,
Radheshyam Radheshyam Radheshyam Bol.

Sadhana is steadying the mind and fixing it on the Lord. It gives you freedom, bliss, peace and immortality. Friend! Plod on patiently like the farmer at his plough. Be persevering, be steady in your daily Sadhana.

Destroy Tandri, Alasya and building castles in the air. Take light food at night and drive off sleepiness. Be regular in your Japa, Kirtan and meditation. Regularity in Sadhana is of paramount importance.

Just as you separate the pith from the Munja grass separate this Atman from the five Kosas.

Peace, cheerfulness, contentment and fearlessness indicate that you are advancing in the spiritual path.

THE GIST OF SADHANA

Remove selfishness	Narayana
Calm the passion	Sadasiva
Control the Indriyas	Narayana
Destroy egoism	Sadasiva
Serve all, love all	Narayana
Concentrate, meditate	Sadasiva
Purify your heart	Narayana
Through selfless service	Sadasiva
Be bold, be cheerful	Narayana
Be generous	Sadasiva
Be tolerant	Narayana
Be sincere	Sadasiva
Do charity	Narayana
Do good acts	Sadasiva
Do kind acts	Narayana

Do simple Tapas	Sadasiva
Do not waste a single minute	Narayana
Do not speak harsh words	Sadasiva
Do not utter vulgar words	Narayana
Do not speak falsehood	Sadasiva
Get up at 4 a.m.	Narayana
Start your Japa	Sadasiva
Meditate regularly	Narayana
On the form of Lord	Sadasiva
Think of His attributes	Narayana
He is Omnipresent	Sadasiva
He is Omnipotent	Narayana
He is Omniscient	Sadasiva
He is all-pervading	Narayana
He is all-merciful	Sadasiva
He is all-loving	Narayana
He is all-blissful	Sadasiva
The secret of renunciation	Narayana
Is killing egoism	Sadasiva
And all desires	Narayana
And all attachments	Sadasiva
You can realise God	Narayana
Remaining in the world	Sadasiva
Be not worldly	Narayana
But be in the world	Sadasiva
Renounce worldliness	Narayana
Preserve Veerya	Sadasiva
This is a real treasure	Narayana
It is all energy	Sadasiva
There is no half-measure	Narayana
In the spiritual path	Sadasiva
Strictly observe	Narayana
All the Yoga rules	Sadasiva
How long you want	Narayana
To remain as a householder	Sadasiva
Grow and evolve	Narayana

Soar high! wake up	Sadasiva
Do not say in future	Narayana
"She is my wife"	Sadasiva
"He is my son"	Narayana
"This is my house"	Sadasiva
Feel the Atman	Narayana
In all forms	Sadasiva
Behold the one Self	Narayana
Everywhere	Sadasiva
Regulate your life	Narayana
Give up idle talk	Sadasiva
Do not read novels	Narayana
And newspapers too	Sadasiva
You will have ample time	Narayana
To do your Sadhana	Sadasiva
Do not visit cinema	Narayana
Do not play cards	Sadasiva
Do not smoke	Narayana
Do not drink	Sadasiva
Even European Sadhakas	Narayana
Have left smoking, meat	Sadasiva
But some Hindu Sadhakas	Narayana
Still keep smoking	Sadasiva
They are still weak	Narayana
What a great pity!	Sadasiva
Do Japa now	Narayana
Meditate afterwards	Sadasiva
Then do Kirtan	Narayana
Then do Asanas	Sadasiva
Then study Gita	Narayana
Then serve the sick	Sadasiva
Then have Satsanga	Narayana
Then go for walking	Sadasiva
Then do Pranayama	Narayana
Then write the Mantra	Sadasiva
Stick to your routine	Narayana

Very tenaciously	Sadasiva
Do not take bribes	Narayana
Even a pie	Sadasiva
It is bad	Narayana
It is very bad	Sadasiva
It is very very bad	Narayana
It is extremely bad	Sadasiva
It will spoil	Narayana
Your name, character	Sadasiva
This will throw you	Narayana
In lower births	Sadasiva
To have a bad name	Narayana
Is more than death	Sadasiva
It is very shameful	Narayana
It is disgraceful	Sadasiva
It is ignominious	Narayana
It is heaven-closing	Sadasiva
Take Sattvic food	Narayana
Give up meat, garlic	Sadasiva
Onions too	Narayana
You will have a pure mind	Sadasiva
Take light diet	Narayana
At night	Sadasiva
Milk and fruits	Narayana
You can easily get up	Sadasiva
In the early morning	Narayana
For meditation	Sadasiva
Keep daily spiritual diary	Narayana
You will evolve quickly	Sadasiva
This will help you	Narayana
To control mind	Sadasiva
Stick to your resolves	Narayana
Don't move an inch	Sadasiva
Stand adamant	Narayana
You will develop your will-power	Sadasiva

PRACTICE OF REAL SADHANA

(*Thars:* Hindustani Bhairavi. *Mettu:* Suna Pyare Mohan)

Do real Sadhana, my dear children
              (Do real Sadhana....)
Sadhana-Sadhana-Sadhana-Sadhana.
To free yourself from birth and death
And enjoy the Highest Bliss
I will tell you the surest way
Kindly hearken with greatest care.
              (Do real Sadhana....)
Acquire first Sadhana Chatushtaya,
Then proceed to the feet of Sat Guru,
After having Sravana and Manana,
Then do practise Nididhyasana.
              (Do real Sadhana....)
Remove first the old, Dehadhyasa,
By repeating Sivoham Bhavana,
Then remove the veil, Avarana,
You will rest in your own Svarupa.
              (Do real Sadhana....)

INTIMATE ADVICE

Have an open mind, A clean Conscience,
A noble character, A clear understanding of Truth;
A broad outlook of life, A new Spiritual vision,
A good receptive mind, A loyal sense of duty to the Preceptor;
A childlike Svabhava, A willing obedience to saints,
A pure, melting heart to the distressed,
A brave spirit to protect Dharma.

SONG OF SADHANA WEEK

Rama Bhajo, Rama Bhajo, Rama Bhajoji.
Rama Krishna Govinda Gopala Bhajoji.

I

You have come to Rishikesh to do rigorous Sadhana,
    Do not think of vegetables and hot Pakkoda.
You have come during Sadhana week to practise Yoga,
    Do not think of milk, fruits and Dahi-vada.

You have come to Rishikesh to practise Yogabhyasa,
    Do not think of Chapathi and Chutai (Kitchadi) Parota.
You have come to Rishikesh to do Tapascharya,
    Do not think of Laddu, Peda, Garama-garam Jalebi.
Are you not ashamed to repeat the same sensuous life?
    Learn lesson from the lower animal kingdom.
Enough, enough, enough, enough of eating, drinking,
    Wake up, wake up, wake up without winking.
Enough, enough, enough, enough of idle gossiping,
    Enough, enough, enough of reading novels, newspapers.

II

Be very punctual in attending meetings and classes,
    Punctuality alone will give you success and prosperity.
Time is fleeting, time is precious, time is all wealth,
    Utilise every second in spiritual Sadhana.
Do not think of good food and comforts for the body,
    Be up and doing in Japa, Kirtan and meditation.
Friends! You are roasted in the fire of this Samsara,
    Take a dip in the Triveni within during meditation.
Sukka rukka thoda khake, Asan me baito,
    Hari Smaro Hari Japo, Hari Dhyana Karo.
Try to rise up in the ladder of Yoga step by step,
    You will soon reach the summit of Nirvikalpa Samadhi.
This is the goal, this is your ideal, this is your centre,
    Here alone you will find Eternal Bliss and Peace.

III

Many cows died this year, there is no milk,
    Try to drink the Ganga water and be happy.
Come back to nature even by virtue of necessity,
    Try to take tea without milk and be happy.
You cannot get even Atta, Dhal; there is control of food,
    The price of all foodstuffs has risen considerably high.
There is severe calamity throughout the length and
                                    breadth of land,
    Let us pray to God now for the peace of this world.
Om Tat Sat, Om Tat Sat, Om Tat Sat OM,
    Om Santi, Om Santi, Om Santi OM.
Hari Om Tat Sat, Sri Om Tat Sat, Siva Om Tat Sat OM.

SONG OF A SADHAKA

I will try to learn one new thing every day.
I will do one good act daily.
I will practise Asanas daily to remove inertia.
I will do Suryanamaskara to get rid of lethargy.
I will practise virtues to make the mind positive.
I will never allow the mind to remain negative.
I will be ever diligent, vigilant and be on the alert.
I will march forward always to attain the goal of life.
I will never indulge in anything in which the worldlings
    indulge.
I will not allow the mind to copy and imitate them.
I will always try to become like Yudhishthira.
I will strive to tread the path which Buddha has trodden.
I will lead the life which Kabir, Nanak, Ram Das led.
I will emulate Bhishma, Sankara and Guru Dattatreya.
I will remember the teachings of Lord Buddha and
    Lord Mohammed.
I will practise the precepts of Lord Krishna and
    Vyasa Bhagavan.
I will not be careless and say 'There is no danger'.
I will not be heedless and say 'I am perfectly safe'.
I will try to fortify myself in all directions,
To resist the subtle working of the mysterious Maya.
I will try to fence myself strongly and powerfully,
To resist temptations and snares of Avidya.
I will not say in future 'I will indulge in this just
    only once'.
This 'only once' will multiply into thousand ones.
This 'only once' will pull me down in the dark abyss.
This 'only once' will cause in me hopeless downfall.
I will never say 'by and by' and put off doing good.
Opportunities come but once and soon slip away.
Through the grace of the Lord and my adorable Guru,
I have found out this clever Maya's Trick,
I will do in future rigorous Tapas and meditation.
I will strengthen my resolves and hold Siva's Trisul.

PHASES OF SADHANA

Be vigilant and destroy the desires,
Be good and do good actions,
Be firm and control the senses,
Be still and realise the Truth.
Be cheerful, smile and laugh,
Be bold and tread the path,
Be humble and kill the pride,
Be pure and slay the lust,
Be regular in your meditation,
Be steady in your Sadhana,
Be sincere to your own self,
Be true to your preceptor.
Be kind to all beings,
Be selfless, 'mind-less' and angerless,
Be rich in your inner life,
Be active in your daily life.
Be truthful in your speech,
Be benevolent to the people,
Be virtuous, gentle and noble,
Be thoughtful, frank and charitable.
Be patient with practising Yoga,
Be balanced in pleasure and pain,
Be peaceful by resting in the Atma,
Be joyful by abiding in the Soul.

TWENTY PRECEPTS FOR PRACTICE

O traveller on earth! Speed up, speed up thy pace,
For many are the pitfalls to impede thy race;
The distance is long, very rough is thy road,
Thy strength will fast fail thee, yet heavy thy load.

Harken, traveller! to these golden precepts,
The Essence of Wisdom of ancient adepts;
In twenty short maxims I'll tell thee the way,
To true Bliss and Freedom from Mayaic sway.

Wake up at four a.m., Brahmamuhurta,
Filled with vibrations of Sattva and Truth,
Sit on Sukha, Siddha or Padma Asana,
Meditate on God and do Brahmachintana.

The most holy Name of the Lord do repeat,
To destroy delusion and to Satan defeat;
Rotating the rosary of hundred-eight beads,
To bliss and perfection this Japa Yoga leads.

In meditation-room with divine vibration,
Take firm, erect pose, practise concentration;
Chant Slokas sublime full with inspiration,
Advance through Dhyana to Supreme Salvation.

A select few Yogasanas without fail do,
A few rounds of vigorous Pranayama too
Health, strength, harmony, will to you accrue,
From such exercises, I assure you.

Elevating scriptures of all religions great,
Study revelations that sages narrate;
Ramayana, Bhagavata and Gita its mate,
Will all purify thee, to Sattva elevate.

Observe a period of silence each day,
Such Mouna the tumult of Rajas will slay;
Speak little, speak sweetly whatever you say,
On firm base of TRUTH thy life's foundations lay.

To 've rigid control over palate do try,
In discipline of diet does true success lie;
Through fasting both body and mind purify,
By restraint of tongue all base passions will die.

Reduce thy wants, and learn plainly to live,
To the poor and needy in charity give;
'Tis a veritable curse and a constant worry,
To possess more wealth than is necessary.

Guard with great care precious Vitality,
In thought, word and deed observe strict purity;
Continence is basis of Spirituality,
Leading to Bliss and Immortality.

Never give way to an angry outburst,
For anger is modified passion and lust;
Wisely over anger do victory gain,
By love and forgiveness 'tis finally slain.

Think daily of God and to Him surrender,
To Him thy whole-hearted allegiance render;
Cutting the Mayaic heart-knot asunder,
He'll raise thee to high heights of Atmic Splendour.

    Always on thyself in all things rely,
    By Purushartha you can Prarabdha defy;
    To stick to righteousness and Svadharma try,
    To twin-steeds of Yama-Niyama life's chariot tie.

Always associate with the good and the wise,
They'll help you from Samsara to Moksha to rise;
The Power of Satsanga will life spiritualise,
And quickly will make you life's Goal realise.

    Of spiritual practices a diary maintain,
    The detailed items of Sadhana 'twill contain;
    Have regular routine, thereby greatly you'll gain,
    An insight and idea of progress obtain.

The motives hidden of thy day to day deeds,
Ungodly traits and of passion the seeds;
Search and remove as the gardener the weeds,
Such self-search to success in Sadhana leads.

    Cling with firmness to these canons divine,
    They're most precious gems out of Wisdom's deep mine;
    The Essence of Sadhana they nicely combine,
    Practise! As dynamic Yogi you'll shine!

CHAPTER TWENTY-TWO
SOME EXPERIENCES OF ASPIRANTS

PURPOSE OF SADHANA

It is because man is not satisfied with his instinctive experience, he seeks the aid of his intellect to widen the sphere of his experience. Reason helps discrimination, discrimination decides the limit and the depth of experience. The restless spirit of man is ever after the quest of perpetual experience of what seems to be pleasant to him.

Real happiness or the joy of life cannot be met in the limited area of instinctive fulfilments. An experience which is to be permanent cannot be met in the object that is not permanent. From the infinite alone can the infinite result accrue. That infinite essence is the inner Self of man. It is the common, indivisible Consciousness in all creations. Realisation of that Consciousness is the goal of life.

A complete transformation of the inner propensities, ideals, thoughts, evaluations and actions of the individual, or the transmutation of the nature of man from the instinctive level of sensual urges to the human level of reason and discrimination, and from the human level to the intuitive level of inner spiritual experience and perception, constitutes the means for the realisation of the Self.

Sadhana or spiritual practices such as concentration, meditation, cultivation of the fundamental virtues like truthfulness, selfless love, purity, holiness, self-restraint, etc., in commensuration to the automatic eradication of their negative counterparts, constitute the main items of the aspirant's effort towards spiritual evolution.

These various practices are attended by occult experiences which are rather dependent on the psychical sensitivity of the individual. These occult experiences are not however, the criterion of Sadhana. What is more important is that the process of the unfoldment of the divine nature in man should find a positive expression in one's intellectual, emotional and physical aspects of life on individual as well as social planes.

The following summary of the spiritual diary of a German student of Yoga, Hans Franke, is interesting to note.

Hans Franke gets up every day at 4 a.m. and practises concentration on his Ishta-devata for fifteen minutes, does 200 Malas of the Japa of his Ishta-Mantra, studies religious literature for half an hour, practises Asanas for 15 minutes and 120 rounds of Pranayama, observes Mouna for one hour, tries to cultivate patience, mental strength and concentration apart from other virtues, and attempts to eradicate haste, anxiety and weakness apart from other defects.

What is more remarkable is the experience of certain psychical forces, which Hans Franke has been able to achieve in a short time. He writes:

"During the evening, when I was praying that God may bestow on me His vision, I saw a brilliant light, as resplendent as the sun, appear from my left and linger on in front of me for a while.

"Eleven days later, during my meditation in the evening, the light appears again. It is very bright. I feel a queer sensation in my legs. The light grows brighter and brighter. I observe that it lasts for two and a half minutes.

"On the next day of this experience, a blue circle of light appears before me as I am about to begin my practice, the room becomes very bright.

"Four days later, as I was meditating on patience, joy and courage, I felt a great silence enveloping me. As my mind wavered on to the question as to what I ought to do, an open book appeared before me, but before I was able to read its contents, two other books of green and yellow colours appeared and obscured the other one. I wanted to see the name of the first book, and when the book turned round by itself I saw that nothing was written on the back of the cover. I had the feeling that I ought to know about it later."

It is not necessary here to go over long interpretations of these experiences. They indicate the progressive trend of the aspirant, and it is enough if he applies himself more assiduously in the practice of his Sadhana without stopping to divert his attention from the goal of life, namely, Self-realisation, to these minor occult experiences.

It will not be out of place to detail here the main points of the reply that was sent to Hans Franke's supplementary enquiries on his Sadhana. They mainly concern the method of meditation for the general class of aspirants to whom the tutelary deity (Ishta-devata) is representative of the Supreme Consciousness, or the Absolute Reality, or God Almighty. I advised the aspirant as follows:

"Concentration on the Ishta-devata, which you have been practising for 15 minutes daily, may be modified as follows, and the period extended.

"Place a picture of the Ishta-devata in front of you. Sit in a comfortable posture. Keep the spine and head erect. Look at the picture with a steady gaze, then close your eyes and try to visualise the picture in the point between the eye-brows. When the mental vision of the picture fades out, open your eyes and concentrate on the picture as before for a short while; close the eyes again and repeat the process.

"You can meditate on the virtues such as joy, holiness, etc., as you have been doing, independent of their association with the Ishta-devata. But it is also necessary to associate these qualities with the tutelary deity while meditating, so as to effect a greater degree of concentration. For the same purpose, mental repetition of the Ishta-Mantra is also combined with meditation.

"Meditation on merely the features of a particular form has no salutary effect on the mind, the physical features alone cannot encompass the entire range of attention. Meditation should, therefore be inclusive of the above associations.

"The *sine qua non* of all spiritual endeavours is to effect a thorough transformation of the nature of the individual, his ideals, urges, thoughts and actions in accordance to the process of Self-realisation.

"The purpose of Sadhana is the unfoldment of the divine nature in man by cultivating and strengthening the divine propensities inherent in everyone. These divine propensities are not an antithesis to the human propensities but a consummation of all that is best in the human propensities which help one to transcend the human propensities."

EXPERIENCES OF SADHAKAS

1. "When I woke up from sleep at 4 a.m. the first flash that went through my brain was the luminous form of Swami Sivanandaji and the feeling that accompanied was of supreme calmness and bliss and I felt as an innocent child would feel happy and secure while inclining on the bosom of its beloved mother. The bliss was intense, and I felt disappointed when I had to pass from that unique state to my usual meditative mood. I think that Swamiji must have sent to me a wave of bliss which the wireless apparatus in me must have been able to grasp...."

* * *

2. "In the dark I see blue dazzling lights in the form of stars. In the morning during my prayer, when I close my eyes, I see one star between my two eyebrows. It is like a blue dazzling star."

* * *

3. "One night I felt that my whole body was vibrating while I was in sleep. I immediately got up and sat for meditation. While I was trying to meditate, I felt the same vibration with greater intensity. It seemed that my lower portion of the body (below waist) was under terrific blaze."

* * *

4. 7th Dec., 1946. "Today is my most surprising experience in my life. It is barely $4\frac{1}{2}$ months since I came to Rishikesh and stayed at Ananda Kutir. When I came here I was suffering from constipation and external bleeding of piles. Not only I have got rid of these complaints completely but I am completely established in my elements.

"Between 4.30 and 6.30 a.m., today I was able to do in one sitting 100 Pranayamas with Japa and full concentration on the photo of Lord Siva with the perfect ease of an adept. During the first 25 Pranayamas my mind was calm. During the next 15 Pranayamas, mind became restless, so that I had to change my Asana twice. During the next 40 Pranayamas my mind slowly separated itself from my senses. During the last 20 Pranayamas my mind was completely subjugated and was following my will like a docile child amenable to reason and direction. There was perfect peace in me. I did not at all feel the biting cold when I came out of my room after this experience."

When the Guru can bring about such marvellous changes of mind in a mediocre like me, how much more he would have brought in an Uttama Adhikari who will follow his instructions to the very letter! Is there any doubt then when he proclaims "Samadhi in six months?" He is the most modern Guru who can work wonders.

Let his sacred feet flower out in my head. Let his sacred feet glisten in my eyes. Let his sacred feet fructify in my heart.

❋ ❋ ❋

5. "When I go to bed, of its own sweet will, the mind drifts away till I forget my body completely. Nothing is remembered or seen or heard. Everything is lost, nay, the very existence is lost in something. Suddenly some mysterious consciousness operates and I experience as if I have opened my eyes and that some figure appears in various forms, each time, like a full size man, a woman dressed like Bhavani, i.e. Kaali Mata or Durga, a figure resembling the enlarged size of five human figures, seven luminous white points, as large as the eye-ball of a child, five paralleled columns, like test-tubes of a science laboratory, a single dazzling ball of light and so on. There is no end to the variety of the forms that appear always to proceed near my body."

COLLECTIVE SADHANA

Holidays are not meant for playing cards, idle gossiping, feasting, sight-seeing or aimless wanderings. It is very difficult to get a human birth. The aim of life is to attain God-consciousness. Holidays must be well spent. Every second must be utilised in worship and meditation only. Start your Sadhana with zeal and enthusiasm and march direct to the Goal.

There is peculiar Santi and Ananda in such a collective Sadhana. Even if there are six members, collective Sadhana must be done. Members will have special enthusiasm and interest in collective Sadhana, otherwise individually they are likely to be overpowered by sleep and inertia, laziness and procrastination.

Collective Sadhana such as common meditation, common prayers, common Sankirtan, Prabhata Pheri, Likhita Japa and Akhanda Kirtan in groups, the Gita or the Ramayana Patha, etc., are more potent or effective than individual meditation, Sankirtan or individual Sadhana. When people join together and practise common meditation or Sankirtan, you get the combined or massive effect produced by the simultaneous efforts of all those who take part in the common spiritual Sadhana.

A large number of people generate and send out a huge thought-form. A corresponding large amount of spiritual force flows in and stimulates the spiritual faculties of those who take part in the common function. Greater the number of persons, greater the thought-forms, greater the flow of inward spiritual faculties. Spiritual entities, Nitya Siddhas are present in those places where common spiritual functions are conducted. Like attracts like. This is the Divine Law. Rishis and Yogis transmit their vibrations to such places. Those who have inner sight can directly behold the spiritual vibratory lines of communication.

Further the simultaneous effort wonderfully harmonises the vibrations of their bodies and minds and consequently makes them more receptive. The five Kosas or sheaths vibrate rhythmically. When there is rhythm or harmony in the vehicles, meditation or Samadhi comes without any effort. Their attention is focussed or rivetted on the same Lakshya or point. They think and feel together, in unison, therefore stimulate one another.

Apart from daily collective Sadhana, special programme should be carried out in a large scale on holidays for a week or three days with the programme of Sadhana Week. In Kali Yuga such a Spiritual Conference or Collective Sadhana is a Maha Yajna. The main object in holding Spiritual Conferences is to create a spiritual awakening in those people who are carried away by the dark materialistic influences, who have forgotten all about their religion and their Divine nature and to reinforce the spiritual force that has already awakened in those who are leading a spiritual life even while living in the world.

When several people join together and practise common meditation or sing the Names of the Lord, a huge spiritual current of Maha Sakti is generated. This purifies the hearts of the practitioners and the atmosphere and elevates them to the sublime heights of divine ecstasy of Samadhi. Common Sadhana has this particular advantage. These magnanimous and powerful vibrations are carried away to distant places and they bring elevation of mind, solace, strength and peace to all people and work as invisible harbingers of peace, harmony and concord. The powerful soothing beneficial vibrations will annihilate hostile forces and quickly bring Peace and Bliss to the whole world.

Further the people are benefited by the valuable discourses and spiritual instructions given by Sannyasins, Yogis and other learned persons who are present on the occasion. Spiritual Conferences tend to produce lasting unity and love amongst people.

In Kali Yuga a Spiritual Conference is tantamount to a hundred Raja Suya Yajnas or a hundred Soma Yajnas. If you weigh the fruit obtained by holding a Spiritual Conference in one side and the fruit of a hundred Raja Suya Yajnas or a hundred Soma Yajnas of days of yore in another side of a scale, the former will go down.

The benefits of a Spiritual Conference are beyond description. You will have a new India, a new Europe and a new world! The spiritual waves will cure incurable diseases and a host of other ailments, overhaul the worldly vicious Samskaras; change the nature of rank materialists and confirmed sceptics and infuse a new religious spirit in people. The Spiritual Conference will take the aspirants and those who take part in the activities with Nishkamya Bhava, with purity and steady devotion directly to the domain of Eternal Bliss or Moksha!

It behoves therefore that all religious-minded or spiritually-inclined persons should try their level best now to hold religious or Spiritual Conferences in different centres, in all villages and towns and cities and carry out the Programme of the Sadhana Week. All members in large numbers should take part in such Conference, and derive the maximum spiritual benefit.

"Brethren! meet together, talk together, let your minds apprehend alike; common be your prayer, common be your purposes; common be your deliberation; I advise you to have a common policy. Common be your desires, united be your hearts, united be your intention, so that there may be a thorough union among all of you. May our Father grant this!"

"May there be welfare to the whole world; may all beings devote themselves to doing good to others; may all evils subside; may the world be happy in all ways."

INSTRUCTIONS TO SADHAKAS

1. When you come to attend the Sadhana week, come with the proper spiritual Sattvic attitude. Do not come to attend Sadhana week as though for a week-end holiday to spend your vacation. Unlike picnics or jolly trips this is a different and more serious occasion. You need not be over-serious or gloomy but holiday mood is out of place at this time. It will spoil the solemn atmosphere and also prevent your reaping the maximum spiritual benefit out of it.

2. You dress yourself in your uniform while on official duty. You put on special clothing on special occasions or during ceremonial events. For the theatre or the park you have informal evening dress. Different functions have their own apparel. For the Sadhana week do not come dressed as though for a marriage party or official gathering. Have simple dress that will be conducive to keep yourself in a religious frame of mind. It would be highly welcome indeed if you have some uniformly simple dress as similar as possible, to other's. This will help to remove feelings of difference, superiority, inferiority etc. Do not have gaudy, flashy or silken dress.

3. At least for that one week all such things like special attention to toilet, elaborate combing and brushing of hair, trimming moustache, applying hair oil, brilliantine, pomade etc., should be given up by men, and ladies should stop scent, powdering faces, nail-polishing, eyebrow pencilling, lip-stick etc. You must have the sole consciousness that you are a Sadhaka and have come specially to do some solid Sadhana. Do everything you can to help to create this feeling in yourself as well as in all others attending.

4. During Christmas Sadhana week you will do well in bringing two extra blankets, sufficient woollen clothes, like sweater, stockings, cap etc., apart from the necessary luggage. All of you are requested to bring one Asana for individual Sadhana purposes, one Japa Mala, one Gita book, a Mantra notebook and pen for Likhita Japa and taking notes during discourses, one torchlight or lantern, a water-vessel and other little articles for personal use for the duration of your stay.

5. Due to the limited accommodation in the Ashram it will not be possible to provide you with individual rooms, but all the

available rooms in the Ashram and the locality nearby will be placed at the disposal of the Sadhakas. Of course, for every family a room will be provided. You are requested to kindly adapt yourself to the accommodation provided for you. During intervals individual Sadhana would be carried on on the banks of the Ganga or in the secluded spots adjoining the Ashram or in individual rooms. Absolute silence and calmness should always be maintained, particularly in the Satsanga Hall, where the general functions will be held.

6. Diet plays a very important part in keeping you in the right condition for all times of the Sadhana programme. Very light and moderate diet will enable you to derive the maximum benefit from the Sadhana week. If you load yourself, you will not be able to get up at the Brahmamuhurta for attending the morning meditation programme. You will be dull-minded and drowsy during the day. Light and simple diet alone will enable you to have an alert mind and follow the discourses etc., and to do all the various other items of Sadhana in the programme. Therefore, do not neglect this point. All Sadhakas should observe Mouna during meals and other intervals.

7. As a measure of tongue-control, saltless diet and other disciplines will be introduced in the diet for a day during the week.

8. In your own interest you are requested to give up habits like smoking, chewing of betel leaves, self-shaving, using intoxicants etc., during the week. This is a measure of self-discipline. Those who take resolve to give up these habits should do Prayaschitta if they break their resolves—do extra Malas of Japa on the Ganga bank or Visvanatha Mandir, pay a fine for each mistake (which will be utilised for poor feeding or temple Puja), or by fasting or any such measure as prescribed by the President.

9. Every Sadhaka should take part for at least half an hour or one hour daily in the Akhanda Mahamantra Kirtan conducted since 1943 in the Bhajan Hall.

10. No Sadhaka should sleep for more than 5 hours a day during the week. He must spend his leisure hours in Japa and meditation.

11. Every Sadhaka should maintain a spiritual diary and fill

up the resolve form and submit it to me, before he leaves the Ashram.

12. Aspirants may do some Nishkama Seva in the routine Ashram work every day under the guidance and instruction of the person in charge of the activities. Everyone should join the Nishkama Seva class without fail, which will be conducted here during the week.

13. (a) As regards instructions for attending the class, you should restrain your desire to get into conversation with your friends when you attend the classes. This is a practice towards restraint. To indulge in conversation when class is going on is likely to be taken as an indifferent or disinterested attitude. That is not becoming of you. If a particular item of the day's agenda or any discourse does not interest you, bear it with a little patience and wait for the next which will interest you. A little disturbance caused by you might impair the other man's attention or put others to inconvenience.

(b) It is wrong to interrupt a person while he is talking. If by chance you feel compelled to speak something, you have to request permission for the intrusion and then say what you have to say. And that is also when something important crops in, a matter which cannot be put off conveniently to another moment.

(c) Kindly do not interrupt a speaker by way of repartee, or offer a jest. It is unbecoming of one to resort to anything frivolous and such conduct is likely to lower the seriousness of the function.

(d) At intervals between the items do not demonstrate tendency to talk. Withhold your desire a little longer as part of discipline.

(e) Sometimes discussions lead to unpleasant words inadvertently uttered; words derogatory to the prestige of the Society. Be brief in your talk and to the point and avoid answering to the members who would have spoken previously. Avoid personality and be particular that you use mild and courteous language. Harsh words will generate heat and heat will retard or nullify progress.

(f) Come with a memorandum notebook and pen. Note down important appealing portions of the discourse which you hear during the week. Do not just come and return and allow ideas to evaporate away.

14. Those who come with their family should make it a point to explain the proceedings and discourses to ladies or children, who may not be able to follow them. The ladies are also requested to intimate to the President if they wish any lecture to be translated in their vernacular.

15. He who is not punctual, who does not attend the Mantra-writing class or the Morning common meditation class or Havan and other items of the programme without any reasonable excuse, who talks unnecessarily in the Satsanga Hall during the class, who leaves the Satsanga Hall in the middle, or arrives late, must pay an appropriate fine, as it may be imposed by the President on each occasion. The fine will be utilised for either poor feeding or temple Puja or Jnana Yajna.

Appendices

APPENDIX—I

A DRAMA IN SADHANA

Synopsis of a Drama staged by the Divine Life Bala Mandali, under the direction of Sri Swami Chidanandaji Maharaj during the Sadhana Week, Christmas 1952.

THE PATH OF A SADHAKA

THE STORY OF TWO SADHAKAS' EXPERIENCES

Two young men, Subodh and Vivek, have been receiving scriptural education at the Ashram of their Guru, a Sannyasin. They are nearing the completion of their studies. Quite early in life they both have come to the Guru and since boyhood have been serving the Master with true devotion. The austere life they had led in the Gurukula, the Satsanga they enjoyed with the saintly Mahatma, their Guru, and the theoretical knowledge of the Sastras, had generated in them an aspiration to lead the Nivritti-Marga, to dedicate their life to wholetime Sadhana for Self-realisation.

On a Guru Purnima day, they approach the Guru with their request to be "initiated and taught the mysteries of higher Yoga and spiritual attainment." The Guru expresses his joy at their aspiration; and whilst congratulating them on their discrimination, counsels a little caution in taking such a drastic step in sudden haste. "Sannyasa is blazing fire; and you should prepare yourself well before embracing it. You have as yet had no first-hand knowledge or experience of the world. The Vairagya (dispassion) that you have now got from study of scriptural texts and by remaining in this pure and holy atmosphere may or may not be real; may not be deep-rooted in you; it may or may not last till the end of your life. At some later period in your life, temptations might assail you and take you astray. I, therefore, think that a little experience of the true nature of the world would fortify and make firm your Vairagya which would then be unshakable. Today is the auspicious Guru Purnima day. Now go out into the wide world. Roam about the country for one year. Pass through different places, move amidst diverse men and things. You will learn many lessons. The world is your best teacher. Keep your eyes and ears open; learn and learn. But keep your mouth shut. Do not take part in worldly activities; just watch and learn. Learn some valuable lessons from every place, person, object and experience you come across. As far as possible live in the company of the wise; if this is not possible, live alone. Then come back to me after a year. You will have gained rich experience during this one year; and I will also be reassured that your dispassion is real and unshakable. May the blessings of my Gurudev grant you strength and wisdom!"

The two young men leave the Ashram after bowing to their Guru.

IN THE DULLARD'S DURBAR

Hearing that the Raja of a nearby State had a number of learned men in his Durbar, the two Sadhakas went there. They were very well received by the Raja; and the Court Pandit was giving expositions of scriptures for the enlightenment of the people who attended Durbar; the Raja himself was interested only in gluttony, fun and frolic and so took no pains to learn.

A clever scoundrel with a smattering of literature was tempted by the Raja's ignorance to play upon his love of the vulgar and to earn a fortune. He went to the Durbar and bragged of his extensive learning and deep wisdom.

"Give me proof of your learning," asked the Raja.

"Maharaj! You must surely have heard the Sloka: *Shuklambaradharam Vishnum Shashivarnam Chaturbhujam Prasannavadanam Dhyayet Sarvavighnopasantaye.* Do you know what is it that is referred to by this Sloka?"

"Surely. Lord Mahavishnu who is clad in white cloth is all-pervading and the bestower of bliss."

"No it refers to a glittering rupee-coin! The rupee-coin is white; it pervades the entire world; it never stays at one place with anyone; it is of the form of the full-moon; it has four four-annas; and it removes all our obstacles and makes every person happy."

"You seem to be more learned than our Court Pandit!"

"What doubt is there?"

The Raja promptly drove away the wise Court Pundit and his colleagues and appointed this impostor in his place. This cunning Pundit amassed much wealth and one day took leave of the Raja.

In the meantime the dismissed Court Pundit was beseeched by his colleagues to save them from this misfortune. The senior Pundit volunteered to teach the Raja a lesson by defeating the impostor. This senior Pundit went over to the Raja, in disguise and boasted that there was not one man more learned than himself in the whole world.

"Give us some proof of your wisdom."

"Maharaj! You might have heard the Sloka *Shuklambaradharam.........Shantaye?* Do you know the meaning?"

"Yes, Yes. The first Pundit said it meant Lord Vishnu; the second one who is my Court Pundit now said it meant the rupee-coin."

"Both of them are wrong. It refers to Dahi-Bada, you know—the Bada soaked in curd."

"That seems to be interesting, Punditji. How do you explain it?"

"The rupee-coin is not clothed in white: but the Dahi-bada is. It is actually clothed in curd. It is our protector. It is of the form of the full-moon. It is eaten by the four castes of people. Its very thought makes one joyous. One should therefore meditate upon Dahi-Bada; and eat it regularly."

"Wonderful! Punditji! The other two people were surely wrong. Luckily my second Court Pundit has gone home on leave. I appoint you as my third Court Pundit."

"Well, that man came to loot you; and he has succeeded," said the Pundit and then revealed his identity. "Do you recognise me? I am the friend of your first Court Pundit. He was a wise man. His interpretation of the Sloka alone was correct. The Sloka refers to Maha Vishnu alone. I gave it a twist only in order to please you. But, Maharaja! This won't do. So long as you are ignorant yourself, you will be a pawn in the hands of every praising cunning man. Become wise. Recall the first Court Pundit. Learn the Shastras yourself. Then you will be able to judge for yourself. No one can deceive you."

The Raja was convinced.

Subodh and Vivek learned their first lesson and moved on.

THE FOUR DACOITS

As they walk along the jungle-path early in the morning, they find a Sadhu running along the path: "Death! Worse than death! I am not afraid of a lion or tiger. *But this money, oh the greatest destroyer in the world!*"

Puzzled, they move forward. They find four dacoits with two bags of money, laughing and joking. The chief feels hungry. He sends two of his companions to fetch some food. While the two are away, the chief and his deputy gloat over the prospect of a rich share of the loot. Satan enters their heart: the thought occurs to them that if they do away with the other two, they could get a large share of the money. At the same time, the two who had gone to the bazaar get the very same idea: if the chief and his deputy are killed, they could get all the money to be shared between them. They mix poison in the food that they fetch from the bazaar.

When they return to the hide-out, they place the food in front of the chief and the deputy. Suddenly the chief and the deputy spring upon the other two dacoits and murder them. With doubly gladdened heart at the prospect of a greater share of the money, they fall to eating the food. The poison kills them.

Subodh and Vivek watch this tragedy and pass their way, musing: "Lord Yama is nothing before this killer of the very soul of man—Money!" They learn, money (greed) is the root of all evil.

THE SHASTRI AND THE GENTLEMAN

On another day they are taking rest in a Dharmashala. On the road in front of the Dharmashala, two friends are talking. One is Shastri and the other a fashionable young man. They were obviously once classmates.

"Oh Shastriji! Where are you going?"

"To Calcutta: to attend the Dharma Sammelan. Where are you going?" "I am also going to Calcutta."

"To attend the Sammelan?"

"Oh, you and your Dharma Sammelan. Do you think I am

also an antique like you? No, I am going to attend the International Film Festival. Why don't you give up your old-fashioned outlook and enjoy life? It is only on account of people like you that India is so backward today. Look at America and other Western nations! They are advancing. But you are clinging to your outmoded old traditions. Time is changing; and your views also should change. When your religion, philosophy and outlook on life grow old, you should throw them away."

"H'm! How is your father? How old is he?"

"He is all right. He is eighty-five."

"Old enough to be thrown away. I think?" "What rubbish are you talking, Shastriji?"

The gentleman goes forward to slap Shastriji who runs away in time.

The two Sadhakas watch this in wonderment and move on. They learn that time-honoured traditions have a great intrinsic worth and should not be discarded as old and time-worn.

BLINDED BY CATARACT: BLINDED BY ENVY

When Subodh suffers from coal-dust in his eyes, the two Sadhakas go to a local eye hospital. The doctor is away. They find five eye-patients. They had been operated upon for cataract and been instructed to lie quiet without moving the head. Their eyes are heavily bandaged.

A cat jumps upon the first patient. In an automatic reflex action, he springs up. Then he begins to think: "My God! The doctor told me that if I even moved my head, my eye-sight would be lost for ever. I have sat up. Surely my eye-sight is gone. But why should the man lying next to me be all right? If I am to be blind, he might as well be blind, too." He rudely shakes the next man. He, too, sits up. In this manner all the patients are up and quarreling. The doctor arrives and regrets their action. "You have not only lost your eye-sight, but you have ruined the eye-sight of others, too! What a great foolish thing you have done!"

STATE MOURNING FOR DONKEY

Subodh and Vivek continue their journey and come to a Barber's Shop. They find there several people waiting to have a face-shave. A rich social leader of the place also comes in. While he is having a face-shave, his washerman passes along the road weeping and wailing aloud.

"What is the matter? Why are you weeping?" asks the rich man.

"What shall I say, Sethji? Gandharvasen is dead."

"Who is Gandharvasen?"

The washerman has neither the mood nor the sense to answer calmly: "Oh; Gandharvasen was a great Paropakari. How can I live without Gandharvasen?" And, he went away.

The social leader thought that Gandharvasen, the Paropakari should have been a great Mahatma. "I too, should mourn for the Mahatma," said he and *shaved his head*, too.

As he was returning home, he met the Inspector of Police on the way. The Inspector was surprised to see the mournful face of the leader and questioned him. The Seth replied: "A great calamity, Inspector Saheb! Gandharvasen the Mahatma is dead." The Inspector wanted to follow the example of the Sethji and he, too, had his head shaved.

When, later in the day, he went to see the Raja, he was questioned by the Raja and told him: "Gandharvasen, the Mahatma is dead." The Raja declared State Mourning for the saint and himself put on the mourning dress.

The Queen was intrigued by all this. She asked the Raja: "Who is this Gandharvasen? Is he such a great Mahatma that you should declare state mourning?"

The Raja sent for the Inspector and queried him; the Inspector pleaded ignorance and brought the Sethji; the Sethji, too, did not know and called for the washerman. The washerman cried bitterly in the Court: "Gandharvasen was truly a great soul." When the Raja asked: "Where did the Mahatma live?" the washerman was dismayed and said: "Who said he was a Mahatma? Gandharvasen was my donkey. Oh how can I live without my donkey?" said he and started wailing again. The Raja got furious and rebuked the Sethji and the Police Inspector.

Subodh and Vivek who had been silently watching the episode laughed at the stupid way in which the blind followed the blind and went their way. Ape not others blindly.

THREE STORIES OF THE MAHATMA

A Satsanga was in progress in Rishikesh. Subodh and Vivek joined the gathering. The Guru was discoursing upon Sadhana and Jnana:

Beloved aspirants!

Bhakti is the greatest in this world. A Bhakta is equal, if not superior, to the Lord Himself. I will illustrate this with a story.

The Glory of a Bhakta: There arose a question once: "Who is the greatest person in the universe?" Earth answered first: "It is I, because I hold the entire humanity, besides all the plants and beasts, all the sacred places and holy rivers." Adisesha, the Great Serpent, could not remain silent: "I am greater than Earth; for, I hold the Earth itself on my hood." Lord Siva gave a hearty laugh that shook the universe and said. "And, I wear this serpent around my neck, and so I am greater than Adisesha." Mount Kailas got the turn now and said: "I hold on the crown of my head, Lord Siva and His entire family; I am greater than Lord Siva Himself." Ravana of Lanka roared with his ten mouths: "I uprooted Kailas with my superhuman strength; I am greater than Kailas." Vali, the great monkey, came forward and said: "This little ten-headed beast! I caught him in my arm-pit and gave him to my son as a plaything. I am infinitely greater than Ravana." Now, it was Sri Rama's turn: "Did I not kill Vali with an arrow? I am greater than all others." A humble devotee of Lord Rama who was immersed in Bhava-Samadhi got up from meditation when Sri Rama spoke, and quietly added: "And this Sri Rama is my captive; I have bound Him with the chords of my supreme devotion and imprisoned Him in my heart. How can my prisoner be greater than myself?" No one contradicted the devotee! No one dared to come forward to claim superiority over him. It was agreed on all hands that he was indeed the greatest of all, greater than even the Lord Himself! Such is the glory of Bhakti or supreme devotion to the Lord.

False identification: Due to ignorance man identifies his self with the body, mind and Vital Principle (Prana). Listen to this amusing story of a deluded man. A man addicted to drinking Bhang (*cannabis indica*) used to carry the mortar and pestle with which the intoxicating drink has to be prepared, tied to his waist. One day he was walking along the banks of a river; and the lure of the drink made him halt beneath a tree. He prepared his drink, gulped it down and then after tying the mortar and pestle to his waist went into the drunkard's slumber. Another adorer of Bhang happened to pass that way. He carried Bhang with him and was eager to have a drink, but did not have the mortar and pestle. He saw the vessel tied to the waist of the sleeping drunkard. Quietly he removed the mortar and pestle from the slumberer's waist, prepared the Bhang and drank it; in that mood of intoxication, he could not remember that the instruments belonged to the other man and so tied them around his own waist! After a while, the first drunkard woke up and his eyes fell upon the mortar and pestle tied to the waist of the second drunkard. He began to reflect: "The mortar and pestle were tied to my waist. If that be the truth, then I must be that sleeping person. But, I was wearing a black shawl; and I find a red shawl on that person: if I am the man-with-the-black-shawl, I must be this person. Oh, I am confused. Am I the man-with-mortar-and-pestle or the man-with-the-black-shawl?" He could not solve this riddle, till the intoxication passed off. Then he realised that he was unnecessarily worried over some superficial extraneous factors which did not at all belong to his own self and were mere cloaks and possessions.

Guru's Grace: When a man has forgotten his real identity, and when through wrong identification with the body and mind suffers grief and pain, the Guru awakens him to the nature of his real Self; that is the end of ignorance and its countless evil effects. Listen to this hair-raising story of a Dhobi and a lion.

A Dhobi (washerman) was instructing his son who was washing clothes: "My son! It is nearing nightfall. Get ready to return home. I am very much afraid of night. I am not afraid of tiger or lion; but night makes me sick with fright." A lion was hiding itself in a nearby bush, and it heard the Dhobi's remarks. It mused within itself: "What kind of being is this Night? Judging from this man's remarks, it must be greatly superior in strength to even me, the King of the Jungle." Fear of the Unknown Night crept into its heart.

The Dhobi was searching for his donkey which had not returned home that evening. In the dusk, he could not see clearly; but he espied an animal crouching in the bush. He thought it was his donkey and gave it a couple of good blows with his stick. The lion was confirmed in its fear: "This must be the Mighty Night. Thank God, I am let off with only two blows." It got up and followed him to his house. The Dhobi did not notice it was a lion, but simply tied it in the yard and went to sleep. The lion was greatly worried.

Early in the morning, the Dhobi put a big load of clothes on the back of the lion (It was still dark and so he could not discover it was a lion) and led it to the river. The poor lion meekly followed him. Another lion met this lion on the way and laughed: "What is this that you are doing? Are you not ashamed that, being a lion, you are doing the work of a donkey? Throw away that burden and come with me." But this lion would not: "Brother, you don't know what this terrible creature night would do to me. Keep quiet or it will beat you also." The new lion laughed at this lion's foolishness: "Look, just roar once and see what happens." It did so. The Dhobi looked back; and in the dim light of the dawn he saw the lion. He bolted away without even caring for the cloth-bundle! The two lions bounded away into the forest.

When the Guru thus opens the aspirant's inner eyes to his real nature, delusion vanishes and with it, fear and grief, too.

Subodh and Vivek rejoice at this opportunity given to them to attend the Satsang. They recollect that Guru Purnima was nearing, and so return to the Ashram of their Guru.

The Guru explains to the two disciples the moral of all the incidents. Before reforming others, reform yourself. Before attempting to judge others, acquire the Highest Knowledge yourself. Only then will you know what is good and what is evil. You cannot know by proxy! You have to do your own Sadhana, become wise yourself.

You have understood the untold misery that money brings upon man. Money is Maya's most powerful weapon: the other is lust. Maya has put a few drops of sweetness in a potful of the most virulent poison—wealth and lust. Man is tempted by those few drops of sweetness, drinks the poison and courts endless sufferings. Remember: death kills only your body. Lust and wealth (greed) go much deeper and blacken your very soul. It will take several lifetimes to retrieve the purity of your soul.

They make you an animal. And God, finding that you have not deserved the glorious human birth He has granted you, will throw you in lower births to wallow in the filth of sense-indulgence, till His Mercy again grants you a human birth. If you wish to tread the Path of the Good, shun lust and wealth.

Do not belittle our ancient spiritual culture. Modern materialistic civilisation has brought nothing but disharmony, misery, poverty and universal unhappiness, and has only transformed man into worse than a beast. Do not be carried away by the external glitter of science. The ancient Rishis were our real well-wishers. We even now claim ancestry to one or the other of these great ones; yet we take pride in decrying their wholesome teachings. This is not conducive to our welfare. Materialistic science can never bring about our real welfare and prosperity.

What did you learn from the mad behaviour of the eye patients? The low bestial levels to which man has descended. He cannot bear to see anyone rise higher than himself, anyone shine better than himself, anyone more prosperous than himself. He will strive more for harming others than for promoting his own welfare. A beautiful ancient utterance comes to my mind: "He is a great man who does good to others at the cost of his own welfare. He is a human being who does good to others without jeopardising his own welfare. He is a devil in human garb who harms others for his own good. He who harms others to no purpose—what to call this man we do not know!" A large section of today's humanity belongs to this last abominable class. Is it difficult to understand what the condition would be when everyone is intent on harming everyone else? There could only be chaos and misery everywhere; and that is what we find in the world today.

And, the wonder of wonders is: no one stops to think even for a moment! Everyone follows everyone; each man tries to outshine his neighbour; every man follows the beaten track, blindly without bestowing a thought whether he is doing the right thing or not! A young man goes to school because his father went to school, and because his neighbour goes to school. He seeks employment because everyone seeks employment. He gets married because his father, grandfather and great grandfather got married. He earns wealth because everyone does so! He wastes his life because he does not know what else to do! Life to him has come to mean being born, begetting children, growing old, and so to the grave. This is just as we have in the story that when Gandharvasen is dead, one after another, up to the King everyone observes mourning! But the real seeker is not like that. He will halt every step and think. He is reflective. He does Vichara and gains Viveka. Then, he abandons the worldly life and embraces the spiritual life. He is a wise man.

This Sadhaka takes to the practice of devotion; for, as we have seen in the story of the search for the greatest person, even the Lord is the real devotee's own!

When devotion and Viveka grow apace in the Sadhaka, he discovers that he had so long been wrongly identifying himself with illusory covering sheaths—viz., the body, the Prana, the mind, etc. He has an intellectual conception of his essential nature and of the nature of delusion that obstructs the realisation of this essential nature. That is what we learn from the story of the Bhang-eaters.

Lastly, we learn from the story of two lions that the grip of nescience over us is so strong and powerful, like the lion's dread of Mysterious Night, that it needs a Guru, another lion, to point out to us our own essential nature and to stand by as our support and guide while we roar "Sivoham, Satchidananda Swarupoham." The load of miseries and grief, of delusion and despair, that we have so long been carrying—as the lion was carrying the Dhobi's clothes—will drop away from us as we leap forward to reach our native Abode of Bliss!

Children! Having successfully been through these soul-awakening experiences and having acquired a thorough knowledge of the nature of the world and the nature of spiritual life, you are really fit for initiation into the Mysterious Atma-Jnana! Come, I will initiate you into the Holy Order of Sannyas. And I pray to my Gurudev H.H. Sri Swami Sivanandaji Maharaj to shower his blessings on you and bestow on you strength of will and enduring discrimination that will take you to the Realms of Immortal Bliss!

APPENDIX—II
A GARLAND OF PRECEPTS IN SADHANA

FOUNDATIONS OF THE LIFE DIVINE

1. When the mind is dull, rouse it by Kirtan; when it is distracted, bring it back to calmness through Pranayama, worship and meditation; when it becomes attached, get it detached through dispassion and discrimination.

2. Do not indulge in worldly talks. By talking on sensual things, mind becomes sensually disposed. Talk always of spiritual matters and God. Go back to the Source. You will attain Immortality and Bliss Eternal. That Source is Parabrahman or the Absolute.

THE DISCIPLINE OF DETACHMENT

3. If you wish to obtain God-realisation, the control of the unruly emotions is of paramount importance. Do not identify yourself with your emotions. By this non-identification, the spirit of detachment is achieved.

4. When the attraction towards external objects ceases you will attain peace. The mind will become firm and steady and you will have wonderful power of concentration.

5. By this power of concentration your will becomes one with the Divine Will, and you will be no more attached to your body, your wife, your children, your property, your country, to the manifold forms of empirical experience.

6. Attachment, aversion and delusion are the roots of evil and suffering. Pains will not, in the least, affect those wise men who regard as a mere paltry bubble all the perishable objects of the world.

7. Detachment is the freeing of ourselves from that to which we are attached. Freedom of detachment is freedom from attachment. Generate the thoughts of the Divine, and stand above the turmoil of life and the trifles of the earth.

PRACTICE OF YOGA SADHANA

8. A long discipline and an intense struggle have con-

ferred upon Saints and Sages, the power of seeing that Reality which the worldly people cannot see. Therefore, take to strenuous spiritual discipline.

9. The practice of Yoga will strengthen your character and help you to gain mastery over any circumstances by facing them fairly and solving them honestly.

10. Constant remembrance of the Lord, constant recitation of His Name, will fill your heart with Sattva or purity and immense strength and peace to face the most trying conditions of life with perfect calmness and serenity.

11. Yoga-practice purifies the mind and bestows insight. Equality with all and even-mindedness is Yoga.

THE EASIEST FORM OF SADHANA

12. Japa is the best of all spiritual practices in this modern age. It is the easiest too. Make the repetition of the Divine Name the sheet-anchor and prop of your life.

13. Om Tat Sat is the most excellent of Mantras. One becomes a Siddha by Japa of this Mantra, Om Tat Sat. By repetition of this Mantra one becomes the conqueror of death.

14. That which one attained through meditation in Satya Yuga (the golden age), through sacrifice in Treta Yuga (silver age) and through worship in the Dvapara Yuga (bronze age) is attained in the Kali Yuga (iron age) by reciting the Names of the Lord.

QUALIFICATIONS OF ASPIRANTS

15. Those who have realised that the sensual pleasures of this world are transitory, illusory, hollow and worthless are fit for the spiritual path.

16. Real aspirants, who thirst for Self-realisation, should be absolutely honest in every dealing.

17. The aspirant in the path of Yoga should be humble, simple, gentle, refined, tolerant, merciful and kind.

18. Unflinching faith puts the aspirant in touch with the Infinite.

19. A man of patience, perseverance and iron-will alone can tread the spiritual path.

20. Without burning renunciation and burning desire for liberation, the other practices, viz., Sama, Dama, Titiksha, etc.,

may be swept off by a strong impulse of passion or some strong blind attachment.

21. A student of Bhakti Yoga should possess abundant pure emotion, a student of Jnana Yoga should possess abundant serenity, calmness or tranquillity and a student of Karma Yoga should learn to merge his heart in others.

22. The aspirant should be free from hope, desire and greed.

23. He who is steadfast and balanced in pleasure and pain, is the fittest person for attaining Immortality.

24. Just as the coloured water penetrates freely and nicely in a piece of cloth when it is pure white, so also the instruction of a sage can penetrate and settle down in the hearts of the aspirants only when their minds are calm, when there are no desires for enjoyment and when the impurities of their minds are destroyed.

25. That man who is sweet, kind, free from irritability, who is adaptable, humble, who knows the science of how to enter into the hearts of others (through constant service with love and humility) can be happy and peaceful.

26. He who ignores his pleasures and comforts and tries to help others always is really an advanced student in the path of spirituality.

27. There must be unshaken faith in God during trials, disappointments and difficulties. Hope and help come from within when one feels utterly helpless.

28. Perfect mental detachment, rigorous self-discipline, perfect self-restraint are essential for the attainment of the *summum bonum*.

29. A qualified aspirant is one, who has purified himself by selfless service and who has controlled his senses, who has faith in the words of his Guru and scriptures and who has acquired the four means of salvation.

30. Righteousness, frankness, amiable disposition, kindness, benevolence, service and mercy are the foremost qualifications of an aspirant.

31. Immortality and eternal bliss are not the fruits of a happy-go-lucky spirit of adventure. Eternal and unremitting vigilance and intense self-effort are necessary.

32. He who possesses physical, mental, moral and

spiritual strength, is an ideal soul. He can easily achieve success in the spiritual path.

33. The desire to know Brahman springs only in the person whose mind is pure, who is free from desires and who, freed from deeds in this birth and in the previous ones, becomes disgusted with external ephemeral perishable objects.

34. If a Yogi is not careful, if a Yogi is not well-established in the preliminary practices of Yama and Niyama, he is unconsciously swept away from his ideal by temptations, Mara or Satan.

35. A gross mind with selfishness and lust is absolutely unfit for spiritual life.

36. Hatred is the deadliest foe of an aspirant, whereas love is the pivot of his spiritual life.

37. Aspirants do not make any progress in the spiritual path, because fault-finding nature is ingrained in them.

38. In one whose nature is corrupt and whose controlling faculties are weak, progress in the spiritual line is very hard and intuition is sluggish.

SENSE-CONTROL AND SELF-PURIFICATION

39. Self-purification is the passport to the glorious foreign land of Eternal Bliss. Divine Life is not possible without self-control and self-purification. Self-control augments energy, vitality, vigour and mental strength.

40. Just as you can clearly see the bottom of a lake, when the ripples and waves on the surface subside, even so you can cognise your real Self, when the modifications of the mind subside.

41. Purity of mind leads to perfection. There must be constant endeavour to keep the mind ever pure. You will have to check the rising Vrittis of the mind and keep them under your control.

42. Service to Guru, Sadhus, poor and the sick persons, is a sure remedy or sovereign specific for rapid purification of oneself. Kind charitable acts with Bhava are of paramount importance for the purification of heart for the evolution in the spiritual path.

43. Keep your Pranas and senses under your control with the help of the intellect strengthened by Sattva.

44. Renunciation of desire, control of breath and right enquiry will counteract the actions of the mind and consequently check the rise of passion and illusion.

45. Do rigorous Tapas. There is nothing more powerful than Tapas to curb the turbulent Indriyas. By constant Tapas, Indriyas become weak and eventually subside.

46. A piece of iron remains red-hot so long as it is kept in fire. When it is taken out, it becomes cold, and loses its red colour. If you want to keep it always red-hot you must always keep it in the fire. Even so, if you want to taste the Divine Consciousness always, you must keep the mind under perfect control. You must dissolve and melt it in the spiritual fire of Brahman.

47. Purify yourself. Silence the bubbling senses. Quiet the mind. Silence the thoughts. Still the outgoing tendencies or energies of the mind.

48. It is very easy to control the mind if you know the right technique. You must have strong faith in God. Analyse your mind and your own nature. Watch your Vrittis and pray. Study your own nature and defects and try to remove them by suitable methods.

49. Discipline the Indriyas. Keep them under perfect control. Subjugate them through Viveka and Vairagya. Lead the life of a Sannyasi at home. Train yourself to hardships and sufferings. Reduce your wants. Do not spend much on your personal expenses. Make the mind free from egoism, desire, craving, attachment. You will attain self-purification.

50. There are two ways for the control of mind, viz., one is Yoga through shutting up the outgoing tendencies of the mind and the other is Jnana through Brahma-Vichara. For some Yoga is favourable. For others Jnana is favourable. It depends upon the taste, temperament and capacity of the Sadhaka. It depends upon pecuniary matters also. He who has a permanent residence, food and other Yogic requisites can practise Yoga. He who is a Virakta and leads a wandering life can have the Vichara, i.e., enquiry.

51. Ram! your mind is still raw and crude. It needs thorough overhauling and drastic regeneration. It is still full of worldly thought-waves and mundane vibrations. Beware. Be vigilant and circumspect. Awake. Be careful. Be on the alert.

52. Never give indulgence or leniency to the mind. Spare the rod and spoil the child. You will have to punish it for every

serious mistake it does, and keep the organs at their proper places. Do not allow them to move an inch. Raise the rod of Viveka, whenever any organ tries to raise its head. By practice get sense-control or self-purification.

OBSTACLES IN SADHANA

53. The spiritual path is thorny, rugged, precipitous, steep and slippery. But it is nothing for a man who has virtuous qualities and a Brahma Nishtha Guru to guide him.

54. The spiritual path is doubtless beset with various difficulties. It is the razor path. You will fall down several times, but you will have to rise up quickly and walk again with more zeal, boldness and cheerfulness. Every stumbling block will become a stepping-stone to success or ascent in the hill of spiritual knowledge.

55. Every aspirant will have to face various sorts of difficulties in the spiritual path. You need not be discouraged. Muster all your strength and courage and march afresh in the path with redoubled vigour and energy.

56. If worldly thoughts try to enter the mind, reject them. Have steady devotion to the spiritual path.

57. Depression, doubt and fear are some of the main obstacles even for an advanced student in the spiritual path. They should be removed by right enquiry and good association.

58. Sometimes depression will come and trouble you. The mind will revolt. The senses will pull your legs. The undercurrent of Vasanas will gush to the surface of the mind and torment you. Sensuous thoughts will agitate the mind and try to overwhelm you. Be bold. Stand adamant. Face these passing obstacles. Do not identify yourself with these obstacles. Increase your period of Japa. All these obstacles will pass away.

59. Doubt or uncertainty is a great obstacle in the path of Self-realisation. It bars the spiritual progress. This must be removed by good company, study of religious books, right thinking and right reasoning. It should be killed beyond resurrection by certainty of conviction and firm unshakable faith based on reasoning.

60. The Vasanas are very powerful. The senses and mind are very turbulent and impetuous. Again and again the

battle must be fought and won. That is the reason why the spiritual path is called the razor path. There is no difficulty for a man of strong determination and iron-will even in the razor path.

61. Passion is lurking in you. It is the deadliest enemy of a spiritual aspirant. From passion proceed anger and other evil qualities, which destroy the spiritual wealth of an aspirant.

62. Leakage of energy, hidden under-current of Vasanas, lack of sense-control, slackness in Sadhana, waning of dispassion, lack of intense aspiration, irregularity in Sadhana—are the various obstacles in the path of Self-realisation.

63. Overloading the stomach, work that produces fatigue or overwork, too much talking, taking heavy food at night, too much mixing with people are obstacles for a spiritual aspirant.

64. Give up arguing. Become silent. Do not indulge in sundry talks and miscellaneous thoughts just to ease the mind. Be serious. Think and talk of God and God alone.

65. Desire for power will act like puffs of air which may blow out the lamp of spirituality that is being carefully tended. Any slackness in feeding it due to carelessness or selfish desires for Siddhis will blow out the little spiritual light that the Yogi has kindled after so much struggle and will hurl the student down into the deep abyss of ignorance. Temptations are simply waiting to overwhelm the unwary student. Temptations of the astral, mental and Gandharva worlds are more powerful than the earthly temptations.

66. Various psychic Siddhis and other powers come to the Yogin who has controlled the senses, Prana and mind. But these are all hindrances to realisation. They are stumbling blocks.

67. Stop the Vrittis. Still the mind. Overcome the Vrittis that rise up from the bed of impressions. Face all the obstacles boldly and come out victoriously with the crown of success, i.e., Self-realisation.

EGOISM—THE SEED FOR BIRTH AND DEATH

68. Egoism is the most dangerous weakness of man. It brings downfall to the spiritual aspirant.

69. On account of egoism, one thinks that he does everything and so he is bound.

70. The moment egoism comes in, there will be immediate blocking to the free flow of the Divine Energy.

71. It is under the influence of egoism that man commits evils and wrong actions.

72. Ego is a mysterious gas which evaporates into nothingness for an enquirer but appears like a granite rock for a man of indiscrimination and worldliness, which cannot be blown out even by dynamite and atomic bombs.

73. One can become a Jivanmukta by annihilating the egoism and the two currents of attraction and repulsion, likes and dislikes, and by identifying oneself with Brahman.

74. Humility is a bomb of infinite potency which can only destroy the invincible citadel of egoism.

75. Practice of Ahimsa is really the practice of killing of egoism.

76. He who neither desires nor dislikes anything, who preserves the serenity of his mind at all times is not affected by the feeling of egoism.

77. Those who are free from egoism have nothing to gain by doing what is declared good, nor have anything to lose by doing an improper act or acting to the contrary.

78. A desire to know one's own Self, to attain liberation, to lead a virtuous life, is born of Sattvic ego.

DESIRE—THE ROOT-CAUSE OF ALL MISERIES

79. Desire is the enemy of peace. Desire is the enemy of devotion. Desire is the enemy of wisdom. Sexual desire is the most powerful of all desires. Kill this desire ruthlessly through dispassion, discrimination, enquiry of 'Who am I?' and regular meditation and attain Immortality and eternal bliss.

80. Desire is the cause for rebirths and all sorts of pains, miseries and sorrows. It is desire that creates various sorts of Sankalpas or thoughts, fancies and imagination.

81. Desires are innumerable, insatiable and unconquerable. Enjoyment cannot bring in satisfaction, but strengthens, increases and aggravates the desires.

82. Craving generates ego-consciousness. From ego-consciousness arise name and form, mind and body. From name and form arise the senses. From the senses arises contact. From contact arises sensation. From sensation arises grasping. From grasping comes birth. From birth arise old age, death, grief, sorrow, pain. These cravings are a mass of pain. Quench this flame of craving through dispassion, renunciation,

self-restraint and meditation on the pure, all-blissful Brahman or the Self within.

83. The Lord is attained by annihilation of desires. Desire leads to attachment. Desire is the cause of rebirth. Shatter this network of desires and hopes and thus clean the mind. Fix the pure mind on the Supreme Self and attain the blissful seat of eternal bliss.

84. The mind is bound to the earth by its desires and freed by its freedom from earthly attractions and expectations. It is the desire in the mind that causes attraction towards objects and brings about bondage.

85. He who is free from desires alone reigns supreme, be he a king or a beggar. One who has many desires is really a most miserable being on this earth.

86. Wherever there is desire, there is world. Destruction of desires is the state of bliss, for a desireless man is the mightiest king, who can command even the elements.

87. Desire to know Brahman is the fulfilment of all desires.

88. Desires for powers will act like puffs of air which may blow out the lamp of Yoga that is being carefully tended.

89. You will not be benefited much, even if the Kundalini is awakened when subtle desires, subtle attachments and ties, personal desires, ambitions, etc., remain in the subconscious mind. Rather you will have a downfall.

90. Serenity can be attained by the eradication of desires.

91. The mind is ever vibrating. The vibration is sometimes low and at other times high. The degree or rate of vibration generates the sensation of heat or cold, pleasure or pain.

92. Weary is the round of births and deaths. Extinguish the fire of desire through dispassion, discrimination, renunciation and meditation on the Lord. You will soon attain the abode of eternal joy.

THE THREE PRINCIPAL ENEMIES

93. Triple are the gateways to the abyss of hell: Lust, anger and greed. A wise man should eradicate these and take to the path of evolution.

94. There is no fire like lust, no evil like anger, no vice like hatred and no sword like abuse.

95. To look lustfully is the adultery of the eyes; to hear

anything that excites passion is adultery of the ears; to speak anything that excites passion is adultery of the tongue.

96. He who indulges much in sensual pleasures, who has an uncontrolled mind, who is immoderate in his food and who is idle will soon come to destruction.

97. To eradicate any evil habit or tea habit which has taken possession of a man only a few months back, man finds it extremely difficult. Then what to speak of the powerful and age-long internal enemies of man, viz., lust, anger and greed. It is only by constant practice of dispassion that one can conquer the mind, which is the seat of these vices.

98. Sex-attraction, sexual thoughts, sexual urge are the three great obstacles in the path of God-realisation. Even if the sexual urge vanishes, the sex-attraction remains for a long time and troubles the aspirants. The organ of sight does great mischief. Destroy the lustful look, the adultery of the eye. Try to see God in all faces. Again and again generate the currents of dispassion, discrimination and enquiry. Eventually you will be established in Brahman or the Eternal. Again and again generate sublime divine thoughts and increase your Japa and meditation. The sexual thoughts will be annihilated.

99. Lust cannot take hold of the man who has real discrimination, dispassion and faith in the words of Guru and Scriptures.

100. Repetition of sexual act intensifies the sexual craving and then annihilation becomes difficult.

101. Passion makes one beggar of beggars.

102. One cannot sacrifice a noble ideal, Self-realisation for the sake of pleasing a bewitching woman. What a pity! O man, open your eyes now! Behold the utter vanity of the world. Everything is transitory, except the All-pervading Brahman. Know this and be wise. Know Him and be happy for ever.

103. Wherever there is Kama, there is no Rama. Wherever there is Rama, there is no Kama.

104. Lust should be checked at all costs. Not a single disease comes by checking passion. On the contrary you will get immense power, joy and peace. There are also effective methods to control the lust. One should reach the Atman which is beyond nature by going against nature. Just as a fish swims against the upstream in a river, so also you will have to move against the worldly currents of evil forces.

105. After checking lust you will enjoy real bliss from within, from Atman. Throughout the Gita, the one ringing note that arrests the imagination and mind of the readers is that the man who has calmed his passion is the most happy man in this world.

106. It is also very, very easy to control the lust, which is your deadliest enemy if you take this subject very seriously and apply yourself to spiritual Sadhana whole-heartedly with a single-minded devotion and concentration. Dietetic discipline is of paramount importance. Take Sattvic food. Do self-enquiry. Do meditation on the divine form and divine attributes such as Omnipotence, Omnipresence and Omniscience, etc. Do not look at ladies with a lustful heart. Look at your toes, when you walk along the streets and meditate on the form of your deity.

107. Avoid looking at ladies with evil thoughts. Entertain Atmic Bhav or the Bhav of mother, sister or Devi. You may fail many times. Again and again try to realise this Bhav. Whenever the mind runs towards beautiful ladies with lustful thoughts have a definite, clear-cut photo in the mind of the flesh, bone, urine and faecal matter of which the body of ladies is composed. This will induce dispassion in the mind. You will not commit again the sin of unchaste look at a woman.

108. Inflict self-punishment if the mind runs towards ladies with a lustful look. Give up night meals. Do twenty Malas of Japa more.

109. Anger is a modification of passion. If you can control lust you have already controlled anger. Control of anger will bring in its train supreme peace and immense joy.

110. Anger is a modification that arises from the mind-lake when the Gunas, Rajas and Tamas predominate. It is a wave of unpleasant feeling that arises from the Antahkarana, when one gets displeased with another. It is the formidable enemy of peace, knowledge and devotion.

111. Anger begets eight kinds of vices. All evil qualities and actions proceed from anger. If you can eradicate anger, all bad qualities will die by themselves. The eight vices are injustice, rashness, persecution, jealousy, taking possession of others' property, killing, harsh words and cruelty.

112. From anger arises delusion, therefrom confusion of memory, from confusion of memory loss of reason, reason gone, the man is destroyed.

113. In the light of modern psychology all diseases take their origin in anger. Rheumatism, heart-diseases, nervous diseases are all due to anger.

114. Too much loss of semen is the chief cause for irritability and anger. Passion is the root and anger the stem. You will have to destroy the root passion first. Then the stem of anger will die by itself.

115. The root-cause of anger is ignorance and egoism. Through Vichara or right enquiry, egoism should be removed.

116. If an aspirant has controlled anger, half of his Sadhana is over. Control of anger means control of lust also. Control of anger is really control of mind. He who has controlled anger cannot do any wrong or evil action. He is always just.

117. Whenever there is a little irritability stop all conversation and observe Mouna or the vow of silence. Practice of Mouna daily for one or two hours is of great help in controlling anger. Always try to speak sweet or soft words.

118. You must try to remain cool even under the most provocative conditions. If you are hungry and if you suffer from any disease, you generally become more irritable. You should control your anger.

119. Do not identify yourself with the Vritti of anger. When a wave of anger arises in the mind-lake, stand as a witness of the Vritti. Identify yourself with the Self. Stand as a spectator of the mental menagerie.

120. Be careful in the selection of your company. Have congenial company. Move with Sannyasins, Bhaktas and Mahatmas. Do not waste your semen. Give up intoxicant drinks. Do not take tobacco.

121. Even if you are a man of great erudition you must be free from greed.

122. Control of tongue is more difficult than the control of sex-Indriya.

123. One cannot become master of his organs until he controls the organ of taste.

SELFISHNESS—A DEADLY VICE

124. Selfishness is the source of all vices. It is born of ignorance. A selfish man is greedy and unrighteous. He is far from God. He will do anything to attain his ends. He injures others, robs their property and does many sinful actions to satisfy

his selfishness. He has neither scruples nor character. Peace of mind is unknown to him.

125. Man lives in vain if he is selfish and miserly. Man lives in vain if he has not got a generous heart, if he has no mercy and sympathy, if he does not lead a life of virtue, austerity and meditation and if he does not help and serve religious institutions and religious teachers with uniform and artless courtesy and devotion.

126. Selfishness retards spiritual progress. If anyone can destroy his selfishness, half of his spiritual Sadhana is over. No Samadhi or meditation is possible without eradication of this undesirable negative quality. Aspirants should direct their whole attention in the beginning towards the removal of this dire malady by protracted selfless and disinterested service.

127. A selfish man is unrighteous. Attachment and separateness are present in him to a remarkable degree. He cannot develop those qualities which Yoga needs. A desire to become a Yogi and to learn Yoga can only arise in a man who is free from selfishness, who is righteous, and who has a religious disposition.

128. Selfishness constricts the heart and forces a man to do injury to others and to get hold of the property of others by foul means. It is selfishness that prompts a man to do evil acts.

129. Through selfishness you have created a boundary wall only round the members of your family. You always think: "Let my family-members duly prosper. Let us only be happy. Why should I bother about the welfare of others?"

130. Do not be much intimate with anybody nor be wanting in friendship. Too much of everything is bad. Therefore always follow the golden medium.

CARDINAL PRINCIPLES OF PRACTICAL SADHANA

131. Be a little more patient, a little more forgiving, a little more charitable, a little more loving, and a little more devoted to the service of your Guru.

132. Mind needs the soap of wisdom to wash off the dust of illusion. Cultivate good habits. Old evil habits will vanish.

133. Love never fails. Love does not envy. Love suffers long. Love is kind. Love is not puffed up. Love is the greatest power on this earth. Love unites. Love always gives. Love never bargains.

134. The life of a student must be a period of intense Tapas, dedication to the building of character through self-discipline, devotion and purity.

135. You cannot attain God-realisation, if there is the slightest trace of pride, desire and egoism.

136. All diversities, all differences, all distinctions are utterly false because they are born out of illusion.

137. Without the cloud, where is the rain; without the rain, where is the grain; without the seed, where is the flower; without the grace of the Lord, where is bliss; without meditation, where is peace?

138. Within you is the key to every problem, the wisdom to guide you in every situation and the strength to rise to magnanimous heights of divine splendour and glory.

139. In the cultivation of the cosmic love is individual spiritual progress, the welfare of the community and the peace of the whole world. Set to work, therefore, and spread its gospel of cosmic love throughout the whole world.

140. Love is the essential quality of the Spirit in man. It is the condition prerequisite to his entering into the Kingdom of Heaven or the supreme abode of immortal bliss.

141. Love is dynamic. It always expresses itself through untiring selfless service.

THE INNER SPIRITUAL DISCIPLINE

142. Understand the mind; study the mind, and know its ways thoroughly. Learn to manage it, to control it, to conquer it. He who has controlled the serpent mind will reach the dominion of Moksha or Eternal Bliss.

143. By constant practice and sustained Vairagya, the victory over the mind is established. This conquest is not a matter for a few days or a few months.

144. Withdraw the senses from their objects. Collect the rays of the mind. Direct the mind towards the Ajna Chakra, the space between the two eyebrows and fix it there steadily.

145. Moksha means nothing but the destruction of the impurities of the mind. If the mind is destroyed by dint of discrimination, then Maya will not affect you.

146. Tame the mind. Collect all your thoughts. Keep the mind serene. Think not of evil. You will enter the realm of deathlessness.

JNANA YOGA SADHANA

147. 'Svarupa' means your real Sat-chit-anandatvam. The goal of life is to realise your real Svarupa. Realisation of one's own real Self is termed as *Svarupa Sakshatkara*. This can be achieved through Viveka and Vichara. Viveka is the discrimination between real and unreal, permanent and impermanent, sentient and insentient (*Atman* and *Anatman*). Vichara is the right enquiry: "Who am I? What is my real Svarupa? What is Atman?"

148. The knowledge that you get from college cannot give you peace of mind. It is mere husk. Ask for that instruction, my child, by which the unheard becomes heard, the unperceived becomes perceived and the unknown becomes known. Then only will you get real knowledge.

149. What is the use of reading too many Vedantic books, Chitsukhi, Khandana-Khanda-Khadyam, etc.? They will intoxicate you and get you out of the way. There is much Vedantic gossiping nowadays; no real practical Vedanta. People talk of unity, oneness and Samata (equality) but fight for a little useless thing. They are full of Irshya and Dvesha. They are extremely mean and narrow. I cannot imagine, I am stunned.

150. Why do you read many books? It is of no use. The great Book is within you in your heart. Open the pages of this inexhaustible Book, the source of all knowledge. You will know everything. Close your eyes. Withdraw the senses. Still the mind. Silence the thoughts. Make the mind waveless. Merge deep in the Atman, the Supreme Soul, the Light of lights, the Sun of suns. The whole knowledge will be revealed to you. You will have intuitional knowledge, Divine Wisdom, by direct perception, Sakshatkara. Doubts will vanish. All mental torments will disappear. All hot discussions, heated debates, will terminate now. Peace and Jnana alone will remain.

151. The world is a mental *Jaalam* (jugglery), *Bhrama* (mere appearance) and *Deergha Svapna* (long dream). You are Vyapaka Atman (Spirit). Be established in this one idea.

152. Vedanta must enter your bones, nerves, cells and interior chambers of the heart. Moha in its various forms either for son, wife, daughter or the so-called intimate friends or thick chums or bosom comrades, must be ruthlessly cut asunder. Whatever you have—physical, mental, moral and spiritual possessions—must be shared with all. This is real Vedanta. I do

not believe in lip Vedanta. This is pure hypocrisy. Even a little of real, practical Vedanta will elevate a man quickly and make him immortal (*Amara*) and fearless (*Nirbhaya*).

153. Get by heart the Slokas of the Isavasya Upanishad. This is for your daily Svadhyaya. This is a wonderful Upanishad. Repeat the Slokas during meditation also.

154. You will have to destroy the Jiva Bhava by entertaining an opposite 'Aham Brahma Asmi' Bhava. The Jiva Bhava is created by the Vyavaharika Buddhi. You will have to destroy this kind of Vyavaharika Buddhi by developing the Suddha Buddhi or pure reason.

155. You will get real rest only by resting in the Atman or Supreme Self that shines in your heart through meditation. The rest that you get by lying in an easy chair or from rolling in the bed is no rest at all.

156. I believe in practical Vedanta. I believe in solid spiritual practice. I believe in thorough overhauling of worldly nature, worldliness of various sorts. We should become absolutely fearless. That is the sign of life in Atman. No more words. No more talk. No more arguments, heated debates or discussions. No more study. No more wandering. Live in OM. Live in truth. Live in one place. Enter the silence. Become a Maha Mouni. Maha Mouna is Brahman. There is Peace. Peace is silence.

157. There is within easy reach, within the heart, the comforting ocean of nectar (Brahman), for those who are suffering from the fire of three kinds of Taapa. They will have to tap the source through Sravana, Manana and Nididhyasana and drink the nectar of immortality.

158. Raise thyself by thyself. Introspect thyself by thyself. Analyse thyself by thyself. Examine thyself by thyself. Purify thyself by thyself. Bridle thyself by thyself. Realise thyself by thyself. For Self is the Supreme Lord of thy little self. Self is the sole refuge, source and support.

159. All feet are the feet of Lord Virat, Lord Vishnu. Feel this. You will have realisation this very moment. Struggle hard.

160. Feel the Indwelling Presence (Antaratman). Be true to the Indweller of our hearts (Antaryami). Remember OM. Soham. Live in Truth. Live in OM. You are Vyapaka Atman. Everything is Atman (*Atmaiva Idam*)—Aitareya Upanishad.

161. Understand your real, essential Atmic nature through Viveka and Vichara. Get rid of the three Bhavanas—Samsaya Bhavana, Asambhavana and Viparita Bhavana—entirely. This is Jnana Abhyasa. Rest in Sahaja Avastha now and realise the fruit of the Jnana Abhyasa. You are now a Jivanmukta (liberated soul).

162. Understand the Eternal Law, the Grand Plan, the Highest Law. Know and feel the Immortal Place, your Original Abode, OM, Atman, Brahman or the Divine Source. Drive the mind back to its Original Home by Sama, Dama, Pratyahara, Dharana, Dhyana and Samadhi.

163. Disconnect yourself from the five senses. Leave the five. Rise above the five. Destroy the five (fetters). Withdraw yourself from the five, by meditating on the Divine Essence that is hidden in the chambers of the heart. These five are illusory superimpositions on account of ignorance. They are the five jugglers of Maya. They are mere false appearances like snake in the rope, water in mirage. That which gives light and power to these five is Self or pure consciousness. That is your own Self. Self is the Indriya of Indriyas, Eye of eyes. Know thyself and be free, my child.

164. I know you have already understood the above point well. I know this. Yet let me remind you again. The force of Maya, the force of Avidya and Moha is very great. You very often forget the Atmic idea or Atmic Bhava. Frequent hammering on the mind is very necessary.

165. This alone is your duty. For this alone you have taken this body. All other duties are only mental creations (Kalpana). You have no duties to perform. You have no responsibilities. You are already free. You are ever free. You are Nitya Mukta. There is neither bondage nor freedom for you. There is neither birth nor death for you. The names and forms are not in you. You are in reality the all-pervading Essence, the Light of lights.

166. *"Tat Tvam Asi*—Thou art That." You are all-pervading Atman. You are the Immortal Soul. Realise the Self by meditation. Mind cheats and tempts you. Destroy this powerful enemy—mind.

167. Repetition of OM (Pranava Japa) with meaning and Bhava is one method of Nirguna meditation. Hear the other method. It is the Sakshi method. You separate yourself from the

outside objects and the various Vrittis inside. You become the Sakshi of the Vrittis. You can work also during practice of this kind of Sadhana. Repeat constantly *"Om Sakshi. Om Sakshi."*

168. Think that all bodies are yours. Do not have any particular attachment for your body. Do not confine yourself to one particular body alone. Say, "All bodies are mine." Expand. Identify yourself with the Cosmic Virat. This is the first step in Vedantic Sadhana. This is Sthula expansion.

169. Identify yourself with Hiranyagarbha (Cosmic Prana). This is the second stage in expansion (*Sukshma*). Identify yourself with Isvara, the sum total of all Karana Sariras. Finally identify yourself with Brahman which transcends Virat, Hiranyagarbha and Isvara. Melt the gross in the Sukshma, Sukshma in the Karana, and the Karana in Atman or Brahman. This is *Laya Krama*.

170. *"Tat Tvam Asi*—That thou art." You are Brahman. Be established in this one idea, though you are a poor clerk in any office. The latter idea is a mental creation. Be cheerful always. Be fearless (Abhaya). You are diferent from body and mind. Separate and remove your Atman from the five Kosas just as you draw the reed from the *Munja* grass.

171. There is a hidden, true treasure in Atman or Supreme Self that shines in the chambers of your heart. Search. It is in your heart. Before you start the search, you must give up Kamini-Kanchana (sex and wealth). You can hardly worship mammon and God at the same time.

172. Do not forget the Atman. Do unselfish, pure, virtuous deeds. Restrain the Indriyas. Walk in the path of righteousness according to the laws of Manu. Then you will become peaceful, strong and powerful. You will become a beacon light, a brilliant spiritual star.

173. I see nothing but God (Narayana) everywhere, within and without, above and below, and all around. Change your Drishti also and mental attitude. You will have heaven here. Be sure of this.

174. In stillness feel the Atman. In activity manifest the Atmic glory and Santi. Remain unruffled amidst troubles and tribulations. Stand firm as a rock. A Jnani has adamantine firmness. Your life and meditation should become one. Life should tally nicely with your meditation.

175. How can you realise the Self (Atman)? By Satyam, Tapas, Samyag-Jnana and Brahmacharya.

176. If you go above the body-consciousness, if you can abandon the body idea and if the mind rests in the Atman, then doubtless you are *Sukhi, Santa* and *Mukta* (happy, peaceful and free).

177. Say boldly—"I am God. I am Brahman." Assert. This is your birthright. Do not be afraid, my child. Stand up. Realise. Proclaim the Truth. Make others realise the Truth. Help them.

178. When you repeat the Mahavakya 'Aham Brahma Asmi,' do not take the physical body or Ahankara (self-arrogating principle) as Brahman. The Sakshi or Pratyag-Atman must be taken as Brahman. Negate everything external. Peel off layer after layer. You will discover in yourself the eternal, immortal Atman.

179. The chief obstacle to Self-realisation is Trishna. Eradicate all sorts of Trishnas to have Nirvana this very second. Remember that Trishnas are inveterate or deep-rooted. They manifest themselves in various forms. They are subtle and hidden also in the subconscious mind. Make a careful search.

180. I am "*Asanga, Akarta, Sakshi, Trigunatita*—unattached, non-doer, witness and beyond the three Gunas." Constantly dwell on these ideas. This is Nirguna meditation.

181. From every face see God shining forth. Still the mind. Silence the thoughts. Enter deep into the Divine Source and know you are God.

182. My dear aspirants! Children of Light, nectar's sons, offsprings of Immortality and Infinite Bliss! O Saumya! I am with you always. Fear not. We are inseparable. Peace be on thee. The Light of my Spirit is shed upon you all. My Peace falls as a benediction upon your souls. May that Light, the Divine Flame, never grow dim. May the glory of the Eternal shine through you all to lift the darkness (desire, passion) all about you. May that Divine Light enlighten your spiritual path. May Peace fill your mind and hearts. Om Santi!

183. Give up '*Aham Bhavana*,' identification with the body and 'mineness.' Dwell in the Atman. You will shine as a Jivanmukta in this very life.

184. "I am that all-pervading Atman which is *Eka* (one), *Chidakasa, Akhanda* (without parts, indivisible), the Self of all

beings (*Sarva Bhuta Antaratma*)." Try to get established in this Bhava with great effort (*Prayatna*). Then only will the Chanchalatva (restlessness) of the mind vanish. You will get eternal bliss. You will become a Jivanmukta. There is not an atom of doubt.

185. You are fully aware that the reflection of your face in the mirror is false. You feel "I alone am real." Even so, this world, body and mind are unreal. Existence (Brahman) alone is the solid Reality. In reality, you are the real Supreme Self. You are identical with Existence. Remember this Drishtanta (example) always. The world will have no attraction for you. You will have Sahaja Avastha always even while working.

186. There must be a combination of head, heart and hand (Jnana, Bhakti and Karma Yoga). That is perfection. You must have the intellect of Sankara and heart of Buddha. *Sushka Vedantins* (people who make mere Vedantic gossips) are incorrigible.

LIGHT ON THE PATH

187. Why not you also, my dear friends, become great spiritual personages? In this Kali Yuga God-realisation can be attained in a short period. It is the Grace of the Lord. You need not do severe Tapas now. You need not stand on one leg for 1,000 years. In the light of theosophy there is much evolution of mind in the present root race.

188. Make 21,600 times Japa of any Mantra daily. Speak the truth. Control your anger. Do charity. Serve elders, Sadhus, Sannyasins, Bhaktas, poor and sick persons with Bhava. You will get Peace, Ananda and Immortality.

189. Sleep alone in a separate room. Whenever passion troubles you, increase the number of Japa. Do 200 Malas or even more. Fast for one day completely. Take only milk and fruits on the second day. Do simple Pranayama. Retain the breath till you count 60 OMs. Study one chapter of the Gita. Observe silence; do not talk to your wife. Do not laugh. Remain in a separate room. Keep the mind fully occupied with something or other. This is most important. This is the best Sadhana for maintaining Brahmacharya. Do not use scents and flowers. Touch not romantic novels. Avoid theatres and cinemas. Sleep on a coarse mattress.

190. When you repeat any Mantra, do it remembering the meaning of the Mantra. Rama, Siva, Krishna, all these mean Sat-Chit-Ananda, purity, perfection, all-light, eternity, immortality.

191. Do the Japa in the throat or Kantha for one year, in the heart or Hridaya for three years, and in the navel or Nabhi for one year.

192. When you advance in practice, every pore in the skin, every hair-follicle will repeat the Mantra forcibly. The whole system will be charged with the powerful vibrations of the Mantra. You will be ever in Prema of the Lord. You will experience muscular twitchings and shed profuse tears of Ananda. You will be in exalted Divine moods. You will get inspirations, revelations, ecstasy, insight and intuitions. You will compose poems. You will have various Siddhis, Divine Aisvarya.

193. Go to a lonely garden and spend two or three hours there in silent Japa or in reading the Gita or the Upanishads, or in meditation. When you go back to your house you will feel quite refreshed. You will be renovated. You will be a new man charged with new Prana.

194. The more you increase your Japa, the stronger, purer and calmer you will become.

195. Have Smarana of Siva always. Live in Him. Take a deep plunge in Him. Merge yourself in Him. Give up all other worldly thoughts. Lord Siva will spiritualise and elevate you. Have strong faith. March boldly onwards in your spiritual Sadhana. Do not look backwards. Do not look to the right or left.

196. If any disease is pronounced as incurable by the doctors, begin to repeat the Name of the Lord. Spiritualise the mind and the body with Pranava vibrations by chanting OM loudly. Do Pranayama also. You will be cured. Have faith. The Name of God is a great boat with which we can cross this ocean of Samsara.

197. Mouna for three hours checks the excessive Rajasic nature of Vak-Indriya. By sitting continuously on one Asana for three hours get Asana Jaya and check the excessive Rajasic nature of the legs (constant motion, a desire to move to various places). Asana and Mouna will increase peace and Sattva Guna.

198. Having adopted these two methods live alone for

some hours in the room. Do not mix with anybody. Plug the ears with wax. This is an auxiliary to give you inner life and shut you out from external buzzle and jarring sounds. Or close the ears with thumb (Yoni Mudra). Now seriously do Japa and Dhyana. You will get Peace. Practise earnestly, my dear friends. Be sincere. What more can I tell you? I cannot put grass into the mouth of a cow. She will have to graze herself. Drink the spiritual Nectar yourself.

199. Stay for a week or fortnight every year in places of pilgrimage such as Varanasi, Prayag, Nasik, Haridwar, Rishikesh, etc., and do Japa intensely. Have Satsanga with Mahatmas. This will give you peace of mind, slowly spiritualise you and regenerate your coarse Asuric nature.

SPECIAL SPIRITUAL INSTRUCTIONS

200. Do not mix with others much. Mixing too much with undesirable persons causes jealousy in the mind.

201. Forget quickly the wrongs done to you by others. Remember this couplet as often as you can: "FORGET AND FORGIVE."

202. Try to bear the insults and scoldings of others. This will develop your Will. Praise and respect are poisons for a spiritual aspirant. Censure and disrespect are ornaments and nectars for a Jijnasu or Mumukshu.

203. Reduce your wants. Live in seclusion in a solitary room for two hours daily, and repeat the Name of the Lord or do Japa of any Mantra. Do not argue with others. Give up the desire for name and fame. If you do these for six months, I assure you, you will attain peace of mind. You can laugh at me if you do not gain any spirituality, if your lower nature is not changed to some extent. But first give my words a fair trial.

204. Be slow to promise but quick to perform. Keep up your word at any cost. Love little; love long.

205. Live alone. Do not mix with undesirable persons. Observe Mouna for a couple of hours daily.

206. Stick to one kind of Sadhana. Do not waver. Be steady in your practice. Stick to one Guru, one place, one method. Remember that a rolling stone gathers no moss.

207. You must become a man of fixed resolve. You must think well—once, twice or thrice—the pros and cons, of a thing. As soon as you have made the resolution, you must not change

it. You must carry it out at any cost. You will develop your Will-Power or Atma Sakti.

208. You must have your own ideal, mottoes and principles. You must adhere to them strongly and steadily. You must not deviate from your ideal and principles even a fraction of an inch.

209. If you strictly follow the teachings of the Saints, Smritis and Vedas, if you practise Yama and Niyama, you will be free from miseries and troubles. You will not move in the path of darkness.

210. Respect the moods, sentiments, convictions and views of others. Do not quarrel. Tolerance is an important virtue for a Sadhaka. You cannot have any peace of mind if you are intolerant.

211. There is nothing absolutely right and nothing absolutely wrong in this relative world. There is a grain of truth in every statement of every individual according to his own experience. Remember this.

212. Do not multiply your friends. There is really no sincere friend in the world. People are united for selfish purposes. The only real friend is the Atman in your heart. Isvara is your genuine friend at all times. Even if you forget Him, He has your well-being ever at His heart.

213. O aspirants! Remember these three points daily: (i) Remember the saints who have already reached the goal like Dattatreya, Sankara, Jnana Dev, Ram Das, Tulasi Das and others. This will give you a great impetus and zeal in your Sadhana. (ii) Remember death, disease, old age and other miseries of the world. (iii) Remember that this world is unreal like the blueness of the sky. These thoughts will induce great Vairagya in you.

214. Do not be too familiar with anyone, particularly with any woman. Familiarity breeds contempt. You must know psychology well. Then only can you move and mix with different minds tactfully. Too much familiarity ends in rupture and enmity.

215. You must not show any levity in the observance of Niyama and in religious or Divine topics. You must not joke on Divine matters. You must be very serious. Otherwise you will not improve. You cannot change your old, vicious habits and ways. You cannot get out of your old grooves.

216. Be kind to all. Trust not the Indriyas or senses. These two practices are quite sufficient to give you Moksha.

217. *Satyam vada*—Speak the truth; *Dharmam chara*—Do acts of righteousness. This also will give you liberation from mundane existence.

218. The gist of the Vedas is CONTROL OF INDRIYAS.

219. Your one important duty is to control the senses. This is Mukhya (primary). Supporting family etc., is only Gauna (secondary). You are born to unfold your Divinity that is lurking in you. *Sarvabhuteshu Goodhah*—hidden in all beings, *Sarvabhuta-Antaratma*—the Inner Self of all beings and *Sarvabhutadhivasah*—abiding in all beings.

220. Keep a Spiritual Diary. Note down your progress, daily routine and other particulars.

221. Respect elders, parents, Sadhus, Sannyasins etc., with sincerity and Bhava.

222. Even Isvara cannot give Kaivalya Moksha to anybody. Everybody should do Pururshartha for himself. Purushartha is Isvara Svarupa itself. This will lead to Asanga Jnana, wisdom that you are unattached to body, mind and Indriyas.

223. You must get rid of all sorts of mental weaknesses, and superstitions, false and wrong imaginations, false fears and wrong Samskaras. Then only can you be really happy.

224. When you move about on the road do not look hither and thither. It will distract you. Always look at the tip of the nose. Practise daily. Then you will develop a habit.

225. Do not spend more than Rs. 10 or 15 on your personal expenses. Simple living and high thinking must be your motto.

226. It is very easy to control the mind if you know the right technique. You must have strong faith in God and sincerity of purpose. Even though the Sun may rise in the West, you must not have the least wavering in your determination. Your faith must be unshakable as the adamantine rock.

227. The company of a worldly-minded man is as dangerous for an aspirant as the company of a woman. Be careful.

228. Why do you get a disease? It is a blessing from God to purge out the evil effect of your bad Karmas, to infuse in you more Sattva and also the virtues, power of endurance (Titiksha), mercy and love towards human beings and to make

you remember God. Pain is the only best thing in this world. It opens your inner eyes. Philosophy takes its origin from pain, finds out the cause of pain and ignorance and tries to reduce it by the eradication of ignorance.

229. All people are not benefited by pain and adversities. The egoism thins out a bit during sufferings. It asserts itself with redoubled force when they get back their original health. The veil again comes back. It is only a Viveki who is really benefited. He remembers his sufferings.

230. Do not waste time. Do not waste even a minute. Time is very precious for aspirants. Meditate. Realise. Drink the Spiritual Nectar of Immortality.

231. Who can command? He who knows how to obey. Obedience is better than sacrifice.

232. Drink gruel and water alone and be happy and contented. A contented mind is a continual feast. Even Brahma and Indra will be jealous of you.

233. Do not belittle others. Do not treat others with contempt. Respect the sentiments and words of others. Praise others and expose your faults before others.

234. Hide yourself. Do not show your skill and ability to others. Do not care for name and respect. Treat name and respect as straw, dung, dust and poison because they are false and worthless. Then only you will get Peace.

235. Scrutinise your motives. Sit alone. Analyse your mind and your own nature. Watch your Vrittis and pray. Study your own nature and defects and try to remove them by suitable methods.

236. Think of yourself as nothing in the world. You can remove your pride and egoism by doing so. Always sit on the ground. Shun chairs, sofas, benches and bedsteads. Do always menial service. Serve others. Speak well of others. Do not expose faults of others.

237. When a man speaks ill of you, excuse and pity him. Pray for him. Do good to him. Love him. Bless him who despises you. Bear insult and injury. This will develop your will-force.

238. Hatha Yogins start their Sadhana or Abhyasa with body and Prana, by practising Asanas, Mudras, Bandhas and Pranayamas. Their theory is that by control of Prana, the mind can be controlled. This is only for the dull type of students.

239. Raja Yogins start their Sadhana with the mind direct. They control their Vrittis. They make the mind blank. They make Samyama (Dharana, Dhyana and Samadhi at one stroke). They improve the quality of the mind by practice of Yama and Niyama. Hatha Yoga without Vichara cannot improve the quality of the mind.

240. Jnana Yogins start their Sadhana with Buddhi and Will. Tantrikas start their Sadhana with Sakti.

241. Bhaktas start their Sadhana with devotion, Sraddha, faith and self-surrender. Higher emotions play a conspicuous part in them and they forget the body and the world.

242. Be established in Brahmic feeling and consciousness. "*Brahma Satyam*—Brahman or God is real." "*Jagat Mithya*—The world is unreal." Have these two ideas well grounded in your minds.

243. Sin is only a mistake. Sin is ignorance. Try to go above sin by getting knowledge of Brahman.

NIVRITTI SADHANA

244. Renunciation of all attractions for sense-objects and breaking up of the ties constitute real Sannyasa. It is a state of mental non-attachment, self-annihilation. Real Sannyasa can be obtained by destroying the Vasanas, selfishness and attachment for children, body, wife and property.

245. Renunciation of all selfish acts and their fruits constitutes real Sannyasa. To abandon the idea of doership is Sannyasa. To rise above all pairs of opposites is Sannyasa.

246. Mere emotion and bubbling enthusiasm will not serve you in the path of renunciation. A Sannyasin must be a living example of silence and an embodiment of everlasting courage.

247. Taking to seclusion, one should observe the vow of silence, non-mixing and disciplining the senses. It will help oneself in the attainment of the highest renunciation and pave a long way directly to the realms of bliss and Immortality.

248. The world is full of miseries. The mind tempts and deceives you at every moment. Through illusion caused by the mind, pain is misunderstood as pleasure. Reflect deeply. The world is a ball of fire. All pleasures, sweet in the beginning, give the bitterest possible taste in the end.

249. Indriyas deceive you at every moment. Senses are very powerful and are able to overcome even the wisest. They give you momentary pleasure, which is mixed with eternal pain, worry, anxiety and illusion.

250. Sages emphatically declare that Immortality cannot be attained either by rituals, or by progeny or by immense wealth; but verily it is attainable through renunciation alone. It is only through renunciation, they attained the highest Seat of Brahman, in the cave of their heart.

251. Sensual life is no life at all. It is attended with pain, various sorts of sins, weaknesses, attachments, slave mentality, weak will, severe exertion and struggle. Sensual life cannot bestow upon you everlasting happiness. It will bring you down to the abyss of hell. The more you run after sensual pleasures, the more you become restless and painful.

252. Shun honour, respect, degrees, name and fame. They are worthless. They will never give you eternal satisfaction. They will only intensify your vanity. They are all intoxicants of the mind. They will bring mental disturbance. That is the reason why Raja Bhartrihari, Raja Gopichand and Lord Buddha deserted their kingdom, wealth, honours etc.

253. Is not a kingdom valuable to be owned? Is not a summer-palace in Kashmir or a pleasant garden with sweet-smelling flowers of various colours, nice to live in? Is not the company of young Maharanis with tender waists and lotus-like eyes dear as life itself, very pleasing? Yet, wise, dispassionate men retired into forests, kicking off all these things as worthless as straw, to realise the Self.

254. Have a strong determination and a strong will. Never think of returning home after taking to the Nivritti Marga. Have courage, fixity of mind and a definite purpose in life. If you are prepared to renounce all possessions, including body and life, you can take to Nivritti Marga and take to Sannyasa.

255. The path of renunciation is not a rosy path. It is beset with countless difficulties and hardships. Obstacles are many in this path. But it can make you a King of kings, an Emperor of emperors.

256. Those who want to take to the path of renunciation should train themselves to a laborious hard life, coarse food. Then alone can they bear the rigorous austerities of an ascetic's life. They should not become lazy. Mental energy

should be utilised properly. Then alone quick progress is possible.

257. The attraction for objects and ties of various sorts make a man bound to this world. Renunciation of all attractions and breaking up all ties constitute real renunciation. That man who is free from attraction and ties, enjoys infinite bliss and supreme joy.

258. The same five kinds of enjoyment of sensual pleasures prevail in the heaven worlds also. But they are more intense and subtle. This cannot give real and lasting happiness to a Viveki. He shuns all enjoyments of the heaven also. He kicks them mercilessly. He is keenly aware of the pleasures of the three worlds and is convinced that they are only a mere drop in the ocean of Brahmic Bliss.

SCIENCE OF YOGA SADHANA

259. Yoga is union with the Lord. It is a spiritual science that teaches the method of joining the individual soul with God by regular practice of Yoga. The conjunction of individual and Supreme Soul is called Yoga.

260. The aim of Yoga is to free man from the thraldom of matter and the fetters of Prakriti and make him realise his absolute independent nature.

261. The practice of Yoga will help you to control the emotions and passions and will give you power to resist temptations and to remove the disturbing elements from the mind.

262. Yoga is a not a system which can be taught and learnt by lectures or correspondence courses. The Yogic student should live under a preceptor for some years and lead a rigorous life of austerity, discipline and practise meditation. Only then he can become a Yogi.

263. There are a good number of persons, who, from eight in the morning to eight at night are good business men. From eight to ten at night they are good Yogis. They perform some Asanas, some Kriyas, a little Pranayama, study some books on Hatha Yoga and Kundalini Yoga and interpret Yoga in their own manner. Be in the world, but be out of the world. This is the highest Yoga.

264. Eat sparingly. Eat simple food. Observe Brahmacharya. Control the senses. Breathe pure air. Live in a quiet

place with high spiritual vibrations under a Guru. Then practise Yoga. Only then will you attain success in Yoga.

265. See God in everything and transmute evil into good. This is real Yoga. This will bring the glorious realisation and will rend asunder all fetters of ignorance. You will abide in Eternity.

266. The essence of Yoga Sadhana is to behold the Supreme and rest in Divinity.

SELF-EFFORT AND DESTINY

267. One can achieve anything in this world through right endeavour or Purushartha.

268. Sit not idle, craving God to help thee, but be up and doing, for God helps only those who help themselves.

269. "*Uddhared-atmana-atmanam*—the self should be raised by the Self." The aspirant will have to do every bit of Sadhana by himself. He cannot attain spiritual illumination by mere jugglery.

270. Men who have insight into the true nature of the world, who have truly discerned the truth about the world, lift up their self and free themselves from evil inclinations and cravings for worldly objects by their own self-efforts and exertion.

271. Work out your salvation yourself in right earnest. The Guru can only guide you in the right direction. You will have to place yourself each step in the ladder of Yoga.

272. Never complain about the lack of opportunity. Where there is a will, there is a way. If you are really sincere in your endeavours, the opportunities will be created by themselves. Lord's grace comes to those, who exert in right earnest.

273. Prarabdha and Purushartha are identical. Prarabdha is indeed Pururshartha of the previous life. It is an unending chain. Right exertion always gives you a good harvest of happy results. It was by exertion that Markandeya got immortality, Savitri got back her husband from the clutches of Yama. Mere resignation to Prarabdha produces fatalism in man, which is by far the worst enemy of spiritual progress. Such a resignation weakens the aspirant considerably. Will-power takes leave of him.

274. Never brood over your destiny. Destiny is created by man's thoughts, habits and character. You can verily mould your destiny according to your heart's desire through right exertion. In reality, man is the master of his destiny.

275. Throughout the Yoga Vasishtha you will find the ringing note that man can attain immortality by Purushartha. Prarabdha is the body and its associates which man carries over from one birth to another. Lord Buddha also stressed this: right exertion alone can bring about success.

BRAHMACHARYA—THE BASIS OF ALL SADHANA

276. Brahmacharya is the keynote of success in every walk of life. It is absolutely necessary for spiritual advancement.

277. There is no panacea more potent than Brahmacharya to eradicate the dire malady, lust, of ignorant persons and to make the aspirants well-established in Brahman.

278. Brahmacharya is the vow of celibacy in thought, word and deed, by which one attains Self-realisation or realisation of Brahman.

279. Virya is the essence of thought, intelligence, life and consciousness.

280. The energy that is wasted during one sexual intercourse is tantamount to the physical energy that is spent in physical labour for ten days, or mental energy that is utilised in mental work for three days.

281. A Yogi always directs his attention to the accumulation of the divine energy in him by unbroken chastity and perfect celibacy.

282. Those who have not observed the vow of celibacy become slaves of anger, jealousy, laziness, fear, etc.

283. He who has completely eradicated lust, is Brahman Himself.

284. There cannot be two opinions in the matter of Brahmacharya. No Viveki thinks of having many children. The life of a householder is not inconsistent with the maintenance of celibacy. As soon as the householder has one child to continue the line, the wife becomes his mother.

285. Brahmacharya includes not only control of sex-Indriya, but also all other Indriyas.

286. The practice of keeping the mind fully occupied is the best of all practices for keeping up physical and mental Brahmacharya.

287. The Japa of any Name of the Lord, Sattvic food, Satsanga, study of religious books, Pranayama, prayer, Kirtan, Vichara, Viveka, etc., will go a long way in the eradication of sexual desire and sex-impulse.

288. A proper understanding of Brahmacharya is possible when one lives in seclusion for some time.

289. Always wear a Kaupeen or Langotee or suspender bandage. This will help Brahmacharya and make you healthy, wealthy and wise.

290. Remember the pains of the world, the unreality of objects and the bondage that comes from attachment to wife and children.

291. Constantly remember, "Through the grace of God, I am becoming purer and purer, every day. Pleasures come but not to stay. Mortal flesh is only clay. Everything will pass away. Brahmacharya is the only way."

GOODNESS, PURITY AND TRUTHFULNESS

292. The noble soul who always does good to the world and entertains sublime, divine thoughts is a blessing to the world at large.

293. A person of good deeds and good, pleasant, sweet speeches has no enemy. If you really want spiritual growth and salvation, do good to those men who attempt to poison or hurt you.

294. Purity leads to wisdom and Immortality. Purity is of two kinds, internal or mental and external or physical. Mental purity is more important. Physical purity is also needed. By the establishment of internal, mental purity, cheerfulness of mind, one-pointed mind, conquest of Indriyas and fitness for the realisation of the Self are obtained.

295. Purity is the best jewel of a Yogi. It is the best and the greatest treasure of a sage. It is the best wealth of a devotee.

296. Practice of compassion, charitable acts, kind services, purifies and softens the heart, turns the heart-lotus upwards and prepares the aspirant for the reception of the Divine Light.

297. Japa, Kirtan, meditation, charity, Pranayama can burn all sins and purify the heart quickly.

298. Truth is the highest Wisdom. Truth stands even if there is no public support. Truth is eternal. Truth reigns

Supreme. Those who are truthful and pure, do not die. Those who are untruthful and lustful are as if dead already.

299. You must have a pure mind if you want to realise the Self. Unless the mind is set free and casts away all desires, cravings, worries, delusion, pride, lust, attachment, likes and dislikes, it cannot enter into the domain of Supreme Peace and unalloyed felicity or the Immortal Abode.

300. Mind is compared to a garden. Just as you can cultivate good flowers and fruits in a garden by ploughing and manuring the land and removing the weeds and thorns and watering the plants and trees, so also you can cultivate the flower of devotion in the garden of your heart by removing the impurities of the mind such as lust, anger, greed, delusion, pride, etc., and watering it with divine thoughts. Weeds and thorns grow in the rainy season, disappear in summer; but their seeds remain underneath the ground. As soon as there is a shower, the seeds again germinate and sprout out. Even so the Vrittis or modifications of the mind manifest on the surface of the conscious mind, then disappear and assume a subtle seed-state, the form of Samskaras again become Vrittis either through internal or external stimulus. When the garden is clean, when there are no weeds and thorns you can get good fruits. So also when the heart and the mind are pure, you can have the fruit of good deep meditation. Therefore cleanse the mind of its impurities first.

301. If you do not clean a plate daily it will lose its lustre. It is the same with the mind, too. The mind becomes impure if it is not kept clean by the regular practice of meditation.

302. Speaking truth, frees one from worries and bestows peace and strength.

303. Speaking truth is the most important qualification of a Yogi. If truth and one thousand Asvamedha Yajnas are weighed in a balance, truth alone will outweigh.

304. God is Truth. He can be realised by speaking the Truth and observing It in thought, word and deed.

305. Truthfulness, self-control, absence of envious emulation, forgiveness, modesty, endurance, absence of jealousy, charity, thoughtfulness, disinterested philanthropy, self-possession and unceasing compassion and harmlessness are the thirteen forms of truth.

306. Some persons hold that a lie, that is calculated to bring immense good is regarded as truth. Suppose an unrighteous king has ordered a sage to be hanged without any cause. If the life of this sage can be saved by uttering a falsehood, the falsehood is only truth.

307. By speaking truth always in all circumstances, the Yogi acquires Vak-Siddhi. Whatever he thinks or speaks, turns to be true. He can do anything even by mere thought.

308. "This Atman is attainable by the strict observance of Truth." "There is nothing greater than the Truth" is the emphatic declaration of the Srutis. Take the life of Yudhishthira and Satyavrata Harischandra. They did not part with truth even at the critical junctures.

CHARITY—AN ASPECT OF SADHANA

309. Charity must be spontaneous and unrestrained. Giving must become habitual. You must experience joy in giving.

310. You must not think: "I have done a very charitable act. I will enjoy happiness in heaven. I will be born as a rich man in the next birth. The charitable act will wash away my sin. There is no charitable man like me in my town or district. People know me that I am a charitable man."

311. You should have a large heart. You must throw money like stones to the poor people. Then alone you can develop Advaitic feeling, Samadhi and cosmic love.

312. Some people do charity and are anxious to see their names published in the newspapers. This is a Tamasic form of charity.

313. The left hand should not know what the right hand is giving. You should not advertise about your charity and charitable nature. There must not be an exaltation in your heart when people praise your charitable nature.

314. You should be thirsting to do charitable acts daily. You should not lose any opportunity. You should create opportunities. There is no Yoga or Yajna greater than spontaneous charity.

315. Develop Udara Vritti (generous heart). Then you can become a King of kings. If you give, the whole wealth of the world is yours. Money will come to you. This is the immutable,

inexorable, unrelenting law of nature. Therefore give. Share with all. The best portion must be given to others.

316. Charity should be given with respect, humility and joy. You must give with right mental attitude and realise God through charitable acts.

SUFFERING—A STEPPING-STONE TO SUCCESS

317. There can be no strength without suffering. There can be no success without suffering. Without sorrows, without persecution, none can become a saint or a sage. Every suffering is meant for one's uplift and development.

318. Suffering augments the power of endurance, mercy, faith in God and removes egoism. Calamity is a blessing in disguise to instil power of endurance and mercy in the heart and turn the mind towards God.

319. Poverty infuses humility, strength, power of endurance and the spirit of struggling and persevering, whereas, luxury begets laziness, pride, weakness, inertia and all sorts of evil habits.

320. Trial is a crucible into which nature throws a man whenever she wants to mould him into a sublime superman.

321. Every difficulty that comes in the spiritual path is an opportunity to grow stronger and stronger and to develop our will. He who knows how to suffer, enjoys much peace.

322. Uncongenial atmosphere, unfavourable environments and obstacles will help one only in carrying on the struggle more vigorously and diligently. Even a weak man acquires a mass of energy, becomes strong and sublime from terrible trials and adversities.

323. A real hero rejoices in suffering. He willingly undergoes pain and suffering in order to serve and please others as well as to mould himself in the proper path.

SADHANA AND SELF-REALISATION

324. Spiritual life is a journey over an unknown path which is as sharp as the edge of a razor.

325. March forward steadily in the spiritual path courageously and perseveringly.

326. A great illumination surely awaits the sincere aspirant at the journey's end.

327. The aspirant must travel alone in the dark, but the light of faith will guide him and the strength of devotion will sustain him.

328. The tract ahead cannot be seen, going is uncertain and many pitfalls await the unwary, but the divine grace and light guide the true seeker at every step.

329. Spiritual life is the conquest and subdual of the animal nature and the sublimation of the human into the divine nature.

330. Truth becomes real to the aspirant. This is Self-realisation.

331. Hold fast to the supreme light of Truth. It will illuminate you on your spiritual journey.

332. O Ram! Look thou not back, but march forward. Thou wilt surely attain bliss immortal.

333. Come out victorious, O Ram! Wear the laurels of peace and enter the self-effulgent, infinite realm of immortal bliss, which is beyond time and space.

ESSENTIALS OF SPIRITUAL LIFE

334. Purity of mind, Vairagya, annihilation of ego, burning aspiration and steadfastness are essential for God-realisation.

335. Without purity, faith, devotion, dispassion and unceasing effort, freedom or emancipation cannot be attained.

336. If you are established in purity of heart, all defects and weaknesses will vanish by themselves.

337. You must have faith, devotion, serenity, humility, dispassion and earnestness. Then alone you will obtain peace everlasting, spiritual enlightenment, and full union with the Lord.

338. Selflessness is the alpha and omega of all Sadhanas and Yogas in all religions.

339. Detach and attach. Detach the mind from worldly objects and attach it to the Lord. This is the essence of religion. This is the essence of all spiritual Sadhanas.

340. The whole meaning of the spiritual life is to get rid of egoism and live in the Eternal.

341. Devotion, dedication and discipline are the means to the attainment of wisdom, eternal bliss and everlasting peace.

342. Eradicate all sense of distinction, difference and separateness. Be all-inclusive.

343. Keep company with saints and sages, with the devout and virtuous. You will be elevated and inspired.

344. In Brahma Vidya or the Science of the Atman, or Reality, no progress is possible without the active co-operation of the Preceptor and the disciple.

345. The disciple must have absolute faith in the Preceptor.

346. Each individual, by his own efforts, draws to himself the Lord.

347. O Ram! Let thy life be a radiance of purity now and for ever. Purify thy mind in the flame of devotion and wisdom.

348. The path by which the sages reach perfection is the path of Truth. There is no other way to freedom or emancipation.

349. You need neither art, nor science, neither study, nor erudition for God-realisation, but faith, purity and devotion.

350. Faith, hope and love will animate and vitalise you. Therefore, have faith. Be hopeful and cultivate love.

351. Purity of heart is a gateway to God.

352. Have a living faith, an unshakable, unswerving faith in God, in the scriptures, and in the words of your Guru. Then alone you will attain God-realisation.

353. With simplicity and love in your heart, with truth, fearlessness and purity, with devotion and meditation, you can reach the realm of immortal bliss and everlasting peace.

354. Become pure; be good, humble, faithful and devoted. Then you will know what God is.

IMPORTANCE OF SPIRITUAL PRACTICE

355. Spiritual life, or spiritual discipline, is the key to Self-realisation.

356. Unremitting and regular efforts on the aspirant's part are indispensable.

357. Sadhana should not be neglected under any circumstances.

358. It should become part of your life and natural life breathing.

359. Equip yourself with self-control and other virtues which are the means to liberation.

360. Stop all discussions and quarrels. Be practical. Act. Find out your relationship with the Absolute.

361. Self-realisation is not possible without renunciation, selfless service and devotion.

362. Pray and meditate. You will obtain the key to blessedness.

363. Selfless service, generosity and meditation lead to God-realisation quickly.

364. Become proficient in meditation through regular practice. Check the wandering mind. Dwell in the Supreme Self. You will attain Self-realisation.

365. You should strive long and rigorously. Then alone you can attain mastery over the lower self.

366. Whether you will attain Samadhi tomorrow or after many births depends upon the purity of your mind, intensity of Sadhana, dispassion, discrimination and aspiration.

367. Argue not. Ask no more questions. Practise. Discriminate. Meditate. Realise.

368. Purushartha is self-effort. It is specially used in the meaning of effort for Self-realisation.

369. The practice of moral and spiritual disciplines culminates in the realisation of the Self or wisdom of the Atman.

370. You will have to place yourself each step in the ladder of Yoga.

IMPORTANT SADHANAS

371. Shun sense-enjoyments. Conquer the objects of the senses. Meditate and freely drink the nectar of the knowledge of the Upanishads.

372. Practice of virtues such as self-control, serenity, dispassion and study of the Upanishads is very necessary till you get a firm understanding of the sentence "I am Brahman."

373. Purify your heart first. Get rid of selfishness, greed, jealousy and hatred.

374. When the mind is thoroughly purified, when all the Vasanas (desires) are destroyed and when you transcend the three Gunas, you will attain Nirvikalpa Samadhi.

375. The path of devotion or Bhakti Yoga is for those who

are not yet thoroughly indifferent and also not too much attached.

376. In whatever name and form you adore the Lord, you will realise Him through that name and form.

377. Karma and Upasana are steps that lead to Jnana or wisdom.

378. The body becomes steady and firm, the mind becomes calm and unshaken and the aspirant becomes fit for the higher Vedantic meditation through purification attained through Karma and Upasana.

379. Study of scriptures, Satsanga, Vairagya, intense yearning for God, increase the Bhava.

380. With the increase of Bhava, the results of Japa are infinite.

381. The attempt for Self-knowledge or Self-realisation, should be preceded by the longing for the same, as the result of renunciation and discrimination.

382. Humility is your guide. Humility is your teacher.

383. Have a balanced mind that is constantly permeated with wisdom and everlasting discrimination between what is right and what is wrong.

384. Cultivate serenity, silence and cosmic love.

385. Practise truth, cosmic love, purity and humility. Meditate regularly, vigorously and seriously. You will have luminous intuition and glowing experiences.

386. Be pious. Eat a little. Sleep a little. Talk a little. Be virtuous. Meditate vigorously. You will attain God-realisation.

387. Purity of heart is the key by which the door of intuition that leads to the abode of Supreme Bliss, is opened.

388. Let your faith be sincere and steadfast. You will grow in spirituality.

389. Aspire ceaselessly. Strive sincerely. Practise regularly. Serve untiringly. Meditate spontaneously. You will reach the goal quickly.

390. Wish nothing. Want nothing. Desire nothing. Hope nothing. Expect nothing. You will be blessed. You will be the King of kings. You will attain Perfection.

391. Meditation, prayer and single-minded devotion will help you to have the vision of God, His Beauty, Greatness and Grandeur.

392. Constant repetition of God's Name mentally and verbally, and meditation on Him and His attributes, will lead to the attainment of God-realisation.

393. Lose all sense of duality in the supreme experience of love.

394. Stop the mind-wandering through dispassion, discrimination and meditation.

395. Mentally repeat always: Prema, Ananda, Santi. All evil, negative thoughts will die.

396. You are tempted, disturbed and defiled by sensual objects. The only remedy is meditation on the Lord with a dispassionate heart.

397. Crucify the flesh. Lead the life divine. Realise the Atman or the Spirit.

398. The road to the abode of God is long and arduous. There is no short-cut or royal road.

399. Everyone must undergo the same disciplines. Everyone must purify one's mind through selfless service of humanity and recitation of the Lord's Name.

400. Obedience, punctuality and cleanliness are the three ingredients of discipline.

401. Stand up, be bold, be cheerful. Be strong. Rely on your own self. Get the power and strength from within.

SECRET OF SUCCESS IN SADHANA

402. Sincerity and regularity in Sadhana are the secrets of success in the spiritual path.

403. Sadhana is impossible without Brahmacharya.

404. The aspirant who carelessly neglects the all-important Yama or self-restraint, never progresses in the spiritual path.

405. Brahmacharya expresses itself as perfect purity in thought, word and deed.

406. Every thought, every feeling and sentiment of the aspirant must be pure as crystal.

407. The character of the aspirant must be spotless.

408. Even the least or the slightest trace of sensuality ought not to taint the nature of the Brahmachari.

409. The aspirant must be inspired by a positive passion for purity.

410. There must be the burning desire to be spotlessly pure.

411. The idea of lust should be completely eschewed.

412. This should be the standard that the aspirant should strive to attain.

413. The glory and the grandeur of the Brahmacharya ideal should never be lost sight of.

414. Absolute purity is essentially the quality of Divinity.

415. A true Brahmachari is a veritable God on earth.

416. When all the impurities of the mind are annihilated, then Self-knowledge dawns.

417. Be judicious and cautious in restraining the mind. Do not identify yourself with evil Vrittis.

418. Open yourself to the Divine in you. This is an essential condition of divine perfection.

419. The life of an aspirant is one long series of renunciation and daily sacrifice.

420. He lives to serve others and make them happy.

421. The door of Immortality is open to that man who is endowed with dispassion, discrimination, devotion and who meditates regularly and constantly.

422. He who is humble and forgiving, who has controlled his senses, and who remembers the Lord at all times, goes to the region of Supreme Peace.

423. He who is sincere, patient, persevering and earnest, will make great progress in the spiritual path.

OVERCOME TEMPTATIONS

424. Temptations will assail even a very advanced aspirant. Cultivate more dispassion and do more rigorous Sadhana now.

425. Every temptation is a test of your spiritual strength.

426. Every difficulty is a test of your faith in God.

427. Every disease is a Karmic purgation.

428. An undisciplined man is one who leads the cave-life, builds castles in the air, gathers wool, and constructs a bazaar in the mind.

429. It is useless to go to forests or caves before dying to the lower nature of oneself.

430. The ambition and cravings which have been suppressed or forgotten due to preoccupations and diverse pleasures of life, show their heads in silence and seclusion.

431. There is a terrific rebellion of the inner, lower forces as soon as the aspirant shuts himself up in absolute seclusion in forests.

432. Temptation tempts even the advanced Yogi, but he is protected by the grace of the Lord, and the power of his good Samskaras.

433. Bring your mind under perfect control. Make it a perfect instrument for the reception and expression of the highest spiritual experience.

434. In this world of sense-desire, Maya is the Lord. But more powerful are the grace of the Lord, power of meditation, devotion, discrimination and dispassion.

435. Courage, fortitude, perseverance—these are the companions of resolution.

436. If you know yourself well, you will find no elation when people praise you.

437. When you are assailed by temptations during meditation, your guiding Deity will form a protective circle around you. Fear not. Be bold. March on heroically. Have faith.

438. You will have to cross a vast Void and a region of darkness during meditation. Fear not. You will get radiant light through the grace of the Lord. Be patient. Push on.

439. The elemental forces will try to harm you in meditation through the force of Maya. God will give you strength to overcome all obstacles. Stand firm. Be adamant. Victory is yours.

440. A bed of iron will become a bed of roses for you. The hostile elements will be transformed into flowers. Only you should have absolute faith in God.

441. You will be attacked from within through the projection of dark thoughts from your subconscious mind.

442. Dark thoughts will take various terrible hideous forms. They will frighten you. Lower astral entities will terrify you. But they will perish through the grace of God and the power of your meditation.

443. You will be tested whether you are free from fear, ambition and passion.

444. Even the superior celestial forces will tempt you. Do not yield to them.

445. Beautiful celestial damsels will appear before you. They will sing, dance and smile. They will try to seduce you. Beware!

446. Be dispassionate. Detect their impurities, hollowness, imperfection and impermanence. Use the sword of discrimination and the axe of dispassion.

MEDITATE AND REALISE

447. Be truthful. Meditate. Strive. Reach the goal of perfection.

448. Resort to seclusion. Detach yourself from externality. Meditate on the Self. Establish yourself in the Supreme Being.

449. The priceless jewel of Atman is hidden in the depths of your heart. Realise this Atman and be happy.

450. Take this jewel by diving deep into the recess of your heart in profound meditation.

451. Dive deep into the chambers of your heart and taste divine essence.

452. Wipe the world out of your mind through meditation on the Self or the Atman.

453. Deny the body and identify yourself with the all-pervading, immortal, fearless Atman.

454. Identify yourself with everything that lives. This will lead to cosmic Consciousness, Visvarupa-Darsan, and Advaitic realisation.

455. If you wish to become immortal, destroy the personal consciousness.

456. Crush the ego. Melt the mind. Tear the veil of ignorance. Become one with Brahman or the Absolute.

457. Realisation of the oneness of Existence will root out selfishness and egoism, and you will begin to feel that your Atman is the Atman of all.

458. Perform worship of the Atman by meditating on Soham—"I am He," by offering the flowers of peace, mercy, forbearance, humility, discrimination and dispassion and by sacrificing the beasts of lust and anger.

459. Realisation is the awakening to your real, divine nature.

460. When all thoughts subside, the Atman reveals Itself.

461. You will find abiding peace in your own Atman.

462. This is real independence when you realise "I am the Supreme Consciousness, which alone exists."

463. The path to Kaivalya Moksha lies through the practice of selfless service, devotion and meditation on the immortal Atman.

464. Selfless service and devotion rub the ego on either side and destroy it.

465. Destruction of the ego is the realisation of Consciousness.

THE IDEAL ASPIRANT

466. The aspirant who possesses discrimination and dispassion, checks the outgoing tendencies of the mind, curbs the turbulent senses and reaches the abode of immortal bliss.

467. A seeker after Truth or liberation must have absolute faith in his teacher and the Upanishads.

468. He who is steadfast, pure, destitute of passion, beholds the Supreme Brahman through wisdom and penance.

469. Violence, in any form, is not permissible to the spiritual aspirant under any circumstances, at any time, or place, or for any purpose whatsoever.

470. O aspirant, do not even hiss. Mind's natural tendency is downward. Be sweet. Be gentle. Be soft always.

471. Self-restraint and pure character are the prime essentials for progress in Yoga or spiritual life.

472. To be perfectly truthful is the most important qualification of a Yogi or a Sadhaka.

473. Not a partial but a perfect and comprehensive adherence to truth is the first element in forming the foundation of the Sadhaka's life.

474. To realise the Truth, you must live in Truth. You must grow into the very form of Truth.

475. An aspirant should develop divine virtues such as serenity, compassion, etc., for attaining success in the spiritual life.

476. Be simple. Be pure. Be childlike. Walk and talk with the Lord.

477. It is very difficult to find an aspirant who cares for nothing but final emancipation, and who treats the whole world and its contents as mere dry straw, and who meditates incessantly upon how to attain salvation from embodied existence.

478. Eat anything that comes before you. Live in any condition of life. Pray and meditate. Aspire and be dispassionate. Then alone you are open to the currents of the spiritual flood of the transcendental Divinity.

LIGHT ON SADHANA

479. Sadhana is spiritual movement consciously systematised.

480. Sadhana is the process of transforming the imperfect, limited human personality into the original unlimited splendour of perfect Divinity.

481. Sadhana is the secret of success in the spiritual path.

482. Control over passion constitutes the essence of truth and spiritual Sadhana.

483. Feel the spiritual impetus before starting a life of Sadhana.

484. Sit in a lonely place. Withdraw the senses, restrain the lower self, centre yourself in the Atman, and thus win the spiritual victory.

485. Think constantly of the immortal, all-blissful Self. You will reach the goal quickly and surely.

486. The more you detach yourself from the world, the more will be the joy and bliss you experience in the Atman within.

487. The more your heart is emptied of its worldly contents, the greater will be the desire to love God.

488. Learn to discriminate. Aspire fervently. Remember the Lord ceaselessly. This will lead to quick God-realisation.

489. Strong and fiery determination, firm resolution, intense application, tenacity, patience and perseverance will bring sanguine success in any undertaking, including spiritual evolution.

490. Learning is one thing and practical realisation is another.

491. Hear not the voice of the mind, but hear the voice of the Supreme Soul in silence, in meditation.

492. Asceticism is a means to Enlightenment as it prepares the mind for meditation.

493. Bodily mortification alone cannot lead to Enlightenment, without the calming of the passions and discipline of the mind.

494. Standing in the sun in summer, and in water in winter, is foolish Titiksha of the dull-witted.

495. Just as striking at an ant-hill will not destroy the snake within, so also no amount of bodily torture can kill the mind within.

496. Tapas is concentration and meditation.

497. Concentrate all your strength in driving away from the mind all sense-objects.

498. Sacrifice egoism as a goat, and anger as a buffalo.

499. Putting an orange-coloured robe, besmearing with ashes, shaving of head, wearing of rosaries, carrying Kamandalu and Yoga-Danda, cannot make one a Yogi or Sannyasi or a saint.

500. The first possible step to intense spiritual Sadhana is right resolution.

501. When this is made, the next step, right exertion, should be immediately taken up.

502. To restrain the senses, to speak the truth, to love all as one's own self, is the essence of Sadhana.

503. To be dispassionate and pure in thought, word and deed, to be contented and cheerful, to be undeluded, ever vigilant and to remember God ceaselessly is the essence of Sadhana.

504. "Discipline" and "Progress" are the watchwords of Yoga-Vedanta.

505. Think rightly, speak truthfully and act righteously. You will attain the kingdom of everlasting peace.

506. Collective Sadhana will bring the power of all to the aid of each.

507. Take recourse to that which raises you to the height of Divinity.

508. Carefully nurture and protect the spiritual plant. It will yield you the fruit of Immortality.

509. Leniency to the internal lower tendencies will land you in the region of suffering.

510. Excuses will not be of any help in this respect.

511. Always bear in mind the grandeur of Self-realisation and its unlimited glory.

512. Side by side, remember the evils of worldly life.

513. Abandon all that goes to fasten you to the earth.

514. Worldly talk is a great hindrance to spiritual progress.

515. Luxury is a hindrance to the process of budding or unfolding of the Self.

516. Foods like meat, fish, wine, etc., that tend to render one's nature gross and subhuman, are an enemy to one's spiritual growth.

517. O Basket of Vanity, throw away your learning. Negate your individuality. Deny your separateness. Efface your ego.

518. The glutton, the talkative man, the sensualist, the slothful, the indolent, can have no knowledge of the Eternal.

519. Vairagya due to mere failure in life or death of relatives will not help one to attain spiritual progress.

520. Japa or repetition of God's Name, and meditation on the Lord help the mind not to retain in itself the remembrance of anything other than God.

521. Japa and meditation drive away all thoughts of objects from the mind, and establish in it the one thought of God.

522. The aspirant relinquishes all thoughts of objects other than God, and forgets his own existence.

523. The Jnani sees the one Self in all; the Bhakta visualises his tutelary Deity in all; and the Karma Yogi or the Raja Yogi subscribes to either of the above two, as the basis of Sadhana.

524. Peace is attained through discipline, mental equipoise and insight.

525. All paths lead to the same goal.

526. The ways of realisation differ according to the temperament, tendencies and capacities of the individual.

527. Different stages of mental development and varying degrees of spiritual evolution require, naturally, different phases of religious thought and practice.

ADVICE TO ASPIRANTS

528. March forward, O spiritual hero! O divine soldier! Let your steps be firm, your resolution strong, your vision undimmed.

529. Despair not. Be courageous. Think and feel that you are not this perishable body, but the Immortal Atman or the Self.

530. The Divine within you is stronger and closer to you than anything else.

531. Wake up! Feel the living presence of God within and about you.

532. Your limitations and sufferings are mere accidents. They, in no way, pertain to your essential divine nature.

533. Be like Bhima in your strength. Be like the Himalayan snow in your purity. Be like the mother Earth in your patience.

534. Be patient. Persevere. Do your best and leave the rest to the Lord. Rely on Him. Pray. He will look after you.

535. Spiritual path becomes easy to tread on, as you advance.

536. Watch and pray. Walk in the Light.

537. Be wakeful. Be thoughtful.

538. Start your spiritual life in right earnest this moment. Be up and doing. Concentrate and meditate.

539. Conserve all your energies. Release all your energies for a higher purpose, for spiritual attainment.

540. Do not fall in carnal love with anyone.

541. Meditate and create inner silence.

542. He who has an iota of lust, pride and selfishness cannot attain the kingdom of God.

543. Work out your salvation. No one can save you. You must save yourself.

544. A well-disciplined mind will do you the greatest service.

545. It is only by living a life of purity, chastity, truth,

non-violence and austerity that one becomes fit enough to tread the path of spiritual realisation.

546. No one can free you from birth and death. You have to attain salvation by your own effort.

547. Keep the divine flame ever bright by regular Sadhana, company of the wise, study of religious scriptures and meditation on the Atman.

548. Even a little spiritual Sadhana confers peace and bliss.

549. Within you is the Teacher of teachers. If you still your thoughts and bubbling emotions, and listen intently to this Teacher within, He will teach you and guide you towards the goal.

550. He who is pure and truthful, can hear the inner voice.

551. The inner voice is generally drowned in the din and noise of worldly life, due to a ruffled mind. Purify. Concentrate. Meditate. Still the senses. Hear the inner voice. March forward in the spiritual path.

552. Be positive always.

553. Fear nothing. Thou art immortal Atman. Be at peace.

554. What you have to do tomorrow, do today; what you have to do today, do this minute.

555. Thou art Brahman! Thine is the strength infinite. Meditate and realise this.

REALISATION OF THE SELF

556. Awake friend! Shake off ignorance. Death is standing near your head.

557. Awake! Arise! Sleep no more. Realise the Truth-Consciousness.

558. Aspire and draw strength from within. Grow. Expand. Evolve.

559. Fear not, have faith. Meditate. You will reach the goal surely.

560. Aspire. Know the Self. Regain your lost Divinity. Acquire the Knowledge of the Reality.

561. Keep the spiritual flame within you always burning steadily.

562. March forward courageously. Yield not to temptations.

563. There is only one path, and that is the path of Truth.

564. There is no easy path to spiritual attainments.

565. You have to sacrifice much to attain eternal bliss.

566. You must suffer great loss to attain the inexhaustible spiritual treasure.

567. Draw up courage and spiritual strength from the inner Atman through meditation.

568. Become a master of the senses. Lead a balanced life of matter, mind and Spirit, and find the Self.

569. March courageously with Sraddha and Vairagya, and meditate constantly on the Atman. You will attain Self-realisation.

570. The Light of lights is in your heart. Realise this and be free.

571. Aspire intensely. Be cautious but bold.

572. Practise self-restraint and selflessness. You will experience spiritual awareness and illumination.

573. Fear not, abandon desires. Waste not a minute. Depend on God.

574. Purify your mind. Meditate on the Indweller of your heart. This is the only way to be happy and free from all afflictions.

THE WAY TO KAIVALYA

575. Identify yourself with the finite body; you become a mortal then. Identify yourself with the infinite Brahman; you become immortal therefore.

576. Withdraw and expand. Detach and attach.

577. Clothe yourself with contentment and use the pillow of serenity to rest in peace.

578. Offer the incense of discrimination. Pour the oil of dispassion. Light the lamp of knowledge.

579. Apply the collyrium of discrimination. You will have a new, magnanimous vision.

580. Take the mind from the body and fix it on the Atman. You will not experience any heat or cold. This will give real Titiksha or power of endurance.

581. Discriminate between the right and the wrong, and tread the positive path.

582. Have this mental attitude: "I may give up my life, but I will not swerve from the spiritual path. I will not break my vow."

583. Make no plans. It is only the worldly-minded that plan; it is only those who have to progress materially, who have to plan.

584. Thou art Divine, live up to it. Feel and realise your divine nature.

585. Know the supremely effulgent Being. Cross the darkness of ignorance and transcend death.

586. Practise selflessness. Do self-sacrifice. Effect self-surrender. Practise self-denial. Have self-restraint. Practise self-analysis. Have self-purification. You will attain Self-realisation.

587. Selflessness expands the heart, kills attachment to objects, curbs the ego and draws God's grace.

588. Self-surrender and supreme love to the Lord are the shoes which save the aspirant from the thorns and pebbles that lie on the road.

589. Egolessness, humility and purity are the shady, fruit-bearing trees that line the path and relieve the pilgrim of the weariness of the spiritual journey.

590. The path is steep, but the real, sincere aspirant is not disheartened. He experiences the divine grace at every step.

591. Know the source of all knowledge. In the silence of communion, listen to the voice of the Soul. Feel the wisdom-radiation from the depth of your heart.

592. The Lord is within you. Strengthen your resolution. Become one with the Eternal.

593. Knock within; attain life's goal.

594. Without the conviction about the unreality and worthlessness of earthly life, without burning dispassion and self-restraint, you will not be benefited by taking to the spiritual path.

595. Self-realisation is the highest aim.

596. Be still. Be quiet. Be silent. Realise the Atman or the Self.

597. There is neither monopoly nor copyright nor "All Rights Reserved" on God or divine wisdom. Every thirsting aspirant can enjoy the Lord's Aisvarya or Vibhutis. He can surely abide in Him.

598. You are essentially immortal. Qualify yourself for the path.

599. To know yourself is to know all.

600. Aim at perfection. Fight the life's battle bravely.

601. Live wisely. Search within. Have intensity of purpose.

602. Climb the peak of Perfection. Self-realisation is here to be attained.

603. Divine illumination and oneness with God is the end or the goal of spiritual path.

604. When the veil of ignorance is lifted during meditation or Samadhi, the individual self melts in the overwhelming glory of one, true Light or the Supreme Self.

605. The world will listen to you eagerly if you possess divine knowledge and spiritual force; the world will follow you and obey you; the world will adhere to your message faithfully; and humanity will find the royal road of peace, bliss and prosperity.

606. Practise sequestration, silent meditation and devotion with iron-determination and leech-like tenacity. You will soon attain Self-realisation.

607. In the case of the Pundit, his life-long exposition of the scriptures ought to have purified, to some extent, his mind. But he would have been more benefited if he had preached to himself what he had read and discoursed upon and practised rigorous Sadhana.

PROGRESS ON THE PATH

608. Practise renunciation. Apply yourself diligently and seriously to spiritual practices. You will attain Moksha or the final emancipation.

609. Train observation, thought, memory and will. Meditate regularly. You will be in harmony with the Universe.

610. Experience and subtle contact with beings on the Fire-world is a very good indication of the inward spiritual progress. It indicates thy ascent into a higher state of purity.

611. Visions are indeed very good and encouraging

signs. Pray to the Lord and express thy sincere heart's gratitude for the Grace bestowed.

612. Most of the dreams are symbolic. The crossing of the river would denote overcoming obstacles in the path of Yoga.

613. No soul can grow without aspiration, renunciation, discrimination, dispassion and meditation.

614. By restraining the senses, by annihilating likes and dislikes, by extending compassion to all creatures and by meditation you can attain immortality.

615. Devotion, freedom from ignorance and desires, God's Grace, wisdom, selflessness, service will make you equal to God.

616. Discrimination, dispassion and discipline are the three spiritual jewels.

617. Selfishness, pride and hypocrisy are the greatest obstacles in the spiritual path.

618. Divine wisdom is available to those alone who are courageous, patient, persevering, tenacious and steadfast, who are regular in meditation and whose eyes are fixed on the object aimed at.

619. A harmonious and happy balance of Sadhana and Seva must be kept up by an aspirant.

620. When Brahmavidya is imparted to those who have a pure heart, who are learned in scriptures, who intensely aspire for Brahman, who have faith and devotion and who do their duties scrupulously, it becomes fruitful.

621. Atma-Vichara, enquiry of the Self, is the best and highest form of Sadhana.

622. Spiritual fire is churned out of the two sticks of the body and the Pranava.

623. In quietness and confidence shall be your strength.

624. Even to visualise the Lord in meditation just once, to utter the Divine Name of the Lord with Bhava even a single time, has surely got a tremendous, transforming influence upon the soul.

625. The divine nature is Perfection. To be nearest to the divine nature is to be nearest perfection. You are free here and now. Only you are not aware of it through ignorance or the force of Maya.

SADHANA—THE ONLY PURPOSE OF LIFE

626. Sadhana is the real wealth. It is the only thing of real and everlasting value. There is butter in milk, but it can be got only after churning. Similarly, if you want to realise God, do Sadhana and worship constantly in right earnest.

627. Whatever spiritual practices you do, either Japa, practice of Asanas, meditation or Pranayama, do it systematically and regularly every day. You will attain Immortality or eternal bliss.

628. If you persist in your Sadhana vigorously and diligently, if you are regular, systematic and punctual in your Sadhana, you will attain success.

629. Be contented with whatever you get by chance and apply yourself to Sadhana with a dispassionate mind.

630. Regularity in Sadhana is of paramount importance. He who meditates regularly gets Samadhi quickly. That man who is irregular and does his actions by fits and starts, cannot reap the fruits of his efforts.

631. Keep your mind always busy in doing Japa, concentration, meditation, study of religious books, Satsanga or in doing something useful to others.

632. Little acts of virtues, little acts of purity will help you a lot in your Sadhana. Removal of Vrittis and impurities is the most important Sadhana. The wandering mind must be controlled by sticking to one place, one preceptor and one progressive method of Sadhana.

633. That Sadhaka who has turned the mind inward by the practice of Sama and Dama and who has keen longing for liberation sees the Self in his own self by constant and deep meditation.

634. You can move the whole world by your spiritual force.

635. A spiritual diary is a whip for goading the mind towards righteousness.

636. Selfishness retards spiritual progress. If anyone can destroy his selfishness, half of his spiritual Sadhana is over.

637. You must get up at 4 a.m. and start meditation first. Have concrete meditation in the beginning. Feel the indwelling presence in the form and think of the attributes—purity, perfection, all-pervading intelligence, bliss, absolute omnipotence,

etc. When the mind runs, again and again bring it to the point. Have another sitting for meditation in the night. Be regular in the practice.

CONCENTRATION AND MEDITATION

638. Meditation shuts worldly thoughts, increases Sattva, gives good health, makes you divine, kills pain and sorrows, destroys rebirths, gives peace and bliss.

639. The ultimate truth or Brahman can be experienced by all persons by regular practice of meditation with a pure heart. Meditation on the Immortal Self will act like a dynamite and blow up all thoughts and memories in the subconscious mind.

640. Just as copper is transmuted into gold by the process of alchemy, so also the sensuous mind is transmuted into pure mind, by the process of meditation. Regular meditation opens the avenues of intuitional knowledge, makes the mind calm and steady, awakens an ecstatic feeling and brings the aspirant in contact with the Source or the Supreme Purusha. Just as you take the pith from the grass, the butter from the milk, take the essence of Brahman through the churning of meditation.

641. Meditation is the only way to get rid of the worldly miseries and tribulations. You will develop divine virtues, and a spiritual road will be constructed in the mind by regular meditation. Mind will remain ever clean, if it is polished by the regular practice of meditation.

642. There is no use of jumping to meditation without having the preliminary practices and purification of the heart. Those people who have not practised any Yogic discipline or curbing of the senses, Vrittis or impurities, will find it difficult to practise meditation as well as concentration.

643. Just as you take food four times, morning, noon, afternoon and night, so also you will have to meditate four times a day if you want to realise God quickly.

644. When the outside sounds are not heard, when the ideas of the body and the surroundings disappear, when inner unruffled peace manifests, one is said to enter the first degree of deep meditation. Various kinds of lights, red, blue, green, etc., may come and go during concentration and meditation. The vision of lights etc., in meditation is a great encouragement

and a sign of progress. Ignore the lights and march forward to the goal which is the source of all these lights and all phenomena, which transcends all lights.

645. During meditation you should try to have one continuous flow of thought of God alone. Control the thoughts during meditation. Develop concentration by fixing the mind on the form of Lord Hari or any Deity according to your liking. Again and again try to call up this mental image of the picture. All unholy thoughts will die by themselves.

646. You must have cheerfulness without hilarity. If you practise concentration and meditation amidst unfavourable environments, you will grow strong, you will develop your will-force quickly, you will become a dynamic personality.

647. Sleep is a great obstacle in meditation. You will have to be careful and vigilant. Take light diet at night. This will help you in your meditation.

648. Restlessness, scepticism, sleep, laziness, mind-wandering, ill-will, hatred, anger, desire for sexual enjoyment are all positive hindrances to meditation.

649. Concentrate on your Ishta Devata. Repeat your Mantra by constant Trataka (gazing on the Deity). The form will become clear in your mind. You can continuously meditate on that form of the Lord.

650. The practice of meditation will lead a Sadhaka to the summit of Samadhi or super-consciousness, wherein all worldly miseries are destroyed *in toto*, and the aspirant ever rests in the blissful state.

BRAHMIC CONSCIOUSNESS

651. The mind should be made to think of the only worthy thing, Paramatman, by means of Yama and other practices of Yoga or by a correct and thorough examination of the two categories and the knowledge gained thereby (reflecting on the true significance of *'Tattvamasi'* Mahavakya) but by no other means.

652. Realisation of Brahman can be effected through the mind alone after abandoning its *Sankalpas* and *Vikalpas*.

653. Just as the iron rod, which is placed in the fire, assumes the qualities of fire through '*Tadatmya Sambandha*,' and just as the water that is mixed with the milk assumes the properties of the milk, so also the mind, on account of its

contact with Brahman, receives its intelligence and power from Brahman.

654. Just as the waves are dependent on the waters of the sea, so also the mind is dependent on the Supreme Soul.

655. Bitterness or sweetness do not lie in the leaves, but they are in the subject. They are created by the mind. It is the mind that gives colour, shape, qualities, etc., to the objects. The mind assumes the shape of any object it intensely thinks upon.

656. Friend and enemy, virtue and vice, pleasure and pain are in the mind only. Every man creates a world of good or evil, pleasure and pain, out of his own imagination only.

657. The running of the mind outside through the avenues of the senses and the resultant experience of the mind by external objects are produced by the Jiva's identifying himself with the body, because of delusion or ignorance.

658. The whole of experience consisting of perceiver and perceived is merely an imagination of the mind. That which exists only in imagination does not exist in absolute reality.

659. It is the action of the mind that is truly termed as Karma. Liberation results from the disenthralment of the mind. Maya havocs through the mind and its power of imagination. If the mind is destroyed, one will come to know the reality *in toto*.

660. Pain and pleasure are Dharmas of the mind. Restraint of the mind frees oneself from all pairs of opposites and leads him to the path of Jnana. The highest end is attained by the restraint of the mind.

661. This world consisting of friends, neutral and enemies, is a delusion of the mind caused by ignorance. There is no world in deep sleep. This goes to show that if there is a mind, there can be a world. If you can consciously destroy the mind by concentration and Samadhi, the world will vanish.

662. The impure mind is no other than the subtle desires that generate countless births. When the mind is freed from the desire for objects and when it rests in the Atman, the world vanishes totally. The tendency to think of sense-objects is indeed the cause of bondage on transmigration. Liberation means nothing but the destruction of the impure mind. The mind becomes pure when the desires are annihilated.

663. This universe and other objects have their substratum in the mind. They do not exist at any time apart from the mind. Renunciation of attachment and sensual thoughts will

bring in destruction of the lower mind. Equanimity of mind brings about real, lasting happiness to a disciplined man.

664. If the mind is pure and free from distraction, you will behold the Supreme Self within and everywhere.

665. There is no other vessel on this earth to wade the ocean of Samsara than the mastery of the lower instinctive mind.

666. Through the play of the mind in objects, proximity appears to be a great distance and *vice versa*. The mind has the potency of creating or undoing the whole world in the twinkling of an eye.

667. Never allow the mind to be tainted by desires and run out through the channels of the senses. Senses cannot do anything independently if the mind is not connected with them. The world is beautiful and pleasant or ugly and miserable, just as the mind chooses.

668. If one is free from desires of sensual objects, attraction and repulsion, egoism, anger, lust, mineness, pride, one can clearly understand that he has got destruction of mind. Right understanding weakens the sensuous mind.

669. Conquest of mind will enable one to go to the source of Brahman and he can realise his own essential nature—*Satchidananda*. Equilibrium of mind brings about real, lasting happiness to a disciplined man.

670. The whole wealth and enjoyment of the whole world are nothing when compared to the bliss enjoyed by the great soul who has serenity and calmness of mind.

671. True freedom will come only if the mind agrees to work as an obedient servant of the Atman or Soul. When the mind is annihilated, when it becomes free from all desires, cravings, longings, it can be said to be an emancipated one. The Sadhaka rests in peace and enjoys the everlasting bliss in the kingdom of the Self.

THE KEY TO BLESSEDNESS

672. Strength is life. Weakness is death. Have strength born of wisdom of the Self. Destroy all weaknesses by identifying yourself with the Supreme Self, the source of all powers and strength. Strength is the key to blessedness.

673. Eat meat; drink wine; live in the hotels; you will become a demon. Take milk and fruits; live on the banks of the Ganga; do Japa and meditation; you will attain Self-realisation. You will become Brahman.

674. Eradicate all evil. Cherish good. Purify your heart. Cleanse your thoughts. Serve all. Love all. Meditate on God. Have devotion to the Lord. Hurt none in thought, word and deed. Dwell in solitude. Reflect. Enquire. Meditate. This is the teaching of the sages and seers.

675. Desire for nothing. Look for no return. Give always like the Ganga, the fruit trees, the sandal trees.

676. Receive everybody in this world with love, respect, kindness and cheerfulness. You do not know in what form the Lord may appear before you.

677. He who lives for others alone lives. A selfish man is a dead man though he is alive.

678. To do good to others and serve others should be your motto. To serve the poor and oppressed is your duty. You should not care a pin for your personal gain or remuneration.

679. Serve the poor. See God in them. Here is a great field for you. Why do you go to build Dharmasalas, choultries and dig wells?

680. Even dacoits have become great Rishis or sages. A sinner is a saint of tomorrow. Therefore exert, purify, approach the saints.

681. Burn all passions when you wave light before the Lord.

682. Practise pure unselfish love in your daily life. Embrace all living beings. Crush all forms of hatred. Expand your heart. This is the real culture or civilisation.

683. All life is one. The world is one home. All are members of one human family. All creation is an organic whole. No man is independent of that whole. Man makes himself miserable by separating himself from others. Separation is death. Unity is eternal life. Cultivate cosmic love. Include all. Embrace all. Recognise the worth of others. Destroy all barriers, racial, religious and natural prejudices that separate man from man. Recognise the non-dual principles, the immortal essence within all creatures. Protect animals. Let all life be sacred. Then

this world will be a paradise of beauty, a haven of peace and tranquillity.

684. Move about freely in peace with a loin cloth. Roam about care-free living on whatever is obtained by alms. Enjoy the bliss of meditation and drink the elixir of contentment. Is there any drink or beverage more delicious than the cool, refreshing waters of the Ganga? Sleep on the green pasture, the Nature's mattress. Let the hands be your cushioned pillow. The kingdom of the three worlds cannot tempt you now.

685. Follow not the joyless quest of the mind. Do self-surrender. Repeat the Name of the Lord regularly. Your heart will blossom soon.

686. To serve the poor, the sick, the saints and the country, to raise the fallen, to lead the blind, to share what you have with others, to bring solace to the afflicted, to cheer up the suffering are your ideals. To have perfect faith in God, to love your neighbour as your own Self, to love God with all your heart, mind and soul, to protect cows, animals, children and women should be your watchword. And your goal should be God-realisation.

SADHANA AND SOME EXPERIENCES

687. When you obtain glimpses of the Self, when you see blazing light, when you get some other extraordinary spiritual experience, do not fall back in terror. Do not give up the Sadhana. Do not mistake them for a phantom. Be brave. March on boldly with joy.

688. Sit in a proper posture. Shut your eyes. Imagine that nothing exists. Next imagine that there is nothing but God everywhere.

689. In the beginning of meditation and concentration you will see in the centre of the forehead a resplendent, flashing light. This will last for half or one minute and then disappear. The light will flash either from above or sideways. Sometimes a Sun of 6 inches or 8 inches in diameter with or without rays will be seen. You will see the form of your Guru or Upasya Murthy (Ishta Devata) also.

690. If you want to enter into Samadhi quickly, cut off all connections with friends, relatives, etc. Observe Akhanda

APPENDIX—II 673

Mouna for one month. Live alone. Take very little but nutritious food. Live on milk alone. Plunge in deep meditation. Dive deep. You will be immersed in Samadhi. Have constant practice. Be cautious. Use your common sense at every step and at every turn. Do not make violent struggle with the mind. Walk alone. Deal very gently with the mind. Allow the thoughts of the Divine and divine feelings to flow gently into your being.

APPENDIX—III
SIVANANDA SADHANA SARA

FUNDAMENTAL ASPECTS OF SADHANA

1. Sadhana or spiritual practice should make you ever cheerful, more concentrated, joyful, balanced, peaceful, contented, blissful, dispassionate, fearless, courageous, compassionate, discriminative. reflective, unattached, angerless, I-less, desireless, mineless. Sadhana should give you rich inner life, introspective inner vision and unruffled state of mind, under all conditions of life. These are the signs of your spiritual growth. Seeing of visions, lights, hearing of Anahata sounds, Divya Gandha or supersensuous fragrance, feeling of the movement of current upwards and downwards have not much spiritual value, although they indicate you have attained the first degree of concentration.

2. Bhakti is essential for everybody. However strong the individual efforts may be, it is impossible to eradicate the subtle Vrittis in the mind, viz., subtle form of lust, anger, jealousy, Moha or delusion, pride etc. You may do Sadhana in crores of lives and yet you will not be able to burn the roots or seeds of the evil Vrittis that are lurking in the corners of your mind from time immemorial without the grace of the Lord. God selects or chooses that man whom He wishes to elevate and liberate. The Kathopanishad says, "Not by spiritual discourses, not by intelligence, not by study of many scriptures this Atman is attained; that man who is chosen by the Lord attains the Supreme."

3. Sincerity in Sadhana is the key to success. Self-realisation has to be attained only through rigorous Sadhana. Sadhana should not be merely a routine. There must be the earnestness to see God face to face, to drink the nectar of immortality through Samadhi and to entertain the pure Advaita Bhavana always. The path is easy for one who is dexterous, who is firm in his resolve and who has that undying aspiration to attain the highest peak of truth.

4. Regular concentration and repetition of the Lord's Name will remove scepticism and infuse faith and devotion. Sadhana of any kind produces deep Yoga impression and strengthens the spiritual momentum. Nothing is lost when the candle burns. So is the case with Yoga also. Spiritual progress is slow. Hence it becomes difficult to gauge it in the beginning. The effect is there already. After sometime, it will become quite tangible and perceptible.

THE NATURE AND PROCESSES OF SADHANA

5. Desire and egoism resist surrender, at every step. When there is total, unreserved, ungrudging true surrender of the whole being without the least demand, then the Divine Grace or the Divine Power comes flooding down into the being of the Sadhaka and does Sadhana. The Divine Power takes complete possession of the mind, will, life and body. Then the Sadhana goes on with tremendous speed.

6. Sadhana is at first mechanical and in the later stage alone it becomes a part and parcel of one's own life. It looks as a drudgery in the beginning. Later on it imparts joy, peace, strength, courage and freedom.

7. If you have no Vairagya or dispassion, if there is no strong aspiration, if there is no purity of heart, there will be a failure in your Sadhana. Practice of Asanas, sitting in one Asana for three hours, practice of Pranayama, Bandhas and Mudras cannot produce much spiritual progress, if you are lacking in the aforesaid three virtues.

8. Even a ray of inner light during meditation will lighten your path. It will give you a great deal of encouragement and inner strength. It will goad you to do more inner Sadhana. You will experience the ray of light when the meditation becomes more deep and when you rise above body-consciousness.

9. All that happens has His Sakti as the basis. He has His own reasons for bringing about everything. Do not identify yourself with anything. Stand aside as a witness and enjoy the fun. God-realisation is your goal. All else is false and fit only to be negated. Come. Gird up your loins and plunge in Sadhana. Realise God in this very life. May God bless you!

10. You can fly with the two wings of Vairagya and Abhyasa to the summit of knowledge of the Imperishable or Nirvikalpa Samadhi or the supreme abode of eternal bliss. Both wings must be equally strong. If Vairagya wanes, energy will leak, the senses will again be turbulent and mischievous. You will have downfall. If you slacken your Sadhana, you will also have downfall. It will be difficult to rise again to the original heights of deep and intense meditation and Samadhi.

11. A man in the world sometimes cannot keep up to his Sadhana on account of his varied engagements. In those circumstances, he need not do all items of Sadhana. Whenever he finds it convenient he may write Likhita Japa at any time of the day.

CONCENTRATION AND NEED FOR VIGILANCE

12. Do not be slack in your Sadhana. It is Sadhana that will help you in the long run. It is the only asset in this life. Be regular in your Sadhana and attain Self-realisation in this very birth.

13. If you give up reading of newspapers and playing of cards, if you reduce your sleep, and if you reduce your time spent in playing tennis, football, cricket, billiard etc., you will have ample time to do Sadhana.

14. Contemplation is of two types, one of remembrance, the other of deep meditation. Constant remembrance of the Lord or the qualities of the Brahman (Nama Smarana) is fit to be practised always. This can be practised without the sitting pose. But deep meditation is possible only in the sitting posture. This is possible only for him who sits up in complete wakefulness, but not for him who is lying in bed overcome by sleep, or standing or walking; for him distraction would necessarily set in. Meditation is far superior to mere remembrance. This is beyond a doubt. Hence the necessity for the sitting posture in meditation is proved.

15. The form of the Lord does not come to the mind vividly because of lack of good concentration. Develop concentration to a great extent. Bring the rays of the mind to fall upon the object. Collect them around the form of the Lord for a long time. This is concentration. If you go on like this for more

time, you will have a clearer idea of the Lord and will remain in God-consciousness for a long time. This is meditation.

16. Come out of the dungeon of ignorance. Bask in the sunshine of wisdom of the Self. Take a dose of recitation of the Lord's Name and Kirtan daily. This will bring down the fever of lust and the scorching heat of greed and Moha. Close your eyes for ten minutes and meditate on the form of Lord Krishna, Lord Rama or Lord Siva. The cool breeze of spiritual peace will calm and refresh you quickly.

17. The final stage of all meditation is to merge the individual self into the Supreme Self. The experiences that come and go are sure signs of spiritual advancement. You should not think of them in high terms. You must achieve the final union wherein all the three states vanish and the supreme fourth state of Turiya, the superconscious state alone shines.

CONDITIONS FOR YOGA SADHANA

18. You cannot practise Yoga living in Wall Street or Piccadily or Esplanade, Mount Road or Mall, breathing contaminated air of these places, eating unnatural, heavy foods, attending cinemas, theatres and ball-rooms, wasting of the vital energy, with nerves under high tensions and with ears dinned by the sounds of motor-cars and machinery. Lord Krishna says, "Let the Yogi constantly engage himself in Yoga remaining in a secret and pure place by himself."

19. Stability and strong will-power will come after facing the opposing movements in life. The waves should be buffeted before the other shore is reached. There is no easy path to salvation except through small improvements, corrections, purity, Japa, celibacy. Do not go astray by believing your lower mind.

20. A Sadhu tried to save a scorpion from flowing down a stream three times. He was stung twice but he succeeded in getting it out in the third time. The spectators asked the Sadhu why he did not learn a lesson from his first experience. He gave the answer that when the scorpion, a lower creature did not leave its nature of stinging, it would have been disgraceful for him to leave his nature of doing good, even to those who did harm to him. Therein lies true strength, power and glory.

21. That is the tongue with which one sings the Lord's excellent attributes; those are the hands which do service unto the Lord and to the humanity. That indeed is the mind which constantly remembers the Lord present in all mobile and immobile beings. That is the ear which hears the Lord's sacred stories.

22. That is the head which always bends before saints, the idols, and all forms of the Lord. That is the eye which looks at the form of the Lord. Those are the limbs which always resort to the waters that wash Lord Vishnu's feet and those of His votaries.

SADHANA, THE DIVINE NAME AND EQUANIMITY

23. Keep balance and harmony between hand, heart and head; actions, feelings and thoughts. *'Samatvam'* (equilibrium or equanimity) is called Yoga. You may fail several times to keep up the harmony. Stand up and struggle again and again. You are bound to succeed eventually. Perseverance, tenacity, courage, determination are needed to achieve success in Yoga.

24. An ignorant man was searching in the street in the moon-light for something. A passerby asked, "O man! what are you searching here?" He replied, "I lost my needle in the house and so I am searching for it here." The passerby said, "O fool! why do you search for the needle here when you have lost it in the house? Search it in your house. You will find it." The man replied, "There is clear moon-light here and so I am searching here." Such is the case with the worldly-minded persons. The ocean of bliss is within their heart in their own Atman, but they are searching for happiness in external, perishable objects, which can give only pain and misery.

25. Mortify the lower nature. Crucify the flesh. Subdue the passions. Have self-control. Then alone you will have strength to bear the Cross, in whatever form it may be ordained for you by the Lord.

26. Choose one virtue for every month and keep it before you as an ideal to be achieved throughout. Meditate on it morning and evening, just after getting up from bed and just before retiring at night. I would advise you to take up "PURITY" this month.

27. I hand you this Master-key to success in life and God-realisation, the Lord's Name. Repeat the Name of your Ishta Devata from this moment whenever you have leisure. Have regular Japa-sitting, morning and evening. Pray to God at bedtime also. Sing the Mahamantra,

Hare Rama Hare Rama, Rama Rama Hare Hare;
Hare Krishna Hare Krishna, Krishna Krishna Hare Hare.

THE RESULTS OF REAL LOVE

28. If you are established in Ahimsa or non-violence, you will become incapable of doing any evil. You will never be harsh, rude and haughty even for a moment. No thought of evil or injuring others will ever occupy your mind even for a moment. Your heart will be filled with love, kindness and affection.

29. If you become incapable of doing any evil to other people in thought, word and deed, and if no evil thought occupies your mind, even for a moment, you can move the hearts of the people of the whole world, you will be endowed with tremendous will-power or soul-force.

30. A boy is taught in the school that 5+5=8. When he comes to his house, his parents and brothers also say that 5+5=8. When he plays with his friends, they also say 5+5=8. This goes on for some years. If anybody tells him now that 5+5=10, he will never believe it. He will at once contradict him and begin to dispute with him. He will say, "I am correct. My parents and teachers also are in agreement with me. You are entirely wrong." Even so, you will doubt if the preceptor and the scriptures say, "You are immortal, all-pervading Atman. You are not this perishable body." You will fight with the Sannyasins and sages, because you are thinking for a long time, "This world is real. This body is the Self."

31. Constant Satsanga with the wise and study of Srutis under a Guru will slowly wipe out the old, wrong, worldly Samskaras.

32. Feel that you are separate from the body. This requires constant mental effort. Sometimes when you relax yourself you will become mixed with the body, senses and

objects. It does not matter. Again try to separate yourself from the five sheaths.

FORMULA IN HIGHER SADHANA

33. When you are engaged in any action, be a witness. Repeat the formula, "I am silent witness or Sakshi, OM OM OM." Even if you have no sufficient time to watch the mind, note what the mind is doing, what particular Vritti or Guna is operating at a particular time, at least once in an hour. This is the best method to find out the defects and weaknesses of one's own mind. Then you should use suitable methods to remove them. Come what may, with asinine patience, with great perseverance like that of a bird which ventured to empty the ocean with its beak or a blade of grass, with leech-like tenacity, gigantic, adamantine will, you will have to apply yourself to Tapas and meditation. The Lord has said, "Remember Me and fight, O Arjuna!" So remember Him and go on with your Sadhana with increased enthusiasm and intense faith.

34. Your vessel must be strong enough to hold the Divine Light. Otherwise it will break at any moment. That vessel is your own mind or Antahkarana or inner instrument. The vessel can become strong only if you purify it through constant, untiring selfless service, Japa, Kirtan, Satsanga, study of holy scriptures, meditation and Pranayama. How hard it is to bear the light of even lightning! You tremble and shiver with fear. Even Lakshmi was not able to bear the effulgence of Lord Narasimha. She trembled. It was only Prahlada, who had a very pure heart filled with supreme devotion to Lord Narayana, who was able to bear the formidable light through His grace. Therefore prepare your mind first to receive the Divine Light. Purify it. Make it perfectly taintless or spotless.

35. Subconscious life is more powerful than your ordinary life of objective consciousness. Beneath your conscious life there is a wide region of subconscious life. The subconscious life can modify and influence your conscious life. Through the practice of Yoga you can modify, control and influence the subconscious depths. All habits originate from the subconscious. All habits are imbedded in the subconscious. The super-conscious experience is Turiya or the fourth state. It is Nirvikalpa

Samadhi or state of perfect awareness or oneness with the Supreme Being.

SADHANA AND THE SPIRITUAL DESTINY

36. You do not come into the world in total forgetfulness and in utter darkness. You are born with certain memories and habits acquired in the previous births. Desires take their origin from previous experience. We find that none is born without desire. Every being is born with some desires which are associated with the things enjoyed by him in the past life. The desire proves the existence of his soul in the previous lives.

37. Open yourself to the Divine through purity, faith, devotion, aspiration and total, ungrudging self-surrender. The Divine grace will descend on you. You will be conscious of the Divine force working in you. Do not obstruct the descent of the Divine grace and Divine force through your own egoistic ideas, subtle cravings and old habits.

38. Man alone has the will to release himself from the bondage. Piercing the veil of ignorance with the sword of true knowledge attained through intense Sadhana, he realises his Real Self.

39. Man gets knocks and blows. He thinks and reflects. He discriminates and meditates. He enquires, "Who am I?" Ultimately he attains Self-realisation. He finds that all that has happened—the ignorance, the veiled state, the births and deaths, suffering and enjoyment—all that has happened has been a long dream.

40. You have not made even an iota of spiritual progress so long as your tongue can offend others. There is a sword or atom bomb in the tongue. Watch. Speak sweetly. Discipline the organ of speech again and again. Observe Mouna, practise Pranayama and thus control the impulse of speech. Prayer, Japa and meditation also will help you a great deal in this direction.

SADHANA AND THE MIND

41. The mind is the creator of all fancies, concepts, and through these of worries. A little control over the mind should be exercised when small ripples of disturbance pass over the surface. Close yourself in the room, and forcibly drive out the

thoughts through Nama Japa. When the mind rests in the calm, some good decision, as to the future action to be taken, comes to the forefront. This will be often the voice of the Soul.

42. Change your vision, attitude or outlook. You will see good in evil, beauty in ugliness, life in stone, pleasure in pain. Everything is good, everything is beautiful, everything is alive, everything is delightful. Feel this. Realise this.

43. The subconscious mind will rake up all thoughts hidden under its veil and throw them up on the surface of the mind. Take only those good, helpful thoughts and destroy the evil thoughts. Leave the good thoughts again to rest in the mind, and drive the bad thoughts to fly off from the mind.

44. Let your spiritual zeal grow steadily. Let the lamp or light that is burning within you be more steady than before. The result of spiritual Sadhana can only be gauged by the heart. Purity in thought, purity in action, widening of love towards others, shedding of tears at the thought of the Lord, horripilation, a sort of attraction for one and all without the distinction of caste, creed or sex, humility, sincerity are some of the outward signs of true spiritual progress.

45. Sit calmly and watch the mind-wanderings carefully. Find out what are its habitual likings and thoughts. Find out on what objects it dwells upon constantly. Slowly withdraw it from those objects by fixing it on the form of the Lord again and again. Place your foot step by step in the ladder of concentration. Be patient. Struggle hard.

46. He who seeks the Eternal, brushing aside the evanescent, he who clings to the good, avoiding the pleasant, he who returns good for evil, he who loves even those who hate him—this one who leads the Divine life, is no doubt a veritable God on this earth.

REQUISITES FOR SPIRITUAL PROGRESS

47. Without ethical perfection there is no spiritual progress. Without spiritual progress there is no emancipation. Ethical perfection comes through the practice of Yama and Niyama. Asanas and Pranayama form the second stage. Concentration and meditation form the third step, Samadhi is the *summum bonum*. Thus the human soul aspiring after

perfection goes from stage to stage and finally merges itself in the blissful glory of the highest union. Aim therefore at moral perfection. Spiritual success is half achieved through strong moral foundation.

48. Meditation enables you to overcome the obstacles which may come from your mind. Do not become dissatisfied with the results. You will gain concentration little by little. When your mind wanders bring it back. Think that you are on the drill ground. When your eyes wander here and there, you officer will call out "attention." Then you will assume the posture of attention. Even so, when your mind wanders, become your own officer and call out "Attention." Your mind will soon fix itself on the image of the Lord. Practise this for some days, even months. Gradually you will develop concentration. Each defective step in the spiritual line will be a step towards progress. Be patient.

49. Aspirants think that they have advanced very much in meditation and Samadhi by sitting in a closed room for a very long time. But they are upset by trifling things. They expect respect, nice treatment, fine seats to sit on. They are irritated and annoyed by petty things. They are slaves of superiority complex. They cannot adapt with others. Hence they wander from place to place without peace of mind. Cultivation of virtues such as humility, adaptability, spirit of selfless service, love, is of paramount importance. If one has these virtues, then Samadhi will come by itself.

50. Blissful is freedom from jealousy and hatred. Blissful is absence of lust, greed and pride. Free yourself from the tangled net of sorrow, misery and bondage. Abandon the erroneous notion of Self in the body. This is a treacherous pillow to rest upon. Errors lead you astray on account of ignorance and attachment to the body. Illusions beget miseries.

51. You have enjoyed the sensual objects in millions of births. You have enjoyed the sensual objects for the last several years in this birth. If there has not come satisfaction in you till now, when will it come then? Do not run after the mirage of sensual objects. The senses are deluding you. Develop dispassion and renunciation and realise your Atman. Then alone you will get eternal satisfaction, everlasting peace and immortal bliss. Wake up from your slumber of ignorance.

52. The aspirant in the olden days used to approach the Guru with a bundle of sticks (Samit) in his hand for spiritual initiation. What does this indicate? He prays to his preceptor, "O adorable Guru! Let my bundle of sins and worldly Vasanas be burnt in the fire of wisdom through Thy Grace. Let the Divine flame grow in me. Let me attain the highest illumination. Make me realise the inner self-effulgent Atman. Let my senses, Vasanas, mind, Prana and egoism be given as oblation in the fire of wisdom. Let me shine as the Light of lights."

53. To aspire to lead a pure Divine life amidst lustful, vicious material life, to yearn for the realisation of the Atman, to be born in a noble family of Sattvic people—these are rare gifts of God which ought to be zealously guarded. Be vigilant. Take shelter under the cool shade of Yoga. Take the fullest advantage of God's gift and grace. Repeat His Name. Sing His glory with family and friends.

54. A real devotee knows that God does everything for his own good. If a man undergoes loss and sufferings, this will produce Vairagya in him and turn the mind more and more towards God and will develop in him the power of endurance, patience and strong will-power. A foolish, worldly man is not aware of this.

55. Until man recognises the fact that in essence he is the immortal Soul, he will not know himself. Through ignorance he identifies himself with the body. When knowledge dawns through annihilation of ignorance, identification with the body vanishes. He becomes one with the Supreme Soul and attains knowledge of Brahman.

56. If the mind is not focussed during meditation, if it wanders wildly, if it builds castles in the air, plans and schemes and entertains or generates irrelevant, nonsensical thoughts, it is better to get up from concentration and do some useful work or study of holy scriptures. It is only waste of time and energy by continuing to sit with closed eyes with such a state of mind.

GUIDANCE IN SADHANA

57. Have perfect mastery over the emotions. Never be carried away by the emotions. Control them. You can enjoy supreme peace. Pranayama, Japa and regular meditation will help you to keep the emotions under control.

58. The Sruti declares, "He who sees the one Atman or the Supreme Self in all beings, how can there be delusion or grief for him? How can he be afraid of anybody?"—Isavasya Upanishad. "The Self harmonised by Yoga sees the Atman in all beings, and all beings in the Self; everywhere he sees the same"—Gita, VII-29. "Sages behold the one Atman in a Brahmana adorned with learning and humility, a cow, an elephant and even a dog and an outcaste and thus have equal vision"—Gita, V-18. Behold the one Atman in all beings. This is equal vision.

59. Thinking of sensual objects is Sanga or attachment. Non-thinking of sensual objects is Vairagya. Stop thinking of objects by thinking of Brahman or the Eternal or your Ishta Devata (Tutelary Deity).

60. Keeping the Vasanas in the mind is keeping a black cobra within, and feeding it with milk. Your life is ever in danger. Kill these Vasanas through Vichara, Vairagya and meditation on the Atman.

61. Do not be highly emotional and over-sentimental. Do not be swayed by emotions. Sympathy and mercy must be there, but you should not be swayed by feelings when anybody is sick. Sickness and death are quite common in this world. Everyone suffers from some malady or other to exhaust or purge out some Karmas. Do not be attached to anybody. Attachment brings pain and restlessness.

62. When you happen to live in a Dharmasala or public inn, if there is a single woman in your neighbouring room, leave the place at once. You do not know what will happen. It is always advisable to leave the danger zone immediately, however strong you may be through the practice of Tapas and meditation. Do not expose yourself to temptation. Remember the story of Sri Vyasa and his disciple Jaimini. Even highly developed Rishis who used to live on leaves, roots, air and water had succumbed to temptation.

63. All your troubles and miseries are due to your egoism. It is egoism that has limited you. The cause of your misery does not come from without. Annihilate this egoism. You will enjoy infinite bliss and a life of expansion.

64. Your enjoyments are the source of your pain. Your desires and ambitions allure you to your own ruin. Your senses and mind are your enemies. All objects tempt and delude you. There is nothing permanent in this world. The splendour of all objects is flickering. Nothing in this world can give you everlasting bliss. There is nothing in this mundane life which can give real solace and perennial joy for the enquirer and thinking man. There is something which is above the sufferings and sorrows of life, which is eternal, pure and all-blissful. If you attain this state of existence alone, you will be ever happy and peaceful.

65. The secret of renunciation is the renunciation of egoism, mineness and desires. Abandoning wife, children, property, house, relations and friends does not constitute real renunciation. Objects do not bind you. It is mineness (Mamata) that binds you to this Samsara or cycle of births and deaths.

66. Seek thou the hidden, inexhaustible treasures of the Self within. You will realise that the empire of the whole world, even the empire of gods is dust before the splendour of the knowledge of the Self. Terrible is the bondage of this world. Go beyond mundane life and live in the Eternal.

67. When you attain the intuitive eye of wisdom, you will surely be able to see the grand panorama of your past lives and your steady evolution towards that God, at the threshold of which thou art now. Stick to the path of Yoga. Practise diligently. Be regular in your meditation. Keep yourself above the allurements of the world. You will soon attain the Knowledge of the Self. I shall serve you and guide you.

THE PRINCIPLES OF SPIRITUAL PROGRESS

68. Discipline the mind and the senses. Cultivate noble virtues. Try to know the nature of the soul. Practise regular meditation. Then alone you will attain immortality and deep, abiding joy.

69. When you know your real nature, then you will understand that the world is a mere dream and all the names and forms are mere mental imaginations. He who is steadfast and balanced in pleasure and pain is the fittest person for attaining Immortality.

70. Do not be dejected. You have got immeasurable

strength and power within. There is a glorious future awaiting you. Face all difficulties with a smile. Pain is the real eye-opener and real guide. God is putting you to this severe test to make you more strong and more powerful. Understand this secret well. Never be despondent. Ever laugh, jump, whistle and smile.

71. There should be unshaken faith in God during trials, disappointments and difficulties. Hope and help come from within when one feels utterly helpless. There can be no strength without suffering. There can be no success without suffering. Without sorrows, without persecution, none can become a saint or a sage. Every suffering is meant for one's uplift and development. Suffering augments the power of endurance, mercy, faith in God and removes egoism.

72. Things which are not in use daily such as knives, copper and brass vessels become rusty. Even so, if the limbs and muscles of the body are not properly used through exercise and work, they get degenerated. Man becomes Tamasic. He becomes a victim of inertia. Hence aspirants who lead a life of Nivritti or renunciation should be very careful. They should not allow themselves to be overpowered by Tamas. They should daily practise Asanas, Suryanamaskaras, etc.

ELEMENTS OF SADHANA

73. Even the most virulent of poisons is no poison but the sensual objects are truly so. The former kills one body only, whereas the latter kills many bodies in successive births. Conquer the mind through love and service.

74. That virtuous man only will attain Moksha or emancipation who from his early boyhood trains himself in Atma-Jnana or spiritual lore, who associates himself with the sages and develops compassion, humility, courage and other good qualities.

75. Do not cause injury by thought, word or deed to any living being. Speak the truth. Practise Brahmacharya. Lead a simple life. Acquire just those things that are necessary to life. Study the scriptures. Bear patiently all afflictions that come with the pursuit of virtue. Worship the Lord. Concentrate and meditate. This is the Path to Supreme Blessedness.

76. Observe Mouna or silence for 2 hours daily. Acquire steadiness through firmness of posture. Withdraw the senses from the objects. Control the breath. Bring the mind into a state of equanimity. This is the path to Infinite Bliss.

77. Give yourself wholly to God. Renounce for the love of the Lord everything that is not He. Live as if there is none but the Lord and you in the world.

78. Take pure food in moderation. Abandon sensual pleasures. Do virtuous actions. Dwell in solitude. Meditate seriously and rigorously. This is the way to Self-realisation.

BACKGROUND OF THOUGHT

79. Make intense inner Sadhana the keynote of your life. Base your life upon the ceaseless remembrance of the Divine Ideal and constant feeling of His Presence.

80. The Name of the Lord is Divine Nectar. Name is your sole refuge, prop and Treasure. Name and Nami (God) are one. Always chant His Names with devotion. Do Kirtan. This is the principal Sadhana in Kali Yuga.

81. Constantly repeat some inspiring verses (praises of God's glory) or some Mantras, or the Name of God. This will be your Divine Background of thought.

82. Pray to the Lord from the core of your heart:—

> "I am Thine. All is Thine.
> Thy Will be done.
> I am an instrument in Thy hands.
> You do everything. You are just.
> Grant me faith and devotion."

83. He who practises Brahmacharya is a Dheera or a hero. He can face easily the dangers and difficulties of life. Without Brahmacharya, education is quite hollow and shallow.

84. From this moment engage your mind and body so incessantly all day and night during the waking hours that the mind will not have the time to think of the evil habits. If evil thoughts attack you, quickly take out the pocket Gita and start reading it; or write a few Mantras in a notebook, which you should always keep with you; or roll a few beads of Japa. Assert: "I have been chosen by God to tread the spiritual path. I

have a very strong will. I will not be conquered by these evils." Do not sleep till sleep overpowers you. Do not overload your stomach at night.

85. Every Mantra is very powerful. The Durga Mantra will invoke the Mother's grace for thy salvation very speedily. Kindly cling to it. Meditate day and night on that Omnipresent Power, Mother—the Cause and the Support of everything. Maya will vanish. True light will dawn in you. Worry not about birth, life and death, but stick to Truth.

86. Only those who have cosmic vision can understand the real import behind the happenings. They know that even a dry leaf cannot be wafted by the strongest gale without His Will. The "why" and "how" of events are transcendental questions. Rack not your brain with problems beyond the reach of the intellect. Repeat the Name of the Lord. Pray for Visvakalyan. This is the opportunity provided by Him for earnest souls to evolve rapidly. Radiate love, spirit of service and sacrifice to all. You can transform the world into a veritable heaven.

87. Plunge in Sadhana. Assert that you are the One, Indivisible Brahman. Identify yourself with the universe through Yoga. All doubts will be cleared. There will then remain no question to ask.

88. How can you ever feel lonely when the only true friend, God, resides in your heart? His company, through prayer, Japa, Kirtan, meditation, Mantra-writing and the practice of Raja Yoga, is elevating. It will give you unending peace, bliss and power, whereas the company of the so-called human friends will lead you astray, will ruin you. True, in the initial stages there may be an internal struggle; but by and by, you will find delight in the company of the sweet Lord and will shun the company of worldly-minded people. Whenever you feel gloomy, read some good spiritual books or write your Ishta Mantra or Guru Mantra in a notebook with one-pointed mind.

SADHANA AND SAMADHI

89. Pain, suffering, misfortune and ill-luck are all mental creations. In fact, they do not exist there at all! Everything is done by the Blessed Lord, our Beloved Father and Mother, for your own good. Try to meditate on this great Truth; and realise the wonderful results. When you learn to reach in the same way

to pain and pleasure, when you greet both as blessings from the Lord showered on you for the purpose of reminding you of Him, and when you use both as God-sent opportunities for remembering Him and repeating His Name and singing His glories, then Infinite Bliss and Supreme Peace will be yours.

90. Approach the Lord with "Sarvabhava," with all your heart, mind and soul, with your whole being. Do not keep any reservation. Do not keep any desire for your secret gratification. The mind, Chitta, intellect and ego should all agree to do the surrender wholly. You will be supremely blessed. You will obtain His full grace.

91. When you write the Mantras, always observe Mouna or silence. Feel that the Divine Sakti is entering your whole being. Do not change your seat till you finished the day's number of pages. There is an Achintya Sakti (indescribable power) in Mantra-writing. It helps the concentration in the Sadhaka. If the two join together, a thrill of joy pervades the whole being. The inner calm is then felt by the Sadhaka. Often he feels himself also lost in the one thought of God.

PHASES OF SPIRITUAL PRACTICE

92. Every attempt in the spiritual path, however feeble it be, will add to your inner spiritual strength. Prayer, Kirtan, Japa, meditation and Svadhyaya will open before you the gates to the domain of inner freedom and eternal bliss. Strive ceaselessly and attain success.

93. Never mind repeated failures in your Sadhana. *Nil desperandum.* Despair not. Do not give up the struggle or the Sadhana. Stand up and again fight, again struggle. You are nearer to success each time. Every failure is a stepping-stone to success. You will succeed in the long run.

94. The mind cannot exist without desire, attachment and egoism. It will cling to some form or other. It will entertain some desire or other. There will be ego in some form or other. Entertain Sattvic desires. Have a strong desire for attaining salvation. Through this you can destroy all worldly desires. Instead of allowing the mind to get itself attached to the form of wife or son, try to fix it on the form of Lord Krishna or Lord Rama. Let it be attached to this form. Develop Sattvic egoism by asserting "I am the servant of Lord Krishna."

95. If you wish to become one with the Universal Consciousness, you must expand your heart. You must be one with the universe. You must eradicate egoism, selfishness, jealousy, hatred, greed—the barriers that separate you from the rest of the world. Become a Karma Yogin and work for the well-being of the world. You will merge yourself in the Universal Consciousness. You must do universal services in order to attain that state of being one with the Universal Consciousness.

96. Be serene and tranquil under all circumstances. Cultivate this virtue Sama again and again through constant and strenuous endeavour. Serenity is like a rock. Waves of irritation may dash on it, but cannot affect it. Meditate daily on the ever-tranquil Atman or the Eternal which is unchanging. You will attain this sublime virtue gradually. The divine light will descend on a calm mind only. An aspirant with a calm mind only can enter into deep meditation and Nirvikalpa Samadhi. He only can practise Nishkama Karma Yoga.

APPENDIX—IV

ONLY WITH AN INVINCIBLE AND POWERFUL ARROW OF YOGIC CONCENTRATION CAN YOU KILL THE SEVEN FACULTIES THAT TROUBLE YOU

(ADAPTED FROM THE MAHABHARATA)

There was a royal sage named Alarka who was a great Tapasvin. He did many rigorous penances. He had full knowledge of duty and morality, and was truthful. He was very firm in his vows. This is how he attained Self-realisation.

One day he was sitting at the foot of a tree and began to reflect on subtle things. He reflected within himself thus: "My mind has become unsteady and turbulent. The real victory is when the mind is conquered. The result of this conquest becomes permanent only, if one gains victory over one's mind. It always wanders. It goads me to do acts for the gratification of my desires. I shall henceforth shoot very sharp-pointed arrows at the mind."

The mind said: "O Alarka! These arrows can never cut me through. They will pierce only your own vital parts and you will die. Try to find out other arrows to kill me."

Alarka heard these words and reflected thus: "The nose troubles me. It always hankers after scents. I shall discharge sharp arrows at the nose."

The nose said: "O Alarka! These arrows can never pass through me. They will pierce only your own vital parts and you will die. Look for other arrows to kill me."

Alarka heard these words and reflected thus: "My tongue is very mischievous and troubles me much. It always craves to taste palatable things and savoury dishes. I shall discharge sharp arrows at the tongue."

The tongue said: "O Alarka! These arrows will not cut me through. They will pierce only your own vital parts and you will die. Find out other arrows to kill me."

Alarka reflected thus: "The skin troubles me. It runs after soft things. It always hankers after objects which are delightful to the touch. I shall discharge sharp arrows at the skin and tear off the skin."

The skin said: "O my dear Alarka! These arrows can pass through me. They will pierce only your own vital parts and you will die. Look for other arrows to kill me."

Alarka heard these words and reflected thus: "The ear troubles me much. It wants to hear all kinds of music. It hears various sounds and hankers after them. I shall discharge sharp arrows at the ear."

The ear said: "My dear Alarka! These arrows will not pierce me. They will pierce only your own vital parts and you will die. Find out other arrows to kill me."

Alarka reflected: "The eye is very troublesome. It longs to see various colours and beautiful forms. I shall destroy this eye with sharp arrows."

The eye said: "These arrows will not, O Alkarka, pass through me at all. They will pierce only your own vital parts and you will die. Find other arrows in order to kill me."

Alarka reflected thus: "This intellect only troubles me much. It forms many determinations with the help of reasoning and in consequence leads me astray. I shall discharge sharp arrows at the intellect and kill it."

The intellect said: "O Alarka! These arrows will not pass through me at all. They will only pierce your vital parts and you will die. Search for other arrows to annihilate me."

Alarka underwent rigorous penance to overcome the seven faculties, viz., mind, nose, tongue, skin, ears, eyes and intellect. But in vain! He then began to reflect for a long time on this subject. At last he found out the real powerful arrow, viz., control of mind which would kill all the seven. He could not obtain anything better than this. He engaged himself in Yoga, fixed his mind on one object and remained perfectly still and calm. He quickly killed all the senses, the mind and the intellect with one arrow, viz., the concentration of the mind in Yoga. He entered into his innermost all-blissful Soul or Brahman and thereby acquired the highest success.

He was struck with wonder and said, "Alas! it is a pity I wasted my life trying to acquire domain over earthly possessions which are transitory. I wasted my energy in sensual enjoyments. I did not know up to this time how to control the mind and the senses. I performed acts that are external. I courted power, wealth and sovereignty till now. I had no right understanding and discrimination. I had no idea of the immortal Soul or the Atman. I had no idea of the efficiency of Yoga. There is no happiness higher than control of mind by Yoga practices. There is no wealth higher than the spiritual wealth. There is no bliss higher than the bliss of the Soul. This is the Supreme state. I have learnt this truth at last! I have realised this only now!"

Arrows cannot really destroy the senses. The senses are located in the astral body or subtle Linga Sarira (Sukshma Deha). Even if the external ears, eyes, nose, etc., are destroyed, the senses still retain their life, strength and vitality. What you see outside are external instruments only. The Indriyas or the senses should be withdrawn and absorbed in the mind itself, through dispassion, discrimination, practice of Dama (self-restraint) and Pratyahara (abstraction). Then only can the senses be destroyed.

All the Vasanas (desires) and Trishnas (cravings) should be destroyed and the mind should be absorbed in its source, viz., Brahman. Then only the mind can be annihilated. You will have to kill these senses and the mind with the help of spiritual arrows, i.e., Dama, Pratyahara, dispassion, eradication of Vasanas and cravings and the practice of Yoga or meditation. That is the reason why the senses and the mind said to Alarka: "You cannot kill us with these ordinary arrows. Do look for other arrows with which to kill us."

As Alarka was a Tapasvin and firm in his vows, he found out the one true arrow of Yogic concentration and killed the seven faculties with this invincible and powerful arrow.

May you all take recourse to this spiritual arrow of Yoga and enjoy the eternal bliss like sage Alarka. God bless you all.

APPENDIX—V

SIVANANDA'S SYNTHESIS OF SADHANAS

(Sri K.S. Ramaswami Sastri)

We have had in India many resounding battles about the superior efficacy of Karma or Bhakti or Prapatti or Jnana or Dhyana. The Advaitins exalt Jnana; the Dvaitins exalt Bhakti; the Visishtadvaitins exalt Prapatti over even Bhakti and Jnana; and the Yogins exalt Dhyana and Samadhi. And yet Sri Krishna says that each one of these, leads us to Him, though the late teachers give that power only to one Sadhana and deny it to the others.

ध्यानेनात्मनि पश्यन्ति केचिदात्मानमात्मना ।
अन्ये सांख्येन योगेन कर्मयोगेन चापरे ॥

अन्ये त्वेवमजानन्तः श्रुत्वान्येभ्य उपासते ।
तेऽपि चातितरन्त्येव मृत्युं श्रुतिपरायणाः ॥

(Some behold Him by Dhyana, others by Sankhya or Jnana, yet others by Karma Yoga, yet others by Upasana or Bhakti, not knowing Him thus but hearing about Him from others. They, with full faith in Sruti, cross death.—Gita, XIII-24, 25.)

The words *Kechit*, *Anye* and *Apare* are decisive and clearly show that each Yoga by itself or in combination with others can lead to Moksha. Though ordinary Karma is connected with a sense of doership and possessiveness (Ahankara and Mamakara) and with a desire for results, i.e., the fruits of Karma are a source of bondage and sure to cause recurrent births and deaths. Karma Yoga in which such elements are absent and Karma is done to carry out God's commands and please Him and offering the fruits of Karma as a dedication to Him and for the welfare of the world, has a powerful Bhakti and Dhyana and Jnana element also. Such Karma Yoga will destroy the binding power of the present and the future Karmas while the Bhakti-Dhyana-Jnana element will destroy the force of Sanchita Karmas (acts to bear fruit in future births) also, leaving the

Prarabdha Karmas (acts which have begun to bear fruit in this birth) to be worked out by enjoining the fruits. This truth is clearly stated in the Isavasya Upanishad Verses 9-11:

अन्धं तमः प्रविशन्ति येऽविद्यामुपासते ।
ततो भूय इव ते तमो य उ विद्यायां रताः ॥

अन्यदेवाहुर्विद्यया अन्यदाहुरविद्यया ।
इति शुश्रुम धीराणां ये नस्तद् विचचक्षिरे ॥

विद्यां चाविद्यां च यस्तद् वेदोऽभयेँ सह ।
अविद्यया मृत्युं तीर्त्वा विद्ययाऽमृतमश्नुते ॥

Mere Karma (Avidya) leads to darkness if it is done with expectation of fruits. Swami Sivananda says: "Avidya means here Karmas or Vedic rites such as Agnihotra, etc., that are performed with expectation of fruits" (*Principal Upanishads*). So does mere Vidya (i.e. knowledge of the inferior deities or book-knowledge of God divorced from Lokasangraha Karma) lead into even greater darkness and will not lead to the radiance of God-realisation. But when we have Vidya (knowledge and love of God), and do acts to carry out God's commands and without a sense of doership and possessiveness and realising that the Gunas of Prakriti do the actions and offering the fruits to Sri Krishna in a spirit of Asanga (detachment) and Krishnarpana (dedication to Sri Krishna) for the welfare of the world (Lokasangraha), the Karma Yoga prevents the present and future Karmas from leading us into Samsara while the Bhakti-Dhyana-Jnana element in such Karma Yoga destroys the force of past Karmas.

ज्ञानाग्निः सर्वकर्माणि भस्मसात्कुरुते तथा (IV-37)

Why then have any battles about the Yogas? In the Karma Yoga we have to obey His orders and offer the fruits to Him and work as His servants. Does not this imply Bhakti and Prapatti and Jnana also? Bhaktas and Jnanis and Dhyanis also have the duty of Lokasangraha laid on them. In the Gita XVIII, 51 to 55, the Lord gives us a complete fusion of the Yogas.

Swami Sivananda's *Yoga of Synthesis* is a treasure-chest of wisdom. "To behold the one Self in all beings is Jnana, wisdom; to love the Self is Bhakti, devotion; to serve the Self is Karma, action. When the Jnana Yogi attains wisdom, he is endowed with devotion and selfless activity. Karma Yoga is for him a spontaneous expression of his spiritual nature, as he sees the one Self in all. When the devotee attains perfection in devotion, he is possessed of wisdom and activity. For him also Karma Yoga is the spontaneous expression of his divine nature, as he beholds the one Lord everywhere. The Karma Yogi attains wisdom and devotion when his actions are wholly selfless. The three paths are in fact one, in which three different temperaments emphasise one or other of its inseparable constituents. Yoga supplies the method by which the Self can be seen, heard and loved." (*Yoga of Synthesis*)

"Synthesis is the hallmark of Indian Philosophy. Hinduism is renowned for its universality. You can find a synthesis of all paths in the Upanishads too. The Upanishads are intentional revelations and hence do not fall short of the all-round approach that may be tried by various kinds of men towards the ultimate goal of life." (*do*)

"The Yoga of synthesis is the most suitable and potent form of Sadhana. The Yoga of synthesis alone will bring about integral development. Just as will, feeling and thought are not distinct and separate, so also work, devotion and knowledge are not exclusive of one another." (*do*)

"The Yoga of synthesis alone is suitable for this modern age. The four Yogas are interdependent and inseparable. Love is endowed in service. Service is love in expression. Knowledge is diffused love and love is concentrated knowledge. Karma Yoga is always combined with Bhakti Yoga and Jnana Yoga. Bhakti Yoga is the fulfilment of Karma Yoga. Raja Yoga is the fulfilment of Karma Yoga and Bhakti Yoga. Jnana Yoga is the fulfilment of Karma Yoga, Bhakti Yoga and Raja Yoga." (*do.* See also *Light Divine*)

"There must be integral development. Vedanta without devotion is quite dry. Bhakti without Jnana is not perfect. How can one who has realised his Atman remain without serving the world which is without doubt Atman only? Devotion is not divorced from Jnana, but Jnana is rather exceedingly helpful to its perfect attainment. Para Bhakti and Jnana are one." (*Religion and Philosophy*)

"These paths are made in accordance with the temperament or tendency that is predominant in the individual. One path does not exclude the others. The path of action is suitable for a man of Karmic tendency. The path of love is adapted for a man of emotional temperament. The path of Raja Yoga is fitted for a man of mystic temperament. The path of Vedanta or Jnana Yoga is suitable for a man of will or reason. Each path blends with the others. Ultimately all these paths converge and become one." (*do*)

"I believe in integral development of synthetic Yoga." (*Sure Ways for Success in Life and God-realisation*)

This idea has the full support of Sri Krishna in the Bhagavata, XI-20, 7 and 8:

निर्विण्णानां ज्ञानयोगो न्यासिनामिह कर्मसु ।
तेष्वनिर्विण्णचित्तानां कर्मयोगस्तु कामिनाम् ॥
यदृच्छया मत्कथादौ जातश्रद्धस्तु यः पुमान् ।
न निर्विण्णो नातिसक्तो भक्तियोगोऽस्य सिद्धिदः ॥

Nay, Sri Krishna says in the Gita, VI, 29-32, that the Jnani who sees his self in all beings and all beings in himself becomes conscious of the Lord in all beings and all beings in the Lord and loves the Lord with the supreme love and shares in the joys and sorrows of all beings.

In his *Yoga in Daily Life*, Swami Sivananda says: "There are four Yogas, viz., Karma Yoga, Bhakti Yoga, Raja Yoga and Jnana Yoga. Karma Yoga is suitable for people of active temperament, Bhakti Yoga for people of devotional temperament, Raja Yoga for men of mystic temperament and Jnana Yoga for people of intellectual temperament with bold understanding and strong will-power. Bhakti Yoga is suitable for the vast majority of persons as they are emotional. Ladies can realise God quickly as their hearts are filled with devotion."

Swami Sivananda has explained each of the four Yogas at great length in various books. In Section IV of *Yoga in Daily Life* he describes Karma Yoga. The Gita is the supreme manual of Nishkama Karma Yoga in the whole world. Swamiji says: "Think that Lord Siva is working through your hands and is eating through your mouth."

तस्मात्सर्वेषु कालेषु मामनुस्मर युध्य च ।

("At all times do your duty of fighting, remembering Me." Gita, VIII-7)

Swami Sivananda warns us against the Karma Yogi

becoming proud of his Nishkama Karma and forging thereby a more powerful means of bondage. He says: "Seva Abhimana is more dangerous than the Abhimana of worldly persons—Seva Abhimana is more difficult to eradicate than the ordinary Abhimana of worldly-minded persons. This is a very subtle Abhimana which lurks in the corners of the mind" (*Karma Yoga Is the Best Yoga—Jnana Surya Series No. 5*)

Swami Sivananda has boldly declared that Karma Yoga by itself can lead to God-realisation, though Advaitins regard it only as bringing Chittasuddhi and say that Raja Yoga will lead to concentration of mind (Chitta-ekagrata) and that Bhakti Yoga will lead to Jnana and that Sravana, Manana and Nididhyasana alone will lead to Jnana and that Jnana alone can bring salvation and though Visishtadvaitins and Dvaitins will give only a subordinate place to Karma and even Jnana and say that Raja Yoga has become non-existent and that Bhakti Yoga alone will give us salvation. He says: "Karma Yoga is not only a means but also the end in itself like Bhakti Yoga. It is quite independent. A Karma Yogi need not study the Upanishads. He need not practise Sravana, Manana and Nididhyasana (hearing the Srutis, reflection and meditation). He plunges himself in the service of humanity alone one-pointedly. He is a Karma Yoga Parayana. He has taken sole refuge in this Yoga. When his heart is perfectly purified he gets illumination and Self-Knowledge through Lord's grace just as a devotee gets knowledge through Lord's grace without the practice of Sravana, Manana and Nididhyasana. There is a mysterious power or Achintya Sakti in the practice of Karma Yoga which transforms the mind of the aspirant and helps him in the attainment of knowledge of Brahman." (*Karma Yoga Is the Best Yoga*)

"He who attends on a helpless man when he is in a dying condition does more Sadhana than a man who does meditation in a closed room. If he does service for one hour it is equal to meditation for six hours." *(do)*

He points out also how "those who take to Jnana Yoga without the purification of the heart by Karma Yoga remain as debaters as dry Pandits." *(do)*

Swami Sivananda 's exposition of Raja Yoga has been described by me above. He expounds Bhakti Yoga in various books (*Bhakti and Sankirtan, Essence of Bhakti Yoga, Treasure of Teachings,* etc.). Bhakti Yoga is the easiest and sweetest of all Yogas and even in its Bhajan and Sankirtan are the sweetest of all. Sri Krishna says in the Gita:

राजविद्या राजगुह्यं परित्रमिदमुत्तमम् ।
प्रत्यक्षावगमं धर्म्यं सुसुखं कर्तुमव्ययम् ॥

("It is the King of Vidyas. It is the King of secrets. It is pure. It is Supreme. It can be easily known. It is pure Dharma. It is easy to do. It yields perennial results."—Gita, XI-4)

भक्त्या त्वनन्यया शक्य अहमेवंविधोऽर्जुन ।
ज्ञातुं द्रष्टुं च तत्त्वेन प्रवेष्टुं च परंतप ॥

("By supreme love alone I can be truly known, seen and realised in union."—Gita, IV-2)

The various aspects of Bhakti are clearly enumerated in the Bhagavata, XI-3.

श्रवणं कीर्तनं विष्णोः स्मरणं पादसेवनम् ।
अर्चनं वन्दनं दास्यं सख्यमात्मनिवेदनम् ॥

In his *Treasure of Teachings* Swami Sivananda says:

"Sankirtan Yoga is the easiest, surest, quickest and safest path to attain God-realisation."

"In this iron age Japa is the easiest way of God-realisation."

"Bhava is the main basis of Rasa. Rasa is the nectarine transcendental bliss."

"Sankirtan is an exact science. The harmonious vibrations produced by singing the Name of the Lord help the devotee to control his mind easily." *(Akhanda Kirtan)*

In *Bhakti and Sankirtan* he expounds elaborately Sandilya's wonderful Bhakti Sutras. He has expounded Narada's Bhakti Sutras also. To be with him is to be immersed in Bhajan and Kirtan, in Prema and Om. He says: "Prayer has tremendous influence. I have many experiences." He emphasises also worship or Upasana. All Puja (worship) is holy but Manasika Puja (mental worship) is the holiest of all. Faith, Love and Bliss are inseparable. At the same time Swamiji has warned us against the devotee becoming proud of his devotion and against Bhakti leading to any moral corruptions. The crown of Bhakti is Prema. A very faithful idea of Swami Sivananda on Bhakti is found in his *Essence of*

Bhakti Yoga. It is in fact an exposition of Vyasa's exposition of the philosophy of Bhakti in the Gopi episode in Skanda X of the Bhagavata. There Vyasa equates Bhakti and Jnana and says that as Atma Jnana burns up all Punya (religious merit) and all Papa (sin), the supreme Bhakti of the Gopis had a like effect.

दु:सहप्रेष्ठविरहतीव्रतापधुताशुभाः ।
ध्यानप्राप्ताच्युताश्लेषनिर्वृत्याक्षीणमंगला ॥

(Their sins were burnt away in the fire of the grief of their unbearable separation from Krishna. Their religious merits were overborne by the supreme bliss of their embrace of Krishna in meditation.)

Swami Sivananda says: "The illustration of the two varieties of Samadhi is found in the Rasa Lila of Sri Krishna. At first the Gopis perceive that all is Sri Krishna alone. This is equal to Savikalpa Samadhi. Afterwards they feel that even they themselves are Krishna only. This is equal to Nirvikalpa Samadhi where sense of ego is absent. The Srimad Bhagavata is the Bible of the devotees. It illustrates the various kinds of Rasas and modes of developing Bhakti." (*Essence of Bhakti Yoga*) Swamiji describes elsewhere in the same work the five kinds of Bhakti Bhavas, viz., Santa, Dasya, Sakhya, Vatsalya and Madhurya, the Madhura Bhava of the Gopis and especially of Radha Devi being the highest Summit of Bhakti Rasa. Swamiji also gives an exalted description of Sri Ramanuja's eleven suggestions for developing and intensifying Bhakti, viz., Abhyasa (repeated Bhakti), Viveka (discrimination), Satya (truth), Arjava (straightforwardness), Kriya (doing good to others), Kalyana (wishing the well-being of all), Daya (compassion), Ahimsa (non-injury), Dana (charity) and Anavasada (cheerfulness).

अहिंसा प्रथमं पुष्पं पुष्पमिन्द्रियनिग्रहः ।
सर्वभूतदया पुष्पं क्षमा पुष्पं विशेषतः ॥

ध्यानं पुष्पं तपः पुष्पं ज्ञानं पुष्पं तथैव च ।
सत्यमष्टविधं पुष्पं विष्णोः प्रीतिकरं भवेत् ॥

[Ahimsa, Indriyanigraha (sense-control), Sarvabhoota-Daya (compassion to all beings), Kshama (forgiveness), Dhyana (meditation), Tapas (austerity), Jnana (wisdom) and Satya (truth) are the eight flowers which are dear to Lord Vishnu.]

Swami Sivananda has expounded Jnana Yoga with great elaboration in many of his writings. In *Yoga in Daily Life* he gives a list of the books which a beginner in Vedanta and an advanced student should study. He gives a clear enunciation of Vedanta formulae and especially Soham Dhyana for meditation. His books *Vedanta for Beginners, First Lessons in Vedanta, Philosophy and Meditation on Om, Secret of Self-realisation, How to Get Vairagya, First Lessons in Vedanta, Vedanta in Daily Life, Jnana Yoga,* etc., are the books which must be studied by us to realise the glory of Jnana Yoga. In the *Voice of the Himalayas* he says: "The Upanishads constitute the life-breath of India...... Vedanta is a system of life itself. It represents the fundamental basis on which alone a universal religion, or a 'Universal Congress of Faiths' can be built." In regard to Jnana Yoga Swami Sivananda warns us against our becoming proud of our Knowledge and vain about our intellect and contemptuous and contentious in our dealings with others. *(First Lessons in Vedanta)*

Hari Om Tat Sat